The Life and Letters of
Emily Chubbuck Judson
{Fanny Forester}

VOLUME 2

Endowed by
Tom Watson Brown
and
The Watson-Brown Foundation, Inc.

The Life and Letters of
Emily Chubbuck Judson
{Fanny Forester}

Volume 2

1826-1845

EDITED BY
GEORGE H. TOOZE

Published in cooperation with the American Baptist Historical Society

Mercer University Press
Macon, Georgia

MUP/H783

© 2010 Mercer University Press
1400 Coleman Avenue
Macon, Georgia 31207
All rights reserved

First Edition.

Books published by Mercer University Press are printed on acid free paper that meets the requirements
of American National Standard for Information Sciences—Permanence of Paper for Printed Library Materials.

Mercer University Press is a member of Green Press initiative (greenpressinitiative.org), a nonprofit organization
working to help publishers and printers increase their use of recycled paper and decrease their use
of fiber derived from endangered forests. This book is printed on recycled paper.

ISBN 13: 978-0-88146-149-7
Copyrights for the original letters and pictures are held and reserved as listed below.
No part of this publication may be reproduced without the prior permission of the copyright owner.

Letters:
The American Baptist Historical Society, Atlanta, Georgia (1,217 letters)
The Hanna family files, Dr. Stanley Hanna, Palo Alto, California (392 letters)
Jerome Walker Chubbuck Collection, Wisconsin Historical Society Archives, Madison, Wisconsin (24 letters)
The First Baptist Church, Malden, Massachusetts (3 letters, 1 poem)
Franklin Trask Library, Andover Newton Theological School, Newton Centre, Massachusetts (3 letters)
Special Collections, Colgate University, Hamilton, New York (1 letter)

Pictures:
The New York Public Library, New York, New York (12 portraits)
The Hanna family files, Dr. Stanley Hanna, Palo Alto, California (16 pictures)
The American Baptist Historical Society, Atlanta, Georgia (14 pictures)

Library of Congress Cataloging-in-Publication Data

Tooze, George H.-
The life and letters of Emily Chubbuck Judson (Fanny Forester) / edited by George H. Tooze.—1st ed.
p. cm.
MUP/H772—T.p. verso.
Includes bibliographical references and index.
ISBN 978-0-88146-131-2 (acid-free paper)
1. Judson, Emily C. (Emily Chubbuck, 1817-1854
2. American Baptist Historical Society. v. 1. Biographies and timelines I. Title.

2010292236

Book design by Burt&Burt

To Connie (Constance Taylor Tooze)
With loving and heartfelt thanks—
For your love, encouragement, and support
over these forty-seven years we have wondrously shared together—
And for the wonderful life that is our present and future.

Contents

Preface
xi

Acknowledgment
xv

LETTERS

1826–1839
1

1840–1843
67

1844
191

January–June 1845
293

July–December 1845
433

Index
525

⁂ This engraving appeared as a front plate in *Alderbrook*. It was attributed to J. Sartain, one of the most famous engravers of the mid-nineteenth century.

In a letter dated May 8, 1846 to the Reverend Mr. A. D. Gillette, Emily Chubbuck wrote:

> "I received yours, together with the engraving and newspaper, this morning. You are so very kind that I do not know how to thank you enough. I like your suggestion about curving the neck more. There is also too much of a dimple in the chin, though perhaps not more than in the painting.[1] The nose, as I have often said before, is too pointed, a little too long, perhaps, at the tip, and, where it joins the face, a little bit too narrow. It gives the whole face a sharp look. Yet I do not know as it would be best to touch it. I wish, however, that something could be done to subdue and soften down the expression of the whole thing. It is quite too spirited—not so meek-looking as I fancy myself to be. The amount of the whole is, the picture is a grand one—beautifully painted and very beautifully engraved—but precious little, if at all, like me, except in the outline—not the least particle in the expression. However, I do not care; it is as like, I suppose, as engravings usually are, and I would rather be flattered than caricatured, as Dr. J. is. Please have no name attached to it; neither my old true name, nor my intended new one. I have concluded not to have any loose engravings out (at least until I leave the country), but reserve the picture for my "Fanny Forester" sketches. For the same reason I do not wish it to appear in any magazine."

On May 23, Adoniram Judson wrote to Emily from Philadelphia, "Even'g—We have had a meeting at Mr. Gillette's, by appointment—Mr. Sartain and I—and we discussed the alterations you proposed in the engraving—He is to give me an amended proof, before I leave, which I shall forward to you—probably with this letter."

---

[1] We believe that the original painting upon which the engraving was based was by P. F. Rothermel, a well known portrait artist in Philadelphia.

At the end of that same letter, written Monday morning, he says, "I am just going out to Gillette's and Sartain's, and will take this letter though unfinished, to deposit in the post office, if I pass that way."

At the post office, twelve o'clock, he writes, "I start at half past 4 for N.Y. Sartain is still working on the engraving and will give me a copy before I leave."

On May 26, 1846, Adoniram Judson wrote to Emily from New York:

> I send you, darling, a copy of the improved engraving with one of the old, that you may see the difference—I think the improvements are very considerable. The sleeve was done last, as Sartain waited for Rothermel (who was not at home) to sketch it, before he would alter the engraving. How do you like it? If you have any further alterations to suggest, write immediately to Sartain through Mr. Gillette. I had an idea of a closer sleeve, more like what you wear, but that would probably not have been on good keeping with the rest of the costume—and perhaps not easily done, as you will perceive—he has made the new sleeve out of the old.

A similar, if not identical, engraving appears in the front of *The Lives of the Three Mrs. Judsons* by Arabella W. Stuart, printed in 1854. In that edition the engraving, no doubt a copy of the Sartrain engraving, is attributed to J. C. Buttre.

Preface

This is volume 2 of *The Life and Letters of Emily Chubbuck Judson [Fanny Forester]*. It encompasses Emily Chubbuck's letters, life and work from 1826 when she was nine years old, through 1845 as Adoniram Judson entered into her life.

The original intention of these volumes was to cover only her correspondence—the letters she sent and received. It became quickly obvious, however, that the poetry and stories she had written could equally illuminate her life. For this reason we have included both where they are informative. In this volume we begin with the actual material from her pen—some as Emily E. Chubbuck, some as Fanny Forester.

This volume will cover:

—the early years of Emily E. Chubbuck

—the poverty of her childhood; the necessity of her working in the mill to help provide resources for her struggling family; and the impact that the death of two of her older sisters, Lavinia and Harriet, had on her entire life

—her earliest writing for the local newspapers

—her enrollment at the Utica Female Academy in October 1840, an event that shaped the rest of her life

—her developing friendships at the Utica Female Academy and the enduring relationships with Miss Cynthia Sheldon (in charge of administration and finance); her sister Mrs. Urania Sheldon Nott (the literary principal); and their niece, and eventually Emily's best friend, Anna Maria Anable

—her writing books for the American Baptist Publication Society, starting a series on the Ten Commandments which included *Effie Maurice* and *Anna Bailey*

—her growing literary career as she began to write for *Graham's Magazine*, the *Knickerbocker Magazine*, the *Columbian Magazine*, and the *New Mirror*

—her discovery in June 1844 by Nathaniel Parker Willis of the *New Mirror* in New York and his subsequent promotion of her career as she became Fanny Forester

—her correspondence with N. P. Willis which indicates their relationship most certainly would have brought them together in marriage had not Adoniram Judson entered her life

—her correspondence and association with the literati of the mid-nineteenth century

—her wintering in Philadelphia in late winter/early spring 1845 and then again beginning in November 1845; Emily was a guest in the home of Rev. and Mrs. A. D. Gillette, which made possible her meeting with Adoniram Judson on Christmas Day 1845, but the correspondence does not describe this event and its unfolding consequences until January 1, 1846. It is here that the material of volume 3 will begin.

During work on the final draft of this document for publication, we received some newly released poetry from the archives of Dr. Stanley Hanna, a grandson of Adoniram and Emily Judson. One of the items released was a notebook in which Emily had copied some of her earliest poetry, written between 1826 and 1831. Some of the other poems we were able with some confidence to date to this early time.[1]

In young Emily's musings, we find the seeds of brilliance and expression, facility with words and creativity, and sensitivity to eternal human thoughts and values able to touch the heart and emotion of the reader, all of which were to come to fruition some fifteen to twenty years later in the work of Fanny Forester.

Though it is not included in these pages (saved for a later volume because of its length), Emily at the age of thirteen wrote a drama which she titled, "The London Merchant." It covers in her handwriting fifteen pages of one of her notebooks. A friend of mine who is a poet and Shakespearean scholar was looking over some of her material for me one night, and as he read through this drama he exclaimed, "Why she has captured Shakespearean meter perfectly!" Again I was reminded of the genius in this young lady that was to bloom as Fanny Forester.

[1] As Dr. Hanna moved into a retirement home, his son David found this notebook and some other single poems and letters, and it was David who sent these items to me. Later he was to find three more notebooks, each with priceless material.

It is appropriate to Emily's life story that the first letter in 1834 was written during a time of personal religious awakening, which was to result in her baptism in the Morrisville Church by Dr. William Dean, soon to be an American Baptist missionary to Hong Kong. This letter was written to her youthful friend Marie Dawson, later to become Marie Dawson Bates. This religious commitment was foundational to all that would follow.

It is easy to miss her greatness in the humanity of her everyday life. Her enormous capability and fame really struck us, however, when we were able to secure a copy of *Graham's Magazine* for 1846. As she was winding down in her writing because of her new marriage and missionary commitments, Fanny Forester had four stories in the magazine that year. Most notable, however, was the company she was in. The other writers included Edgar Allen Poe, Frank Forester, N. P. Willis, Frances Osgood, James Russell Lowell, James Fenimore Cooper, John Inman, Henry Wardsworth Longfellow, William Cullen Bryant, and Charles Fenno Hoffman. In other words, she was counted amongst those who have come to be known as some of the greatest writers of the nineteenth century.

At the same time her literary friends were writers, publishers, literary critics, songwriters, and poets such as George Graham of *Graham's Magazine*, John Inman of the *Columbian*, Charles Fenno Hoffman of the *Evening Gazette*, Joseph Clay Neal of the *Saturday Gazette*, Rufus W. Griswold, author of numerous anthologies, Nathaniel Parker Willis of the *New Mirror*, and Horace Binney Wallace of *Literary Criticisms*. These names were among the preeminent writers, publishers, and editors of that period, and they were her social circle, the origin of letters to her and the recipients of letters from her.

I write these words as I am finishing a careful edit of this volume, and I have been astounded (once again) as I have been touched and moved by a tidbit here, a thought there, an expression, a passion, a defense, an aggressive statement. They are like nuggets of gold to be found in careful perusal of these pages.

Emily E. Chubbuck *is* well worth knowing. My hope and prayer in sharing these pages of letters, poetry, and stories is that you will, in getting to know her, be as moved and blessed as I have been over these many years and that you will find delight, inspiration, and encouragement through these pages.

George H. Tooze
Indianapolis, Indiana

Acknowledgment

The editor wishes to express his deepest appreciation to the following for granting permission to use original letters and pictures for these volumes.

Letters
: The American Baptist Historical Society, Atlanta, Georgia

  The Hanna Family Files, Dr. Stanley Hanna, Palo Alta, California

  Jerome Walker Chubbuck Collection, Wisconsin Historical Society Archives, Madison, Wisconsin

  The First Baptist Church of Malden, Massachusetts

  Franklin Trask Library, Andover Newton Theological School, Newton Centre, Massachusetts

  Special Collections, Colgate University, Hamilton, New York.

Pictures
: The New York Public Library, New York, New York

  The Hanna Family Files, Dr. Stanley Hanna, Palo Alta, California

  The American Baptist Historical Society, Atlanta, Georgia

We note that volume one, *The Life and Letters of Emily Chubbuck Judson (Fanny Forester)*, has biographies of all letter writers and of those mentioned in the letters; it also has descriptions of places and events.

Additionally it has timelines of Emily's life and events important to her life story. Volume one is a descriptive companion to all the other volumes.

Letters

—⁐—

1826-1839

Emily E. Chubbuck to her Cousin Mary, 1826[1]

Here is something dated 1826—I have this moment found it on the back of an old letter sent me by a cousin whom I had never seen.

A portrait drawn for my cousin[2]

Mary, you say you'd like to know
How cousin Emma looks, and so,
She, having nothing else to do,
Will send to you a portrait true.—
She's thin and slender—By the by,
You seem to think the "soul-like eye"
The truest index of the mind,
But verily that's too unkind,
For hers are small and black—and more,
She cannot see an inch before
Her nose, though that is not so bad
As though a shorter one she had.
Her hair is dark, a glossy brown,
Sometimes bound up but oftener down,
In wild confusion o'er her face,
And destitute of every graies [sic].
Her forehead is neither high nor low,
Her cheeks oft light up with a glow,
Which passes very soon away
And leaves them pale, uncoloured clay.
Then, she is crooked, and her gait,
Is what I fear you'd surely hate.
Walker[3] compares me to a hare,
But mother[4] says if I would dare
To trust myself I'd walk much better—
Timidity, she calls my fetter.—
Now, pretty coz, don't turn away,
And say you hope I'll always stay,
In Morrisville[5] for you don't care,
To look on such a hog den [sic] fair.—
Don't say my eyes ought to be blue,
My cheek of laughing rosy hue,
Complexion lily and my mien
As airy as a fairy queen.

[1] This work is Emily Chubbuck's earliest known poem, writing, or letter, written at age nine. Interestingly, it is a somewhat personal self-portrait written for her cousin, Mary, as Emily described herself. It seems appropriate that Emily's self-portrait begins these volumes chronicling her life and work.

[2] This is the fourth of six poems that Emily copied into a notebook. She had dated it as 1826.

[3] Born September 24, 1815, John Walker Chubbuck was twenty-three months older than Emily. Trained as a printer and having worked for a newspaper, Walker established a newspaper with a partner upon arriving in the Wisconsin Territory. He moved to Wassau in 1857, establishing the Central Wisconsin. In 1863 he became Clerk of Circuit Court. He was married in 1855 to Caroline Sanborn, and they had three children, one of whom, a daughter, died at the age of twelve. As this was written, Walker would have been eleven years old.

[4] Lavinia Richards Chubbuck, b. June 1, 1785 at Goffstown NH.

[5] Morrisville, Emily's childhood home, is a part of Eaton NY.

I moulded [sic] not the face nor eye,
Nor form.—My gentle coz, good-bye.

Emily E. Chubbuck, 1827[6]

First Version

The Little Girl's Soliloquy

The March winds blow
So loud!—and I,
What cold and stormy weather!—
I thought that spring,
Would surely bring,
The birds and flowers together.

Heigho! heigho!—
It plagues me so,
I scarce can keep from crying,
Here I must sit,
And sew and knit,
Old Rover by me lying.

It seems so strange!
I used to range,
The pleasant fields all over,
For hours I've sung,
Low, hid among,
The buttercups and clover.

And then I'd bound,
Away around
The fields, in search of berries;
And often stay
Along the way,
To pick the red, ripe cherries.

I us'd to deck
Old Rover's neck,
With violets and wild roses,
And laugh to see,
How 'shamed he'd be,
To wear such pretty posies.

[6] This work must be one of the earliest poems of Emily Chubbuck, probably composed in 1827. We have the original finished poem as it was completed, in Emily's handwriting, from the Hanna Family Files. Actually, we have two versions of the poem, and both are presented here. The only overlap is that the second stanza of version one is identical to the first stanza of version two.

We believe that the simplicity of these poems places them early in Emily's life, as does the reference to her "baby brother." This would be Wallace Chubbuck, born January 1, 1824; Emily was approximately six and a half years old at the time of Wallace's birth. If we place this poem in winter 1827, Wallace would have been three years old and Emily would have been nine-and-a-half years old.

Second Version

Heigho! heigho!—
It plagues me so,
I scarce can keep from crying,
Here I must sit,
And sew and knit,
Old Rover by me lying.

And louder still
From yonder hill,
The bleak winds now are blowing.—
'Tis wrong to cry,
So I must try,
To keep the tears from flowing.

Tis surely bad,
To feel so sad,
And keep up such complaining,
This vain regret
makes me forget,
The blessings still remaining.

This roof so warm,
Keeps off the storm,
The fire burns bright and cheerful
While many roam,
Without a home,—
O such a thought is fearful.

Here I might lay
My work away,
And play with puss or Rover,
Or go and swing,
Or read, or sing,
Or look my playthings over.

If all of these,
Should fail to please,
[ ] [ ] I could seek my mother,[7]
And with me bring,
Some offering

[7] Lavinia Richards Chubbuck, Emily's mother. Lavinia was born June 1, 1785, at Goffstown NH, and was the eldest of thirteen children. She married Charles Chubbuck on November 17, 1805, at Goffstown. Together they had seven children.

To soothe my baby brother.[8]

Dear mother tells
Of God, who dwells
Far, far away in heaven,
Who loves the child,
That's meek and mild,
And seeks to be forgiven.

I love to be
Upon her knee,
And hear her sigh so lowly,
[ ] gaze into
Her eye of blue,
So kind, and sweet, and holy.

What should I do,
And brother too,
Without so kind a mother?
For Mary there,
Has none to care
About, and now to love her.

I'm sure that I
Should never cry,
About the stormy weather,
Since God above,
Keeps those I love,
In happiness together.

Source: Hanna family files.

[8] Born January 1, 1824, William Wallace Chubbuck was six years younger than Emily. During these years of Emily's correspondence, Wallace was living at home, or near home, working at different occupations including printing, office work, and teaching. Emily wrote of him as very capable in many areas but seeming to lack ambition at times. He proved to be a strong support for the Chubbuck family over these years, and, at the time of her death in 1854, Wallace had become one of Emily's primary care-givers. After February 1854, he wrote, at her dictation, all of her letters because of her failing strength.

[9] This same year Emily wrote another poem which she titled, "On finding a gold coin." It may be that she was enraptured by gold coins because she never would have seen them in her life at that time with the poverty of her family. The first two stanzas read:

> Ha! thou'st mine, dear glittering bauble!
> Welcome, welcome to my hand;
> For tho' thou causes care and trouble,
> Thou are still in great demand.
>
> Not only bring'st thou food and clothing,
> But thou raisest influence high;
> Makest man feel a noble loathing,
> For his brother shivering by.

Emily E. Chubbuck to "the coin in her purse,"[9] 1828[10]

Hast thou tossed upon the billows?
Guarded by the watchful eye,
Of the owner, 'neath his pillow,
All the night long doom'd to lie?

Perhaps by murderous hands directed,
For thee the glittering daggers flashed,

[10] This whimsical poem is the first of six poems Emily copied into a notebook. Because four of the six are dated between 1826 and 1830, we place this undated piece in the middle of that period. The notebook has lost its cover, so it is possible that this is the ending of the poem, with beginning material on a prior page, though it does seem complete.

Maybe too, thou hast protected,
Many from the cruel lash.

Then perchance the beggars snatched thee,
Thou hast saved his worn-out life;
Or the gamester reckless dashed thee,
From him for a chance at dice.

Thou mayst have been the price for satin,
Some young bride's fair gown to deck,
Or proudly in her white hand glittering,
Purchased a bauble for her neck.

But eagle since thou wilt not answer,[11]
I know not what's been thy lot—
Thou'st doubtless sway'd both sense and fancy,
And many wondrous doings wrought.

Now lie there, quite free from danger,
In a little maiden's purse;
And think no more to be a ranger,
Since she's told thy praise in verse.

Source: Hanna family files, poetry notebook 1.

[11] The U.S. Mint coined the first "golden eagle" coins in 1795. These ten dollar coins had an eagle on one side.

Emily E. Chubbuck, 1828

Apostrophe to the Moon[12]

Sweet Moon, I love to gaze
Upon thy smiling face,
And give my fancy wings,
Thy mystery to trace.

I wonder what thou art,
So beautiful and fair,
Hung like a silver lamp
In yonder halls of air.

Tell me, if on thy sphere
A tear is ever shed;
If pallid mourners bend
In grief above the dead.

[12] When this poem was published in *An Olio of Domestic Verses*, Emily C. Judson added this note to her youthful work: "Written at the age of eleven, after a 'first grief.'"

Knowest thou that fearful One,
He of the iron hand,
Whose shadow mingles here,
In every love-knit band?

Ah no! by that calm smile,
I know thou hast but bliss;
Sure there's no other sphere
So full of woe as this!

Source: Emily Judson, An Olio of Domestic Verse, 25–26.

Emily E. Chubbuck, 1829

A Dialogue[13]

[13] Dated 1829, this work is the fifth of six poems Emily copied into a notebook.

Celia.
    What! weeping still! Come Mary, dry these tears
    And smile. I cannot bear to see you ever thus.
Mary.
    Nay, Celia, talk not thus: these tears I love,
    They are a balm to this poor wounded breast.
    I can't exist unless I weep: this heart
    Would burst if its deep misery had no vent.
    Tears seem to this lone bosom like a draught,
    To a poor trav'ller o'er Arabia's sands.
Celia.
    You almost make me smile. *You* talk of misery;
    You who scarcely know its name! Mary, fie!
    Your disappointments are but trivial, your—
Mary
    —My disappointments trivial!
    Celia, you're happy, and you cannot feel
    For one like me—so miserable, so sad.—
    I've had bright dreams, have painted visions gay,
    Had towering hopes which raised me to the clouds,
    But now alas! how low.
Celia
    Dear Mary, do not pain me so. You have
    No cause to weep.—You were not wise
    To do as you have done and list to fancy's voice.

Mary
> I know it, but my evil genius said,
> These tales were true and so I drank them in
> Imagination's been my direst foe.
> I've follow'd her, but she's a phantom guide,
> And now behold me, miserable indeed.

Celia.
> Well then, discard her now, for still she reigns,
> As despot-like as heretofore she did,
> Though in a different way.

Mary.
> No, Celia, no, I'm deeply read in all,
> The sad realities of life, and thus I weep.

Celia.
> Life is not sad, if you'll not make it so.

Mary.
> Perchance 'tis not for you, but mine, alas!
> Is but a wayward heart.—I feel I'm not
> As others are; ne'er was I born to be
> Content in such a humble sphere.

Celia—What would you have?

Mary—Knowledge!

Celia—Would that suffice?

Mary.
> Yes, give me that and I will be content.
> O let me quaff from the Pierian [sic] spring,
> Quench this deep, burning thirst at Wisdom's well,
> And I will ask no more.

Celia
> If you had all the wisdom of the king
> Of ancient Jewry, added to the love,
> Of all she sages, it would be in vain.

Mary—Indeed!

Celia
> You'd want your name to sound thro'out the world
> To be on every tongue, and handed down
> To earth's remotest age.—

Mary.
> I think if I had wealth I might attain

>   To some high eminence, but hope is vain,
>   Chill penury has bound me firmly down
>   And I must labour to support,
>   That life which oft I wish I'd ne'er possessed.
>
> Celia.
>   'Tis honourable to be poor and—
>
> Mary.
>   Yes, woundrous honourable! Canst tell me why
>   You butterfly [sic] neglects me thus, tosses her empty head
>   So scornfully, whene'er she casts a glance,
>   Towards me?
>
> Celia—You're jealous.
>
> Mary.
>   No, indeed, I'm not! for I have eyes to see,
>   And heart to feel neglect. But it is *gold*!
>   Gold makes her blind to simple puny me!
>   'Tis gold that lifts her empty head so high,
>   And fawning sycophant around her draws
>   To sue for favours, bask within her smiles
>   Or sink all scar'd beneath her fickle frown.
>
> Celia—And do you envy her?
>
> Mary.
>   Oh no, it is not her, nor such as her I envy
>   It is the learn'd, the wise, 'tis the refined
>   In thought, and soul, and such as wealth
>   To their society admits.
>
> Celia.—But Mary, wealth cannot be yours,
>   So be content with what you do possess.
>
> Mary.
>   Celia, have you a lesson you can teach
>   To make me rest content as now I am?
>
> Celia
>   Sober your fancy, and subdue your pride,
>   Give place to common sense—
>
> Mary
>   Go—tell the winds, and hush the ocean's roar!
>   Go make the veriest jibbering idiot wise,
>   And make a dreamer of the yeoman stern,
>   Then come and still my buoyant fancy down,

And give me what you call plain common sense.

Source: Hanna family files, poetry notebook 1.

Emily E. Chubbuck, 1830

To Sarah,—Love[14]

[14] Dated 1830, this work is the second of six Emily copied into a notebook.

There is a char[ ] I can't describe,
In one little word contained;
That word's far sweeter when applied,
To one, who all its soul has gained.
Did you ere walk at eventide,
Beneath fair Cynthia's silvery ray,
Where crystal streamlets softly glide,
And fragrant breezes lingering stay?
O then did not a feeling creep
Around your heart you can't define?
Sarah, I think the *word* is sweet,
But rather let the *soul* be mine.

Source: Hanna family files, poetry notebook 1.

Emily E. Chubbuck to Adoniram Judson

Notes of My Early Life, Prepared Partly from Memory, and Partly from Letters and Papers. (for My Husband.)[15]

John Chubbuck was a native of Wales, though of English parentage. He emigrated to the American colonies somewhere about the year 1700. The vessel in which he sailed being wrecked off Nantucket, he landed and subsequently took up his permanent residence in that vicinity. His son Jonathan, born near Nantucket, was married to Hannah Marble, a worthy and pious woman, by whom he had several children. Among them was Simeon, my paternal grandfather. Simeon Chubbuck was born at Bridgewater, Massachusetts. At the breaking out of hostilities between England and her colonies, he, though only sixteen years of age, enlisted as a volunteer in the colonial army, and continued in the service until peace was restored, and the army disbanded. He afterward married Lydia Pratt, a

[15] Though Emily wrote this early history of her life for Adoniram Judson, we include it here for the background information it provides us about her childhood and adolescence. Originally it was thought that Emily might have written this before her marriage to Adoniram Judson, but she included in it the date of her brother Benjamin's death in September of 1846, which was while they were on the way to Burmah.

native of Bridgewater, by whom he had five sons and five daughters. Charles, the second son, was born at Bedford, New Hampshire, March 3, 1780.

James Richards, the father of my maternal grandfather, was a native of England, and a dissenter. His son Amos married Catharine McCartney, whose father was an Irishman, and her mother, Mary Bois, a French Huguenot. My maternal grandfather was also a boy-volunteer in the war of the Revolution, and a commissioned officer in the last war of the United States with England. Lavinia Richards, the eldest of the thirteen children of Amos and Catharine McCartney Richards, was born, June 1, 1785, at Goffstown, New Hampshire. She was piously educated by an excellent mother, and at an early age united with the Presbyterian church.

Charles Chubbuck and Lavinia Richards were married November 17, 1805, at Goffstown, New Hampshire. They subsequently removed to Eaton, Madison county, New York, where they arrived September 27, 1816. While on a visit preparatory to removal, my father gained a hope in Christ, and was baptized May 19, 1816, and my mother followed him in the same ordinance the ensuing November. They brought with them to New York four children.

Lavinia Richards Chubbuck was born at Bedford, New Hampshire, September 28, 1806, and died at Pratt's Hollow, New York, June 22, 1829, after a lingering illness of about five weeks. She evinced from childhood singular energy and strength of character, which qualities increased as trials thickened round her path, and through her last years of suffering[16] her activity and cheerfulness never failed. She was converted and baptized at the commencement of her illness, and from that time she daily grew in grace until the end of her life. Materials for a memoir (a journal, several poems,[17] letters, etc.) were placed in the hands of the Rev. Dr. Nathaniel Kendrick, who arranged them for the press, and left them at a publishing house, but they were never heard of afterward.

Benjamin Chubbuck was born at Bedford, New Hampshire, March 25, 1809. When about seven years of age he had an alarming attack of inflammation of the brain, from the effects of which he never fully recovered. His nervous system was permanently deranged, and some of the mental qualities entirely suspended, while others remained in full and healthful operation. He was on this account a source of constant anxiety up to the time of his death, which took place at the house of our mother's sister in Michigan, September 1, 1846. He left a wife and two children.

---

[16] A family letter from Charles Chubbuck written in May of 1827 to a relative stated that Lavinia "was almost gone with consumption."

[17] One of Lavinia Chubbuck's poems was included in the book, *Emily C. Judson: A Memorial*, by Walter N. Wyeth (15):

> Oft have I sat, in moonlit hours,
> Beside the brook where sweet wild-flowers
> Perfumed the evening air;
> Beside the alders, as to trace
> Soft mysteries on the water's face
> And I was free from care.

Harriet Chubbuck was born at Goffstown, New Hampshire, November 18, 1811, and died at Morrisville, New York, December 6, 1831. She was very beautiful in person, and fascinating in manners, and for a time was the pride of the family. After her conversion, less than a year previous to her death, her natural gaiety was to a great extent subdued; and so beloved had she rendered herself, that her death, which was sudden, threw a gloom over the whole community, and the funeral services were disturbed by sobbings from different parts of the house. Her mind was much exercised on the subject of missions; and she once told me, in strict confidence, that she had consecrated herself solemnly to this cause—had made a vow which nothing but death could break.

John Walker Chubbuck[18] was born September 24, 1815, at Goffstown, New Hampshire. He learned the business of printing at Morrisville, New York, and afterward conducted newspapers at Hamilton and Cazenovia. He removed to Milwaukee, Wisconsin Territory, in 1834, where he established, in connection with another man, a newspaper which has since been permanent. While residing there he was converted, and united with the Presbyterian church.

Sarah Catharine Chubbuck was born at Eaton, New York, October 25, 1816. She was baptized at Morrisville, April 1840.

William Wallace Chubbuck was born at Eaton, New York, January 1, 1824. He learned printing, but has devoted his life principally thus far to editing papers and to teaching.

I was the fifth child,[19] and the first born out of New England: I was born August 22, 1817, at Eaton, Madison county, New York. I was an exceedingly delicate child, and my mother was often warned that she could "have me with her but a short time." I remember being much petted and indulged during my first years (probably on account of the fragility of my constitution), and also being several times prostrated for a week or more after a day's visit with my little cousins. The first event of any importance which I remember is the conversion of my sister Lavinia, when I was about seven years of age. My little cot was in her room; and as she grew worse after her baptism, the young members of the church were in the habit of spending the night with her, partly in the character of watchers, partly because of a unity of interest and feeling. She and her visitors spent the greater part of the night in conversation and prayer, without any thought of disturbing so sound a sleeper as I seemed to be. I was a silent, sometimes tearful listener when they talked; and when they prayed, I used to kneel down in my bed, and with hands clasped and heart

---

[18] In later years, when he lived in Wisconsin, John Walker Chubbuck was identified as Jerome Walker Chubbuck. The Wisconsin Historical Society has a Jerome Walker Collection of Emily's letters to him, and the census of both 1870 and 1880 identifies him as Jerome Walker Chubbuck. We have no information as to this change of name. Here, Emily clearly identifies him as John.

[19] Though this is clearly what is written, Emily actually was the sixth of the Chubbuck children (following Lavinia, Benjamin, Harriet, John Walker, and Sarah Catharine.

uplifted, follow them through to the end. I can not [sic] recall my exercises with any degree of distinctness; but I remember longing to go to heaven, and be with Christ; some moments of ecstasy, and some of deep depression on account of my childish delinquencies. My sister used often to converse with me on religious subjects; and I remember on one occasion her going to the next room and saying to my mother, "That child's talk is wonderful! I believe, if there is a Christian in the world, she is one." For a moment I felt a deep thrill of joy, and then I became alarmed lest I should have deceived them. The effect was to make me reserved and cautious.

April, 1828. Removed with my parents to Pratt's Hollow, a small village, where there was a woolen factory, and immediately commenced work at splicing rolls. We were at this time very poor, and did not know on one day what we should eat the next, otherwise I should not have been placed at such hard work. My parents however, judiciously allowed me to spend half my wages (the whole was one dollar and twenty-five cents per week) as I thought proper; and in this way, with numerous incentives to economy, I first learned the use of money. My principal recollections during this summer are of noise and filth, bleeding hands and aching feet, and a very sad heart.

December, 1828. The ice stopped the water-wheel; and the factory was closed for a few months.

January, 1829. Entered the district school, and, I believe, acquitted myself to the satisfaction of everybody, my poor sick sister especially. She had taken great pains with my education while I was at work in the factory, though, as we worked twelve hours a day, and came home completely worn out with fatigue, I was not a very promising subject.

March, 1829. The factory reopened, and I left school and returned to my old employment.

May, 1829. It was some time in this month, but I do not recollect the day, that the carding-machine broke, and I had the afternoon to myself. I spent all my little stock of money in hiring a horse and wagon, and took poor Lavinia out driving. We spread a buffalo robe on a pretty, dry knoll, and father carried her to it in his arms. I shall never forget how happy she was, nor how Kate[20] and I almost buried her in violets and other wild spring flowers. It was the last time that she ever went out.

June 23, 1829. This was the day of poor Lavinia's death. They released me from the factory four days on this occasion, and O, how long they seemed to me! The first day she was in great agony, and I crept as much out of the way as I could, and scarcely moved. The next day she rallied, and took some notice of me; but the women (very many neighbors had come in) appeared just as busy and anxious as ever, and mother wept incessantly. Every thing appeared strange and unnatural

---

[20] Sarah Catharine Chubbuck, b. October 25, 1816.

about the house, and I thought it must be unpleasant for her. She kissed me, and told me I must be a good girl; but her voice sounded hollow, and her lips were cold. I longed to do something for her, and remembering her extreme fondness for flowers, I went to a neighbor's and begged an apron full of roses. When I returned the house was still as death. I entered the room; they were kneeling around her bed, and no one took any notice of me. In a moment, however, she beckoned to me with her finger, and when I put the flowers upon the bed she smiled. She tried again to turn her eye upon me, but it would not obey her will. She tried to speak, but her lips gave no sound. She lay quietly a few moments, then suddenly exclaimed, "Glory! Glory! My Father! Jesus!" and never breathed again. She was buried at Eaton, being a member of the church there.

August, 1829. My health failed very perceptibly after my sister's death, and at last mother called in a physician. He said that I could not live where I was, but must have my freedom and fresh air—a home on a farm, if possible.

1828–9. I believe there was not a decidedly vicious person in the factory, and there were several, both men and women, who were pious. Indeed, there was less courseness and vulgarity among them than would be supposed, though they were certainly far from being the society one would select for a child. The girls were, most of them, great novel readers, and they used to lend their novels to me, first exacting a promise that I would not tell my mother and sister. When I had finished one I used to carry out the story, and imagine my favorite character going on, on—but it always would end in death. Of what avail, then, was the beauty? Of what use the wealth and honor? At other times, while at my work, I used to make a heroine of myself. My Uncle Jonathan, (who was lost twenty years before on a voyage to India) would come home and make me an heiress; or my face, which people used sometimes to praise, would become so beautiful as to bewitch the whole world; or I should be a brilliant poetess (my verses were greatly admired by my brother and sisters), and my name would be famous while the world stood. But nothing satisfied me. Whatever I became, I should die and lose it all. Then common sense told me that these great things were unattainable, and I would moderate my plans, and confine my wishes within narrower limits. But all ended in the same way; death would come at the end, and then, what good?

One day I took up a little, dingy, coarse newspaper—the *Baptist Register* in its infancy—and my eye fell on the words: "Little Maria lies by the side of her fond mother." I had read about the missionaries, and my sister had told me respecting them; I knew, therefore, at once, that the letter was from Mr. Judson, and that his little daughter was dead.[21] How I pitied his loneliness! And then a new train of thought sprang up, and my mind expanded to a new kind of glory. No, thought I,

---

[21] Maria Judson had died in Burmah on April 24, 1827.

though the Burmans should kill him, I will not pity him; and I—yes, I will be a missionary. After this I had my romantic dreams of mission life; but they were of a different cast—of suffering, and toil, and pain; and though they, like the others, ended in death, somehow death in such an employment came pleasantly. I read the "Pilgrim's Progress," and thought of the golden city; then I read the Bible more, and novels less.

November, 1829. Removed to a farm in the vicinity of Morrisville; Walker entered a printing-office in the village; and Harriet[22] returned from Courtland county, where she had been spending half a year with some cousins. We suffered a great deal from cold this winter, though we had plenty of plain food. Indeed, we never were reduced to hunger. But the house was large and unfinished, and the snow sometimes drifted into it in heaps. We were unable to repair it, and the owner was unwilling. Father[23] was absent nearly all the time, distributing newspapers; and the severity of the winter so affected his health that he could do but little when he was at home. Mother, Harriet, and I, were frequently compelled to go out into the fields, and dig broken wood out of the snow, to keep ourselves from freezing. Catharine and I went to the district school as much as we could.

January, 1830. There was a revival of religion among the Methodists in the immediate neighborhood, and one evening, at a meeting, those who wished the prayers of Christians were requested to rise. It was something new to me, and I trembled so that I shook the seat, and attracted considerable attention. A girl next me whispered that I had better arise--she was sure she would if she felt as I did; and a class-leader came and took me by the hand, so that I succeeded in getting upon my feet. After this I attended all the class-meetings, and thought it a great favor to get talked with and prayed for.

February, 1830. A "three days' meeting" was commenced by the Baptist church in Morrisville, and we all attended. The revival among the Methodists had previously prepared our minds, and Harriet, especially, was deeply affected. This meeting was followed by a similar one in the Presbyterian church, not one hour of which was lost to Harriet and myself. A great many young persons were added to both churches, among the most joyful of whom was my sister Harriet. They baptized her, while I looked on almost broken-hearted. We joined two weekly bible-classes [sic] at the village (a mile distant), and attended all the meetings we could hear of, walking when father was away. When he was at home, though ever so much fatigued and ill, he was too happy to see us interested in religious things not to go with us. I recollect feeling myself very heart-heavy, because the revival had passed without my being converted. I grew mopish and absent-minded, but

---

[22] Harriet Chubbuck, b. November 18, 1811, Goffstown NH.
[23] Charles Chubbuck, b. March 3, 1780, Bedford NH.

still I did not relax my efforts. Indeed, I believe my solemn little face was almost ludicrously familiar to worshipers of every denomination, for I remember a Presbyterian once saying to me, as I was leaving the chapel, after having, as usual, asked prayers: What! this little girl not converted yet! How do you suppose we can waste any more time in praying for you?"

March, 1830. Benjamin came home (he had been for five years in the employ of a farmer), and he and father commenced building fences and other spring work. Our house had always, especially after Lavinia's conversion, been the resort of very pious people, and a favorite home for Hamilton[24] students. We had now a large house, and they made it a place of frequent resort. I remember several whose society was very improving. We were also well supplied with choice books, a luxury which, even in our deepest poverty, we never denied ourselves. For we had been taught from our cradles to consider knowledge, next after religion, the most desirable thing, and were never allowed to associate with ignorant and vulgar children.

April, 1830. Commenced taking lessons in rhetoric and natural philosophy of Miss L.W.F. C.F. also volunteered to train me in English composition, but she proved a dangerous teacher. She had read novels till her head was nearly turned, and had, moreover, imbibed infidel sentiments from a young man of better mind than morals, with whom she was too well pleased. She was, however, supposed to be a safe companion, and as my health was the principal thing that brought us to the farm, I was allowed to spend as much time with her as I pleased. She introduced me to Gibbon, and Hume, and Tom Paine; but more especially to Voltaire and Rousseau, whose style pleased her better.[25] She read the French writers in the originals, though she had access to translations. She was very insinuating, and I not only loved her most sincerely, but really believed her one of the wisest persons in the world. I did not embrace her sentiments, however, though I felt my confidence in the Bible weakened, and lost, to a great extent, my religious impressions. Still I was constant in my attendance upon divine worship, remained a member both of the Bible-class and Sabbath-school, and, I think, never neglected secret prayer. C. F. was a great admirer of the misanthropic school of poetry; Byron, especially, she was always repeating, and used actually to rave over his Manfred. When she mounted her stilts I always trembled, for though fond of being with her, I still feared for her. She was seven or eight years older than I.

November, 1830. Father's attempt at farming proved as might have been expected, an entire failure, and for want of a better place, he determined to remove to the village. He took a little old house on the outskirts, the poorest shelter we ever had, with only two rooms on the floor, and a loft, to which we

---

[24] Hamilton College, later to become Madison College and then Colgate University.

[25] Emily would have been several months shy of thirteen years of age. These books would have been an impressive challenge to her.

ascended by means of a ladder. We were not discouraged, however, but managed to make the house a little genteel, as well as tidy. Harriet and I used a turn-up bedstead, surrounded by pretty chintz curtains, and we made a parlor and dining-room of the room by day. Harriet had a knack at twisting ribbons and fitting dresses, and she took in sewing; Catharine and Wallace went to school; and I got constant employment of a little Scotch weaver and thread-maker, at twisting thread. Benjamin returned to his old place, and Walker was still in the printing-office.

April, 1831. A new academy had been erected in the village, and it now opened with about a hundred pupils. I was one of the first to attend. As soon as I came home at night, I used to sit down to sew with Harriet; and it was a rule never to lay the work aside, until, according to our estimation, I had earned enough to clear the expenses of the day-tuition, clothing, food, etc. I have since thought that I was any thing but a help to my poor sister, as she always gave me the lightest and easiest work.

June, 1831. Were surprised by a visit from a maiden sister of my mother, an elegant, dashing, gaily-dressed woman, who contrasted oddly enough with our homely house and furniture. Harriet and I estimated that the clothing and jewelry she carried in her two great trunks would purchase us as handsome a house as we wished. She was quite surprised to find us in such humble circumstances, and wondered that we could be so happy. She told me a great deal of my mother as she was in former days, and frequently wept at the contrast.

August, 1831. The first term of school closed, and I lost no time in going into the employ of the thread-maker. While standing alone in his house, turning my little crank all day, I had much time for reflection, and I now began to think more of the books C. F. had taught me to read. If I was to be a missionary, which vocation I had never lost sight of, I must understand how to refute all those infidel arguments, and I now set about it with great earnestness. When I was puzzled with any thing, I used to go to Harriet, or father, or some of our visitors; and sometimes I startled them with my questions, which showed any thing but an orthodox train of thought. I knew they were a little alarmed, but as I was constant in attending the meetings, and had begged to be admitted into the more advanced Bible-class, as well as that of the youth, they were somewhat appeased. About this time, Walker purchased a share in a town library, and gave me the privilege of drawing one book a week. The first thing I drew (for the library was a heterogeneous mass) was Paine's "Age of Reason." This I pored over carefully, then took some notes, and returned the book without any of the family's knowing that it had been in my possession. Father, however, discovered my notes, and I remember that he looked pale, and his hand trembled, when he showed them to me, though I afterward partly succeeded in reassuring him.[26]

October, 1831. My parents concluded it would be impossible to spend the winter where we were without suffering, and so we removed to a nice house, in a pleasant part of the village, with the intention of taking academy boarders.

November, 1831. Aunt Jane, who left our house in June to visit another sister in Michigan, returned, and again spent a week with us. When she left for her home in New Hampshire, father and mother accompanied her about eighty miles, to visit a common friend. They had been gone only two or three days, when Harriet remarked to me, one morning, "I am afraid I am going to be ill; I never felt so strangely in my life." As she spoke, I observed that her eye glared wildly and her cheeks were crimson. I took her hand, and it felt like fire. She snatched it away, laughing, and said, "Now don't be alarmed, child; there is nothing the matter;" and then she went on talking in a strain perfectly delirious. I was alone in the house, and dared not leave her to call for help; and for a few moments I was almost stunned with terror. At last I succeeded in inducing her to put her feet into warm water, and drink some bitter herb tea; but before I got her into the bed I was immensely relieved by a call from her most intimate friend, M. G. I immediately ran for the physician, who pronounced it a case of violent inflammatory fever. By the time my parents returned the fever had taken the typhoid form, but after a time it abated, and reasonable hopes were entertained of her recovery. She was thin, but her fine face was never before so spiritually beautiful, and she conversed most brilliantly, using the choicest language, and overflowing with poetical conceptions.

December 6. Two or three days previous to this, the doctor had pronounced poor Harriet on the verge of the grave from pulmonary consumption; and now we all knew that she was dying. Her reason was disturbed by the disease, though occasionally she would rally and speak a rational word. M. G. had never left her side from the morning when she called so opportunely, and now Harriet exhorted her, in the most glowing language, to remain steadfast and meet her in heaven. She bade us all farewell separately, but although her words breathed of hope and trust, and she seemed full of Christ and heaven, she expressed herself, during most of the time, incoherently. At first she was in great agony, but gradually her sufferings abated, till we scarcely knew when she ceased to breathe. Her funeral sermon was preached from a text chosen by herself—Eccles. xii. 1.[27]

January, 1832. We could not enjoy the privilege of quiet mourning, for a great number of boarders, came in upon us; so we took a maid, and I went to school. On Monday morning I used to arise at two o'clock, and do the washing for the family and boarders before nine; on Thursday evening I did the ironing; and Saturday,

---

[26] Reading this we are aware that Emily was never one to simply accept things. She had a questioning mind and she was unafraid to express these questions to those she thought might be able to teach her.

[27] "Remember now thy Creator in the days of they youth, while the evil days come not, nor the years draw nigh, when thou shall say, I have no pleasure in them." (KJV)

because there was but half a day of school, we made baking day. In this way, by Katy's[28] help, we managed to get on with only one servant. I also took sewing of a mantua-maker close by, and so contrived to make good the time consumed in school. My class-mates had spent all their lives in school, and they now had plenty of leisure for study. They were also, all but one, older than myself, and I therefore found it a difficult task to keep up with them without robbing my sleeping hours. I seldom got any rest till one or two o'clock, and then I read French and solved mathematical problems in my sleep.

March, 1832. My health again failed under my accumulated labors, and the physician was consulted. He said study disagreed with me, and I must leave school.

April 1, 1832. Mother insisted on my giving up my studies, and hinted that I might make millinery a very lucrative business. I had considered it all very well to work in the factory, twist thread, and take in a little sewing now and then, as a means of help for the time being, because I could stop when I pleased. But to devote my life to making bonnets was not in accordance with my plans, and I rebelled most decidedly. "But what do you intend to do?" asked my mother; "here you are almost fifteen, and you can not go to school always." That was true enough, and I went away to *think*. At length I proposed attending school one year more, and preparing to be a teacher. But our boarders had proved less profitable than we anticipated; father had been underbid, and so lost one mail route; and then another year in school might kill me. I must think of something else.

April 5, 1832. Mother spoke to Miss B. about taking me into her shop, and as I was already expert with the needle, she was able to make very good terms. I cried all night.

April 6. Went to Mr. B—, my Academy teacher, and after some awkward hesitation, ventured to ask if he thought me capable of teaching school. "Yes," said he, "but you are not half big enough." He, however, gave me a recommendation, and promised to keep the matter secret.

April 7. Told mother I wanted to make the F-k's a visit, which she was pleased to hear, as they lived on a farm, and she thought a little change would do me good.

April 8. Father carried me to the F-k's before breakfast, a drive of about two miles. As soon as he had left me, I inquired if their school was engaged. It was; but the J. district had not yet obtained a teacher, they thought. I took a short cut [sic] across the lots, and soon stood trembling in the presence of Mr. J. He was a raw-boned, red-headed, sharp-looking man, in cow-hide shoes, and red flannel shirt. "Is your school engaged?" I timidly inquired. He turned his keen gray eye upon me, measuring me deliberately from head to foot, while I stood as tall as possible. I saw at once that it was not engaged, and that I stood a very poor chance of getting it.

---

[28] Sarah Catharine Chubbuck.

He asked several questions; whistled when I told him my age; said the school was a very difficult one, and finally promised to consult the other trustees and let me know in a week or two. I saw what it all meant, and went away mortified and heavy hearted. As soon as I gained the woods, I sat down and sobbed outright. This relieved me, and after a little while I stood upon my feet again, with dry eyes, and a tolerably courageous heart. I went back, though with great shame-facedness, to Mr. J., and inquired the way across the woods to Mr. F.'s, which I reached soon after sunset. Here I found my old friend, C. F., and others of the family, very glad to welcome me; and without stating my errand, I went to bed, too tired and anxious to be companionable.

April 9. Told C. F. my errand, and she at once volunteered to go to the trustees with me and do what she could in my behalf. When we arrived at Mr. D.'s, she spoke of the Morrisville Academy, inquired if they knew the principal, Mr. B-, and then presented my recommendation, which I had not ventured to show the day before. Mr. D. was pleased, said he had heard of me, and did not know of anyone whom he should like so well for a teacher. He hoped his colleagues had engaged no one, but did not know, as Mr. B. was the acting trustee. To Mr. B.'s we went, a frank, happy-looking young farmer, with a troop of children about him, and made known our errand. "Why, the scholars will be bigger than their teacher," was his first remark. "Here, An't, stand up by the schoolma'am, and see which is the tallest; An't is the blackest, at any rate," he added, laughing. He would not make any definite engagement with me, but said I stood as fair a chance as anybody, and he would come to the village next week and settle the matter. You have got it," said C., as soon as we were out of the house. I was not so sanguine, but I was too far from home to think of going further, and so I had nothing to do but to wait.

April 10. Left the F.'s, and without seeing the F-k's again, walked home, a distance of three miles and a half.

April 14. Mr. B. made his appearance, and announced to mother (much to her surprise and a little to her embarrassment), that he had come to engage her daughter to teach school. We were told that they never paid over six shillings (seventy-five cents) a week, besides boarding; and though I could earn as much with the milliner, and far more at twisting thread, we were all very happy in the arrangement. Mother had intended putting me with Miss B. only for want of something better, and now she was highly pleased, particularly with the ability I had shown to help myself.

May. On the first Monday in May father took me in his wagon to Nelson Corners. The school-house was a little brown building on the corner, all newly cleaned, and in good repair. About twenty children came, some clean, some pretty, some ugly, and all shy and noisy. I got through the day tolerably well, and after school went to Mr. B.'s. I was to "board round," and so took my first week with the leading trustee.

The first evening at Mr. B.'s passed off tolerably well; but I was very timid, and not very fond of visiting, and I had neglected to provide myself with either work or books. The B.'s were not a reading people; their whole library comprised only a Bible and Methodist hymn book, and there was not a newspaper about the house. I had been trained in habits of the severest industry, and before the end of the week was completely miserable. I had no congenial society, nothing to do, and I had intended, when I left home, to be absent six weeks. I was downright home-sick, and after the third day could neither eat nor sleep. On Saturday I closed my school at noon, and without taking leave of the B.'s, hurried away over the hills to Morrisville. I think there was no happier being on earth than I when I bounded into the old dining-room; and I wept and laughed together all the evening. On Monday morning father carried me back in his wagon, and after that he came for me regularly every Saturday night, and left me at the schoolhouse Monday morning.

August, 1832. Closed my school and returned home. I had been much less industrious this summer than during any three months of my life heretofore; had not been very conscientious in the discharge of religious duties, and began to like attention and praise. I had been partly under the influence of C. F., and there were two other families of gay young people with whom I had been on terms of intimacy. I was happy, however, to be at home again, and none of the family seemed to remark any change in me.

November, 1832. Entered the Academy again, sewing out of school hours as before. I began to think more of my personal appearance, and of intercourse with my fellow-students; hence I advanced less rapidly in my studies than formerly, though I still made very respectable proficiency.

January, 1833. A dancing-school was set up in the village, and I became very anxious to attend. Walker volunteered to break the matter to my father and mother, and solicit their permission for me; but without success. They maintained that dancing was in no way essential to the most accomplished education; and that this step, if not the first in a course of ruin, would, in all probability, exert a determining and permanent influence on my character and habits. I could not understand their reasoning, and I had set my heart on attending the school, not because I cared in the least for dancing, but because the other village girls went, and I wanted to be like them. I believed what I had often heard and read about the usefulness of this accomplishment, and I knew that pleasing personal presence, and elegance of manner were valuable to a woman; I therefore used all my powers of persuasion, and harped upon the subject so continually, that father lost all patience, and commanded me never to allude to it again in his presence. I now considered myself very ill-used, and thought that my father's obstinacy stood directly in the way of my advancement. Fixing my eye on a single point, and thinking of nothing else, I behaved with more foolishness than would have been believed possible. I told mother that I thought I had better get a boarding-place in the village; for, as I had my own fortune to look after, I ought to be allowed to follow my own plans. She was exceedingly distressed, and said she would much rather have me attend the dancing school than do so wild a thing. I suppose she talked with father; for he came to my room one evening, and said he thought he had been unwise in laying his commands upon me. He spoke most feelingly of having been able to do so little for his children, and of his strong desire to see them virtuous and respected; and said I would one day learn that the village girls whom I wished to imitate were by no means the lady-like models that I supposed. He then removed every obstacle to my attending the dancing-school, and said that though he and my mother disapproved of it in their hearts, I should be subjected to no annoyance. I said but little, though I inwardly resolved that I would *never* learn to dance, and never, while I lived, grieve my father and mother again. I think I have kept both of these resolutions—the first certainly.

Source: A. C. Kendrick, *The Life and Letters of Mrs. Emily C. Judson*, 12–32.

Emily E. Chubbuck, April 1831[29]

Written on the day I left school.[30]

'Tis done! I leave my school today,
This much lov'd spot and go away,
Alas! I know not where!
I go to search a heartless world,
Where Vi[ ]he's banner is unfurled,
Where all is pain and care.
Farewell, farewell then happy home,
I'll recollect thee when I roam,
Far from this much loved spot,
The friends I loved in early youth,
Should they but prove my friends in truth,
Shall never be forgot.

Source: Hanna family files, poetry notebook 1.

[29] In her diary, Emily E. Chubbuck had written: "April, 1831. A new academy had been erected in the village, and it now opened with about a hundred pupils. I was one of the first to attend. As soon as I came home at night, I used to sit down to sew with Harriet; and it was a rule never to lay the work aside, until, according to our estimation, I had earned enough to clear the expenses of the day—tuition, clothing, food, etc. I have since thought that I was any thing but a help to my poor sister, and she always gave me the lightest and easiest work" (A. C. Kendrick, *The Life and Letters of Mrs. Emily C. Judson* (New York: Sheldon and Company, 1831) 23.

[30] Dated April 1831, this work is the third of six poems Emily copied into a notebook.

Emily E. Chubbuck, 1833[31]

The Salem Murder[32]

It is a lovely evening, and the stars,
Look down from their blue vaults and sweetly smile,
As if the earth a spot celestial was.
The moon, now crescent, sails majestic through
The azure vault of heaven while breezes cool,
Come bearing on their wings the rich perfumes
From lilach [sic] blossoms, and from rosy bowers,
And all the fragrant flowers, which this part[ ]
So beautifully adorn.
But what is that rustling the silken leaves,
That quietly and peaceful lay but now,
As if beneath so fair a covering,
Some secret danger lurk'd?
There! there he comes, with stealthy cautious step,
His eyes look wild;—there now! they deadly gleam,
As if some demon power possess'd his soul.
And now he casts them anxiously around—
Sure guilt is in that wile and hurried glance!
The polished blade he holds within his hand,
Tells of the horrid deed he contemplates;
The power within, that [ ] him to perform
This hellish deed, sits on his countenance,
As demons laugh, when fear and malice join.
Now see him slowly lift the lattice, where,
His victim lies, wrapt in the arms of sleep,
And see him start, then crouch like panther wild
And steal along to seize upon his prey.

Eternal God! Ye Power Omnipotent!
If there is mercy at thy holy throne,
If Heaven ever pitying looks on erring man,
Preserve, preserve his life! My prayer is vain!
I see the weapon flashing o'er his head—
'Tis plung'd into his aged bosom now—
A groan! A fainter sigh now snaps life's chords.
One long, last, deadly groan, and all is o'er!—

Source: Hanna family files, poetry notebook 1.

[31] This sixth of the six poems copied into a notebook is undated, though likely from 1833. The rest of the notebook was written between 1826 and 1831 but this poem seems to be from a more mature hand.

[32] This work of unknown date is the last of six poems Emily copied into a notebook.

Dr. William Dean[33] to Dr. A. C. Kendrick, Spring 1834[34]

You are quite welcome to my memories of Emily Chubbuck, so far as I am able to record them. Soon after I rose to the dignity of school-teaching, and "boarded round," I was employed in her father's district for the winter of 1827, and was often in her father's family, and saw much of the timid little pale-faced Emily, both in the family and in the school-room. She ever appeared dutiful to her parents, cheerful in her home duties, and diligent and successful in getting her lessons. I recollect to have been especially interested in finding one of her slender frame and sensitive temperament so successful in arithmetic. Accuracy characterized all her lessons, and propriety all her deportment.

In the spring of 1834, before leaving the country, I had occasion to baptize some dozen or fifteen young persons in my native town, and Emily Chubbuck was among the number. In conversation, during her serious impressions, she was not communicative, but in answer to questions gave clear views of sin, and her sole trust in the atoning sacrifice of Christ for salvation. In relating her Christian experience before the church, she discovered her accustomed coy manner, but gave satisfactory proof that she had been renewed by the spirit of God.

Not long before this event she had witnessed the death-bed triumphs of an older sister, who had in her person presented a lovely example of piety.[35] This sister had cherished a warm sympathy for a suffering world, and expressed a desire to go in person to teach the heathen.

Source: A. C. Kendrick, *The Life and Letters of Mrs. Emily C. Judson*, 37–38.

---

[33] William Dean had been born in Morrisville NY, and in 1827, had taught in that area. He was active within the community, and the Chubbuck family was well known to him. Appointed to the mission field September 17, 1832, he was ordained in Hamilton NY in June 1833, and while waiting to be sent, he served the local Morrisville church where he baptized seventeen-year-old Emily Chubbuck. Dean departed for Bangkok, Siam, on July 2, 1834.

Dean resumed correspondence with Emily after her marriage to Adoniram Judson and her appointment to Burmah. There is considerable evidence that, in the time after Judson's death, Dean had an interest in marrying Emily himself. For more information on Dean and his relationship with Emily Chubbuck Judson, see the biographical notes on him in the "Cast of Characters" in volume 1.

[34] This letter has been placed by the approximate date of Emily E. Chubbuck's baptism, and not by the date the letter was actually written, which is probably several years after Emily's death in 1854, when Kendrick was gathering materials for his memoir of her. Because Emily, writing as Fanny Forester, had been considered a secular writer, there was considerable public comment, and even opposition, within the church to her marriage to the venerable Dr. Judson. Certainly her religious credentials as expressed here, and a record of her baptism, would have been of great interest for such a memoir.

[35] Emily's sister, Lavinia, had died on June 22, 1829. Her sister, Harriet, had died on December 6, 1831. This reference seems to be to Harriet's death.

Emily E. Chubbuck to Marie Dawson,[36] May 2, 1834[37]

Perhaps you have heard that I have learned, as I trust, to love my God. O would that I could have your company! Would that you, too, could know the peace there is in believing! Would that you would engage in this glorious cause in which my every feeling is enlisted, and for the promotion of which my every future effort, I *hope*, will be made. I have loved you, Maria,[38] as I never loved another human being who was not bound to me by the ties of relationship, and I shall never cease to love you till "the silver cord be loosed, and the golden bowl broken." But the purpose of my life is changed. Hitherto I have lived for myself, and now I mean to live for God.

Source: A. C. Kendrick, *The Life and Letters of Mrs. Emily C. Judson*, 36–37.

Emily E. Chubbuck, July 4, 1834[39]

Parting Ode

Farewell.—
The parting sunlight sits
On hill and tree;
The zephyr, as it flits,
Lisps "Liberty,"
With gentle swell.

Farewell.—
May the rich robe of peace
Enfold us o'er;
May plenty's golden fleece
Find every door;
Health with us dwell.

Farewell.—
The Father's blessing rest
Upon us all;
Love's voice, in every breast,
To labor call,
Our duty tell.

Farewell.—
It is the hour to part;
And circling round,

---

[36] Marie Dawson was one of Emily's childhood friends. In October 1839, she became Marie Dawson Bates. We have ten letters from Marie to Emily, written between 1839 and 1846. In them there are many references to visit invitations and reflections on the actual visits.

[37] This letter was written when Emily Chubbuck was seventeen years old; it was a time in her life when she was experiencing a personal religious awakening. It coincided with her baptism by William Dean at the Baptist church in Morrisville NY. Her membership remained in that church until an unknown time in 1844, when, as she said in a May 6, 1846 letter to Anna Maria Anable, she "removed to Bethel." Dr. Dean reflected on that time and his perception of Emily's "renewable by the spirit of God" in the letter prior to this in the correspondence. Because of Adoniram Judson's missionary fame, and because Emily was seen as a writer of more secular, though popular, literature, Emily's religious credentials were of enormous importance to the church and to American Baptist Missionary Union, that she might be seen as a worthy and suitable companion for the venerable Dr. Judson.

[38] A. C. Kendrick, in *The Life and Times of Mrs. Emily C. Judson*, always referred to Marie as "Maria."

[39] Emily noted when this was published in *An Olio of Domestic Verses*, that it was "sung at a 'celebration,' July 4, 1834."

As by angelic art,
Echoes the sound,
Farewell—farewell!

Farewell.—
Till we shall join the choirs
Of saints above;
And tune our golden lyres,
To thoughts of love.
Farewell—farewell!

Source: Emily Judson, *An Olio of Domestic Verse*, 55–56.

Emily E. Chubbuck, November 1834[40]

Thanksgiving

Hail, cheering day! but let us bring
A richer, purer offering
Than mirthfulness unmeaning;
In gratitude to Heaven raise
The word of thanks, the note of praise,
For blessings we are gleaning.

Thanks for the basket and the store,
With harvest wealth still flowing o'er;
Thanks for the roof's protection;
Thanks for the friends that 'neath it dwell,
And thanks that love's unchanging spell
So hallows the connection.

Thanks, thanks for all that time has wrought,
Howe'er with grief or pleasure fraught;—
'Twas Heaven, our footsteps guiding,
That gave the smile, that woke the sigh,
Or broke the too-endearing tie,
For pleasures more abiding.

Thanks that the last departed year
Pealed not its requiem o'er our bier;
Thanks for this morning given;
And pray that God, whose eye of love,

[40] Emily Judson, in ordering her poetry in *An Olio of Domestic Verses*, says that she placed them in sequence as written, to the best of her ability. In that publication, "Thanksgiving" immediately followed "Parting Ode," written for July 4, 1834. This gives us reason to place this Thanksgiving poem in November of that same year.

Beams ever on us from above,
May guide our steps to heaven.

Source: Emily Judson, *An Olio of Domestic Verse*, 57–58.

Emily E. Chubbuck, July 1835[41]

The Spirit Voice

'Tis June—'tis gladsome, gorgeous June,
The rich, warm flush of summer noon
Rests on the golden hills;
And far and wide a Spirit Voice
Rings out, "Young heart, rejoice! rejoice!"

But all this glow will soon be passed,
And silvery mists their mantles cast
Wide o'er the flushing fields ;
Then will the sorrowing Spirit sigh,
"'Tis sweet with autumn flowers to die."

When Nature wears her icy shroud,
And winds are piping long and loud,
Adown the rugged plain,
The Spirit Voice shall softly call,
But on my ear no whisper fall.

I love the warm, wet summer sky,
When gems on every flower-bud lie,
Nor dread the autumn pale;
But know, ere winter, I shall be,
Where fresh flowers bloom eternally.

Source: Emily Judson, *An Olio of Domestic Verse*, 67–68.

[41] When she published this poem in *An Olio of Domestic Verses*, Emily Judson noted that it had been "Written in Illness." She also noted the date as "July, 1835," even though the first line of the poem says "'Tis June."

[42] At this time Emily was teaching at a school in Brookfield.

[43] See the poem "Stanzas" dated August 7, 1838, which Emily wrote about her brother Walker and his absence from their family life. In the last stanza she wrote:

> Then come to us. 'tis but a little hour
> That we may spend in this dark world of woe;
> Let us together cling—a sister's dower
> Is but her brother's heart—and thine, we know,
> Is all our own—then why, why dost thou roam?
> We wait thee, deeming thou wilt soon *come home*.

Emily E. Chubbuck to J. Walker Chubbuck, October 18, 1837—Morrisville

Very dear brother,

Little did I think when we parted last winter that I should not see you again for so long—perhaps never on earth. I have but just now returned from Brookfield[42] and you cannot think how I miss you, how lonesome I am without a brother,[43] for I suppose you know B.[44] is married and Wallace[45] has gone to work in the office and boards with James.

Joseph is here but I scarce dare speak to him since the whole village are angry with us for helping him. Poor Jose—he sees trouble plenty. Do you recollect the letter that was found in the street last winter and that I told you I believed H. Bicknell's wife wrote him. Well I shall probably be telling you no news when I tell you that my surmise was correct. Some time in the fore part of summer Harrison found in Joseph's trunk a packet of letters all written by Sarah and by what I can learn and even Joseph's own confession very, very improper. He took those out into the woods and with Nat Palmer at his elbow read them. He then returned to the house and showed them to Sarah. *He* says she immediately showed some of her old symptoms of derangement and declared if he did not give them to her she would kill herself before night. Thus threatened he gave them up and she burnt them. Harrison saw Joseph and promised if he would leave the place all should be kept secret and relying in this promise he went. Soon after Sarah took a journey for her health and seeing Joseph at the cars endeavored to persuade him to return. At the same time he received a letter from Norton requesting him to return and one from Harrison allowing him the privilege and promising that all would be forgotten. He came and his return was signal to awaken all the demon in the Bicknell tribe. You would have thought the furies were let loose.

He received frequent intimations that plans were being laid against his liberty and many even trembled for his life. Even now he dare not appear alone after dark. They have tried to get Norton to dismiss him but he has engaged with him until Spring and Joseph *will not go*. He thinks it would be equivalent to a confession of guilt. He acknowledges that they have been foolish and imprudent but not criminal. They have written to the old Major and he is not expected soon. They say their [sic] will be a "blow up" then. Poor Sarah is treated with the utmost rigor. One day in particular Harrison fastened her in the chamber and came to the village. She tore up several boards, but finding she could not free herself in that way she let herself down from the window by means of blankets. She has sometimes remained in the woods all night afraid to go home.—But enough of this. It sickens me to think of it.

I expect sister Ann[46] will be here tomorrow, she is a good little sister. I wish *you* had so good a wife. They are not preparing to remove to Hamilton. The stage now

---

[44] Emily's older brother Benjamin or "Ben," was born March 25, 1809. In the personal biography she wrote for Adoniram Judson, Emily wrote that as a young boy, Ben sustained some kind of brain inflammation, which seemed to seriously impair his judgment and behavior. See Emily's letter of February 18, 1838, for some very sharp comments on Ben. Then, on April 2, 1839, Emily wrote to her brother Walker that Ben had been sent to state prison for stealing a horse, blanket, and saddle. Later correspondence had litanies of such problems—stealing a cow, difficulties holding jobs, problems with his marriage, situations exacerbated by character flaws. He died in September, 1846, shortly after Emily left for Burmah.

[45] William Wallace Chubbuck, Emily's younger brother, born January 1, 1824.

[46] Ann was the wife of Benjamin Chubbuck.

runs from Chittenango to [Note: "Brookfield" is written and crossed out.] Hamilton every day except Sunday. Pa has got the mail on the Brookfield rout which "old loon" bid off and I expect we shall remove to Hamilton next spring so that he can carry it himself.

We do not receive your papers at all regularly.[47] Do you send them? The village papers have been sent to you every week but for fear you have not seen all the weddings I will tell you of a few. Palmer Hall and Luretta Lewis: Seymour Curtiss and I've forgot who: Westley Hickcox and Clarindas Story ("O dear!" say you): Alden Dean and Lucitta Cole: Wm Stilwell and Mary Ann Blaksler: Mr. Babbot and Sarah Gaston: Mary Gates, Caroline Sumner, and to put on the climax Elhanah Peckard. We also heard that Otis P. Esq. was married on Monday, but I presume it is not so. However it will be the next news.

Mary Stilwell will be married in a few weeks. I shall be at the wedding—Catharine[48] had been keeping company with Harvey Roger and people generally approved it would make a match but she has ship'd him now.

I don't know what to do Walker. I wish you would write and tell me. Shall I take a school this winter or go to Hamilton board with Ben and go to school (sic) and then come out to you in the spring? Could I obtain an advantageous situation there? I should like, well, to go provided I could have good company on the journey and a good situation near you. I wish you were married and then I could depend on your remaining in one place but now you are such a wild bird I don't know as I should dare trust myself with you. Be sure you write as soon as you conclude what I better do. By spring I should be prepared to teach beside Geography, Grammar and Arithmetic: History, Natural philosophy, Chemistry, Botany, Rhetoric, Logic, Moral and Intellectual philosophy, Astronomy, French, drawing and painting. Write and tell me how profitable a school would be, whether the place is healthy, the state of society, the cost of the journey and the best mode of getting there.

O you can't imagine what bad dreams I have had about you. They almost made me superstitious. Are you really doing well? Are you steady? How often do you attend church? Do you enjoy good health? Are you bless'd with your situation? Answer these and as many more as you suppose I would be glad to ask.

---

[47] John Walker Chubbuck, Emily's older brother who ran a newspaper in the Wisconsin Territory.

[48] Sarah Catharine ("Kate," "Kit," or "Kitty") Chubbuck, Emily's older sister by ten months. Outside of the two terms at the Utica Female Academy that Emily arranged for her, Catharine always lived with her parents in Hamilton NY. The letters indicate opportunities for marriage, but Catharine remained single. She later helped care for Henry and Edward Judson when, after their return from Burmah in fall 1851, they moved in with their "aunt" and "grandparents." Her nephews remembered her as "a dear friend." In this paragraph, we find one of the references to Catharine being, or having been, in a "relationship."

Pa[49] labours [sic] like a slave but his health is quite good considering etc. I do not see as Ma[50] is much different from usual. The rest of the family are well. My health never was better—no, nor so good since I can remember.—*Marion Munger says she would "give a dollar to see Walker."* Don't blame her, I'd give two. And kisses more than she would dare. Good night.

Emily E. Chubbuck

Written along the left margin of page 1: "I was half angry with you for not writing or even mentioning my name when you wrote to Pa, but I concluded it would [ ] good without I told you so I concluded to write and tell you of it. Write me soon and tell me all about the pretty girls and smart beaus of the 'Far West.'"

Written along the left margin of page 2: "They are about getting up an exhibition here. I don't know any thing about it but judging from the committee of arrangements, vis. Henry Bicknell, Scott Sloan, and Edward Norton, it will be a wonder.—E"

Written along the left margin of page 3: "Taylor is gone and Wm Farwell teaches in the Academy. Taylor won't pay for that bass-viol. Rascal! Is there an Academy in your town? If so secure me a place in it."

Source: Jerome Walker Chubbuck Collection, Wisconsin Historical Society Archives, Madison, WI.

Emily E. Chubbuck to J. Walker Chubbuck, February 18, 1838—Syracuse[51]

Very dear Brother,

I know not that you care to hear from us as you have not answered our numerous letters but when I was home last Pa[52] advised me to try once again and have you direct to me here. I am now on the second term of my school but as it is not very healthy here I think I shall teach in Hamilton next summer.

Our folks are in trouble I can assure you. You know the business they went into last summer. It has just about ruin'd them. Pa moved to Hamilton about three months scince [sic] and I rather think he is pretty dog'd by creditors. Dwight Williams sued him and took away his best coach last fall and sold it for 75 dollars.

---

[49] Emily's father, Charles Chubbuck, was born at Bedford NH on March 3, 1780; he married Lavinia Richards in Goffstown NH on November 17, 1805, and together they had seven children. Though he held varying jobs over the years, Charles failed at many of them. Emily became a main financial support for the family, purchasing a home for them in fall 1842.

[50] Lavinia Richards Chubbuck, Emily's mother, was born June 1, 1875, in Goffstown NH, the eldest of thirteen children. She married Charles Chubbuck on November 17. 1805. They were the parents of seven children.

[51] Emily Chubbuck was teaching in a school in Syracuse at this time.

[52] Charles Chubbuck, Emily's father. Though he held varying positions over the years, he failed at most of them. With the purchase of the house for them, Emily was to continue as a significant financial contributor to the support of the family.

It was worth 250. A horse had his leg broke not long since and Ben[53] has broke more coaches than he will ever be worth while the world stands. But this is the easiest to bear. *Ben has got to be a poor worthless, drinking fellow not to be trusted with anything and his wife is a crazy extravagant ill-natured simpleton. They are nothing but torments to their friends on both sides. She knows he drinks and yet she will do her best apparently to lead him into temptation. All she appears to care for is balls and the lowest of all company.*[54] You know Catharine is not very proud and apt while she lived in Hamilton she mortified her dreadfully. You know Pa and him[sic] were in company. That was broken up a little while ago and Ben seem'd to consider it very hard indeed after Pa had lost all he had in his account that he could not still hang on his hands and prevent his doing any thing to retrieve the past. I can't but pity *Ben his* wife makes him much worse. Take warning and beware of the girls. They are *all deceitful.* For my part—I have made up my mind to be an old maid for I can take care of myself quite well and I don't know as I could take care of two. If you will form the same resolution and come home I will keep house for you.

By the by I am doing pretty well and never enjoy'd the world better in my life. I have obtained a footing in the highest circles of society which astonishes Ruth and Lucy very much. To tell the truth I was somewhat astonished myself to find my society so much courted by those who were so much my superiors but I have lately discovered the mighty secret. I have written of late for several publications over the signature of E. E. C.[55] People were quite curious to find out who it was and the Editor of the "Whig" at last bribed a little boy who carried my communications to the office and he betray'd me. People at once believed because the letters were my initials and so I got to be an "authoress" before I was aware of it.

You can't think how I do want to see you. I have dream'd of you now three nights in succession. Isn't that a sign you are coming? Now for once obey me. Go this instant and find a paper of some kind in the P. O. I don't care if it is as old as Methuselah and send it to me then write as quick as you finish this and make a pen. I have got a most excellent compliment for you and from *a handsome lady*, too, but you sha'n't have it until you write and ask for it.

They say your trunk of books is at Cazenovia[56] yet where you boarded and the gentleman says he shall not open it until he receives orders from you. He says he

---

[52] Benjamin "Ben" Chubbuck, Emily's older brother. Ben suffered a head injury as a child, and his subsequent behavior throughout his life reflected some mental impairment.

[53] This is significantly different from Emily's comment in her October 18, 1837 letter when she said of Ann, "she is a good little sister. I wish you had so good a wife."

[54] Emily would have been just a little over twenty years old as this was written, and this is the first evidence available that she had been writing for the public press. Following this letter is a poem which A. C. Kendrick noted in *The Life and Letters of Mrs. Emily C. Judson* had appeared in the public press. A second poem and story available to us Emily dated 1840, and those pieces appear in this volume under that date.

[55] Before moving to the Wisconsin Territory, John Walker Chubbuck had worked at a newspaper in Cazenovia.

believes you mean to pay him as soon as you can but if you are a rogue he will not commit a mean action. I think he acts honourable [sic] and deserves his pay. At least I wish you would enclose me money enough to redeem your trunk. I saved money enough of my own last summer but when I came here I was oblig'd to use it for it costs me a great deal to live. I board at Luceins Cheney's.

Our people have been somewhat afraid scince [sic] Mr. O. Rourke died that you had commenced publishing the paper. When you send that paper to me write the name of the proprietor on it.[57] Ma's[58] health is poor, Catharine[59] is well and at home. Wallace[60] is at work for Norton. Ben is at our house [written in the left margin of page three] and Ann down with her mother. I don't know what will bear me of the creatures. Write, write, write, do, do, do. I am sure you would if you knew how anxious we all are to hear.

Emily E. Chubbuck

Written along the left margin of page 1: "Elhanah is married and so is [ ]lmer. I have not heard from M. A. [ ]—Aunt Betsy the sweet Darling was at our house not long since with [ ] of the dear little cousins. E. E. C. [written along the right margin of page two] Pa got a letter from Joseph a little while ago he is with his brother Henry. I saw M. Munger a few weeks scince [sic] on her way to Buffalo. Morrisville[61] has got to be this most dubious place I ever saw. The young people are quarreling continually. Mr. Stilwell's people are going to Manlius in the spring. Mary is not to be married until after they remove."[62]

Source: Jerome Walker Chubbuck Collection, Wisconsin Historical Society Archives, Madison, WI.

---

[57] John Walker Chubbuck, Emily's older brother who ran a newspaper in the Wisconsin Territory. Previously, he worked at a newspaper in Cazenovia NY.

[58] Lavinia Richards Chubbuck, Emily's mother, was born June 1, 1875, in Goffstown NH, the eldest of thirteen children. She married Charles Chubbuck on November 17. 1805. They were the parents of seven children.

[59] Sarah Catharine ("Kate," "Kit," or "Kitty") Chubbuck, Emily's older sister, born October 25, 1816.

[60] William Wallace Chubbuck, Emily's younger brother, born January 1, 1824.

[61] Morrisville, Emily's childhood home, is a part of Eaton NY.

[62] See Emily's October 18, 1837 letter to her brother Walker, in which she told him that Mary Stillwell was "to be married in a few weeks."

Emily E. Chubbuck to the Hamilton Village Newspaper, 1838[63]

The midnight air is filled
With rich-toned music, and its deep wild gush
Sweeps strongly forth, and bids the earth to hush
Its din—and it is stilled.

Then with low whispering tone,
Like the last sigh of a departed one
That, all unmurmuring that his task is done,
Breathes out his life alone.

The soft sound floats along;
Or like a harp with one unbroken string,
Which still its plaintive notes around may fling,
Breathes forth this spirit song.

Now fainter than the sigh
Of the last faded rose-leaf when it falls,
As its departed sister softly calls,
The low sweet strains move by.

And then again they burst
In rich, deep strains of melody untaught,
Stirring the spirit's depths, and kindling thought
Pure as in Eden erst.

I may not read the spell
Flung on my soul, but I may feel its power,
And twine bright thoughts around this hallowed hour,
On which alone to dwell.

Source: A. C. Kendrick, *The Life and Letters of Mrs. Emily C. Judson*, 42–43.

[63] On February 18, 1838, Emily wrote to her brother, Walker, mentioning to him that some of her material had appeared in the local papers. A. C. Kendrick, on pages 42–43, *The Life and Letters of Mrs. Emily C. Judson*, said that the following was "from a series of contributions to the Hamilton village paper."

[64] This letter is a combination of two—one letter from Wallace Chubbuck to his brother Walker, and added to it a letter from Emily Chubbuck to Walker. Emily's letter immediately follows this in the correspondence. She obviously added to the original for, after she filled a single sheet, she wrote all over Wallace's letter, in every margin or opening left blank.

[65] Charles Chubbuck, Emily's father. Though he held varying positions over the years, he failed at most of them. Emily was soon to become a major financial contributor to the support of the family.

[66] Lavinia Richards Chubbuck, Emily's mother, was born June 1, 1875, in Goffstown NH, the eldest of thirteen children. She married Charles Chubbuck on November 17. 1805. They were the parents of seven children.

Wallace Chubbuck to J. Walker Chubbuck, February 27, 1838—Morrisville[64]

Walker—

I have got news enough to tell you to cover two sheets of paper, so you must not expect to get it all this time, but I will tell you the rest *when* you write to me. Father's[65] health and mother's[66] are both very poor. All the rest are well as usual. I aim to work for Jimmy in the office and have been for 18 months. The Major built a new house between the store and his house about two years ago and the office is in the upper part of that. There is a press room and reading room which makes it twice as large as the old office. The lower part is occupied by aunt Betsey for a milliners shop and tattle house and by M. Bicknell for a post office. There has been a distillery built here since you went away by M. B. E. Co. Charles Fairbanks was killed in it a few weeks ago. Morrisville[67] is just as it used to be—*as dull as an old hoe*. The printing office is now carried on by P. & E. Norton. Ed feels as big as *an old turkey cock*. They have one journeyman to work in the office so that we do not have to work evenings this winter. Polly Stillwell was married last spring and had a boy about six months after she was married—Strange wasn't it. That gives the finishing up touch to Morrisville news.

I will now tell you about the Cazenovia[68] folks. Fonila fussed round Awhile [sic] after you went away till the neighbors had to get up a begging paper for him. He then went to keeping grocery and got in debt what he could and then ran away. Dwinell broke down a little while after you went away. J. C. Marvin is now keeping the Linctuen [sic] House. He has got your trunk but has never opened it.[69] You ought to pay him if you can. I want that you should write to me as soon as you get this or else *you need not open it*. We have not had but one letter from you since you went there and have not had a paper for three months until the one you sent me last week. Now don't fail to send a paper every week and sit down this evening and write me a letter. Don't fail.

W. W. Chubbuck[70]

Source: Jerome Walker Chubbuck Collection, Wisconsin Historical Society Archives, Madison, WI.

Emily E. Chubbuck to J. Walker Chubbuck,[71] February 27, 1838[72]

I never intended to put my pen to paper for your sake again but Wallace[73] has growled until I was obliged to. I say I never intended to write you—Cause why? Why you have never written me. Last evening I sat down to count the letters I have sent you scince [sic] you have been in Milwaukee. Would you believe I have written nine and never received a line from you. O you rascal! if [sic] I don't pay

---

[67] Morrisville, Emily's childhood home, is a part of Eaton NY.
[68] John Walker Chubbuck, Emily's older brother who ran a newspaper in the Wisconsin Territory.
[69] See Emily Chubbuck's letter of February 18, 1838 for more information on the trunk that is mentioned here.
[70] William Wallace Chubbuck, Emily's younger brother, born January 1, 1824.
[71] John Walker Chubbuck, Emily's older brother who ran a newspaper in the Wisconsin Territory.
[72] This letter is the second part of a letter sent by Wallace Chubbuck to his brother Walker—his letter immediately precedes this letter. Emily has added a note of her own, and then filled in all of the blank spaces with bits and pieces of news. Wallace reiterated much of the news that Emily had written of on February 18.
[73] William Wallace Chubbuck, Emily's younger brother, born January 1, 1824.

you sometime for if I can't see you otherwise I will come out on purpose to torment you. Pa[74] came within one of writing to the Post Master at Milwaukee to learn where you was [sic]. Ma[75] imagined you dead and I—why I thought you had run [ ]. Seriously Walker, if you care anything for your friends, if you would relieve the anxiety of those who think and talk of you every day—I had almost said every hour, write—do write. I want to know how you are getting along, and what you are doing. I know you cannot care a fig for us or you would write.

I am teaching this winter. Do you have any Academies in Milwaukee or high schools? If you have just send for me.—I won't tell you one word of news—no not if our side of the world should turn over and leave yours standing still until you write. Good night.

Emily E. Chubbuck.

Written along the left margin of page 3: "The Whigs nominated Dan'el Hovey for constable last week. ha. ha. Guess he'll '*catch*' himself first."

Written upside down to the text on the bottom of page 2 of Wallace's letter: "Wallace is so afraid I'll read what he has written that he has to keep both hands on the paper so don't make me accountable for his trash—don't."

Written upside down to the text at the top of page 1 of Wallace's letter: "Send me a paper in two minutes and write in there or I'll—I'll—what? Why write you of course to pay you for this. What should I do? Nancy is as *pretty* and h*umble* as ever"

Written upside down to the text at the bottom of the first page of Wallace's letter: "Wallace is afraid I shall spoil the looks of his letter ha. ha. ha. Shouldn't you think there was danger of it."

Written in the left margin of the first page of Wallace's letter and the right margin of the address page: "I have just thought why you don't write. You think my letters are not worth .25 but I value them much so instead of paying the postage I shall get the post master to charge six pence more. Are you ever coming home? Eh? I suppose you won't answer."

Written across the top of the address page: "I have put a *york-six pence* on this month's west corner of this [ ] for you. For *you* now mind so don't give it to any of the Milwaukee *gals*. Do ye find it? Eh?"

Written across the bottom of the address page: "Do you keep a kind of animal [ ] beaux? If so I'll *come out*."

Source: Jerome Walker Chubbuck Collection, Wisconsin Historical Society Archives, Madison, WI.

---

[74] Charles Chubbuck, Emily's father. Though he held varying positions over the years, he failed at most of them. With the purchase of the house for them, Emily was to continue as a significant financial contributor to the support of the family.

[75] Lavinia Richards Chubbuck, Emily's mother, was born June 1, 1875, in Goffstown NH, the eldest of thirteen children. She married Charles Chubbuck on November 17. 1805. They were the parents of seven children.

Emily E. Chubbuck to Catharine Chubbuck, May 21, 1838[76]

Monday eve. Hamilton May 21st 1838

I don't know sister, better how to spend this lovely evening and so I will write you a few stray thoughts. Mr. Reed has just been here and told me about you and promis'd to call and carry anything I had to send. I felt rather queer when I saw that handkerchief for I did'nt mean *that*, I meant the old one that I spoiled last winter. I wonder if mother[77] thought I was going to give her the old one and then send home and beg the other? What would *she* wear in such a case?—Catharine[78] is'nt it strange that with all my success in other respects (and I do begin to think I have remarkable success) I have not the nack [sic] of money-making? I never have a penny to spare and really I don't think I dress more than I should or am wasteful. My going from place to place prevents my wearing clothes that I should if I lived at home, and I can't take quite so good care of them. Now here for instance I have to change my dress every day before going to the tea-table or wear my best in school.[79] Then again I am very hard on shoes and that costs me a great deal. Now I stand absolutely in need of two pairs of shoes and don't know what I shall do—I wish Wallace[80] could come down after me some Saturday morning and carry me back Sunday evening for I feel very anxious to see home for a variety of reasons. Mr. Reed says mother has worried about my health. You minded my caution greatly I *must* say. Didn't I tell you not to say anything about it, you rat? I am well enough, only growling round a little just as every body does in the spring. You know what a cold I had when I first came here? Well it clung to me as close as a burr to a stocking until I got pretty well wore down and it brought on a slight fever which pays me a visit every day. But it's only the effects of the cold and I shall get over it soon. Indeed I am better now than I was last week so tell mother to not worry for I believe am getting to be tough as hickory. I suppose you will want to know how I like Mr. Reed. I don't know for he did'nt stay more than five minutes, and that in the dining room for I had got through Marilla's lessons and my room was in such confusion I could'nt admit him there. I guess however he's a loafer for he sat and gaz'd, as much as to say "well old lady, I'll know you next time I see you." *Old* I say for you must know Hamilton folks think I am about 27.[81]

---

[76] There is an addendum to this letter dated May 25, 1838.

[77] Lavinia Richards Chubbuck, Emily's mother, was born June 1, 1875, in Goffstown NH, the eldest of thirteen children. She married Charles Chubbuck on November 17. 1805. They were the parents of seven children.

[78] Sarah Catharine ("Kate," "Kit," or "Kitty") Chubbuck, Emily's older sister, born October 25, 1816.

[79] At this time in her life, Emily was teaching school in various villages, and she would board with local families as a part of her compensation.

[80] William Wallace Chubbuck, Emily's younger brother, born January 1, 1824.

[81] As Emily wrote this letter, she would have been twenty years old.

Kate how do you suppose Hamilton folks ever heard of me? It is the strangest thing in the world. Every body [sic] knows me. Mr. Spear called me by name last Sunday without an introduction and he had'nt [sic] been here but a week and so have a good many folks. When Mr. Reed came here to get me to take a class in Sabbath School and I told him I did'nt know enough to teach it, he laughed and said "I have heard of Miss Chubbuck before." And when Miss Payne called and I made the same excuse she said quite a number had told her to get me if she possibly could and she should'nt [sic] let me go. What made me think of it now was, a gentleman call'd with Mr. Reed and in the course of conversation told me he had two of my scholars in his Sabbath School class. Now how did he know they were my scholars? I never saw him before in my life or he me that I know of. Whew! if my name goes my evil deeds go with it and I don't much like that. How should they hear of me? No smart people send to school, not even Mr. Clark's. They are all loafering [sic] folks and Paddies and I should'nt [sic] suppose folks would scarcely know I had a school and there was such a little back here. Is there no such thing as my remaining a stranger but must I be [ ]ed into day light [sic] every where. A stranger I say I have all the disadvantages of a stranger without any of the advantages. Every body knows me and I don't know any body [sic].—

I saw Mathews last Sunday and he said he should call soon. I guess Lamb will think it is not profitable to come very often for we got into a real [ ] last week and I did'nt [sic] know as he could act so bad. Marilla and I got into a scuffle and don't you think he held *me* to help her. I don't think much of him anyhow.—Slafter or Slenghter called here last week but he could scarcely look down on such a little fellow as I am. O I don't like him, he grows too fast he's no more the fellow he was.—I should have told him about Lucy but I did'nt [sic] know but it might hurt his conscience to be reminded of those days.—There. I've said enough now I'll go to bed. Good night.

Source: Hanna family files.

Emily E. Chubbuck to Catharine Chubbuck, May 25, 1838[82]

It is Friday evening now and if the rain did'nt [sic] come down like flour through a sieve I should expect Mr. Reed[83] after my letter but as it is I am afraid he will go off without it and that would be a pity you know.—I was very much disappointed because you did'nt [sic] write for I want all the particulars how you get

---

[82] This letter is an addendum to a letter dated May 21, 1838.

[83] In previous letters, Mr. Reed had been bringing Emily mail and articles from home and returning letters and articles from Emily to her family.

along with your studies and every thing [sic] else—I will enclose a bit of poetry for the paper[84] and if is published tell Wallace[85] to send one to Walker[86] with my name to it so he will know where it comes from.

Day before yesterday I left school at eleven A.M. and have not been in again until today because I was sick but I am well again now and think I shall be. I don't want the story to get all around Morrisville[87] that I am sick. Mrs. Clark is one of the best women in the world and if I should take a notion to [ ] a little I should be in a good place.—I've not seen *my* students *yet*. I guess I should give him the privilege of calling again—old rut.

Yesterday Mrs. Clark had company for the first time since I've been here and as there were no boarders here but me I was invited into the room. When the boarders come pouring in again and that is next week I shan't expect any peace. I dread it. But I must draw to a close for I have got to hear Marilla's lesson in a few minutes.

E. E. Chubbuck

Written in the margins between pages two and three: "If mother[88] made a mistake about the handkerchiefs and will send me the old one I will send this back. The reason I don't send it now is because I want to wear it once—Are [ ] Stilwell's people gone from Morrisville yet? Do tell me what is going on and if you are like to come upon the town. Well these are queer times."

Written in the left margin of the first page: "I have just now heard that Mr. [ ] is dead. He died this morning about 6 o'clock. O it is strange 'how unsearchable are thy judgments and thy ways past finding out!' His father went home only a few days ago.—It is not yet determined when the funeral will be. I hope Sunday."

Written in the left margin of the address page: "Do you wear your hat just as I did, and have you fix'd over your [ ] dress? If you don't have any thing new you must brush up the old and try to make it shine. O I am sick of life fixing and fussing—eventually it is vanity and worse than vanity. Do you recollect Mr. Weary-of-the-world? Well I am not him for I am weary of *this* life without his strong hope of a better. O Kate. Kate, what will become of me. Should I live many years all is dark should I die there is a deeper more deadly darkness. What then? but [sic] I will not complain. I meant this letter should not...."

Written in the right margin of the address page: "...have any thing of the kind in it, but I forget myself. Conceal it how I may the iron is still cankering and fes-

---

[84] A February 18, 1838 letter to her brother Walker Chubbuck had also mentioned her submitting material to the local Morrisville newspaper, and their accepting the material for publication.

[85] William Wallace Chubbuck, Emily's younger brother.

[86] John Walker Chubbuck, Emily's older brother who ran a newspaper in the Wisconsin Territory.

[87] Morrisville, Emily's childhood home, is a part of Eaton NY.

[88] Lavina Richards Chubbuck, Emily's mother.

tering in the soul. But my wayward destiny is ma[ ] out. I may not fight against fate, nor will I.—Nonsense. I forget and and [sic] remember forget and write again. Now re[ ] for I shall be obliged to stop because I've filled my sheet.—Write. Write. Write, write. do. do. do, and [ ] [ ] [ ]."

Written in the top margin of the address page: "Do have Wallace come after me some Saturday as soon as he can without it costing any thing.—Send me now and then a paper from Walker.[89] Have'nt [sic] you had a letter from him yet? E. E. C.—O I forgot to enquire about our folks."

Source: Hanna family files.

Emily E. Chubbuck to Catharine Chubbuck,[90] May 30, 1838[91]

Dear Kate,

I received your letter last evening and right glad was I to get it. I can assure you *I am sorry* Wm. thinks you a fool for I don't by a great deal. The teachers that you shall take—why I don't know what to say about them. Philosophy is the best and the reason I did'nt [sic] mention it before was, I somehow got it into my head that you were acquainted with it. Botany if you can attend to so much you better study. Do you want my Adam's Arithmetic? I forgot to send it you [sic] when I sent the other books. If you don't want those—that is if you wouldn't use them at all send them by Dr. Kendrick.[92] Also that money—seventy five cents in the cocoa-nut shell in my trunk for I am penniless as a rat. The plan I had in my head I shan't tell you anything about at present for I don't know—that is I rather think it will be blown over. And now sis for a word of real sober advice. You *must* have your whole mind on your book you must think neither of work nor company. And you mustn't expect to learn anything without hard labor. A person that thinks gaining knowledge from books easy and study no task is most woefully mistaken. And here perhaps you have a wrong idea of me. It has always been said I learn easily and I know I do in comparison with many but you don't know—you can't conceive how much the little

---

[89] Emily's brother, Walker, regularly sent copies of the newspaper he published in the Wisconsin Territory, though Emily complained that they would rather have had a letter.

[90] The initial paragraph of this letter is an extremely interesting and revealing section on Emily's philosophy of learning as she speaks to her sister about education.

[91] This letter is undated. Comparing its content with Emily's letter of May 21, 1838, and its May 25 addendum, it is quite obvious that this was written soon after; just under a week would give Catharine time to receive Emily's letter and respond to it.

[92] When Emily Chubbuck was in her teens, Nathaniel Kendrick had been the pastor of the Baptist church in Eaton and also a theological professor in a local theological school; he eventually became the president of the Hamilton Literary and Theological Institution. At that time, Emily spoke with him about becoming a missionary. Kendrick had given her the wise counsel of discernment, patience, and waiting. Kendrick officiated Adoniram and Emily's marriage. A. C. Kendrick, in *The Life and Letters of Mrs. Emily C. Judson*, says that the marriage of Emily and Adoniram Judson was the last service for which Kendrick was able to leave his home. Other correspondents mention his continued frailty. He died on September 11, 1848.

knowledge I am now possessed of, has cost me. I have studied hard when every other eye was closed and when my aching head seemed almost bursting and as you well know materially injured my health but I can assure you I never saw the moment I regretted it. I find that by the little learning I have and more still by the information obtained by general reading I posses an ascendancy over minds superior to mine I never hoped for. There is no study that is "easy" and perseverance is more essential in forming a good scholar than any for any other object in life. You mustn't be discouraged because others learn easier than you for there are those that learn much *harder*. About writing compositions you must select a subject you understand perfectly and do your best on it. Don't get some hard abstract subject a philosopher could scarcely *handle* for of course you would fail. I have taken upon myself to instruct Mrs. Clark's daughter and I wish you were here to study with her. It would make a nice *pair*. You are as like as two black beans.

My school—I don't know what I shall do with it but I will try not be discouraged.[93]

Kate, what would you say if I should tell you I had got a beau? I shan't tell you anything about it but last evening a fellow I never saw untill [sic] scince [sic] I came here asked the privilege of calling. Of course I di'nt [sic] refuse for he's a pretty spruce chap. Seriously Catharine I don't know but the fellow is *in earnest*. And he's a *student*.

They have all been teazing [sic] me to take a class in Sabbath school—ever since I have been here and last Sunday I consented. Esther Payne is going (tomorrow morning) to Homer to school and I've got her class—I am very well contented though I don't know a rat of a human *being*, not even Eld. Perkin's people. "It is vacation" now in the Academy and so I shall room all alone for a fortnight. I wish you could come down here in that time for after the loafers get back I don't expect to have any peace.

Mr. Whipple remains "about so" but I believe they have no hope of his recovery. I have seen Mathews at church but no where else.—Mr. Lamb said Mia expressed much anxiety about the state of my mind. Perhaps if I understood it myself I could tell her something of it, but all is dark, *dark. dark* although I will acknowledge that I take rather more comfort than I did formerly. Possibly because I *think* less. And now Kate I can't bear that you should stay where you are. Mr. Lamb says he never conversed with anyone that gave a better evidence and Miss Payne says she was very much interested in your care last winter and could'nt have you stay back so. I don't tell this to flatter, you know, but to encourage. And why do you wait? What base ingratitude is it to withhold the hand from doing because the blessing is not all you expected, and because a voice from heaven had not

[93] Emily was teaching school in Hamilton NY.

audibly called you to refuse to acknowledge the faint calling you have received, and to appear before the world in the garb of Him who has blessed you.—Write every opportunity you get and I will do the same. Don't forget the *money*.—I should like to see Reed right well—

Written along the right margin of the page: "Send a letter by him so he'll come while I'm alone.

"The superscription of my letter looks so bad. I will print a wrapper over it and try to better it. I have not heard from Syracuse yet. Have you?

"Mr. Lamb thinks you (at Morrisville[94] I mean) like Mr. Reed too well.

"My health is much poorer than it has been before scince [sic] I went to Brookfield,[95] but you need'nt [sic] tell anybody of it .—I don't want to go home for I held down my head long enough when I was there. (Here I can carry it as high as any body [sic]) to make my neck ache but I want to see you all hands. I don't know as you will get this letter for I [ ] [ ] Dr. Kendrick but *if you don't you must answer it.* 'Now Goodbye'—

Q. M

"I had something more to say but I've forgotten what it is, so I'll save it til next time. If Ma[96] doesn't want that velveteen dress handkerchief that is if she can do without it as well as not send it [ ] for I don't know but I shall have to go bare-naked or wear a stocking round it."

Written in the right margin of page 2: "Mary Ann Stilwell used my Chemistry. Make her lend you the Botany—teaze *her* [sic] —"

Written along the left margin of the first page: "If you knew how *spry* I have written this you would not wonder it looks bad."

Source: Hanna family files.

---

[94] At the time of this letter, Emily's family was living in Morrisville NY.
[95] Earlier, Emily had been teaching at a school in Brookfield.
[96] Lavinia Richards Chubbuck, Emily's mother, was born June 1, 1875, in Goffstown NH, the eldest of thirteen children. She married Charles Chubbuck on November 17. 1805. They were the parents of seven children.

Emily E. Chubbuck[97] to J. Walker Chubbuck

To my brother[98]

Brother, I love thee yet—I have not lost
Our early feelings save my joyousness
For now my heart beats lowly, or is toss'd
On the caprice of strangers, for the bliss
Of being lov'd—But *thou*, dost thou forget?
O dearest brother, say thou lovest yet.

Our early feelings! no, they are all there,
Save that they have assumed a deeper tone,
Ay, gather'd deepness from the very ( ),
Which its dark mantle round my heart has thrown
And oft my cheek with tears for thee is wet—
O dearest brother, say thou lovest yet!

Source: Hanna family files, poetry notebook 2.

Emily E. Chubbuck to J. Walker Chubbuck, August 7, 1838[99]

Stanzas[100]

I am home once again but it seems all unlike
The home of other days. My brother, my own

---

[97] This is from page 6 of a notebook 2, a notebook with eighty-four intact pages, all with poetry in the handwriting of Emily Chubbuck. The notebook was originally larger; there are some pages missing. This is the second of three poems on this page.

[98] We are not sure of the date of this poem. It is the second poem on page 6 of poetry notebook 2, with the first dated September 1828. The poem on page 7 is dated 1838. We believe that this poem is written to her brother J. Walker Chubbuck, who was approximately two years older than Emily. As a youngster, he took training in local newspaper offices, and in 1834, at the age of nineteen, he went to the Wisconsin Territory where eventually he started his own newspaper. Beginning in 1837, there are a number of letters from Emily to Walker, and in many of them, she reflected some of the sentiments offered here. It is obvious that she felt very close to him, and she often wrote of what they had shared and how much she missed him. She also castigated him for the fact that very seldom did he return her correspondence, though he often sent her copies of the paper for which he worked or which he published. Emily had another older brother, Ben; something had happened to him as a child, a case of brain fever, and he was somewhat impaired the rest of his life. With this he was often a source of powerful problems to the family. In the correspondence Emily expressed far different views on Ben than what are expressed here in these poems. Her third brother was Wallace Chubbuck, who was a number of years younger than Emily; to our knowledge, Wallace never left the Hamilton, New York area. He was there in 1854, for he took care of Emily's correspondence in her final illness.

See the next poem in this volume, "Stanzas," a poem to her brother Walker, which A. C. Kendrick included in *The Life and Letters of Mrs. Emily C. Judson*.

[99] See the poem in this volume prior to this, "To My Brother."

[100] This poem is found in two sources. Six of the stanzas are found in A. C. Kendrick, *The Life and Letters of Mrs. Emily C. Judson* and he has given in the title "Stanzas." Another version of it, with an added introduction and an extra stanza, is found in one of Emily Chubbuck's early notebooks, from page 11 of what we have identified as notebook 2. This copy of the poem is untitled. Dr. Kendrick either copied from a later version of this poem, or he made many editorial changes for publication. There are many changes in the punctuation and many pronoun changes from "my" or "me" to "our" or "us."

Brother dear, why art thou away. Come back
And we will be again happy.[101]

And I again am home;—again I hear
The thrilling tone of voices early loved;
And all I love on earth, but *he*, are near,
All whom I have so long and deeply proved:
But *he* is absent—ah! that he should roam;
It must not, must not be—*Brother*, come home.

Come to the hearts that love thee—come and bless
The fleeting moments of a *mother's* life;
To her fond love what is the world's caress?
What its ambitious hopes? its maddening strife?
What seek'st thou there that thou alone shouldst roam
From those that love thee? Brother, come, come home.

Come, for thy *sire* awaits thee—though he's shrunk
From the proud world since Heaven has bowed his head,
Of sorrow's bitter cup has deeply drunk,
And looks upon this life with almost dread,
Yet even there, brother, *thou* art not forgot;
Though *hope*, though peace be gone, yet *love* is not.

Come to a *sister's* arms—thou'rt almost all
Her heart may cling to in this sunless day;
O let thy hand remove this fearful pall,
Which wraps her heart while thou dost thus delay.
O gaze no longer on Fame's rainbow dome;
Cheat not thyself with meteors—come, come home.

We've naught but hearts to offer—but there's there
A depth of richness thou hast long since proved;
Our web of life is darkly dyed with care;
But shrink thou not, thou'rt e'en more deeply loved
Than when the stream of life unruffled flowed,
And hope our pathway with bright visions strewed.

Then come to us. 'tis but a little hour
That we may spend in this dark world of woe;
Let us together cling—a sister's dower
Is but her brother's heart—and thine, we know,

[101] This is an opening sentence found on page 11 of Emily Chubbuck's notebook number two. It is not found in the A. C. Kendrick version.

Is all our own—then why, why dost thou roam?
We wait thee, deeming thou wilt soon *come home*.

Source: A. C. Kendrick, *The Life and Letters of Mrs. Emily C. Judson*, 44-45. Hanna family files, notebook number 2, pages 11-12.

Emily E. Chubbuck to J. Walker Chubbuck, December 26, 1838—Morrisville

Dear Bud,

I don't expect you will answer me if I do not write you but I do not believe you will get much peace any longer if you don't, for I have set my heart to tormenting you out of your senses, you *scoundrel*. Why what do you mean? Would you convey the idea that my letters are not worth answering? *Master Impudence!* better take care!

But seriously Walker, why will you not take the trouble to just drop us a line now and then? Do you think we care nothing about your welfare or do you not care to let us know about it. You don't know how anxiously we have watched the western mail stage now expecting a letter, now a fragment, and again half-hoping to see the boy himself. But we were always doomed to disappointment.[102]

The family affairs are rather more prosperous than they were when we wrote last. Pa[103] is in remarkably good spirits. Tillinghhast says if he will pay him 50 dollars per year for six years he may have the place and he thinks he can do it. That you know is but little more than the rent. Ma[104] is about as usual. Catharine[105] is attending my school (by-the-way I have a fine school in the Academy now) and Wallace[106] is still in the office.

Ben[107] is teaming for Darling and boarding his wife at her mother's. His little girl Annette now six months old is a sweet little creature as handsome as may be. Let me think of some news. I don't know what you may have heard. But Augustine Leach and Sophronia Burdwin have jumped over the broomstick. Harrison Bickwell has got a bill from his wife. She is now at her father's neglected and despised by almost every body [sic]. I pity her sincerely—I suppose you have heard that Mrs. Fry and Joseph are dead. It is not expected that Sarah Fry will live long—

[102] See the poem Emily had written to her brother Walker, dated August 7, 1838.

[103] Charles Chubbuck, Emily's father. Though he held varying positions over the years, he failed at most of them. With the purchase of the house for them, Emily was to continue as a significant financial contributor to thesupport of the family.

[104] Lavinia Richards Chubbuck, Emily's mother, was born June 1, 1875, in Goffstown NH, the eldest of thirteen children. She married Charles Chubbuck on November 17. 1805. They were the parents of seven children.

[105] Sarah Catharine ("Kate," "Kit," or "Kitty") Chubbuck, Emily's older sister, born October 25, 1816.

[106] William Wallace Chubbuck, Emily's younger brother, born January 1, 1824.

[107] Benjamin "Ben" Chubbuck, Emily's older brother. Ben suffered a head injury as a child, and his subsequent behavior throughout his life reflected some mental impairment.

Did you ever know Edwin or Franklin Rush of Woodstock? (perhaps they lived in Cazenovia[108] when you were there). The former is now our minister. I think he is one of the best men that ever lived he possesses such a noble generous heart. I know you would like him—Oh how do you like Mr. Matthews? We had a box of letters to send out to you by him but he did not call to get them. Scornful! By the paper that we last received from you we suppose that you have changed your place. Write and tell us particulars with your prospects etc. etc. Pa says "write once more now if you ever mean to" and I say do, do.

Your sister

Emily Eloise Chubbuck

Source: Jerome Walker Chubbuck Collection, Wisconsin Historical Society Archives, Madison, WI.

Emily E. Chubbuck,[109] January 1839—Morrisville NY

"Why not attend church?"[110]

I would be there—I would be there,
But 'tis no place for one like me,
I've lov'd this world so passing fair,
And yielded to its witchery,
Till heaven has cast me far away,
Far, far beyond the reach of day.

The rocks, the flowers, the stars, and trees,
I've lov'd—ay, 'twas idolatry—
And still my spirit clings to thine,
And these my altars needs must be,
I think of Him who these has given,
And then I almost worship Heaven.

I almost deem I love the hand,
Which showers these blessings in my way,
But when I see life's ebbing sands,
So carelessly all thrown away—
What is it but the world I love?
Since worldly things I'm not above.

O yes, I love the world too well,

[108] John Walker Chubbuck, Emily's older brother, had worked at a newspaper in Cazenovia NY before moving to the Wisconsin Territory.

[109] This is from page 8 and the top of page 9 of a notebook with eighty-four intact pages (It was originally longer; there are some pages missing.) all with poetry in the handwriting of Emily Chubbuck.

[110] This poem would be considered blasphemous by the Church who questioned the piety of Emily E. Chubbuck upon her engagement to Adoniram Judson. Emily Chubbuck Judson often lived on the edge with her creative thoughts and reflections, and her view of the Church, which she loved and which she had joyfully joined as a young girl, often reflected the darkness which could come from what she perceived as its sternness and judgment. This was her lighter, playful, if not "pushy" side, which many find to be her most endearing trait.

And I have never worship'd Heaven,
'Tis not for such as me to tell,
Of holy joys and sins forgiven.
No longer dare I self deceive,
No more dare deem that – I *believe*.
There's one wish when a high hope dies!
Sure I have had my share of woe,
And still do bitter thoughts arise,
If where I've been I dare to go,—
Yet I'd be there their peace to see,
But 'tis no place for one like me.

Source: Hanna family files, poetry notebook 2.

E. M. Griggs[111] to Emily E. Chubbuck,[112] March 14, 1839—Worcester

Dear Friend

A long—long time has lapsed, and I have heard nothing from you. It may seem strange to you that after being [Note: Most of line is lost.], yet desiring to hear from an old friend and know where she is and what she is doing. The girls have gone to the chemistry lecture and I am seated by my table all alone and where could my thoughts better stray than on an absent acquaintance—perhaps no where—I have been in Hamilton this winter—in our old rooms at Fathers [ ] I have entered it but once since I came here nothing looked natural than save the old man who had just completed the letter A. I was occupied by new inhabitants [ ] [ ] [ ] [ ] furniture. I have boarded at Mr. Treet's who lived in a house [ ] found it pleasant [ ] [Note: Two lines are lost.] [ ] what a delightful time we had [ ] [ ] just completed our compositions for [ ] examination, when informed that we must prepare an enter-tainment for the Sons of literature belonging to the temple of science the next Wednesday. A short [ ] this to prepare for those great [ ] who are so much farther [ ] in ascending the hill of science than the daughters of this temple find themselves to be. But this difficult task we thought could be performed with a degree of pleasure were it not that the [ ] students were permitted to darken our doors, and we must be doomed to read not only before Academics but Collegiates and even theology [ ]. Now imagine to yourself that Wednesday afternoon nearly sixty girls were seated on one side of the room and what were the feelings and

---

[111] Miss Griggs, in this first of two letters, appears to be a teacher, someone who had known or perhaps taught with Emily in former years.

[112] This is a two-page letter—the cramped handwriting, blurred copy, and very thin and faded copy, make it difficult to transcribe in places.

thoughts which were passing through the minds of each. O if you had been there you would have heard the heart go pit pat and a whispering I can't read—what shall I do I can't read. Thus the afternoon passed away and some very good compositions were read but enough of this perhaps you are already wearied with what I have now written. But stop while [ ] such a vivid description of our [ ] I [ ] the one which they prepared [ ] [ ] with a [ ] walk [ ] she [ ] indeed to get there. The room was filled with spectators. The exercises commenced by a speech from Mrs. E. Clark. A number of dialogues were spoken among which was a tragedy the poor woodchoppers. [ ] made lord of the soil and last of all a gentleman married to [ ]. This closed the [ ] exercises of the day and we all retired to our dwellings through the mud and rain, and now subjects a plenty for conversation about this one's and that one's composition and about that and the other one's speech. It is a privilege indeed that we can converse with each other on paper but I have confined myself long enough to this mode and would now that I could be [ ] your presence but no such boon for me at present, so I will converse a few moments longer. If you would like to see me employ your imagination and you will see the same [ ] [ ] Griggs you saw last winter. She acts just as she did then sometimes brooding over a lesson and sometimes harassed with a composition and making just as hard and long a job [ ] [ ] but [ ] tired of this employment [ ] teaching this summer [ ] [Note: Three lines are lost.] are leaving but others do not come in [ ] [ ] [ ]. Thus we are almost daily reminded that though [ ] [ ] have the pleasure of meetings [ ] [ ] of life, and [ ] our [ ] must be interrupted by the pain of parting. We [ ] the [ ] [ ] must be spoken and the frail bark will launch out of sight [ ] sail on and perhaps forever—but to those whose highest and [ ] affections are centered on the [ ] springs parting considered [ ] [ ] another path towards the haven of eternal felicity where they will soon meet each other [ ] to part and then hearts will [ ] with [ ] of friendship, and learn to love with [ ] of the [ ] it in [ ] light [Note: The rest of the line is lost.] [ ] upon your path, [ ] Although much of the time I am doubting, there are times when [ ] some degree of consolation to think I shall meet some of our acquaintances in that bright world above where sin will [ ] me to close and perhaps your patience [ ] My best wishes and love to you [ ] [Note: Line is lost.]

Source: American Baptist Historical Society, AJ 24, no. 1187.

John Blair to Emily E. Chubbuck, March 9, 1839—Syracuse

My Dear Sister,

Your communication is before me, and having attended to the subject named I hasten to answer. I am sorry to be compeled [sic] to inform you that [Note: The remainder of this line is lost in the letter fold.] in the school to which you allude. Mr. and Mrs. Welling think now that it will be doubtful about the continuance of the school, and if it is continued doubtful about there being any vacancy. We should very much rejoice to have you find a home in Syracuse,[113] and we trust that the Lord will at some future time provide you a place where you may be profitably and pleasantly employed.

The Lord is doing a good work amongst us for which we feel grateful, and so trust you are leaning on that blessed arm from which is derived all spiritual blessings.

Let us hear from you frequently, and be advised that any favour [sic] I can do you shall be cheerfully and promptly done.

Mrs. Blair joins in much love.

May the Lord abundantly bless and comfort you on earth and finally place you

"As a gem
In his bright crown, to shine forever there."

[Note: Between these lines Emily had written, "Heaven grant it may be so! Emily."]

Yours in the Lord,

John Blair   Source: American Baptist Historical Society, AJ 24, no. 1215.

Emily E. Chubbuck to J. Walker Chubbuck, April 2, 1839—Morrisville

Very, very dear brother,

I am about to become the bearer of distressing tidings, yet although repeatedly advised so to do. I will not withhold from you what has so nearly crushed our own hearts. Last Sabbath morning our brother (*our* brother) left here for Auburn State's Prison. Three weeks ago last Thursday he left here to look him a place and said he was going to Oxford, Cincinatus, Sherburn, etc. The next Sabbath morning we heard that D. T. Williams had had a horse taken from his stable the night before, and then they were looking for the thief. It was frequently mention'd and with others we too wondered who it was. Imagine our surprise, our consternation, nay, our horror when we heard it was Ben.[114] Such a house as ours was for one week you

---

[113] Emily had taught in Syracuse; see her letter of February 18, 1838.
[114] Benjamin "Ben" Chubbuck, Emily's older brother. Ben suffered a head injury as a child, and his subsequent behavior throughout his life reflected some mental impairment.

never saw and I pray Heaven you never may. I couldn't live through it again. Handbills were out Tuesday bearing his name and describing his person and dress so that people should'nt [sic] mistake. He was brought back Thursday evening and placed in jail. Eld. Bush went to see him on Friday and also his wife and Pa. I went up the next morning. He was in great distress and wept constantly. He confessed his crime when first taken and endeavored to settle but it was too late. Things had proceeded too far. He took at the same time Curtis Lewis' saddle and Donaldson's blanket. He had exchanged the horse for another. After he left he kept himself intoxicated on brandy nearly all the time and whenever we heard of him he was in "*on scale.*" On account of the respectability of his friends, being the first crime, and his not standing trial he was sentenced for as short a time as the law would allow viz: two years. Ma[115] has not been able to step out the door scince [sic] she first heard of it and Pa[116] is broken in spirit—as well as health. O how much trouble can one make! If you had seen our poor old father whose firmness death has never been able to shake groaning and weeping as a child you too would have wept and been almost tempted to curse the cause. Yet we all pitied him and you too must pity. Had you seen you could not have had a heart to add by one reproaching word another pang. People have been very kind and even Dwight has acted like a gentleman. The neighbors came in and wept with us even to Mrs. Williams and Mary. [Note: Written here in another handwriting is "Draw your own inference and *warning.*"]

You will think Walker that we are doing strange things out here and begin to disown us, but it is not so. We occupy about the same position in society we formerly did, at least we are no lower. Catharine[117] (now nineteen as you know)[118] is [ ]—a good looking genteel sort of an interesting girl and universally liked. We can have any society we please and instead of being obliged to seek it, society seeks us. I have been teaching in the Acd. the past winter and intend to remain during summer which will complete my year. Wallace[119] is as tall as you are—a boy of sound judgment and splendid talents (though a very clown in appearance) but a spendthrift withal and de[ ]ted to some bad habits. I wish you would write to him (you would have double the influence over him of any of *us*) and warn him against bad, low company, rouse his pride (for by the way he has plenty of it) and tell him to learn his trade and lay up all he can and you will then take him into partnership.

---

[115] Lavinia Richards Chubbuck, Emily's mother, was born June 1, 1875, in Goffstown NH, the eldest of thirteen children. She married Charles Chubbuck on November 17. 1805. They were the parents of seven children.

[116] Charles Chubbuck, Emily's father. Though he held varying positions over the years, he failed at most of them. With the purchase of the house for them, Emily was to continue as a significant financial contributor to the support of the family.

[117] Sarah Catharine ("Kate," "Kit," or "Kitty") Chubbuck, Emily's older sister, born October 25, 1816.

[118] While this is clearly what Emily wrote in the original letter, Catharine had been born October 25, 1816. At the time of this letter she would have been twenty-two years old.

[119] William Wallace Chubbuck, Emily's younger brother, born January 1, 1824.

Advise him to study and become an Editor. He thinks everything that Walker[120] says must be so.

Now about Pa. He got rid of that K. and C. rent I suppose you know by L. and T. paying Allen $100 per year more than they rec'd. Allen got sick of it and [ ] [ ] P. O. Department till he got rid of his contract so you see has saved his 100 a year. Well that is not all; Jonny bid on the [ ] [ ] and got it to go from C. to K. twice a week so that he can stay at home every night—for $320 per year. Not a bad job either!

Written in the left margin of page 1: "Write me immediately and let me know whether or not you receive this for of course I shall be anxious to know. Drop a paper[121] into the office box for us, it will come quicker than a letter."

Your sister, Emily E. Chubbuck

Written upside down in the top margin of page 1: "Don't be discouraged while *we* do right all is well."

Written upside down in the bottom margin of page 1: "I want to write a great deal more but you see my sheet is full. We want to know how you are getting long."

Written upside down in the bottom margin of page 2: "Wilber has been condemned for the murder of Barber and sentenced to be hanged on the 28th of May. Poor, poor fellow he is to be pitied."

Written in the right margin of page two: "Nathan Shepherd and Dr. Barnett confessed yesterday and Williams and Clark Tillinghast, Amariah Williams and a number of others appear to be under deep convictions."

Written in the left margin of page three: "There is a protracted meeting in progress here and indications of a great reformation about 50 went forward for prayers last evening among which were Mary Ann and David Havey, J. Treat, S. Smith etc."

Written along the right margin of the address page: "I am sorry you have been sick but you must keep *up* good courage. When a spider begins to crawl up the wall and gets brushed off she don't [sic] crawl into his nest but tries again and again and that is the way with us [ ] spiders. We are placed here to be busy. But I would to heaven you would busy yourself about what you should [ ] would give the world [ ] [ ] you a Christian."

Written along the bottom of the address page: "Ruth Bicknell, Harriet Cooper and about 20 such loafers [sic] have attended my school this winter—They are all scolding me for telling you this *bad* word but I know if I were in your place I should not want it kept from me."

Source: Jerome Walker Chubbuck Collection, Wisconsin Historical Society Archives, Madison, WI.

---

[120] Walker, Emily's older brother, was publishing a newspaper in the Wisconsin Territory.
[121] Emily's brother, Walker, regularly sent copies of the newspaper he published, though Emily complained that they would rather have had a letter.

Emily E. Chubbuck,[122] 1839

Mr. R. Randall[123]

A slender flower, that we fear to crush,
A silvery voice, that a breath might hush,
A dew-drop quivering on a flower,
The deep'ning blush of the sunset hour,
The chain of pearls round the brow of night,
That will melt away at morning's light,
All things gentle, and pure, and free,
And fragile, bring me thoughts of thee.

Source: Hanna family files, poetry notebook 2.

[122] This is from page 13 of a notebook with eighty-four intact pages (It was originally longer; there are some pages missing.) all with poetry in the handwriting of Emily Chubbuck. It is the second poem on this page.

[123] There is a single letter in the correspondence from Roswell Randall to Emily Chubbuck; it was written in August 1839. The letter, which follows this poem in this volume, assumed a relationship between Emily and Randall, for he spoke of the illness of his sister, and of the death of his grandmother, people Emily would have known. He also spoke of having "occasionally seen an article from you in the public prints."

Roswell Randall to Emily E. Chubbuck, August 1, 1839—Brookfield

My dear Miss C.—

Need I an apology for writing to you? I do not know that I can frame a suitable one unless indeed I plead the gratification of my own feelings. Sister Desdemona has however requested me to write you for she remembers with thankfulness a letter from you and says she ought long ago to have answered it, but alleges as an excuse why she did not that she was unaccustomed to writing.

I have hard news to tell you of her, for 6 mo she has been ill, unable for the most part of the time to raise her head from the pillow. She was attacked very suddenly and the disease appeared to be simple fever—the symptoms, however, soon became less strongly marked until it was difficult to determine what class of symptoms predominated. This is precisely the case now—she is scarcely better but hopes are entertained of her ultimate recovery. She has, for the most exhibited a remarkable degree of resignation and complacency—but hers, *is* indeed a sad lot—more so for being experienced at such a season of life—when hope is the most ardent and worthy enjoyments possess their highest relish.

The mortality in this neighborhood for a few weeks past has been much greater than usual. Among the number whom I have been called upon to follow to the tomb was my aged grandma, who I doubt not has entered upon that "rest which remaineth for the people of God." In the midst of the scenes which have been passing before me I cannot but be sensible of the debt of thankfulness I owe to a kind Providence for having spared so many of my friends—those family friends in particular who are more than half the world to me.

I have occasionally seen an article from you in the public prints but beyond that I have seen and heard nothing for a very long time. And I have asked myself if these printed words were *all* the memorial I was to have of Miss C? That if a half-begun yet unforgotten and unforgettable friendship was thus to pass away? Shall indeed earths [sic] dearest ties like all things else bright and beautiful, die and be "forgotten all"?

Were "minnie words" capable of embodying the Language of my heart I should delight to write you, but it is my misfortune to be unfortunate! misunderstood even in conversations—how then shall I *dare to write?*

If I could recollect the "news"—I will confess frankly I cannot remember any items which I think could be interesting to you. So I will pass over the department by simply saying that Miss Julia A. B. is neither dead nor married and "*don't want to be*"!

I *would* write you a good letter—"take the [ ] for the [ ]" and forget not your "two sided" Yet ever affectionate friend

Roswell R

Miss E. E. Chubbuck

Source: American Baptist Historical Society, AJ 26, no. 1288.

Emily E. Chubbuck to J. Walker Chubbuck, August 8, 1839—Morrisville

Dear brother,

I have no time for a very long letter, but a letter of some kind you deserve and shall have to pay for yours—that, what you wrote by the "next mail." O shame! what a promise breaker. If you were to tell me it was your intention to *live by eating* I should expect the next report of you would be that you had *died of starvation.* [ ] why? You have such an incorrigible propensity to break your promises.

I have just sealed a letter for a beau (I shdn't tell you his name, if you do want to know—it is some one you never saw) and so feel in the very best mood of scolding you. I like *him* best for I get a letter from him every few days and you have never written me—I mean I never have received a line from you—since you left Fayetteville. Look out! Or I will "get married off out of the world" before you think of it, if you don't give me some of your sage counsel. That scare you? Eh? Catharine[124] says "ask Walker if there are any pretty beaux, *west* for me." But you need'nt [sic] look, they wouldn't have her I can assure you, she is so homely. If you don't believe me, just step out here and see for yourself

[124] Sarah Catharine ("Kate," "Kit," or "Kitty") Chubbuck, Emily's older sister, born October 25, 1816.

Elijah Chubbuck and his wife and boys were here from Lockport last week. Elijah is as great a *fop* as ever with his [ ] boots and black tasseled cane and fine whiskers. I would give a *york six-pence* (to you of course) if you could see him. *Your friend Jonathan* is *in* the sea or *on* it, I don't know which—sometimes they said one and sometimes the other.

You never have told me whether I might go west or not—now tell me.[125]

Ma[126] has never fully recovered since her extreme illness, and it is the general opinion that she is in a decline but you know I always hope for the best.

I tell you Walker I don't love you "at all—at all" you won't write nor pay the least attention to my letters—save once you did, indeed, make a paltry promise that you would write by the "next mail." Next mail, indeed! I shall petition to Uncle Sam that poor Milwaukee be allowed a mail officer there once in two or three months. Why if you should all have the cholera out there I suppose we shouldn't hear of it till it was all over. But as I said, I don't intend to write much only plague you all I can. So Good-bye and be sure to keep your promise and write by the next mail and I will give you two york-sixpences when I see you. This from-*Guess who.*

J. Walker Chubbuck

Source: Jerome Walker Chubbuck Collection, Wisconsin Historical Society Archives, Madison, WI.

Lydia Ann Allen[127] to Emily E. Chubbuck,[128] August 8, 1839—Wampsville

Ma chere ami Emilie [sic]

Rejoice with me dear Emily for my heart *once* oppressed with sorrow, and disappointment, is *now* elated with *joy* for the obnoxious *Lydia* is not *entirely* banished from the remembrance of her dear Emily, you know not how your kind letter (just arrived) raised my drooping spirit.

O Emily. I can hardly compose myself enough to write and want to see you so. *Do* come and see me.

How foolish I am but I cannot help it.

---

[125] See the letter of Emily Chubbuck to J. Walker Chubbuck dated October 18, 1837.
[126] Lavinia Richards Chubbuck, Emily's mother, was born June 1, 1875, in Goffstown NH, the eldest of thirteen children. She married Charles Chubbuck on November 17. 1805. They were the parents of seven children.
[127] See also the September 25, 1840 letter from Lydia Allen to Emily; that letter was one that changed Emily's life completely as it set her future course and the events which were to follow.
[128] This letter was addressed to Emily in Morrisville NY. We note that in this newsy letter mentioning a number of names, many of them are identical to names mentioned by Emily in her letters to her brother Walker, as she told him news of local interest.

I had indeed concluded that I was entirely forgotten. I wrote you last winter and have never received a line from you since and have sent you one or two papers since I came home but not having any returned had concluded not to send any more but as I feel myself reinstated in my former possessions my hand shall [ ] [ ] only to send them.

You write that trouble deep and dark has overshadowed your path but do not name it. Can you not confide it to your friend Lydia? She is ever ready to extend her sympathy—however I would not urge to pain yourself by recalling the past.

How I would like to be with you this summer and assist you in the duties of your school and soar aloft on "Science wings" with you. Have you finished Algebra? Are you studying this summer? if so, What? I have given up going to Utica before winter of fall [sic] certain as I expect to journey this fall if nothing prevents. Shall visit Newport and Boston probably. Will you not go with me? Do. But I suppose that entirely will be in vain.

You write E. Clark is in Syracuse. The first I have heard particular from him since last summer, excepting a word Mr. Lamb has dropped now and then as I never have inquired about him. Thanks to Venus I've no more to do with him. He may go where he pleases I care not but Miss Bicknell ought not to ridicule him I think even if he is ridiculous. I received a paper from Marilla a few days since. I have not heard a word from Seiley since Spring he was then at Hamilton. Do you hear from Len Brook. Church Gillette or that promising Ladd? Do you remember our run-away walk to the grove of Mr. Wipple? Where is Snow—do you hear from her? Why did you not meet me in Clinton at the Commencement of College? I did not go with Clark this year and had a much pleasanter time than last too. I saw no one there from H. but Y. Land. Are you going to the commencement? meet me there will you?

Did the protracted meeting in Morrisville have any effect upon you in drawing you from that lethargic state of mind in which you were last summer? I was glad when I heard Eld Kingsley was going to M. on your account. I was not at home while he was in Hicksville but I hope it was not altogether lost upon me. I have been baptized and united with the church and I thot [sic] I might be a bright and shining light in the world.—I have spent the summer thus far at home very pleasantly too, in the solitude of my own room often thinking of dear absent ones. My thoughts ha[ ] become very expert in traveling as they fly with wonderful rapidity from Morrisville to Hamilton, to Clinton, and elsewhere.

Now Emilie you wished me to write immediately and I have, and I shall request the same of you that you do not wait three or four months before I hear from you again. Send me a paper as soon as you receive this, and a letter soon, and do not be so remiss again, and you shall ever find

That Lydia is ever yours

Miss Emilie [sic] Eloise Chubbuck

P.S. Are you going to be married? A pretty girl you are Lydia Ann Allen to wish one who is so much older than yourself such a question as that but never mind it is just like her. Do write a *longer letter next time.*

Source: American Baptist Historical Society, AJ 22, no. 1085.

Marie L. Dawson to Emily C. Chubbuck,[129] August 27, 1839—Cazenovia

Dearest Emily

I cannot describe to you my feelings upon the reception of your *very unexpected* yet more than welcome letter. A thousand thanks for that dear little boon which has brought so many hallowed remembrances around me—and shed a heavenly lustre o'er happy hours, long since past, and dimmed by times [sic] oblivious touch.—I have read it o'er and o'er again and yet again for I can "weary" ne'er become when drinking at the fount of love and joy. Bright scenes of the sacred unforgotten *Past* are brought before me in all their pristine purity and joy—the deep fountain of feeling is unlocked, and the ardent affection which I once cherished for Emily, has awakened again into life recolouring [sic] the portrait of the past with life and warmth more thrillingly beautiful than ever. It is as the soft sweeping of some spirit hand among the chords of my affections and vibrates there with the most sacred melody. It is as the harp-like breathings of memory where with heavenly sweetness she calls back the mind to the contemplation of other days and other years. I love you Emily, and have ever loved you, but I thought you changed, my last letter was unanswered and I could not stoop to retain the friendship even of one whom I had learned to love as my better self, Emily dearest. The Marie of other days is Marie still, and most happy will she be to convince you that she has been true in all the changes which has brightened and claimed in turn life's diadem.

I have been attending school at the Seminary during the Summer, left last week, and shall probably not commence again until winter. I regretted very much to leave before the close of the session, but circumstances rendered it necessary. Among other branches I have attended to French with which I am delighted. I suppose you taught it in your school. You think of attending the ensuing winter I believe, have you any school in contemplation? I think you would enjoy yourself in Cazenovia and there are several excellent schools. I wish you would conclude to

---

[129] In this letter there is suggestion of a relationship fracture, Marie feeling that Emily had not been responsive to the relationship.

try one of them. *Do come*, and we will make [Note: The entire line is lost in the blur of the paper fold.]. How is your dear Mother[130] and Sister Katherine[131] [sic]—my best love to them, also if you please to Miss Mary A. Williams etc. How soon may I hope *dear Emily* to hear from you again? Please remember that I am an impatient little body, and very selfish too, therefore please favor me with a *long letter*.—I was about on a visit (out of town) when your letter arrived, and improve the first opportunity of writing since my return.

Most affectionately yours

Marie L. Dawson

Miss E. E. Chubbuck

Source: American Baptist Historical Society, AJ 23, no. 1155.

Emily E. Chubbuck to Marie Dawson,[132] September 5, 1839—Morrisville

My Dear Maria,[133]

I am alone to-day—all, all alone, for the first hour since I received your dear, kind letter; so I hasten to improve the precious moment. I am exceedingly happy just now. Maria has not forgotten me: We are friends again-old, tried friends; we will meet and kiss, and the past with its years of alienation shall be buried in oblivion.

Maria, I will tell you the truth; Emily is changed. You would not recognize, I presume, either her face or her character. But her heart remains the same. Years could not change that, save, perhaps, to call up some deeper feeling, to unseal some hitherto undiscovered fountain. I have said that I am changed. You could hardly suppose that years would make no alteration, and I think that I should even look for some changes in your own dear self. I am not diffident and shrinking as I used to be, but perhaps approaching too much the other extreme. The world has given me some heavy brushes; disappointment has cast a shadow over my path; expectation has been often marred and hope withered; the trials of life have distilled their bitterness; care spread out its perplexities, and all this has served to nerve up my spirits to greater strength, and add iron to my nature. There is but

---

[130] Lavinia Richards Chubbuck, Emily's mother, was born June 1, 1875, in Goffstown NH, the eldest of thirteen children. She married Charles Chubbuck on November 17. 1805. They were the parents of seven children.

[131] Sarah Catharine ("Kate," "Kit," or "Kitty") Chubbuck, Emily's older sister, born October 25, 1816.

[132] In this letter Emily gives to the reader a very remarkable presentation as to the state of her mind at the moment. This letter was in response to Marie's August 27, 1839 letter, in which she questioned their friendship, as Emily had not answered several of her letters.

[133] This is "Marie L. Dawson" (later Marie Bates)—A. C. Kendrick, in *The Life and Letters of Mrs. Emily C. Judson*, consistently has her as "Maria."

little of the poetry of life about me now; little of the bright, rich coloring of a warm imagination. In short, I am a plain matter of fact little body, somewhat stern and "quite too positive for a maiden," as the quaker said. The neighborhood calls me proud; my mother, rough; my sister, coarse; my brother, old maidish, and my dear good father,[134] *rather too decided for a girl*. I have said this much of myself that you may know what it means, and that it is really I that write, should you happen to find something in my letters that does not fully coincide with your former ideas of Emily. What an egotist I am! But then I have nothing else to talk about; you, of course, do not care to hear the news.

Source: A. C. Kendrick, *The Life and Letters of Mrs. Emily C. Judson*, 48–49.

Emily E. Chubbuck to Marie Dawson Bates,[135] October 1839

Although, I believe, somewhat my junior, Maria, yet your heart is older, and has learned a lesson in which mine can not sympathize; yet be assured I shall ever be interested in your welfare, and should the "dark hour" ever come, in Emily you will find a faithful friend, and, Maria, then she will know how to sympathize. She is well instructed in the love of care and trouble, for the hand of the world has touched not lightly. Sometimes in the hour of trouble and anxiety, when obliged to wear a smile to cheer my mother and sister, I have longed for some loved bosom on which to rest my aching head, and pour out the pent up anguish of my heart.

Talking of "rhyme," I will give you a little, if you will excuse the "reason." I profess no proficiency in that:

To Maria on Her Marriage.

'Tis past, that thoughtlessness of care—
Bright girlhood's gift is thine no more;
And though a smile thy lips yet wear,
It seems not gladsome, as of yore.

Thou may'st not be a girl again,
That fascinating, foolish thing;
Restless and joyous, light and vain,
Free as the wild bird on the wing.

---

[134] This family litany would have included Emily's mother, Lavinia Richards Chubbuck, her sister Catharine Chubbuck, her brother Wallace Chubbuck, and Emily's father Charles Chubbuck.

[135] This is "Marie L. Dawson Bates"—A. C. Kendrick, in *The Life and Letters of Mrs. Emily C. Judson*, consistently has her as "Maria." This letter and the poem it contained were written at the time of Marie Dawson's marriage to E. A. Bates.

Thine is a new and holy tie,
Bound with a sacred, solemn trust,
To live, and live all lovingly;
To die, and mingle dust with dust.

Yet say not, dearest, we must part;
For, while new ties with old ones blend,
Though other loved ones claim thy heart,
Thou'lt not forget thine *early friend*.

Source: A. C. Kendrick, *The Life and Letters of Mrs. Emily C. Judson*, 49–50.

Lydia Ann Allen to Emily E. Chubbuck,[136] October 8, 1839—Wampsville

Ma chere Emilie

Again I resume my pen to address one who has thus far proved a friend, but for what I am sure *I* cannot tell for there is truly nothing worthy of love, or even a thought unless indeed it be my mind, weak, and imbecile, or a heart as black as sin and Satan with all his machinations can make it.

O Emily, if you could but look within my heart and see what—but I will not tell you else you will hate me—I will leave it for the day of final account to exhibit; when I shall cover my face for shame. Whichever way I turn, I sin. It mixes with all I do or say whether in school converse, or the house of God, or in silence or meditation, or in prayer. O why have [Note: The next line is lost in the blur of the letter fold.] sinned so long. Pray for me dear Emily.

How often have I thought of my visit to your home since I came home. Not one word of our eternal welfare passed between us but all was "vanity," will you forgive me? I pray that God may forgive me.

Have today visited the house of mourning and seen the young and lovely committed to the dust. A youth of 19 who had long been afflicted with a distressing disease which has finally borne him to his Maker and to Eternity. Now he *knows* the realitie [sic] of another world, his destiny is fixed forever [ ] for happiness or worry. Oh, is it not strange that Christ [Note: Several words are lost in the fold.] such sinful rebellions worms of the dust and makes them heirs of eternal glory? O

---

[136] It is noted that this is a very depressive letter, and we take note of her August 8, 1839 letter in which Allen stated that she was spending a lot of time alone in her room. Much of this seems to be related to recent deaths, and her own religious reflections on the state of her own soul. Though we only have three letters from her to Emily (this is the second), and the third letter written in September 1840 will prove to be a transformational letter in Emily Chubbuck's life, we understand that Lydia and Emily were very good friends, though we do not know for how long. This letter was mailed to Emily at Morrisville NY.

amazing love, how can *I* be so stupid, I live as though I had not power to move, and surely I have not of myself.

Dear Emily, do not condemn me as an egotist for I am not *always* so, but *self* now occupies a great share of my mind and it is not strange that it should prou[ ] the words I utter.

Saw Caroline Hopkins of Vernon today, she says she is acquainted with you, and sends her love to you, what a careless, heedless, affectionate girl she is. She visits here next week. Cannot you come and spend the week with me?

[Note: The first line of this paragraph is lost in the blur of the letter fold.] of his death. Where *is* he now? Lord and worthy Saviour [sic], how awful the thought, may we live faithful" then Heaven and Christ will be our home. How brief is our time below, and surely 'tis but a moment.

Have you concluded where you shall attend School? When you do please let me know, and if you have no objections I will go with you.[137]

Now you *will* come and spend a week or two with me will you not? I will expect you, write soon and let me know your [ ] if you think me not too inquisitive. Remember me to Mr. Read and lady also your sister[138] and mother,[139] and shall I ask too much if I request an interest in your prayers?

Your unworthy but affectionate friend

Lydia

Miss E. E. Chubbuck

NB Do please excuse this ill looking scrawl for it was written in haste I can assure you. Sit not upon the critic's chair else commit this to the flames without a perusal or at least a seccond [sic] perusal write soon Lydia.

Source: American Baptist Historical Society, AJ 22, no. 1084.

---

[137] See Lydia Allen's September 25, 1840 letter to Emily, in which Lydia made arrangements for Emily to attend the Utica Female Academy. Entering the academy would be a transformational life experience for Emily with the friendships she made and with the opportunities that were opened up to her.

[138] Sarah Catharine ("Kate," "Kit," or "Kitty") Chubbuck, Emily's older sister, born October 25, 1816.

[139] Lavinia Richards Chubbuck, Emily's mother, was born June 1, 1875, in Goffstown NH, the eldest of thirteen children. She married Charles Chubbuck on November 17. 1805. They were the parents of seven children.

Hannah Randall to Emily E. Chubbuck, October 29, 1839—Brookfield

My dear friend,

You will perhaps think by this time my letters are like angels visits, "few and far" between.

But I know you will excuse, my seeming neglect, when I tell you that, I have been gone from home, ever since I received yours, until within a few days, and those *few days* we have had so much company that I could not steal a moment to write you. I have only written one to Mrs. Carpenter in answer to one I had received, which required an immediate answer. Your letter reached me on the 20 Sept: and I can assure you [ ] truly acceptable [ ] [ ] what a [ ] [ ] cold [ ]—but I trust your own heart has seen and [ ] the delight with which are received these silent messengers of love. You cannot think how desolate everything looked out of doors when I came home after an absence of only two or three weeks. When I left I had a great many bright, and beautiful flowers, which still lingered, notwithstanding the lateness of the season. They each seemed like myself to dread the parting scene and therefore I have fancied they availed themselves of my absence to make their exit and save us the natural pain of separation. But I will not mourn that nature is for a season disrobed of all her loveliness for it shall only enhance "the beauty of returning brightness." I have frequently thought if things of nature were unfading life would loose half its poetry. Who would purchase an unfading summer, by a sacrifice of those feelings of rapture which pervade the heart at the approach of Spring when every green leaf every bursting bud possesses a magic charm. Scenes like these even while the [ ]ness of winter, is upon us, pleases more than the full luxuriance of summer.

This is one of autumn's happiest days; the weather is unusually warm and pleasant—the light breeze is lightly sighing among the dry branches, but so late disrobed of their beautiful foliage—and the earth is litteraly [sic] covered with pale yellow leaves—and although the air is destitute of the odour [sic] of Summertime there still seems a kind of inspiration more than earthly and something which whispers as to look beyond the transitory etc.

Can you tell what M. W. White meant when she says I am pleased and yet [ ] said [ ] [ ]. I rejoice to hear you are in good health and spirits and am happy to hear you express a love of domestic enjoyment for this is a sentiment I can truly reciprocate. I have ever been accustomed to find my dearest enjoyment my most unaffected happiness in the *home circle*. Oh how much is comprised in a Mother's love. Often when absent from home have I wept to hear the kind accents of maternal love addressed to another and to feel that I too might not share.

Sister and myself have [ ] [ ] attending school somewhere this winter but I have within a few days pretty much decided to stay at home and let her go alone, although [ ] much she wants to but then I am so fickle minded there is not much knowing where I shall be.

Perhaps even before this, you have left Morrisville[140] and are again engaged, in some pleasant school or perhaps—perhaps—you are preparing to take your farewell, of all "your youth's unconsciousness, of all your lighter cares." Ere this reaches you the pale orange wreathe may have encircled your emotion and you may now be taking your farewell of loved ones. If so well may you "turn aside, to weep, as you cross the parental threshold—well may you indulge feelings to [sic] deep for utterance"—but I will not anticipate.

Yesterday we had company from Hamilton, a Miss King and brother. She is just such a girl as you would love. She has a cultivated mind and refined taste—and in short possesses all the qualifications we would wish for in a friend if I have judged correctly from a short acquaintance.

Cousin Louise has gone to Hamilton to spend the winter. She had taken Miss Sheel's place as Assistant in the Academy. She had anticipated remaining at home until a few days since when she received a letter from Miss Treadwelling [sic] requesting her to come immediately, and so you see I am again disposed of the society of a dear friend. Her two younger sisters are attending school, at [ ], and so aunt Brown is left alone—I had anticipated attending the association at North Brookfield but was unavoidably absent from home the week it was held, and consequently was deprived of the pleasure of attending the meeting and the still greater pleasure of seeing you. I had hoped I should visit Morrisville this fall, but the season is so far advanced I presume I shall be deprived of the privilege. Oh by the way Emily I have just seen a young gentleman (since I commenced this) who says he saw you in Hamilton Village about two weeks since, and that he wanted to speak to you "*the worst kind*" but did not. I commended his gallantry—but he said well I will go to Morrisville and see her one of these days.—Would you not thank me to [ ] lines when I write again?

Pray who was this friend who reminded you of me? must have been indescribably interesting—[ ] [ ] in danger of looseing [sic] your heart—Oh, but while I think of it—Louisa was here a few days before she left and says tell Miss C. when you write her again that I saw a gentleman a few weeks since with whom I instinctively associated the idea of Emily—I have just seen the Chap myself and must acknowledge his first appearance rather prepossessing—but possibly you may have seen him yourself as he is a tract agent and may have visited your section—his name I cannot recollect.

Saw A. A. Bailey a few days since, she seemed unusually happy—she expects to spend the winter at home I believe. Hariot Levison [sic] too is at home

---

[140] Morrisville, Emily's childhood home, is a part of Eaton NY.

surrounded by [ ] as usual. Hariot [sic] is a dear girl—and finally we have a great many fine girls—yet after all few "kindred spirits." I hope my dear friend you will answer this in less time than I have taken to answer yours as I shall wait impatiently to hear from you.

Good bye. May you be happy as my wishes would make you

Hannah Randall

Love to your Ma[141] and sister.[142]

Written along the left side of the first page: "Allow me to assure you, that your [ ] [ ] your letters. Being seen is entirely uncalled for: I must reprove your want of confidence as a friend. Etc. I like Young's idea of friendship. 'Reserve will wound it—and distrust destroy.'"

Written along the left side of the third page: "Sisters desire to be affectionately remembered to you."

Source: American Baptist Historical Society, AJ 25, no. 1217.

Marie Dawson Bates to Emily E. Chubbuck, December 29, 1839—Cazenovia

My dearest Emily

I can scarcely realize that so many weeks have flown by since I rec'd that kind, affectionate letter[143] from you, and which I intended to answer immediately, but day has succeeded day, and still *procrastination* with his syren [sic] voice has persisted in declaring, "there's time enough yet" and I have lent a willing ear, but I am now resolved to dig a grave for that troublesome individual, and henceforth be guided by my *own free will*. Charming resolution is it not?—It is Sabbath evening, dreary and desolate. I am seated in my room alone, a cheerful fire blazing in the stove and as I gaze around I congratulate myself upon the comfortable appearance which my room presents, compared with the dreary scene without.—I have been thinking of *other days, other scenes* and as memory has presented them to my mind's eye, I have smiled and wept at the bright and glowing past. I could almost fancy that I had held high encounter with many who in other days were boon companions. O! there is a kind of pleasure, deep, thrilling, exquisite pleasure, which few enjoy, arising from the train of thought in which I have just been engaged. Memory

---

[141] Lavinia Richards Chubbuck, Emily's mother, was born June 1, 1875, in Goffstown NH, the eldest of thirteen children. She married Charles Chubbuck on November 17. 1805. They were the parents of seven children.

[142] Sarah Catharine ("Kate," "Kit," or "Kitty") Chubbuck, Emily's older sister, born October 25, 1816.

[143] See the letter of Emily E. Chubbuck to Marie Dawson dated September 5, 1839.

is a never failing source of delight, to me at least and I delight to picture in any colours [sic] of my own creation, on the canvass of imagination—old Friends—old times—old scenes—and old associations—not that I am much of an *antiquarian*—but I derive as pure and unalloyed happiness from this source as from any other—of an earthly nature. There is something sweet even in the recollection of unpleasant events as they come mellowed by the lapse of time, bringing with them a kind of uncommon, indefinite sensation, which creeps with restless influence over the soul, softening down the sterner attributes of humanity as the "lovely and luxuriant light of evening mellows the rougher parting of a rugged landscape." Do you not remember dearest, when we were daily associates, our spirits light and buoyant, as we joyously pursued our studies and our amusements. Since then we have both experienced the *lights* and *shades* of life, and have been taught how transient are all earthly joys and we have both I trust been led to seek for happiness where alone it can be found—in the bosom of religion. Here are joys which can never decay—and while the pleasures of earth are fleeting as the rainbow hues, we have I trust secured the diadem which will shine with increasing luster throughout the unceasing ages of eternity. I am happy, inexpressibly so; I sometimes fear my happiness is of too deep, too ardent a nature to be lasting, but my heavenly Father knows what is good for me. Therefore I will not distrust that being who is "too wise to err, too good to be wicked." You ask if I think it is time for you to settle down in the calm quiet life of the Sisterhood—No! My dearest Emily, I am not willing to have you do that, but I think if you can find a *good kind-hearted gent* whose feelings seem consonant with your own, and could bring your mind to *marry* you would find more real happiness in the married life than you ever did in the single. Look closely E. There are few such; I would not have you give that dear confiding heart of yours, into the possession of a *selfish* "Lord of creation" (N.B. one who feels himself such) for worlds—but if you can, I say, find one to whom you can impart each thought and impulse of the heart, to whom you can…

    Written in the left margin of page 3: "look for guidance and consel [sic] [ ] HIM—You must allow your *matronly* friend the prerogative of giving you a little advice, 'cause as how' you know she has tried both states of existence viz. married and single, she ought to know."

    Written in the left margin of page 1 and across lines of text: "Please make my best regards to your mother,[144] Sister,[145] Mary, Willie [ ] etc. How is your Mama's health? I hope you and friend Mary are spending the winter very pleasantly. I think you will get this letter about Jan. 1st, 1840—therefore allow me to anticipate a little and wish you a 'happy New Year.' O may you be ever happy! May we be good

---

[144] Lavinia Richards Chubbuck, Emily's mother, was born June 1, 1875, in Goffstown NH, the eldest of thirteen children. She married Charles Chubbuck on November 17. 1805. They were the parents of seven children.

[145] Sarah Catharine ("Kate," "Kit," or "Kitty") Chubbuck, Emily's older sister, born October 25, 1816.

friends! May the bright chain which now unites my heart to yours be never broken."[146] [Note: Written here, in Emily's handwriting is: "*Be it so my own Marie dear, Emily.*")

Most affectionately yours

Marie

Written half way down the top margin perpendicular to the text: "Heaven grant my sweet friend that you might ever be happy as now. O I would not have that fair brow saddened by care for all the" (Note: Sentence ends.)

Written in the right margin of page 2: "Do not my dear girl—follow my example but write soon and often. A thousand thanks for your last letter and the poetry,[147] my husband admired it very much as well as I."

Written upside down in the bottom margin of the address page: "I am about as unsettled as the wandering Arab, this winter as I am in Nelson a few days at a time and then here a few days—but they are unusually long and when in Cez. fond Emilius [sic] is not with me. I am now a 'poor love widow' as I am in Cazenovia and E. A. Bates[148] in Nelson, quite too bad is it not?"

In extreme haste,

Yours M. L. B.

Source: American Baptist Historical Society, AJ 23, no. 1154.

---

[146] One can see the depth of this enduring relationship when Marie closes her letter with these tender words, and the letter shows that Emily has written an addition in her own handwriting, "Be it so my own Marie dear. Emily"

[147] Emily had composed and sent a poem on the occasion of Marie's wedding to E. A. Bates. See Emily's letter of October, 1839.

[148] Mr. Emilius A. Bates was the husband of Marie Dawson Bates.

Letters

—⚜—

1840–1843

Emily E. Chubbuck to Marie Dawson Bates,[1] January 1840

The evening I saw you at C—, safely landed us at Morrisville,[2] at a not very late hour. The next day I received an invitation to take a school in Pratt's Hollow, and accepted it without hesitation. Behold me then the Monday evening after, at the head of a little regiment of wild cats. Oh, don't mention it, don't. I am as sick of my bargain as—(pardon the comparison, but it will out)—any Benedict in Christendom. I am duly constituted sovereign of a company of fifty wild horses "which may not be tamed." Oh, Maria, Maria,[3] pity me. But the half has not yet been told you. Immediately after coming here, I caught a severe cold, and have ever since been afflicted with something like inflammation in the eyes, so that I have been obliged to keep them bandaged, save in school hours. This evening is the first time I have ventured to take the bandage off, and I may rue it. My school is almost ungovernable. They have dismissed their former teacher—an experienced one—a married man, and it seems a hopeless task to attempt a reformation among them. I receive three dollars per week, and board.

Source: A. C. Kendrick, *The Life and Letters of Mrs. Emily C. Judson*, 50–51.

Emily E. Chubbuck to the Morrisville, New York, Newspaper,[4] March 1840[5]

The following "adventure" occurred while on a visit in the far country, and although not at all remarkable either for incident or humour [sic], it [Note: "Had its" is written and crossed out.] excited no small degree of laughter, and even the relation of it had its day! The account, slightly caricatured, particularly in the description of the actors, was written the next morning and sent to the Morrisville paper not for any supposed merit, but merely for the purpose of surprising my friends and carrying on the fun.

---

[1] Marie Dawson was one of Emily's childhood friends. In October 1839, she became Marie Dawson Bates. We have ten letters from Marie to Emily, written between 1839 and 1846. In them there are many references to visit invitations and reflections on the actual visits.

[2] At this time, Emily was living in Morrisville NY.

[3] This is Marie Dawson Bates, one of Emily's childhood friends—A. C. Kendrick, in *The Life and Letters of Mrs. Emily C. Judson*, consistently has her as "Maria."

[4] This fragment of a story and its introduction was found on a piece of paper that had on the front page and part of the back, a poem titled "Morning thoughts." The heading on the paper stated, "Published in the Madison Observer." This note and story start was placed on the bottom half of the second page.

[5] We date this in March 1840, because 1840 was a Leap Year. We know also from earlier letters that as early as 1838, Emily had been sending materials to the Morrisville and Hamilton Papers, materials which had been published. Note the reference in the letter of Roswell Randall to Emily dated August 1, 1839, where he says he had noted her writings in the public press.

A Leap Year Adventure

The scene of the following adventure is one of those retired and happy places where black-berries grow in all their ebony beauty, and the ladies are not afraid to soil their fingers by picking them; and where *Sunday evening* has been from time immemorial a word which young damsels blush to speak.—Here there lived Simon Day, not in luxurious [...]

Source: Hanna family files.

Emily E. Chubbuck for the *Hamilton Observer*, 1840[6]

Published in the *Hamilton Observer*[7]

Morning Thoughts

Gay morn has come—Aurora peeps,
Out from the light grey mists,
Hailing each low bow'd flower that weeps
By nights chill vapour kissed;
And o'er her cheek and on her brow,
The rosy blush is deeper now.

And now the golden girdle lends,
Its glorious splendid sheen.
And softer colours with it blend,
To deck the lovely scene.
And widely flows the purple robe,
This drapery shading half the globe.

Oft have I stood at such an hour,
And borne on fancy's wing,
[ ] not that clouds could ever lower,
Or woe the light heart wring.
But now I faze not as when erst,
Gay visions on my young heart burst.

My heart is sad and o'er my soul,
A sickened feeling creeps,
Corroding fast life's golden bowl,
While fancy from it reaps.
A wing which farther soars and high,
But dark as was young Egypt's sky.

---

[6] On February 18, 1838, Emily wrote to her brother Walker, mentioning to him that some of her material had appeared in local papers. In May of that year (May 21), Emily enclosed a poem in a letter to her sister Catharine and asked her to send it to the local newspaper. On August 1, 1839, Roswell Randall said that he had noticed some of Emily's articles "in the public prints." Then on April 28, 1840, Emily enclosed some of her poetry that had been in the local paper in her letter to Walker, and asked if he would print it in his Wisconsin paper. With all of this, we place this poem in the later part of that time period, 1840.

[7] This was the heading on the paper, in Emily Chubbuck's writing. On the bottom half of the second page of this paper, Emily had written the beginning of a story—that piece we dated March 1840, and it precedes this poem in this volume.

The earth is beautiful and fair,
And bright as heaven-born dreams,
And 'tis these charms make childhood wear,
The sunny smile which seems
To usher in the bitter tears,
The blighted hopes of coming years.

I love this fair this *too* fair earth.
My spirit fondly clings,
To the sweet spot that gave me birth;
I only hate the stings
Whose venom rankles in the heart,
I only hate the ever poisoned dart.

Which ever points at the young hearts,
Hushing the voice of hope and joy,
Winding its coils with subtle art
Among the heart-strings to destroy
Those springs of life—and spirit free,
A soul unscathed, a heart of glee.

But "it is well." Did storms ne'er rise,
Our sky would be too bright and fair,
'Twould be too hard to read those ties
Which [ ] half worn out by care
And easy broken. But away,
Aurora yields to deeper day.

Source: Hanna family files.

Dr. James W. Redfield to Emily E. Chubbuck,[8] March 7, 1840—Huron

Dear Friend,

I hope you will not think it an unwarrantable freedom in this to address you as a friend for I should not [ ] likely to write you at all if I were not [ ] [ ] [ ] by the appellation. Should [Note: Four lines are lost in the fold of the letter. They are unreadable.] soon who planted the seed and hastened its growth. I do not mean to charge you with having had any such intention for I dare say you know nothing about the susceptibility of the soil, neither can you charge me with any willful free-agency in the case. What if Nature having made happiness the desire of man and

---

[8] This is the first of four letters to Emily from James W. Redfield, dated March 7 and 23, May 14 and 22. In a letter to her brother Walker on March 22, 1840, Emily said:

> But, I think some of getting married myself. How would you like such a place? I have had several what some would call pretty good chances since you have been gone and now another says he will take me under his sheltering using 'for better, for worse,' if I will only speak the 'yes'. But—oh, this but, it will come up, however—I am not quite ready. Good friends say I don't act very wisely and that if I go on at this rate I shall be an 'old maid'. Horrid! Is'nt [sic] it? The Damon in question is a young physician of Wayne Co. by the name of Redfield, a fine face and figure, genteel, pleasing manners, a good address, some talent, and the heart of a turtle dove. Nothing great, nothing small—about on a level with the rest of mankind. But I don't care a fig for him. Then what shall I do. I don't love him and I don't hate—and I don't believe I ever should do either. Shall I then tie myself to a person towards whom I feel perfect indifference for the sake of a home and a protector? You know my disposition well, you know how unhappy I should be in such a situation and I will wait until you write and abide by your decision. But—be in haste. I must give an answer soon…

Later in that same letter she says: "If you have any young congressmen or governors that are in want of a 'better half' just send them here. I will give up the Dr. any time for a better."

In a letter to Walker on June 28, 1840, she says: "I don't know what I shall do this summer as I had said the 'no' to Dr. R. before the receipt of your letter."

harmony the source of happiness, adapts the mind to active sympathy with every thing purely her own and to that which it supposes to be congenial, it is to herself that all is to be ascribed. True it is that the mind often deceives itself and imagination supplies the deficiency of experience and knowledge but it is reality to the mind 'till the falsehood is discovered and what [ ] [ ] [ ] [ ] to act accordingly. It may be moreover that my acquaintance with you is greater than my apparently slight brief opportunities would indicate—at least Miss C., it has been sufficient to make me regret its shortness and wish its continuance and how can that be with these long miles between us without the use of "this noble art of painting words speaking to the eyes."

"Well—so—"if I have made out the case to your satisfaction whereby I assert and maintain my right to be your friend. I hope you will acknowledge it in *writing*, so that I may have a warrantee deed of the same and if you were here I would confirm by a shake of the hand as the [ ] of some is and perhaps seal it also [ ] [ ] I will take [Note: The next three lines are lost in the letter fold.] Madison to Wayne County. At [ ] [ ] [ ] [ ] [ ] [ ] visit with your friend [ ] who entertained me with the politeness which is well defined "kindness kindly expressed" and showed me agreeable and wonderful things in the city, to mention in particular that friend in our evening [ ] for I approve of *Frank*'s taste very nicely. But you are already better acquainted with Syracuse than I am. Nothing worthy of mention happened to me on the remainder of my way unless it might be the "pomp and circumstance" with which I occasionally traveled when I chose my own private conveyance—for the sake of greater expedition, comfort, and independence. By this you will justly suppose that I do not stand [ ] the roads when I say they were very *bad*, and [ ] [ ] was I to arrive at the end of [ ] [ ] [ ] [ ] are blest with a delightful Spring [ ] you that [ ] [ ] I have heard the remarkable phenomena of the [ ] accounted for on the principle if its being Leap Year—but whether it is a philosophical reason or not no female has informed me. However that may be I imagine this fine weather will force you to yield your pretended preference for that still, cold, rough cruel fellow Winter if his own fierce aspect is not sufficient to condemn him. I do not wish to fall into another [ ] [ ] with you on this subject for [ ] [ ] [ ] but really you must admit that Summer presents moot objects of comfort to the body, [ ] pleasure and instruction to the mind [Note: The next two and a half lines are lost in the fold of the paper.] shall not be disposed to abridge very much an agreeable visit at my brother's. Sordus Bay is a romantic spot. I hope you are not prevented the weekly gratification of your love of home and that you enjoy yourself at "Pratt's Hollow"[9] which has better association for me than "Sleepy Hollow" and Rip Van Winkle. There is not in this wide world a valley so sweet." I shall cherish [ ] pleasant

---

[9] Emily Chubbuck had been teaching in Pratts Hollow NY. See Emily's letter to Marie Dawson Bates dated January 1840.

recollections of its muted [ ] whose "delightful task" it is "to rear the tender thought and teach the young idea how to shoot" whose words no doubt are a terror to evil doers and a prize to those that do well. I should like to see the buding [sic] and flowering of the bushes, shrubs and trees in your nursery but the [ ] [ ] [ ] mind—the "feast of season and the [ ] of soul" I should relish more. I perceive that I am fast advancing to that limit of my paper whose seams can "no further go" and my "grey goose quill" tho' won't (in my brother's hand) "to soar above this Soman mount" must not be ambitious to pass beyond. I trust you will be too kind to read with critical severity this letter which needs your charity so much but will rather reciprocate the sincerity which dictated it. Always your friend.

James W. Redfield

Miss E. Chubbuck

Source: American Baptist Historical Society, AJ 26, no. 1286.

Emily E. Chubbuck to J. Walker Chubbuck, March 22, 1840—Morrisville

Dear *bub*,

I have no paper but this and it is Sunday evening so that I can't get any so I suppose you will take up with a sheet of foolscap if I only put a great many good things on it. O Walker, Walker why don't you write? Run away from us so long and only sent us *one letter* and that not to *me*. You used to say you loved me—I don't believe it now or you would write. What can you mean? I should think you quite forgot us if it were not for your papers.[10] But papers are not *letters* and though they tell us you are yet alive they say nothing of your prospects—our hopes and fears—your pleasures and your troubles. Write bub write. But I'll not teaze [sic] you any more. And now for the news.

First and greatest (in my own estimation) is myself. I continued in my school in this place until last fall when I stepped out to make room for a gent. by the name of Clark. The Acd. is in rather a flourishing condition now. At first I thought of not teaching last winter and contemplated fine fun in the visiting line. Went out to Madison, down to Hamilton, spent a week or so at Mr. Leach's where you know Augustine keeps his Sophronia and to crown the fun went to Syracuse and spent a most delightful week. Attended Lucy Bicknell's wedding on New Years day and the

---

[10] Born September 24, 1815, John Walker Chubbuck was twenty-three months older than Emily. Trained as a printer and having worked for a newspaper, Walker established a newspaper with a partner upon arriving in the Wisconsin Territory. He married Caroline Sanborn in 1855, and they had three children, one of them a daughter who died at the age of twelve. In 1857 he moved to Wausau and established the *Central Wisconsin*. In 1863 he became the Clerk of Circuit Court.

next a splendid rich and in the evening a [Note: Line is lost.] had been there. After my return from S. I engaged a school in Pratt's Hollow[11] and have now two weeks longer to stay. They pay three dollars per week and board.[12] I have not yet decided on what to do next summer but I am tired to death of school teaching. Ruth Bicknell intends to say "love, honour, [sic] and obey" on the 21st of next month and I have an invitation to go out to Syracuse as bridesmaid. I will invite you. You will be there—won't ye? eh?

Bub, I think some of getting married myself. How would you like such a place? I have had several what some would call pretty good chances since you have been gone and now another says he will take me under his sheltering using "for better, for worse," if I will only speak the "yes."[13] But—oh, this but, it will come up, however—I am not quite ready. Good friends say I don't act very wisely and that if I go on at this rate I shall be an "old maid." *Horrid*! Is'nt it? The Damon in question is a young physician of Wayne Co. by the name of Redfield, a fine face and figure, genteel, pleasing manners, a good address, some talent, and the heart of a turtle dove.[14] Nothing great, nothing small—about on a level with the rest of mankind. But I don't care a fig for him. Then what shall I do. I don't love him and I don't hate—and I don't believe I ever should do either. Shall I then tie myself to a person towards whom I feel perfect indifference for the sake of a home and a protector? You know my disposition well, you know how unhappy I should be in such a situation and I will wait until you write and abide by your decision. But—be in haste. I must give an answer soon and I can assure you I am greatly teazed. When are [Note: This is the bottom of the page. The line is lost.]

Mother[15] says "tell Walker if he ever means I shall see him to come home quick." Her health is miserable and she is dreadful low-spirited. After all bub what is the use of staying there when you are so much wanted here? Are you getting rich, or famous? They say the West is a capital place for such like business. If you

---

[11] See Emily's letter of January, 1840, to Marie Dawson Bates for more information on her teaching position in Pratt's Hollow.

[12] In a narrative written for Adoniram Judson about her early life, Emily spoke of her first teaching position in April 1832, for which she was paid seventy-five cents a week and board.

[13] At some time during this period, Emily had written a poem to which she gave the title "Maiden Resolve":

> They tell me thou lovest—beware! beware!
> Love whispers of bliss, but he traffics in care;
> Illusions all glowing around thee he'll fling,
> But woes in his foot-prints forever upspring.
>
> They say thou wilt marry—'tis well, 'tis well!
> Though the chain may be heavy, thou're under Love's spell;
> But I—*I am free, and no Cupid shall task me*,
> I never will marry—till *somebody ask me*!

[14] There are four letters in the collection from James Redfield to Emily. For a more complete explanation, and a listing of the letters, see the footnotes written in his letter of March 7, 1840.

[15] Lavinia Richards Chubbuck, Emily's mother, was born June 1, 1875, in Goffstown NH, the eldest of thirteen children. She married Charles Chubbuck on November 17. 1805. They were the parents of seven children.

have any young congressmen or governors (in[ ] of course) that are in want of a "better half" just send them here. I will give up the Dr. any time for a better. Pa[16] is more down than ever and I don't know what he will do. Kate[17] is a poor girl but no more capable of taking care of herself than a baby. I don't know but they will starve. But Wallace[18] is in a printing office in Syracuse. We don't hear from Ben[19] and I am glad of it. His silly wife is here at her mother's and doing better than could be expected of her. You would be proud of your little sister Annette.[20] O she is a little beauty and echos [sic] all our words with the prettiest lisp imaginable. I don't go there much though—don't like to acknowledge relationship.

No bub, in good faith how are you getting along? Are you so bad a boy that you are afraid to tell what you are about. You know I am not naturally suspicious but really your unaccountable silence alarms me. O so many times as I have written you and so many times, sent, and sent to the office for an answer and met with nothing but disappointment. Walker you don't care for any of us I know you don't and I would'nt love you if I could help it just out of revenge. But it is getting very cold and late so good-night—and tomorrow—no to-day send a letter to [ ] [ ]

Emily

Written in the left and top margins of page 1: "A sad looking letter to be sure, but then you know I can write better when I try and if you will only ask me in writing I will give you a fine specimen of penmanship one of these days—O I forgot to tell you that little Ed. Norton and Kate are good friends and I mistrust will be better sometime. Ha! Ha! How would you like a Norton or a brother?[21] I wish I knew how to fold a *sheet of foolscap*. Kate needs love and a kiss. Good-bye."

Source: Jerome Walker Chubbuck Collection, Wisconsin Historical Society Archives, Madison, WI.

---

[16] Emily's father, Charles Chubbuck, was born at Bedford NH on March 3, 1780; he married Lavinia Richards in Goffstown NH on November 17, 1805, and together they had seven children. Though he held varying jobs over the years, Charles failed at many of them. Emily became a major financial support for the family and purchased a home for them in fall 1842.

[17] Sarah Catharine ("Kate," "Kit," or "Kitty") Chubbuck, Emily's older sister by ten months. Outside of the two terms at the Utica Female Academy that Emily arranged for her, Catharine always lived with her parents in Hamilton NY. The letters indicate opportunities for marriage, but Catharine remained single. She later helped care for Henry and Edward Judson when, after their return from Burmah in fall 1851, they moved in with their "aunt" and "grandparents." She was remembered by her nephews as "a dear friend."

[18] William Wallace Chubbuck, Emily's younger brother. During these years of Emily's correspondence, Wallace was living at home, or near home, working at different occupations including printing, office work, and teaching. Emily wrote of him as very capable in many areas but seeming to lack ambition at times. He proved to be a strong support for the Chubbuck family over these years, and, at the time of her death in 1854, Wallace had become one of Emily's primary care-givers. After February 1854, he wrote, at her dictation, all of her letters because of her failing strength.

[19] Emily's older brother Benjamin, or "Ben," was born March 25, 1809. In the family biography she wrote for Adoniram Judson, Emily wrote that as a young boy, Ben sustained some kind of brain inflammation, which seemed to seriously impair his judgment and behavior. See Emily's letter of February 18, 1838, for some very sharp comments on Ben. Then, on April 2, 1839, Emily wrote to her brother Walker that Ben had been sent to state prison for stealing a horse, blanket, and saddle. Later correspondence had litanies of such problems—stealing a cow, difficulties holding jobs, problems with his marriage, situations exacerbated by character flaws. He died in September, 1846, shortly after Emily had left for Burmah.

[20] Annette Chubbuck, Ben Chubbuck's daughter.

Dr. James W. Redfield to Emily E. Chubbuck,[22] March 23, 1840—Huron, Wayne County

Dear E.

I cannot tell you with what pleasure I hailed the arrival of your letter, for in it you have made me the possessor of a precious gift [ ] think that while I prize it for its intrinsic value I am [ ] to the kind "welcome" which it informs [ ] [ ] received at your hand and the honor of that very respectable [ ] [ ] you enumerate, all of which save one unfortunate stranger received your favor. While you have *belief* in such ready exercise surely I shall need [ ] argument to [ ] [ ] your language [ ] only the negative assertion that my friendship was no "bad news" but an "invaluable treasure" to you. O this is too good news to believe but I will believe it because I love to-day, I am emboldened by success and will even trust that it will need no argument to make you believe that I indulge in my heart a feeling beyond that of mere friendship for you, which while I would not have it [ ] [ ] it would be [Note: The next fifteen lines of this letter are lost in extended damage by the letter fold.] [ ] [ ] [ ] three fold cord "is not soon broken"! It is too much to hope that in this also you will find no reason for conscientious scruples for having [ ] [ ] in my heart—say what will you call this better than "a pearl so rare in this selfish world!" and will you not give me a pledge of this also? But I would not for the price of my happiness which I may love but will not sell, defeat by my haste and precipitate my object and forfeit the great favour [sic] I desire from you [ ] is better than [ ] [ ] [ ] [ ] to ask me "where is the harm." I would reply in disappointments. Nevertheless let me open my heart with exceeding frankness "with the curtain of ceremony drawn up to the very sky." I will not like you by pardon for not being an *old friend* for if "that life is long which answers life's great end" that friendship must be long which answers the purposes of friendship. Do not judge [ ] this vine [ ] [ ] [ ] other sentiment you have engrafted upon it, like wine and physicians by their old age, but by their qualities, and think not that tho' nurtured by genial influences, they are precocious and short lived. My nature seeks the confiding

> "bosom of a friend
> Where heart meets heart reciprocally soft
> Each others pillow to repose divine"

a mind not all understood and learned at once, where one's thousand thoughts as they spring up diffident to the eyes of others response assistance or correction.

---

[21] In spring and summer 1841, there are references to the future marriage of Catharine Chubbuck and Edward Norton, which was to take place in September. Nothing was ever said of it, until a letter of March 25, 1842, when Emily mentioned that the relationship of the Chubbucks and Nortons was still very good, in spite of the break up of Catharine and Ed.

[22] This is the second of four letters from Redfield to Emily Chubbuck. See the Footnote in his letter of March 7, 1840.

[ ] [ ] heart whose freshness [ ] up from the deep fountain of domestic [ ] [Note: The next five and one half lines are lost in the letter fold.] —but, for one who could find [ ] pleasure in a "Washer's cabin" as in a palace , possibly even a [ ] [ ] [ ] whose only capital is his profession, or longing to that [ ] class who as Franklin says "attempt to live by their will but often [ ] [ ] of stock" might not [ ] despair of finding some [ ] which she would consent to make her home. Such an one Love would not fly out at the window because poverty entered the door and with wealth in such an our what [sic] [Note: The letter ends at the end of page 2.]

Source: American Baptist Historical Society, AJ 26, no. 1285.

E. M. Griggs to Emily E. Chubbuck, April 13, 1840—Hamilton[23]

Dear Emily,

I received your letter in a busy time, of course a speedy answer could not be expected but the sem. is over with now. I must tell you what it was, preparing for examination and you well know at such times every heart is beating high with hope and fear but every thing went well and was quite interesting. The exercises were in the Presbyterian Church on Wednesday evening the house was crowded as many were anxious to attend it being Miss Treadwell's last examination. The audience were entlerned [sic] by the reading of six compositions, music, and an address by Miss Treadwell which was in the true sense of the word *good*. It was a solemn evening. Many of us then gave the parting hand and spoke the word farewell for the last time.

> "The last, the last, the last,
> O how this little word stirs the mind,
> And whispers of the past."

and are now separated from those we love and with whom we have enjoyed pleasant interviews and mingled with each other in varied scenes of delight, but the time has rapidly passed away and the period has arrived as we have just began to lose each other as friends, that we must past and the silken cord which has united our hearts [Note: "Together" is written and crossed out.] be broken.

Source: American Baptist Historical Society, AJ 24, no. 1186.

---

[23] There is an addendum to this letter dated April 18, 1840.

E. M. Griggs to Emily E. Chubbuck, April 18, 1840[24]

Saturday eve 9 o'clock—I commenced this letter Monday evening and wrote a few lines and was obliged to lay aside my pen until the present. Sister has been quite sick but is now gaining and Pa's health is very poor. Thus my attention has been directed to the serious occurencies [sic] of a week that is now numbered with the past. It has gone never more to return, but the thoughts and deeds may be recalled at pleasure as a source of pleasure or pain to the mind. Miss Treadwell has left H. to return no more as a teacher. Her absence from the school is deeply regretted by all. They have engaged a teacher who is very highly recommended, by Miss Phelps. Perhaps she will in the true sense of the word fill her place and this is all one could ask. I see Miss Wickwise frequently she is well at present. I received a letter from Nancy Jones the other day she is at school in Penfield and her sister is teaching there. [sic] Miss Mathers has been at school the last half of the term, and is going to return next term and take Music lessons. She is as the same creature as when you saw her. While reading yours the scenes of the past were brought to mind with the freshness of yesterday's occurrences, and be assured, believe when I tell you are not forgotten, by me, No! I never shall forget you, nor the many pleasant scenes of that winter. It was a memorable season. It passed happily away but I think I have scene [sic] as happy days since. I have past [sic] this winter pleasantly in school, I have formed acquaintances I sincerely *love* (but do not forget the friendships formed by previous acquaintances) but I have parted with them now. It is hard to part from those we love, and have the silken cord which has united our hearts be broken, though by it we may learn that this life is a continual scene of meeting and parting, and it ought to remind us of the frailty of menkind [sic], and the coanessence [sic] of all earthly pleasure, and turn our attention to the immutable One of the universe, and lean upon the Saviour as our only true and never failing friend.

I have been intending to teach this summer and shall now probably if an opportunity presents if not I shall spend the summer at home.

I *did care* to receive your letter and was happy to hear from you and hope you will write a longer one soon.

I must close for I already find the effects of [ ] being up so much previous nights so good bye Dear E—and pleasant dreams to you this night.

Source: American Baptist Historical Society, AJ 24, no. 1186.

---

[24] This letter is an addendum to a letter dated April 13, 1840.

Emily E. Chubbuck to J. Walker Chubbuck, April 28, 1840

Morrisville, June 28th, 1850

My own brother dear

Your two letters were very joyfully rec'd a few days since and I know you would be "werry" much flattered if you knew how many kisses they got. What! bub have you no more perseverance than to commence a letter and not finish it—why you are not half so much of a man as I, for I always "carry my pint." It will never never do—so next one you serve in that style please send along and I will finish it. We were very sorry I can assure you to hear of your sickness but you have not told us where you staid [sic], or if you had good care, what the disease was, etc. Write particulars. You may say you have an "empty purse"—well that is better than no purse at all—but is your land paid for?

"Father's[25] prospects." Eh? O [ ]inry! you shouldn't ask that question. Dark, dark, dark! You know he lost all and involved himself in debt by that silly stage business. He put too much confidence in B.[26] who killed the horses, made friends of all the drivers (low wretches! by-the-way) against paid interests, contracted brandy debts, broke down carriages and in *short* acted more like a spirit of darkness than a rational man. Hard talk I know but it is every word true. Well, after that was over he had nothing—[ ] back to the old place and is still staying there considering whether it is best to *buy* it. Buy! what with? He don't do any thing but carry a few papers for James and keep boarders. His health is miserable. He fails every day. He is quite deaf—and gray-haired—and clumsy—appears like a man worn down by age. Mother[27] is worse yet—though her inexhaustible ambition keeps her up. She has a very bad cough and [ ] at the [ ]—[ ] done, [ ] symptoms. They are both mere children in judgment and I don't know what will become of them. Catharine[28]—I hardly know what to say of her she is not so happy and contented as she wants to be—still she is a first-rate good girl. We thought if she could learn piano music, teaching would be a fine business. She has therefore commenced taking lessons but I can't help feeling somewhat fearful of the result as you know she has no energy. However all may be well. Wallace[29] is delighted with Syracuse—and it is indeed a delightful place. I should love to live there. I don't know what I shall do this summer as I had said the "no" to Dr. R.[30] before the receipt of your

---

[25] Charles Chubbuck, Emily's father. Though he held varying positions over the years, he failed at most of them. With the purchase of the house for them, Emily was to continue as a significant financial contributor to the support of the family.

[26] Benjamin "Ben" Chubbuck, Emily's older brother. Ben suffered a head injury as a child, and his subsequent behavior throughout his life reflected some mental impairment.

[27] Lavinia Richards Chubbuck, Emily's mother, was born June 1, 1875, in Goffstown NH, the eldest of thirteen children. She married Charles Chubbuck on November 17. 1805. They were the parents of seven children.

[28] Sarah Catharine ("Kate," "Kit," or "Kitty") Chubbuck, Emily's older sister, born October 25, 1816.

[29] William Wallace Chubbuck, Emily's younger brother, born January 1, 1824.

[30] See the letter of James Redfield, March 7, 1840, and the footnotes to that letter.

letter. I've got tired of teaching and guess I shall not this summer. I have a few pence—that may not last [Note: Last line at bottom of the page cannot be read and transcribed.]

Sarah M. B. is now in Madison on a visit to her relatives. Poor girl! She has seen her best days and whatever are her faults her punishment has already been sufficient. No one here will associate with her, or scarcely speak—she is not allowed to see her children, and you would think she had lived an age of woe in two short years. Well be it so! her persecutors will not always triumph for "with what manner they meet it shall be measured to them again." Yet she sometimes appears lively though it is manifestly forced mirth. I will treat her well in spite of the tongues of slander. She lives at her fathers [sic]. I suppose you know that Harrison was married again. Don't you think he's made a pretty bargain to have Sarah for Eliza Ann Cloyd? Joseph C. is in Rochester and the last we heard, he was on the point of being married to a pretty Quaker girl.

"The hill folks"—eh? Marion M. has gone to Rochester (her parents live there) and they say she is engaged to Chrison Chamberlain. L. A. Lewis keeps a milliner's shop on the hill they say she has a beau from Lebanon by the name of Sheldon—rather a good fellow. We expect every day when J. Tillinghart (he belongs to the firm of Tillinghart & Co) and M. J. Fox will be married also. D Hovey and Ann Crandall (a tailoress [sic] girl). A. Thompson every body says (and of course it must be) is about to be married to a young lawyer by the name of Fowler. He is genteel in his person and manners, a graceful speaker and a talented man. He is decidedly superior to any man in the village except Foster who by-the-way is a first rate lawyer. Is'nt [sic] it strange he should fancy that empty-pated thing? But you know the old maxim. Lucinda Lewis is teaching school. Thompson L. is in Hamilton to work at his trade. He was engaged to Cynthia Gage who died last fall. It is understood he felt very bad. *Nancy* is stepping round as pert and independent as ever. Don't you wish you could be her? Mr. Fox is not expected to live. J. H. and J. C. Lewis have left the tavern and Darius Morris has taken it. Curtiss was married last winter to Mary Morris—old Tom's daughter. At the same time Frank Cloyd to a lady in Cherry Valley. Dwight and Ann Jenette live across the way in the Smith house. I saw David Atwood the other day (there being a grand Whig convention). His health is not very good at present. He is in H. working for his brother in the "H. Palladium" office. Brad Williams has got to be a Methodist. His health is poor and he is "very nervous." Little Ed has got to be quite a gentleman but J. grows clownist every day. It was a joke about [ ] [ ] he calls often. Weld and Phila live in Hamilton they have a nice boy two years old. M. L. Dawson is Mrs. E. A. Bates[31]—she was married last fall—I visited her a few weeks previous,

---

[31] Marie Dawson Bates, childhood friend of Emily's. In October 1839, Emily enclosed a poem she had written for Marie's marriage. For more on their relationship, see Marie Dawson's letter of August 27, 1839, and Emily's letter of September 5, 1839.

and called on her in January on my return from Lucy Bicknell's wedding. Marie is a sweet creature. "The compliment!" nonsense! Do you suppose I keep a compliment for you in my head so long when I get so many for myself. No, no. If you want to get a compliment, you must answer my letter in less than two years.

I went to Ruth's wedding a week ago.[32] Rode out to S. with Rev. E. D. Rud and his sister from this place. She is a sweet girl and you would love her 'cause *I* do. A delightful wedding! Louis Cheney was there and Caroline. I was bridesmaid and a Mr. Dunning groomsman. We were dressed in white—new styles for weddings here—and made things go off about right. Whew! The next morning went shopping. Got me a brown silk dress and a beautiful chali—just the thing for a bride and it's Leap Year you know. We all rode out here Tuesday and they returned Wed.—R. has done very well—he is a painter (first rate workman) and industrious etc.—Now, Walker, as I can't "scr[ ] up"—wedding on the 4th of July mayhaps we can [ ] it into another shape. I have, agreeable to your request, selected said wife and the [ ]. Now, then come and have that job done up and we'll both go back with you—would'nt [sic] that be admirable? But I must describe the bride elect. Sophia N. Rud is about my size with somewhat larger face and broader shoulders. She has a fine forehead, large gray eyes, a decent nose, and an exceeding pretty mouth and chin. In disposition and manners she resembles M. Dawson. Her complexion is rather dark. She is a very superior girl, warm-hearted and kind. She says she loves you because I do—*now* you must love her because I do and when you see her for herself. Won't you? Earnestly, "bub" I'd give all my old shoes if you were acquainted—I know you'd think of her just as I do. Poor girl, I! I have'nt a sign of a beau now and I expect Dr. R.[33] is offended, but—I don't care. What could I do *with you*? Have they an academy? I don't know what beau you referred to in the P. S. of your letter—I have so many you know. Give my love to Mrs. Brown—I'd send a kiss if I *did*'nt [sic] think there was some danger in having it pass through your hands. Tell her however I'm a capital "sister" and love her—why. Cause you do. E.

Written along the left margin of page 1: "They have given pardon for B.[34] and Pa has started to go after him today. He is expected back Thursday night and people think he will settle down here. What an eye-sore. Perhaps he will be sick or dead. Ma thinks I better not close my letter till we know the result but I'm in a hurry for you to get it because I think I should be likely to get an answer quicker. Write, boy, write and I'll love ya."

---

[32] On the weddings of Lucy Bicknell and then that of her sister Ruth, see Emily's letter to her brother, J. Walker Chubbuck, dated March 22, 1840.

[33] Dr. James Redfield had written two letters to Emily Chubbuck indicating his interest in a friendship that would develop into a deeper relationship of marriage. See his letter of March 7, 1840. Earlier in this letter, Emily had told Walker that she had said "no" already to Dr. Redfield.

[34] Emily's brother Ben had been sent to state prison for two years for stealing a horse, blanket, and saddle.

Written along the right margin of page 2: "Lucy W. Hay was married to Mr. Lathon about a year since and [ ] this last winter in Hamilton. Sarahs [ ]—George French's wife died in Illinois about the same time."

Written along the right margin of page 2, upside down to the above: "I can't get in the '*werrys*' now but I'll [ ] [ ] [ ]."

Written along the left margin of page 3: "If it don't make my letter look too thick I'll put in a bit of poetry that was written for you and published in the Caz. paper over the signature of 'Eloise' about two years ago.[35] I never could get a paper to send you. It got some pretty compliments from the Editor. You may republish it if you please and send me a paper."[36]

Source: Jerome Walker Chubbuck Collection, Wisconsin Historical Society Archives, Madison, WI.

Emily E. Chubbuck to J. Walker Chubbuck, May 12, 1840—Morrisville

Dear, dear bub,

I shan't make any excuse for writing to [sic] soon again for I know you don't want me to, yet I have no news. Ma[37] wanted me to tell you about Ben.[38] He got home *a little too safe* week before last (Apr. 30th) and has been sauntering around here not ashamed to stick by me all the time. It seems as though he don't [sic] know half as much as he used to. Poor fool! I don't know but I'm wrong—sometimes I think I'm wicked but I don't put any confidence in anything he does or says. He's lost all his pride but I don't care for that if he only would keep away from us. He and Ann go to meeting every Sunday and don't you think sit in our pew [sic]. I haven't been yet since his coming home and won't go. He even *pretends* (is that wicked?) to be pious, but I think true piety or even common sense would lead him to attend some other meeting and so save our feelings—though I don't think it hurts any one much but Pa[39] and me. I'd get away if I could. Pa wants to know about your concerns. He says if you don't come home soon you'll never see him (discouraged you see). He wants you to write all about the country and what your

---

[35] On February 18, 1838, Emily had written to J. Walker Chubbuck, and told him that material of hers had appeared in several publications over the signature of E.E.C. and that the editor of the "Whig" had found her out.

[36] John Walker Chubbuck, Emily's older brother who ran a newspaper in the Wisconsin Territory. Though he regularly sent copies of the paper to Emily, she often reminded him that a paper was not a substitute for a real letter and that his family longed to hear a personal word from him.

[37] Lavinia Richards Chubbuck, Emily's mother, was born June 1, 1875, in Goffstown NH, the eldest of thirteen children. She married Charles Chubbuck on November 17. 1805. They were the parents of seven children.

[38] Benjamin "Ben" Chubbuck, Emily's older brother. In her letter of April 28, 1840, Emily mentioned that her father had gone to pick Ben up as he was being released from prison.

[39] Charles Chubbuck, Emily's father. Though he held varying positions over the years, he failed at most of them. With the purchase of a house for them, Emily was to continue as a significant financial contributor to the support of the family.

calculations are for the future. I don't know but he thinks of going first [Note: or "fast"]—but don't *be scared Ma won't let him. I'd go for a six-pence (york) any minute.* Sophia Bird says she loved you and she'll be on the ground July 4th if you'll only come. She's the best girl in the world. Send her a paper (with compliments of J. W. C.) Earnestly bub, when do you mean to be married? Get you a good little wife and then I'll come and live with you. I shall make a good "Aunt Emily" the best old maid in Christendom don't you believe it. Tell me all about the pretty Milwaukee girls—ay, and the beaux too if you have any—Ain't [sic] you sorry Marion is married? I am for I always meant to have her for a sister, Lazy boy! But Sophia is as good only not quite so "gently sweet." I think L, the smarter of the two. But I don't know as you can get her she is very particular and has smitten a score of beaux.[40] But you love me best after all don't you! well have me then for I learned lately to be quite a tidy house-keeper and I'm sure I love you best of any body [sic]? O bub dear, I had a sad dream a few nights since—I thought you came home and when we met only very coldly shook my hand. I wept bitterly and when you inquired the reason I told you I did not believe you loved me as well as you used to do. "Well" said you very demurely, "that is all very true. I have been gone so long and seen so many different faces that you must not expect me to feel as I used to. All the world changes and why not brothers?" I thought I tried to speak but words choked me, and I strangled, which was true enough for Sophia awoke half frightened out of her wits. But I know you don't change so I shan't cry about it. This is the most unhappy spring I ever saw for everything goes wrong—especially since Ben came home. But you know the old adage—"The darkest time before day" and so I am expecting better things." "It's a long road that never turns" and "the darkest day is not all clouds" etc. etc. are fine comforters. I asked Catharine[41] just now what I should tell W. for her, and she said "Tell him I don't care for nothin' nor nobody." Mother says "she wants to see you so that it seems she could take wind and fly to you. She says she would give all the world for half an hours chat." Do you love me, bud? Kiss me then. Good-bye, and good luck attend you ever.

Emily

Pa says you must be a "good boy"

Written along the left margin of the letter: "Glad to hear you behave so well. You must read solid books and grow as fast as you can. The poetry I told you of I will enclose. If they republish it send me a paper. I suppose you got our paper and

---

[40] See Emily E. Chubbuck to J. Walker Chubbuck, June 28, 1840. In that letter she mentioned a Miss Sophia N. Rud as a wife for him. She had "personally" chosen her.
[41] Sarah Catharine ("Kate," "Kit," or "Kitty") Chubbuck, Emily's older sister, born October 25, 1816.

know my signature.[42] (E. E. C. Ellen—Leila—H. L. etc. etc. etc.) My love to *our sister*. Write often."

Source: Jerome Walker Chubbuck Collection, Wisconsin Historical Society Archives, Madison, WI.

Dr. James W. Redfield[43] to Emily E. Chubbuck,[44] May 14, 1840

I can resign. I believed you one who could make me happy, but the cup would be dashed to the ground were I not capable of making yourself so. Altho' I would choose the best, and be always gratified in its attainment, it is not absolutely indispensable to my happiness. To bring good out of evil, and make the best of every thing, is good philosophy in such a world as this. What a wretch is man without it! We are told that "the gods do not fight against necessity"—much less should mortals. Yet it is hard to sacrifice a fondly cherished hope. Miss C., if I am obliged to bid you adieu, the friendship I bear you, and you your[ ] self will [ ] [ ] in my recollections—and may [Note: The next two lines are lost in fold of letter.]—is poorly qualified for its embassy being written perhaps too much like its predecessors, and with the intellectual assistance of a tooth-ache, which has punished me these few days, mayhap for the injury I might have done that at "family of pain" in times past. This letter I was speaking of—if it secure the forgiveness I so humbly crave, and say something in reparation of the injury I may unintentionally have done your feelings, and to myself in your just estimation by my headlong impetuosity—and as an assurance and token of it procure another letter from you, it shall here thank you in my name. I cannot ask for one of your letters for this poor thing, but may I not hope for a gratuity at your hand—one more precious remembrance of my friend? [Note: Written here in what is likely Emily's handwriting is, "Poor child, it should have one."][45]

Always yours, truly

Jas W. Redfield

Miss E. E. Chubbuck

P.S. I expect to remain here a few weeks—Perhaps I may learn through you whether my friends in Morrisville are alive and well, as I hear nothing from them.
(Thank you for the paper just come to hand) J

---

[42] Some of Emily's poems had been published in the local newspapers over her initials, E. E. C.
[43] See the first footnote on the March 7, 1840 letter from Dr. Redfield.
[44] This is a letter fragment—only the last page survives.
[45] We note that in two places in this letter, and in several places on the May 22, 1840 letter, Emily had added notes in her own handwriting, some of them quite impish. We suspect that she might have had enough of Dr. Redfield.

Written along the left margin of this page in the handwriting of Emily E. Chubbuck:

I have the very [ ] of love—the meaning [ ] [ ] [ ]

O I am well yet we [Note: The rest of the line is lost.]

I love my own family friends and [ ] [ ] [ ] is all I [ ] [ ] [ ]

Owns such treasures but I will not [Note: The rest of the line is lost.]

Emily

Source: American Baptist Historical Society, AJ 26, Number1284.

Dr. James W. Redfield[46] to Emily E. Chubbuck,[47] May 22, 1840—Huron

While you have denied me the richest boon I ever asked and the only one of that nature I ever desired, next to that you have granted me the highest favor in your power to confer in allowing me to call you *sister*. That I have *not known you*, you have quite satisfactorily demonstrated and yet if it is not paradoxical, very little to my satisfaction. I cannot *comprehend* the fact of which you have assured me, that you are "incapable of a sentiment warmer than friendship" while I believe human nature susceptible of no "sentiment stronger, deeper, or holier" than you are capable of feeling. I would rather think that you never saw one whom you thought worthy of your love. If you really possess a "heart so cold" and me so *incapable* of an affection indispensable to happiness in a state" ordained by Heaven, then indeed have I been wonderfully mistaken and am very thankful to you for having had the frankness to inform me of my error. Such reasons for a decided negation I consider quite deficient. While I expected only to learn that I was not pleasing to you, "her heart it is another's and never can be mine," or that "Fool's haste is no speed," how surprised was I at such a strange disclosure. Altho' some whose ideas of attachment are founded on interest and cold policy may look upon the "tender passion" as a weakness, I could never more than partially sympathize with a heart destitute of it. But there seems to me to be an incongruity in this, that one should appreciate so well a feeling which is the spring of the greatest happiness arising from the human heart, and still profess no foundation for it in her nature. Not my friend that I have any more desire to influence your mind in respect to myself; [Note: Above this line Emily has written, "Good."][48] since you choose to have no such regard for me—I am now a brother, and as such I feel inclined to speak my thoughts to you as a

---

[46] See the first footnote on the March 7, 1840 letter from Dr. Redfield.

[47] It is obvious that this letter is in reply to Emily's letter to him letting him know that she had no interest in pursuing a serious relationship with him.

[48] This is the first of several personal (and sometimes impish) notes that Emily had added to this page. See also the letter of May 14 where she made some notes also. This is the last of four letters we have in the files from Redfield.

sister. I must confess that your declarations to which I have alluded were rather shocking to me, [Note: Above this line Emily has written, "Of an electrical nature probably."] and the resolution *"never to marry"* I have always been accustomed to consider as a gross violation of nature's laws and a vow not binding. [Note: Above this line Emily has written what appears to be "[ ] of it."] Can it be so, that there is a casket of the affections destitute of the richest and purest gem of all, neither its own or pledged to another. Is it not possible Miss C. that you are mistaken in supposing yourself possessor of no intrinsic feeling by which the First Author of our being has designed us for conjugal bliss! [Note: Above the line beginning with "supposing yourself" Emily has written, "Is it not possible, Mr. R., that we girls may fix upon excuse to answer our purpose and suit your characters. How credulous!"] and is it not implied in the expression that you "have learned the art of living within yourself"? Perhaps it is not right to question your self-knowledge, but it is far more pleasant to believe that your love is of an order with the rest of your nature, and that you may one day find an object that may "inspire it" [Note: Above the line here Emily has written, "Hope [ ] [ ]."] where affection shall be founded on merit, intellect and taste, and *subservient* to them. I cannot believe that Heaven smiles upon so unnatural a state as celibacy, and if it were proper I might point out some of its evil consequences, where its "only motive" [Note: Above this line Emily has written, "Thank you."] is the one you mention—but "a mon is weel o'wae as he thinks himself sac" [sic]. For my own part I hope nothing will ever deprive me of the power of loving what is lovely. Enough of this.

I am very sorry to hear of your illness while you were obliged to inform me of it on a pillow. The window by which I write is shaded (when the sun shines) by a pleasant little grove of cherry, pear and peach trees which have been filled with blossoms and swarms of honey bees with their murmuring busy hum soothing the mind to contentment and cheerful musing. Its analeptic virtues on a poor invalid are like an enchantment or I too am a valetudinarian. "The spleen is never found where Flora reigns."

My sisters (and I believe I have some of excellent taste) have never succeeded in choosing what I deemed a "proper mate" for me, and with the poet I now almost "Expect to find / Two of a face as soon as of a mind." Yet I thank you for your kindness and advice, and am interested to know who it is that "has not forgotten me" as I supposed that no kind heart in your part of the world had thought me worth a remembrance, and I would like to know what "she said." Now I think I "have met you half way." If you choose to "act the sister's part" to me, be sure I shall feel a brother's gratitude, and that it is with fraternal interest in your welfare that I have endeavored to convince you that "Happiness was born a twin." If you "understand something of my character and disposition" as you fancy, you will not fear to tell me any thing you feel inclined to with perfect confidence and freedom—and I cannot doubt the friendship which would prompt any suggestion or piece of information you might give. You describe *nearly* every thing I desire in a lady and say that my "wish is not unattainable." Yet it still seems to me that I have lost it, notwithstanding I am a rational and practical believer in the truth that "love and love only is the loan for love."

As a "traveling companion" of your letter, I received one from brother Herd. I hope to be so happy as to meet him with Sister, and under the paternal roof at Watertown—at "my own dear native home." He professes to be at W. on the 3rd or 4th of June. I may hear from you before that, or may be I shall not go at all.

Good night and believe me ever your friend and brother

James W. Redfield

Miss E. E. C.

Source: American Baptist Historical Society, AJ 26, no. 1283.

Marie Dawson Bates to Emily E. Chubbuck,[49] July 14, 1840—Pleasant Hall

My dear friend

I received a few days since a paper from you containing a magical word—magical it must be since it has induced me for once to lay aside every employment and thought save those which will enable me for a few moments to converse with *Emily*, the friend of my early days—*Early days*—how many dear associations rush in as I repeat again those cherished words—how many "thick coming fancies" crowd around me as I again linger at memory's shrine and recall that happy period of my life when *we* together laughed away the very hours—even now I can almost fancy myself seated with my chosen friend at Morrisville, two light-hearted buoyant creatures in some unobserved corner, pouring into each others ears the gladsome thoughts and witching dreams of early youth; or perchance rambling in the glittering sunlight o'er natures garden in pursuit of some rare plant to analyze—or conning over the lessons of the day—say, my friend do you remember those happy scenes—or have the cares and pleasures of more mature life obliterated them?

I cannot forget them nor would I—they are woven with my existence and at times they come thronging round me with all the freshness and beauty as events of yesterday.

—Were I writing to one experienced in all the duties cares and pleasures of housekeeping I would not apologize for a silence of *months*, and indeed upon

---

[49] This letter is addressed to Emily E. Chubbuck, Morrisville, Madison NY.

second thoughts I will not to you for you are convinced I am sure, it has not arisen from forgetfulness and that my time has been fully occupied—Our family is small but—come and see us please and judge if there is not business enough to keep one pretty busy.

You recollect I presume that I mentioned in a former letter something about a select school in Cazenovia taught by a Miss Davenport—that her health was poor and well having been informed that her health was too poor to admit of her teaching and that she wished to engage some young lady to supply her place, I mentioned to Mr. Bates that it would be an excellent situation for my friend Emily, and he accordingly took the first opportunity of calling on Miss D. and mentioning to her Miss Chubbuck, but had already engaged a Miss Beckwith who had then been in school a week—Mildred D. said if she had known anything respecting it you could have had the school. You will think perhaps my dear friend I was taking quite a liberty not knowing how you were situated or employed this summer, but I thought it would be a pleasant and lucrative situation and wished to secure your society in Caz.—Probably you have recently seen a notice in the Moniter of the death of Miss C. E. Beckwith of Caz.—she was the teacher of said school and I do not know whether it is now in operation or not—if not and you wish to engage address Miss D. soon and I presume you will be successful—or if you would like to have me call on her I will, though not at all acquainted. But enough of this—I must finish my letter, it is some time since I commenced it, but I have so little time to write. All my correspondents have been sadly neglected for a few months back.

Dearest come and see me, I think we would have a good visit and I shall be very very happy to see you. I am enjoying much happiness this summer. I should be happy perhaps if my health were perfect.

Written along the left margin of page 3: "Mr. E. A. Bates[50] regards to you and please accept my warmest love—most affectionately yours, Marie L. Bates."

Written along the left margin of page 1: "Please do not [ ] after my long silence. I shall hope to hear from you soon. Tell me how you got along with your flock of wild cats that you told me about last winter.[51] Marie."

Source: American Baptist Historical Society, AJ 23, no. 1153.

Emily E. Chubbuck to Marie Dawson Bates, September 1840

O this is a sad world, where we must hope and weep, then hope again, and find even that in vain. I have spent the day alone, and I have almost felt as though I

---

[50] Emilius A. Bates, husband of Marie Dawson Bates.
[51] See the letter of Emily Chubbuck to Marie Dawson Bates, dated January, 1840.

was alone in the world. And now, Maria[52] dear, my heart as it is. I love my friends, and am grateful to them for regarding me; but I would have them altogether mine. O there is a fearful sense of loneliness comes over me when I think that none among my numerous friends love me as I would be loved; that I love no one with all the strength and capability of my nature. I would lay down my heart at a mortal shrine, and be, next to God, the supreme object of affection….

Wednesday, September 9, P.M. I have been making embroidered butterflies and needle-books until I begin to think it small business for such a "big girl;" so I have taken my pen to tell you how much happier I am to-day than I was yesterday—happier, because I will be.

>Happy, happy! Earth is gay;
>Life is but a sunny day.
>Lightly, lightly flit along,
>Child of sunshine and of song
>Happy, happy, earth is gay,
>Life is but a sunny day.
>
>If perchance a cloud arise,
>Darkly shadowing o'er thy skies,
>Heed it not 'twill soon depart;
>Bar all sadness from thy heart.
>Happy, happy, earth is gay,
>Life is but a sunny day.
>
>Drink the cup and wear the chain,
>But let them weave their spell in vain;
>Lightly, lightly let them press
>On thy heart of happiness.
>Happy, Happy, earth is gay
>Life is but a sunny day.

Source: A. C. Kendrick, *The Life and Letters of Mrs. Emily C. Judson*, 51–52.

---

[52] This is Marie Dawson Bates, one of Emily's childhood friends—A. C. Kendrick, in *The Life and Letters of Mrs. Emily C. Judson*, consistently has her as "Maria."

Lydia Ann Allen to Emily E. Chubbuck,[53] September 25, 1840—Wampsville

My dear, dear Emily.

My project has succeeded, and our most glowing anticipations are almost to be realized. I have but a few minutes since received a letter from Miss Sheldon[54] saying she will receive you and wishes you to come immediately; I will transcribe her words.

"Your friend Miss C. can come into my school as a pupil for one term for the expense of which time I will wait upon her, until she can pay—and when she is here we will make further arrangements for the rest of the time that it may be necessary for her to be in school.

"Please say to her that I shall be happy to see her as soon as convenient, the sooner the better for her, and will afford her every facility in my power for the accomplishment of her laudable project." Miss Sheldon says at the close of her letter, "Miss Chubbuck I hope will come immediately, the necessity of this you will understand."

Now Emily is not Miss Sheldon good, O I *do* love her, and I know you will.

You will find her a kind, and faithful friend. I shall visit Utica next week and I shall hope to meet you there, do'nt [sic] delay any longer than is positively necessary as the classes will be advancing.

O Emily I do want to see you and can talk so much faster than I can write. I write as though a cannon ball were attached to my pen. You asked me if you could take as many studies as you choose. Yes, if you do not choose to take improper hours to study, the young ladies are required to be in bed *quarter before ten*, and lamps *extinguished. Not at midnight!!*

Now Emily do not think of waiting until next term before you attend—As to

---

[53] In October 1839, Lydia had asked Emily in a letter if she had made a decision as to where she would be going to school. Apparently Emily had been thinking after having taught in village schools for several years, that she needed more personal education to advance her career.

The opportunity Lydia Allen offered in this letter would become one of the pivotal turning points in Emily's life. Her experience at the Utica Female Academy shaped her future in every way imaginable. The academy opened up new and more mature friendships to Emily, it gave her opportunities for teaching in her special field of composition, it provided financial security as a salaried teacher, and above all, it gave her personal time to pursue her writing and launch her career as Fanny Forester.

In *The Life and Letters of Emily C. Judson*, A. C. Kendrick says:

> Providence, meantime, was ordering an unlooked-for and grateful change in Chubbuck's destiny. Toward the close of the summer term of the Utica Female Seminary, Allen of Morrisville, one of its best pupils, and a warm friend of Emily, laid before the principal, Urania E. Sheldon, the subject of her admission to its privileges. The proposition was, that she should be allowed to spend two or three years in pursuing higher studies in the school, and subsequently make payment when she should become established as a teacher. Similar favors had been already extended by Sheldon, acting conjointly with her sister, Cynthia, to many young ladies, who were now filling important posts as teachers in different sections of the country. The application was successful. (53)

[54] This is either Urania Sheldon—a mentor, advisor, and friend to Emily—who was the literary principal when Emily was at the Utica Female Academy, or Cynthia Sheldon, who was responsible for executive and financial departments.

"security" Miss Sheldon says nothing about it, and I presume requires none. Now let me give you a little advice. Make a *confidant* of Miss Cynthia Sheldon,[55] Miss Urania's sister, who has care of the financial department, for she is a dear good creature, and of Misses Susan Look, and Eliza Gird, for they are dear good friends of *mine*, Mary Lavis. Also Misses Sarah and Sophia Hastings you will find to be noble girls, also become acquainted with Charlotte Whipple if possible, she is intimate with Susan Look and Sophia W. O that I were going to be with you. It seems to me that I *cannot* cannot [sic] stay away.

One thing more, do attend the Broad St church with Susan Look, where Mr. Eldridge preaches rather than the Bethel Ch.

Good bye, to you tonight, dear Emily. May blessings attend you through life, the path of the humble self-denying Christian be yours, also the triumphant death of the righteous.

Remember at the mercy seat
Your unworthy servant[56]

Lydia Ann

Miss Sheldons [sic] letter was written today.

Source: American Baptist Historical Society, AJ 22, no. 1083.

Marie Dawson Bates to Emily E. Chubbuck, October 3, 1840

Dear Emma [sic][57]

Mr. Bates[58] is going to Morrisville and I cannot deny myself the pleasure of saying just a word or two, all I can possibly have time as he did not think of going till a few moments since. How do you do Emma dear and how are all the rest? How did you get home,[59] and where is your friend Miss Reed, that you think your social intercourse with her is at an end. Have you seen Mr. Brown again? I am sorry to inform you (lest I spoil your [ ] in his favour [sic]) that he made himself quite ridiculous in his deep regrets relative to your friend Marie, at our neighbours [sic]—I wish I could see your sunny face—I'm sure it looks happy and why should it not?

---

[55] The subsequent relationship with Miss Cynthia Sheldon was to become an enduring one; Miss Sheldon, later known as "Aunt Cynthia," became both mentor and friend.

[56] This theme of "unworthiness" in Lydia Allen was especially expressed in Allen's letter of October 8, 1839.

[57] Emily sometimes referred to herself as "Emma"; in fact, in her first poem, written at age nine, she wrote to her cousin, "Mary you say you'd like to know/ How cousin Emma looks."

[58] Emilius A. Bates, husband of Marie Dawson Bates.

[59] In a letter to her brother Walker, dated April 28, 1840, Emily spoke of several visits she had made with Marie Dawson Bates. This may suggest a more recent visit.

Earth is happy, earth is gay.
Life is but a sunny day![60]

Tis even so dear E. I am *happy* too. Come and see me again this fall if you can do. Is your brother W returned—my compliments and best wishes if he has— Love to Pa,[61] Ma,[62] and Catharine;[63] how does "pussy" do? Mine grows interesting ever day [sic].

I wish you would call out and take dinner with me, am going to have some *samfe* [sic]. You see I am full of wishes as ever.

Many thanks for your good letters. Please write
Written along the left margin: "A line by Mr. B."
In extreme haste
Adieu dear Emma

Marie   Source: American Baptist Historical Society, AJ 23, no. 1152.

Emily E. Chubbuck,[64] October 8, 1840—Utica Female Academy[65]

Miss U. Sheldon[66]

A kindly star whose widely beaming rends
On many a budding flowret sweetly shine,
A spirit high – beyond the reach of praise,
A priceless gem from nature's richest mine.

Utica Fem. Acd.—Oct. 8th, 1840
6 o'clock P.M.   Source: Hanna family files, poetry notebook 2.

---

[60] In a September, 1840 letter to Marie, Emily had enclosed a poem which she had written, and these lines are a fragment of that poem.

[61] Charles Chubbuck, Emily's father. Though he held varying positions over the years, he failed at most of them. With the purchase of the house for them, Emily was to continue as a significant financial contributor to the support of the family.

[62] Lavinia Richards Chubbuck, Emily's mother, was born June 1, 1875, in Goffstown NH, the eldest of thirteen children. She married Charles Chubbuck on November 17. 1805. They were the parents of seven children.

[63] Sarah Catharine ("Kate," "Kit," or "Kitty") Chubbuck, Emily's older sister, born October 25, 1816.

[64] This is from page 51 of a notebook with eighty-four intact pages (It was originally longer; there are some pages missing.) all with poetry in the handwriting of Emily Chubbuck. It is the second of two poems on this page. There are a number of pieces which follow from Emily's life at the Utica Female Academy.

[65] This is the very first piece we have from the hand of Emily E. Chubbuck from the Utica Female Academy. This would have been written within the very first days of her arrival.

[66] Urania Sheldon had been the literary principal of the Utica Female Academy in fall 1840 when Emily Chubbuck came to study there, able to afford this wonderful education through the generous offer of Urania, along with her sister Cynthia, the executive and financial head of the academy, to defer tuition. Urania Sheldon was to leave in late summer 1842, with her marriage to the Reverend Doctor Eliphalet Nott, the president of Union College in Schenectady NY. Though, because of the distance separating them, Emily's relationship with Urania Sheldon Nott did not develop the intimacy that Emily grew into with Cynthia Sheldon, Urania Sheldon Nott was to remain a mentor, advisor and friend to Emily in the years of her writing, her missionary endeavors, and upon her return to America in 1851. She was also the aunt of Anna Maria Anable.

Emily E. Chubbuck Composition Book,[67] October 9, 1840

E.E. Chubbuck's Composition Book
Utica Female Academy 1840

A Sketch of Female Character

She was a rare creature—that Fanny Landon—*rare* I say, because qualities like hers are seldom centred [sic] in one person. But then they were beautifully blended, all soften'd down and half-shaded by a reserved modesty. It is seldom we meet a character where self-respect wears not a tinge of pride and a desire to please does not degenerate into inordinate vanity—when cheerfulness borders not on levity, and seriousness on sternness, or melancholy. Yet such a character was Fanny Landon's. Firmness was united with gentleness, energy and perseverance with a quiet retiring demeanour [sic] and a conscious integrity with that forgiving meekness which characterizes a true Christian.—Her life had not been one of continued sunshine; but trials if rightly improved are blessings in disguise and those through which she had past [sic] although they had imparted to her a singular power of endurance, had not detracted from her sensitiveness. Heaven had gifted her with a brilliant intellect but not at the expense of feminine delicacy and her heart was a rich mine of affection which often overflowed-not only for "kindred spirits" but for the smallest work of the Deity she worship'd.

Ay, Fanny loved everything—everything good, and pure and holy. The flowers, the rocks, the trees, the hills and sky—the light-winged butterfly, and wild-wood bird—all these she lov'd and not purely that they were passing beautiful, but because they had issued from the hand of the great Creator.

There was a depth of thought and feeling about her, unnoticed by the casual observer, and she passed in the crowd as a being of no superior mould. A character like hers to be appreciated must be fully known, and few there are that can read a page so veiled. Goodness must sit enthroned on the brow, or perchance be proclaimed by the tongue—and genius must flash from the eye, or clothe itself in the garb of eccentricity, to be understood by a common mind, and counterfeit jewels glitter with all the brilliancy of the true.

But Fanny sought not the praise of man. True, the approbation of the good was dear to her, yet dearer still the approval of high Heaven. The Author of her being was her guide, her director, the keeper of her heart, and in him centred [sic] all her hopes, not only for this life but for an immortality of blessedness.

Emily E. Chubbuck   Source: Hanna family files.

[67] Emily had received Lydia Allen's letter about the Utica Female Seminary on September 29, 1840, and the willingness of Urania and Cynthia Sheldon to take her on as a student on a deferred tuition basis. Emily must not have wasted any time in getting there, for this composition is dated ten days later.

Emily E. Chubbuck, October 16, 1840

The Old Man

Or

A Description of My Grandfather[68]

The old man's eyes are dim and cold,
And his pulse is faint and low;
The wind lifts up his thin grey hairs,
And his steps are weak and slow.
His voice is broken, and his thoughts
Are the thoughts of a simple child,
And by a smile, or a fragile toy,
Are the old man's woes beguil'd.

He remembers the day when an idle boy,
He careless rov'd and free;
And tells of the tiny brook that flow'd,
Beside the button-wood tree.
Each shrub that grew the old cabin near
Has its tale, and every tree,
And the old man laughs as he cons them o'er,
And claps his hands in glee.

Of boyhood's freaks he loves to tell,
And how his mother smil'd
Then shielded him from his father's wrath
When a reckless, happy child.
Again he tells of dark'ning days,
And rumors strange and wild,
And that kind mother's gathering tears,
As she look'd upon her child.

He remember well the rude old church—
He was in that house of prayer,
When a stranger brought a fearful scroll,
And the mild priest read it there.
He speaks of the throbbing pulse and brain
And the wildly flashing eye;
As their little band that day went forth,
To "conquer or to die"

[68] This is a variation on the undated poem with the title "Grandfather" which was published in the Revised Edition *Alderbrook*. One does notice the simplicity of this earlier poem, and the complexity of the later one. For the sake of comparison, the *Alderbrook* version is included at the end of this earlier version. This version was found in poetry notebook four, page 1.

The old man then forgets his tale,
And his thoughts are broken things,
But there's* a name will call him back,
In his wildest wanderings.
But speak of that, and his eye will beam,
With a newly kindled ray;
For memory clings to his country's friend,
In that dark and perilous day.

He knows not things of later years,
He lives but in the past,
And his dreams so long have cherish'd been,
He dreams they'll ever last.

He's going downwards to the grave—
—The good and kind old man—
Yet dreams of many years to come,
Nor knows his life a span.

He stands like the wreck of a fabric proved,
A bird with broken wing,
A rifted rock, a sever'd chain,
Or a harp with a single string.
O I love the old man with the wrinkled brow,
And the dimm'd and faded eye,
There's a holy spell around him cast,
That I feel as I pass him by.

Emily E. Chubbuck

*A *name.*—Every soldier of the revolution cherishes the name of Washington as the dearest of his treasured memories.

An anecdote is often told of a man whose mental powers had been so worn out by age, that he had even forgotten his children's names, and yet at the mention of Washington, his mem'ry would return, and his kindling eye and earnest tone plainly show the place the "father of his country" occupied in the soldier's heart.

Source: Hanna family files, poetry volume 4, page 1.

The Alderbrook Version of "The Old Man" or "A Description of My Grandfather"[69]

Grandfather

The old man's eyes are dim and cold;
His pulse beats fitfully and low;
He whispers oft, "I'm old—I'm old!"
And brokenly the sad words flow;
But, like the troubles of a child,
The old man's griefs are all beguiled.

The hair above his wrinkled brow
Is braided like a wreath of snow;
Years have not made his shoulders bow,
But his worn foot is weak and slow;
And totteringly the old man moves
Among the things his fond heart loves.

His boyish fears are o'er and o'er
In pride recounted every day;
And then he sighs that all who bore
A share, have mouldered back to clay;
A tear just wets his eyelid's rim,
Making the pale eye still more dim.

But soon another memory wakes,
Of prank wild, mischievous, and bold;
His trembling voice in mirth oft breaks,
While merrily the tale is told;
And then he laughs, long, loud, and free,
And claps his withered hands in glee.

But tales of darker, sterner days,
The old man loves the best to tell,—
The rumor wild, the dumb amaze,
The struggling bosom's fitful swell,
While liberty was yet in bud,
And e'en the bravest shrunk from blood.

The rude old church within the wood
Must in his rambling tale have share;
He tells how one blithe day he stood

[69] This is found on pages 281–83 of volume 1, the revised edition of *Alderbrook*.

Within that solemn place of prayer,
When with a scroll a stranger came,
Which turned the latent fire to flame.

How throbbed the pulse! how low leaped the heart!
How flashed the valor-lighted eye!
What tears from close-shut lids would start,
Though maiden pride suppressed the sigh!
How many a cheek forgot its glow,
And many a voice was choked with woe!

Now hastes the old man in his story,
Thick-coming memories on him crowd,—
The proud array, the battle gory,
The buried chieftain's starry shroud,
The midnight march, the ambush sly,
The savage yell and victim's cry.

The deed of daring proud, the word—
Here soaring memory stays her wing;
Some melody within is stirred,
And tears are trembling on the string;
For dearer meed the brave ne' er won,
Than praise from lips of Washington.

Around the things of later years
A veil of shadowy mist is cast;
The clearest, deepest voice he hears,
Steals upward from the distant past;
And as the lengthening vista grows,
Each far-off vision brighter glows.

He's going downward to the grave,
The good, the kind, the dear old man;
A worn bark drifting on the wave-,
Which the soft breeze, that comes to fan,
May wreck, while other vessels lie,
With canvass spread, scarce rocking, nigh.

He's going downward to the grave,
Yet bears a palm-branch in his hand;
Pauses his standard high to wave,

Ere treading on the blood-bought stand;—
Ah! church and hearth will mourn thy loss;
Thou brave old soldier of the cross!

I love that dear, kind, wrinkled brow;
I love the dim and faded eye;
I love to see the calm saint bow,
With those he loves all kneeling by;
For some strange power must sure be given
To prayers breathed on the verge of heaven.

Anna Maria Anable to the Reverend Rufus Wilmot Griswold,[70] October 1840[71]

I remember well her first appearance in Utica as a pupil.[72] She was a frail, slender creature, shrinking with nervous timidity from observation; yet her quiet demeanor, noiseless step, low voice, earnest and observant glance of the eye, awakened at once interest and attention. Her mind soon began to exert a quiet but powerful influence in the school, as might be seen from the little coterie of young admirers and friends who would often assemble in her room to discuss the literature of the day, or full as often, the occurrences of passing interest in the institution. Miss Chubbuck had a heart full of sympathy, and no grief was too causeless, no source of annoyance too slight, for her not to endeavor to remove them. She therefore soon became a favorite with the younger, as with the older and more appreciative scholars. Her advice was asked, her opinions sought, and her taste consulted. Many things illustrative of her influence over the young at this time crowd upon my memory, but I have no leisure at present to write them more fully.

Source: A. C. Kendrick, *The Life and Letters of Mrs. Emily C. Judson*, 55–56.

---

[70] Reverend Rufus W. Griswold was an ordained clergyman, noted anthropologist, editor, writer, and one of the distinguished literary figures of this period. Griswold originally showed up in an April 2, 1845 letter, in which Emily referred to him as a clergyman who had called upon her. Speaking of her days in Philadelphia, Emily wrote her brother Walker: "I got to be quite a belle while I was gone—gallivanted about with Graham and R. W. Griswold in Philadelphia."

[71] We placed this undated letter in October 1840 because the letter is about Anna Maria's remembrance of Emily at that time when she started her studies at the Utica Female Academy. It probably was written at Rufus W. Griswold's request as a resource for an article he wrote about Emily in 1848.

[72] Emily E. Chubbuck entered the Utica Female Academy in October, 1840.

Emily E. Chubbuck,[73] November 1840

Friday 6 o'clock P.M.

O I feel so alone! The kind and good are around me, but they are kind from principle and not because they love me. No one here loves me[74] and I feel that I could weep my very life away in loneliness[75] and weariness of spirit. "Glad faces are smiling around me" yet their smiles are not for me and they but bring up the image of the lov'd and absent. But there is one beam of brightness one[76]

Source: The Hanna Family Files

Emily E. Chubbuck,[77] November 10, 1840

A morning scene at Utica Fem. Acd.

A smiling band of young and happy hearts
Had gather'd round the well-spread board, but now
Each head was bow'd, and on each youthful brow,
A solemn stillness sate, for one low voice,
With tones of heartfelt, reverential awe,
Ascended up to heaven in grateful thanks
For gifts so oft enjoyed, so oft forgot.—
At length the sound was hush'd, and glances bright
Stole out from half-raised lashes, and the sound
Of merry voices like a murmur rose
And yet subdued, with softness in each tone
And kind forbearance in each playful word
Not like the wit we laugh at while it stings
The sly remark with malice half-concealed,
But all was mirthful truthfulness and joy.—

---

[73] This is from page a notebook with eighty-four intact pages (it was originally larger – there are some pages missing) all with poetry in the handwriting of Emily Chubbuck. This is the second of two pieces on this page. The next page, which would be pages 53 and 54, has been torn from the notebook.

[74] While this is an expression of Emily Chubbuck's loneliness (she had entered the Utica Female Academy in early October of 1840) we know that this was to become her new home, with wonderful friends of fellow students and eventually fellow teachers, and with the faculty (especially with Miss Cynthia Sheldon).

[75] Here Emily had added and crossed out "of Spirit".

[76] This sentence remains unfinished as though Emily was interrupted, left the writing, and never returned to finish her thought. Within a very short time her sentiments were to certainly change, for many of her life-long friends were to come from her friends and students at the Utica Female Academy.

[77] This is from pages 9–11 of poetry notebook 4 with twenty-six intact pages. Twenty-two of the pages are covered with poetry and/or prose in the handwriting of Emily Chubbuck; two of the pages are blank, and two have newspaper clippings of articles and poetry from the life of Emily Chubbuck Judson.

It was a happy throng: on those light brows,
The name of Care had never been engrav'd,
And disappointment with her blighting breath,
Had never sear'd and wither'd up the heart,
Nor Sorrow spread her wing of darkness there.—
It was a scene such as the angels love,
When each bright face threw off its mirthful garb,
And from the lip were drop'd rich gems of truth,
All cull'd with care from that exhaustless mine—
The book where God has registered his will.
O what a well-stor'd casket is a heart,
With the deep love of inspiration rich;
And better still if from its humble depths,
Beams the bright star of faith and truth and love.
But soon the chain of living pearls was strung,
The wreath of fadeless flowers was woven all,
And then the page was spread and on each word
Renounced by that dear lov'd one, many hung
With touching interest, and with hearts subdued,
Yet rais'd above the dross of earthliness.—
And then the song of praise to heaven arose—
—A heart-felt melody, so full of truth,
Each heart unconsciously was wafted back
To her dear childhood's home—far far away—
Where those more deeply lov'd had oft breath'd out
The self-same song at early mornings hour—
And there the wandering spirit was call'd back,
For such fond memories befitted not,
The sacred duties of that solemn home.—
The song of praise swell'd out and died away;
And then there knelt an aged white-hair'd man,[78]
With all those young and lightsome spirits knelt,
And raised his voice in supplication deep,
Pleading for freedom from the stain of sin,
For purity of heart, and thought, and life,
And that the likeness fallen man had lost,
Might be restor'd through Him who died and rose,
To be the lost one's mediating Friend.
He ask'd of Heaven to guard that youthful band

[78] In Emily's future correspondence with Anna Maria Anable, Urania Sheldon, and Cynthia Sheldon, Deacon Asa Sheldon is mentioned frequently as is the fact that he felt it his privilege and responsibility to lead the girls of the academy in prayer. Deacon Sheldon was the father of Urania and Cynthia Sheldon, Alma Sheldon Anable, and he was the grandfather of Anna Maria Anable. Deacon Sheldon died in March 1848.

Against the spell temptation's voice might weave,
For well he knew a thousands evils lurk,
Around the smoothest pathway, to destroy,—
And serpents evil among the brightest flowers,
That ever bloom'd to lure the'unwary f[ ],
Down to the world of death.
He ask'd for blessings on those spirits kind,
Whose task it is to guide, direct and check—
The boon of life, and health and peace for all.
And ask'd the richer boon of future life,
In that bright world where ransom'd spirits meet,
To join with seraph minstrels in the song,
Of "hallelujah to the King of kings."

Emily

Nov. 10th 1840   Source: Hanna family files, poetry notebook 4.

Emily E. Chubbuck[79]

The importance to Ladies of cultivating a Talent for Conversation

I do not propose on this present occasion to examine this subject very minutely, and in speaking of conversation here I shall refer only to that free, unrestrained interchange of thought and feeling, which constitutes the principal charm of social life.

That this talent ought to be cultivated is evident from a variety of reasons, and first for the very obvious one, that it is like all other qualities imperfect without cultivation. The Almighty has bestowed on us various powers but for wise reasons all in an imperfect state, and these we are to improve and strengthen. Among them the one I have taken for my present subject occupies a very conspicuous place.

---

[79] This is from pages 12–14 of poetry notebook 4 with twenty-six intact pages. Twenty-two of the pages are covered with poetry and/or prose in the handwriting of Emily Chubbuck; two of the pages are blank, and two have newspaper clippings of articles and poetry from the life of Emily Chubbuck Judson. Emily probably wrote this piece for her Composition class at the Utica Female Academy between November 10, 1840, and the New Year, as it falls between two poems around those dates. Beginning in fall 1841, when Emily taught the Composition class, essays, such as this one, were the main way that teaching and discussion took place. Emily spoke in letters of time taken to read and correct compositions. They were often presented, both in class and at social events. On April 10, 1844, Rev. D. E. Corey wrote a sharp response in reaction to a composition read at an academy soiree the evening before. The composition was on the subject of "Dancing as Exercise." Emily is often referred to in the correspondence as being extremely talented in this area—her future fame would attest to the writing—but also there was to be great praise for her classroom presence, her demanding requirements, and the life lessons that were taught and learned by her young students. As Emily and Adoniram Judson prepared to leave for Burmah, the issue arose of taking with them Abby Ann Judson, the eldest child and daughter of Adoniram and Sarah Hall Boardman Judson. Emily wanted to take her and made the point to Adoniram that she had been extremely influential in the lives of numerous young ladies during her teacing days at Utica Female Academy. In the end Abby Ann did not go; she remained in the United States.

By neglecting to cultivate this talent, a young lady is often placed in situations peculiarly unpleasant. There are in every society those who spider-like sip poison where the bee would find only honey and often a person of truly amiable disposition and kind heart is obliged to join (passively at least) in this heartless scandal, because she has not the art to change the subject of conversation.

Again she is wearied by the idle words and unmeaning phrases which have been uttered for want of something better and she wishes to introduce some subject of an intellectual or moral nature, but now she painfully feels her deficiency. She knows not how to throw in the few playful, yet meaning remarks which would make the transition easy, some studied thought is abruptly expressed which evidently jars upon the feelings of the company, she is abashed, disconcerted, and perchance gets the title of a *would-be* or *blue*.

Again, it is a moral duty to render those with whom we are associated happy, and next to kind acts and delicate attentions the power of expressing all that the heart feels has an incalculable influence in gaining the affections—and love and happiness are one. She who converses with ease and grace holds in her hands a chord which reaches every heart and produces there by its pleasing vibrations a delightful harmony. Not only has she power to discover *what* should be said, and *when* her idea should be expressed, but she knows *how* to express them. She knows how to soothe the afflicted, cheer the lonely, encourage the desponding, reason with the absurd, smooth the ruffled temper and bring together the discordant elements of a promiscuous assemblage of minds.

Ladies particularly, are expected to possess a talent for conversation, as they are (the De [ ] and Martineans notwithstanding) the ornaments of society rather than the pillars, formed to grace, not support the edifice. Taciturn men (especially philosophers) are sometimes forgiven, as their thoughts are supposed to be occupied by higher subjects, but women, never. There is an incongruity in the thing that strikes every mind, and how often do we see the effect produced by beauty and grace entirely destroyed by the chilling monosyllable, or inelegant expression of perchance the most refined sentiment. In this case a lady has no right to console herself with the thought that she is the only sufferer, for inasmuch as we dismiss our influence we diminish our power of doing good—benefiting our fellow-beings. This is indeed a very powerful argument in favour of cultivating a talent for conversation and when viewed in this light it becomes a duty which we owe not merely to ourselves and society, but to our God. —Our influence over those with whom we associate depends on a right state of feeling, as evinced by word and manner, and the one or the other becomes the more important according to our situation or the nature of the influence to be exerted. But there are few situations where action alone will produce as great an amount of influence as a proper expression of sentiment and feeling. If we wish them to *do good*, we must learn to converse intelligently, to express our ideas with perspicuity—and not only this but in an engageing [sic] manner—without which the most important truths will be like pearls recklessly thrown upon the uncareing [sic] ocean.

E. E. Chubbuck

Source: Hanna family files.

Emily E. Chubbuck to Marie Dawson Bates,[80] December 8, 1840[81]—Utica

My Own Maria[82] Dear

I wrote you last week, but as the letter remains in hand yet, and upon a review I find a very strong tinge of sadness about it, I have concluded to write again, lest you should think me *tres-miserable*, when, on the contrary, I am *tres-heureuse*. O, Maria, this is a happy, happy place, and Miss Sheldon[83] I love dearly.

In my other letter, dear Maria, I talked to you a great deal about our childhood's days, when you were such a bright, busy "humming-bird," and I your shadow; but as I feel now I can not mourn over them. I have been with Miss Sheldon tonight, and she is the dearest comforter in the world, and makes me believe that all will be right with me yet. My health is much better than it was last summer, and my spirits rise in proportion, except when—*n' importe*. I shall not talk of that now. But, O, when I sit down alone, and in my selfishness think there is no woe like mine, then, Maria, I want you by.

Maria, I have half a mind to consult you concerning a scheme which I broached to Miss Sheldon the other day. I have always shrunk from doing any thing in a public capacity, and that has added a great deal to my school-teaching troubles. But O, necessity! necessity! Did you ever think of such a thing as selling brains for money? And then, such brains as mine! Do you think I could prepare for the press a small volume of poems that would produce the desired—I must speak of it—cash?

I wish, Maria, you could see Miss Sheldon, you would so love her. My love for

---

[80] This is the first of two letters written on this date from the Utica Female Seminary; Emily was obviously settling in after several months. We note that her health was better, and that she was talking to Miss Sheldon about the possibility of writing as a source of income for herself. She also mentions here the possibility of a book of poems for publication.

[81] In two December 8, 1840 letters written to her sister Catharine and her friend Marie, Emily wrote of the possibility of a volume of poetry.

[82] This is Marie Dawson Bates, one of Emily's childhood friends—A. C. Kendrick, in *The Life and Letters of Mrs. Emily C. Judson*, consistently has her as "Maria."

[83] Urania or Cynthia Sheldon. Urania Sheldon was the literary principal, and Cynthia Sheldon was the administrative and financial manager. Both were to influence Emily profoundly.

her I sometimes think is almost idolatry. She makes everyone happy about her, and the school is more like a happy family than any thing else. Perhaps you already know that her father's family are [sic] here,[84] and they are all so good and kind to us girls that we look upon them as parents and elder sisters. I sometimes think of home, and then I want to be with my parents and dear Kate;[85] I sometimes think, too, of the past-a few past years. O Maria, how *did* I live?

Yours truly,

E. E. Chubbuck

Source: A. C. Kendrick, *The Life and Letters of Mrs. Emily C. Judson*, 56–57.

Emily E. Chubbuck to Catharine Chubbuck, December 8, 1840—Utica[86]

Dear Kate

Jabez can't get a chance to send you a letter without taxing you with postage and after serious consideration he has resolved to venture for he remembers the old proverb "nothing venture nothing have" so here goes!

You don't know Kate how I want to hear from home for I think of you and poor Mother[87] trudging and trudging away there, and lazy me doing nothing, but "there's a better day coming—" So Miss S.[88] says, and I suppose she knows. How *do* you get along, Kitty though? Any sign of morning in the east? Eh? Has father[89] done any thing about the place? How is Mother's health? Have you heard from Walker?[90]—I am going to make a grand trade with you when I come home so prepare yourself for getting cheated Miss.

The term ends on the 28th have father be sure and come for me that day.[91] If you are too modest to tell Mrs. [ ] what I wrote—just send her the letter and tell

---

[84] In addition to Urania Sheldon and Cynthia Sheldon, their sister, Alma Anable, was also engaged at the academy. Their parents, Mr. Deacon Asa and Mrs. Isabell Low Sheldon lived there with them, and there are frequent mentions in subsequent letters of the girls stopping by their room to visit with them. As they grew older, Urania Sheldon Nott would urge Emily and the other students to stop by and "cheer them up." Anna Maria Anable, a student and future teacher at the academy, became Emily's closest friend.

[85] Sarah Catharine ("Kate," "Kit," or "Kitty") Chubbuck, Emily's older sister, born October 25, 1816.

[86] This is the second of two letters that Emily wrote on this date. In this letter, she was talking about the possible publication of a "volume of poems." Writing for income is also mentioned in the first letter, so we know that writing and the need for income was very much on her mind.

[87] Lavinia Richards Chubbuck, Emily's mother, was born June 1, 1875, in Goffstown NH, the eldest of thirteen children. She married Charles Chubbuck on November 17, 1805. They were the parents of seven children.

[88] Urania or Cynthia Sheldon. Urania Sheldon was the literary principal, and Cynthia Sheldon was the administrative and financial manager. Both were to influence Emily profoundly.

[89] Charles Chubbuck, Emily's father. Though he held varying positions over the years, he failed at most of them. With the purchase of the house for them, Emily was to continue as a significant financial contributor to the support of the family.

[90] John Walker Chubbuck, Emily's older brother who ran a newspaper in the Wisconsin Territory.

[91] Hamilton was about twenty-four miles from Utica.

her there's "meanin' in every word."

I laid a plan a while ago to raise the wind, by publishing a little volume of poems to gain money to keep me in clothes and such like things while I stay here. I broached it to Miss S. and she is now examining my rag-bag, which is all I have with me.[92] If my plan goes into operation I shall have a job of copying for you when I get home, for I have no time for copying. I don't know whether the thing would be profitable or not. What do you think of it? Ask father what he thinks of it.

Attend to your piano music Kate and things will come right sometime.[93] I wish you could come out and spend a week with me. Wouldn't we have nice times? I have a drawing of Ham. Sem. to show you when I get home which I think pretty good. I haven't been very well lately but they have cooked me up and I am quite smart again.

Emily

P.S. You must be prepared to go about with me a great deal when I get home. We must bury the old house in vines and rosebushes until we are able to repair.[94]

Source: Hanna family files.

Emily E. Chubbuck to J. Walker Chubbuck, February 5, 1841—Utica[95]

Dear Bub,

I am very, very tired but having just received a paper from you I find a strong inclination to answer it by a letter even though it must necessarily be a short one. I don't know what you mean by your last two letters for I have not rec'd any from you since I have been here. I can't tell you how disappointed we all were in not seeing you home this fall, but I will not talk of that for I feel completely worn out and my head is aching dreadfully—A glance of my own prospects then!

I am as you well know contracting a large debt here[96] and sometimes I feel distressed about it but Miss Sheldon[97] is universally kind and I am sure I rather be

---

[92] See comments on publishing her poems in Emily's December 8, 1840 letter to Marie Dawson Bates.

[93] See Emily's letter to J. Walker Chubbuck dated April 28, 1840, in which she spoke of finding a career opportunity for Catharine and Catharine's temperament.

[94] Emily was aware of the home's condition in which Catharine and her parents lived. In late summer 1842, Emily purchased a new home for them.

[95] This letter is dated February 5, 1840—but the date is an obvious error. It is written from Utica where Emily was at the Utica Female Academy, and she had not begun her studies there until early October 1840. This letter also picked up themes of her potential writings, which are found in her December 8, 1840 letters to her sister Catharine, and her friend Marie Dawson Bates. For these reasons we have placed it in 1841. We note that Emily would have been 24 years old at this time, and she was just over three years away from her letter to N. P. Willis, the letter which was published in the *New Mirror* and which catapulted her to fame.

[96] Emily had an agreement with Urania and Cynthia Sheldon that they would provide her with an education without immediate cost, and that she, upon finishing her course, would make payments to them when she obtained a teaching position.

under obligation to her than any other mortal. I attend to but one branch besides French, Drawing and Oil-painting and the rest of my time I employ in writing, with what success time will determine and I sometimes dread to anticipate. They will pay me $2 a column for articles for the *Baptist Register* and a dollar a page for the *Mother's Journal*[98] but the style of both these papers is quite out of my vein and I don't expect to do much at it. I am also engaged some in preparing a little volume of stories for children and that too is quite as far from the mark. It perplexes and tires me and I am dissatisfied with every thing I do. If I did not place implicit confidence in Miss S. and know that her judgement [sic] was every thing I should give up at once and—I don't know what I believe if I have any genius it is for things not useful and can never be turned to account. Nonsense! how I go on! Very likely next time you hear from me it will be as an authoress. Pah!

Wallace[99] is in Canton yet but they have promised him the next vacancy in the office here [ ]. I am in hopes—no I can hardly hope anything of him. Wallace has a grand intellect but he is too indolent to properly improve it. He is proud and independent too and at the [ ] awkward and bashful. Few know him and he is very far from knowing himself. His intellect is I think of a superior order. He has the judgement [sic] of a man (with ten-thousand faults) the feelings of a woman, the shyness and self-distrust of a boy, and the roughness of a bear. Strange mixture—isn't it?

I rec'd a letter from him with your paper.[100] They are as well as usual and in better spirits. Kate is engaged to Ed. Norton[101] but I very much doubt whether they'll be married much under a year. Won't they make a capital couple! A very rational sort of love, theirs. Ha! ha! But it is better so. They will take the chances of life easy and perhaps be a great deal happier than the more warm-hearted. As for prospects Ed. is undoubtally [sic] a "rising genius" and besides enjoying a comfortable share of this world's goods may yet be some what [sic] distinguished at least enough to be "corporal" in peace or "scales of weight and measures" in war or *vice versa*.

I won't seal my letter tonight much as I want it to get to you but will wait till I am in better spirits and then perhaps I can speak more encourageingly. [sic]

Well another night has come but that wretched headache has followed me so

---

[97] This is either Urania or Cynthia Sheldon. Urania Sheldon was the literary principal, and Cynthia Sheldon was the administrative and financial manager. Both were to influence Emily profoundly.

[98] Emily would write for both of these publications. There is correspondence in the collection between Eliza Allen of the *Mother's Journal* and Emily, and Alexander Beebee of the *Baptist Register* and Emily. At the time of her marriage to Adoniram Judson and for several years after, Beebee was in a contentious relationship with Emily due to some judgments he expressed about her qualifications to become a missionary.

[99] William Wallace Chubbuck, Emily's younger brother, born January 1, 1824.

[100] John Walker Chubbuck, Emily's older brother who ran a newspaper in the Wisconsin Territory. Though he regularly sent copies of the paper to Emily, she often reminded him that a paper was not a substitute for a real letter and that his family longed to hear a personal word from him.

[101] Sarah Catharine ("Kate," "Kit," or "Kitty") Chubbuck, Emily's older sister. Kate's relationship with Ed Norton is mentioned several times in letters between March 1840 and March 1842.

perseveringly that I fear I should be a no more interesting companion so I may as well be off. Write often—give me our kiss—there I have imagined. My love to our friend Mrs. Brown, when you see her and—good-night, good-night.

Emily

Source: Jerome Walker Chubbuck Collection, Wisconsin Historical Society Archives, Madison, WI.

Emily E. Chubbuck,[102] February 8, 1841

Utica Fem. Acd. Feb. 8th

To Hatty[103]

I hear the sigh of the evening breeze,
The starlight is flicking the distant trees,
O'er the old brown hills play the quivering light,
And the towering church-spire glitters brightly;
While the white cloud laid on the night'winds' breast,
Like a wandering spirit in search of rest,
Is floating [ ] in the ether high,
Or poising awhile in the clear, blue sky.
It is a cold but a glittering eve,
Like the chain of pearls the brain may wear,
When the heart is as glazed and as chill below,
As the crystal ice or the sparkling snow.
O such is the chain we oft may see! –
Not this – not this, I weave for thee.
Nor seek I the[104]

Source: The Hanna Family Files

---

[102] This is from page fifty-nine of a notebook with eighty-four intact pages (it was originally larger – there are some pages missing) all with poetry in the handwriting of Emily Chubbuck. There has been a page torn from the notebook between pages fifty-eight and fifty-nine before the numbering was put in place.

[103] This is probably Harriet or Hatty or Hattie Anable, the sister of Anna Maria Anable, the daughter of Alma Sheldon Anable who worked in housekeeping at the Utica Female, the niece of the sisters Urania Sheldon and Cynthia Sheldon, the literary principal and financial administrator of the Academy. Born in 1823, Hatty was often mentioned in the correspondence over the years between Emily and Anna Maria, as well as with the Sheldon Sisters; beginning in 1842 she was to move to New Orleans and take a position in one of the homes as a teacher for the children. She was to become fluent in French, and in 1849 she returned to Philadelphia and the Misses Anable School, started by her sister Anna Maria with the held of extended family, and she became a teacher in the language department. Abby Ann Judson was to write during her stay there in 1852 – 1853 that she positively adored Miss Hatty.

[104] The poem ends here unfinished.

Emily E. Chubbuck,[105] May 1, 1841—Utica NY

Mo[ ]to written by Miss E. E. Chubbuck for Mrs. Anable[106] and Misses C.[107] and U. Sheldon.[108]

Mary Anable,[109] May Queen. Crowned in the evening in the large school room.

The three sisters— Not the Furies, though furious they may be
against vice—neither, though petrifying offenders, the Gorgons—
Not the Fates, though influencing the future destinies of thousands,
Not the Sirens, though charming all— No—yet, although of all
of the grace of benevolence, are they the Graces—but, but if
not a more renowned, a far more beloved trio—the mother
and Aunts of our respected Queen.

Source: Hanna family files.

Emily E. Chubbuck to J. Walker Chubbuck, May 7, 1841— Utica Female Academy

Dear Bub,

It is very late but I must write just a line to tell you a thing or two. Mr. Hawley[110] one of the publishers of the *Baptist Reg.*[111] starts for Wisconsin a week

---

[105] This is from page 21 of poetry notebook 4, with twenty-six intact pages. Twenty-two of the pages are covered with poetry and/or prose in the handwriting of Emily Chubbuck; two of the pages are blank, and two have newspaper clippings of articles and poetry from the life of Emily Chubbuck Judson.

[106] Alma Sheldon Anable, sister of Cynthia Sheldon and Urania Sheldon Nott. On July 28, 1814, Alma married Joseph Hubbell Anable in Troy NY (Anable's second marriage). Joseph and Alma Anable had nine children: Henry Sheldon Anable, b. June 21, 1815; William Stewart Anable, b. November 6, 1816; Anna Maria Stafford Anable, b. September 30, 1818, Cynthia Jane Anable, January 28, 1820; Samuel Low Anable, b. November 28, 1821; Harriet Isabella Anable, also known as Hatty or Hattie, was born December 18, 1823; Courtland Wilcox Anable, b. July 28, 1825; Frances Alma Anable, or Fanny, b. April 12, 1828, and Mary Juliet Anable, b. February 18, 1830.

[107] Cynthia Sheldon was in charge of the administrative and financial departments of the Utica Female Academy. After Cynthia's sister married and moved away, Cynthia assumed a larger leadership role at the academy. Active and well-known in Baptist circles, Cynthia became an important mentor, advisor, and friend to Emily until the time of Emily's death in 1854. Cynthia was the aunt of Emily's best friend, Anna Maria Anable, and addressed by most as "Aunt Cynthia." In 1848, Sheldon would move to Philadelphia to help Anable with the startup of the Misses Anable's School.

[108] Urania Sheldon Nott was literary principal of the Utica Female Academy and a mentor, advisor, and friend to Emily.

[109] Mary Juliet Anable, daughter of Alma and Joseph Anable. For about a year in the fall of 1846 to early 1848 she taught with her sister Hatty in New Orleans, and in 1849 she joined the staff of the Misses Anable's School in Philadelphia. Hatty said of Mary, "She paints and draws, speaks French, plays the piano, sings, dances and is our mathematician. She laughs from morning till night, and it is really refreshing to be with her. She became the wife of Pierre Jacques Darey in a service officiated by her uncle, the Reverend Eliphalet Nott. She died at the age of 68 in Ottawa, Ontario, Canada.

[110] Horace H. Hawley married Jane Sheldon, the niece of Cynthia and Urania Sheldon. Hawley was a member of a publishing firm and also worked with Alexander Beebee in publishing the *Baptist Register*. Hawley was enormously helpful to Emily as she published her early stories and books. There are numerous references to his help and his generosity.

[111] The *Baptist Register* was a local Baptist paper in central New York that grew into a paper of regional prominence. Published by Alexander Beebee, it had significant influence in Baptist circles. As a budding writer, the *Baptist Register* would have been a

from next Monday for the purpose of being married. His lady is Miss Jane Sheldon[112] daughter of John R. Sheldon[113]—perhaps you know her. He is to be accompanied by Miss Cynthia Sheldon[114] one of the best of good folks and Miss Barber[115] our drawing teacher. They will carry letters both ways and will see you if possible. You must look upon them as real friends for they are the best I have in the world. I don't expect you are overstocked with money but if you can possibly send me a few dollars by them I will agree to make the best of uses of them. I am here getting in debt,[116] out of clothes and shan't earn anything before next fall at any rate. Pa[117] is as poor and a rat and every cent he earns is by carrying Norton's papers. Wallace[118] is in Canton but he has quarreled with Barber and I have just dispatched a letter telling him to come home.[119] Kate and Ed. are to be married next September.[120] I will tell you of my own prospects when I write, next. I wish you could come home with them. Can't you? do!

Emily

Source: Jerome Walker Chubbuck Collection, Wisconsin Historical Society Archives, Madison, WI.

natural outlet for some of Emily's work. Later, in 1846 and the immediate time after her engagement and marriage to Adoniram Judson, there would be a conflict between Emily Judson and Beebee, as he was less than enthusiastic about Emily's suitability for missionary service, reflecting the attitude of many in the wider church. Emily was, after all, a popular, secular writer, and Adoniram Judson was the venerable missionary held in awesome respect. Emily and Beebee were to be eventually reconciled, and Beebee was often mentioned in letters from Cynthia Sheldon as Emily's strongest supporter.

[112] Jane Sheldon, niece of Cynthia Sheldon, Urania Sheldon, and Alma Anable, cousin of Anna Maria Anable, and married to Horace H. Hawley.

[113] John Sheldon was the brother of the Urania and Cynthia Sheldon, and Alma Sheldon Anable.

[114] Cynthia Sheldon was in charge of the administrative and financial departments of the Utica Female Academy. After Cynthia's sister married and moved away, Cynthia assumed a larger leadership role at the academy. Active and well-known in Baptist circles, Cynthia became an important mentor, advisor, and friend to Emily until the time of Emily's death in 1854. Cynthia was the aunt of Emily's best friend, Anna Maria Anable, and addressed by most as "Aunt Cynthia." In 1848, Sheldon would move to Philadelphia to help Anable the startup of the Anable's School.

[115] Mary Barber, mentioned frequently in the Emily Chubbuck Judson letters, was a student and then a teacher at the Utica Female Academy. There were ups and downs to that relationship; in fall 1845, apparently Mary had written to someone expressing what Anna Maria Anable called "ingratitude," and Mary had been banned from the academy until she made proper apologies to Sheldon. In a September 7, 1845 letter from Anna Maria, we learn that her remarks had been about Cynthia Sheldon. In November 1847, Jane Kelly remarked that they had not heard from Mary in over a year. In 1848, Mary was back at the Utica Female Seminary teaching with Jane Kelly. Though at this time Sheldon had moved to Philadelphia, Mary had been able to reconcile with her, and in later years we find Mary very close to the Sheldon-Anable families; later, there was considerable consternation on Cynthia Sheldon's part in her correspondence with Emily about Mary's health, the seriousness of it, and Mary's impending death. These letters were written in April 1852. Sheldon went to help transfer Mary to Albany in June 1852, where she would be better situated and perhaps have access to better doctors. On September 9, 1852, Anna Maria Anable wrote to Emily of Mary's death.

[116] Cynthia Sheldon and Urania Sheldon had agreed to defer Emily's tuition costs until she finished her education and found a teaching position. The debt was a constant burden to Emily and pushed her to find outlets and compensation for her writing.

[117] Charles Chubbuck, Emily's father. Though he held varying positions over the years, he failed at most of them. With the purchase of the house for them, Emily was to continue as a significant financial contributor to the support of the family.

[118] William Wallace Chubbuck, Emily's younger brother, born January 1, 1824.

[119] There is more about this falling out between Wallace and Barber on page one of Emily's letter to Walker of May 17, 1841.

[120] Sarah Catharine ("Kate," "Kit," or "Kitty") Chubbuck's relationship with Ed Norton is mentioned several times in letters between March 1840 and March 1842.

Emily E. Chubbuck to J. Walker Chubbuck, May 17, 1841—Utica Female Academy

Dear Bub,

Our folks start for Wisconsin tomorrow[121] and I suppose I can try to make you out a letter although I scarce know what to say. I rec'd a line from home this morning but no good news. Ma[122] is about worn out, Kate[123] is not able to do anything, and Ben[124] and Annette[125] is [sic] very sick. B. says he is about the "same old sixpence," but I am afraid the old sixpence *will not stand* many more scrubbings from fortune. He has got a mail route from Hamilton to Sangerfield for $140, a year, but has as yet made no arrangements for performing it. Ben conducts himself passably—as well I suppose, as he knows how, for you know he had a soft spot in his head and his wife's wisdom is not likely to harden it. My greatest trouble at present is concerning Wallace.[126] There are not many boys of his age that can surpass him in natural talent (for you know education has done but little for him) but I begin to discover that he has some weak points I had not thought of before. He has worked the past winter in Canton St. Lawrence Co. but this spring has had a quarrel with Mr. Barber and left the office. He gives one version of the quarrel and Mr. B. another so we don't know which to believe but what is worst of all he is in *debt*.[127]

He owes $30.00 and says he will not leave the place until he can pay it and so—what do you think? Why, the silly instead of going to work—ploughing [sic], digging, or anything that would bring the cash is *going to school*. Go to school to pay debts! Why, I'd beg my way to Texas or work my passage to the Indies if there was no other way of bringing things into a better state, or I would work side by side with the slave on a southern plantation before I'd sit down quietly to play the *gentleman* and be in debt. O it worries me almost to death! Nature has done enough for the boy, but this want of energy and perseverance will be the ruin of him. I have tried my very best to get a place for him here (at the Reg. office) but have failed. What can be done? Write to him do—and see if you can't start him out some way or other.

Now for myself. When I came here I calculated to go to school a year and then go out and teach. I have been two terms for which I am in debt about $120, but

---

[121] See Emily's letter to J. Walker Chubbuck of May 7, 1841. Cynthia Sheldon and Mary Barber were going to Wisconsin for the marriage of Sheldon's niece, Jane Sheldon, to Horace Hawley.

[122] Lavinia Richards Chubbuck, Emily's mother, was born June 1, 1875, in Goffstown NH, the eldest of thirteen children. She married Charles Chubbuck on November 17. 1805. They were the parents of seven children.

[123] Sarah Catharine ("Kate," "Kit," or "Kitty") Chubbuck, Emily's older sister, born October 25, 1816.

[124] Benjamin "Ben" Chubbuck, Emily's older brother. Ben suffered a head injury as a child, and his subsequent behavior throughout his life reflected some mental impairment.

[125] Annette Chubbuck was the daughter of Ben and Ann Chubbuck.

[126] William Wallace Chubbuck, Emily's younger brother, born January 1, 1824.

[127] See Emily's letter to J. Walker Chubbuck of May 7, 1841.

this term I shall (contrary to my former expectations) pay my way and in the fall be ready to begin to pay my past expenses.[128] I have written considerable since I came here but I begin to think this business more profitable to the *possessor* of money than to the *seeker* of it. Its promises are very flattering and I have hoped and hoped but never realized a single penny. I *think* now of stopping but am not at all sure of what is the best course. When I came I expected you home and was in hope you would help me to clothing, but I had'nt [sic] been here but a little while before Pa[129] wrote us that you were not well enough to come. Here there was a disappointment, but I have managed along although I have scarce appeared decent all the time. Miss Sheldon[130] is *very* good to me and I love her next to my own mother. She does everything in the world for me. I hope you will manage to see her somehow for she is going to bring me back word all about you. If you can spare any money possibly I wish you would send some and I will pay you with interest in less than two years. I am not very healthy but I *can* work and I *will*. I shall have neither Hough[131] nor Dr. Redfield[132] for I don't like them and can live alone. Besides I calculate to take care of Pa and Ma for I believe I am the only one left to do it.[133] Be a good boy, come home soon, but yet however long you stay forget not your sis,

Emily.

Written in the left margin of page 3: "Come home to the wedding in Sept. if you can."[134]

Source: Jerome Walker Chubbuck Collection, Wisconsin Historical Society Archives, Madison, WI.

---

[128] Cynthia Sheldon and Urania Sheldon had agreed to defer Emily's tuition costs until she finished her education and found a teaching position. The debt was a constant burden to Emily and pushed her to find outlets and compensation for her writing.

[129] Charles Chubbuck, Emily's father. Though he held varying positions over the years, he failed at most of them. With the purchase of the house for them, Emily was to continue as a significant financial contributor to the support of the family.

[130] This is either Urania or Cynthia Sheldon. Urania Sheldon was the literary principal, and Cynthia Sheldon was the administrative and financial manager. Both were to influence Emily profoundly.

[131] We have no information about "Hough," but apparently, with Dr. James Redfield, he had been a recent suitor.

[132] See James Redfield letters of March 7 and 23, May 14 and 22, 1840.

[133] Here again we see the need of Emily's parents, and their dependence on her for support.

[134] In a March 22, 1840 letter, Emily wrote to her brother Walker about a relationship budding between their sister Catharine and Ed Norton. There are several mentions of September wedding plans in letters written in spring 1841. A May 7, 1841 letter specifically says they would be married in September. A May 17 letter invited Walker home for the wedding. A July 6, 1841 letter to Catharine asked about money for the gown and her matrimonial plans. Nothing more was ever said of it until March 25, 1842, when Emily commented to Walker that the relationship of the Chubbuck family and the Norton family was still very good, in spite of the break up of Catharine and Ed.

Emily E. Chubbuck to Catharine Chubbuck, June 16, 1841—Utica

(Ma)[135] Chere Kit,—

I am not in the best possible humor for letter-writing (today), but knowing that you will be obliged to pay the fee before you examine the contents, **here's** (here is) at ye for a scribble. This morning I had a mammoth tooth extracted, and the rest are now dancing right merrily in commemoration of the event; so you must not wonder **at all, at all** if my ideas dance in unison. Kate, you may be sick**,**—for aught I know—**awful sick,** ("dreadful sick;") but **it's** scarce a particle of pity **that** will selfishness **allows** allow me for you, for know **ye** that I too am an invalid. I am growing rich "mighty fast," I can assure you; rich alike in purse and brain, by— doing nothing. **Don't** (Do you not) envy me? I wrote you that I could pay my way this term, study French, draw, and be allowed the use of the oil-paints. Well, first I dropped oil-painting; it was too hard for me. Then I threw aside drawing to save my nerves, and at last French was found quite too much. Afterwards I wrote a little, but have of late been obliged to abandon the pen entirely. What is to become of me I **don't** (do not) know. Here I am doing enough to pay my board, and attending to *one* class, by which I shall earn six dollars; (thus) wasting, absolutely throwing away my time. Miss Sheldon[136] says, if I never pay her she **shan't** (shall not) trouble herself; but she intends, she says, to keep me here as composition teacher, which will be as profitable as any other teaching, and for me, rather easier. **It is easier because** I can attend to **them** (the compositions) when I **happen to** feel like it, and not at particular hours. Miss Cynthia[137] has not **got back** (returned yet),[138] but Miss U**rania** is very **good** (kind) to me, and although I am merely working for my board **and not gaining any, I think**, I feel it my duty to stay;

Now pray, **don't** (do not) think, by what **I've** (I have) written, that I am really **sick** ill. **I'm** (I am) only **sort of** "fidgety"—**that is, nervous** (*i.e., nervous*)—as I used to be in (the) days of babyhood. To be sure, I **don't** (do not) see **kittens** ("kit-

---

[135] We have two versions of this letter—the original as written by Emily E. Chubbuck, and the edited version published by A. C. Kendrick in his biography, *The Life and Letters of Mrs. Emily C. Judson*. Additions made by Kendrick we have placed in parentheses (), and words in the original left out by Kendrick we have added in bold. One will note significant changes and omissions. In a note in his book, Kendrick explained that interest, purpose and propriety sometimes led to these changes and exclusions. "I remark here that in giving Chubbuck's letters, I do not always indicate unimportant omissions. Real letters must always contain much which should not meet the public eye; and Emily's were real letters, dashed off hastily amidst pressing cares and duties. Written also after the exhausting labors of the day, they by no means do uniform justice to her epistolary powers." He later added, "In giving a few extracts from his and Chubbuck's correspondence at this time, I have no wish to minister to a prurient curiosity, not to violate that principle which would generally place letters written during the period of an 'engagement' under the shelter of inviolate secrecy."

[136] Cynthia and Urania Sheldon had agreed to defer Emily's tuition costs until she finished her education and found a teaching position. The debt was a constant burden to Emily and pushed her to find outlets and compensation for her writing.

[137] Miss Cynthia Sheldon was the administrative and finance manager of the Utica Female Academy. She was a mentor, advisor, and friend to Emily.

[138] See Emily's letter of May 7, 1841, to J. Walker Chubbuck. Cynthia Sheldon was in the Wisconsin Territory with her brother John, John's daughter Jane, and H. H. Hawley for the marriage of Horace Hawley and Jane Sheldon.

tens") dance; but then sometimes the whole table full of young ladies **"go it for han'some"** (seem in tumultuous motion). I can walk better than I could last spring; but I can not endure the least mental excitement, and the slight noise that I (now) make with my pen produces a horrid sensation, as if every scratch went deep into my brain. **Sometimes I am almost afraid** (I sometimes almost fear) that I shall be crazy, but that is nonsense.

Why **under the sun don't** (do you) not send the money for your dress?[139] I have not had a new waist to my chale, for I **hav'nt** have not a cent of money on earth, and Miss C., you know, is gone. I had my brown bonnet **fix'd** repaired, and it looks as simple as a cottage-girl's; but **I have not paid for it.** *I have not paid for it.* **I hav'nt worn my white shift yet, but have put it in the wash this week, my light silk I find very handy. My [ ] fitted so badly that I have not done anything with it, especially as I lie on the settee so much that I should have no time to wear it.** My white bonnet I have pulled to pieces and laid [sic] by. If I had any money to pay for the coloring, I would take it to the dyer's, **then swap** and exchange it with you when I come home. **Betsey could make it by my brown.** Miss S. has given me some slips of geranium, but I am afraid they will die, because I can not get any jars to put them in. If they live I will bring them to you. I could get pretty flower-pots for eighteen pence apiece. O poverty! how vexatious thou art!

How do the doctor and Lucy get along? Mary says they are undoubtedly engaged, but I believe after all I have set the critter in [ ] to go home, because she thinks "the society there must be improving." Ahem! She sighs whenever I talk to her of doctor B. Poor man! how is he?

Mary shows herself more and more of a fool every day. I can't tell what Miss S. thinks of her but she's not one of the sort to be taken in. The teachers partly know her—not all—that is impossible. There may be "system in madness" but system in [ ] is I believe beyond most people's comprehension if not credulity. I expect every day when Mary will be off on another grand teaching expedition. I imagine the skin-flint has made Miss S. believe she is poor, I know she has told the girls so.—

I hear the Reeds have journey'd to Jefferson Co. How blows the wind in that quarter? Tell Br. R. he need no longer be afraid of my novels. They are not likely to amount to much.[140] Miss S. had written to New York and I shall probably hear in the course of a fortnight when you shall be duly informed.

This is a wondrously *loving* letter, I must say. But never mind; if I do not write the love I shall have the more for you when I get home. Seven weeks! Whew! **They'll**

---

[139] We wonder if Emily is speaking here of a wedding dress for Catharine. In a March 22, 1840 letter, Emily wrote to her brother Walker about a relationship budding between their sister Catharine and Ed Norton. There are several mentions of September wedding plans in letters written in spring 1841.

[140] *Charles Linn or How to Observe the Golden Rule*, Emily's first book, published in July 1841.

(They will) go like a **whizz** (whiz)! **I'd** (I would) like to have you burn this, for **somehow I've** (I have) something of an idea that it would not look well **sav'd** *saved*.

Eloise[141]

Source: A. C. Kendrick, *The Life and Letters of Mrs. Emily C. Judson*, 60–62; Hanna family files.

Emily E. Chubbuck to Marie Dawson Bates, June 23, 1841— Utica Female Seminary

Very Dear Maria,[142]

I have to commence in a very letter-like manner, viz., by asking pardon for delays, at the same time, however, hoping that your attention has been so much engrossed by your pleasant cares, that my silence has been scarcely noticed. How is the little one,[143] and your own dear self, and Mr. B.?[144] I hope the spring brought back more color to his face than it wore when I was with you.

O, you do not know how much I want to see you; and, Maria, forgive me, but I can but wish that you were a schoolgirl again, and here. How can I help thinking of you when I look out on the sun-lighted hills, and the flowing Mohawk;[145] on the waving shrubbery, and the dark, dense foliage of the distant forests? How can I help wishing you were by me, when I visit, with some uncaring friend, the thousand and one romantic spots that cluster this delightful valley? You do not know how I like the scenery around Utica! The "slop-bowl of the Union" is likely to make itself very attractive to me. I have a most delightful view from my window, and often when my brain has ached with exertion, I have sat for hours and watched the waves of light as they chased each other over the brow of the far-off hills, or sparkled on the waters of the Mohawk.

Shall I tell you what I am about, dear Maria? Well, silencing all the poetic aspirations I may have ever had, and chaining down my thoughts and feelings to—what think you?—stories for children. *You* ought to thank me, for who knows but they may be the means of making your little Edward Francis (by the way, I do like the name) "moral, good, and wise." Seriously, Maria, I am engaged in the very thing that you would least of all expect, and for which, if I am any judge of my own talents, I am least qualified. I have a little volume now in the press of Dayton and Saxton (New York), entitled "Charles Linn, or How to Observe the Golden Rule,"

[141] Eloise was the "E" in Emily E. Chubbuck. She often used this as she did here to sign a letter or a piece she had written.
[142] This is Marie Dawson Bates, one of Emily's childhood friends—A. C. Kendrick, in *The Life and Letters of Mrs. Emily C. Judson*, consistently has her as "Maria."
[143] Edward Francis Bates, son of Marie Dawson Bates and Emilius A. Bates.
[144] Emilius A. Bates, husband of Marie Dawson Bates.
[145] The Mohawk River ran through Utica.

and am preparing another for the same publishers. They settle with me once in six months, allowing me ten per cent on the net price of the books. A number of wise heads have together concocted this plan for me, and I think it, on the whole, the best that could be devised. Poetry, unless of a superior kind, is not saleable, and my present duties forbid my attempting any thing of a higher order. I do not study this term my health is not good enough; but I have charge of a composition class consisting of an hundred and twelve young ladies.[146] Is not that enough?

Now, Marie, I have *I'd* my way through two whole pages, and I suppose you can dispense with anymore egotism; but I shall not promise not to talk of *I* any more. Have you seen the new work by Washington Irving, "Memoirs of Margaret Davidson?" I have just finished reading it, and know not which to admire most, the fond mother, the frail, but gifted daughter, or the justly celebrated biographer.

You ask if Miss Sheldon[147] is all that she was. Aye, more. She is all the world to me now—my guide, my director in every thing. She takes a mother's care of me. If I ever succeed, I shall owe it all to her; and if I fail, I shall care more on her account than that of any being living. Four years ago the encouragements now held out to me, the bright hopes of literary distinction which sometimes I almost feel I am entitled to indulge, would have quite bewildered me. But now I have lost my ambition. Were I certain of the most unparalleled success, without any other inducement than fame, I should lay down my pen for ever [sic], or take it up only for my own amusement. Necessity at present urges me to this exertion, and when the necessity is past, then is the work past also.

Excuse this letter, Marie, dear, for I am an invalid to-day; and to-morrow, if well enough, I must resume my work of story-telling. I am anxious now to complete the volume on which I am engaged before the vacation, which will occur in six weeks.

Yours devotedly,

Emily E. Chubbuck

Write me often; please do, for I have but few correspondents now; and when I am sad and lonely, a letter is, as the Frenchman said, "like to yon oasis in the desert," or, with the penny-a-liner, "balm to the wounded spirit."

Source: A. C. Kendrick, *The Life and Letters of Mrs. Emily C. Judson*, 62–64.

---

[146] This surprising number gives us an idea of the size of the Utica Female Academy under the leadership of the Sheldon Sisters.

[147] This is either Urania or Cynthia Sheldon. Urania Sheldon was the literary principal, and Cynthia Sheldon was the administrative and financial manager. Both were to influence Emily profoundly.

Emily E. Chubbuck to Catharine Chubbuck, July 6, 1841—Utica Female Seminary[148]

Chere
Dear Kit,—

Not a word do I hear from you, notwithstanding all my **teasing** (trying and coaxing), and I suppose you would be "much obliged" if I would follow your example; but **that's** (that is) out of the question. I *will* write if **it's** (it is) only to plague you. And **'cause** (why shouldn't I)? If you **won't** (will not) tell any news, why, I must make up for the deficiency. Well, then, first, the July number of the *Lady's Book* has come, but, **O** terrible to relate! my poor "Old Man"[149] has not the expected place in its columns. If I had not the magnanimity of a-**of—of**—a-oh, dear! I can not think of a suitable comparison; but I do think there is **an awful sight** (a wondrous deal of goodness) in **not stinging** (me not to sting) the undiscriminating editors most scientifically with my powerful pen! But then I lay it to their ignorance; what a soothing unction!

Secondly, the July number of the *Knickerbocker* has brought out with flattering haste my "Where are the Dead?"[150] for it has been in their possession not yet a month; and consider, Kate, the *Knickerbocker* is, (perhaps), the most popular periodical in the United States. Thirdly, my "Charles Linn" has come—a beautiful little volume of 112 pages. It will be worth about five shillings. I have no **volumes** (copies) now in my possession, but suppose I can get some before long; at least I will try to bring home as many as *two* (you know I **shall have** (am obliged) to pay as much for them as any body). **You better be contented about seeing them till then and tell the Morrisvillians they can be obtained by sending to Utica.** I am very much encouraged about the sale of the thing **and think it will go finely**. The publishers **couldn't** (could not) send me the proof-sheets, so there are some mistakes in the volume.

My next book is about half written, but not copied at all. I shall not get it done this term, but mean to bring it home to finish. There is an article of mine in the *Mother's Journal* of this month.

My health is somewhat better than **it was** when I last wrote, and I do hope that it will continue. Miss Cynthia,[151] Miss Urania,[152] and ever so many other good

---

[148] We have two versions of this letter—the original as written by Emily E. Chubbuck, and the edited version published by A. C. Kendrick in his biography, *The Life and Letters of Mrs. Emily C. Judson*. Additions made by Kendrick we have placed in parentheses (), and words in the original left out by Kendrick we have added in bold.

[149] See "The Old Man" or "A Description of My Grandfather," dated October 16, 1840.

[150] "Where Are The Dead?" is printed in this volume following this letter.

[151] Miss Cynthia Sheldon was the administrative and financial manager of the Utica Female Academy. She was a mentor, advisor, and friend to Emily.

[152] Miss Urania Sheldon was the literary principal of the Utica Female Academy and a sister of Miss Cynthia Sheldon. She became a mentor, advisor, and friend to Emily.

folks here are as glad about my success as you will be. **O** (Oh), I love to write when people are interested for me; it makes the **labour** [sic] (labor) ten times lighter; and I have succeeded beyond what I ever expected, or even hoped. "Yet all this," as Haman said, "avails me nothing,"[153] so long as I see my empty wallet lying useless in my trunk, and my bills accumulating. But hope—hope. The publishers **will** settle with me in six months, and next January **comes** (brings), if not "*golden* opinions" exactly, *silver* ones.—**I should think the Nortons would take "Charles Linn." Ain't** [sic] **they book-sellers?**

Now Kate I have detailed my literary speculations at length—how is it with your matrimonial ones?[154] **Why hav'nt I got the money for the gown? I declare I believe you are plotting something in darkness, for not a word can I get out of you. Well enjoy your privacy and I will mine. I will not tell you one word of a certain gentleman that looks just like me, nor another certain gentleman that comes up to my idea of perfection all except in face.**

Do, if you care one cent for me, write immediately; for I have imagined (that) all sorts of things **have** (had) happened to you till I **got** (became) half crazy, and (have) then turned the scale by getting **all-killing mad** (desperately) angry.

I have not heard from Wallace[155] lately and Miss Cynthia did not go near Walker.[156] Now write, and make up friends speedily, or prepare for the everlasting hatred of

Amy Scribbleton[157]

Source: A. C. Kendrick, *The Life and Letters of Mrs. Emily C. Judson*, 64–65; Hanna family files.

---

[153] This partial quote is from Esther 5:13.

[154] In a March 22, 1840 letter, Emily wrote to her brother Walker about a relationship budding between their sister, Catharine, and Ed Norton.

[155] William Wallace Chubbuck, Emily's younger brother, born January 1, 1824.

[156] John Walker Chubbuck, Emily's older brother who ran a newspaper in the Wisconsin Territory. Though he regularly sent copies of the paper to Emily, she often reminded him that a paper was not a substitute for a real letter and that his family longed to hear a personal word from him.

See Emily's letter of May 7, 1841, to J. Walker Chubbuck about the trip that Cynthia Sheldon had made to the Wisconsin Territory with her brother John Sheldon, whose daughter Jane Sheldon would marry Horace H. Hawley. On that trip they had hoped to be able to see Walker, but that evidently had not worked out.

[157] "Amy Scribbleton" was one of the many nicknames or *noms de plume* Emily used for herself. Others included "Fanny Forester," "Nem," "Miss Peakedchin," "Nemmy Petty," and "Petty."

Emily E. Chubbuck to the *Knickerbocker* Magazine, July 1841[158]

Where Are the Dead?
Oh, whither have they fled—
Those spirits kind and warm,
Which, numbered with the dead,
Have nobly braved the storm;
And gained a port at last,
A port of peace and rest,
Where, earthly perils past,
Their happy souls are blest?

In some bright-beaming star,
Do they weave the pencilled rays,
Which, streaming from afar,
Upon our vision blaze?
Or is the flickering light;
Which the varying twilight brings,
As it glimmers on our sight,
But the waving of their wings?

Perchance along the sky,
The far-off azure dome,
They wing them free and high,
In their lofty spirit-home;
And the cooling zephyr's wing
As it fans the brow of care,
In its voiceless whispering,
Many a message from them bear.

I have read a page that tells,
Of a home *beyond* the sky;
Where the ransomed spirit dwells,
With the God of love on high.
There, their crowns of living light,
They cast down at his feet,
To seek this lower night,
And the child of sorrow greet.

---

[158] On July 6, 1841, Emily wrote to her sister Catharine that the recent edition of the *Knickerbocker Magazine* had printed her poem, "Where Are The Dead?"

Low, where dark shadows fall
On the heart and on the brain,
Where earthly pleasures pall,
And the bosom throbs with pain;
There, with kindly lingering stay,
On their ministry of love,
They smooth the thorny way,
And point to rest above.

Source: A. C. Kendrick, *The Life and Letters of Mrs. Emily C. Judson*, 64; Emily Judson, *Alderbrook*, 1:185.

Cynthia Sheldon to Emily E. Chubbuck, August 17, 1841—Utica[159]

My Dear Emily

Your manuscript is highly applauded by Mr. Hawley[160]—he says the dinner of the mo[ ]s is so exquisite as to insure a passport to the book—if it professed nothing more of genius—which is not the case. It will go with him the last of this month. Miss Reynolds[161] says you had it contemplation to add a wreath—if so can you send it before he goes—I cannot say anything about Urania's[162] visit to you as she has not yet returned—her stay in Washington was extended—and her engagement there and at Baltimore far exceeded her anticipations—probable [sic] she is now on her way home—I will write you if she can go visit. Miss R. and Harriet[163]

---

[159] This letter originally had addendums written by Caroline Reynolds and Hatty Anable. They are placed as the next two letters in the correspondence.

[160] Horace H. Hawley was enormously helpful to Emily as she published her early stories and books.

[161] Caroline Reynolds was at the Utica Female Academy with Emily—and here she added to a letter written by Cynthia Sheldon, stating that in Emily's absence she had taken over her room. In a September 1842 letter, Caroline was teaching school in Port Byron, with thirty-five scholars. In a June 25, 1842 letter, Emily wrote to Catharine that "Caroline is too mean and hateful to give me a minute's peace. She is decidedly the most disagreeable thing that I ever saw, but one thing you may be assured, your amiable sister is not quite a martyr for nothing, and can make the [ ] of others somewhat uncomfortable when her own is stuck full of thorns. This I imagine Car. has found out for she has not been ten minutes in the room since breakfast. Good!"

[162] This is either Urania or Cynthia Sheldon. Urania Sheldon was the literary principal of Utica Female Academy, and Cynthia Sheldon was the administrative and financial manager. Both were to influence Emily profoundly.

[163] Harriet ("Hatty," "Hattie," or "Hat") Anable, daughter to Joseph and Alma Anable and niece of Cynthia Sheldon and Urania Sheldon Nott. In this letter, she had added a note to Sheldon's letter. As early as November 1842 she was away, and a letter from Emily to Catharine Chubbuck said that "she expected that Hat would return as accomplished as Anna Maria." Her trips away were both educational, and employment as she worked as a private tutor in families that would bring her into their homes. In August 1843, she had just returned from Beonsen, in the vicinity of New Orleans, and was engaged to go again. A letter from Anna Maria on January 6, 1845 said that she would stay south for another year. About this time Cynthia Sheldon mentioned her concern for Hatty's spiritual health. In May 1845 she was in New Orleans. She was home again in the summer 1846, but a September 27 letter from Anna Maria said she had been asked by Roman with some urgency to return and she thought that she should. She returned home from New Orleans in January 1849 after Anna Maria Anable had started the Misses Anable's School in Philadelphia in fall 1848. Harriet was fluent in French, having placed herself earlier in a French environment in New Orleans. Hatty died in 1858.

are taking comfort—the children too—Mary[164] is at Mrs. Looks. Our Missionaries are expecting to come here before the school commences[165]—Mr. and Mrs. Chandler will be set apart publicly next Sabbath Evg and leave the same week for Boston—

We have succeeded finally in the outfit. My room is filled with finished work for marking—thus you see the Lord opens the hearts of his people to work for his glorious cause in the earth.—poor Mrs. Bennettt[166] does not gain strength—never were my deepest sympathies more enlisted—but God our guide only can lead her in safety.

May kind heaven grant you every blessing which bringeth peace and gratitude to the giver in this vacation—above all prise [sic] is health—do seek it in relaxation

In haste yours truly

C. Sheldon

Source: American Baptist Historical Society, AJ 26, no. 1280.

Caroline Reynolds to Emily E. Chubbuck, August 17, 1841[167]

I have just received your paper and was going down to tell Miss Sheldon[168] you were well, when she met us at the top of the stairs with this sheet, which she wishes Harriet[169] and I to fill, and right gladly do I comply. Dear Emily, you don't know how much we think and talk about you, and we miss you so much.

We are as busy as we can be. What with riding, visiting, studying, scribbling, and repairing our wardrobes, we manage to beguile ourselves of the loneliness we should otherwise feel and make ourselves very happy. We don't hear from the girls

---

[164] Mary Juliet Anable was born February 18, 1830, in Bethlehem NY, daughter of Alma and Joseph Anable. She went to New Orleans with Hatty Anable in 1847, but returned home early in March 1848, and by 1849, she was working with Anna Maria Anable in the Misses Annable's School in Philadelphia. Writing in March 1849, Hatty said of Mary: "She paints and draws, speaks French, plays the piano, sings, dances and is our mathematician. What should we ever do without her? She laughs from morning till night, and it is really refreshing to be with her." On December 26, 1860, she married Pierre Jacques Darey, with her uncle, Rev. Dr. Eliphalet Nott, officiating the ceremony. Mary died at the age of sixty-eight (April 20, 1898) in Ottawa, Ontario, Canada.

[165] See Cynthia Sheldon's letter of September 1, 1841, as she speaks of this ceremony.

[166] Stella Bennett, missionary to Burmah. Married to Cephas Bennett. Cephas and Stella arrived as missionaries to Burmah in 1830; Cephas was a printer for the mission. Stella was from Marcellus NY, and we know that she was home in the United States at this time. Later the Bennetts would send their daughters to the Utica Female Academy and the Misses Anable's School.

[167] This letter was an addendum to the August 17, 1841 letter written by Cynthia Sheldon. There is a second addendum added by Hatty Anable.

[168] This is either Urania or Cynthia Sheldon. Urania Sheldon was the literary principal, and the sister of Miss Cynthia Sheldon. She became a mentor, advisor, and friend to Emily.

[169] Harriet ("Hatty," "Hattie," or "Hat") Anable, daughter to Joseph and Alma Anable and niece of Cynthia Sheldon and Urania Sheldon Nott.

many of them yet. Miss S.[170] is having fine times at W. and A.M.A.[171] is very happy at N. Y. Not a word from Linda or M. B.[172]—your room is "alone in its glory" yet, but I am soon to "follow in the footsteps of my illustrious predecessor" and take possession in fine style, when Old Mary has as she says cleaned it "as clean as a pin." But follow as I will, I may never hope to merit or attain the *laurel wreath* which is destined to encircle your brow; but I am sure you cannot yourself rejoice more in your success than will the friends who love you. May it be yours on earth, and may a crown of never fading glory be yours above. I have so much to say, but I must leave room for H. dear Harriet suffers so much with her face and teeth. I will take care of your cloak and what ever else I can find belonging to you.

Yours ever

Caroline Reynolds

Source: American Baptist Historical Society, AJ 26, no. 1280.

Harriet Anable to Emily E. Chubbuck, August 17, 1841[173]

My Dear Emily

I am almost dead with the face ache yet I must write to tell you how very nicely Sister Reynolds[174] and I get along together.

She has'nt [sic] thought of crying since you left, and indeed now that she knows me better, I believe she thinks I more than make up for the loss of her dear Emily. We are as happy as two pigs. She talks most all the time about you, and says she don't [sic] believe I love you near as well as she does, but I do, don't I Emily? She *talks* a great deal, but I *feel* a great deal more.

Your most obedient nonsensical

Hatty

[Note: This is an insert from Caroline.] Hatty has told a fib C.

Source: American Baptist Historical Society, AJ 26, no. 1280.

[170] Urania Sheldon was the literary principal and the sister of Miss Cynthia Sheldon. In the earlier segment of this letter, Miss Reynolds mentioned that Urania was visiting in Washington.

[171] Anna Maria Anable was the niece of the Urania and Cynthia Sheldon, the daughter of Joseph and Alma Sheldon Anable. Emily first met Anna Maria in fall 1840 when she went as a student to the Utica Female Academy; both Emily and Anna Maria were to become members of the faculty there. In these years Anna Maria became Emily's dearest friend, and the extensive correspondence between the two reflects sensitive, flirtatious spirits, and a deep intimacy. Emily was "Nemmy" to Anna Maria's "Ninny." In 1848, Anna Maria Anable, with the help of her extended family, moved to Philadelphia and started the Anable's School in Philadelphia. At Emily's death in 1854, Anna Maria was given guardianship of Emily Frances Judson, daughter of Emily and Adoniram Judson.

[172] Probably Mary Barber, one of the students, later to become a teacher at the Utica Female Academy.

[173] This letter was an addendum to the August 17, 1841 letter written by Cynthia Sheldon. An earlier addendum had been added by Caroline Reynolds.

[174] Miss Caroline Reynolds, who wrote the earlier part, with an addendum to this letter.

Cynthia Sheldon to Emily E. Chubbuck,[175] September 1, 1841—Utica

My dear Emily,

Oft have I wished you here this past week.—The last week with our dear Missionaries.[176] They left yesterday morning. The enclosed locks of hair and the miniatures on one ivory is all those parents bear as mementos of their six children.

I do wish you would draw the picture—showing the power of religion—and let the world know how strikingly it is demonstrated in this case.—Holy consecration to the requirements of heaven. The superintendence of the same Almighty being over the children's parents all present with Him, and commingling at the throne of grace whatever distance—you would bid them God speed as did the primitive church to Paul when they gave him the hand of fellowship to go the second time to the Gentiles he had been absent on the mission [ ] year—and we know not as the brethren attempted to hold him back, could you have been here I say notwithstanding, the tears and sobs of separation you would say, go.—Childhood feels but momentary—yet they in turn will gaze on the picture and love mama—papa too gave the last look with streaming eyes—dear Emily, if you can but hold up this picture to comfort parents—sooth children—stop the cry of others who decide it is in the wrong—doing more than duty makes them feel that missionaries children have claims where no sacrifice has been made of self or children—[177]

I ask again dear girl if it is possible for you to write suitable length for the Register[178]—in Poetry. Send it to me on Monday—that I may forward the original to them at Boston Tuesday morn'g, it would just reach there the 11th, day for sailing—perhaps a few days later.

I know of nothing that would so much blunt the sting of separation as this course—nothing that would so much subserve the mission cause—and no one but your dearself who can do it.

My prayer is that you will try—firmly believing you will succeed.

I do not think Urania[179] can get there. Say nothing about my writing this—no

---

[175] This letter is a reference to the departure of Mr. and Mrs. Chandler, missionaries who were leaving for the mission field. Apparently they had left six children behind, and Sheldon speaks of the difficulty and sacrifice of this very common practice.

[176] In her letter of August 17, 1841, Sheldon spoke of the missionaries Mr. and Mrs. Chandler, who would be set apart publicly on the following Sabbath, upon which they would leave for Boston and sail to the mission field.

[177] While Miss Cynthia Sheldon speaks nobly of the consecration of missionaries and the children's grief as "momentary," the idea of separating parents and children was controversial. Many missionaries did in fact leave children, feeling a strong call of God's wanting to protect younger lives from the harsh realities of missionary service and wanting their children to receive the best education possible; yet in future correspondence with Emily Judson, many missionaries spoke of this and gave reasons why they would keep their children with them. One spoke of the United States as offering too much in the way of sinful temptation to children.

In 1847, when her niece Anna Maria Anable was contemplating missionary service, Miss Sheldon's feelings were not so noble as expressed here. She simply said "no"—Anna Maria was needed here as an important part of the householld.

The Judson children, especially Abby Ann and Adoniram, spoke out in later years with harsh criticism of the practice.

[178] The *Baptist Register* was published by Alexander Beebee and had significant influence in Baptist circles.

[179] Urania Sheldon was the literary principal of the Utica Female Academy and a sister of Miss Cynthia Sheldon. She became a mentor, advisor, and friend to Emily.

one knows it.

All well—yours truly,

C. Sheldon

Source: American Baptist Historical Society, AJ 26, no. 1279.

Urania Sheldon to Emily E. Chubbuck, September 3, 1841—Utica

I am scarcely reconciled my dear Emily to the disappointment of not visiting you this vacation, but day after day has slipped by, and here I am, and here I am like to be. It is impossible for me [to] visit you and your dear parents now, whom I wish very much to know—but at some future time I will promise myself that pleasure. We are still quite alone—with the exception of Mrs. Mason, Miss Reynolds'[180] particular friend—who will spend a few days with us. Ms Jordan will leave us next week. She will join company for Alabama and Baltimore. Mr. Hawley[181] writes from S.B. that the publishers are delighted with your book[182] and intend bringing it out very soon—We hope to begin to collect our wandering things by the last of this week—and as the long journey generally makes you sick, I shall look for you this Friday and Sat or until you come—to be serious I hope to see you in as good health as [ ].

In great haste

I am my dear girl your affectionate friend

Urania E. Sheldon

Source: American Baptist Historical Society, AJ 26, no. 1277.

Emily E. Chubbuck to Catharine Chubbuck, September 28, 1841—Utica Female Academy

Chere Kit

It is at last decided (Miss U.[183] did'nt [sic] quite think) that you will room with me and I have the nicest little room that ever was. We shall expect you on the day

---

[180] Caroline Reynolds, Emily's schoolmate at Utica Female Academy.

[181] Horace H. Hawley was enormously helpful to Emily as she published her early stories and books.

[182] We believe that this is a reference to Monthly Rose, which, though expectations were high, was unfortunately not published at this time.

[183] Urania Sheldon was the literary principal of the Utica Female Academy and a sister of Miss Cynthia Sheldon. She became a mentor, advisor, and friend to Emily.

proposed all in order.[184] Get your teeth fixed, purchase a green veil and a pair of India rubbers, and have your other things in the best possible order. You had better ride in your merino dress and a muslin or some kind of thick collar, I don't exactly remember what you have, but don't wear lace. I have bargained for you a shawl at four dollars, an imitation brocha [sic] which I think is rather pretty and I will try to hire you a guitar, this is all I can do for you in the money line, as, after I get me a pair of shoes, I shall have only fifty cents left. Ain't [sic] I rich!—You must, at least, bring money enough to purchase pencils, Bristol board, papers etc.—I don't like it at all to think pa[185] did'nt write more. Not a word about business, or who was to stay with mother,[186] or anything but that you had'nt [sic] heard from Wallace[187]—wonder if he thought I didn't care.

I bought a *Charles Linn*[188] to send home by M. Williams but she was so good as not to call. Suppose she forgot.

I have written about thirty pages on foolscap of my new book but I get along rather slow.—I want to write to Wallace and shall if I can possibly get time.—You must bring all the medicine you will want till Jan. with you. Now don't think you won't need much, for it will be very difficult to get the right sort here.

I have made a rough estimate of matters and things and think I don't owe Miss Sheldon[189] over $70.00[190] which with my bill at Dr. Kendall's makes the amount of all my debts $84.00. Your bill will be about $63, per term and this I rather think I can pay in writing.[191] At any rate I shall try. I think if we both have our health we can come out square at the end of the summer term. This however can be done only by the closest application and the strictest economy. Now for a chase Kate, an' what say ye?—O your washing—can you raise money to pay it? I hate awfully to speak about it's [sic] being done in the house, and if [Note: "I do" is written and crossed out.] it is, it must be paid sometime. I wish you would look among my

---

[184] In previous letters to Catharine, and to their brother J. Walker Chubbuck, Emily had spoken of Catharine's future, and encouraged her to study music, and to obtain as much general education as she possibly could. Here Emily has made arrangements with Cynthia Sheldon and Urania Sheldon for Catharine to spend at least two terms at the Utica Female Academy, with the charges to go against Emily's account. As fall unfolded, Emily became ill, and Catharine was obliged to spend considerable time taking care of her; but by the time she returned home in March, she had been able to take classes over several areas of interest.

[185] Charles Chubbuck, Emily's father. Though he held varying positions over the years, he failed at most of them. With the purchase of the house for them, Emily was to continue as a significant financial contributor to the support of the family.

[186] Lavinia Richards Chubbuck, Emily's mother, was born June 1, 1875, in Goffstown NH, the eldest of thirteen children. She married Charles Chubbuck on November 17. 1805. They were the parents of seven children.

[187] William Wallace Chubbuck, Emily's younger brother, born January 1, 1824.

[188] *Charles Linn or How to Observe the Golden Rule*, Emily's first book, published in July 1841.

[189] Cynthia Sheldon and Urania Sheldon had agreed to defer Emily's tuition costs until she finished her education and found a teaching position. The debt was a constant burden to Emily and pushed her to find outlets and compensation for her writing.

[190] Emily's deferred tuition for the year of study at the Utica Female Academy.

[191] Catharine took a year of study at the academy because Emily added the cost to her own personal debt. Emily hoped to pay it off through her writing.

papers for a sheet pinned together in the form of a book with my wash bill for three terms on it, I am afraid it is lost.—How do you settle your bill with Marsh?—I wish you would bring my knitting-needles (tell mother I'll pay her in something better than cash if she will do the stockings—no hurry—sometime in the course of the winter) and the plants—no I hav'nt [sic] any pots and don't know how to buy them. You will want your work-basket and a couple of towels. Bring some cloths that will do for dusting. Miss S. will take the ones we now have away.

If you have plenty of room you may put in that night-gown you were to make, but no great matter, I shan't have time to do it this term. Bring your short night-gown and all, they will come in play. You had better have two prs. drawers of course cloth for winter. I have got cotton flannel and have been buying me some flannel for waists or wrappers. I bought some port wine, [ ], and sugar the other day—a very pleasant medicine by the way—and it is doing wonders for me. I can almost "see myself" grow fat.—Tell mother she must have all the courage of a "man of war" for things are all coming round right.—Now don't you love Miss Sheldon? Miss Cynthia?[192] And all? They may preach about their men-women, neather-spirits, female-brethren, or whatever you chose call them as much as they please, such persons never dreamed of doing the good that these do without making any fuss at all about it. hey Kate?—But I must to my compositions while I jabber here, they are suffering for want of proper attention. Good-bye and come on.

Amy S.[193]

Source: Hanna family files.

Marie Dawson Bates to Emily E. Chubbuck, October 3, 1841, Sabbath Eve

Very dear friend

The "ten days" have passed by and the *eleventh* too, on which you promised to write me and I have been wishing for the letter, though not exactly expecting one for I knew how busily you would be engaged after your arrival at Utica, besides I feared your journey there would unfit you for any employment for a few days at least—How is your health now Emma[194] dear, and how did you find Miss Sheldon?[195] I can't help feeling interested in her and loving her too, for she is such

---

[192] Miss Cynthia Sheldon was the administrative and finance manager of the Utica Female Academy. She was a mentor, advisor, and friend to Emily.

[193] In her July 6, 1841 letter to Catharine, Emily had signed it "Amy Scribbleton," so this "Amy S." is a variation. These are two of several other names used of Emily by herself and her close friends—"Nemmy"—"Nem"— "Nemmy Petty"—"Peakedchin."

[194] In her letter of October 3, 1840, Marie Dawson Bates also addresses Emily as "Emma." In a childhood poem (1826), Emily referred to herself as Emma.

[195] Miss Cynthia Sheldon was the administrative and finance manager of the Utica Female Academy. She was a mentor, advisor, and friend to Emily.

a good friend of yours and taking such sisterly care of you. And I am thankful that she does, for I really am apprehensive if you had not some kind guardian, some ministering spirit near you, you would let your *ambition*—no not *that*—*industry* run away with you—be careful of your health dear E. you know it is of priceless value. Let your progress towards the pinnacle of fame be *slow and steady*, I feel assured it will be onward—indeed I see in the prospective laurels of no ordinary [Note: End of page.]

Source: American Baptist Historical Society, AJ 23, no. 1151.[196]

Emilius. A. Bates[197] to Emily E. Chubbuck, October 3, 1841, Sabbath Eve

Dear friend,

Allow me to express my opinion of your first production for the Press, *Charles Linn*[198]—I have examined it attentively, and taking into consideration the difficulty of clothing one's Ideas, in language suited to the comprehension of the Young reader, I must frankly say to you that you have succeeded beyond my most sanguine hopes—*Charles Linn* is a work, abounding in pure moral sentiment, displaying a through knowledge of the workings of the human heart, making plain that Principle of Forgiveness taught by our blessed Saviour [sic] when here upon Earth and which should be the guiding principle of his followers. "To love those that despitefully use and persecute you." To *forget an injury while we forgive it*—this to me is the most admirable feature of the work. A work which taken as a whole reflects credit upon the head and heart of its author. A work surpassed by none not even by our much loved Miss Sedgewick.[199]

"Press on" Emily nor leave the Paths of Literature until beneath the vine recorded bower which stands upon the very summit of Sciences rugged steep—You can rest on the lap of Genius fanned by fames gentle breeze—inhaling Poetry's rich fragrance—and sustained by Genius' ability, truth and self-respect.

> May peace be yours as calm and sweet
> As the dew on flowers or the waters that meet

---

[196] This is the first of two letters found in file 1151. It is a fragment from Emily's friend Marie Dawson Bates, and we only have the first page. The second letter, of the same date, is from her husband E. A. Bates.

[197] Emilius A. Bates, husband of Marie Dawson Bates. This letter was included in a letter of the same date that had been written by Marie Dawson Bates.

[198] *Charles Linn or How to Observe the Golden Rule*, Emily's first book, published in July 1841.

[199] Catherine Maria Sedgwick was born in Stockbridge MA and later attended Payne's Finishing School in Boston. She was a prolific writer whose works include: *A New England Tale* (1822), *Hope Leslie* or, *Early Times in Massachusetts* (1827) *Married or Single?* (1857), *Redwood, A Tale* (1824), *Clarence: or, A Tale of Our Times* (1830), *The Linwoods: or, Sixty Years Since in America* (1835), *Didactic Tales: Home: Scenes and Characters Illustrating Christian Truth* (1835), *Live and Let Live: or, Domestic Service* (1837), *Tales and Sketches, Second Series* (1844). She was featured in many of the same magazines, which later featured Emily's stories.

In the crystal stream, on the verdant mead
Where the pale moon beam doth the wanderer lead

E. A. Bates   Source: American Baptist Historical Society, AJ 23, no. 1151.

L. S. Swett to Emily E. Chubbuck, December 18, 1841—Boston[200]

Dear Madam

I have repeatedly read *Charles Linn*,[201] with intense, and all absorbing interest, and presented several of them to friends, and weeks since, noticing in N. Y. Evangelist, a proposal for a Periodical, edited by you,[202] applied to my bookseller here, to procure it for me. He tells me (he) has written for it, but does not receive it—I know not your agent here, but wish to read all written by the author of "Charles Linn," and if you will be so good as to have it sent by mail, to "Mrs. L. Swett, care Col. Swett, Boston, Mass," and at your leisure, direct me *where* to pay my $1. I will most gladly do so. I notice that is the price.

Source: American Baptist Historical Society, AJ 26, no. 1258.

Hannah Randall to Emily E. Chubbuck, December 24, 1841

My ever dear friend

If you suppose I have become indifferent to friendship, or that I love E. E. C. less than I used *to did* [sic] you are mistaken. My short acquaintance with you was a happy one and I rejoiced to find one I loved, even while you was [sic] yet almost a stranger. That affection neither absence, or [sic] time, have in the least lessened; but I still think of you, as a dear, and may I add confidential friend. The world might perhaps deems [sic] such confidence, [ ] and presumptuous, but Emily does not your own heart tell you that there is sometimes a sympathy of souls, even

---

[200] We place this undated letter in 1841 because *Charles Linn* was published this year, the same year that Emily and the Utica Female Academy began to solicit subscriptions for the *Young Ladies' Miscellany*, a magazine started and edited by Emily in fall 1842, with the help and cooperation of the students and staff of the Utica Female Academy. Advertisements for subscriptions had been in the religious press as early as December 1841. It was to survive only through the end 1843. In *The Life and Letters of Mrs. Emily C. Judson*, A. C. Kendrick said, "While it drew forth much talent from the school, Chubbuck, of course, under every variety of disguise, figured largely in its columns. Now a Greek 'maiden'—Kore—now a Latin 'nobody'—Nemo—now a reluctantly accepted country contributor—now in all the dignity of the editorial 'we,' she played off both her heavier and lighter artillery on the public. Essays, stories, songs, and sonnets, now grave, now gay, were thrown oft from her facile and fertile pen. The magazine ran gracefully through its single year of existence, and then quietly resigned its breath, having delighted its friends, edified, it is hoped, the public, contained much sound instruction, sparkled with many bright gems of genius, and contributed much to the reputation, and not a cent probably to the purse of the editor. But the dramatic genius of Fanny Forester flashes through its vivacious sketches" (77–78).

[201] *Charles Linn or How to Observe the Golden Rule*, Emily's first book, published in July 1841.

[202] The *Young Ladies' Miscellany*, a magazine started and edited by Emily in fall 1842, with the help and cooperation of the students and staff of the Utica Female Academy. Emily wrote a large percentage of the content, in it showing the true genius of Fanny Forester.

before that friendship has been tested by acquaintance. A healthy an affection [sic] of the stomach which has rendered me unable to write, has alone prevented my answering your letter, written a long time ago. Yes Emily the 5 months which have passed since the receipt of your letter have been to me perhaps the saddest of my life. A cloud has seemed to come over all my sundry feelings not only involving the present in gloom, but forbidding me to hope for the future.

If you have ever been sick, of a lingering disorder, when you hoped, and anxiously expected, you should soon be well—until hope was forbidden and you find yourself after months of solitude, still the same good for nothing useless being—if this has ever been your fate you can perhaps sympathise [sic] in some respects with the depths of my feelings.

Sisters have both been in ill health, for several months and for several weeks past sister R has been confined to her room. Hariot has so far recovered, as to be able [to do] some sewing. So you see I have not had to grieve for myself alone—My anxiety for myself has not I trust been entirely selfish. A desire that I might if possible be useful in the world; that I might be something for the happiness of others, that I might yet breathe the words of consolation, of hope, and encouragement, to the child of sorrow and misfortune. Such thoughts cause me to wish that my life might be prolonged yet a little space, that health might once more be mine. But when I look on the other hand and ask myself, What better is the world for my having lived in it. [sic] Who has been happier for my friendship? The answer has been any thing [sic] but heart cheering. The pleasure of making others happy, is in reality, the only pleasure, worth living for.

Cousin Louisa spends the winter at home and as ever I enjoy her society exceedingly. We contrive to spend together at least one day in a week. You are probably aware that from childhood we have been intimate and confidential friends. That our joys and our sorrows have been shared together—and I had fondly hoped we might not be separated for a long time—But I fear—shall I state what I fear? I fear that ere long another may claim the first place in her heart the place I have flattered myself I was always to retain. Now how can I bear this.—But perhaps my fears are without foundation. There is at present no positive engagement but "coming events cast their shadows before." I can tell you no more for you know we must never reveal such "heart hushed secrets."

Speaking of our confidential friendship reminds me of an idea from *Ponce De Leon* which I have just been reading—by the by I do not allow myself in novel reading—"The brightest part of love is its confidence. It is that perfect, that unhesitating reliance that interchange of every idea—and every feeling—that perfect community of all the hearts [sic] secrets—and all the mind's thoughts, which binds two beings together, more closely, more dearly, than the dearest of human ties: more than the vow of passion, or the oath of the altar." Christmas and New Year holidays are coming on—I wonder what they will bring—weding [sic] parties I presume by the *wholesale*. Oh, dear me; do you know Elisa Denison—and have you heard of her exit—she has gone and left Hariot, and Fidelia, until next time. Her chosen is a Mr. Greene of Clarksville—But F—does not intend being left a long time—You know Lucius Clarke I presume. Well I suppose he is her intended, that is all. Dr. Bailey and his lady were here a few evenings since. I suppose you have never seen his choice. Well, she is a good natured, bright-eyed sort of a girl; rather larger than myself, and about as *common place*. Cheerful and affectionate.

Sister Desdemony remains sick about the same as when I wrote you before. There is no hope of her ever being well again. How sad to see one so young thus deprived of all the pleasures of life uncheered by hopes for the future. How mysterious are the ways of Providence! but I frequently hear a still small voice saying "What I do thou knowest not now but thou shalt know [Note: "Afterwards" is written and crossed out.] hereafter." It should be enough for us to know that it is our Heavenly Father [sic] appointment. Why should we question his designs? Delayon is well and cheerful and frequently says if Sis could only get well enough to talk and sit up a part of the time, he should be perfectly happy. They live in a small house of their own just out of the village. Aunt Betsey Frinke lives with them, and takes the care of him.

I am very anxious to hear from you, to know if you are happy, if hope still sheds its bright [ ] around you. Pray what has been the success of your new publication. [sic] Has the second volume appeared.[203] [sic] I think you might be successful as a *scribler*, for I know you have talent of uncommon order. (deserved praise is not flattery you know)—You speak of faults, or errors committed while in Brookfield—I know not to what you allude, but can assure you that your Brookfield friends love you dearly.

Cousin Esther Clarke spent last week with us—She is a good girl is she not—so pious—so self denying—so kind hearted. She spoke affectionately of you and wished very much to see you. Mr. and Mrs. Carpenter the Ex principals of DeRuyter Institute have gone to R.I. and are by this time I suppose engaged in teaching. I read a letter from her written after her arrival. She found herself in excellent health, and spirits and ready as she expressed herself to go to work—Oh I love Mr. Carpenter; but I don't think him very beautiful. He is so amiable so affectionate and so—every thing that is good, that one can't help loving him.—We have excellent sleighing now and I begin to anticipate some pleasant rides, as my health has been better for the past week than for a long time before—The world

---

[203] The first volume, *Charles Linn, or How to Observe the Golden Rule*, was published in July 1841, and the second book, *The Great Secret, or How to be Happy*, which was finished in November.

has, I fear, too many charms for me. I fear that I love it too much—and I have sometimes thought I was deprived of its enjoyment to teach me to "lean not on earth" [ ] [ ] not our place of rest.

Written in the left margin of page 3: "You should readily excuse this ill-looking scroll if you knew how it was written but I shall not tell you—I hardly know how to close—but my paper as well as trembling hands remind me to stop."

Written in the left and top margins of page 1: "Brother R. spends the winter at home and wishes to be remembered to you—*by the way* he says you gave him the mitten when he saw you at Hamilton in the summer. I regretted that I could not be there for then I hoped to meet you. I wonder if we shall ever meet again. I hope so but time only will determine.

"My letter has been two or three days writing and a great deal has transpired since it was commenced. Yesterday Hariot Denison visited me. She too will be married someday I presume and it may be very soon but perhaps not for a long time yet. Do you know Mr. Caltey—now this is a wondrous secret and you must not *tell no body* [sic] for it has not got out much yet. Do write me as soon as you get this as I am very anxious to hear from you—Do you never intend visiting R again? Do come I will assure you of a warm reception. I don't know where this will find you, perhaps you may have concluded to spend the holidays at Morrisville. Do you teach now? Do not forget to write me if you think me worth the trouble."

Hannah

Source: American Baptist Historical Society, AJ 25, no. 1216.

Emily E. Chubbuck to Marie Dawson Bates, January 11, 1842—Utica

Very Dear Marie,—

When I received your very kind letter dated—tell it not in Gath!—October 3d, I did not think two days would pass ere an answer would be on the way to you. But O the vanity of human expectations, in more instances than one! That very day there came a heavy disappointment. Before I left home I had laid a plan for having Catharine[204] come here if my *Monthly Rose* should meet with success, when lo! a failure. Now you must not tell of this; for we would-be authors are rather sore on such points, and care not to have the world witness our mortification. You will recollect that our hopes of the *Monthly Rose* were rather sanguine, and Mr. Hawley[205] wrote from New York that the publishers were delighted, and intended bringing it out with some eight or ten engravings. Judge, then, of my disappoint-

[204] See Emily's September 28, 1841 letter to Sarah Catharine ("Kate," "Kit," or "Kitty") Chubbuck, Emily's older sister, born October 25, 1816.

[205] Horace H. Hawley was enormously helpful to Emily as she published her early stories and books.

ment when I found it returned upon my hands, fit for nothing but waste paper. It seems that the publishers employ a manuscript reader whose decree upon every work is law, and said critic decided that my humble effort should be laid upon the table, or subjected to the dissecting knife of the poor author! Who would dissect his own bantling? Not I—not I. My heart has "too much of tenderness." Well, after finding fault with the title, the plan, the style of the prose, the poetry *en masse*, and, in short, every thing [sic] but three or four stories, which he deigned to compliment, he sent it back to me for revision. Revision! As well pour water into a sieve, and try to save what is left. I stubbornly declared against the alteration of a single word—even "Alma Mater" which, said critic thought, sounds pedantic—and folded up my manuscript to await a more auspicious moment for introducing it to the world. I laughed and pretended not to care; but it was a disappointment nevertheless, and a severe one; for what now was to become of Kate? My spirit rose in proportion to the difficulties, and having received fifty-one dollars for the first edition of *Charles Linn*,[206] I wrote to her to come,[207] and then sat down to scribble another book. In less than a fortnight I had written about one hundred and fifty pages, besides attending to my duties as composition teacher, and then all at once I failed and poor Kate, instead of studying, was obliged to take care of me. I recovered slowly, but not so as to be able to accomplish much, and so did not finish the work I had commenced *a la Jehu*, until the close of the term. I spent the vacation at home, but was not able to go out while there, and returned to school last Saturday, expecting to do just "nothing at all." Now I have given you a history of the past, and I suspect that you will more readily pardon me for not writing before than for telling this "long yarn" which has filled up so much of my letter. But a word more of these affairs. My new book is entitled *The Great Secret, or How to Be Happy*, and I am not at all confident that it will be successful. Kate is with me and will remain until spring. She takes the guitar, flower painting, and drawing.

Now, how is your health, and how have you been since I saw you at Morrisville? Well, and happy? I doubt it not for why should you not be?

> The flowers around the single side
>   May not the proudest be,
> But they the richest fragrance shed;
>   And these unfold for thee.

Now do not criticize this doggerel; I am sure I do not call it poetry.

Marie, I thank you and Mr. Bates also for your praise of *Charles Linn*,[208] and

---

[206] *Charles Linn or How to Observe the Golden Rule*, Emily's first book, published in July 1841.
[207] See Emily's letter to Catharine of September 28, 1841.
[208] See their two letters of October 3, 1841.

your encouragement. Think how opportunely they arrived! Just when my New York critic had administered his bitter dose. It does not speak very highly for my ambition—(and, after all, I doubt if I was ever formed for such a rough-and-tumble, soap-bubble chase)—that I was very glad that the partial friends approved, and that the impartial stranger was the critic. I would rather receive the approbation of the few I love, than of the whole world and "England into the bargain." Tell Mr. Bates I thank him for his piece of a letter, and should be glad to see as much in all of yours, and the number of yours "multiplied by twelve." I remain, dear Marie

Yours truly,

Emily E. Chubbuck.

Source: A. C. Kendrick, *The Life and Letters of Mrs. Emily C. Judson*, 67–69.

Marie Dawson Bates to Emily E. Chubbuck, January 23, 1842—Nelson

Jan 23rd, 1842

Very dear friend,

Your long wished for letter has at length arrived[209]—matters not, now, how anxiously I expected, nor how long a time I was forced to wait its coming. 'Tis here! Thank you for that. Need I tell you it was perused with deep interest—with affectionate solicitude, you already know how sincerely I enter into all your plans, and that anything which adds to your happiness is ever hailed with joy by me, while aught that can tend to throw a cloud upon your moral horizon casts also a shade upon the sunlight of my enjoyment. It grieved me much, that your *Monthly Rose*[210] was no better appreciated, that our sanguine hopes of its success were destined to perish. I could have wept with vexation to think that the decision of a self-conceited *critic* should be *law*, and that enlightened and probably well cultivated minds should bow in meek subjection to his fiat, when perhaps a cursory glance at its contents was all the trouble he bestowed upon the work.

The *title* it seems, said critic did not like, and *Alma mater* he thought *pedantic*! Weighty objections surely, yet such as would serve to exalt the work in my opinion rather than otherwise. But dear Emily why not make arrangements with some other Publishers and bring forward your book without loss of time.

Mr. Bates earnestly recommends it and feels almost certain you will be

---

[209] See Emily's letter to Marie Dawson Bates of January 11, 1842.

[210] Originally Emily's book *Monthly Rose* had received a favorable review from a publisher obtained by H. H. Hawley, but then their manuscript reader and literary critic suggested that it would need major revisions, revisions that Emily was not willing to make because, in her opinion, the revisions would strip the book of all of its character. Yet another publisher later offered to publish it, but offered so little compensation that it was not worth the effort.

successful. For myself I feel very solicitous to see your *Monthly Rose* in *blossom*. My bouquet is not complete without it. I was never born to "blush unseen and waste its sweetness on the desert air." I should not be half so confident of its success had I never read *Charles Linn*.[211] I am heartily glad you did not attempt *revision* for the gentleman's gratification and admire the firmness manifested in making the resolution, and adhering to it.

Success attend your new work! All I know of it is its title and that is admirable. I always delighted in an appropriate title to a work—for instance, "Hope on, hope won" by Mary Howith. This is a charming one, and *The Great Secret, or How to be Happy*[212] by Emily Chubbuck sounds quite as sweetly, and as if it would "*take*" with the world.

You have been ill! and among strangers too—poor E. would I could have been with you—Yet you had kind friends around and dear Kate[213] hovering like a ministering spirit near, to cheer your loneliness and with her sunny face and gladdening tones beguile the weary hours. And best of all you had another Friend better better far and kinder too than any earthly friend could be, to "make your bed in sickness" and sustain you by his love. How constant how rich and varied the Christian's joys. In sickness or in health when prosperity gilds his pathway, or when adverse fortune frowns upon him, to feel that he has a Friend in Heaven who will never forsake, never leave him, and who has assured us that *all things* shall work together for good to those that love him. This dear E. is happening which I trust we have both experienced. Is it not so? Then let us go on our way rejoicing, "hoping all things, believing all things, and enduring all things."

You ask if I am well and happy—Yes dear friend I am well and happy as 'tis permitted us to be in this world. 'Tis true.

"The flowers around the single side
"May not the proudest grow.
"But they the richest fragrance shed
"And these do unfold for me.

I wish you could see my little Edward[214] (accept a kiss from him in return). He prattles a little (his voice is music to us), and he runs about a good deal. Emilius[215] is pretty well—he wished to be remembered to you, I think I shall not give him room to write in this. Pray let me hear from you oftener, dear Emily—wish you

---

[211] *Charles Linn or How to Observe the Golden Rule*, Emily's first book, published in July 1841.

[212] Started in the fall and delayed because of illness, Emily had finished *The Great Secret* by the end of the term. Emily had mentioned to Marie in her letter of January 11 that the book was ready.

[213] Sarah Catharine ("Kate," "Kit," or "Kitty") Chubbuck, Emily's older sister, born October 25, 1816.

[214] Edward, the son of Marie and Emilius Bates.

[215] Emilius A. Bates, Marie' Dawson Bate's husband.

would write 2 or 3 to my one for letter writing is such a task to me nowadays that I am not held punctual with any of my correspondents, although their number is considerably diminished since I first became a wife.

My best love to Kate (that is the best name she ever had or I would not call her so) also to your dear Mother[216] when you write to her.

When is there another vacation? Will you not try to visit with me at that time? Do if possible and write to me very soon—that's a dear girl.

May our Heavenly Father guide and protect you ever is the prayer of your ever Affectionate friend

Marie L. Bates

Written in the left margin of page 1: "I hope you will [ ] the paper dear E—'tis all there is in our house just now and it is Sabbath Evening Music."

Source: American Baptist Historical Society, AJ 23, no. 1150.

Emily E. Chubbuck,[217] March 1842

For Miss Damaux[218]

Preliminary Remarks

An elegy! O yes, my muse is ready,
To shed the ink, if not the pitying tear,
And well she knows her pinion how to steady.
And droop, and sigh, when themes like this are near.

She sung a song, as was her bound duty,
When, like a shadow, passed "a nation's pride",
She's touch'd the lyre for ugliness and beauty,
O'er wrinkled [ ], and infant buds has sigh'd;

The dog, the birdling, and the stricken kitty,
Have claim'd alike her elegiack [sic] strain—

---

[216] Lavinia Richards Chubbuck, Emily's mother, was born June 1, 1875, in Goffstown NH, the eldest of thirteen children. She married Charles Chubbuck on November 17. 1805. They were the parents of seven children.

[217] This is from pages 81 and 82A of a notebook with eighty-four intact pages (It was originally longer; there are some pages missing.) all with poetry in the handwriting of Emily Chubbuck.

[218] Eugenia Damaux was associated with the Utica Female Academy. One letter said that Miss Cynthia Sheldon would have to make other arrangements about a teacher for the French class as Miss Damaux had another position and was not available. An 1849 letter from Sarah Hinkley says that she had married Johnny Edmonds, who had been described as "rich and pious." A letter to Emily suggested that the couple would be happy as they had been praying for four years about the possibility of marriage. After her marriage, she remained in Emily's circle of friends from her days at the Utica Female Academy.

I mention this, to show she's practis'd pity,
And so should this attempt prove weak and vain.

'Twil be the fault of the amanuensis,
Whose pen cuts capers just as it may choose
So never lay its failures and offences,
Up in your heart, against *my* gentle muse.

Source: Hanna family files, poetry notebook 2.

Emily E. Chubbuck to J. Walker Chubbuck, March 25, 1842—Utica Female Academy

My dear brother,

It is a long, long time since I have heard a word from you, and really I think it is quite too bad. What on earth can you be about? Are you sick, or married, or tired of your friends, that you fling them aside like a cast-off coat, and grow to a new soil? Oh! oh! you are a sad renegade from early principles!

I suppose I shall have to go back a long ways in order to make you understand what I am about just now. Well for a beginning! You know when I came here, and you know for what and how I came. Last summer I was duly installed as teacher, but as I do not perform the usual duties, my salary is proportionately small. I teach composition-writing only (mistress of belles-lettres—don't you feel afraid of my pen?) and so have a great deal of time to devote to my own amusement, or improvement as I choose. Last summer I had a little book published by Dayton and Saxton, N. Y. and in eleven weeks after, the 1 ed. being all sold out I rec'd $51, as my share of the profits.[219] I expected a 2. ed. would follow immediately, but, owing to a press of new works, it has not yet appeared and I don't know when it will. I sent them another little affair last Dec. but this for the same reason has been postponed, although I suspect it is not in press.[220] Then in addition to this I have got to be quite a poetess, so where-ever [sic] you find anything the signature "E. E. C."[221] you may claim a kind of relationship. A poem covering some dozen sheets and entitled, "Astonrogo, or the Maid of the Rock," is the last effusion of "my muse," though in my humble opinion not least. This is now in the hands of S. Gaylord Clark, Esq. for examination, but not publication, as it is quite too long for the

---

[219] *Charles Linn or How to Observe the Golden Rule*, Emily's first book, published in July 1841.

[220] After *Monthly Rose*, which seemed to have great promise but in the end was rejected for publication, she wrote *The Great Secret or How to be Happy*—that was finished by the end of the school term in late 1841.

[221] On February 18, 1838, Emily wrote to J. Walker Chubbuck and told him that material of hers had appeared in several publications over the signature of E.E.C. and that the editor of the "Whig" had found her out.

pages of the *Knickerbocker*.[222] Kate[223] is with me and has been since last Sept., but will leave next month. She has been taking lessons on the guitar and in drawing and painting. Wallace[224] is at Hamilton, boarding at home, and working for the Atwoods. Between ourselves, that boy has the talent—ay, and even *genius* necessary to make a great man, but he is too indolent and capricious, his head is too full of air castles, and I am afraid he will never do any thing. Ben[225] has become a wanderer on the face of the earth I believe, but I can't tell you where he is. His wife is a poor miserable thing, and I suppose is now living on the charity of her relatives. Ben. went westward in Jan. to look for work and a place.

Father[226] and mother[227] are keeping house in Hamilton, where they removed last Jan.[228] Kate will live with them next summer. We are all of us in as good health as could be expected from natural constitution etc.

And now as to pecuniary concerns—ah! there's the rub! If "riches take to themselves wings," I should think some of them might fly this way ere long. But no, that's out of the question. The disappointment in the publication of my books, together with the expense incurred on Kate's account ($130) has embarrassed me in no small degree. Yet if I am well I hope I shall weather the storm. Father is the same old sixpence precisely—digs and jogs, lives comfortably and rather happily, but never has a penny in his pocket. Wallace is no money getter, or rather no money *saver*, for he has good wages, and keeps in debt. I wish you would give him a lecture on the occasion.

And now, mon cher frere, just write a good long letter and tell us what you are about—what you enjoy, what troubles you, what you hope, what you fear, and all these every-day [sic] things that although they look mighty common-place on paper are no small things after all. Kate and I talk about you everyday and wonder if you look and act as you used to, and if you ever think of us. Are you never coming home? never?

---

[222] This poem was not published at this time, but the *Knickerbocker* did publish it after she had achieved her fame as Fanny Forester. This led A. C. Kendrick, in *The Life and Letters of Mrs. Emily C. Judson*, to muse about how fame and popularity was able to change the perspective even of publishers.

[223] Sarah Catharine ("Kate," "Kit," or "Kitty") Chubbuck, Emily's older sister. Emily had brought Kate to the Utica Female Academy for a year of study and had added the cost of that education to her own personal debt.

[224] William Wallace Chubbuck, Emily's younger brother, born January 1, 1824.

[225] Benjamin "Ben" Chubbuck, Emily's older brother. Ben suffered a head injury as a child, and his subsequent behavior throughout his life reflected some mental impairment.

[226] Charles Chubbuck, Emily's father. Though he held varying positions over the years, he failed at most of them. With the purchase of a home for them, Emily was to continue as a significant financial contributor to the support of the family.

[227] Lavinia Richards Chubbuck, Emily's mother, was born June 1, 1875, in Goffstown NH, the eldest of thirteen children. She married Charles Chubbuck on November 17. 1805. They were the parents of seven children.

[228] Emily's mother and father moved to Hamilton from Morrisville NY. In fall 1842, Emily would purchase a permanent home for them there. When they returned from Burmah in 1851, Henry and Edward would live there with Emily's sister Catharine and her parents, until she bought a house there for herself in 1852. This was spacious enough to accommodate her entire family—mother and father, sister, Emily, Henry and Edward, and then A. C. Osborne who boarded with the family and helped with the discipline and care of Henry and Edward. At one point it was hoped to have all of the Judson children together under one roof.

Do write, do, or I will never subscribe myself again,
Your loving sis,

Emily E. Chubbuck

An after-thought

The people in Morrisville I know but little about. Notwithstanding the break-up between Kate and Ed. the Nortons are very friendly.[229] Aunt Dinah and old Rider are still in existence and the last time I saw the former she gave me as many consoling flings as usual, particularly upon *pride*. Betsy Crandal is the best friend "this young woman" has, and I have got a mighty fine opinion of her. Mrs. Caroline Barnett is some twenty years older than her mother. There is still considerable scandal afloat in them diggings [sic], and several new gossips have come to town. Did you ever hear anything equal to Uncle Bacehus's marrying Rachel Chubbuck? Only think of her being Ma to Augustine! Cynthia has settled down into a really "dutiful daughter" and useful old maid. Write, write I tell ye! write!

Source: Jerome Walker Chubbuck Collection, Wisconsin Historical Society Archives, Madison, WI.

Emily E. Chubbuck to Marie Dawson Bates, May 20, 1842— Utica Female Seminary

My Dear Marie,—

I ought to commence this letter with an apology, but if I should apologize to the end of it, I could not convince either you or myself that I had not been unpardonably negligent in allowing your valued letter of—I dare not mention the date[230]—to remain so long unanswered. The truth is, Marie, writing has become such a matter-of-fact, dollar-and-cent business with me, that I have as complete a horror of the pen as a sweep of his chimney on a holiday. Oh, there is nothing like coining one's brains into gold—no, bread—to make the heart grow sick. But enough of this; only I beg of you just to take notice that though writing, from a pleasure, has become an intolerable bore, *reading has not*; so do not, pray, do not withhold your letters.

Kate[231] went home in March, and I am lonely enough without her; but so is mother,[232] and I must be content. Did you know that our people have removed to

---

[229] In a March 22, 1840 letter, Emily wrote to her brother Walker about a relationship budding between their sister, Catharine, and Ed Norton.

[230] Marie Dawson Bates had sent Emily a letter on January 23, 1842.

[231] Sarah Catharine ("Kate," "Kit," or "Kitty") Chubbuck, Emily's older sister, born October 25, 1816. Emily had paid tuition for Kate at the Utica Female Academy for about six months, so she could learn some practical skills in music and art.

[232] Lavinia Richards Chubbuck, Emily's mother, was born June 1, 1875, in Goffstown NH, the eldest of thirteen children. She married Charles Chubbuck on November 17. 1805. They were the parents of seven children.

Hamilton, and Wallace[233] is boarding with them? I suppose they are only too happy; why can not I join them? This is a delightful place; both of the Misses Sheldon[234] are extremely kind to me, and I love the teachers very much; but *mother is not here.*

My affairs in the business line are not very prosperous—the hard times having put a great check on book-publishing. *The Great Secret* (Newman & Dayton; publishers) went to press some five or six weeks ago, and I am expecting it very soon. Appleton offers to take my *Monthly Rose*[235] under the new name of *Buds and Blossoms*; but the price he would allow is too small to pay for copying, so I prefer keeping it. I have a manuscript of about fifty pages in the hands of a publishing committee in Philadelphia,[236] but its fate I can conjecture only from a consciousness of its deserts.

Last term I perpetrated a sort of a poem called "Astonroga, or, the Maid of the Rock." It consisted of about one hundred and fifty Spencerian stanzas, and was divided into four cantos. It was not intended for publication.[237] Now, I believe you have a full account of my past literary labors; and as you may wish to know what I have done this term (four weeks of it have passed), I will tell you. I have written one letter home, covering almost one page; written three lines of a temperance song, which jingle most beautifully; and. written thus much of a letter to you, which latter effort I am sure you will pronounce *comme il faut*. Yet I have not been very idle. My composition class (consisting of all the young ladies in the school), toe the mark admirably, and of course I claim the credit. I have read "Tecumseh," a new poem, by George Colton; it has many faults, but is, after all, a fine thing. "Cranmer and his Times," by Miss Lee, I have read with the greatest pleasure; also the life of Aaron Burr, and find it vastly interesting. I have on the table before me an "American Eclectic," with a splendid article from the *Edinburgh Review*, written by Macaulay-a sketch of the life of Warren Hastings. So you see I have "plenty enough" to keep me busy and as the hard times make writing of little or no pecuniary avail, I mean to do what I please....

Your affectionate

---

[233] William Wallace Chubbuck, Emily's younger brother, born January 1, 1824.

[234] Miss Urania Sheldon was the literary principal of the Utica Female Academy, and Miss Cynthia Sheldon was the administrative and financial manager. Both were to influence Emily profoundly.

[235] Originally Emily's book *Monthly Rose* had received a very favorable review from a publisher obtained by H. H. Hawley, but then the deal fell through. The publisher's editor and literary critic wanted changes that Emily was unwilling to make. Now, we learn here, a second publisher has offered to publish it, but offered so little compensation that it was not worth the effort.

[236] In May, *Effie Maurice*, a book for Sunday school use, was published by American Baptist Publication Society in Philadelphia. (According to A. C. Kendrick, *The Life and Letters of Mrs. Emily C. Judson*.)

[237] In fact, Emily had submitted this long poem at least to the *Knickerbocker* for publication, but they considered it too long. They did publish it when she achieved her Fanny Forester fame, leading A. C. Kendrick, in *The Life and Letters of Mrs. Emily C. Judson*, to muse: "It is, doubtless, a rightful prerogative of acknowledged literary reputation that its productions find an instant and unquestioning reception, while the unknown candidates for favor must await the slow processes of trial."

E. E. Chubbuck

Source: A. C. Kendrick, *The Life and Letters of Mrs. Emily C. Judson*, 72–74.

Minnie to Emily E. Chubbuck, June 21, 1842—Williamsburg[238]

My dear Miss Chubbuck.

It was quite a treat for me to receive your letter and it was a good long one too and that is the kind I like to get. It must certainly have been a great task to you, to begin and clear house after going home and especially when you saw the garden so much in need of your care also. I really don't see how your strength held out until you had completed it all.

Your letter quite refreshed my memory about Mr. Varley's meetings—not that I had forgotten them, but it is good to have some one to talk to about these even on paper. I wish more and more every day as I feel the need of it, that I had the Varley's faith—it was not only resigned [sic] to God's will, but a cheerfulness with this—happy even in the midst of affliction. O what a blessing to feel this way. My mother is in Troy at present. I miss her so much. I have the blues all the time when she is gone.

I do not feel very strong at present, and the Dr. says I must go away somewhere and make a good visit this Summer. I should so much have liked to have gone to Hamilton for commencement but I could'nt [sic] leave while mother was away, so if you will extend your invitation into July I think it very likely I can accept it. I must go somewhere, and I would rather go and stay quietly with you, than any place I know of.

Maggie Liadgren told me the other day, she saw that motto in this city that you want so if I go I will take it with me, and, also a frame for it if you wish.

Emily, Tom and the children are quite well. Miss Anable[239] has been visiting there for these several days past but I believe she is to return home tomorrow. Mr. Connor's father came here on a visit about seven weeks ago—he likes this country very much—and if he got a good situation would remain, and bring his family. I tell you as a secret, I'd not like him at all and would rather hear of his going back—but this is private of course—I can explain to you when I see you.

We have had delightful weather in the city for the past two weeks but it bids fair to be very warm again. Thomas gave his lecture on the Holy Land called "Walks about Zion" at the Lansingburg Church—also Willie's church in Troy—he

---

[238] This letter is undated as to the year in which it was written. The writer speaks of Anna Maria Anable, so it is in a time when Emily was at the Utica Female Academy. At the same time there is nothing in the letter speaking of Emily's books or writing, so we would place it fairly early in her career. The year 1842 seems to fit all of the categories for a guestimate.

[239] Anna Maria Anable was the niece of the Urania and Cynthia Sheldon, the daughter of Joseph and Alma Sheldon Anable.

is to go next Wednesday to Newburg, and next Sabbath to East Orange. He was away in Connecticut yesterday preaching—but perhaps Emily has given you all this news before.

Mr. Oakley has resigned from our church and I have heard is talking fearfully about us all—but what of that when we know just all about his history with the church. We do not yet know who we shall have but we will probably have supply for awhile.

Mrs. Liadgren and Maggie are about as usual going about their usual routine every day Maggie at school and Mrs. L. in the house. I have a bad headache today, and my hand shakes, so you will excuse me from saying any more. I shall be looking for a letter from you very soon.

Ever your loving friend

Minnie

Source: Hanna family files.

Emily E. Chubbuck to Catharine Chubbuck, June 25, 1842—Utica Female Academy

Dear Kate,

The secret is at last out, and Miss U. E. S. is to be married next vacation[240]—this however is to be kept private on your part, as I suppose not a teacher in the house but myself knows it. The teachers are most of them going away and new ones coming in their places—and I—Oh dear! Mr. and Mrs. Nichols are expected to take Miss U's place.[241] I cannot bear the idea of this change if I stay, but it seems there is an *if* even there; I may not stay. There are so many things to be thought of, in the issuing of the proposed magazine,[242] (and there Miss U. thinks it highly improper) that I do not believe it will go off well, and it is very doubtful whether we even commence it.[243] Unless this plan is put in execution, I suspect my services can be dispensed with, as the trustees will not consider my office a very important one in their new arrangements. However I hope to stay, and still don't want to, for it will be very, very awful here, when Miss U. is gone. Hav'nt [sic] heard from Phil.[244] Yet now N. Y. Mr. H[245] says that firm[246] is perfectly safe so that removes one

---

[240] Urania Sheldon Nott was literary principal of the Utica Female Academy and a mentor, advisor, and friend to Emily.

[241] James Nichols and his wife. He and his wife would assume the position of literary principal at the Utica Female Academy upon the marriage of Urania Sheldon to Eliphalet Nott in fall 1842.

[242] The *Young Ladies' Miscellany*, a magazine started and edited by Emily in fall 1842, with the help and cooperation of the students and staff of the Utica Female Academy. Emily wrote a large percentage of the content, in it showing the true genius of Fanny Forester.

[243] It was published from fall 1842 into January 1844.

[244] American Baptist Publication Society had *Effie Maurice* for publication as a Sunday school book.

[245] Horace H. Hawley was enormously helpful to Emily as she published her early stories and books.

trouble from my mind, and they wrote him the other day that the *Great Secret*[247] and 2. Ed. of *Charles Linn*[248] were both in press. I should think they'd get *press'd* to death—fear there is danger of their coming out decidedly *flat* don't you? —Tell W.[249] that I beg leave to insinuate in the gentlest and politest manner possible that he is the *fool* instead of Mr. H. Here he has given me two most surprising lectures on a subject over which I have about as much control as he has and finally concludes that I've had enough of N. Y. publishers, when upon my word and honor I have never had but $50, and that I don't call quarter enough. But now for a full explanation. In the first place Mr. H. is only one man while B.B. and H.[250] are three. <u>N.WH</u>[251] would like to go into the publishing business deeply but B. and B. like the safe side of the fence and prefer confining their operations to school books, and others for which they are paid by the job. It was first proposed that they should do my work and they were consulted and agreed to do it—at what rate I don't know for I was a stranger then, but Miss C.[252] thought it wasn't fair and Mr. Hawley said if I agreed I should make a bad bargain. He then wrote to Boston and they offered fifty cents for a page of 1000 letters—that he didn't like. About this time he went to New York and took a great deal of pains to make good terms for me, but the hard times have made business backward and I have'nt [sic] done so well as I expected. Other publishes are doing no more than D. and N.[253]—they are all republishing European works. I should be glad to get my work done here, but I don't want to give it away and then coax them to do it. If we go into the mag.[254] I shan't write any more books, and if we don't I shall write for the Phil. folks.[255] Why under the sun don't you tell me whether you got your things, and how you like your bonnet?

I expect to have to borrow my share of the money in Aug. if it is to be borrow'd, as Miss C. is [ ]ing every way to scrape the purse together, and I suppose will not have a particle to spare until after the wedding. Write and let me know how

---

[246] The reference is to the Publishing firm of Dayton and Newman.

[247] *The Great Secret or How to be Happy* had been finished in November 1841. In May Emily had written that it had been at the press for five weeks.

[248] *Charles Linn or How to Observe the Golden Rule*, Emily's first book, published in July 1841 Emily had received $51 that fall for the sold out edition; a second edition was slow in coming because of a slowdown in the economy and in the publication business.

[249] William Wallace Chubbuck, Emily's younger brother, born January 1, 1824.

[250] Publishing firm of Bennett, Backus and Hawley.

[251] This letter is taken from a transcription of the original; the original was unavailable. We suggest that an error was made and that this should read "Mr. H," referring to Horace Hawley.

[252] Miss Cynthia Sheldon was the administrative and finance manager of the Utica Female Academy. She was a mentor, advisor, and friend to Emily.

[253] Publishing firm of Dayton and Newman, successors to Dayton and Saxton.

[254] In the end, Emily focused more on writing for the magazines. They were agreeing to pay her the unheard of sum at that time of five dollars a page. With this she would receive fifty dollars for a ten-page story, whereas we note that for the first edition of *Charles Linn* she had only received a total of fifty-one dollars.

[255] American Baptist Publication Society, located in Philadelphia.

father[256] is getting along, what he says, and so on. Have they begun to fix the house? Tell me how all the things go off.

E. E. C.

"To what high honours [sic] do we come at last?" What think you Kate?[257] A collector of autographs sent yesterday for mine and I sent it to him to-day. Ha, ha, haw!

My health is a constant source of trouble to me so much so that I think of dispensing with it altogether and Caroline[258] is too mean and hateful to give me a minute's peace. She is decidedly the most disagreeable thing that I ever saw, but one thing you may be assured, your amiable sister is not quite a martyr for nothing, and *can* make the [ ]sts of others somewhat uncomfortable when her own is stuck full of thorns. This I imagine Miss Car. has found out for she has not been ten minutes in the room since breakfast. Good! A fellow can have a little peace when she's away. S.S. is just too good—she does everything for me. E. Douglas and Mary S. just called—both send love. Ever so many of the girls enquire for you almost every day and think you are the worst correspondent in the world[259]—be hanged if I don't agree with them! I had some strawberries the other day as big as my thimble. Jane Hawley[260] brought them over. Miss S. wants awfully to see W. I suspect she thinks he is a prodigy. Hope he won't come (tell him) for fear she'll find him out. Your comps get a great deal of praise—some say you beat me all to nothing—s'pose ye do. Do you hear anything about me "up to Hamilton"? How does Ann[261] get along? Miss S. called on the bride (long-nosed jigger) yesterday—says she's mighty nice. *I* haven't seen the critter yet.—Shall I put my name on the magazine cover as editor? Eh? Do you believe father could distribute any?[262]

Emily

Source: Hanna family files.

---

[256] Charles Chubbuck, Emily's father. Though he held varying positions over the years, he failed at most of them. With the purchase of a house for them, Emily was to continue as a significant financial contributor to the support of the family.

[257] Sarah Catharine ("Kate," "Kit," or "Kitty") Chubbuck, Emily's older sister, born October 25, 1816.

[258] We believe that this is Caroline Reynolds, who was with Emily at the Utica Female Academy.

[259] Beginning in September 1841, Catharine had spent some time at the Utica Female Academy. The intention had been for her to take some courses, which she had been able to do; but early on Emily had been ill, and Catharine had taken care of her. From this stay of some six months, many of the girls had gotten to know her.

[260] Jane Sheldon, daughter of John Sheldon, niece of Cynthia Sheldon, Urania Sheldon, and Alma Anable, cousin of Anna Maria Anable, and married to Horace H. Hawley.

[261] Ann was the wife of Emily's brother Ben.

[262] The *Young Ladies' Miscellany*, a magazine started and edited by Emily in fall 1842, with the help and cooperation of the students and staff of the Utica Female Academy. Emily wrote a large percentage of the content, in it showing the true genius of Fanny Forester.

Jane Blodgett to Emily E. Chubbuck, June 1842[263]

My dear Miss C.

I send you the book as I promised. If it contains any thing [sic] you fancy, you will honor me much by accepting it. Any alterations you may choose to make cannot be otherwise than pleasing to me, trusting as I do to your exquisite taste, and perfect knowledge of those "petite mours" of the literary world, of the which I am so profoundly ignorant.[264] I shall never forget your kind praises of my first uncouth lines—waking as they did a new life within me, which had not yet lost its sunshine, or its joys. Your kind words were the key which opened to me a new, and beautiful though, ideal world, and if my pen trys sink to oblivion without raising one joyous emotion in the hearts of those around one, yet they have cast a golden light on my lifes pathway, they have made one heart happy. And is it not happiness for which the soul still pleads, however ambition may strive to stifle its "still small voice."

In great haste, I remain gratefully yours,

Jane

Afterthought. The subscription[265] enclosed is from Miss Butterfield. I hope, as soon as the weather will permit, to procure more subscribers. J.

"Will you have the kindness to inform me of the time when the term commences."

Source: American Baptist Historical Society, AJ 24, no. 1214

H. M. Dodge to Emily E. Chubbuck, July 4, 1842—Cazenovia

Dear Miss Chubbuck,

You will probably be surprised to receive a letter from me,—a personage who no doubt floats but indistinctly in your recollections, but to me *you* have never been forgotten.

To my heart, genius or talent has an all-absorbing interest, and when once found is never lost sight of. I have kept my eye upon your track as much as possible, until I find you taking a noble and decided stand among the female writers of our

---

[263] We place this undated letter in June 1842 because Emily was actively soliciting material and subscriptions for the *Young Ladies' Miscellany*, a magazine that she published with the Utica Female Academy beginning in fall 1842. Emily wrote a large percentage of the content, in it showing the true genius of Fanny Forester.

[264] We wonder if Emily was soliciting material for the *Young Ladies' Miscellany* from her former students.

[265] The *Young Ladies' Miscellany* is a magazine started and edited by Emily in fall 1842, with the help and cooperation of the students and staff of the Utica Female Academy. Emily wrote a large percentage of the content, in it showing the true genius of Fanny Forester.

dear expanding country. *And may God bless you.* Oh, Emily, I cannot tell you the deep yearning of my almost crushed mind, after literary pursuits, *even now*, though people with cares innumerable, and tied down to a family of small children! Once, like yourself, I loved study, and my time, as much as possible, was devoted to it. Solitude and meditation were ineffably sweet to my heart, and society could offer me no charm when that which I found in being alone with my book and pen. The enchanting ladder of literary enterprise stood before me, a bright sunlight enveloped it,—and I had ascended a round or two, when suddenly it crushed beneath my unsteady feet, and I groaned hopelessly amidst the ruin my own decision had made.—Years have rolled along, but my faltered spirit has longed for liberty—longed for the promise of my early youth, and I *cannot* give up this delicious dream while hope is utterly crushed.

Even now, to-day, I am indulging desires and hopes of still enjoying my strong propensity for study. A few weeks ago I sent two small manuscripts to Mr. O. Hutchinson for his examination; he was pleased with them, and was soon to publish them, when he failed in his business and will not get under way again until some time. Now, my dear girl, I mention this to you wholly confidentially, and in strict confidence would request some thing of you. In the first place, how would publications be received by the publick [sic] if issued from his press? I knew not that he was a Universalist until I had sent him my mss.—Did he publish for you? Is there any other publisher in Utica to whom I could apply to publish for me? If I can but get a start I intend to lay my cares upon the shoulders of another and make a tremendous effort to go ahead.

The above mentioned mss were written several years ago, and in my opinion, are in old-fashioned style, but Mr. Hutchinson approved them well. Now I want to get from you exact information of *who* and *what* he is etc. etc.—And I want to get assistance from you in starting in my second literary career. If your publisher lives in Utica, I wish you would call on Mr. Hutchinson, get my mss from him, tell him I do not know how to wait so long a time for him if I can start sooner, submit them to your publisher and tell him I do not consider them much, but should be glad to make stepping stones of them to something more important. My dear girl, you will fully comprehend me in every respect; and I shall freely and confidentially rely on your assistance, if you can render me any.

I have tried much to obtain your *Charles Linn*,[266] but without success. Please tell how much you have published, what you are now preparing for the press, what are your prospects etc. etc. Every item on this subject will interest me deeply, and most certainly so kind a heart as yours will not refuse me this qualification.

Dear Emily, you cannot think how much I love a mind like yours,—so stu-

---

[266] *Charles Linn or How to Observe the Golden Rule,* Emily's first book, published early in 1841.

dious, so [ ], so full of filial love and gratitude—again I say *God bless you*; and you will be blessed. Such a mind as you possess, and such a use as you are making of your talents cannot fail of finding a rich and complete blessing.

I feel that I could write a whole day to you, would time permit but I must here bring my hasty lines to a close. I want you to write me as soon as consistent, and shall then expect a long and very agreeable letter.

Yours with much respect and affection,

H. M. Dodge   Source: American Baptist Historical Society, AJ 24, no. 1205.

M. I. Rhees to Emily E. Chubbuck, July 5, 1842—Philadelphia

Miss Emily E. Chubbuck,

I rec'd from Rev. A. D. Gillette[267] a Mss. which you had forwarded to him for the Am. Bap. Pub. S.S. Society. After examination I submitted it to our Com. and Board, by whom it has been approved and ordered for Publication, provided the copy rights [sic] can be satisfactorily obtained. I would have written to you at once, but your address was not given, and I only received it from Mr. Gillette a few days since.

As we have not published many small works for S. Schools, we have not fixed any regular prices to give for copy rights. After a little more experience we shall be able to do it. I am desirous therefore of ascertaining from you, what amount will be considered satisfactory by you. Will you inform me as early as convenient? If the proposed sum shall be considered satisfactory by us, we will at once put the book in the printers' hands.

Different Societies vary in their compensations for copy, but I am informed by the Secr. of the A.S.S. Union that they always refer the question first to the Author. If the sum named is approved, the work is received. If not, they make an offer for it. The above is in accordance with this course, and they say, their experience has convinced them of the expediency of this course.—

Our Board not only approved of the work now submitted to them, but are desirous of a series on the commandments in similar styles, and about the same size. Will you be willing to undertake this preposition?

---

[267] Rev. A. D. Gillette was the founding minister of the Eleventh Baptist Church in Philadelphia. He had a distinguished career there for another decade, when he left to take another pulpit in New York. Prominent in Baptist circles, he served on the Board of American Baptist Publication Society. Gillette was educated at Hamilton College, and he was known to Cynthia Sheldon. We can be sure that it was at her suggestion that Emily asked the Reverend Gillette to submit her book to the society for approval. In April and early May 1845, Emily stayed in Philadelphia at the home of this same Rev. Gillette, and she returned again that fall for winter 1845–1846. On Christmas Day 1845 Gillette had introduced Emily Chubbuck to Adoniram Judson in the parlor of his home. Just prior he had traveled to Boston to bring the revered missionary to Philadelphia for meetings with the churches. Gillette was to be a stalwart friend and supporter throughout it all, not only to Emily, but to the Sheldon and Anable families.

Your early reply will oblige.

Yours very respectfully

M. I. Rhees

Source: American Baptist Historical Society, AJ 22, no. 1082.

M. I. Rhees to Emily E. Chubbuck, July 23, 1842—Philadelphia

Miss E. E. Chubbuck,

Yours of the 7th inst[268] was duly rec'd but as our Board did not meet till the 21st I was not prepared officially to reply. Meanwhile I have written the Agent of the A.E.S.S. Union, to ascertain on what terms they purchased Mss. for their publications, and after your letter was rec'd, I rec'd one from him containing the information desired.

He says, "Our uniform price is 50 cents for a page, counting 1200 letters. We never deviate from this, unless the book has been prepared with uncommon care, and has been of more than ordinary expense to the author. We always purchase the copy right [sic], and do not like the plan of percentage. We estimate the amount of matter in a book thus: count the number of lines upon any full page of the book, then the average no. of letters in a line, and multiply the latter by the former, which will give you the number of letters upon the page. Count the number of pages and multiply as before, and divide by 1200 which will give the no. of pages for each of which we pay 50 cents. Deduct blank pages, half pages etc. We pay in six months after the book is published." He adds, "The above terms correspond with the A.S.S. Union and the [ ] S.S.Socy prices for Mss."—

I submitted your letter, and his communications to the Board, and they resolved, to adopt the system and terms of the N.E. Union, as our standard price for S.S. Mss. I am therefore authorized to propose to you the foregoing terms for the Mss. we have of yours, and which has been approved, and the same terms for such others as you may prepare, and shall be approved by the Board.[269]

I suppose a page of 1200 letters would not vary much from one of 700 or 800 wrs.— In regards to the remaining commandments,[270] we should be glad to have them all contained in the series, and tho' as you suggest the 2nd might not be so practical, still I think it would be better to have a complete series, and it has

---

[268] Rhees had first written to Emily on July 5, 1842, so Emily's reply to him must have been immediate.

[269] In subsequent years, Emily was to command the unheard of compensation of five dollars a page from the Magazines for which she wrote, a princely sum in comparison to the fifty cents a page offered here. It easily becomes obvious why Emily turned from books to magazine stories.

[270] *Effie Maurice*, her first book published by the society, had been on the first commandment.

appeared to me, that the image worship of Popery might be well rebuked, and its evils exposed in such a work as you could propose. You have also omitted in your suggestion the 7th, which ought by no means to be omitted, tho' great care should be used in its illustration. The purity of our children seems to require that its prohibition should be illustrated and enjoined, and a female pen would do both more delicately and powerfully than it could well be done by another.

I submit these suggestions to your consideration, and shall be glad to receive the Mss. of any of the series from you, at your own convenience. There is no immediate haste, and you can use the most favorable time for yourself.

I shall be glad to have your answer soon to the proposal for the Mss now in hand, as if accepted, I will at once put it in the printers' hands. Your early attention will therefore oblige

Yours truly

M. I. Rhees, Cor. Sec.   Source: American Baptist Historical Society, AJ 22, no. 1081.

Caroline Reynolds[271] to Emily E. Chubbuck, September 6, 1842—Port Byron

My Dear Emily,

Yours of the 1st I received Saturday morning in my School room (make your best curtsy to the "School Ma'rm" quick) and right glad I was to hear from you though it was only "a business letter"—it would have been still more welcome had it *told* me anything of your *health*, (an important item) or about C. and the rest. I shall expect in your next a detailed relation of all omissions in this. You ask about my affairs—well I never could jump at a conclusion, so I'll go back and up through the intermediate events to the present. The week after you left us was like other *lost weeks*, only it was like nothing else I ever experienced—I didn't know which way I should bend my course, or what I should do—however after seeing Mrs. Nott's[272] departure, the next day Lou. and I started for her home.

Miss C.[273] gave me "Life as it is,"[274] before I left and it excited a good deal of attention on the Packet—so you are in a fair way for fame—Oh! you should have been here to see the delightful home to which we came and the pride and pleasure of Mr. M. in showing us his grounds, taking us walking, riding etc. It is one of the

---

[271] In a June 25, 1842 letter to her sister Catharine, Emily describes Caroline as "decidedly the most disagreeable thing that I ever saw," the result we suspect of a very bad day. There is no indication here that Caroline was aware of any such feelings.

[272] Caroline Reynolds had been a guest at the marriage of Urania Sheldon to Eliphalet Nott.

[273] Miss Cynthia Sheldon was the administrative and finance manager of the Utica Female Academy. She was a mentor, advisor, and friend to Emily.

[274] *Life As It Is* was one of Emily's books; she had sent her brother Walker a copy in September 1842.

happiest families I know. I found that the lady who had engaged the house we wanted had relinquished it and people were expecting me to open school soon. So in little more than a week I commenced with 29 scholars—the number is now 35—it is a pleasant room and very agreeable scholars—I board at Mr. Graham's (father of the Mr. G. opposite the Acad;) and see nothing to prevent being very happy—and last, though not least, I think *some* 5, or 6, or more of my young ladies will take your paper!![275]

With regard to what you say about my Composition Book, I hardly know what to do—you are perfectly welcome to it such as it is, but I should be glad to have time to fix up some things[276]—I see a good many things that need alteration or re-writing—however that is impossible now, and so I believe I'll send it. Some things may do to fill out a page, perhaps if they were longer they shouldn't in their present state—I wouldn't put it in many people's hands any way [sic]. I haven't lain awake a night; or lost a meal! Or got out of patience with a scholar! Or refused to receive a call! On account of my ignorance respecting the opinion of J.W. W. on that poetry!!!!! I don't think I'm descended from Eve. I won't be sui'generis. [sic] I *shall be* distressed though, if that paper don't [sic] come to hand soon—I thought Miss C. would send me a specimen no. and so have been watching every mail—the new engraving is fine, only a little flattered. Tell Miss B.[277] I've a fine class in Drawing, I wonder what she'll think of that—such an awkward piece as I? Please give my love to *all* the good folks, I can't name them all and so will stop before I commence. It would be fine fun to peep into your house a little while and see what you're all about, next week—send if you'll be nicely settled and others just coming with bag and baggage. Do write *soon* and *often*. You can hardly realize how lonesome I am here and expect to be more so when Lou is gone.

Caroline

Written in the right margin of the address page: "Oh! you naughty girl you! I thought when I commenced I'd write about five words to you [ ] to Miss C. and find time to scribble a little to the rest, but here you have kept me talking to you till my time is yours. I am busy, busier, busiest, all the time. Company, company, constantly out of school."

Written in the left margin of the address page: "The next opportunity I shall send a package of letters to the girls, and would now had I time. All of you write

---

[275] The *Young Ladies' Miscellany* was a magazine started and edited by Emily in fall 1842, with the help and cooperation of the students and staff of the Utica Female Academy. Emily wrote a large percentage of the content, in it showing the true genius of Fanny Forester.

[276] We would suspect that Emily was looking for materials for the new magazine, The *Young Ladies' Miscellany*. See a similar letter from Jane Blodgett dated June 1842.

[277] Mary Barber was the art instructor at the Utica Female Academy.

me when Mrs. Marble returns, which will be in about two weeks after you receive this. C."

Source: American Baptist Historical Society, AJ 26, no. 1282.

Marie Dawson Bates to Emily E. Chubbuck, September 6, 1842—Nelson

My dearest Emily

I had intended giving you a practical lesson in *punctuality* by writing immediately on the reception of your last dear letter, but I am reminded by the date that I have failed in that respect. Therefore I must beg one from you, for my especial benefit. How much I wish you, my beloved friend, were with me this evening. My husband is absent, my little one asleep, and I am writing you to keep off *ennui*. How calm and quiet all things seem about me this evening. The harp-like music of the autumnal breeze falls sweetly on the senses, and seems as pure and holy as the gentle breathing of a sleeping child.

I received your paper yesterday[278] (thank you) and suppose from the Post-mark that you are now at Hamilton[279] with your dear Mother[280] and all other friends. I should be delighted to visit you there, but hardly dare promise myself that pleasure—and still I cannot bear the thought that you will return to Utica again and I be denied the inestimable privilege of seeing—Can you not come here?[281] Say I may expect you for a visit, and a long one too. Well then I'll look for you—so do not disappoint me. Where is Kate[282] dear? My best love to her and tell her she must come with you, without fail.

When was *Life as It Is*[283] published, and where shall I be able to procure a copy? I am very anxious to see it. The more *Charles Linn*[284] is read, the more it is admired. Allow me to make a short excerpt from the letter of a friend who has often heard me speak of you.

Norwich, Chenangs Co,

---

[278] Ibid.

[279] On September 16, 1842 Emily was to write to her brother J. Walker Chubbuck that, at the end of the summer, she had purchased a home in Hamilton Village for her parents and sister. She had paid four hundred dollars for the house, to be paid in four yearly installments.

[280] Lavinia Richards Chubbuck, Emily's mother, was born June 1, 1875, in Goffstown NH, the eldest of thirteen children. She married Charles Chubbuck on November 17. 1805. They were the parents of seven children.

[281] Previous correspondence indicated that Emily and her childhood friend Marie Dawson Bates had visited back and forth with each other on a fairly regular basis.

[282] Sarah Catharine ("Kate," "Kit," or "Kitty") Chubbuck, Emily's older sister, born October 25, 1816.

[283] This was Emily's most recently published book, which had been published in summer 1842.

[284] *Charles Linn or How to Observe the Golden Rule*, Emily's first book, published in July 1841.

I trust she writes not in vain at least I feel that she has done me much good. Last winter I went to the Bookstore to purchase something to present as a donation to the Presbyterian Clergyman's daughter—Well my eye fell upon *Charles Linn*, so for the sake of patronizing the worthy, I purchased it. About two months since I borrowed the book and gave it a careful perusal, and the good work it wrought upon my heart, I trust will be lasting as my life, never before did I understand the true nature of forgiveness. Like little Charles, I have often said I will forgive, but can never forget, and like him I have learned to know and feel what true forgiveness is, and oh how sweet, sweet is the peace it brings! Still I am not a Christian, or a good girl; but trust I shall grow better as I become master of my evil passions, and still will I pray for power to extirpate from my own heart every desire of wickedness and every germ of vice, that my heart may become a fit temple for the Abode of that Pure Spirit whose dominion is the Universe—whose rule is justice and whose law is love!—[285] I think I will constitute myself an agent for the *Young Ladies' Miscellany*—do not know as I shall meet with very good success—as there is but little interest manifested by the inhabitants of this place *generally* though there are some who pay a good deal of attention to the Literature of the day. My health has been poor all summer, and my phiz[286] has become so elongated (as the Dr's say) that you would scarcely know me—however I am rather better now, and hope I shall soon be as well as ever. I have taken two short journeys this summer as far as Powaga at one time, and the other we rode to Lineklaen where my brother Lucius lives. Sister Lucia Kinney arrived here from Illinois about the middle of July, having been absent 4 years. She thinks some of returning there this fall yet it is possible she may not. Her health is poor. Mr. Bates has gone with herself and daughter, to Madison to-day—he will be back tomorrow I expect. Be assured of his best wishes and warm regard. You remember Sister L. I presume, at any rate she had not forgotten my *early friend* and would be much gratified at having her here. Do try to come, now won't you? And as an earnest of this let me receive a letter from you Thursday morning, this week. Accept my best love. Please make my regards to your Pa[287] and Ma and dear Kate dearest E. together with the kindest wishes of my heart for your success and happiness. As ever, Your aff'ate

Marie L. Bates

Source: American Baptist Historical Society, AJ 23, no. 1149.

---

[285] This is the ending of the letter Marie Bates had copied.

[286] The editor believes that "phiz" is a reference to Miss Marie Dawson Bates's face.

[287] Charles Chubbuck, Emily's father. Though he held varying positions over the years, he failed at most of them. With the purchase of the house for the them, Emily was to continue as a significant financial contributor to the support of the family.

Emily E. Chubbuck to J. Walker Chubbuck, September 16, 1842—Utica Female Academy[288]

Sept. 16, 1841

Dear Brother,

It is a long, long time since I have heard from you and now I doubt whether it will do any good to write, as you seem to have forgotten us entirely, and may not take the trouble to answer.

I left home last week—our folks are all well, well as could be expected in their circumstances, I mean. They live in Hamilton village. I have just purchased a little place for them on Broad Street.[289] I sent you a "Young Ladies' Miscellany"[290] last week, of which I have the honour [sic] of being both editor and publisher, so I will appoint you a sort of general agent there, and hope you will show a sort of brotherly interest in my affairs. Do ya [sic] take?

Mr. John P. Sheldon[291] is here and will be going out on Monday, but is not sure that he will pass through Milwaukee, so I thought of committing my letter to other hands. The book by which this is accompanied (that is if the lady will leave room for it) is my own work,[292] and is I think better than its predecessor *Charles Linn*.[293]

---

[288] The original of this letter is clearly dated September 16, 1841. We believe, however, that it was misdated by the author, something we have seen several times in the correspondence. We believe that a careful analysis of the letter's contents demands that it be dated September 16, 1842.

The first reason we believe this date change must be made has to do with the second paragraph, where Emily told Walker that she had purchased a home for their parents on Broad Street, in Hamilton Village. A. C. Kendrick, in his *Life and Letters of Mrs. Emily C. Judson*, (76) has this home purchase taking place in the late summer 1842. Then in October 1842, Emily wrote to the newly married Urania Sheldon Nott (the wedding had taken place in August 1842): "I have not told you what (perhaps unwise) thing I did during vacation. My poor old father and mother have had no home for about five years, and they have felt their lack of one severely. I hesitated, measured my own resources, that is, my head and hands, and made a very humble purchase for which I am allowed four years to pay. I am sure you would not think the act unwarranted if you could see how happy it made them."

The second reason we believe this date change must be made has to do with the copy of her publication (she was editor and publisher), *The Young Ladies' Miscellany*, a copy of which she had included for Walker to evaluate. There are letters in the six to nine month period before this in which the prospect of such a publication was announced in a Baptist periodical, and subscriptions were solicited; and in several letters she spoke of the plans being made for publication (one dilemma she mused upon was whether or not she should have her name prominently placed on the cover as the editor). But the records indicate that no actual copies were printed until late summer/early fall 1842.

The third reason we believe this date change must be made is her inclusion in the letter to Walker of a copy of her latest book *Life As It Is*. Again, this book was not published until the summer 1842.

[289] In this letter to her brother Walker, and an October letter to Urania Sheldon Nott, Emily told them that she had purchased a home for her parents on Broad Street in Hamilton Village. She was able to do this from the proceeds of her writing. Emily had paid four hundred dollars for the home, payable in four payments over four years, and she was to often mention this debt, and the pressure it put upon her for continued writing, and the income derived from it.

[290] The *Young Ladies' Miscellany* is a magazine started and edited by Emily in fall 1842, with the help and cooperation of the students and staff of the Utica Female Academy. Emily wrote a large percentage of the content, in it showing the true genius of Fanny Forester.

[291] John Sheldon was the brother of Urania Sheldon, Cynthia Sheldon, and Alma Sheldon Anable. He was the father of Jane Sheldon Hawley.

[292] Later in this letter Emily identifies this book as *Life As It Is*.

[293] *Charles Linn or How to Obey the Golden Rule*, Emily's first book, published in July 1841.

I have also a small (very small) Sunday School book in press, called *Effie Maurice*. In the meantime I am composition teacher here, and have a salary of $150 per year beside my board. However my affairs are not the brightest that might be as I have expended a great deal, and the hard times have prevented my raising as much on my books as I expected. Now, I may have told you all this before, and very likely have, but how do I know what I have written when you never take the trouble to answer my letters? It strikes me that you must be a good deal changed during the five years that you have been a westerner or you would show a little interest in your "own flesh and blood" anyhow. Fie on you, for an unnatural, good-for-nothing—never mind the rest, I forgot what a tremendous fury I was in.

I don't know what Ben is about—he is a poor miserable fellow and is loafing round somewhere, a disgrace to us all.[294] His wife is in Morrisville—she ought to take a ride over the Rocky Mountains, and then I should pity the cave that was destined to hold her. Wallace[295] is a fine fellow I can tell you, and will do us credit yet—he is already more manly than some fellows at twenty-five, but he has one defect that I believe is constitutional, he lacks economy. He is just now out of business and talks of setting up a job office in H.—if he does, I predict a failure, and so I hope he won't.

Now do write and tell what you are about—how many farms you own etc. etc.

Really do you never mean to come home? now I should think a young chap like you (come to think though you're not so wondrous young are you?) could make nothing at all of a trip out to "York State," even if he had to go back again. Come, just think of it! Why, dear me! if I had'd a finger in every body's pie so that I could neither raise the money nor be spared I should step over your way myself one of these days. Father[296] and mother[297] would be the gladdest to see you of any body in the world. Mother shakes her head and says "No, no, I never shall see him again! I would'nt have believed it of *Walker*."

Don't forget now to get me at least twenty subscribers for some predict that the "Young Ladies' Miscellany" will be a losing concern, and to tell truth I am more than half convinced of the *fact* myself. However, be that as it may, I will keep it up a year.

I mus'nt [sic] write another word for I have got to go down to the bookstore for "Life as it is," as I suppose I can't make you believe I am an author till you have proof positive, and notwithstanding the *excellence* of the work it may not have

---

[294] Benjamin "Ben" Chubbuck, Emily's older brother. Ben suffered a head injury as a child, and his subsequent behavior throughout his life reflected some mental impairment.

[295] William Wallace Chubbuck, Emily's younger brother, born January 1, 1824.

[296] Charles Chubbuck, Emily's father. Though he held varying positions over the years, he failed at most of them. With the purchase of the house for them, Emily was to continue as a significant financial contributor to the support of the family.

[297] Lavinia Richards Chubbuck, Emily's mother, was born June 1, 1875, in Goffstown NH, the eldest of thirteen children. She married Charles Chubbuck on November 17. 1805. They were the parents of seven children.

found its way into your benighted region.

Now pray don't forget to write, and try to brush up your memory so as to realize the fact that you have a sister by the name of

Emily

Source: Jerome Walker Chubbuck Collection, Wisconsin Historical Society Archives, Madison, WI.

Emily E. Chubbuck to Urania Sheldon Nott, October 10, 1842—Utica

Dear Miss Urania,—

I have just received your kind note by Dr. James,[298] and although 1 wrote you last evening, find there are a few questions which I neglected to answer.

Mr. Hawley[299] seemed to hesitate about the propriety of trying to get the copyright out of D. & N.'s[300] hands, and I shall not have an opportunity to see him again before Mr. S. goes. I heartily wish somebody else had it, but do not know who. It would make a great deal of trouble, and involve some risk, for me to hold the copyright; and I should think it would be difficult, now that the chance of the first edition is lost, to dispose of it to any bookseller.

Dayton & Newman took the MSS., secured a copyright, and agreed to pay me ten per cent [sic] on all that were sold. The percentage is not increased for a new edition, and they are under no obligation to get out a new one at all unless they choose. The first edition of "Charles Linn"[301] was only 1500 copies, and my receipts $51. I do not know how large an edition of "Life as It Is"[302] they have issued, but the volume being larger than the other, if the edition is equally large, I shall receive about $70. Mr. H. says these sell well, but he does not know how many are sold, and, of course, he does not know how many remain on hand: the first is out of print. The reason of their acting so strangely about the business ever since last fall I can not [sic] guess. I wish I had time to write something purposely for the district-school library; but I am afraid I shall not.

Many thanks to you and your kind friends for the interest you take in the affairs of a simple girl, without money, without influence, and almost without friends.

---

[298] Dr. James was a trusted physician in Utica, who attended the students and faculty of the Utica Female Academy. He is mentioned frequently in the correspondence as having been consulted for varying medical complaints and his advice was always welcomed and highly regarded.

[299] Horace H. Hawley was enormously helpful to Emily as she published her early stories and books.

[300] Publishing firm of Dayton and Newman.

[301] *Charles Linn or How to Observe the Golden Rule*, Emily's first book, published in July 1841.

[302] *Life As It Is*, another of Emily's books, was published in late summer 1842.

I rejoice to find that you do not dislike the Miscellany.[303] It is just the kind of labor that suits me, and gains a great many compliments; yet I am by no means sanguine concerning its success. The number of subscribers is constantly increasing; yet they come one by one, and it seems to me rather slow work. Only think of this child's being compared with Miss Sedgwick[304] and Miss Mitford![305] Dew-drops are diamonds, and pinchbeck may well be taken for gold. I wish—but no, I will take what I can get thankfully, though the best compliment I ever received was my father's[306] sitting up till midnight to finish "Life as It Is." I have a magazine, containing a notice of this last, which I will send you.

I am very much ashamed of this careless note, but I have written to-day till my shoulder aches and my hand cramps. As for good pens, you know *Lydia*[307] *has gone*. Please write after Dr. Potter has seen the books, and advise me what to do about them; for I do not think—is altogether disinterested (I may be wrong there), and you well know how little I am qualified to judge.

Yours truly,

Emily

Source: A. C. Kendrick, *The Life and Letters of Mrs. Emily C. Judson*, 79–81.

---

[303] The *Young Ladies' Miscellany* is a magazine started and edited by Emily in fall 1842, with the help and cooperation of the students and staff of the Utica Female Academy. Emily wrote a large percentage of the content, in it showing the true genius of Fanny Forester. Mrs. Nott had originally discouraged Emily as to the magazine's feasability.

[304] Catherine Maria Sedgwick, born in Stockbridge MA, attended Payne's Finishing School in Boston. She was a prolific writer whose works include A New England Tale (1822), Hope Leslie or Early Times in Massachusetts (1827), Married or Single? (1857), Redwood, A Tale (1824), Clarence: or, A Tale of Our Times (1830), The Linwoods: or, Sixty Years Since in America (1835), Didactic Tales: Home: Scenes and Characters Illustrating Christian Truth (1835), Live and Let Live: or, Domestic Service (1837), Tales and Sketches, Second Series (1844). She was featured in many of the same magazines that later featured Emily's stories.

[305] Mary Russell Mitford, a British novelist and dramatist. Publishing a book of poems as early as 1810, she was published by London Magazine and other periodicals, achieving significant fame.

[306] Charles Chubbuck, Emily's father. Though he held varying positions over the years, he failed at most of them. With the purchase of the house for them, Emily was to continue as a significant financial contributor to the support of the family.

[307] We believe that this could be Lydia Lillybridge, who was one of Emily's closest friends at the Utica Female Academy. When Emily made the decision to go to Burmah with Adoniram Judson as a missionary, Lydia offered to go with them, and with Emily speaking to Adoniram Judson and to Solomon Peck and the Board of American Baptist missionary Union of her extraordinary abilities, she was commissioned to go with them, in spite of the fact that she remained single. Always independent and outspoken, unafraid to cause ripples in the missionary community, Lydia would serve on the mission field for twenty-eight years. She married missionary Thomas Simons in May 1851. See the timeline on the life and service of Lydia Lillybridge Simons in vol. 1.

Emily E. Chubbuck to Urania Sheldon Nott, October 1842—Utica Female Seminary

My Dear M—

There it is again! I can not [sic] write to "Miss Sheldon,"[308] and I am sure such a bashful body as I could not be expected to address so dignified a personage as Mrs. Nott.[309] So what shall I do? I am very lonely just now, and feel inclined to be somewhat sentimental; for I have been up the hall, and found a certain corner room, looking—not desolate—O no, it is wondrous cozy and comfortable—but as though it ought to be desolate. Yet I will spare you all the things I *could* say, and turn to some other subject. F- and I are exceedingly quiet and happy together, and as for the rest of the house, things seem to go about right; at least when I put my head out into the hall I see nothing to the contrary. One new boarder has come today, and I hope the number will increase. I find the much dreaded task of giving out composition subjects not so bad after all, though I should not like a spectator any better than formerly.

I am very grateful for the interest you took in my affairs when in New York, and should of course be but too ready to avail myself of any thing [sic] that Dr. Potter was willing to do in my behalf.[310] I think D. & N.[311] act very strangely; for Mr. H.[312] says they told him that the second edition of "Charles Linn"[313] was in press several weeks ago. It has been out of print for a long time, and Mr. H. says he has had a great many calls for it. I was obliged to take the copy belonging to the library to send to you, for I could get no other. It can be replaced if the second edition ever appears. I have marred both books by corrections; but that is the fault of the most careless of all proof-readers. The publishers own the copy-right [sic], and if it could be obtained I do not think it would pay for the trouble. Placing the books in the district-school library might, by creating a demand for them, induce the publishers to bring out a new edition; but I suspect that they have about had their day, and am content to let them pass. There is but one thing that would induce me ever to see another line of mine in print, and that is, the necessity which is the mother not only of invention, but of many follies. If I were in other circumstances I should undoubtedly be a scribbler, but not a professed one.

---

[308] See Emily's letter to her sister Catharine June 25, 1842. Urania Sheldon who was the literary principal of the Utica Female Academy, was to marry Eliphalet Nott, the president of Union College in Schenectady NY. The thought of this loss made Emily so distraught that she wondered if she could even stay as a faculty member of the academy.

[309] To celebrate and commemorate the marriage of Sheldon and Nott, Emily Chubbuck wrote a multi-stanza'd poem. That untitled poem is published as the next piece in this volume.

[310] See Emily Chubbuck's letter to Urania Sheldon Nott dated October 10, 1842. See also Urania Sheldon Nott's letter to Emily Chubbuck dated October 21, 1842.

[311] Dayton and Newman, the successors to Dayton and Saxton.

[312] Horace H. Hawley was enormously helpful to Emily as she published her early stories and books.

[313] *Charles Linn, or How to Observe the Golden Rule,*, Emily's first book, published in July 1841.

I have not told you what (perhaps unwise) thing I did during vacation. My poor old father and mother have had no home for about five years, and they have felt their lack of one severely. I hesitated, measured my own resources, that is, my head and hands, and made a very humble purchase for which I am allowed four years to pay. I am sure you would not think the act unwarranted if you could see how happy it made them; and if I fail to pay, it is but to fail. Kate[314] is at home, quite well and happy.

I have not heard from Philadelphia[315] since I wrote that I could not prepare that short Sunday-school series. I suspect that they can not [sic] publish for lack of funds. As soon as I get time I mean to commence a new book; but I hardly know whether to write one of the same character as the others, or something different; for I do not know how it could be published. However, I shall not waste much time in deciding.

I know this is a very tiresome sheet, and brimfull of selfishness; but you will know how to pass that over, for you have looked away into the writer's heart and will expect the fruit to resemble the tree.

F. sits studying close by; somebody is thumping Miss F.'s piano over our head tremendously; M. B. is passing the door—there! the bell rings—study-hour is over; there is a general increase of sound in the house, and I know by the voices in the hall that many a door has been flung open within the last half minute. How I wish—but no, there is no use in wishing! I will go to bed and dream (I have few day-dreams now) of pleasant things, and wake in the morning and see every thing pleasant; for this *is* a happy world in spite of its perplexities. Fine dreams to you too, both waking and sleeping; yet now and then intermingling may there come a little (though it were the least in the world) thought of

Your truly affectionate

Emily

Source: A. C. Kendrick, *The Life and Letters of Mrs. Emily C. Judson*, 81–83.

---

[314] Sarah Catharine ("Kate," "Kit," or "Kitty") Chubbuck, Emily's older sister, born October 25, 1816.
[315] American Baptist Publication Society, who, after *Effie Maurice*, had asked Emily to write a series of books on the Ten Commandments.

Emily E. Chubbuck to Urania Sheldon Nott,[316] October 1842[317]

For (inter-nos) I'll bet a pigeon,[318]
She'll sometime join the camp of Gideon.—
Then-but I'll pass that Martin-bird,
Without a solitary word,
For she's well nigh an interloper,
And if I ventured to soft-soap her,
Like all the rest, I am not pure,
But she would take my words for truer
When was intended, and grow vain,
And how can my poor muse sustain
The weight of the responsibility
E'en now incurred by her civility
Next-pray don't turn your eyes this way!—
Next is a damsel blind and gray,
That sometimes tried to mount Pegasus,
And take a trip upon Parnassus,
But finds her steed a stupid donkey,
Unruly as an untamed monkey,
And so by rising not-all-all,
She's saved a most tremendous fall.

These constitute a group respectable,
And to my thinking quite delectable;
But there's a chord that cuts the circle,
With power to set the rest at work all,
While for herself there's *Nott*[319] can move her,
For certes, she boasts *Nott* a lover,
But when for *Nott* we're all forsaken
She'll find that she's been *Nott Miss-taken*,
In thinking she'll be *Miss'd* no more
As she's been ever heretofore.
She can't be *eclips'd* she's *Mrs*. Nott—
Sure 'tis a very unique lot,
Thus to exist without a title,
Yet be assured it will be right-all,
For when one *Nott* is closely tied
There's two will hold the willing bride,

[316] This poem has been put together from separate pages, and while we believe we have a correct order of pages, we are not sure. We have stated our reasons and the reader can decide for her/himself.

[317] This poem was written to celebrate and commemorate the marriage of Urania Sheldon to the Reverend Doctor Eliphalet Nott in the late summer–early fall 1842. Sheldon had been the literary principal of the Utica Female Academy, and had been instrumental, with her sister Cynthia Sheldon, in bringing Emily into the academy with tuition deferred, to be paid when she had found a teaching position. For an expression of the depth of her feeling, see the letter of Emily E. Chubbuck to Urania Sheldon Nott that appears prior to this poetry in this volume. That letter is dated October 1842.

[318] At first, we did not believe this stanza to be a part of this poem, but the third line from the stanza end ("But finds her steed a stupid donkey") and the last two lines of stanza 3 ("Lest by another step, my mule / May chance to prove himself a fool") connected the two stanzas.

[319] This, and the lines that follow, are all word plays on Miss Urania Sheldon's new married name, Urania Sheldon Nott.

And I have heard grammarians say,
These were equivalent to yea,
So while the marriage knot or tie
One title to her does deny,
And While the other can't be got,
Since though a wife she married Nott,
The truth, I think, is very clear,
And must to everyone appear,
That she'll be *miss'd*, and *Mrs.'d* too,
And so with little more ado,
I hope before she rings the bell,
To make my bow and my farewell,
Lest by another step, my mule,
May chance to prove himself a fool.

Source: Hanna family files.

Urania Sheldon Nott to Emily E. Chubbuck,[320] October 21, 1842—Union College

My dear Emily,

I am always glad to receive your notes or letters—and hope you will ever improve any opportunity that may occur to drop me a line. I have conversed this mor'g with Prof Potter—he has read "Life as it is"[321] to his wife and children—and thinks it one of the best books for the kind he has ever seen—he has gone to Albany and taken them both to put in the hands of Col G. who will read them—and if he thinks so too, they will be required for the Library—he thinks you had better let Mr. Hawley[322] ask Mr. Dayton[323] if he will dispose of the copy right of both books to you—and upon what terms—if they are cramped for means—he thinks they will be glad to do it—if they will not on any terms—then let them know what is proposed to do with them by Col G—and ascertain when they will publish them—If you are very certain that Mr. Hawley is not in their interest in any way—he can manage the matter well—but if he is—let him do nothing. Mr. P will attend to it. The Harpers or Appleton's would be glad to take them.[324]

Source: American Baptist Historical Society, AJ 25, no. 1241.

---

[320] This is a letter fragment, with only the first page.

[321] *Life As It Is*, Emily's latest book, published at the end of the summer 1842.

[322] Horace H. Hawley was enormously helpful to Emily as she published her early stories and books.

[323] The publishing firm of Dayton and Newton.

[324] This is a fragment; the letter ends here.

Jane Blodgett to Emily E. Chubbuck,[325] October 29, 1842—Kingston

Dear Emily,

You are doubtless surprised that your kind line should they remain unanswered, and be assured this should not have been the case, had it come to hand earlier, but through some mistake it did not reach me until this week. You are very kind in offering to continue your Magazine,[326] and believe me the perusal of its interesting pages adds not a little to my happiness while away from home, as well as those rendered dear by associations connected with my school days. But I like not thus to tax your generosity. Should I succeed in securing other publishers, I will let you know and claim the several copies at your hand, otherwise shall scarcely feel myself justified in receiving them.

I am very glad to hear you are all so happy and I love to think of you as forming the same merry group as in days gone by, before I laid the *romping school girl* for the staid and sober *school marm*. Yes, and I would again love to sit in the same old seats and receive instruction from the same efficient source, but change has not lef [sic] the Old Sem. untouched, with its once young and happy inmates. During the short space of little more than one year, he has taken your head so that she is *Nott*,[327] and with his ruthless hand has scattered to the four winds of heaven the little flock once so contented and cheerful under the [Note: "Fond" is scratched out.] guidance of a fond and loving Preceptress. Yes, some are tossed on the waves of temptation and driven by the fierce winds of adversity, and since the Shepardess [sic] has thus been smitten the Lambs of the flock, have many of them expired, and their frail barks have been driven on the dangerous rocks of matrimony; while these few are still wandering in the fields of hope and expectation, and while thus journeying onward leaving some good word of advice to those around them, or perchance "Teaching the young idea how to shoot" (or shout) [sic]. Thus is it with all; each views with wonder the vast changes which are wrought not only with ourselves, but those with whom many happy moments have been spent.

You did not mention the name of Mrs. Nichols,[328] so I know nothing of her or the dear little *Luly*. I have looked and anxiously for even one word from her since

---

[325] We note that the second paragraph of this letter is a wonderful nostalgic soliquey on student life at the Utica Female Academy, and the changes that take place both in the staff and in the student body as years pass.

[326] The *Young Ladies' Miscellany* is a magazine started and edited by Emily in fall 1842, with the help and cooperation of the students and staff of the Utica Female Academy. Emily wrote a large percentage of the content, in it showing the true genius of Fanny Forester.

[327] In this clever play on words, Jane Blodgett was speaking of Urania Sheldon, the literary principal of the Utica Female Academy, who that summer had married Eliphalet Nott, the president of Union College, in Schenectady NY, and speaking to the fact that Nott had left Utica to live in Schenectady. See the letter of Emily Judson to Urania Sheldon Nott dated October, 1842, and the untitled poem that Emily had written about the loss of Urania Sheldon Nott to the staff of the academy.

[328] James Nichols and his wife had assumed the position of literary principal at the Utica Female Academy upon the marriage of Urania Sheldon to Eliphalet Nott in fall 1842.

she left Kingston, but thus far I have been disappointed, and am almost inclined to think she has forgotten me. If there are any with you who remember me and should chance to ask after me, give them my best love—Particularly, Miss Cotrander. I suppose you have become acquainted with her before now. Much love to Miss Cynthia[329] and all.

If it is not asking too great a favor, I would be exceeding happy to hear from you often, at any rate let it be once in a while at least. Let no one see this to excuse haste.

Yours affectionately

Jane C. Blodgett   Source: American Baptist Historical Society, AJ 24, no. 1213.

Emily E. Chubbuck to Urania Sheldon Nott, November 1842—Utica

My Dear Mrs. Nott,—

It is a splendid morning, and if I had not my bed to make and my floor to sweep, and all this sea of papers which escaped from my portfolio last night when I was so sleepy, to pick up, I should undoubtedly write some poetry about the golden clouds hovering above the Deerfield hills, and the broad sheets of silver—(i.e., thinly scattered snow just a little bit tipped with sun-light)—now and then peering out through the openings. But beds and floors are very arbitrary things, and never would think of stopping getting tumbled or dirty, though the poetical world should suffer ever so much thereby.

I should have written you before about Mr. Hawley's[330] negotiations in New York, but I have been expecting every day that Miss Cynthia[331] would write and tell you all about it. Dayton & Newman[332] will let me have the copy-right [sic] of the two books for a hundred dollars, fifty dollars apiece. Now as I could have had it for a mere trifle a year ago when the manuscript was in my own hands, and as they have had the advantage of a whole edition, of course making the right less valuable, I do not feel inclined to accept the offer. Besides, it would not be a very pleasant thing, even if I were sure of making money by it, to hold the copy-right [sic] myself, and have the books printed; and disposing of it otherwise is in the

---

[329] Miss Cynthia Sheldon was the administrative and finance manager of the Utica Female Academy. She was a mentor, advisor, and friend to Emily.

[330] Horace H. Hawley was enormously helpful to Emily as she published her early stories and books.

[331] Miss Cynthia Sheldon was the administrative and finance manager of the Utica Female Academy. She was a mentor, advisor, and friend to Emily.

[332] Dayton and Newton had published *Charles Linn or How to Observe the Golden Rule*, and *The Great Secret or How to be Happy*. Because of their inability or lack of interest in published second editions of her book, previous correspondence had indicted Emily's interest in controlling the copyright herself. See Emily's letters to Urania Sheldon Nott dated October 10, 1842 and October 1842.

present case out of the question. They say that they can sell it for more than fifty dollars to publishers in New York. So, assuming that I could dispose of it for ten or twenty dollars more, it would be of little use, as I should cut myself off from the percentage which I am now to receive. They promise to republish "Charles Linn"[333] before January; but I shall not depend much upon any profit from either of the books.

According to your suggestions I have commenced a new book designed exclusively for district schools, but I have written as yet only about a dozen pages. My time seems completely occupied, and though I have prepared and laid aside copy enough for two numbers of the Miscellany,[334] yet there are little hindrances constantly arising to prevent me from accomplishing anything. However, I shall do what I can, and hope to finish something by the middle of next term.

The very flattering compliments which I received from Schenectady a few days ago encouraged me not a little. You can not [sic] imagine how they lightened my heavy foot, and straightened my bent shoulders. I need not say, my dear Mrs. Nott, how grateful I feel for all the interest you take in my little affairs, for you must know it all, must know that I could not feel otherwise. And now—and now for a little more motherly counsel—but I have no room, and "there is time enough yet."

Yours truly,

Emily.

Source: A. C. Kendrick, *The Life and Letters of Mrs. Emily C. Judson*, 83–84

H. M. Dodge to Emily E. Chubbuck,[335] November 1842—Cazenovia

Dearest Emily,

I have but a very few moments to write, as the bearer of this is about leaving. I received your last summary but have not time to tell you here, how much pleasure it gave me. Also your "Young Ladies' Miscellany."[336] [ ] since that time I have indeed through afflictions [ ] and [Note: Two lines are lost here because of a fold in

---

[333] *Charles Linn or How to Observe the Golden Rule*, Emily's first book, published in July 1841. The publishers had been promising her a second edition for many months, and none had been forthcoming.

[334] The *Young Ladies' Miscellany* is a magazine started and edited by Emily in fall 1842, with the help and cooperation of the students and staff of the Utica Female Academy. Emily wrote a large percentage of the content, in it showing the true genius of Fanny Forester. Urania Sheldon Nott had originally disapproved of the project, but in more recent letters she had been more favorable.

[335] This letter seems unusually "pushy" in asking Emily for personal information. It is important to read it along with Mrs. Dodge's letter to Emily dated July 4, 1842. Mrs. Dodge seems to be on a mission to get herself in business as an author, and strongly pushes Emily for her help as an expert.

[336] The *Young Ladies' Miscellany*, a magazine started and edited by Emily in fall 1842, with the help and cooperation of the students and staff of the Utica Female Academy.

the paper and very indistinct copy]. I was sick myself many weeks, and have scarcely yet recovered. My sweet babe was born July 15th, and lived about eleven weeks, but God has taken her to himself.

I write at this time to get some particular information respecting your method of publishing your books. You say the Publishers know nothing about you, how then do you manage? I wish you would be very explicit on this subject, as it may be of great importance to me. Besides, could you send by any means mss to N. York for me, if I should send them to you? I have some opportunity now for writing, and am anxious to publish, if I can produce anything worthy. I am perfectly enraptured with your books, which I have obtained through the kindness of your intimate friend, Mrs. M. Bates.[337]

I should like to know how much you have received from your books, and also how you succeed with the "Miscellany." I hope you will write at your earliest convenience, and give me that information which your discriminating mind will at once perceive I am reaching after. I trust you will not deem this an intrusion but be willing to do what you can to help a sister of the quill.

Yours with much affection

H. M. Dodge   Source: American Baptist Historical Society, AJ 24, no. 1204.

Emily E. Chubbuck to Catharine Chubbuck, November 30, 1842—Utica[338]

Dear Kate,

I did'nt [sic] receive yours until after the package had gone, so I could'nt [sic] send mother's gloves but I will get them to bring home with me. As to the cambric and wadding, they are not of much consequence and we'll talk that over then. I shall be ready to come a fortnight from next Fri the 17. I believe.—Misses Buel and Knapp are coming next term. I wish father[339] would write and let me know whether he can come after me, as I suppose there will be no accommodation line then. My health is very good and if I had ever so much to trouble me, I should'nt [sic] have time to be troubled. The Miscellany[340] is liked I believe, but I have rec'd

---

[337] Marie Dawson Bates was one of Emily's childhood friends.

[338] The original copy of this letter does not have the year in which it was written. I have placed it in 1842 because that is the year that Emily did the *Young Ladies' Miscellany*. Also, in an earlier letter to Urania Sheldon Nott, dated November 1842, Emily spoke of the book she was writing intended exclusively for district school libraries.

[339] Charles Chubbuck, Emily's father. Though he held varying positions over the years, he failed at most of them. With the purchase of the house for them, Emily was to continue as a significant financial contributor to the support of the family.

[340] The *Young Ladies' Miscellany* is a magazine started and edited by Emily in fall 1842, with the help and cooperation of the students and staff of the Utica Female Academy. Emily wrote a large percentage of the content, in it showing the true genius of Fanny Forester.

only $100, yet, and that as you may well believe is all spent. What with my debts[341] and what with my wants it is no easy thing to pay the printers. My salary however for this term is untouched, and Miss Cynthia[342] notwithstanding her own troubles will stand between me and the printers. I believe my popularity as a teacher is increasing all the time and I am allowed to go on in my own way since I have given a certain couple to understand[343] it is the only way I will go, unmolested. I do think Miss Cynthia is the best woman in the world, and if it was'nt [sic] for her some of us teachers would come out slim.

I have commenced a book intended for district-school libraries, and written about 30 pages. I think it will be a capital thing and the Schenectada [sic] people promise that it shall be brought out favourably [sic]. It is different from either of the others, and if less interesting is I think more useful.

Don't you think it is queer we don't hear from Walker.[344] John P. Sheldon Esq.[345] is coming through here on his way to Washington this winter, and if he don't [sic] bring letters I shall give up.—Do tell Wallace[346] to stick to his business—he who does a small thing ill will never do a large one well, and if he fails now he will be ruined, at least for years to come. I hope you practice a great deal—you must.[347] Lou Campbell is going to Rochester to teach—when she goes we shall all hold jubilee–I never saw such a very *devil* in one little body as is wrapt [sic] up in hers.

Does father expect me to bring home any money? If he does, I wish he would write and let me know how much.

It is doubtful to me whether I get anything for my book this winter until the first ed. is all sold—if I do it will go towards the Miscellany. Julia Holmes sent her subscription the other day—wonder why she don't [sic] take of the Nortons. Did'nt [sic] you tell Aunt Dinah all the good things the Reg. had said about it? I should think that would gain her heart of course. I mean to go up to M. and raise a row when I get home—Did'nt [sic] you give Mrs. Laselle a hint upon the subject of

---

[341] Emily Chubbuck's debts at this time included the cost of her original tuition at the Utica Female Academy for the school year beginning in fall 1840, the tuition for her sister Kate who spent two quarters there beginning in fall 1841, and the cost of the new home which she had purchased in Hamilton Village for her parents and sister in late summer 1842.

[342] Miss Cynthia Sheldon was the administrative and finance manager of the Utica Female Academy. She was a mentor, advisor, and friend to Emily.

[343] James Nichols and his wife. He and his wife had assumed the position of literary principal at the Utica Female Academy upon the marriage of Urania Sheldon to Eliphalet Nott in fall 1842. Emily found Mr. Nichols difficult, and characterized him in other letters as having a very judgmental personality which was hard on both teachers and students.

[344] John Walker Chubbuck, Emily's older brother who ran a newspaper in the Wisconsin Territory. Though he regularly sent copies of the paper to Emily, she often reminded him that a paper was not a substitute for a real letter and that his family longed to hear a personal word from him.

[345] John Sheldon was a brother to the Sheldon sisters, Urania Sheldon Nott, Alma Sheldon Anable, and Cynthia Sheldon. He was the father of Jane Sheldon Hawley.

[346] William Wallace Chubbuck, Emily's younger brother, born January 1, 1824.

[347] In the two terms Catharine spent at the Utica Female Academy beginning in fall 1841, she took a course on playing the guitar, giving her a background in music that would translate into something that she could teach from her home in Hamilton.

subs and C. Castle would'nt know who sent it or who was the editor I am afraid.

Just heard from Hat. Anable.[348] She is only too happy—expect she will return to us as accomplished as Anna Maria[349] is. The girls enquire for you every few days[350] and I suppose would be sending love now if they knew I was writing. Jane Hawley[351] gave me a beautiful geranium the other day—One slip of bridal rose that I brought from home is alive and my other rose has begun to send out new leaves. My geranium will spread all over the house yet.

Why did'nt you tell me what my "nice little present" was? I hav'nt [sic] had but one new thing this term except shoes and gloves, but that is a very extravagant one and I shant [sic] tell what it is till I come home. It is'nt a dress—oh no! I'm as ragged as a beggar.

"So write it be."

Emily

Source: Hanna family files.

Cynthia Sheldon to Emily E. Chubbuck, December 21, 1842—Utica[352]

My dear Emily,

Your family letter came to hand in due time, and was rec'd with as much zest as the writer evinced—

They were in full glee to pay you off the next mail—but I am most certain it was neglected—those very girls you may divine their apology for such neglect, when I tell you they all moved towards Schenectady, on Tuesday—that is Anable,[353] Barber,[354] Dorland, Dameux,[355] Mr. Nichols[356] and Henry were snugly piled into a fine sleigh—with the intent to have a two days visit there and return

---

[348] Harriet ("Hatty," "Hattie," or "Hat") Anable, one of the five Anable sisters.

[349] Anna Maria Anable was the niece of the Urania and Cynthia Sheldon, the daughter of Joseph and Alma Sheldon Anable; she was Emily's closest friend at the Utica Female Academy.

[350] Catharine Chubbuck had spent several terms at the Utica Female Academy, studying guitar, flower painting, and drawing. She had left to return home to her parents in March 1842.

[351] Jane Sheldon Hawley, daughter of John Sheldon, niece of Cynthia Sheldon, Urania Sheldon, and Alma Anable, cousin of Anna Maria Anable, and married to Horace H. Hawley.

[352] This letter is undated. We place in on December 21, 1842. We know it was winter because of the sleigh rides, we know Emily left Utica for Hamilton on December 17, and this would be the following Wednesday, and 1842 was a time when the *Young Ladies' Miscellany* was being published.

[353] Anna Maria Anable was the niece of the Urania and Cynthia Sheldon, the daughter of Joseph and Alma Sheldon Anable; she was Emily's closest friend at the Utica Female Academy.

[354] Mary Barber, mentioned frequently in the Emily Chubbuck Judson letters, was a student and then art teacher at the Utica Female Academy.

[355] Eugenia Damaux, part of Emily's intimate circle of friends at the Utica Female Academy. Living in New York City, Eugenia suffered from some kind of eye problem that at times made her life very difficult; this was a matter of comment in many of the letters exchanged between the girls themselves and with Cynthia Sheldon. In 1848, Eugenia was in New York living "at Mrs. Brown's—the same warm-hearted French girl as ever." In 1849, she married Johnny Edmonds, described as rich and pious, and they lived in Utica.

on Saturday—their teachers are scattered—the dozen girls left do various things to kill time—On Monday Evening father[357] was taken very ill with an attack of Cholera Morbus—we were much alarmed, but it has happily passed over—although he feels very weak—the rest are well—we have had a house full of company—the meetings continue with interest—deeply [ ], still the multitude cares for none of these things—

I have six names for the Miscellany,[358] one paid—Mr. Hawley[359] said the number for next month could not well come out before the 15th.

I must send this to the office. I was interrupted yesterday, before three lines were done—and staying friends fermented my writing last night—much love to all.

In haste yours truly

C. Sheldon   Source: American Baptist Historical Society, AJ 26, no. 1276.

N. Luce to Emily E. Chubbuck,[360] December 27, 1842—Guilderland[361]

My dear Miss Chubbuck,

Business before pleasure—Sophronia [sic] could not have expressed herself very clearly relative to the "Miscellany."[362] When you sent me a number I, like the great *coot* as I am, never observed the direction to return it if I did not wish to take it,[363] and when Sophron mentioned it to me, I immediately transferred my numbers to Maria, for such poor wretches as we, can't afford to take "Miscellanies"—I made a mistake in the direction (for it should be Miss L. M. Nott) and also in the back number—You sent the September No. instead of August,[364] and Maria is very

---

[356] James Nichols, literary principal at Utica Female Academy.

[357] Deacon Asa and Mrs. Isabell Sheldon, parents of Cynthia Sheldon, Urania Sheldon Nott, and Alma Sheldon Anable. Mr. and Mrs. Sheldon lived with their daughters and grandchildren as a part of the Utica Female Academy community. For many years, Mr. Sheldon led mealtime prayers for the academy family. Mr. and Mrs. Sheldon were very popular with the students. When Mrs. Sheldon died January 29, 1847, Mr. Sheldon continued to have a room at the Utica Female Academy until he died in March 1848.

[358] The *Young Ladies' Miscellany* is a magazine started and edited by Emily in fall 1842, with the help and cooperation of the students and staff of the Utica Female Academy. Emily wrote a large percentage of the content, in it showing the true genius of Fanny Forester.

[359] Horace H. Hawley was enormously helpful to Emily as she published her early stories and books.

[360] This letter is the first page of a letter of three pages. At the bottom of the page are the initials "N.L."; the second and third pages of the letter are written by and signed "Harmony Luce." We believe this first page to be a letter written by a sister or family member, so we have it as from "N. Luce." The letter from Harmony Luce immediately follows.

[361] The original letter has the month and year, but not the day it is written. We have assigned it this date as it has a reference to children playing with their Christmas gifts.

[362] The *Young Ladies' Miscellany* is a magazine started and edited by Emily in fall 1842, with the help and cooperation of the students and staff of the Utica Female Academy. Emily wrote a large percentage of the content, in it showing the true genius of Fanny Forester.

[363] We learn here that Emily made an attempt to market the *Miscellany* by sending multiple copies to her former students.

[364] Up to this reference, every indication has been that the first issue of the *Miscellany* was in September 1842. The first mention of a copy was in a September letter to Emily's brother, Walker, when she enclosed a copy. Prior to that, all the references were to

anxious to have that as it contains the commencement of the "Boarding School"—You must not send us any more for altho' I could wish to encourage "*rising geniuses,*" still the curse of Adam rests on us and we must have *raiment*; (*food* I can dispense with,) therefore to sum up the whole, if Adam had not sinned I would take your Miscellany, but as he did, I am compelled to "Veto" it a la John Tyler.

N. L.

Harmony Luce to Emily E. Chubbuck,[365] December 27, 1842

How do you flourish? Do you still persevere in the blissful employment of correcting the "old compositions"—Can it be possible that I had to string a certain quantity of words together weekly, *purely* for your edification?[366] It seems like a dream—to think how I used to get my locomotive pen, and steam across the paper Monday mornings, as though I had taken writing by the job and my only object was to save time—the ideas were utterly beneath my consideration (as you undoubtedly perceived), and thereby spared you considerable trouble; for if there had been an idea, you would have had to arrange it in a civilized form, but as it was, the only thing necessary was to correct the ungrammaticality—A coined word, Madam.

The children are displaying their Christmas presents in great glee but Alas! I have got none—It is my luck—I never had but one present, and that was my "grass skirt." I find people give presents to those who can make some return, and as I cannot, why of course I must go without them. I have, however, one thing to give away, big rag knit caps. I wish you would advertise for some *small* person who will give me something for it, as I cannot wear it, on account of its size.—I have just been down stairs to make some cider syllabub, and it was delicious. Allow me to help you to a glass—do now, for it is perfect nectar—"essential juice of pineapple" etc. etc.

I have heard from Caroline[367] once—she seemed in fine spirits—wrote us in the usual strain—

If you see Helen Munson,[368] will you ask her if she received a letter from me some time since?—I wrote her and requested an immediate answer but as usual my

---

subscriptions.

[365] The first page of this letter was written by and signed "N.L.," and it appears immediately prior to this letter. We have assigned it to a sister or family member of Harmony Luce. The month and year are on the first page, and we have assigned the date, as the letter mentions children playing with Christmas presents.

[366] Harmony Luce had been a student of Emily's at the Utica Female Academy. Emily became the teacher of composition in fall 1841.

[367] Caroline Reynolds, formerly a student at the Utica Female Academy.

[368] Helen Munson was part of the Utica Female Academy community. In December of 1840 Emily had written a poem dedicated to "Miss H. Munson." The first two stanzas read: Go gather flowers, ay gather flowers / To deck thy sunny brow, / And garlands twine in summer bowers, ---- / 'Tis fit employment now. / Tune, tune the lyre! / Thy musick [sic] breathe, / Fair child of light and song: / Dream fairy dreams, gay visions wreathes / Though they must fade ere long.

request is disregarded—Strange that no one thinks my letters worth answering!—I wrote to Miss Dorland ages ago, but that's the end ou't [sic]. I wish I could think of some poetry expression of my "feelings," but I never knew but two lines—Ah! here they are—

> The world is before me—I'll never repine,
> But why I'm desolate, I cannot divine.

Will you say now that I can't write *poetry*? and the real genuine article too, disdaining both metre [sic] and sense—Speaking of poetry reminds me of Kate[369]—what has become of her? I conclude however, she is at *home*, enjoying *that*, if nothing more—I would be willing to rise on air, and lie in bed all day for want of clothes if I could only be at *home*, but such is not my destiny—"Kihn kirosh kithemock pithine" [sic]—do you understand that quotation? Well, neither do I—and so we are equally wise, but I feel like talking in some unknown tongue—Now, Miss C. if you have waded to this spot, take courage, for you can "see land." Do write to me if you will, but if you don't wish to you need not—I'll not feel slighted—love to all

I have the honor to be

Harmony Luce

Written along the left margin of page 1: "May the winds of heaven visit you gently and the rain wet you slightly. May the hail fall harmlessly, and your sun ever shine gloriously. Adieu."   Source: American Baptist Historical Society, AJ 25, no. 1246.

Emily E. Chubbuck to Urania Sheldon Nott, January 4, 1843—Utica Female Seminary[370]

My Dear Mrs. Nott,—

The "blind harper" has been entertaining us this evening, and those simple airs are of all things the "open sesame" to the heart. While listening I have been back, not many years, it is true, but in the review singularly long, over the whole ground of my past life, visited every nook, sat down awhile by every friend, and acted over again what distance has robbed of almost all bitterness.

Source: A. C. Kendrick, *The Life and Letters of Mrs. Emily C. Judson*, 85–87

---

[369] Sarah Catharine ("Kate," "Kit," or "Kitty") Chubbuck, Emily's older sister. Kate spent two terms in fall 1841 and winter 1842 at the Utica Female Academy, and was well known to many of the girls who were there at the time.

[370] This letter has an addendum dated January 7, 1843, and a second addendum dated January 11, 1843.

Emily E. Chubbuck to Urania Sheldon Nott, January 7, 1843[371]

Tuesday, January 7. I was interrupted on Saturday evening; so you are relieved of the "association of ideas" which brought me up to the time of my first landing in Utica, not quite "friendless and homeless," but certainly very forlorn.[372] Well, you can judge from that of whom I last thought, but not how pleasant were those thoughts; for even you can not comprehend all you have done for me, nor how unwilling I should be to be able to say, "I owe her nothing." But let that pass; however much the subject may be in my thoughts, I know you will not care to hear it talked of, so I will turn to other topics.

The school this term is very pleasant. There is no one to head mischief among the young ladies, so they are all remarkably correct. True, we feel a lack of something; but that can not [sic] be helped, and I believe in all cases the true philosophy is to "take it easy."

And now for myself;—egotism is pardonable in a letter. I am doing just nothing this term, and am as busy about it as though I was servant-general to the whole world. You know I never had much time to read; I have taken the matter in hand now, and hope I shall make something of that, if nothing else. I have not written a line of poetry, this term; for, saith the poet Sands,

> "Thou who with the eagle's wing,
> Being a goose, wouldst fly, dream not of such a thing;"

a caution worth observing. My district school book[373] stands right where I left it last term, and I have not the courage to touch it. I can not [sic] write as I could before people expected me to succeed; and when I now take up the pen I feel the same embarrassment that I do before company. I do not *say* this, for people would consider it affectation; but I feel it none the less, while making other excuses. You may tell me that it is foolish to feel so about those simple little books that nobody but children reads, and sometimes I try to laugh myself out of it in the same way. But I care more for my small circle of friends than for a hundred critics, and they, if nobody else, read them. I heartily wish I had never touched a pen but to write letters; may be then I should have been more expert in this line. Mary comes to say that a man wishes to see me in the hall. It is the printer after copy, no doubt; so my letter must have another beginning.

---

[371] This letter is an addendum to a letter dated January 4, 1843. There is a second addendum dated January 11, 1843.

[372] In fall 1841, Emily had decided that she needed additional education upon which to build her future. On September 25, 1840, she had received a letter from her friend Lydia Allen, telling Emily about the Utica Female Academy, and the sisters Urania and Cynthia Sheldon. The Sheldon sisters agreed to defer Emily's tuition payments until she could afford to pay them, and Emily was enrolled in early October. It was to be one of the transformational experiences of her life.

[373] In her November, 1842 correspondence to Mrs. Nott, Emily had mentioned several times that she was working on such a project. Mrs. Nott had been encouraging Emily to do this work.

Source: A. C. Kendrick, *The Life and Letters of Mrs. Emily C. Judson*, 85–87

Emily E. Chubbuck to Urania Sheldon Nott, January 11, 1843

Saturday morning. Mr. and Mrs. Sheldon[374] are going this morning, and I have concluded to send this by them, if you will excuse its age. I heard from home yesterday; I am afraid my poor old father[375] is failing, and will be before long confined entirely to the house. The rest of the family are in usual health….

The little Sabbath school book that I sent to Philadelphia last summer is in print.[376] There are sixty pages, for which they have paid me thirty dollars. Do please write to me at your first leisure, and believe me, with the greatest affection and respect,

Yours truly,

Emily E. Chubbuck

Source: A. C. Kendrick, *The Life and Letters of Mrs. Emily C. Judson*, 85–87

Emily E. Chubbuck to Catharine Chubbuck, January 18, 1843—Utica[377]

Dear Kit,—

The Miscellany[378] is very late this month, but I expect it out to-morrow. Have not yet heard from New York.[379] There is an article on neurology in the *Democratic Review* which I wish Wallace[380] to read. I begin to believe in it; it is no more mysterious than our breathing and thinking. All is mystery, and if we believe in nothing which we can not comprehend, we may as well go back to the scholastic philosophy, or disbelieve the existence of matter. Dr. and Mrs. Nott[381] were here when I

---

[374] This is probably a reference to John Sheldon and his wife; a previous letter had mentioned that they would be stopping by Utica in their travels. John was the brother of Miss Cynthia Sheldon, Urania Sheldon Nott, and Alma Sheldon Anable.

[375] Charles Chubbuck, Emily's father. Though he held varying positions over the years, he failed at most of them. With the purchase of the house for them, Emily was to continue as a significant financial contributor to the support of the family. He would remain healthy, and in fact, would outlive Emily.

[376] Emily had been in conversations with Rhees of American Baptist Publication Society about such a work. The title was *Effie Maurice*, and it had been released in December.

[377] There is an addendum to this letter dated January 23, 1843.

[378] The *Young Ladies' Miscellany* is a magazine started and edited by Emily in fall 1842, with the help and cooperation of the students and staff of the Utica Female Academy. Emily wrote a large percentage of the content, in it showing the true genius of Fanny Forester.

[379] Emily, in previous letters, had been speaking of the copyrights to her earlier books and the possibly of purchasing them, as well as the possibility of second editions and new publishers for her books. In October 1842, Emily had written to Urania Sheldon Nott: "I am very grateful for the interest you took in my affairs when in New York, and should of course be but too ready to avail myself of any thing that Dr. Potter was willing to do on my behalf."

[380] William Wallace Chubbuck, Emily's younger brother, born January 1, 1824.

[381] Eliphalet and Urania Sheldon Nott. Dr. Nott was the president of Union College.

came back, and we had a delightful visit. Did Wallace write the notice of Dr. N.'s lecture in the *Whig*? It was capital.

I understand that Mr. Miller[382] (he left town yesterday morning) has created quite a sensation in the city. One merchant has dismissed his clerks, and shut up his shop. We do not know much about it in the Seminary,[383] but I learn that some families are nearly crazy. I went to hear him once, and must own that I was a good deal disappointed. He was more visionary than I expected to find him. However, they *say* that his lectures are characterized by sound reasoning and good common sense, and that positions in which I thought him visionary he had previously established. He is evidently sincere and very pious, and—deluded or not—I would rather be in his place than in that of those who sneer at him. I do not wonder that wicked men do it, but I think it awful in ministers.

My plants thrive beautifully. I have commenced an article, "Our Village," for Wallace, but do not know that I can finish it; I get so little time. Can't write his story, "no how." Don't expect ever to get my book done.

Source: A. C. Kendrick, *The Life and Letters of Mrs. Emily C. Judson*, 87–88.

Emily E. Chubbuck to Catharine Chubbuck, January 23, 1843[384]

Monday morning. Have been sick, but am a good deal better. I am pretty much discouraged about earning any thing, but don't care much. What is the use of money when one has enough to eat, drink, and wear, as I am sure I have? The commercial article in the *Democratic Review* predicts a change of times in the spring—hope it will be verified. Write, *do*, immediately to

Your very loving sister,

Emily

Source: A. C. Kendrick, *The Life and Letters of Mrs. Emily C. Judson*, 87–88.

---

[382] Commenting on this, A. C. Kendrick, in *The Life and Letters of Mrs. Emily C. Judson*, said: "The allusion is to William Miller, formerly of Hampton, Washington county, the celebrated lecturer on the millennium, and originator of the 'heresy' known as 'Millerism.' The sensation which he produced will be remembered by many. Had Chubbuck heard more of his lectures her sound judgment must have confirmed her estimate of the visionary character of his views."

[383] The Utica Female Academy (or Seminary).

[384] This letter is an addendum to a letter dated January 18, 1843.

M. I. Rhees to Emily E. Chubbuck, January 24, 1843—Philadelphia

Miss E. Chubbuck,

Accompanying this, you will receive 12 copies of "Effie Maurice," which has been out of press since December 7, 1842.

I have made an estimate of the matter it contains, and find in it according to the average I have made 62 1/2 pages of 1200 letters each, which at our terms, as agreed upon, for the copy right, [sic] entitles you to $31.25, payable June 7th, 1843. If our Treasury should be replenished sooner than that, we would rather settle it earlier, but at present money is hard to be got.

I regret the delay which occurred in its publication, but it was unavoidable on my part. I put it to press as soon as I could consistently with previous [Note: The last of this sentence is lost in the blur of the paper fold.]

I hope you will be pleased with the style in which thez [sic] are got up. The binding is in the usual style of S. S. books.[385] I hope also you will go on with the series on the Commandments, as I believe such books will do much good.

I am
Yours truly

M. J. Rhees

Source: American Baptist Historical Society, AJ 22, no. 1080.

Urania Sheldon Nott to Emily E. Chubbuck, February 24, 1843—Union College[386]

Dear Emily—

I was indeed very much gratified with your kind letter[387]—and I beg you once for all to write me freely about yourself—your family and about anything that interests you. Tho' I am not daily and hourly brought in contact with you and the dear sisterhood—as in bygone days—still you are all very dear to me—and when I see or hear, in the course of my peregrinations, anything that deeply interests me—the wish [ ] arises that you could one and all enjoy it with me.

---

[385] See the letter of Mr. Rhees dated July 23, 1842.
[386] This letter has an addendum dated March 2, 1843.
[387] See Emily's letter to Urania Sheldon Nott dated January 18, 1843.

Why is your pen idle this winter? Your District School book[388]—I had hoped was nearly ready for the public—your talent lies in that direction Emily—and I hope you will not bury it—"Ministering Angels"[389] is sweet—very sweet.

Source: American Baptist Historical Society, AJ 25, no. 1240

Urania Sheldon Nott to Emily E. Chubbuck, March 2, 1843[390]

I have been compelled to take this scribbled sheet of paper for the want of another dear Emily—though as I have seen you since the above was written, I did not intend to inflict it upon you—I look back upon my stolen visit of a few hours as upon a pleasant dream in which I can trace with the vividness that sometimes belongs to our dreams, loved forms and faces—and listen to words of kindness and affection, almost as distinct as if this vision of the past were before me.

I had a pleasant journey—as I had no one to whom I was obliged to talk—and

---

[388] According to the correspondence Emily had been writing, at the urging of Mrs. Nott, to write a book specifically for district school.

[389] *Ministering Angels*

Mother, has the dove that nestled
Lovingly upon thy breast,
Folded up its little pinion,
And in darkness gone to rest?
Nay; the grave is dark and dreary,
But the lost one is not there;
Hear'st thou not its gentle whisper
Floating on the ambient air?
It is near thee, gentle mother,
Near thee at the evening hour;
Its soft kiss is in the zephyr,
It looks up from every flower.
And when, Night's dark shadows fleeing
Low thou bendest thee in prayer,
And thy heart feels nearest heaven,
Then thy angel babe is there.

Maiden, has thy noble brother,
On whose manly form thine eye
Loved full oft in pride to linger,
On whose heart thou couldst rely,
Though all other hearts deceived thee,
All proved hallow, earth grew drear,
Whose protection, ever o'er thee,
Hid thee from the cold world's sneer,—
Has he left thee here to struggle,
All unaided on thy way?
Nay; he still can guide and guard thee,
Still thy faltering steps can stay:
Still, when danger hovers o'er thee,
He than danger is more near;
When in grief thou'st none to pity,
He, the sainted, marks each tear.

Lover, is the light extinguished,
Of the gem that, in thy heart
Hidden deeply, to thy being
All its sunshine could impart?
Look above! 'tis burning brighter
Than the very stars in heaven;
And to light thy dangerous pathway
All its new-found glory's given.
With the sons of earth commingling,
Thou the loved one mayst forget;
Bright eyes flashing, tresses waving,
May have power to win thee yet;
But e'en then that guardian spirit
Oft will whisper in thine ear,
And in silence and at midnight,
Thou wilt know she hovers near.

Orphan, thou most sorely stricken
Of the mourners thronging earth;
Clouds half veil thy brightest sunshine,
Sadness mingles with thy mirth.
Yet, although that gentle bosom,
Which has pillowed oft thy head,
Now is cold, thy mother's spirit
Cannot rest among the dead.
Still her watchful eye is o'er thee
Through the day, and still at night
Hers the eye that guards thy slumber,
Making thy young dreams so bright.
O! the friends, the friends we've cherished
How we weep to see them die!
All unthinking they're the angels
That will guide us to the sky!

[390] This is an addendum to a letter dated February 24, 1843.

the day was very beautiful. I was quite vexed the next day, to learn that a comet or planet was distinctly seen from 12 till 2 o'clock with the naked eye. It was very near the sun—and there I sat gazing within a few inches of it a long time, without dreaming that any such wonder was to be seen by my eyes—and could just as well as not be seen by mine.

I have a request to make dear E. of you, and through you of all the teachers—that they will each one sit a few minutes of every day in mother's room. Do not all go together—but drop in when you can do it for my sake—and as my representative.[391] I am aware that you are all very much charged with your [ ] duties—still without interfering with them—you can take a little time—to cheer and enliven the hours of my dear father and mother—and I know you will cheerfully do it.

Will you ask Cynthia[392] to send my keys to me as soon as she can—and also to make my apology to Doct James[393] for not sending for him—she can tell him that old Mrs. Jackson is failing, it is thought rapidly as she has never recovered from her fright on the night of the fire,

Mr. and Mrs. Pearson have dined with me sociably today and just left me—Mary counts the days till she shall go to Utica—if Utica were only within calling distance—we should see each other oftener—but then—this is about as reasonable as if—as was that of the little girl who thought she should be so very happy if she could be a fairy. It is a great lesson to learn this—to be cheerful every where [sic]—and yet why do we not learn it—we who have daily proofs of the care and goodness of God—We should be willing to trust, not only our own affairs with Him, but our absent friends—The attention to religion seems to be increasing in our city—and in every direction—I have no doubt but the doctrines of Mr. Miller[394] have had much to do in producing this effect—We cannot think of this great event, seriously think of it, without finding that whether near at hand to the whole world or not, it is very near to us. God grant that our lamps may be trimmed and burning.

Tell Fanny[395] to keep up good courage—and aim very high—a perfect report may yet be achieved—I feel very grateful to you dear Emily, for all the interest you have manifested in her—and hope she will reward you for it, by new improvement.

---

[391] Deacon Asa and Isabell Low Sheldon, parents of Cynthia Sheldon, Urania Sheldon Nott, and Alma Sheldon Anable.

[392] Miss Cynthia Sheldon was the administrative and finance manager of the Utica Female Academy. She was a mentor, advisor, and friend to Emily.

[393] Dr. James was a trusted physician in Utica, who attended the students and faculty of the Utica Female Academy. He is mentioned frequently in the correspondence as having been consulted for varying medical complaints and his advice was always welcomed and highly regarded.

[394] William Miller, founder of the sect of "Millerism" and celebrated lecturer on the millennium. See Emily's letter of January 18, 1843 to her sister Catharine. Apparently Miller was generating serious discussion at the Utica Female Academy.

[395] Fanny Anable was one of nine children born to Joseph and Alma Anable and was a niece of Cynthia Sheldon and Urania Sheldon Nott. By 1845, Fanny had moved to Philadelphia to study and work in the home of the Reverend A. D. Gillette and his family. In fall 1848, she became a part of the teaching faculty at the Misses Anabel's School in Philadelphia.

Love to all the teachers and family from
> Your affection friend.

Urania E. Nott   Source: American Baptist historical Society, AJ 25, no. 1240

Louisa B. Marble to Emily E. Chubbuck, May 16, 1843—Port Byron

My Dear Miss Chubbuck

Caroline[396] leaves this afternoon and I hasten with pleasure to fulfill the promise which I made in part, of writing to you after my arrival home. It is now a month since I left Utica, and I have never known the time pass more swiftly or pleasantly. But I must tell you what I have been about so that you may believe me and give me all the credit I deserve. "Well," where to begin; after arriving safely home again and passing through the affecting scenes of meeting old friends, beaux, etcetera, I began to reflect upon the dignity and importance of my station as a young lady graduate, and to summon to my aid all the wise sayings and doings that could possibly be of use in adopting a course of conduct conformably thereto. The plan was laid, and I can assert with perfect safety that it was acted up to, in every respect for three whole days successively, after which time I regret to say (probably owing to some mysterious movement of the stars) there was a rapid falling off, and has been ever since. I have played a little, sang less, and sewed least, but have been seized with a sudden mania for reading, which my Father thinks is likely to prove fatal, as I have already devoured the contents of numberless periodicals, novels, etc. and am now deeply engaged in the "Lincali" and "The bible in Spain" which I like very much.

When you should see Miss "Jeanne," when occasionally she plies her hand at housekeeping. [sic] Many a laugh is raised at her expense, and many a kind face turns away to suppress a smile, and of fear you would be inclined to do the same, my dear Miss C—, could you witness the patience with which she endeavors to bear these sufferings.

I have not mounted my Pegasus once since my return. Poor fellow! I fear he must hobble most sadly by this time for want of exercise, but then when I left school it was with the serious determination to drive a more sober paced nag hereafter, and endanger my character no longer by the tricks he is wont to play.

I am very anxious to see the next number of the "Miscellany"[397] and suppose it will be forth-coming soon. I forgot in my haste while at Utica to ask you to please

---

[396] Caroline Reynolds was at the Utica Female Academy with Emily.

[397] The *Young Ladies' Miscellany* is a magazine started and edited by Emily in fall 1842, with the help and cooperation of the students and staff of the Utica Female Academy. Emily wrote a large percentage of the content, in it showing the true genius of Fanny Forester.

direct my numbers, Port Byron. Cay Co —But Caroline reminds me that I have but a few moments more and I must close. Please give my best love to Miss Kelly,[398] Miss Damaux[399] and the girls. Oh! how I would love to see them all again! I trust you will excuse the manifold errors of this scrawl as my only plea is very great haste.

Please write me soon and believe me ever,
Your sincere and affectionate friend,

Louisa B. Marble

Source: American Baptist Historical Society, AJ 25, no. 1245.

Lydia Lillybridge[400] to Emily E. Chubbuck, May 21, 1843—Annsville

Dear Emily

I hardly know how to address you. Death has again come very near to us. "Another from our ranks hath passed. The dearest and the loveliest." My second eldest brother expired on Monday morning the 15th inst after an illness of two weeks and four days. His sickness proceeded from a slight wound about half an inch in length just below the knee of the right limb. He kept about his usual work for nearly three days after receiving the cut, when in consequence of taking cold, the limb became much inflamed, and disease spread rapidly through his whole system. On the day before his death, his physician concluded that the only hope of saving his life was in amputating the limb, and even then the hope was very faint. It was left for him to decide whether it should, or should not be done. After conversing with the family he wished Doc. Pope of Rome, to be consulted before that step was taken. When Dr. P. arrived he told my brother that amputation would be useless—that there was no remedy—that he could not continue long, perhaps not till morning.

His replay was—"I am ready to go." He had expressed the same sentiment many times before. During his whole illness he talked of death with the greatest composure settling all his accounts with much carefulness.

After Dr. Pope was sent for, he thought it doubtful whether he lived until he arrived, and requested those standing about him to sing. Among other hymns he

---

[398] Jane Kelly was Emily Chubbuck's friend at the Utica Female Academy. Jane later became a teacher with Emily at the academy. Kelly became the literary principal in 1844 with the retirement of James Nichols and his wife from that position. During a period of Kelly's illness in 1844, Emily filled in the position for her. Then, in 1848, when Cynthia Sheldon moved to Philadelphia to help start the Anable's School, Kelly became the "headmistress" of the academy and successfully brought the academy into the future, though not without some initial disparagement from the Sheldon-Anable families.

[399] Eugenia Damaux, part of Emily's intimate circle of friends at the Utica Female Academy.

[400] Lydia Lillybridge, who in 1846 would go to Burmah with Emily and Adoniram. Lillybridge would serve the missionary field for twenty-eight years. See Lydia Lillybridge Simmons time line in vol. 1.

mentioned the one commencing "What is this that steals upon my frame? Is it death, is it death?" and joined the others in singing the last line "All is well, all is well." After the hymn was ended, he requested us to have it sung at his funeral.

His sufferings were very great from the first and reduced him as much in two weeks and a half, as we should commonly expect in six weeks. So said the physicians.

O Emily, it has been a great satisfaction to me to be able to attend upon the wants of this dead, dying brother day and night. I have seen more of the power and efficacy of Religion within the last four weeks, than during my whole life before. Life seems more uncertain than ever before. Though now in perfect health it would nothing strange [sic] or uncommon if the next week should find us in our graves.

About one month ago we attended the funeral of a cousin of ours, an amiable girl nineteen years of age, who died after an illness of five or six days.

There is so much sickness and death in this town, that it makes one feel gloomy to think of it.

My dear Mother's health is better than it was last winter.

I have not forgotten what was said between us with regard to our old accounts. I have ascertained, to my own satisfaction just how they were left, and will say more about it at another time.

The favor you put into my satchel secretly is not lightly esteemed.

My love to the dear friends Miss Cynthia,[401] Mrs. Anable,[402] with their parents[403]—also to dear Miss Dorland, and Miss Dismang, and all the rest.

I wish to hear about a great many thing [sic] that I cannot speak of now. Do write soon.

Yours truly

Lydia Lillybridge

E. E. Chubbuck

Written along the left margin of page 3: "Please don't leave this where every body will see it. I have not written before in three months I think."

Source: American Baptist Historical Society, AJ 25, no. 1250.

---

[401] Miss Cynthia Sheldon was the administrative and finance manager of the Utica Female Academy. She was a mentor, advisor, and friend to Emily.

[402] Alma Sheldon Anable, sister of Cynthia Sheldon and Urania Sheldon Nott. On July 28, 1814, Alma married Joseph Hubbell Anable in Troy NY (Anable's second marriage). Joseph and Alma Anable had nine children: Henry Sheldon Anable, b. June 21, 1815; William Stewart Anable, b. November 6, 1816; Anna Maria Stafford Anable, b. September 30, 1818, Cynthia Jane Anable, January 28, 1820; Samuel Low Anable, b. November 28, 1821; Harriet Isabella Anable, also known as Hatty or Hattie, was born December 18, 1823; Courtland Wilcox Anable, b. July 28, 1825; Frances Alma Anable, or Fanny, b. April 12, 1828, and Mary Juliet Anable, b. February 18, 1830.

[403] Deacon Asa and Isabell Low Sheldon, parents of Cynthia Sheldon, Urania Sheldon Nott, and Alma Sheldon Anable.

B. R. Loxley (A.B.P.S.) to Emily E. Chubbuck, June 28, 1843—Philadelphia

Dear Sister,

Above you have two drafts drawn to your order one on N. York Bank for 19.5/100 Dollars and the other on Bennett Bachus and Hawley for 12.20/100 Dollars which is the payment for the copy right on *Effie Maurice* as per agreemt [sic] with our Cor. Sect. Mr. Rhees. I regret I could not have forwarded it sooner but we have had such hard times to get money. I sent to the care of Baker and Thompson, N. York a small package of the books for you, which I hope you have received, they were requested to forward them.

Yours truly

B. R. Loxley, Asc.
(Please send me a receipt)

Source: American Baptist Historical Society, AJ 22, no. 1079.

Emily E. Chubbuck to Cynthia Sheldon, July 31, 1843—Hamilton

Dear Miss Cynthia,

I arrived at a certain cozy little nest, down on the corner, at about 8 o'clock Sat. Eve. and found all but my poor mother[404] well. Her health is very miserable indeed. The day was perfectly lovely, neither too hot nor too cold, and I had my usual luck in the company line. Tell Mary Barber[405] she need'nt [sic] say any more about widowers,[406] for did'nt [sic] just the finest one that ever was play the agreeable to me all the way? A six-footer, "and which is more" rich as Croesus, and which is more with only *two sons*. Then did'nt [sic] I get a compliment from him afterwards? And *such* a compliment! Not my face, beautiful as it is, nor my exceeding gracefulness, nor even my enthusiasm and romance—no more of that, but my practical common sense, and (now, Jane Kelly,[407] hide thy diminished head,) *my conversational powers*.

I should think Miss C., there might be a place for somebody at Norwich. Mr. Taylor, the principal of the school, was inquiring of Wallace[408] about me last week

---

[404] Lavinia Richards Chubbuck, Emily's mother, was born June 1, 1875, in Goffstown NH, the eldest of thirteen children. She married Charles Chubbuck on November 17. 1805. They were the parents of seven children.

[405] Mary Barber, mentioned frequently in the Emily Chubbuck Judson letters, was a student and then a teacher of art at the Utica Female Academy.

[406] "Widower" refers to widowed older men and usually suggested availability and interest in marriage. The academy girls and their teachers were always referring to "the widower" or to "widowers" in their conversations and correspondence.

[407] Jane Kelly was Emily Chubbuck's friend at the Utica Female Academy. Following the departure of Mr. and Mrs. Nichols, Jane became the literary principal in early 1844. Then with the departure of Cynthia Sheldon to Philadelphia in fall 1848, she became "headmistress."

[408] William Wallace Chubbuck, Emily's younger brother, born January 1, 1824.

and said they should lose their lady principal this fall. I don't know what kind of a situation it is, not anything about the salary, but should think it might be respectable.

I see that it will not do for Kate[409] to leave Mother and I shall try to get up something for her to do here but don't know how I shall succeed.

I haven't said anything yet about the discouraging state of matters and things, but tell father it is time enough to worry when the day comes. We have a fine garden and some other little improvements have been made, so that I think it very pleasant here.

Mother thinks the antimony that I sent her has done wonders, as she is troubled with fever every day. Will you please send out some when E. Knapp comes and also one of those cheap sun-shades at Doolittle's. I believe they can be had for six shillings.

I saw Helen Nye's mother at Madison and she says she has concluded to not send H. to Utica before the winter term. She thinks she can't spare her this fall. I am to go to Mad. tomorrow to eat cherries and promised myself a grand time. I wish some of the girls were with me—no *all*—would'nt [sic] we strip the boughs, though?

The widower, of whom I have made mention, owns a large cream-coloured [sic] house just in sight. Would'nt [sic] be funny if I should mistake it for the Academy, when the vacation is over? Oh, if you could see the delicious fruit there you would'nt [sic] wonder. Love, ever and ever so much to all (yourself of course included) from

Yours truly

E. E. C.

Source: Hanna family files.

---

[409] Sarah Catharine ("Kate," "Kit," or "Kitty") Chubbuck, Emily's older sister, born October 25, 1816.

Eliza C. Allen to Emily E. Chubbuck,[410] August 22, 1843

My Dear Miss Chubbuck,

Your very valuable communication was rec'd after the matter for the Sept. No. of the *Mothers' Journal*[411] was sent to the Publishers, but I very cordially avail myself of it for the Oct. No.

The subject is one of great and increasing importance and difficulty. I know not how mothers are to end with us in reference to it. Your views are just and forcible. There is great weight in the remarks upon the necessity of mothers sympathizing with their children in their literary pursuits, and *reading with them*. Instead of this parents too often treat their children as if they had no common ground, and did not belong to the same species.

I took up the subject of fictions and light reading in the course of the last volume of the jour.—in two articles in, perhaps, the May and June Nos., or thereabouts; and hope that others would pursue it, and throw upon it more light. It must not be permitted to sleep.

I hope you will, by all means, favor me with the story to which you allude, and I shall feel greatly indebted.

I read with much interest the Y. L. Misc'y,[412] and doubt not its effect will be happy upon those who are favored with it.

It will always give me pleasure to hear from you.

Truly yours,

Elisa C. Allen

Lebanon Springs
August 22, 1843

I have desired one of the publishers to obtain your permission to allow your name to be attached to the article—I hope you will not object.

E. C. A.

Source: American Baptist Historical Society, AJ 22, no. 1091.

---

[410] This letter was sent to Emily in response to an article sent to her by Emily for publication in the *Mother's Journal*. Apparently Eliza Allen's letter went to the Utica Female Seminary and was opened by Cynthia Sheldon, who then added her own note on the back of the letter. That letter is found in the collection under Cynthia Sheldon, August 26, 1843.

[411] In the archives of the Hanna family, we were privileged to find two pieces—one a poem "The Caged Robin," and one an essay "The Works of God the Best Teachers." Both were in the handwriting of Emily Chubbuck, and both were identified by her as "For the Mother's Journal." This poem and essay are the next two pieces to be found in this volume.

[412] The *Young Ladies' Miscellany* is a magazine started and edited by Emily in fall 1842, with the help and cooperation of the students and staff of the Utica Female Academy. Emily wrote a large percentage of the content, in it showing the true genius of Fanny Forester.

Emily E. Chubbuck for the Mother's Journal, August 1843[413]

The Caged Robin[414]

Child
Sing, sing, pretty robin!
I love thy sweet song;
And fein would I listen,
All through the day long.
Sing, sing pretty robin!
'Twas long ago day,
And now I must go,
To my lesson away.

Mother
O it pines for the woodland,
So green, and so fair;
For the blue, smiling heavens,
And cool summer air.
It is sad,—for the pinion,
Once active and free,
Is useless, and droops—
And all [ ] for thee.

Child
But, Mama, I bring flowers,
The sweetest that bloom,
And boughs from the green-wood,
I have round its room,
And the clear, crystal water,
That comes from the spring,
Both morning and eve,
To my robin I bring.

Mother
Yet thinkest thou, Mary,
All this will repay,
For the rich gem of freedom,
Thou'st stolen away?
No, it longs to spread out
Its glad wing, and to fly,

---

[413] This date is an approximation. We know that Emily Chubbuck was writing for the *Mother's Journal* as early as fall 1843, and we place this letter with the first letter from Eliza C. Allen, the editor of that publication. There are six letters in the correspondence from Allen; they begin in August 1843, there are two in 1844 (January and February), one in March 1845, and two in 1846 (February and April).

[414] The original of this poem is in Emily Chubbuck's handwriting, and was found on the back of the second sheet containing an article, "The works of God the best teachers," also written for the *Mother's Journal*.

From this lone, gloomy crate,
Far away in the sky.

Child
Then, mama, it shall go,
Though I love it so well.
With other sweet birds,
In the woodland to dwell.—
Adieu, pretty robin—
See! it rises so high,
That it fades and is lost,
In the [ ] of the sky.

Mother
Yes, child—'tis like this.—
This world is the chain,
That binds thee to sorrow,
To sin, and to pain;
But death will release thee,
Then may'st thou arise,
Like the bird thou has freed,
To a home in the skies.

E. E. C.

Source: Hanna family files.

Emily E. Chubbuck for the Mother's Journal,[415] August 1843[416]

The works of God the best teachers

There is no better way in instilling truth into the minds of children, and fixing on them habits of virtue, than by teaching them to love the beautiful things of God's creation. A mother would find her task materially diminished, if she would but make use of the teachers a kind Providence has placed all around her, to guide her children in the path of virtue.

Take for example a flower—every child loves it for its intrinsic beauty, but without the mother's assistance it becomes insipid, and is cast aside as the toy that

---

[415] The original of this article is in Emily Chubbuck's handwriting, the front and back of one sheet of paper, and two thirds of a page on the second sheet of paper. On the back of page two is "The Caged Robin."

[416] This date is an approximation. We know that Emily Chubbuck was writing for the *Mother's Journal* as early as fall 1843, and so we place this letter with the first letter from Eliza Allen, the editor of that publication.

familiarity has made worthless. There are many things that contribute to make children love even a simple flower. It is necessary that the mother enter into their feelings, participate in their enthusiasm, and point out the beauties that escape their careless eye. Another thing which contributes much to interest them is a kind of feeling of *ownership*. This principle of human nature which has not escaped the notice of philosophers, we discover in the infant mind almost as soon as it is capable of thinking. I have known some parents who gave their children a spot of ground, to cultivate for themselves exclusively, and I have never known this plan to fail of producing the most admirable effects. I am speaking now of little girls, particularly, for no one would doubt its happy effects on boys. A little girl can display as much taste in arranging her flower garden, as in dressing her doll—at the same time she acquires habits of industry, regularity, and order, with something of a feeling of responsibility, that it is often very hard to gain in after life. It is well known that amusements requiring exercise in the open air, besides being conducive to health, impart an activity, a freedom and grace of manner, and a character to every movement, never gained in the nursery or even parlour. But anything of this kind must not be enjoined as a task. The love of freedom, so active in every bosom, is manifested in children by their impatience of restraint, and natural dread of anything like a command, and it is better in managing them that coercion be used as little as possible. Oblige a child to read a little book, for instance, and however calculated to interest, she will become weary, yawn over it, and not be able to tell you a single word she has read. Offer the same book as a favor, or reward, and tell how delightful "Mama" was with it, and the tables are turned at once. She will remember a great deal, to which you can add a personal application, and it makes a lasting impression on her mind. Then in the one case she is contracting a careless mode of reading and thinking, with a dislike for books in general, while in the other she acquires a habit of attention, and she will understand and remember more of the next book she reads than of this, and be able with a little assistance to make the application herself. Parents err in not knowing how to manage these little caprices more frequently than in any other way.

But to return to our flower-garden, and its last great lesson. It affords an admirable opportunity of leading the tender mind upward to the great Director. The child learns by experience that all her efforts, without the rain, the dew, and the sunlight, would be unavailing, and thus if you early make the application, she learns confidence, and dependence on the Supreme Being, and through life her mind is continually going "from nature up to nature's God." Children discover a great many important truths, but they always need a more thinking mind to reduce them to practice.

Again, children may be taught to love birds, and listen delighted to their music. A bird upon the wing is I think one of the most beautiful things in nature, and the same little creature at rest, seeming the very emblem of innocence and peace, is an object of universal admiration.

But it is not my intention now to point to particulars. I know of nothing beautiful or curious, from the worlds that flash and glitter above us, down to the merest pebble, that may not be made interesting, and at the same time, have a direct influence on the moral character of the child.

And speaking of pebbles, reminds me of a little circumstance that occurred last summer. Walking in the country, I met two little girls carrying a basket filled with very common petrifactions, such as impressions of shells, etc. On asking them some questions concerning their load, I found as in most cases of the kind, that the mother was the instigator of the thing, "and" added one of the little girls with peculiar animation, "Mama is going to tell us a nice story about petrifactions when we get home." I longed to see that happy mother, for I thought there was coming a day when "her children would rise up and call her blessed."[417]

The hearts of children thus taught by the works of the great Creator, will be doubly barr'd, not only against the vices and follies of the world, but against the trials that beset the pathway of the most favoured. If the Christian's life is a warfare, the spiritual nature cannot be too early prepared for the conflict. The husbandman does not sow his seed in midsummer, neither should the parent wait till the weeds of sin and folly have twined their roots so deeply in the ready soil, as to call for a harsh hand to remove them as she gives her children the key-stone [sic] of happiness in this world, which rightly used may unlock the portals of a glorious immortality.

E. E. C.

Source: Hanna family files.

---

[417] This quote is from the good wife narrative in Proverbs 31.

Cynthia Sheldon to Emily E. Chubbuck,[418] August 26, 1843

Dear Emily

This note was said to be from Mrs. Allen[419] and I could not resist the temptation to get inside—*feel exceedingly gratified*—

Harriet[420] has returned from Beonsen, and engaged to go again, but really I know not what to think about our Fanny.[421] It is quite time she was home. If no opportunity is to come, will you say to her that we think she had best come in the stage on Tuesday,—I will however leave it with [sic] to judge about her remaining longer—Hawley[422] went down to N. Y. with Mr. and Mrs. Bright[423] Wed'y—He wished me to say to you he thought the book thus far was just *the thing*—and they will take hold of it when he returns—I will send this to the office this E'g—Urania[424] came up from N. Y. last night in good spirits—we hope to see her next week, [ ] is probably in Detroit tonight.

Mr. Anderson from Hamilton with Mr. Corey[425] are to keep us from being

---

[418] On August 22, 1843, Eliza Allen, the editor of the *Mother's Journal*, responded to Emily's letter. Allen sent the letter to the Utica Female Seminary, where Cynthia Sheldon opened it, added this note to it, and forwarded the dual letter to Emily in Hamilton.

[419] Eliza C. Allen was the editor of the *Mother's Journal*, which included Emily's material as early as 1843. In a letter to Emily during their courtship, Adoniram mentioned that he had met Eliza Allen and had written: "I am afraid I shall get to dislike her. She is a woman that I could make some use of. She has a sharp, strong intellect—is a good critic in the rough, but not in the nice. No heart—no amiability—very severe and what is worse, glaringly envious." Judson went on to say that the *Mothers' Journal* was considered to be a very prestigious publication for the church. After June 1844, Emily seemed to turn her literary attention to commercial publications such as the *New Mirror*, *The Columbian*, and *Graham's Magazine*, which would pay Emily five dollars a page, an unheard of sum at the time. There are six letters in the correspondence from Allen; they begin in August 1843, there are two in 1844 (January and February), one in March 1845, and two in 1846 (February and April). Later letters reflect a dialogue between Emily and Allen with Allen's expectation that Emily should write for her magazine and find her reward not in lucrative financial reward, but in the ministry of *Mother's Journal* to mothers and children. Emily replied frankly that she had financial burdens needing to be met. In December 1848, Emily received a letter from Eliza Allen's husband, the Rev. Ira Allen, describing in some detail the death of Eliza Allen.

[420] Harriet ("Hatty," "Hattie," or "Hat") Anable, one of the five Anable sisters. She had been teaching in the New Orleans area, located in a private home.

[421] Fanny Anable, one of the five Anable sisters. She was born April 12, 1828.

[422] Horace H. Hawley was enormously helpful to Emily as she published her early stories and books.

[423] Edward Bright was, at this time, one of the publishers of the *Baptist Register*, a very popular Baptist paper in the New York region. In 1846, Bright became the American Baptist Missionary Union's corresponding secretary, and at the time of Adoniram Judson's death, he was instrumental in helping Emily and her family settle back in the United States. He worked with Emily on the business details of the Judson Memoir, and after Emily's death, was one of the executors of her estate. Beginning in October 1851, Adoniram and Elnathan lived with the Brights in Roxbury MA.

[424] Urania Sheldon Nott, formerly literary principal of the Utica Female Academy, was a mentor, advisor, and friend to Emily.

[425] Elder Corey was the pastor of a Baptist church near the Utica Female Academy, and Miss Sheldon and many of the girls from the academy worshiped there. In April 1844, he wrote to Emily expressing dismay that at a school program one of the girls had read a composition justifying dancing as exercise; he spoke of this as a roadblock to the salvation of many. Then on March 10, 1846, Emily indicated in a letter to Anna Maria that Corey had been very critical of her relationship and impending marriage to Adoniram Judson. Cynthia Sheldon wrote a number of times expressing Corey's regret and support, and in 1847 there were letters of reconciliation between Emily and Corey. In spring 1848, we learn that Corey's wife had died of consumption, her condition exacerbated by recent childbirth. She had left behind four children, the youngest a baby. Then in July 1849, Anna Maria Anable wrote of his impending marriage to Jane Backus, a good choice for this "rising man." Corey remained popular with the Sheldon-Anable families even after their move to Philadelphia in 1848. A March 2, 1852 letter from Charles B. Stout told of

lonesome until Monday—thus providence provides—painters and cleaners are progressing, and we all feel a good weeks work [sic] is done, some very favorable applications give me courage to *trust*—C. S.

Do you know we shall want your council on the 6th or [ ].

Source: American Baptist Historical Society, AJ 22, no. 1091.

Charles Fenno "Hoffy" Hoffman to Laura Linden,[426] October 15, 1843[427]

She was fair enough and an heiress, kind-hearted though cold, and sufficiently intelligent though common-place. Others in their kind wish to reclaim a Batchelor [sic] to domestic life, had wooed and won her for me. I had but to speak and there was ample opportunity. I did not speak. She married another. Fifty times since when suffering from my own vehement passions, or cowering with pity for the beloved one who sympathised [sic] in nature with me—have I bitterly regretted that I had not made the placid lady the mother of children. [ ] worldly-wise and sensible then myself—a man shelved years back as "a respectable [ ] man" a "useful member of society." Laura I often now regret it—not the lady—not her wealth. But I regret that I did not slide into the safe comforts [ ] [ ]—approving condition of calm and healthy, though but half developed, life in which such a marriage would have planted me!—

Read the previous page over twice Laura my Sister fondly loved. I have repressed this aplation [sic] in which thy letter threw me in [ ] to write it the first thing. For Laura by the God that made I cannot advise thee about this marriage. Such a responsibility I would not undertake were it my own brother's daughter who asked for counsel. I give thee only my own experience of thought in the only thought I ever addressed to the subject. It makes my blood curdle to think of one so fun so gentle and loving as thou art being consigned to a husband who might only recognize cherish and [ ]sted to a part of her nature. Yet such I do [ ] believe my Laura is the destiny of nine-tenths of God's creatures in marriage, which when

---

Corey's call to the Stanton Street Church in New York City, a call that Corey did not accept. Finally, in 1854, there was a pastoral letter from Corey to Emily on her illness and her possible death.

[426] Charles Fenno Hoffman was a prominent literary figure in Philadelphia and New York, who was well known in those literary circles as an adventurer, an editor, a poet, and a writer of exceptional talent. In fall 1843 he had written three letters to Emily Chubbuck addressed to "Laura Linden," for Emily had written to him under that name, asking his advice about love, fame and fortune. Only one of these letters is in the correspondence. Hoffman was not to learn of Emily's identity until spring 1845; in a letter we have dated April 7, 1845, he spoke of Laura having taken off her mask and revealing herself to him. There were four letters from Hoffman in this April period when Emily was in Philadelphia. There were another three in December 1845 when Emily again was in Philadelphia. See vol. 1, "Cast of Characters," Hoffman, Charles Fenno. Anna Maria Anable frequently intimated in her letters that Emily was interested in "Hoffy" as a beau.

[427] All of the Laura Letters are undated.

not a co*mpro*mise is half the time a *mistake*; and therefore are there no marriages in Heaven—when sympathy of soul makes propinquity of [ ] and when Spirits blend in proportion as they are of kindred nature. Milton in his strange but powerful paper on Divorce would make us acknowledge *only* such marriages *here*. But God as well as man has ordered the earth difficult and both [ ] and law universally recognize only the external covenant,—a solemnized partnership of parentage interest and reputation. Laura my child, oh most prayerfully would I consider thy vocation for thee—but I am not equal to it. Thou must ask thyself if such partnership would bring thee comfort or not even though thy soul had no share in it. As far as the fullness of the other marriage in this world "the union of wedded souls"—thy hope must be [ ] [ ] and stronger than thy brothers if thou looksest [sic] for it. Cannot Mr. G. play the guardian the wise and filial advisor to thee in this solemn [ ]. I must stop dear. But I will write to other parts of thy most moving letter tomorrow. I kiss thee fondly—affectionately—obligingly, my Laura kiss thee as a do[ ] would who could not assist his child at her [ ] and most solemn exigency. Bless thee girl. God bless thee and guide thy decision to the peace and approval of thy latest years. Thy suitor—I wish I knew him. Laura he may be more worthy of thee in spite of his cold exterior than any of those thou wouldst refer. God grant it may be so if thy decision gives thee his name. Put up thy [ ] so sweet—[ ] eyes—another kiss on them Bless thee.

Source: Hanna family files.

Emily E. Chubbuck to Catharine Chubbuck, November 10, 1843[428]

Dear Kitty,

A letter that I supposed had reached you more than a week ago has just returned upon my hands and so I suppose you must be wanting to hear from me by this time.

I have been enjoying a charming episode in the dry book of a teacher's life—a correspondence with C. Fenno Hoffman.[429] I had written three letters and rec'd three in return under the signature of "Laura Linden."[430] He has no idea of who I am, but it seems to make no difference his whole soul appears on the page. His letters are delightful and I should be glad to get more of them, but prudence said stop

---

[428] This letter is undated. We place it on Monday, November 10, 1843, because of the reference to the proof sheets of *Allen Lucas, The Self Made Man*. In a letter to Urania Sheldon Nott placed towards the end of November, Emily enclosed some of the published copies of *Allen Lucas*. Obviously the proof sheets would predate the publication by at least several weeks.

[429] Charles Fenno Hoffman, a prominent literary figure in Philadelphia and New York, well known in literary circles as an exceptionally talented editor, poet, and writer.

[430] *Nom de plume* of Emily E. Chubbuck.

and we both obeyed. The little affair has ended and I alas! am the prosing school ma'am again.

I have an invitation out to-night—am not certain whether I shall go or not—it is at Mrs. Warner's to meet Miss Spencer and Miss Sprague, daughter of Doct. Sprague, Albany. Mrs. Judge Denio called upon me last week—she is very civil and agreeable—wishes me to visit her without ceremony, and of course I shall accept the flattering invitation. This dull, dragging teacher's life grows more and more distasteful to me every day and I grasp at anything to vary its monotony.

I have another box of dirty clothes ready and shall send them the first opportunity. Don't you get any chance to send and I am getting somewhat needy. Put all the pieces like my cloak in the box for I want to fix it. I wish too you would give me back the chali frock—I can't afford to buy anything new this winter and by lining that it may do for covering. Send all the pieces—Tell father[431] there is but little hope of getting Miss D.'s money, her mother is likely to want it, but he must'nt [sic] be discouraged. I expect a windfall of some sort or other, though I can't for the life of me tell what, or where it is to come from.[432]

> "The darkest day,
>   Live till to-morrow, will have passed away."

I have had the first proof-sheet of "Allen Lucas"[433]—they are doing it handsomely and intend to have it out before or about Christmas. I wish I could strike out some plan for money-making—to help us out of this difficulty, but nothing seems to be worth trying—n'importe, "every dog must have his day" and ours will come by and by.[434] I hope you are all well and behaving well. [Note: Six lines are blacked out.] Write, do—it is such a very ling time since I have heard.

I hav'nt [sic] heard from Walker[435] since the receipt of the letter which I immediately answered—what do you suppose is the reason? Have you any drawing scholars? How does Leonora manage?—Mr. M. is wonderfully civil to me but I don't place any confidence in him—I know he is a snake in the grass.—We have

---

[431] Charles Chubbuck, Emily's father. Though he held varying positions over the years, he failed at most of them. With the purchase of the house for them, Emily was to continue as a significant financial contributor to the support of the family.

[432] In a September 16, 1841 letter to her brother Walker, Emily told him that she had purchased a home for her parents on Broad Street in Hamilton Village. She was able to do this from the proceeds of her writing. Emily had paid four hundred dollars for the home, payable in four payments over four years, and she was to often mention this debt, and the pressure it put upon her for continued writing, and the income derived from it.

[433] This is Emily's latest book; she was able to send a copy of it to Urania Sheldon Nott by the end of November.

[434] Over several years Emily Chubbuck had amassed what would have been a significant debt. She was still paying for her tuition which had been deferred when she was a student at the Utica Female Academy, beginning in October 1840. When her sister Catharine came for two terms of study in fall 1841, Emily assumed that debt. And then in late summer 1842, Emily paid $400 for a home for her parents and sister in Hamilton Village.

[435] John Walker Chubbuck, Emily's older brother who ran a newspaper in the Wisconsin Territory. Though he regularly sent copies of the paper to Emily, she often reminded him that a paper was not a substitute for a real letter and that his family longed to hear a personal word from him.

had a young winter out here, I hope it will be succeeded by a delightful Indian Summer—I don't know what has got into me lately, I dream of home every night, and wake in the morning—O *so* disappointed and lonely. But every thing [sic] is pleasant here and we are all like *own* sisters to each other—we teachers, I mean. It *does* seem *too* bad though that poor I must always be away, there are [ ] few of us too—how comfortable and [ ] a few hundreds would make us—the hundreds that some are spending so carelessly.

By the way, Kit, how comes on our friend Re[ ] Don't you think he was a good deal flattered by our maneuver? Does he call?—Where is Lawton? I don't think much of him now-a-days. But the widower![436] the widower! Where *is* he? What *can* he be about? Write and tell me everything.

Your homesick sister

E. E. C.   Source: Hanna family files.

Emily E. Chubbuck to Urania Sheldon Nott, November 1843—Utica[437]

Dear Mrs. Nott,—

The girls are about starting, so I have only time to say, "How do you do? And good-bye. We closed up last night, and to-day are feeling exceedingly free. To-morrow I leave for home. Delightful thing—a stage-coach ride in this mud! "The Self-Made Man"[438] made his appearance yesterday, and I enclose a copy. You must wink as you read, but I shall not trouble myself about that; you have seen the like a time or two before, and would not undertake to read with your eyes open. I should feel complimented by some of the little newspaper puffs if I did not happen to know that the writers of them could not have read the book. So if you see them, estimate them at their proper worth. Please remember me to the doctor,[439] if he would recollect me, and believe me,

Yours ever and truly,

Emily   Source: A. C. Kendrick, *The Life and Letters of Mrs. Emily C. Judson*, 88–89.

---

[436] "Widower" refers to widowed older men and usually suggested availability and interest in marriage. The academy girls and their teachers were always referring to "the widower" or to "widowers" in their conversations and correspondence.

[437] The dating on this letter is from Kendrick's book, *The Life and Letters of Mrs. Emily C. Judson*. An earlier November letter to her sister Catharine told us that Emily had just received the proofs for *Allen Lucas: The Self-Made Man,* and that they hoped for a publication release before Christmas. Here in this letter she has received copies, would put this letter in late November.

[438] The book was *Allen Lucas: The Self-Made Man*.

[439] Reverend Doctor Eliphalet Nott, was the president of Union College in Schenectady NY. An ordained Presbyterian minister, he was married to Urania Sheldon Nott, the sister of Cynthia Sheldon and Alma Anable, and the aunt of Anna Maria Anable.

Urania Sheldon Nott to Emily E. Chubbuck, November 29, 1843—Union College[440]

Nov. 29, 1843

My dear Emily

I return you the letters you were so good as to loan me, and which, notwithstanding your fears and my difficulties, I did make out to read, very much to the satisfaction of my dear husband. Indeed we both enjoyed them vastly, by our fireside on Saturday eve'n. And who knows what may grow out of them was the enquiry that arose spontaneously in *my* mind?

That you will be able to presume your incog, I do not believe, if the gentleman in question has any mettle in him, he could with little difficulty find out the real Laura Linden.[441] But you can, if that should be the case, have many a merry laugh with him (for he is a merry fellow I ken well), should you ever see him, and you may make *a friend* for life, though you might not wish a lover—With your talents, a literary friend like Mr. H.[442] might be of great service to you and he seems to have heart as well as head.

May your future be as bright as your past has been dandy, dear Emily, is the wish of your friend,

U. E. S. N.

Source: American Baptist Historical Society, AJ 25, no. 1243.

Cynthia Sheldon to Emily E. Chubbuck, December 18, 1843

Dear E.

A very few moments for you—not a scrap yet—to "L. L." Mr. W. has gone to Waterville to preach—the people there are looking out for a minister—from his conversation with L. Look Friday E'g [evening] I am really in hopes he will resign this week. My plan is fully matured if he does so favor us—and mind fully made up to bring it about in some way. Now my girl no time to explain—but I want you should return home on Tuesday for certain—let us look for help from on high as tho' we knew our prayers were heard for good. I cannot know any thing certain

---

[440] Urania Sheldon Nott had this dated as 1834—but that is clearly in error as the content places it in November 1843.

[441] This is the introduction to what we know as "The Laura Letters." They were written by Charles Fenno Hoffman, one of the prominent literary figures in the Philadelphia of this time. Emily, in trying to protect her identity, led Hoffman to believe that she was "Laura Linden." In return he wrote three letters to her as "Laura" before discovering the secret. In the first paragraph, Urania Sheldon Nott is right—the letters have a scrawling handwriting and they are very difficult—in fact, extremely difficult, to read. There were to be five more letters by the end of 1845. With his great talent, Charles Fenno Hoffman was to end the decade, committed to an insane asylum for the remainder of his life.

[442] Charles Fenno Hoffman, a prominent literary figure in Philadelphia and New York, well known in literary circles as an exceptionally talented editor, poet, and writer. He was later to be considered a romantic possibility by her friends.

probably before a Trustee meeting Sat'y E'g,—will write you if any thing definite in the mean time but either way it will be important for you to come on Tuesday—with love from all to you—in haste yours truly,

C. Sheldon

Source: American Baptist Historical Society, AJ 26, no. 1275

Emily E. Chubbuck to Cynthia Sheldon, December 29, 1843—Hamilton

Dear Miss C.,

I cannot say how glad I am at the happy prospect you mentioned in your letter.[443] I hope the thing will go off and am very anxious to hear.[444] I have had my old luck and have been on my back all the week with a cold ten times worse that that I had before the term closed. It has spoiled all my fun, but I hope I shall get over it before Sunday. Miss Weston has concluded to raise the money and go out next week—she is pretty sure of the situation I should think, having seen Mr. Edmond's letter, but she will have to work pretty hard to get fitted for it. She is good-hearted as I told you before, but vain and noisy. However she seems determined now to behave herself and set about study in good earnest. She wanted my advice about a room-mate—I spoke of H. Hinckley and found she had heard of her and would be very glad to go in with. If Hannah is not already provided for, I think it would be a capital idea to put Miss W. in with her. I shall try to come on Tues. but should be glad if no change takes place in school to stay over a day or two longer. My affairs are so arranged that I might, under common circumstances [Note: There is no completion to this sentence. A page may be missing.]

I hope to hear from you again and if all is going as last term shall hope I can stay a little longer, if I am needed, though, say so, and I will come. Excuse my horrible writing—I believe my pen was made before the flood. With a thousand good wishes which I think are just now *all* needed. I remain as ever

Yours truly

E. E. Chubbuck

Source: Hanna family files.

---

[443] See Cynthia Sheldon's letter to Emily E. Chubbuck dated December 18, 1843.

[444] Cynthia Sheldon had written on December 18, 1843 of her interest and her plan to settle a "W." to the pulpit of the Waterville Church.

Letters

1844

Eliza C. Allen to Emily E. Chubbuck, January 4, 1844—New York City

Dear Miss Chubbuck

I embrace an unexpected opportunity of sending to Utica, hastily to write a few lines, which I must beg you to accept in place of a full letter which my feelings would dictate.

In a line written upon the margin of your article contained in the M. Jour.[1] for this month, you acknowledge the receipt of a note from me 'by due course of mail'—I regret it, if you had postage to pay upon it. I sent it in a parcel to B.B. & H.,[2] supposing they would place it in your hands. From your remark, I infer that you were not in Utica; and if that was the case, perhaps they had no opportunity to consult you in regards to the use of your name.

In a note to the firm, I desired them to ascertain if you would permit your name to stand at the head of the article of yours published a few months since,— as I had placed it,—altho' I did not feel at liberty thus to use it without your consent. I also, as you may recollect requested of you permission to insert it.[3] But the article was printed without the name—from which I inferred that you did not consent to its use. Perhaps you were not consulted.

As your last piece had no name or signature, and I had no evidence that you were willing to place your name over it, I did not venture, tho' I much desired, to do so. I have been anxious to make this explanation, since it has occurred to me that you might have been out of Utica at the time I desired the publishers to see you, and thus you might have had no opportunity to give the assent I desired. Permit me to hope that you will in future allow your name to be attached to any communications with which you may favor me.

Permit me also to beg that you will [ ] me with your pen as far as you shall make it practicable. I shall most readily compensate you in a pecuniary sense, and gratefully acknowledge the favor. I have desired the former publishers to pay for the matter furnished for the last volume, and to supply you with the Journal the present year. Should they neglect to do either, I trust you will feel no hesitation as to reminding them.

---

[1] The *Mother's Journal*, a Baptist publication ministering to mothers and children, included Emily's material as early as 1843 and continued periodically until 1849. Eliza C. Allen was the editor until her death in 1848. Mary Clarke became the editor upon Allen's death, and in 1851 would request additional material from Emily.

[2] Bennett, Backus, and Hawley, the publishing firm in which H. H. Hawley, one of Emily's publishing mentors, had been a partner.

[3] See Eliza Allen's letter to Emily dated August 22, 1843.

I wish I had time to speak of the subject of your last article—it is one which distresses me. We must all do what we can to lessen a great and growing evil.[4]

Do let me hear from you soon. If, as I presume, you are in Utica, please present my regards to Miss Sheldon[5] and her family.

Yours affectionately,

Eliza C. Allen

Source: American Baptist Historical Society, AJ 22, no. 1090.

J. Watson Williams to Emily E. Chubbuck,[6] January 12, 1844

Miss Chubbuck,

I take the liberty of sending some volumes concerning the early history of New York, which are at your service so long as you may have occasion for them. The two volumes of Bancroft contain something on the subject, as you will perceive by referring to the index, at the end of the last, under the head of *New Netherlands*.

I have a strong impression that there is a volume published, devoted to Hudson and his voyages. If so, I can find it, and will see that it reaches you.

I send also the seventh volume of Deha Rochefoucauld's Travels, in 1797, which is a book of authority. At the 91st page you will find a Chapter devoted to N. York; but it may not be full enough, nor early enough as to time, for your purposes.

In the collections of the New York Hist. Society, there are doubtless many articles of value respecting our early history; but they are not within my reach.

You will find, in the school Dist. Library, Dunlap's Hist. of N. York, numbered on the Catalogue, 370, 371. Perhaps these volumes contain something that might be of service.

Yours *to serve*,

J. Watson Williams

Source: American Baptist Historical Society, AJ 27, no. 1294.

---

[4] From Eliza Allen's August 22, 1843 letter: "The subject is one of great and increasing importance and difficulty. I know not how mothers are to end with us in reference to it. Your views are just and forcible. There is great weight in the remarks upon the necessity of mothers sympathizing with their children in their literary pursuits, and *reading with them*. Instead of this parents too often treat their children as if they had no common ground, and did not belong to the same species." The article was "The Works of God, the Best Teachers" and it encouraged mothers to interact with their children in nature as teaching opportunities.

[5] Cynthia Sheldon was in charge of the administrative and financial departments of the Utica Female Academy and an important mentor, advisor, and friend to Emily.

[6] This letter is one of several in these months; we surmise that Emily had been writing others looking for background resources for her writing.

E. T. Josslyn to Emily E. Chubbuck,[7] January 15, 1844—Centreville

My dear Emily

This week I have resolved to devote to letter writing and here it is only Monday morning and I have seated myself at my *agreeable duty*. Your name stands first on the list of the devoted ones, on whom I intend to inflict an epistle. One thing I find I must do in order to accomplish much and that is to omit all excuses—but after I have told you my experience for the last two or three months, I shall have no objections to your making as many for me as may be necessary.

About the first of November Mr. Chipman (a lawyer here of some celebrity) came to my husband urging him in the strongest terms to rent his house, as he would be obliged to be absent most of the winter and his wife's health was so delicate that she would prefer to leave. Of course we were very glad to find a house that could be rented and gladly acceded to his proposition. But as Mrs. C. had an infant only a fortnight old she could not be moved and moreover a new family were [sic] daily expected to move into the village Hotel where Mrs. C. was to board. Both Mr. and Mrs. C were very anxious we should move into the house immediately (leaving her merely one room for herself and two children) and insisted on our using any and every article of furniture with which we were not provided until we could supply ourselves. We accordingly did so more to accommodate *them* than to suit ourselves for a week or even two. I therefore hired a "Help" and we went to work brushing, sweeping, scrubbing and cleaning, taking up carpets and shaking them and nailing down again. Well my "help" would stay only a week so I had only Will for a substitute, so when I wanted to bake bread, cook meat, or do indeed any kind of cooking I would take the ingredients into Mrs. C's room and receive instructions from her. You would have laughed to see me shoulder a quarter of beef and start to find which part was for steaks, which to bake and which to make into soup, and then back it out again and laying it on the kitchen table begin to cut it up. Do you ask why Will did not do it—why he had gone to Indiana on business which kept him from home for a week. We had been under a successful tide of operation for about four weeks when it was ascertained that the family who was to have come into the hotel had given up the design and consequently Mrs. C. had no where to board—for you must know all this time she was sick and could not leave her room and I had to make her bed—keep her room—prepare and carry her her meals separately and nurse her, and in the meantime Miss Bacon a young lady (a cousin of mine) from New York had come to spend the winter with me by invitation on the strength of my going to house-keeping. But I am making a *dreadful* long yarn of this. Well finally things came to this shape—either Mrs. C.

---

[7] E. T. Josslyn lived in Michigan. From the content of this letter, and especially in the names of the people mentioned, we know that she formerly was associated with Emily at the Utica Female Academy.

with her three children and her husband (for he did *not* go south as he expected) and all her furniture must leave her own house and take board wherever she could find it or we must. To be sure had we not been *very amiable* we might have persevered and stayed in spite of them but *entre-vous*, house-keeping under such circumstances (to use an elegant expression) was "not what it is cracked up to be"—and I was not particularly chagrined to give up the title of "Mistress of the house" and "head of the family"—I mean *one* of the heads, for I am afraid my husband would [ ] if I arrogated to my self the supremacy over him. Will finally found a family in which Cous Will and I could be nicely accommodated better than we were at Mrs. Brown's. As we were expecting to make an excursion of a week or two to Hillsdale, Jonesville, Marshall and so forth, we concluded not to move our effects till after our return, and now here I am in my own pleasant parlour [sic] as happy as a queen. We have a parlour and bedroom out of it and Cous has a room upstairs. Now when you hear of all my trials and tribulations Emily, don't "take on" about it and say "poor Eloise when she went way off to Michigan she little knew what she was coming to—how I do pity her," for I do assure you that my health was not injured in the least and I really think there are women *now living* who have suffered as much as I did. One oasis in my desert I forgot to mention. Abby Bagg came and stayed a week with me and whilst she was there I had a *young lady* who helped me work in the kitchen. One word more and I will leave the subject of house-keeping. Notwithstanding circumstances were so unpropitious [ ] and I were both pleased with the experiment and we would gladly have obtained another house if it had been possible. There was an independence about it we liked. I *guess* he thinks I will make a more valuable wife than "he had reference to"—and I am sure I had little reason to expect to find him as familiar with his part of the business as he proved to be. He not only made fires but milked (our beautiful new milk cow) and ground coffee. I wish, my dear Emily, you could come to Mich. I am sure you would like it. I used to think Mich was out of the world tho' I now think Centreville must be in the very middle of the world as its name indicates, tho' my sister Kate maintains Hillsdale is. I love to see our little village growing in population and intelligence. My home now is Ladies' School and Lyceum here and you cannot doubt we are important folks when I tell you *my* Cousin teaches the school and *my* husband the president of the Lyceum. There has not been a party since I have been in town till last Christmas evening the Rev. Mr. Hotchkiss had a donation party[8]— but we have lectures on all subject and *circuses and shows of learned pigs*. In the same street with us are two or three families of the kind of people I like and we

---

[8] A "Donation Party" encouraged members of the church and community to bring a "donation" to the pastoral household; Abby Ann Judson was later to study in Philadelphia at the Anable's School, and she wrote at some length about a "Donation Party" the church had held for the Rev. A. D. Gillette, and she spoke of what she and a friend had given. Its origin was probably in trying to supplement the paltry salaries paid to most clergy.

have resolved to have sociables among us at least once a weak. I mean to begin it this week.

Where and how did you spend the Holidays? Did you go home, or did you go with some of the girls to their home. Where did Eugenia[9] go? It seems like an age since I have heard from Utica. I have been wanting to write for a long time—but have been in such an unsettled state I really could not compose myself enough to write. What are your literary occupations now-a-days. I regretted exceedingly your being obliged to give up your interesting little periodical.[10] Our children read it with much pleasure and I could find plenty of readers, but no subscribers. Have you ever had your Poem published? Your sketches of the breaking up of school and of teacher's meeting have been the source of much amusement. They have however irrevocably established the names of "Ken" upon me—and made Monsieur "Bill" very vain of his influence over me.[11] Em—if Eugenia told great stories about me on her return, remember Dr. Nott's[12] rule of making a deduction of 00 percent on some folks and of 75 on others. I wonder if it is true that the organ of exaggeration lies in the nose? It is a remarkable fact that big nosed people are queer sort of folk. Did any of the teachers leave at the close of the last term? Where are Jane Kelly,[13] Jane Damaux, Lou Look, Molly Barber, Anna Maria,[14] and Eugenia? Why

---

[9] Eugenia Damaux had been part of Emily's intimate circle of friends at the Utica Female Academy. Living in New York City, Eugenia suffered from some kind of eye problem that at times made her life very difficult; this was a matter of comment in many of the letters exchanged between the girls themselves and with Cynthia Sheldon. In 1848, Eugenia was in New York living "at Mrs. Brown's—the same warm-hearted French girl as ever." In 1849, she married Johnny Edmonds, described as rich and pious, and they lived in Utica.

[10] The *Young Ladies' Miscellany* was a magazine started and edited by Emily in fall 1842, with the help and cooperation of the students and staff of the Utica Female Academy. Advertisements for subscriptions had been in the religious press as early as December 1841. It was to survive only through the end of 1843. In *The Life and Letters of Mrs. Emily C. Judson*, A. C. Kendrick said; "While it drew forth much talent from the school, Chubbuck, of course, under every variety of disguise, figured largely in its columns. Now a Greek "maiden"—Kore—now a Latin "nobody"—Nemo—now a reluctantly accepted country contributor—now in all the dignity of the editorial "we," she played off both her heavier and lighter artillery on the public. Essays, stories, songs, and sonnets, now grave, now gay, were thrown oft from her facile and fertile pen. The magazine ran gracefully through its single year of existence, and then quietly resigned its breath, having delighted its friends, edified, it is hoped, the public, contained much sound instruction, sparkled with many bright gems of genius, and contributed much to the reputation, and not a cent probably to the purse of the editor. But the dramatic genius of Fanny Forester flashes through its vivacious sketches" (77–78).

[11] This comment would give us a glimpse of some of the content in the *Young Ladies' Miscellany*.

[12] The Reverend Doctor Eliphalet Nott was the president of Union College in Schenectady NY. An ordained Presbyterian minister, he was married to Urania Sheldon Nott, the sister of Miss Cynthia Sheldon and Mrs. Alma Anable and the aunt of Anna Maria Anable.

[13] Jane Kelly was Emily Chubbuck's friend at the Utica Female Academy. Jane later became a teacher with Emily at the academy. Kelly became the literary principal in 1844 with the retirement of James Nichols and his wife from that position. During a period of Kelly's illness in 1844, Emily filled in the position for her. Then, in 1848, when Cynthia Sheldon moved to Philadelphia to help start the Misses Anable's School, Kelly became the "headmistress" of the academy and successfully brought the academy into the future, though not without some initial disparagement from the Sheldon-Anable families.

[14] Anna Maria Anable was the niece of the Urania and Cynthia Sheldon, the daughter of Joseph and Alma Sheldon Anable. Emily first met Anna Maria in fall 1840 when she went as a student to the Utica Female Academy; both Emily and Anna Maria were to become members of the faculty there. In these years Anna Maria became Emily's dearest friend, and the extensive correspondence between the two reflects sensitive, flirtatious spirits, and a deep intimacy. Emily was "Nemmy" to Anna Maria's "Ninny." In 1848, Anna Maria Anable, with the help of her extended family, moved to Philadelphia and started the Misses Anable's School in Philadelphia. At Emily's death in 1854, Anna Maria was given guardianship of Emily Frances Judson, daughter of Emily and Adoniram Judson.

don't they write me. Don't they know that letters from either of them are "like apples of gold in pictures of silver." Sarah with her husband and child I can excuse, but they have no such troubles. I had a letter from M. Adams[15] last week, she too complains but alludes to A. M. Anable [ ], proving she writes to one of her poor absent sisters and not to another. I expect too Eugenia has been writing her, from some information she had, that sounds as if E. had written it. Tell Molly Barker I wish she would take a sheet of paper and write until she gets tired some of these dark cold evenings when she can't go out any where [sic] and Jimmy[16] can't come to see her—for I hear even from N. Orleans that he continues his attentions to her yet. I would fain send messages to our dear Miss Cynthia,[17] Grandpa and Grandma,[18] the second edition of teachers, and all the dear scholars, but the time would fail me. But do assure them, judging of what your own feelings would be, of my earnest and sincere affection. I would like to inquire about the little Bennettts

---

[15] Mary Adams had been related to the Utica Female Academy. Her letter to Emily in October 1845 was almost a whimsical piece of fantasy with literary pretensions. It would reflect a fairly close and whimsical relationship. A second letter in December 1845 was similar. The letters were written from New Orleans, and she spoke of Hatty Anable as being near to her. On January 29, 1849, Anna Maria Anable wrote: "Hatty says Mary Adams is going to marry Gardner Green of Norwich,—a very fine young man, of invention, fortune, piety and all that Mary's heart was sighed for." On July 8, 1850, Urania Sheldon Nott spoke of attending this wedding in New York.

[16] Jimmy Williams was often mentioned in Anna Maria Anable's letters, mostly simply as "Jimmy." He was around the Utica Female Academy, and she spoke of their conversations, what he was doing, his interests. She often referenced him as being with "Helen." Writing to Emily on April 29, 1845 Anna Maria had some interesting comments to make. In a paragraph of gossip she said, "[and now] I'll turn to Jimmy and Helen." She went on to talk about a party:

> It was one of the most elegant parties that has been given in a long time. Jimmy's three sisters were there—all elegant women. (Also) all the flowers of Utica Society—and among them—no not among *them* but in the rooms was [sic] poor dowdy looking little Helen giggling when she showed any animation with [ ] and girls of that class and stamp. Jimmy tried to bring her forward as much as he could—but it would not do. She will never shine in society, and what is worse Jimmy will feel her deficiency in that respect very much. He would like very much to have a wife but would entertain his guests handsomely—and yet—he loves Helen very much I have not doubt and the one hundred thousand will make up for some deficiencies or ought to. I may abuse my pity I dare say.

Then on November 14, 1845, Anna Maria said to Emily: "Do you know Jimmy is really engaged to Helen M? He hasn't been to see me yet, and he came home last Sat. Oh, love! love! Even a seven-year friendship must fade before thy potent spell. Little did I think tho' that Jimmy would be faithless."

[17] Miss Cynthia Sheldon was the administrative and finance manager of the Utica Female Academy. She was a mentor, advisor, and friend to Emily.

[18] Deacon Asa and Isabell Low Sheldon, parents of Cynthia Sheldon, Urania Sheldon Nott, and Alma Sheldon Anable. Mr. and Mrs. Sheldon lived with their daughters and grandchildren as a part of the Utica Female Academy community. For many years, Mr. Sheldon led mealtime prayers for the academy family. Mr. and Mrs. Sheldon were very popular with the students. When Mrs. Sheldon died January 29, 1847, Mr. Sheldon continued to have a room at the Utica Female Academy until he died in March 1848.

[19] Cephas and Stella Bennett were missionaries to Burmah. They had arrived in Burmah in January 1830, and Bennett was to remain superintendent of the Baptist press there for more than fifty years. From the Utica area, they sent their children back and the girls were educated at the Utica Female Academy. The girls included Elsina (April 1828), Mary (November 1829) Ann (August 1833), Ellen (June 1835) and Sarah (June 1837).

[20] Mary Jones was married to Morven Jones. They lived in the Utica area and were intimately familiar with Cynthia Sheldon, and the staff and student body of the Utica Female Academy. Morven and Mary Jones, as well as Sheldon, were members of the Baptist church where Corey was the pastor. In a December 1848 series of letters to Emily, Morven Jones described a terrible accident; a group from the church was standing on a bridge overlooking the Mohawk River, there to witness a baptism, and the

[sic][19] and their Aunt, Mrs. Jones,[20] Mr. Bright,[21] Dr. James,[22] Mrs. Dr. Nott,[23] Mary[24] and Fanny Anable[25] all, all but cannot. I do wish Emily you would not wait a week before you write me. Don't say "you have waited a year" but show your forgiveness and generosity by your promptness in writing.

Where is your sister Kate?[26] And what is she doing? I expect I shall hear every day of her marriage[27] and yours.[28] After I have been married a year I may advise about marriage I suppose—and as it will be a year day after tomorrow I have half a mind to anticipate and tell you when you find the right sort of man "don't say nay." How does your brother the printer[29] come on? Is he realizing your hopes? I hope so.

---

bridge collapsed. At least one person died in that accident, and Mary Jones was severely injured.

[21] Edward Bright was, at this time, one of the publishers of the *Baptist Register*, a very popular Baptist paper in the New York region. In 1846, Bright became the American Baptist Missionary Union's corresponding secretary, and at the time of Adoniram Judson's death, he was instrumental in helping Emily and her family settle back in the United States. He worked with Emily on the business details of the Judson Memoir, and after Emily's death, was one of the executors of her estate. Beginning in October 1851, Adoniram and Elnathan lived with the Brights in Roxbury MA.

[22] Dr. James was a trusted physician in Utica, who attended the students and faculty of the Utica Female Academy. He is mentioned frequently in the correspondence as having been consulted for varying medical complaints and his advice was always welcomed and highly regarded.

[23] Urania Sheldon Nott, formerly literary principal of the Utica Female Academy, was a mentor, advisor, and friend to Emily.

[24] Mary Juliet Anable was born February 18, 1830, in Bethlehem NY, daughter of Alma and Joseph Anable. She went to New Orleans with Hatty Anable in 1847, but returned home early in March 1848, and by 1849, she was working with Anna Maria Anable in the Misses Anable's School in Philadelphia. Writing in March 1849, Hatty said of Mary: "She paints and draws, speaks French, plays the piano, sings, dances and is our mathematician. What should we ever do without her? She laughs from morning till night, and it is really refreshing to be with her." On December 26, 1860, she married Pierre Jacques Darey, with her uncle, Rev. Dr. Eliphalet Nott, officiating the ceremony. Mary died at the age of sixty-eight (April 20, 1898) in Ottawa, Ontario, Canada.

[25] Fanny Anable was one of nine children born to Joseph and Alma Anable and was a niece of Cynthia Sheldon and Urania Sheldon Nott. By 1845, Fanny had moved to Philadelphia to study and work in the home of the Reverend A. D. Gillette and his family. In fall 1848, she became a part of the teaching faculty at the Misses Anable's School in Philadelphia.

[26] Sarah Catharine ("Kate," "Kit," or "Kitty") Chubbuck, Emily's older sister. Outside of the two terms at the Utica Female Academy that Emily arranged for her, Catharine always lived with her parents in Hamilton NY. The letters indicate opportunities for marriage, but Catharine remained single. She later helped care for Henry and Edward Judson when, after their return from Burmah in fall 1851, they moved in with their "aunt" and "grandparents." She was remembered by her nephews as "a dear friend."

[27] In a March 22, 1840 letter, Emily wrote to her brother Walker about a relationship budding between their sister, Catharine, and Ed Norton. There are several mentions of September wedding plans in letters written in spring 1841. A May 7, 1841 letter specifically says they would be married in September. A May 17 letter invited Walker home for the wedding. A July 6, 1841 letter to Catharine asked about money for the gown and her matrimonial plans. Nothing more was ever said of it until March 25, 1842, when Emily commented to Walker that the relationship of the Chubbuck family and the Norton family was still very good, in spite of the break up of Catharine and Ed.

[28] In a lighter moment, Emily had written a poem which she titled "Maiden Resolve":

> They tell me thou lovest—beware! beware!
> Love whispers of bliss, but he traffics in care;
> Illusions all glowing around thee he'll fling,
> But woes in his foot-prints forever upspring.
>
> They say thou wilt marry—'tis well, 'tis well;
> Though the chain may be heavy, thou'rt under Love's spell;
> But I—*I* am free, and no Cupid shall task me,
> I never will marry—till somebody ask me!

[29] Born September 24, 1815, John Walker Chubbuck was twenty-three months older than Emily. Trained as a printer and having worked for a newspaper, Walker established a newspaper with a partner upon arriving in the Wisconsin Territory. We know that he married and was active in his church.

Written along the left margin of the address page: "Eugenia wrote me you were expecting a visit from Sophia Ward? Has she been to Utica yet? It really seems to me I must go and see you all in the spring—and I am sure I would if Will was able—and if he can sell whip-lashes enough. Perhaps tho' you did not know he was making a fortune in the manufacture of lashes—but it is sure so. He says I ought to make myself useful, and that if I will braid a dozen a day as I might, it would save his hiring a man for the purpose. Don't you think it would be a good plan? And I might save enough to visit Utica next fall on my own hook. Once more I beg of you to write soon. Tell Eugenia for me that we are boarding at Mr. Hampson's, the last house on Main Street—the one the Exchange is on and next door to Judge Stevens. Be a good girl and love ever your sincere and affectionate friend

E. T. Josslyn"

Source: American Baptist Historical Society, AJ 24, no. 1173.

Emily E. Chubbuck to Urania Sheldon Nott, January 25, 1844[30]

Dear Mrs. Nott,

The Doct. has not been here this morning yet, and as I am afraid of being too late for the cars, I will not wait for him. Poor little Rosa is certainly no worse than yesterday—probably about the same. Miss C.[31] took care of her last night. She says her fever was not very high, but she was quite restless—slept but little.—The Doct. has just come and I will wait for his decision.

The doctor says Rosa is decidedly better, her symptoms are all favourable, and Miss C. is going to write the news to Mrs. Pitcher. He says he assured Doct. P yesterday, that there was nothing in the case at all alarming.—Eugene is quite comfortable this morning and Mr. B recovered his head-ache in due time—S. Anable[32] and "Aunt Rhoda" (I don't know her other name) arrived last night. In great haste,

Yours truly,

Emily

Source: Hanna family files.

---

[30] This letter is undated. The letter was post-marked January 25, which was a Thursday.

[31] Miss Cynthia Sheldon was the administrative and finance manager of the Utica Female Academy. She was a mentor, advisor, and friend to Emily.

[32] Samuel Anable was one of four sons born to Joseph and Alice Anable; he had five sisters.

Emily E. Chubbuck to Urania Sheldon Nott, January 26, 1844[33]

My dear Mrs. Nott,

Rosa had a very good night's rest, and appears better this morning. The doctor is now with her[34]—May I trouble you to get for me a particular account of the burning of Schenectady? And also anything else in the history of N. Y. from 1690 to 1698 or thereabouts. Especially should I like particulars of Leider and Milborne. I have already Smith, Upham, McAuly and Bancroft, furnished by Mr. W,[35] but they are too general for my purpose. I want to find all I can concerning the manners and customs of the Dutch etc. You may think this a heavy commission, but if they are not at hand, do not mind about them. I shall get along very well without.[36]

The doct. says Rosa is getting along very comfortably indeed—she sends a great deal of love to you, but we can't induce her to do such a very improper thing as to remember Sipley. She seems to take an interest in what is going on about her for a few moments and then shuts up her eyes as though tired. The doct. has left us new medicine.

We had the usual teacher's meeting last night and that you must know is now-a-days quite a wearisome thing. Mr. N[37] is quite tired of this "conscience-hardening business," that is requiring young ladies to answer for their own transgressions. It was impossible not to say that there was a time when the system was very effective. I suspect he would institute a kind of espionage—a catch-them-at-it system, and so lest they should harden their consciences by using them, save them the trouble of acting and thinking for themselves at all. He would be peculiarly fitted for the business; the very king of spies and key-hole guard. But after all he is right in the present state of things—his own inefficiency is placing truth below fear in the school and what will be the result no one can tell. The subject is a disturbing one—the worst feature in the system of mismanagement. My head was so full of this matter, that I could not let it alone and so I have gone on forgetful of the lateness of the hour—Grandmother[38] is feeling nicely this morning; and all the rest are in as good health as usual.

Yours aff.

E. E. C.   Source: Hanna family files.

---

[33] This letter is undated. It picks up on the themes of the January 25, 1846 letter which Emily wrote to Urania Sheldon Nott, and since Nott had asked Emily to update her on Rosa's condition daily, we place this on Friday, January 26.

[34] See Emily's prior letter to Urania Sheldon Nott dated January 25, 1844.

[35] See the letter dated January 12, 1844 from J. Watson Williams to Emily giving her historical information over a number of topics.

[36] This is one of several letters in this time period where Emily was looking for historical resources, background, we assume, for her writing.

[37] James Nichols. He and his wife had assumed the position of literary principal at the Utica Female Academy upon the marriage of Urania Sheldon to Eliphalet Nott in fall 1842.

[38] Isabell Low Sheldon, mother of Cynthia Sheldon, Urania Sheldon Nott, and Alma Sheldon Anable.

Urania Sheldon Nott to Emily E. Chubbuck, January 27, 1844—Union College[39]

My dear Emily,

Allow me to thank you for your favour [sic] so promptly written, and punctually received. They have indeed been a very great relief to me and I can but hope that our sweet little Rosa is still on the recovery—tho' your letter has not come tonight. I believe I mentioned to Cynthia last night that I would not trouble you longer to write daily, unless she should relapse. May a good providence restore her soon.

I have enquired of Mr. Potter about the books that would be of use to you. The most particular account of the period you refer to is to be found in Dunlap's "History of New York"—Leider and Milbourne figure largely in it—but Mr. Potter says that you cannot rely on Dunlap in their case, as he was much prejudiced in their favour [sic]. Mr. P. is writing a work that has brought to light many facts that throw the whole subject of their reign into a new position—I should hardly think them the most interesting characters of that day—For a minute and accurate account of the manners and customs of the Dutch, particularly at Albany, nothing is better, Mr. P says, that Mrs. Grant's "Memory of an American Lady" not her letters—I have tried to day [sic] to get them for you—but cannot—Probably they are not to be found this side of Albany or New York. Mr. Backus would get them for you—and you may tell Mr. Williams[40] that they ought by all means to belong to their library—as also Dunlap's History—in 2 vols—not the abridgment.

I send you a poem that is said to be very accurate in its facts of the burning of S. but you will find the whole thing in Dunlap.

My friend Miles Gates the greatest antiquarian of our state is out of town—I will see him when he returns and try to get something for you. He is a large contributor to Dunlap's History.

Mrs. Pearson child [sic] is quite ill again—and singularly affected by his teeth—say to Eugenia[41] that her friend Maggy Bell Brown had a son night before last weighing eleven pounds—it is not expected to live.

Monday mor'g

I will send tomorrow by the bride whom Ian K. is to meet at the cars—all well—much love to all

In great haste

Yours affectionally

Urania Nott.   Source: American Baptist Historical Society, AJ 25, no. 1239.

---

[39] See the two letters dated January 25 and 25, from Emily Chubbuck to Urania Sheldon Nott that preceded this letter. This letter answered many of Emily's questions on historical resources found in her letter of January 26.

[40] J. Watson Williams, who had written to Emily on January 12, 1844, in answer to many of her historical questions.

[41] Eugenia Damaux, part of Emily's intimate circle of friends at the Utica Female Academy.

John Inman[42] to Emily E. Chubbuck, February 26, 1844—New York City

Miss Chubbuck has by this time seen, I hope, the March number of the *Columbian Magazine*; and in that event she will also have seen that her offering is acceptable to the editor. It is indeed a more different letter of recommendation than even the printed credentials by which it was accompanied; and it will appear in good company in the April number.

Miss Chubbuck's future contributions will be heartily welcome if she keeps her promise "never to do worse." As much bel[ ] as she pleases; but will she permit the editor—an old stoger in literature—to warn her against the hazard of losing her easy and natural vein in efforts to surpass what she has already done so well?

As to compensation, the editor begs leave to say that he had no rates of payment to propose in any case. He pays for good articles what the writers ask, if they do not ask too much; if they do, in his judgment, he says so very frankly. The time of payment is in the receipt of the manuscript.

Very Respectfully,

J. Inman

Please have the goodness to let me know what I shall send for "The Game of Chess," and how.

Source: American Baptist Historical Society, AJ 24, no. 1180.

Eliza C. Allen to Emily E. Chubbuck, February 28, 1844—New York City[43]

Dear Miss Chubbuck,

I have only time by the present opportunity to acknowledge your favor, with thanks, and to say that I have since written again to B. B. & H.[44] to supply you with the Journal.

I write without the least trouble, send the work to you by mail, but do not wish to cause you to pay postage when, as our agents, the firm are under obligations to

---

[42] John Inman was the editor of the *Commercial Advertiser* and the *Columbian Magazine*—responsibilities which failing health forced him to give up early in 1845. He was Emily Chubbuck's initial contact with the *Columbian Magazine*, which began to publish some of her stories early in 1844. He strongly encouraged Emily in her writing, said that they would publish everything they could get from her, hoped that she would consider writing exclusively for them, and when she asked for it, gave her the unheard of rate of five dollars a page for her articles. When he did that, he very candidly stated that with this, they would not consider it fair if she continued to write for N. P. Willis and the *New Mirror* without charge.

[43] This is the third letter from Eliza C. Allen, editor of the *Mother's Journal*, trying to make sure that Emily receives a copy of the magazine each month.

[44] Publishing firm of Bennett, Backus, and Hawley, of which H. H. Hawley, Emily's publishing mentor, was a member.

furnish it to you. If, however, you do not get it of them, and prefer it, I will send it. Have the kindness to inform me if you wish it.

Affect Yours E. C. Allen

Source: American Baptist Historical Society, AJ 22, no. 1089.

B. R. Loxley to Emily E. Chubbuck, February 29, 1844—Philadelphia

Dear Sister,

Yours of 13th is at hand and I would in reply say that the manuscript refrd [sic] to as sent to Mr. Gillette[45] was received, and after much delay it has passed our Publishing committee and being approved, it is ordered for Publication, and is in the printers' hands; I expect it will be out in a week or two.—[46]

The present manuscript I will put in the hands of the Committee[47] at once, and hope that there will not be so much delay.

Yours truly B. R. Loxley
Am Bap Pub Society

Br Peck[48] our Cor Secretary is absent in Illinois and will not be here for several weeks.

Source: American Baptist Historical Society, AJ 22, no. 1078.

J. Watson Williams[49] to Emily E. Chubbuck, March 1844

Miss Chubbuck,

Many of my supposed criticisms were designed as mere suggestions; and had I had leisure, I should have explained them on paper. I am not sure that I would adopt them all myself, more particularly those which disturb the frame of sentences. My suggestions of that sort were intended as intimations, that improvements might be made, rather an as improvements.

I will endeavor to answer the inquiries contained in your note.

Potato. I cannot say why it should take an *e* in the plural, unless it be that it was formerly spelt with one in the singular. *Wo* is split indifferently *wo* or *woe*, but in the plural it is always spelt with an *e*. *No* is spelt, in legislative proceedings, with an *e* in

---

[45] Rev. A. D. Gillette was a stalwart friend and supporter of the Judson, Sheldon, and Anable families. Emily met Adoniram Judson in the parlor of the Gillette home in Philadelphia. He was the pastor of the Eleventh Baptist Church in Philadelphia.

[46] This would be the manuscript for *John Frink*.

[47] In 1843, American Baptist Publication Society had published *Effie Maurice*.

[48] John Mason Peck.

[49] See J. Watson Williams's letters to Emily E. Chubbuck dated January 12, 1844, and July 14, 1845.

the plural,—*noes*. I think the general rule is that nouns ending in *o* form the plural by adding *es*. But the usage of the best writers settles such matters, whether with or without reason.

> 'On choicest melons and sweet grapes they dine,
> 'And with *potatoes* for their wanton swine!
> —Waller

> 'The families of farmers live + + + upon buttermilk and *potatoes*.'
> —Swift.

> 'After *potatoes* have germinated, the quantity of starch in them is found diminished.
> —Dr. Playfair's Liebig's Chemistry.

Snugged. I cannot say that this is objectionable for any other reason that that it seems to require an adjunct,—*snugged down*,—and is rather too colloquial for the place it occupies. The other word is not liable to the same objections, and expresses your idea quite as accurately and a little more neatly.

"If she were driven from Holland, etc." I suggested this because I thought it according to the *best usage*, which is the grammar I generally follow. My own rule is, to be governed by the *if*, *though*, etc. I do not know what distinction the grammarians make.

"If so be there *were* no resurrection." Atterbury.
"Oh, that my head *were* waters!" Jeremiah
"Would God my lord *were* with the prophet that is in Samaria." Kings
"Though his father die, yet he is as though he *were* not dead." Ecclesiastes.
"Oh, that the salvation of Israel *were* come out of Zion!" Psalms
"If I *were* you" is a common expression.

Still the strict grammatical rule may be against me. I have no grammar at hand to examine.

In regard both to the rhymes at the close of the first Chapter, I suggested *lofty*, instead of *dainty*, as more characteristic epithet. The truth is, *dainty* is made, nowadays, to do too much service, and out of its proper sphere. I do not think it more characteristic of an eagle, than a song is.—The *screech* or *scream* is the eagle's music, and for that very reason, either of those words would drop more naturally from the lips of a crazed woman than the word *song*. Your mad people generally speak strongly and descriptively; they use the wildest and most expressive words.

Body in counsel. I hesitated a little about the change I suggested. If you had written *council*, I should not have hesitated at all, but should have passed on as if every thing [sic] were right. It is very usual to speak of men "in council."—But I cannot explain myself well without re-perusing the manuscript. *Counsel*, meaning deliberation, is right.

Proprietary. This noun is frequently misused. It never meant the property, but the owner of it. My substitute for the word may not be the best that could be suggested; but it was the only one that occurred to me at the moment.

I was the more critical in perusing the Ms. and pointing out trifles because it was submitted to me for that purpose. I think I could undertake to expose as many inaccuracies in almost any two chapters of Dickens' works, as in your two chapters. Perhaps it would not be venturesome to say as much of Scott, for he is far from nice.—Both he and Dickens raise brutes to the level of human beings by misusing the pronoun *who*.—My sort of criticism is but tithing mint and cumin; and those who are not capable of great things, are very apt to make much ado about nothings. Though I catch you nodding occasionally, I am confident I could not have written your two chapters.

Yours very truly,

J. Watson Williams

Monday

Written in the right margin of the address page: "P.S. Since writing the within I have consulted Brown's Grammar and Fellon's. They confirm my opinion. Brown says 'The subjunctive mood is generally preceded by a conjunction; as *if, that, though, lest, unless*, etc. It does not vary its *termination* in the different persons. It is used in the present, and sometimes in the imperfect tense; rarely in any other. It can be used only in a different clause.' Felton calls it, more expressively, the Conditional Mood. Brown quotes the following authorities for

J.W. Williams Esq.
March 1844"

Written in the left Margin of the address page: "The use of the imperfect tense. 'If therefore perfection *were* by the Levitical priesthood, what further need was there' etc. Hebrews. 'If the whole body *were* an eye, where were the hearing?' Corinthians. 'If it *were* possible, they shall deceive the very elect.' Matthew. He gives the imperfect sense thus: If I were, if thou were, if we were. Etc."

Source: American Baptist Historical Society, AJ 27, no. 1293.

John Inman[50] to Emily E. Chubbuck, March 28, 1844—New York City

My dear Contributor,

If I were not happily in possession of a sweet little wife and a double pair of nice little children, I should certainly fall in love with you "unsight unseen" as the schoolboys say, for the sake of your wise head and cheerful heart. There is no "worse" at all about "Grandfather Bray,"[51] but a great deal better; a tone of deeper though not more genuine feeling, and altogether more loveableness [sic] (in the little peace-maker) than even in charming "Fanny Fay."[52]

I hope you have received Fanny in her typical dress; and have appreciated my compliment to the sex in giving up the whole number to ladies. I think the two best articles are "Fanny Fay" and the "Chapter on Woman"; and the writer of the latter is alas a lady in Utica; whereat my natal pride is somewhat flattered for [ ]—not [ ] but a Utica boy; though I left the village, as it was then, probably some years before you were born.

I confess to the possession of some curiosity and I should like to know something about *you*. I like to have a good understanding *of* as well as *with* all my contributors. Will you promise not to be shocked if I ask you to tell me how long you have lived in Utica, where you came from, how old you are (!!), what you have studied, what you teach and all those other things that make up personal appreciation? I may come to Utica in the course of the Summer on my way to Lewis County where I have a sister, and then I will let you see *me*. Yours very truly,

J. Inman

Written in the top margin of the letter: "P.S. There are forty* dollars waiting for you at Mr. Post's[53]—but I believe a gentleman is to call for it.

---

[50] John Inman was the editor of the *Commercial Advertiser* and the *Columbian Magazine*, responsibilities that failing health forced him to give up early in 1845. He was Emily Chubbuck's initial contact with *Columbian Magazine*, which began to publish some of her stories early in 1844. He strongly encouraged Emily in her writing, said that they would publish everything they could get from her, and hoped that she would consider writing exclusively for them, and when she asked for it, he gave her the unheard of rate of five dollars a page for her articles. When he did that, he candidly stated that with this, they would not consider it fair if she continued to write for N. P. Willis and the *New Mirror* without charge.

[51] "Grandfather Bray" was to be one of Emily's stories to be printed in the *Columbian Magazine*. It was reprinted later in *Alderbrook*. It's first lines read:

> Dear lady—thou that reclinest so gracefully upon yon sofa, I mean—lady, for a moment close thine eyes upon that handsome volume, though its dress of gilded morocco was certainly invented on purpose to be pressed by thy dainty fingers, and the printed words may make thy heart palpitate almost as much as did the whispered ones of the giver. Nay, turn them not upon the brilliant chandeliers, not the voluminous folds of crimson that shut in the rich, warm light, flecking the heavy drapery with changing gold and purple; nor let them fall upon the soft, yielding carpet, almost yielding enough to bury up thy tiny, slippered foot.

[52] We interpret this to read that "Fanny Fay," Emily's story that was in the current *Columbian*, is the one that John Inman was compensating Emily for at the end of the letter.

[53] J. Post worked for the *Columbian Magazine*; at the end of 1844 he picked up some of the responsibilities that John Inman had relinquished because of failing health and other commitments. There are two letters in the correspondence from Post.

*Supposing G. B. to be of the same length as F.F. If longer we will add the surplus in paying for *the next*."

Source: American Baptist Historical Society, AJ 24, no. 1179.

Rev. D. G. Corey[54] to Emily E. Chubbuck, April 10, 1844—Utica

Miss Chubbuck.
Dear Madam,

In compliance with an invitation I attended your *Soiree* this Evening to be entertained with music of which I am exceedingly fond. But to my grief and astonishment the assembly were [sic] presented with a defense of the practice of dancing. I address this note to yourself, because you have the charge of the compositions and as I suppose, designated what should be read—if so, for all the influence such a production is capable of exciting you are most certainly responsible.

With your own views upon this subject, I have never before been acquainted; but suppose it [ ] just to infer, that you are favourable [sic] to the practice. And those who were present, regarded the School as giving countenance to such an amusement.

Were it necessary, I could give you my reasons for regarding the practice of dancing decidedly sinful. Permit me to name a few. It is a prominent hindrance to the salvation of the Soul. Not a few under the influence of the Spirit of God, and deeply convicted for Sin, have found it so. Said an [ ] in tears… I am willing to give up all [ ] the pleasures of the dance. But why this struggle if it be perfectly harmless? Who would be willing to defend dancing in the presence of such a person? And yet there may have been such present this evening.

It also detracts from the piety and usefulness of those disciples who have been brought under its influence. If it is perfectly in accordance with a life of devotion to Christ and his cause, why do we not witness in those who practice it bright evidence of love to God? But invariably the opposite is true. I could name were it necessary, more than one young lady known to yourself in whom this truth has

---

[54] Corey was the pastor of a Baptist church near the Utica Female Academy, and Sheldon and many of the girls from the academy worshiped there. In April 1844, he wrote to Emily expressing dismay that at a school program one of the girls had read a composition justifying dancing as exercise; he spoke of this as a roadblock to the salvation of many. Then on March 10, 1846, Emily indicated in a letter to Anna Maria that Corey had been very critical of her relationship and impending marriage to Adoniram Judson. Cynthia Sheldon wrote a number of times expressing Corey's regret and support, and in 1847 there were letters of reconciliation between Emily and Corey. In spring 1848, we learn that Corey's wife had died of consumption, her condition exacerbated by recent childbirth. She had left behind four children, the youngest a baby. Then in July 1849, Anna Maria Anable wrote of his impending marriage to Jane Backus, a good choice for this "rising man." Corey remained popular with the Sheldon-Anable families even after their move to Philadelphia in 1848. A March 2, 1852 letter from Charles B. Stout told of Corey's call to the Stanton Street Church in New York City, a call that Corey did not accept. Finally, in 1854, there was a pastoral letter from Corey to Emily on her illness and her possible death.

been exemplified. It also destroys the line of demarcation between the Church and world. Where is the difference, if professing Christians mingle with the irreligious in all their vain and worldly amusements?

Professing as you do, to be a follower of Him who was holy, h[ ]less and undefiled, and reposing confidence in your ability to investigate, and decide in the light of evidence, I am conscious that a prayerful attention to this subject cannot fail to secure your influence against a practice to which I have referred. However innocent it may be in the abstract, we cannot look at things in such a light; with every act is associated a train of influences. And what are the tendencies of dancing? Do they not violate at least a precept. Shun the very *appearance* of evil? If so, it should not be countenanced by any who profess love to the Saviour [sic]. Who wrote the composition I do not know, but most certainly it was written by one who loves pleasure more than God.

As an individual, I regret that dancing is practiced in the Seminary for exercise. Let us suppose a mother to send her daughter to a boarding school deeply anxious that she should become early pious, and avoid every thing [sic] prejudicial to such a change. In that boarding school for the first time she contracts a love for dancing. On returning home, the mother finds to her grief, that the object of her more early training is defeated. To her the ball-chamber has more attraction than any thing [sic] else. Fashionable and irreligious families, may be willing that their daughters should be exposed to such an influence; but the pious Mothers in our country will never consent to it. They will rather educate them at the fire-side.

You will not I am sure regard this letter as evidence of any unkind feelings. I cherish the warmest regard for you all, and will contribute all in my power to your prosperity. I should not have written what I have but for a feeling and obligation and responsibility not easily removed.

I am yours most respectfully,

D. G. Corey

Source: American Baptist Historical Society, AJ 24, no. 1209

Cynthia Sheldon to Emily E. Chubbuck, June 4, 1844—Utica

My dear Emily,

This is truly a bright morning. I have spent it in various ways, have only a few minutes left in which to say, the Trustees meeting went off finely—no opposition—we all stay past five years if we want to so long—I have since that time been obliged to write to Urania[55]—Harriet and others—the girls were—to tell you the

---

[55] Urania Sheldon Nott, formerly literary principal of the Utica Female Academy, was a mentor, advisor, and friend to Emily.

story, but here it is time to go to the office again, and not a scratch from their pens—too bad.

Mrs. Conant[56] called here Monday e'g, we had a delightful chat with her—she designs to see you—we are all well—another letter from Hatty[57] tells us where she lives—five minutes have gone talking with a poor woman—this must go—your friend

C. S.

Source: American Baptist Historical Society, AJ 26, no. 1274.

Anna Maria Anable to Emily E. Chubbuck, June 7, 1844[58]

Now Nem![59] My poor child!

Your letter has just been handed to me and I am [ ]sed to know [ ] my [ ] [ ] skirt into which I had got engaged "full tilt"—to console you—where shall I begin? According to your [ ] [ ] your [ ] minister so nigh-sighted he can't see the perfections your mother-in-law[60] does—your doctor—a gone [ ]—and your widower[61]—oh Nem, my daughter. Oh! my daughter Nem! That "grieves me [ ]."

---

[56] Anna Maria's comments about Hannah Chaplain Conant in her letter of July 31, 1848 ("Mrs. Conant with all her talent I have found out to be a thoroughly selfish woman, so I don't mean to like her any more"), are quite interesting, if not surprising. In spite of Anna Maria's feelings, we know that Conant was an accomplished scholar. She wrote a number of articles and books about the Bible and was considered very competent in the Biblical field. Earlier letters indicate that she had called on Emily a number of times when Emily was in Hamilton, and the references are always very cordial. When Emily returned to the United States, a warm letter from Mrs. Conant invited Emily to stay with her should she come to Rochester. After the publication of the Judson Memoir, written by Francis Wayland in collaboration with Emily Judson, Emily planned to write an abridgment of those two volumes as a more popular offering. As Emily's health deteriorated in late 1853, and it became increasingly obvious that she would be unable to take on such a task, Conant was asked to take the responsibility for that project and eventually it was to be published as: *The Earnest Man: A Memoir of Adoniram Judson, D.D., First missionary to Burmah.*

[57] Harriet ("Hatty," "Hattie," or "Hat") Anable, daughter to Joseph and Alma Anable and niece of Cynthia Sheldon and Urania Sheldon Nott. In 1841, she had added a note to a letter written by Cynthia Sheldon to Emily. As early as November 1842 she was away, and a letter from Emily to Catharine Chubbuck said that "she (Sheldon) expected that Hat would return as accomplished as Anna Maria." Her trips away were both educational and employment, as she worked as a private tutor in families that would bring her into their homes. In August 1843, she had just returned from Beonsen, in the vicinity of New Orleans, and was engaged to go again. A letter from Anna Maria on January 6, 1845 said that she would stay south for another year. About this time Cynthia Sheldon mentioned her concern for Hatty's spiritual health. In May 1845 she was in New Orleans. She was home again in summer 1846, but a September 27 letter from Anna Maria said she had been asked by Roman with some urgency to return and she thought that she should. She was to return home from New Orleans in January 1849 after Anna Maria Anable had started the Misses Anable's School in Philadelphia in fall 1848. Harriet was fluent in French, having placed herself earlier in a French environment in New Orleans. Hatty died in 1858.

[58] Overwriting on page 1 perpendicular to the original text, and weak copy quality account for the many blanks in this letter.

[59] "Nem" or "Nemmy" was a name of endearment given to Emily by a small group of her intimate friends at the Utica Female Academy. Anna Maria Anable was "Ninny."

[60] "Mother-in-law" was a term Anna Maria often used to describe herself to Emily.

[61] "Widower" refers to widowed older men and usually suggested availability and interest in marriage. The academy girls and their teachers were always referring to "the widower" or to "widowers" in their conversations and correspondence.

I did think that some future day I should behold you in the yellow house—*Don't give up yet*—hold on—are you *sure* he is engaged?[62]

Now Nem, just about this time you must be reading the *New Mirror*![63] What think you! I'd give a good deal to see you perform.

When you first get it—You'll be so hopping mad when you first get it you'll berate Willis[64] and say you never had so much ill luck in a week before. But by the time you get this you'll have made up your mind that on the whole—it's rather complimentary and that you'll be 'up to him' with a good story—Ain't it so Nem?

There—I have given my last lesson, till Saturday morning—congratulate me.

It seems to me, that we have had all sorts of doings since you went away—Mrs. Conant[65] was here Sunday night[66] and we talked all sorts of things—Tuesday night Mastini the great guitar player was here and "concerted" in our school room—and yesterday Aunt C.[67] and Jimmy[68] went off—but James Dorland did not go—neither did Jimmy go with Aunt C. as you might infer from the arrangement of the above sentence—O, I forgot about the trustees[69]—Jane[70] came in with tremendous applause—why Aunt C. wrote you all about it—I am not going to write it over for

---

[62] On July 31, 1843, Emily had written to Cynthia Sheldon of meeting a man—a widower—on the stage coach ride from Utica to Hamilton. He was a "six-footer—rich as Croesus." "Then did'nt [sic] I get a compliment from him afterwards? And such a compliment! Not my face, beautiful as it is, nor my exceeding gracefulness, nor even my enthusiasm and romance—no more of that, but my practical common sense and *my conversational powers*." Emily was to close the letter stating that the widower lived in "a large cream-coloured [sic] house just in sight. Would'nt [sic] be funny if I should mistake it for the Academy, when the vacation is over?" (We are not sure if this house was in sight of her home in Hamilton Village as she wrote the letter or in sight of the Utica Female Academy.)

[63] See the June 8, 1844 letter that Emily sent to the editor of the *New Mirror*. The editor, N. P. Willis, published this letter and subsequently promoted Emily as a literary sensation. This was a time and a letter and an opportunity which was to change the direction of Emily Chubbuck's (now becoming Fanny Forester) life and career. The publication date of the paper was on June 8, but we assume that Emily and Anna Maria had received an advance copy.

[64] Nathaniel Parker (N. P.) Willis, along with George "General" Morris, was the editor of the *New Mirror*, a prominent literary magazine in New York. His "discovery" of Emily in the June 8, 1844 edition of the *New Mirror* catapulted her into literary fame and enabled her to command the highest prices for her articles and stories from the major magazines of that period. It was to begin a new and glorious chapter in her life. He was to become over the next two years her friend—her mentor—her confidant. His black-bordered letter of March 21, 1846, made it abundantly clear that her engagement to Adoniram Judson had come as a "death blow," and that he had expected to marry Emily upon his return that month from England. He later returned several of her letters to Emily to demonstrate to her, lest she had forgotten, why he had felt right in that expectation. In vol. 1 there is a timeline which presents in some detail the substance of their developing relationship, all from the letters which Willis had written to Emily. When she received her letters back from Willis, she had destroyed them, feeling that they would cast a negative shadow on her life, and because of that, the life and ministry of Adoniram Judson.

[65] Hannah Chaplin Conant, an accomplished biblical scholar, wrote a number of articles and books and was considered competent in the biblical field.

[66] In her letter of June 4, Cynthia Sheldon mentioned this visit as well.

[67] Miss Cynthia Sheldon was the administrative and finance manager of the Utica Female Academy. She was a mentor, advisor, and friend to Emily.

[68] Jimmy Williams was often mentioned in Anna Maria Anable's letters, mostly simply as "Jimmy."

[69] On June 4, 1844, Cynthia Sheldon had written of a meeting of the trustees which had gone favorably for her. She said that she could stay in her position for at least another five years if she so desired.

[70] Jane Kelly was Emily Chubbuck's friend at the Utica Female Academy. Following the departure of Mr. and Mrs. Nichols, Jane became the literary principal in early 1844. Then with the departure of Cynthia Sheldon to Philadelphia in fall 1848, she became "headmistress."

you. You ought to have seen Jimmy through that night—He felt 'cute—there's no mistake—and I guess he made *me* a pen too.

We had a grand Whig convention here yesterday. Kedy [sic] delivered a lecture before the young men's association Tuesday eve-g. Poor Jane! I never saw such a struggle between duty and inclination. Duty said, stay at home Jane and make yourself agreeable to the people who will be here to hear Mastini—It will be good for the school.

Inclination said—Can I forget the pleasure of seeing and hearing this beau ideal—Mrs. Hoffman of *my* imagination—But she made the sacrifice. She did. She staid [sic] at home. She wishes me to say that tho' the broomstick is about as companionable as you are, still on the whole she prefers you—I presume she is afraid of the temptation over the way—amiable self distrust. I found at the dinner table that Jane's mind was sorely wrought upon by that pen of yours—She set me to thinking, and if she is not a *Mans[ ]* I very much doubt her [ ] and therefore would give you some ray of encouragement—I just went down into your room to steal this nice pen—and found Jane reclining upon the sofa—pretending to be asleep. I persisted in being heard though—and poped [sic] into the bed-room to accomplish my purpose—Now Nem stop a moment—take a break—summon all your fortitude, before I disclose anything further.

I had no sooner entered the bed room than I heard the back door to your parlor open—and am confident I heard Mrs. Long's voice—remember Jane now lying on the sofa pretending to be asleep—

Written in the right margin of the address page: "On my return to the other room (Jimmy's pen [ ] write so good as mine does—so I'll take it back) Jane was in the act of rising—and looked very much confused at this detection—Don't lisp word of Jane's intrigue at Hamilton as she is our principal. This thing must be hushed up."

Written in the left margin of the address page: "Give my love to your good mother[71] and Kate[72] and thanks for that good opinion of me.

And now Nem—don't take on too hard about that widower[73]—I should not like that you should find and waste your beauty for the like of him—there's plenty as good fish yet in the sea—keep up good courage my daughter. I am going to betake myself to the sofa to finish."

Written in the left margin of the address page and across the text: "Reading the *New Mirror*—I suppose the mail is closed or I'd send this this afternoon—

---

[71] Lavinia Richards Chubbuck, Emily's mother, was born June 1, 1875, in Goffstown NH, the eldest of thirteen children. She married Charles Chubbuck on November 17. 1805. They were the parents of seven children.

[72] Sarah Catharine ("Kate," "Kit," or "Kitty") Chubbuck, Emily's older sister, born October 25, 1816.

[73] "Widower" refers to widowed older men and usually suggested availability and interest in marriage. The academy girls and their teachers were always referring to "the widower" or to "widowers" in their conversations and correspondence.

Wouldn't that be an example of punctuality—I rec'd a letter from Sissy W. yesterday—Marion is to be married June 12th—She sends a great deal of love to cousin Nemmy—She is to be married at 7, receive calls at 8 in the evening and leave the next morning for Ct.—to visit his parents."

Written in the right margin of the address page and across the text: "This is the evening of Harmony Luce's[74] wedding—Sarah Bell[75] and Fan[76] are going out with Mr. Johnson. We haven't got no beau [sic] so we can't go.

We had a letter from Henry[77] yesterday—he is coming up in a fortnight so will be here to our party—I have already put down one hundred and eighty whom I must invite.—"

Written across the text on page 1: "Nemmy dear—do come back—you have no idea how lonesome I am—I went down to take tea with Mrs. Lansing—but as they were going out to spend the evening—came home, directly after tea—and now I go moping round the house without any body [sic] to console me—Jimmy is away and Sarah Bell has gone to the wedding—and Mary[78] is as cross as she can be—I hope Aunt C. will bring Mary Pearson with her tomorrow—and then Miss I guess you'll feel sorry that you left your mother—Maria Ford was married this morning—and there is some wedding cake for you—I have been down to see Jane and she is fretting at you too—I got a beautiful bouquet by going down and I guess you would not think I envy you—for I have no less than seven—and I could have a dozen if I *was* a mind to *split* them.

Mrs. S[ ] has got home [ ] and she has lost her spectacles. I saw them advertised—don't you pity her! No! Don't you *envy* her? To think of Willis calling you an old maid with spectacles—out upon him! I thought he had more gallantry. Punish him Nem in just the cunningest way you can think of. Don't make him feel flat—but as I beg of you outwit him. I am dying to see what you'll do. I am glad you have got in the notion of writing Rothenberg for every thing else seems done up unless you build the work over Willis' yes."

Source: American Baptist Historical Society, AJ 23, no. 1132.

---

[74] See the letter of Harmony Luce to Emily Chubbuck dated December 27, 1842.

[75] Sarah Bell Wheeler was a teacher at the Utica Female Academy, and an intimate friend of Emily Chubbuck, one of the few who addressed Emily as "Nemmy." There are a number of letters from Sarah Bell before and after her marriage to Charles Gould of Boston. They were married in October 1850. There are several letters clustered in the year or two after Emily left for Burmah, and a number of letters at the time of her return to America. Emily stayed with Charles and Sarah Bell Gould in October 1851 when she arrived in Boston, after the long sea voyage from Burmah, and then England. She was to stay there a number of times following that. In 1851, Anna Maria Anable had written of Sarah Bell: "Sarah is grown so lovely in person as well as character that she must assert a blessed influence on all with whom she comes in contact."

[76] Fanny Anable was one of the five Anable sisters. She was born April 12, 1828.

[77] Henry Sheldon Anable, Joseph and Alma Sheldon Anable oldest child. In August 1846, Henry was in the Milwaukee WI area. In a September 27 letter, he said he might leave Utica to join William and Olivia in Sheboygan WI. He married Rosanna Frick in Sheboygan WI on February 13, 1855, and died September 3, 1887, in Flushing NY.

[78] Mary Barber or Mary Anable.

Emily E. Chubbuck to N. P. Willis, June 8, 1844[79]

Introduction of N.P. Willis, Editor of the *New Mirror*

"We are fortunate in a troop of admirable contributors, who write for love, not money-love being the only commodity in which we can freely acknowledge ourselves rich. We receive, however, all manner of tempting propositions from those who wish to write for the other thing-money-and it pains us grievously to say, 'No;' though, truth to say, love gets for us as good things as money could buy—our readers will cheerfully agree. But yesterday, on opening at the office a most dainty epistle, and reading it fairly through, we confess our pocket stirred within us! More at first than afterward-for, upon reflection, we became doubtful whether the writer were not old and 'blue,' it was so exceedingly well done. We have half a suspicion now that it is some sharp old maid in spectacles—some regular contributor to Godey and Graham, who has tried to inveigle us through our weak point-possibly some varlet of a man scribbler-but no; it is undeniably feminine. Let us show you the letter-the latter part of it at least, as it opens too honiedly for print:—"

Text of the Letter from Fanny Forester

You know the shops in Broadway are very tempting this spring. Such beautiful things! Well, you know (no, you don't know that, but you can guess) what a delightful thing it would be to appear in one of those charming, head-adorning complexion-softening, hard-feature-subduing neapolitans; with a little gossamer vail [sic]dropping daintily on the shoulder of one of those exquisite *balzarines*, to be seen any day at Stewart's and elsewhere. Well, you know, (this you must know,) that shopkeepers have the impertinence to demand a trifling exchange for these things even of a lady; and also that some people have a remarkably small purse, and a remarkably small portion of the yellow "root" in that. And now, to bring the matter home, I am one of that class. I have the most beautiful little purse in the world, but it is only kept for show; I even find myself under the necessity of counterfeiting—that is, filling the void with tissue paper in lieu of bank notes, preparatory to a shopping expedition.

Well, now to the point. As 'Bel' and I snuggled down on the sofa this morning to read the *New Mirror* (by the way, Cousin 'Bel' is never obliged to put tissue paper in her purse), it struck us that you would be a friend in need, and give good counsel in this emergency. 'Bel,' however, insisted on my not telling what I wanted

---

[79] This is the letter that Emily E. Chubbuck wrote to N. P. Wills, editor of the *New Mirror*. Though her work had been published previously in other magazines, his publication of this letter, and later his endless promotion of Emily and her work, (and after this any thing Emily would write for the *New Mirror*) brought her fame and recognition, making her, under the name of Fanny Forester, a household name. It allowed her to command top compensation (up to five dollars a page) for her writing. It also brought her friendship with N. P. Willis, their mentoring relationship and romantic interest, into full bloom.

the money for. She even thought that I had better intimate orphanage, extreme suffering from the bursting of some speculative bubble, illness, etc., etc.; but did not I know you better? I have read the *New Mirror* so much (to say nothing of the graceful things coined "under a bridge," and a thousand other pages flung from the inner heart), and not learned who has an eye for every thing pretty? Not so stupid, Cousin 'Bel'; no, no!

However, this is not quite the point, after all; but here it is. I have a pen—not a gold one, I don't think I could write with that, but a nice, little, feather-tipped pen, that rests in the curve of my finger as contentedly as in its former pillow of down. (Shocking! how that line did run down hill! and this almost as crooked! dear me!) Then I have little messengers racing "like mad" through the galleries of my head; spinning long yarns, and wearing fabrics rich and soft as the balzarine which I so much covet, until I shut my eyes and stop my ears and whisk away, with the 'wonderful lamp' safely hidden in my own brown braids. Then I have Dr. Johnson's Dictionary—capital London edition, etc., etc.; and after I use up all the words in that, I will supply myself with Webster's wondrous quarto, appendix and all. Thus prepared, think you not I should be able to put something in the shops of the literary caterers? something that, for once in my life would give me a real errand into Broadway? May be [sic] you of the *New Mirror* PAY for acceptable articles—may be [sic] not. *Comprenez-vous?*

O I do hope that beautiful balzarine like 'Bel's will not be gone before another Saturday! You will not forget to answer me in the next *Mirror;* but pray, my dear Editor, let it be done very cautiously, for 'Bel' would pout all day if she should know what I have written. Till Saturday,

Your anxiously-waiting friend,

Fanny Forester.[80]

Reply by N. P. Willis

"Well, we give in! On condition that you are under twenty-five, and that you will wear a rose (recognizably) in your bodice the first time you appear in Broadway with the hat and balzarine, we will pay the bills. Write us thereafter a sketch of 'Bel' and yourself, as cleverly done as this letter, and you may 'snuggle down' on the sofa, and consider us paid, and the public charmed with you."

Source: A. C. Kendrick, *The Life and Letters of Mrs. Emily C. Judson,* 93–95. This also appears in *Trippings in Author-land,* 2–5. Also *The New Mirror* 3/10 (June 8, 1844): 159–60.

---

[80] There is a story that Emily was one day asked why she wrote under the name of "Fanny Forester." She replied, "Would you purchase something written by Emily Chubbuck?" Indeed, it is all in the name!

Nathaniel Parker Willis to Emily E. Chubbuck, June 1844[81]

I am malicious enough to persist in wishing to see you—even though I entail some future penance on myself for having made use of a bank note compulsion. Out of five thousand mixtures of mind I chance to fancy the compound that is in *you*, and if you were plain as genius *will* sometimes be, you should still be charming stuff for a friend. I address this note to you without confidant, even without the knowledge of my brother editor,[82] and I beg for a live, confidential and to me only, telling me—where the balzarine is to be seen and paid for.

Yours very truly,

N. P. Willis

Source: Hanna family files, Willis to Emily, letter W1.

Emily E. Chubbuck to Catharine Chubbuck, June 27, 1844—Utica[83]

Dear (Katy) Kate,—

I have made an arrangement for you to come on and take lessons of Sarah Bell[84] just as soon as you can get ready. School closes five weeks from to-morrow, and I think you need to be here certainly four weeks.[85] Can you get ready so soon? **I should like it if you could get those night-gowns done so that you could have them to wear. Your petticoat and [ ] too and that is all the sewing you need do.** I have made the arrangement now, because there never will be a better time,

---

[81] This letter is addressed to: " Fanny Forester," (to be called for). Written in the left margin of the address page, in Emily Chubbuck's handwriting, is "N. P. Willis Esq. June 1844. No. 1."

[82] George P. "General" Morris, was N. P. Willis's partner at the *New Mirror* and a prominent literary figure in New York and Philadelphia. The original founder of the *New York Mirror* in 1823, beginning in 1843 with the *New Mirror*, he entered into a succession of publication enterprises with Willis. A writer, poet, and songwriter, he published a number of anthologies of both prose and poetry. After Willis's wife died, he went to Europe in 1845 and asked General Morris to guide Emily in her literary endeavors. Known universally as "General Morris," his title came from his rank as a brigadier-general in the New York militia.

[83] We have two versions of this letter—the original as written by Emily E. Chubbuck, and the edited version published by A. C. Kendrick in his biography, *The Life and Letters of Mrs. Emily C. Judson*. Additions made by Kendrick we have placed in parentheses ( ), and words in the original left out by Kendrick we have added in bold. One will note significant changes and omissions. In a note in his book, Kendrick explained that interest, purpose and propriety sometimes led to these changes and exclusions. "I remark here that in giving Chubbuck's letters, I do not always indicate unimportant omissions. Real letters must always contain much which should not meet the public eye; and Emily's were real letters, dashed off hastily amidst pressing cares and duties. Written also after the exhausting labors of the day, they by no means do uniform justice to her epistolary powers."

[84] Sarah Bell Wheeler was a teacher at the Utica Female Academy, and an intimate friend of Emily Chubbuck.

[85] Beginning in fall 1841, Emily had paid for Catharine Chubbuck to take some practical courses in art and music for two terms at the Utica Female Academy. Catharine was to be there into March 1842, though during that time Emily had been taken ill, and a great deal of Catharine's time had used to take care of Emily.

Wallace[86] being at home with mother,[87] and things here being in a proper train. Come the last of next week, or, if you **can't** possibly get ready, the week after **will do**; but a week is invaluable to you. Do not think another time will do as well. I may not be here another time; another time you may not be able to leave home. You *must* take lessons to run a race with S—.

The *New Mirror*[88] has just come, and you will see what a (splendid) **whopping** compliment N. P. **W.** (Willis)[87] has paid me **darling fellow**. I **shan't** shall not get any money, however, now—that is, from him; but it will put me in a way of making money like smoke. All well.

Write soon. In haste,

Nem

Source: A. C. Kendrick, *The Life and Letters of Mrs. Emily C. Judson*, 101; Hanna family files.

Emily E Chubbuck (Fanny Forester) to the Editor of the *New Mirror*, June 29, 1844[89]

Introduction by N.P. Willis

"Our readers will remember in the *Mirror* of two weeks ago, a very clever letter, written to us by an anonymous lady who wished to conjure a new bonnet and dress out of her inkstand. The inveiglement upon ourselves (to induce us to be her banker) was so adroit and fanciful, that we suspected the writer of being no novice at rhetorical trap—one indeed, of the numerous sisterhood who scatter their burdensome ammunition of contrivance and resource upon periodical literature. We 'gave in,' however—walking willingly into the lady's noose, on condition that she should wear a rose recognizably in Broadway the day she first sported the balzarine and neapolitan, and afterward send us a sketch of herself and her cousin. The 'sketch' we have received, and shall give it next week, and when we have seen the rose, we shall

---

[86] Born January 1, 1824, William Wallace Chubbuck was six years younger than Emily. During these years of Emily's correspondence, Wallace was living at home, or near home, working at different occupations including printing, office work, and teaching. Emily wrote of him as very capable in many areas but seeming to lack ambition at times. He proved to be a strong support for the Chubbuck family over these years, and, at the time of her death in 1854, Wallace had become one of Emily's primary care-givers. After February 1854, he wrote, at her dictation, all of her letters because of her failing strength.

[87] Lavinia Richards Chubbuck, Emily's mother, was born June 1, 1875, in Goffstown NH, the eldest of thirteen children. She married Charles Chubbuck on November 17. 1805. They were the parents of seven children.

[88] This would be the edition of the *New Mirror*, June 29, 1844, which had a second letter from Emily (Fanny Forester), following up her letter of June 8, 1844, and the response to it of N. P. Willis.

[89] Nathaniel Parker (N. P.) Willis was the editor of *New Mirror*, which catapulted Emily into literary fame. He became a friend, mentor, and eventually a suitor.

[90] Emily's first letter to the editor of the *New Mirror* appeared on June 8, 1844 (See letter of that date.); it had an introduction and a response from Willis. This letter was the reply of Fanny Forester to the invitation of Willis to tell more about herself.

not hesitate to acknowledge the debt. In the following parts of her letter which accompanied the sketch, the reader will see that the authoress feels (or feigns marvelously well) some resentment at our suspicions as to her age and quality."

Letter of Fanny Forester

To the Speculations of the Mirror as to who and what the Author might be.

...Have you never heard, my de-(pardon—I fear it is a habit of mine to write too 'honiedly')— but have you not heard that "suspicion is a heavy armor, which, with its own weight, impedes more than it protects?" Suspicion is most assuredly a beggarly virtue. It may, now and then, prevent your being "taken in," but it nips you in the costs most unmercifully. Oh! sharpsightedness is the most extravagantly *dear whistle* which poor humans ever purchased! That you should suspect me, too, when I was opening my heart away down to the core! How *could* you? "Inveigle!" No inveigling about it! I wanted a bonnet and dress, and said so, frankly and honestly. Moreover, I never wrote a line for Graham in my life-no! nor for Godey either. As for *couleur des bas*, your keen-eyed hawk pounced on less than a phantom there. From the day that I stood two mortal hours with my fingers poked into my eyes, and a fool's-cap on my head, because I persisted in spelling "b-a-g, baker," to the notable morning of christening my cousin by her profession, I have been voted innocent of all leaning toward the hue celestial. Indeed, it is more than suspected by my friends (cousin 'Bel' excepted) that I affect dame Nature's carpet, rather than her canopy.

May be I am "some varlet of a man scribbler"— Oh! you are such a Yankee at guessing!

Old! ah, that is the unkindest cut of all! You an editor, and the son of an editor, and not know that "old maids" are a class extinct at the present day, save in the sewing societies, etc., of some western village, subject only to the exploring expeditions of the indefatigable "Mary Clavers!" Have you never heard of five-and-twenty's being a turning point, and ken ye not its meaning? Why, *faire maydens* then reverse the hourglass of old gray-beard; and, one by one, drop back the golden sands that he has scattered, till, in five years, they are twenty again. Of course, then, I must be "under twenty-five;" but as a punishment for your lack of gallantry, you shall not know whether the sands are dropping in or out of my glass. One thing, however, is indisputable; I am not "sharp"—my face has not a single *sharp* feature, nor my temper (it is I, you know, that say it) a *sharp* corner, nor my voice a *sharp* tone. So much in self-justification, and now to the little package which you hold in the other hand.

I send my sketch in advance, because I am afraid cousin 'Bel' and I might not interest you and the public so much as we do ourselves; and then how are we to "consider you paid?" In truth I can not [sic] write *clever* things. 'Bel' might, but she never tries. Sometimes she plans for me; but, somehow, I never find the right words for her thoughts. They come into my head like fixed up visitors, and play "tea-party" with their baby neighbors, until I am almost as much puzzled by their strange performances as the old woman of the nursery rhyme, who was obliged to call on her "little dog at home" to establish her identity. No, no! I can not [sic] write clever things; and particularly on the subject to which I am restricted; but if it is the true sketch that you would have for the sake of the information, why here now it is. You will perceive that I have been very particular to tell you all.

Pray, do you allow us *carte blanche* as far as the hat and dress are concerned? You had better not; for 'Bel' never limits herself. How soon may we have them? The summer is advancing rapidly, and my old muslin and straw are unco shabby.

Yours, with all due affection,

Fanny Forester

Source: A. C. Kendrick, *The Life and Letters of Mrs. Emily C. Judson*, 96–98. This also appears in *Trippings in Author-land*, 16–18 and *The New Mirror* 3/13 (June 29, 1844): 208.

John Inman to Emily E. Chubbuck, July 14, 1844—New York City

My very excellent and dear friend,

You think me, I have no doubt, the most disgracious [sic] person in the world; and in the matter of letter writing I will not say that your judgment of me is very far wrong. I have in truth so great an aversion to writing letters, and sit down to the task at any time with so much reluctance, that I am continually in hot water with those who expect to hear from me; but in the present case I am not altogether without excuse. You know my position in the *Commercial Advertiser*. Mr. Stone, the senior editor, has been unable to do any thing [sic] for the last three or four months in consequence of severe illness, from which there is little hope of his recovery; and therefore the whole burden has fallen upon me occupying every moment of my time (including the going to and returning from the office) from 6 in the morning till 4 in the afternoon; in the remaining fragments of the day you may suppose I have enough to do in reading acres of manuscripts and writing some besides. Add to this the exhaustion and languor attendant upon this horrid hot weather, and I am sure you will feel a compassionate emotion, prompting you to forgive if not to excuse my remissness.

And there has been another reason why I delayed writing to you particularly. I wanted to do something for you in relation to that unhappy old Governor Seisler; but Mr. Stone himself was one of the two sources on which I relied for information, his studies having led him to the investigation of our colonial records and annals; but he has been so very unwell that I did not like to bother him about that or any thing [sic] else; and he was removed some three weeks ago, to Saratoga Springs where his wife's family and friends reside.

My other source of information was Charles Hoffman,[91] and he is as hard to catch as an eel. I did, however, get hold of him, the other day, and straitway [sic] attacked him upon the subject.

He says that there is nothing in print of which use can readily be made. All that is known of Seisler exists in the shape of divers [sic] pamphlets and Mss., mostly contained in the library of the N. Y. Historical Society. Some also are in the archives of private families, to which he has had access. It was by the use of such materials that he prepared his lecture on Seisler. But better news for you is that at the request of Mr. Sparks (to be published in his American Biography) Mr. Hoffman has drawn up a memoir, full and authentic, from the materials above described; and this memoir will be published soon—probably in August. I asked him to let me have the proof sheets, that I might send them to you, and he half-promised that he would; but do not rely upon them; he is apt to forget such promises. You may rely upon my sending you the memoir as soon as it is published. I do not neglect such things, though I am a bad correspondent.

And now what more shall I say? Will you not think me still more disgracious [sic] if I tell you that I don't like the love-story half so well as its predecessors? It is true though, and I'll tell you what I don't like about it—the incompleteness. You raise a mystery, the solution of which is expected to be the grand feature of the tale; which to the solution remains about as great a mystery as the other. We want to know who the ladybird was—where she first encountered her—what was the origin, what the course of their [ ]—what the long Yankee had to do with it—in a word some more complete elucidation of all that is strange and exciting in the earlier part of the story. As for the style, in that there is nothing to "fault," as the Rev. Arthur Corey would say. The story is beautifully written, as is everything you write; but I wish there was more artistical [sic] construction of the plot. Go to work and write me another; and in the meantime, send me your [ ] fifty pages—perhaps I can do something with them. In the meantime again believe me [Note: The signature is cut out at the bottom of page three, probably by some autograph collector.]

---

[91] Charles Fenno Hoffman was a prominent literary figure in Philadelphia and New York, who was well known in those literary circles as an adventurer, an editor, a poet, and a writer of exceptional talent. In fall 1843 he had written three letters to Emily Chubbuck addressed to "Laura Linden," for Emily had written to him under that name, asking his advice about love, fame and fortune. Only one of these letters is in the correspondence. Hoffman was not to learn of Emily's identity until spring 1845; in a letter we have dated April 7, 1845, he spoke of Laura having taken off her mask and revealing herself to him. There were four letters from Hoffman in this April period when Emily was in Philadelphia. There were another three in December 1845 when Emily again was in Philadelphia. See vol. 1, "Cast of Characters," s.v. "Hoffman, Charles Fenno"; and vol. 1, "Places, Events, Organizations, and Magazines," s.v. "Laura Letters." Anna Maria Anable frequently intimated in her letters that Emily was interested in "Hoffy" as a beau.

Written along the left margin of page 3: "Please give my best respects to your aged 'mother-in-law,'[92] and write to me soon. I like to read your letters, though I am so poor a hand at answering."

Written vertically to the script and crossing the text on page 3: "If you grant to oblige me *very* much, let me know, at full length, what you candidly think of the July number. I have seen presses of it, enough and to spare, but I should like to see a criticism of it; a real [ ] notice of the several articles. Will you write such a thing for me? I give you free license to condemn, or damn with faint praise, as your judgment dictates. That indeed is what I want—to see something like a judgment upon it."

Source: American Baptist Historical Society, AJ 24, no. 1178.

Anna Maria Anable to Emily E. Chubbuck, July 17, 1844[93]

Oh! Nem[94] but isn't it hot? Do you feel inclined to go to the West Indies or Lapland this same morning of the 17th July? On the whole tho' I take the heat quite *lovingly*. I have been making bouquets for the parlor and fussing around till it is almost nine o'clock, and now I can't help wondering whether there was rain in Utica last night. Nobody here thinks or talks about anything but the possibility of rain and the signs of the clouds and sunsets.

I wish you could look out of my window for a while. I can scarcely keep my eyes on the paper long enough to write a sentence. On my right between the colleges they have raised two immense circus tents under which a thousand animals are to be fed on Tuesday next at two o'clock P.M. They *do* say, that is my paper. Read whispered to me last evening that a *few ladies* might be admitted (as a special favor) to see the show. From the tents to the road is a gravel walk at the end of which your admirer Gillespie[95] is superintending the erection of a triumphant arch. To the left is the beautiful slope towards the river studded with trees and waving with grain. Beyond the river rise hills like our Trenton hills and—but I must put my head clear out of the window to see what else there is—There! a cloud as fine as I live—and a gust of wind. hurrah! here comes the rain; Pitter patter, down with the window. There, the tent is blown over. What will they do? How the folks run across the plain—I must go and see what they can do about the tents and the arrangements

---

[92] Anna Maria Anable often referred herself to Emily as Emily's "mother-in-law."

[93] This letter was written from Union College in Schenectady NY, where the Rev. Dr. Eliphalet Nott was the president. Dr. Nott was the husband of Urania Sheldon Nott, Anna Maria's Aunt.

[94] "Nem" or "Nemmy" was a name of endearment given to Emily by a small group of her intimate friends at the Utica Female Academy. Anna Maria Anable was "Ninny."

[95] William Gillespie was a professor of civil engineering at Union College. In a July 9, 1845 letter to her sister Catharine, Emily spoke of going to a Union College commencement and that "A man there has fallen in love iwth me—Mr. Gillespie, author of 'Rome as seen by a New Yorker.'"

for the grand dinner for it must be confessed it would not be very agreeable to have the tents blow over with a thousand people underneath.

Afternoon

Well, as I left the tent down I may as well tell you what they are going to do, tho' you will I trust be here to see for yourself. They have concluded to place the tents back in the Dr.'s[96] garden where they will be protected by the trees from the wind. It has cleared off charmingly and I have taken a ride down town with Aunt U.[97] Oh! you must come on Sat; and see how fresh and green and charming the country looks. Aunt U. wants you to come then, for she *may* go to Albany and I shall be here alone, for one reason, and if she does not go she wants a nice visit with you alone on Sat. and Sun. The house will be topsy turvey Sunday, Monday, Tues. and Wed. You want to know about the wedding? Well the bride looked beautiful positively; and the bridegroom is quite a handsome man, something like Prof. Read, and every body [sic] is sounding his praises now that he is married. Such a [ ] and such a hot night I think was never known before. There were hogsheads of lemonade drunk I reckon and every body [sic] looked as if they wished they were home in bed or in some cooler place.

Last night we went down to call on the bride and on Mrs. Willard. While Aunt U. and the Dr. talked to Mrs. W. Mrs. Mumford told I would find the bride in the garden somewhere—and sure enough I came upon her—leaning on the arm of her beloved in the summer house. For a moment I felt [ ] [ ] [Note: two French words.]—but H[ ] behaves like a woman forty years married and we chatted away quite at our ease till I got quite well acquainted with her husband. They remain here till after commencement and there will be I suppose several parties given to her.

Tonight I suppose you go to Mrs. R's. Take care of yourself and don't get fagged out before you come down. Have you heard anything from Willis[98] yet? Or Graham?[99] I think I have written about enough with this horrid scratchy pen and much ink. Do come Sat.—and come on the eight o'clock run so that you can get rested by evening and don't pray *leave your baggage behind*! I will meet you at the

---

[96] Eliphalet Nott, president of Union College, married to Urania Sheldon Nott.

[97] Urania Sheldon Nott, formerly literary principal of the Utica Female Academy, was a mentor, advisor, and friend to Emily.

[98] Nathaniel Parker (N. P.) Willis was the editor of *New Mirror*, which catapulted Emily into literary fame. He became a friend, mentor, and eventually a suitor.

[99] George Graham was the editor of *Graham's Magazine*, one of the pre-eminent literary magazines of Emily's time. He took an interest in Emily Chubbuck as Fanny Forester; he mentored her, he published every piece of writing that she could submit to him, and for it all he remunerated her with the unheard of sum of five dollars a page. When, in April 1845, Emily was staying in Philadelphia with the Reverend and Mrs. A. D. Gillette, Mr. and Mrs. Graham were frequent visitors, often inviting Emily to tour parts of the city with them in their elegant carriage. That relationship picked up again when Emily returned to Philadelphia in fall 1845.

cars. Please send [ ] to Mrs. Memchaus for her corsets and don't forget to bring my clothes. Love to all.

Ninny[100]   Source: American Baptist Historical Society, AJ 23, no. 1125.

Emily E. Chubbuck to Anna Maria Anable,[101] August 7, 1844—Hamilton[102]

Oh Anna Maria! If you *did* know how I want to ride! Why, I am actually suffocating for the want of a breath of air. The house is stuck away down, down, down, and here I am burrowed up in it without the possibility of seeing out. Walk, did you say? O innocent! little do you understand your suggestion! Where shall I go? To be sure, the streets are like a dozen ribbons knotted in the middle; but which to go off on! That is the query. One way you encounter innumerable perils in the shape of students, another, of bogs, another, of barn-yards; all have their *peculiarities*, and Kate[103] has put a veto on each proposal of mine. Besides, I do not want to walk; I want to ride. "Spring-halt"[104] has made me aristocratic. Have I ridden so many times after him, to foot it now? (That blot is a tear-drop of the pitying ink.) I'd pawn my *chemise* for a horse and buggy if men wore such things. I never did so want to *get out* in my life. Tell Aunt Cynthia,[105] if she has a spark of love for me—if she has any bowels of compassion, she will either send out "Spring-halt," or a portion of the needful. And now, mother-in-law,[106] what more shall I say? It is above sixty miles from here to Cooperstown, and fifty to Cherry Valley! I have given up the thought of going anywhere this vacation but I *do* want to stir here. When are you coming? Do come, if you don't want me to turn into a pillar of salt. You and I could manage to kick up a dust, but you know Kitty[107] is like her bulk in lead as far as a project for going out is concerned, and I havn't the spirit to keep myself from moping alone. As for Wallace,[108] he went to Oriskany Monday and has not got back yet.

Source: A. C. Kendrick, *The Life and Letters of Mrs. Emily C. Judson*, 101–104; Hanna family files.

---

[100] Ninny was a name of endearment given to Anna Maria Anable by her most intimate friends at the Utica Female Academy. Emily was "Nemmy."

[101] This letter has beautiful handwriting, Emily certainly at her best.

[102] This letter has an addendum dated August 8, 1844, and another dated August 9, 1844.

[103] Sarah Catharine ("Kate," "Kit," or "Kitty") Chubbuck, Emily's older sister, born October 25, 1816.

[104] "Spring-halt" was the name of a horse at the Utica Female Academy; Emily and Anna Maria often spoke of sleigh rides or carriage rides.

[105] Miss Cynthia Sheldon was the administrative and finance manager of the Utica Female Academy. She was a mentor, advisor, and friend to Emily. By this time, she had become "Aunt Cynthia."

[106] In letters to Emily, Anna Maria often referred to herself as "mother-in-law."

[107] Sarah Catharine ("Kate," "Kit," or "Kitty") Chubbuck, Emily's older sister, born October 25, 1816.

[108] William Wallace Chubbuck, Emily's younger brother, born January 1, 1824.

Emily E. Chubbuck to Anna Maria Anable,[109] August 8, 1844[110]

"Blessings on ye," Anna Maria, for that *New Mirror*.[111] I thought of you all day yesterday while reading it—though I didn't expect such a nice bit for myself. I am crazy to get the letter. Please send to the Express Office and P.O. both, and, *after you have read it*, enclose it in one of your own and send on.—We had a delightful time Sat. part of the way. The air was deliciously fresh, and the scenery magnificent; but as evening came on, it grew "damp, moist, and unwholesome;" [sic] the roads were rough and poor Kate[112] was sick. I made her up a bed on the back seat (my dictionary and shawls for a pillow), and on we came in some tribulation. It was amusing enough to see the men gather around for news at every place we stopped. At Bouckville (a little cluster of houses about as big as your fist) the portico of the inn (the only one there) was swarming with men, and as we came up a dozen voices shouted, "What news?" "Bag full," said the driver, throwing the stuffed leather bag to a little man waiting for it. "Hurrah for Polk!" broke in a pert feminine voice from one end of the portico. "Hurrah for Polk!" echoed a bull frog [sic] at the other. Another—very deliberately, "Hur—r—ra for Henry Clay!" A tall, lean man, rather sheepishly, "Harrah for Birney!" Then a general shout, with but the variation of a name broke from bar and portico, and all scrambled off after the mail, for they saw by the return of the bag that it was assorted. The whole country seemed up in arms about politics. We reached home about ten o'clock. Sunday Kate sick and I tired—neither of us at church. Monday, made mother[113] a cap, and read "Hallam's Middle Ages." Tuesday, made two collars and read same—nothing else to read. Wednesday, too impatient to do much, but in the afternoon coaxed Kate off into the swamp and had a very nice time after all. Got ever so many flowers.

To-day I have been reading the *New Mirror*, and afterwards made Kate a bracelet of beads. Wallace[114] has gone to Morrisville, and what do you guess I have been making for us when he comes back in the evening? Why a set of chess-men. I have checked off a paper for a board, and made all my large men of poppy heads. The difference in the length of the stems distinguishes between king and queen—the castles are made of two heads fastened together—the bishops have split stems for mitres, and the knights are decorated with plumes in the absence of their

---

[109] This letter has beautiful handwriting, Emily certainly at her best.

[110] This letter is an addendum to a letter dated August 7, 1844. There is a second addendum dated August 9, 1844.

[111] The *New Mirror* was a literary magazine published by N. P. Willis and General Morris. Emily had had two pieces in it in June (8 and 29) and that opportunity and the developing relationship with Willis was opening new doors for her. She was to have some of her work in virtually every issue of the *New Mirror* for many months.

[112] Sarah Catharine ("Kate," "Kit," or "Kitty") Chubbuck, Emily's older sister, born October 25, 1816.

[113] Lavinia Richards Chubbuck, Emily's mother, was born June 1, 1875, in Goffstown NH, the eldest of thirteen children. She married Charles Chubbuck on November 17. 1805. They were the parents of seven children.

[114] William Wallace Chubbuck, Emily's younger brother, born January 1, 1824.

horses. Oh! they are a capital set of men! you would be charmed with them. My pawns are marygold [sic] heads, which, set on the flat side, with the little stems sticking up to move them by, are as complete pawns as ever you saw. The two parties are distinguished by a streak of red paint on one. To-morrow we can have father's[115] old donkey—a miserable beast, not half as good as "Spring-halt," and mother and Kate and I are bent on a ride. It is the only day in the week when we can have him, and so I warrant it will rain.

Source: A. C. Kendrick, *The Life and Letters of Mrs. Emily C. Judson*, 101–104; Hanna family files.

Emily E. Chubbuck to Anna Maria Anable,[116] August 9, 1844[117]

Fri. Oh no! it didn't rain—not a bit—but I managed to get up a very real headache this morning and have been hugging the pillow all day; so mother[118] and Kate[119] were dished as well as I, and we must wait for another Friday. Schocking! [sic] I can't sit up yet—my head goes like a spindle—so no more at p*resence*. [sic]. —I have got up again, and carry myself a little more respectably. The mail leaves at nine, and I carry myself a little mo—bless me! I am copying from the line above. I believe I am growing daft; but *n'importe*—I am determined to send off this blotted sheet tonight. Why *don't* you write me, Anna Maria,[120] and let me know what you are about. When are you coming out? Do come, do! I hope Aunt Urania[121] will look in upon us when she comes—I should like to *ask* her, but you have been here, and so know why I can't.—I hav'nt [sic] seen anybody since I came home for the reason that the bells were not rang [sic] on the arrival and I hav'nt [sic] shown my beautiful face out yet.

Written in the right margin of the address page: "Tell Miss C.[122] that Miss Shaply will go back with me, if she can get the better of a humour (a cutaneous eruption I mean) which disfigures her face. Guess Em and Soph hav'nt [sic] done much harm for she is one of the scholars they boasted of getting. And now Anna

---

[115] Emily's father, Charles Chubbuck, was born at Bedford NH on March 3, 1780; he married Lavinia Richards in Goffstown NH on November 17, 1805, and together they had seven children. Though he held varying jobs over the years, Charles failed at many of them. Emily became the main financial support for the family and purchased a home for them in fall 1842.

[116] This letter has beautiful handwriting, Emily certainly at her best.

[117] This letter is the second addendum to a letter dated August 7, 1844. The first addendum was dated August 8, 1844.

[118] Lavinia Richards Chubbuck, Emily's mother, was born June 1, 1875, in Goffstown NH, the eldest of thirteen children. She married Charles Chubbuck on November 17, 1805. They were the parents of seven children.

[119] Sarah Catharine ("Kate," "Kit," or "Kitty") Chubbuck, Emily's older sister, born October 25, 1816.

[120] Anna Maria Anable was the niece of the Urania and Cynthia Sheldon, the daughter of Alma Sheldon Anable; she was Emily's closest friend at the Utica Female Academy.

[121] Urania Sheldon Nott, formerly literary principal of the Utica Female Academy, was a mentor, advisor, and friend to Emily.

[122] Miss Cynthia Sheldon was the administrative and finance manager of the Utica Female Academy. She was a mentor, advisor, and friend to Emily.

Maria may I trouble you or Miss C. with a queer commission? Ask her to get me a dozen of knives and forks such as she uses 'for common' and hand them to Mr. Bennett to send by whoever preaches at Broad-St. next Sunday."

Written along the left margin of the address page: "On second thought, though, they would be too heavy, but if I could get them any time [sic] between now and commencement it would do. I find them an article much needed, and if I had money (I hav'nt [sic] but a sixpence) the right thing could'nt be found here. I have had two presents since I came home—both characteristic of the givers. A cheese about as big over as the top of a coffee cup—a whole cheese as perfect in its make as a mammoth one—and a bag of live geese feathers enough for a pair of pillows 'to rest her dear little head,' so said the good donor. I would send you the first if I had a chance—the cheese not the head."

Written along the bottom margin of the address page: "I suspect you are having wondrous peaceful times. Love to every soul of you and make the most of your comforts of stillness and quietude till the five weeks are passed. I should'nt [sic] think your mother[123] would know how to calculate for breakfast and dining in such a small way."

Written upside down in the top margin of page 2: "Hav'nt [sic] tried my new chess-men yet,[124] for W.[125] has'nt got home. Could'nt [sic] you step over and play a little —though, I'd much rather ride."

Written along the left margin of page 1: "I have just got 'Letters from under a bridge' and promise myself a treat. Oh! —does Jenny *droop* over the departure of Mary."

Written upside down in the top margin of page 1: "I should think A.M. you would consider yourself among the favoured (alias bored) few, for you know I don't write such long letters every day.—If you can't find out who it is from, send it back and I will find a place to sign it."

Source: A. C. Kendrick, *The Life and Letters of Mrs. Emily C. Judson*, 101–104; Hanna family files.

---

[123] Alma Sheldon Anable, sister of Cynthia Sheldon and Urania Sheldon Nott. On July 28, 1814, Alma married Joseph Hubbell Anable in Troy NY (Anable's second marriage). Joseph and Alma Anable had nine children: Henry Sheldon Anable, b. June 21, 1815; William Stewart Anable, b. November 6, 1816; Anna Maria Stafford Anable, b. September 30, 1818, Cynthia Jane Anable, January 28, 1820; Samuel Low Anable, b. November 28, 1821; Harriet Isabella Anable, also known as Hatty or Hattie, was born December 18, 1823; Courtland Wilcox Anable, b. July 28, 1825; Frances Alma Anable, or Fanny, b. April 12, 1828, and Mary Juliet Anable, b. February 18, 1830. Alma Anable was employed by the Utica Female Academy in what would be identified as "food service."

[124] See the letter of Emily E. Chubbuck to Anna Maria Anable dated August 8, 1844. In that letter she described her projects, and one of them was to make a set of chess men.

[125] William Wallace Chubbuck, Emily's younger brother, born January 1, 1824.

Anna Maria Anable to Emily E. Chubbuck, August 13, 1844—Verona Springs

Well Nem,[126] have you exclaimed and stared enough at receiving a letter from me dated from this forlorn part of creation. Well then, I'll tell you—your letter found me in a great "state" packing and fixing off Fan[127] and myself for a week's vacation at this far famed and sweet smelling watering place. I got scared about this swelling in Fan's face—and hearing wondrous accounts of the efficacy of these [ ] waters we started off at a moments warning—Spring-halt[128] brought Cousin Fan I [sic] and the trunk—he did and its sixteen miles from Utica—and he returned the same day—and I have not heard of his death either. What may we not hope for the future.

But to my business—I want you to come out here—There is a Dr. Babcock of your place who has been out here—and I have heard a great deal of his skill in curing Erysipelas—He has been expected here all this week and if he has not left by the time you get this—just bargain for half of his buggy—and come straight out here Thursday—He is and [sic] old bachelor too I hear and so my daughter who knows? ahem!

If he *should* happen to have got his start of [ ] and should come out tomorrow with some Hamilton folks—so that Fan would be contented to stay here—I shall come out to see you by Friday—I wish you would send that Miss Shapery out here to stay a couple of weeks with Fan—The folks here say she was a little fool to go away when the waters were so decidedly beneficial to her.

What do you suppose I do to amuse myself here—why I am of more forlorn [ ] you—for besides the lack of amusement I am away from home—but no—I have had two buggy rides already—one to the Methodist church at Andover on Sunday—and yesterday I borrowed the buggy again to drive Fan over to Verona on a shopping excursion to get a paper of needles—but not succeeding we walked to day [sic] down to Andover about a mile distant on the same pursuit—So have passed the *three days*! The buggy has gone with its owner—and we have taken the only walk that is exciting at all—and so what shall I do tomorrow—O, I forgot—I have the same resources as you—Some benefactor of mankind has made the landlord a present of [ ] by the way—and to that will I resort. What has become of your letter? I sent to the office every day before I came out here and left word to have

---

[126] "Nem" or "Nemmy" was a name of endearment given to Emily by a small group of her intimate friends at the Utica Female Academy. Anna Maria Anable was "Ninny."

[127] Fanny Anable, one of the five Anable sisters. She was born April 12, 1828.

[128] Spring-halt was a horse, owned by the Utica Female Academy for sleigh and carriage rides.

any letters for F. F.[129] sent up to the seminary—I hope you have got (them) by this time—Do write to Graham[130]—I have been reading an excellent story of Mrs. Butters in his magazine—The few boarders who are here are watching with intense interest a game of fox and geese which is going on between Fan and one of the other boarders at the table at which I am writing—I wish I had your chess-board[131] here—in want of another antagonist I think I *could* teach Fan how to play—they want me to play fox and geese so I guess I'll stop. Much love to your Mother[132] and Kate[133]—If you can't decipher this epistle lay it to the pen and ink—for you know I can write beautifully. Anna Maria

Written on the bottom of the address page: "I've finished my game and its about bed-time—I'm going to try and get a wagon to carry this over to [ ] myself tomorrow morning—I'm as crazy to see you—as you can be to see me—Court[134] came home the day you left—I wrote to Aunt Rhoda that you…[135]

Written on the top of the address page: "and I were coming out to see her—I hope you can go—I've hardly seen anything of Jimmy[136] this vacation for I was out almost every evening before I came away—It seems as if I had been here three months instead of thee days—and I feel entirely out of the world with regard to news—I must pick up a little before"

Written in the top right margin of the address page: "I come to see you."

Source: American Baptist Historical Society, AJ 23, no. 1131.

---

[129] F.F., or Fanny Forester, was Emily Chubbuck's *nom de plume*.

[130] George Graham, editor of *Graham's Magazine*, took an interest in Emily Chubbuck as Fanny Forester and paid her with the unheard of sum of five dollars a page.

[131] In her August 8, 1844 letter, Emily had mentioned a chessboard and figures that she had made for her brother Wallace.

[132] Lavinia Richards Chubbuck, Emily's mother, was born June 1, 1875, in Goffstown NH, the eldest of thirteen children. She married Charles Chubbuck on November 17. 1805. They were the parents of seven children.

[133] Sarah Catharine ("Kate," "Kit," or "Kitty") Chubbuck, Emily's older sister, born October 25, 1816.

[134] Courtland Anable, younger brother to Anna Maria Anable. He held several positions over the years and eventually studied at Hamilton College and boarded for a time with Emily's parents. In 1853, he returned to Philadelphia where he preached his first sermon at the Eleventh Baptist Church. He was "Uncle Court" to Emily Frances Judson. In 1880, Anable was listed in the Massachusetts census as an ordained minister serving in a church.

[135] Sentence is finished in the next paragraph at the top of the address page.

[136] Jimmy Williams, often mentioned in Anna Maria Anable's letters, usually just as "Jimmy."

Cynthia Sheldon to Emily E. Chubbuck, August 18, 1844

Dear Emily

My mind was set on going with Urania[137] this morning, but company arrived with the evening cars to remain until aft'n prevents me—besides this number one should be at home—The knives you named would be $4.50 per doz[138]—the fact of the business is I am head and cars minus money for anything. You can write again if you wish. The knives—at that price—they can go out Tuesday.

In great haste—Love to all

Yours truly

C. Sheldon

Source: American Baptist Historical Society, AJ 26, no. 1271.

Anna Maria Anable to Emily E. Chubbuck, August 18, 1844[139]

My dear Nem[140]

Tho' I am most tired to death, I can't help sitting up a little longer to say a few words to you. I am *so* disappointed that I can't come out to see you next week. Aunt C.[141] says I *must* go with her on Monday—and you know when *she* says you must "you must and never ask why." We came back from "The Springs"[142] yesterday very much improved in health and spirits from our residence at that delightful watering place!! Fanny[143] will probably return next week—and I *do* wish some of those Hamilton folks would go out—she will be so lonesome. We have heard that Hatty[144] was not well—had a pretty severe attack of fever—and until we hear again from her I don't think I shall go down to S. We expect to leave Sunday.[145]

---

[137] Urania Sheldon Nott—a mentor, advisor, and friend to Emily—was the literary principal of the Utica Female Academy when Emily arrived in October 1840. In late summer 1842 Urania married Eliphalet Nott, the president of Union College in Schenectady NY.

[138] See the letter of Emily C. Chubbuck to Anna Maria Anable dated August 7, 1844, in which she asks Anna Maria and "Aunt Cynthia" to fulfill "a queer commission" for her.

[139] This letter is undated. We do know that Anna Maria wrote Emily on August 13, 1844 that she was coming to see her from Verona Springs. Since Anna Maria went home instead to go to Schenectady with Sheldon, we place this letter at the ending (Sunday) of that week when she would have been going to Hamilton.

[140] "Nem" or "Nemmy" was a name of endearment given to Emily by a small group of her intimate friends at the Utica Female Academy. Anna Maria Anable was "Ninny."

[141] Miss Cynthia Sheldon was the administrative and finance manager of the Utica Female Academy. She was a mentor, advisor, and friend to Emily. By this time, she had become "Aunt Cynthia."

[142] On August 13, 1844, Anna Maria Anable had written to Emily from Verona Springs.

[143] Fanny Anable was one of nine children born to Joseph and Alma Anable and was a niece of Cynthia Sheldon and Urania Sheldon Nott.

[144] Harriet ("Hatty," "Hattie," or "Hat") Anable, one of the five Anable sisters. She had been teaching in the New Orleans area, located in a private home.

[145] Anna Maria Anable left for Schenectady on Friday, August 23.

Now Nem—what do you think of Willis?[146] He can't get hold of that letter, nor can he get on the track of it[147]—can't be in the *New Mirror* Office at New York? Or had he never written it. He is evidently bewitched to know you—and though he calls on Heaven to forgive you it is plain he don't [sic].

I would write to him and ask him for another letter to pay for his lost one.

Do write soon—if you can't find time to write by Aunt U[148]—write to Schenectady.

Much love to your dear mother[149] and Kate[150]—and if I can get away from Schenectady and Lou's in time I will run down to see you the last week. We have letters from the girls tonight—they went down to N. Y. Wednesday—and Mary B.[151] and her folks are all going out to Union Village—her native place—Jane Kelly[152] went to S. this morning—She got in such a teaze [sic] to get home to see her Ma but she could hardly stop to see Mr. Falls. And so she went from her house and back again like a [ ]—or more properly like herself when she gets "set on"— Good Night.

Write do—AM

Source: American Baptist Historical Society, AJ 23. These undated letters are found in Numbers 1134, 1137, 1139, and 1163.

Nathaniel Parker Willis to Emily E, Chubbuck, August 20, 1844[153]

Dear Lady Fanny,[154]

The lost letter was directed to "Utica Fem. Acad.," and either Cousin 'Bel'[155] is a bad mouser, or my man Summers mis-box'd the letter. But no matter. It was merely a letter of warm thanks for what you had done for us, and an assurance that

---

[146] Nathaniel Parker (N. P.) Willis was the editor of *New Mirror*, which catapulted Emily into literary fame. He became a friend, mentor, and eventually a suitor.

[147] N. P. Willis had written to Emily Chubbuck on August 20, 1844, concerning the whereabouts of the "lost letter."

[148] Urania Sheldon Nott, formerly literary principal of the Utica Female Academy, was a mentor, advisor, and friend to Emily.

[149] Lavinia Richards Chubbuck, Emily's mother, was born June 1, 1875, in Goffstown NH, the eldest of thirteen children. She married Charles Chubbuck on November 17. 1805. They were the parents of seven children.

[150] Sarah Catharine ("Kate," "Kit," or "Kitty") Chubbuck, Emily's older sister, born October 25, 1816.

[151] Mary Barber, mentioned frequently in the Emily Chubbuck Judson letters, was a student and then the art teacher at the Utica Female Academy.

[152] Jane Kelly was Emily Chubbuck's friend at the Utica Female Academy. Following the departure of Mr. and Mrs. Nichols, Jane became the literary principal in early 1844. Then with the departure of Cynthia Sheldon to Philadelphia in fall 1848, she became "headmistress."

[153] This letter was addressed to: Fanny Forester, Hamilton, Madison Co., N.Y. In Emily's handwriting on the letter is "N. P. Willis. Aug. 20. No. 2."

[154] F.F., or Fanny Forester, was Emily Chubbuck's nom de plume.

[155] In the June letters which Emily sent to N. P. Willis, which were printed in the *New Mirror*, she spoke of coming to New York with her "Cousin 'Bel'" (Anna Maria Anable), and lamenting that while they looked in the windows at beautiful things, with empty pocketbooks they could not afford to purchase anything.

tho' we could not pay you, we could make your name so *coinable* by praises that you could sell high to others. Every line your *clever pen* writes should bring you an equivalent *besides* praise, and we will bring that about speedily. You have remarkable talent at writing the *readable*, and if you are not over forty you have a career before you. I esteem you, (authorly), very much, and should be delighted to know you, pretty or plain. A lady told me to-day that you were not pretty, or you would not have so much wit and leisure to *throw* away! Woman's sagacity! Please tell me what you are like, and I beg you to write for us as long as you can afford to. How can I[153] send you the *Mirror* and our *extras*—one and all? How can we serve or please you?

Yours admiringly,

N. P. Willis

Excuse any delay in replies as I am at Rockaway most of the week. I send you next Saturday's *Mirror*. We print it always in advance to dry the plates.

Source: A. C. Kendrick, *The Life and Letters of Mrs. Emily C. Judson*, 104; Hanna family files.

Cynthia Sheldon to Emily E. Chubbuck, August 20, 1844

Dear Emily,

Your note came by Urania.[157] They have left us this morn'g, Anna M.[158] stays at home until we receive tidings from dear Harriet[159]—Fanny[160] was taken sick yesterday too—I wish you to see or cause to be seen. Doct Babcock[161]—Homeopathy, and find when he will be at the Springs, Verona. I wish to meet him there on Fanny's account, we are at a loss to know what course to pursue in her case—I send you a package if we can find a chance—we can as well lend you the knives

---

[156] It is interesting to note the changes in the letter that A. C. Kendrick made as he published them in *The Life and Letters of Mrs. Emily C. Judson*. For one, this "I" was changed to "we." Also the postscript after the name was omitted completely.

[157] Urania Sheldon Nott—a mentor, advisor, and friend to Emily—was the literary principal at the Utica Female Academy when Emily arrived in October 1840. In late summer 1842 Urania married Eliphalet Nott, the president of Union College in Schenectady NY.

[158] Anna Maria Anable was the niece of the Urania and Cynthia Sheldon, the daughter of Joseph and Alma Sheldon Anable; she was Emily's closest friend at the Utica Female Academy.

[159] Harriet ("Hatty," "Hattie," or "Hat") was one of the five Anable sisters. At this time, she was teaching in a private residence near New Orleans. A recent letter had spoken of her being ill, with a high fever.

[160] Fanny Anable, one of five Anable sisters. She was born April 12, 1828.

[161] On August 13, 1844, Anna Maria Anable had written to Emily from Verona, a recreational area with springs where she was vacationing. "There is a dr. Babcock of your place who has been out here—and I have heard a great deal of his skill in curing Erysipelas—He has been expected here all this week and if he has not left by the time you get this—just bargain for half of his buggy—and come straight out here Thursday—He is an old bachelor too I hear and so my daughter who knows? ahem!"

and forks till next week[162]—as anyone wish one were at hand—as neighbors—I send two Dolls[163]—do if you can send me word about the Doctor Thursday. I wish he could be at the Springs Friday—Urania was disappointed in Anna M. giving up, but thought it best—she will if providence permits. We are truly sad—this long delay of the letters gives us great anxiety—in great haste

Yours truly,

C. Sheldon

How did the Doct[164] acquit himself. He and U. were delighted with the visit.

Source: American Baptist Historical Society, AJ 26, no. 1270.

Anna Maria Anable to Emily E. Chubbuck, August 21, 1844

Well Nem[165] my daughter

I think you will need a little motherly[166] advice to help you digest this dose—Can this be an answer to your first letter? If it is I do not understand its pertinency [sic]. He is mighty free and easy in his style. What does his last sentence mean? From his quotations I should think you had been making some demonstration of affection to him. I am completely mystified—I wonder if he ai'nt [sic]. Do write and tell me what you have written to [Note: An ink blot obscures several words.] if you know what he meant—[167]

If Willis[168] had written so I should not have been surprised—but Graham[169] to whom you wrote such a sober sort of a letter to up and be facetious—I don't understand it—It seems as if all the men are determined to make love instead of do business with you. I'd write to Graham and tell him he'd better publish Cousin

---

[162] See the letter of Emily Chubbuck to Anna Maria Anable dated August 7, 1844 in which she asked Anna Maria and Sheldon to perform a "queer commission" for her—i.e. purchasing knives and forks.

[163] We believe this means two dollars.

[164] Eliphalet Nott, president of Union College, married to Urania Sheldon Nott.

[165] "Nem" or "Nemmy" was a name of endearment given to Emily by a small group of her intimate friends at the Utica Female Academy. Anna Maria Anable was "Ninny."

[166] Anna Maria often referred to herself, in letters to Emily, as "mother" or "mother-in-law."

[167] The next paragraph of this letter leaves no doubt but that George Graham, the editor and publisher of Graham's Magazine, one of the great literary figures of the mid-nineteenths century, had written a letter to Emily Chubbuck, a letter that Emily had forwarded to Anna Maria Anable, and here Anna Maria responds with genuine astonishment, with surprising suggestions as to its content.

[168] Nathaniel Parker (N. P.) Willis was the editor of New Mirror, which catapulted Emily into literary fame. He became a friend, mentor, and eventually a suitor.

[169] George Graham, editor of Graham's Magazine, took an interest in Emily Chubbuck as Fanny Forester and paid her with the unheard of sum of five dollars a page.

'Bel'[170] right off, just as it is—to please you—and the wish story you'll write to please him.

Fan[171] is a good deal better today and Frank C. is going out to [ ]with her tomorrow. We do not yet hear from Hat[172]—Love to all your folks AM

Source: American Baptist Historical Society, AJ 23, no. 1129.

Anna Maria Anable to Emily E. Chubbuck,[173] August 22, 1844[174]

Dear Nem[175]

I don't feel this morning like saying anything but how forlorn and anxious I feel—Hatty[176] sick at a distance of two thousand miles and no letter from her or Mary[177]—Fanny[178]again subject to her old attack—I [ ] feel as if you, if your friends are well have the best of it—Yesterday I felt like making a full confession of my naughtiness—but to day [sic] I don't feel called upon—I am crazy to know what you wrote to Willis[179]—and to Graham[180]—He (Graham) has come out with a flaming announcement—all the big names he can get—I suppose he's jealous of

---

[170] In the June letters to the *New Mirror*, Fanny Forester had written that she had toured New York with her "Cousin 'Bel'" (Anna Maria Anable), and that they were discouraged because, as they looked at the costly goods in the store windows, they had no funds to purchase them—and would the editor of the *Mirror* be willing to help them. On October 4, 1844, George Graham wrote Emily that "Cousin 'Bel" would be appearing in the November Number of *Graham's Magazine*

[171] Fanny Anable, one of five Anable sisters. She was born April 12, 1828.

[172] Harriet ("Hatty," "Hattie," or "Hat") Anable, one of the five Anable sisters. She had been teaching in a private residence in the New Orleans area. A recent letter had spoken of her having a high fever and the family was concerned.

[173] We note in this letter that Anna Maria Anable is writing about Emily Chubbuck's relationship as Fanny Forester with four of the most prominent literary figures of the mid-nineteenth century—George Graham of *Graham's Magazine*, N. P. Willis of the *New Mirror*, John Inman of the *Columbian Magazine*, and Charles Fenno Hoffman who like the others, wore a number of different hats in the literary world.

[174] This letter is undated, though likely written on August 22. Hatty's illness would place it after August 20 when Sheldon wrote to say that they were worried about Hatty, and the 23rd when they had an encouraging letter about Hatty. It would also be close after Anna Maria's letter of August 21, when she mentioned a letter from George Graham that seemed to be romantically suggestive—Anna Maria said she would not have been surprised if it had come from N. P. Willis; here Anna Maria wants to know what Emily wrote to reply to each of them. We know also that Anna Maria Anable left Utica for Schenectady NY on August 23.

[175] "Nem" or "Nemmy" was a name of endearment given to Emily by a small group of her intimate friends at the Utica Female Academy. Anna Maria Anable was "Ninny."

[176] Harriet ("Hatty," "Hattie," or "Hat") Anable, one of the five Anable sisters. She had been teaching in a private residence in the New Orleans area. A recent letter had spoken on her suffering a high fever and the family was concerned.

[177] Mary Juliet Anable, daughter of Alma and Joseph Anable. For about a year, late 1846 to early 1848, she taught with her sister Hatty in New Orleans, and in 1849 she joined the staff of the Misses Anable's School in Philadelphia.

[178] Fanny Anable, one of five Anable sisters. She was born April 12, 1828.

[179] Nathaniel Parker (N. P.) Willis was the editor of *New Mirror*, which catapulted Emily into literary fame. He became a friend, mentor, and eventually a suitor.

[180] George Graham, editor of *Graham's Magazine*, took an interest in Emily Chubbuck as Fanny Forester and paid her with the unheard of sum of five dollars a page.

[181] John Inman was the editor of the *Commercial Advertiser* and the *Columbian Magazine*.

Inman[182]—Hoffman[182] has written for him—the *Columbian* has not come—I'd write a desperate letter to Inman—I feel just like having you do it.

Nothing more at present

AM   Source: American Baptist Historical Society, unrecorded.

Cynthia Sheldon to Emily E. Chubbuck, August 26, 1844—Utica

Dear Emily,

Anna M.[183] left for Schenectady on Friday morning,[184] and I suppose is now returning from Saratoga with the Doct.[185] and Urania.[186] As the plan was laid to spend the Sabbath there—I took the liberty to espay [sic] the condiments of your letter before I sent it on to her—that went in a box which I presume she received Sat'y morn'g for it went by the night train.

We received a very encouraging letter about dear Harriet[187] on Thursday, last, it was written in time to save many days anxiety—but delayed some where—Mary Adams[188] wrote. The fever had yielded and the physician pronounced her out of danger of a longer run—thought she would recover rapidly—she assured us too, that every possible attention was given her—we sometimes feel to leave it entirely—but deep solicitude will arise—we are in daily hopes of receiving one from Harriet.

I have found it necessary to arrange for Little Sarah Bennett[189] to come on with the children—on which account some arrangement with a proper person to room with must be made—the thought strikes me you have spoken of some one

---

[182] Charles Fenno Hoffman, a prominent literary figure in Philadelphia and New York, well known in literary circles as an exceptionally talented editor, poet, and writer.

[183] Anna Maria Anable was the niece of the Urania and Cynthia Sheldon, the daughter of Joseph and Alma Sheldon Anable; she was Emily's closest friend at the Utica Female Academy.

[184] As we have dated several undated letters around this sequence of events, it is important to know that Anna Maria left for Schenectady on August 23, 1844.

[185] Eliphalet Nott, president of Union College, married to Urania Sheldon Nott.

[186] Urania Sheldon Nott—a mentor, advisor, and friend to Emily—was the literary principal at the Utica Female Academy when Emily arrived in October 1840. In late summer 1842 Urania married Eliphalet Nott, the president of Union College in Schenectady NY.

[187] Harriet ("Hatty," "Hattie," or "Hat") Anable, one of the five Anable sisters. She had been teaching in a private residence in the New Orleans area.

[188] Mary Adams, a friend of Emily's while at the Utica Female Academy. Her letter to Emily in October 1845 was almost a whimsical piece of fantasy with literary pretensions. It would reflect a fairly close and whimsical relationship. A second letter in December 1845 was similar. The letters were written from New Orleans, and she spoke of Hatty Anable as being near to her. On January 29, 1849, Anna Maria Anable wrote: "Hatty says Mary Adams is going to marry Gardner Green of Norwich,—a very fine young man, of invention, fortune, piety and all that Mary's heart was sighed for." On July 8, 1850, Urania Sheldon Nott spoke of attending this wedding in New York.

[189] Sarah Bennett, born in Maulmain, Burmah, on June 15, 1837, was the daughter of Cephas and Stella Bennett, missionaries working with Adoniram Judson. The Bennetts were from the Utica area, and the girls in the family were sent to the Utica Female Academy and later to the Misses Anable's School in Philadelphia.

[sic] who had taught[190]—and wished to pursue studies here—I would give the board for an equivalent for such attention as necessary, the tuition could stand—a good Baptist girl—I am not certain, but the right one will come from another quarter—of course cannot empower you to close a bargain—still by the time you can reply after finding what can be done—I shall be ready to answer—It is a matter that gives me much concern. Miss Knealand is no better—their family are [sic] sick too, the children will all be here Thursday—you see I have specified one quality—your own judgment would guide me entirely on other qualifications for the charge.

One inkling of news—Jane Dorland is to be married this fall to Mr. Berry, Post Master at Whitesboro—a literary Batchelor [sic] of 45—Mrs. Doct. Thomas says it is capital—now what may we not expect. [Note: Inserted about the line: "She is entirely recovered."] Laura Wheeler and Mary[191] are riding now—poor Miss Holland has gone with them, she is still exceedingly gloomy—we look for her friend next week to take her home—I perceive you are inclined to keep up the steam of the goose quill—and conclude your brother Editors are put to their wits end by the power thereof—that wary Graham[192]—no wonder he is a bachelor.

Mr. Hawley[193] has gone to New York—no progress towards getting possession of the U. Club—O to be a man one week here.

Do tell me if you have returns from Willis[194]—or any other quarter—not a thing through the P.O. for you.

The girls are so much taken up with something or other in their absence as to forget me—not a word from any of them, only Sarah Bell.[195] They have had fine times in New York. She stays in Troy until the last of next week.

Hannah Hinckley is still at the [ ].

10 o'clock at night—Hannah has made her appearance this evening; Mr. Corey[196] and Mr. Wheelock have retired—and all the rest—I have learned Miss

---

[190] On this matter see Emily's letter to Sheldon of August 28, 1844 and September 2, 1844, and Sheldon's letters to Emily of August 31, and September 3, 1844.

[191] Mary Juliet Anable, daughter of Alma and Joseph Anable. For about a year in late 1846 through early 1848 she taught with her sister Hatty in New Orleans, and in 1849 she joined the staff of the Misses Anable's School in Philadelphia.

[192] George Graham, editor of *Graham's Magazine*, took an interest in Emily Chubbuck as Fanny Forester and paid her with the unheard of sum of five dollars a page. He recently had written to Emily and both Emily and Anna Maria had felt it to be out of line. See Anna Maria's letter of August 21, 1844.

[193] Horace H. Hawley married Jane Sheldon, the niece of Cynthia and Urania Sheldon, Hawley was a member of a publishing firm and also worked with Alexander Beebee in publishing the *Baptist Register*. Hawley was enormously helpful to Emily as she published her early stories and books. There are numerous references to his help and his generosity.

[194] Nathaniel Parker (N. P.) Willis was the editor of *New Mirror*, which catapulted Emily into literary fame. He became a friend, mentor, and eventually a suitor.

[195] Sarah Bell Wheeler was a teacher at the Utica Female Academy, and an intimate friend of Emily Chubbuck.

[196] Corey was the pastor of a Baptist church near the Utica Female Academy, and Sheldon and many of the girls from the academy worshiped there.

Cowles is ill of a cancer, know not what can be done—now think of going to see her Wed'y.

Much love to the family—yours truly,

C. Sheldon

Source: American Baptist Historical Society, AJ 26, no. 1269.

Emily E. Chubbuck to Cynthia Sheldon, August 28, 1844— Hamilton[197]

My dear Miss C.

I was glad to get your letter this morning I can assure you, for I had imagined all sorts of bad things about Hatty[198] and Fanny[199] and all the rest. It has quite relieved me. It seems that you did not go to Verona.[200] I hope A. M.[201] will have a good time and that she won't cheat me out of her visit. Your letter came in very good company—one from Mr. Graham.[202] It seems that his other letter[203] was surely an invitation to let him see me, and he thinks I *pretended* not to understand. He says, as a punishment, he will pay me only three dollars a page for what I have sent, but when he *knows me better* he will give more. There will be about seven pages in the two stories—one of them is to come out with an engraving. He says he will see "cousin 'Bel'"[204] at all counts sometime, so A. M. had better be setting her cap for the old bach. We shall have him up to U. I dare say. He declares moreover that the first pretty woman he gets engraved he will christen Cousin 'Bel'! I am terribly afraid A. M. will cut me out.

I got Willis'[205] letter last week Thursday[206]—a charming one. Not a bit like the heartless care-for-nothing fop we took him for, but right good and brotherly. I shall

---

[197] This letter has an addendum dated August 29, 1844.

[198] Harriet ("Hatty," "Hattie," or "Hat") Anable, one of the five Anable sisters. She had been teaching in a private residence in the New Orleans area. Recent letters had expressed concern for Hatty's health, as word had come of her suffering a high fever.

[199] Fanny Anable, one of five Anable sisters. She was born April 12, 1828.

[200] See Cynthia Sheldon's letter of August 20, to Emily. She had asked when Dr. Babcock would be at the Verona Springs—she wanted to consult with him about Fanny.

[201] Anna Maria Anable was the niece of the Urania and Cynthia Sheldon, the daughter of Joseph and Alma Sheldon Anable; she was Emily's closest friend at the Utica Female Academy.

[202] George Graham, editor of *Graham's Magazine*, took an interest in Emily Chubbuck as Fanny Forester and paid her with the unheard of sum of five dollars a page.

[203] See the letter of Anna Maria Anable to Emily Chubbuck dated August 21, 1844. In that letter she comments about the letter referenced here from George Graham to Emily. Of it she said: "From his quotation I should think you had been making some demonstration of affection to him." Then she said later: "I don't understand it—It seems as if all the men are determined to make love instead of do business with you."

[204] In her initial letters to N. P. Willis and the *New Mirror*, Emily had spoken of visiting New York with her "Cousin 'Bel,'" so Anna Maria as "Cousin 'Bel'" was taking on a life of its own.

[205] Nathaniel Parker (N. P.) Willis was the editor of *New Mirror*, which catapulted Emily into literary fame. He became a friend, mentor, and eventually a suitor.

never believe another bad story I hear about him. He says the lost letter was directed to "U. Fem. Acad."—strange what has become of it! He says, tho' they cannot pay me they will make my "name so coinable by praises" that I can "sell high to others."— precisely what I want, you know. He seems particularly anxious to know *what* I am like, and begs me to write for them as long as I can afford to— promises me the *New Mirror* together with all the Mirror Library gratis, and asks how he can *serve* or *please* me. He is evidently a little troubled about the age yet for he says if I am not *forty* I have a career before me. I have taken almost as great a fancy to him as I did to C. F. H.[207]

Inman[208] has come out this month with the "Demon of the Bush," the story he criticized.[209] It has however a very honourable position in the magazine—the first *story*—preceded [sic] only by a review and a piece of poetry. I am looking for a letter from him every day. You perceive, my dear Miss C. that I have had a tide of good luck; yet I can say with Haman, "All this availeth me nothing so long as"[210]— the money don't [sic] come. And not exactly that either—it does avail to keep me in passing good humour, but I do hope Inman will send me some money before the week is out.

Kate[211] has had the ague in her face and has got a cold and a little of most everything bad. I have had another attack of nervous head-ache—shall have to go to N. Y. again—don't you think so?

About S. Bennett[212]—the young lady that I have spoken about to you, altho' good and careful etc. is, I think not quite the thing for S. will need somebody to watch her every moment. I know a girl however that would be exactly the thing, and I think she would be glad to go. She is over thirty, has taught a great many years, knows all about taking care of children, and is just the most faithful disinterested creature in the world. She would be just like to mother to Sarah. She has some disagreeable ways, but there is a good heart at the bottom of all, and she is always cheerful and good-tempered—tidy, active and trusty. She is a thorough-going Baptist too, though not a church member. A few years ago she entertained a hope—I do not know whether she has given it up yet or not, but I should think not for she is always very much interested in religious things. She is teaching near the

---

[206] This would have been Willis's letter of August 20, 1844.

[207] Charles Fenno Hoffman, a prominent literary figure in Philadelphia and New York, well known in literary circles as an exceptionally talented editor, poet, and writer. Emily had started a correspondence with him as Laura Linden before he discovered that she was Fanny Forester.

[208] John Inman was the editor of the *Commercial Advertiser* and the *Columbian Magazine*.

[209] See the letter from John Inman to Emily E. Chubbuck dated July 14, 1844.

[210] This is a paraphrase from the Book of Esther (Esther 5:13) in the Old Testament.

[211] Sarah Catharine ("Kate," "Kit," or "Kitty") Chubbuck, Emily's older sister, born October 25, 1816.

[212] Sarah Bennett, born in Maulmain, Burmah, on June 15, 1837, was the daughter of Cephas and Stella Bennett, missionaries working with Adoniram Judson. The Bennetts were from the Utica area, and the girls in the family were sent to the Utica Female Academy and later to the Missess Anable's School in Philadelphia.

village now, and in the morning I shall go to see her. If she wishes to go, and I think she would be glad to, I hope you will make no other arrangement, for I have known this Miss Gilman[213] from the cradle and I should consider Sarah as well off under her care as that of her Aunt Persis.

Jane Dorland![214] Shocking! What next? *Don't* you think it is my turn? Do you keep Mr. Corey[215] with you? What makes his wife choose the vacation to go away in? I shall have to look into it a little.—Will you believe it, Miss C., I have been in a wagon but once since I came home. Father's[216] old horse gave out yesterday, and he is in a peck of troubles. "A horse! A horse! My kingdom for a horse!" I meant to have sent by H. Henderson (your knives etc.)[217] but she played me the slip this morning, so I must wait another opportunity. I didn't see much of H. for it rained constantly keeping the streets so wet that it was imprudent to go into them—hav'nt [sic] been beyond the gate since commencement day.—I think it will be very nice for us all to get together again, and the time will come now shortly but I *do* dread to think how near cold weather will be. Why I curl over the stove now. Please give a deal of love to grandpa, grandma,[218] Mrs. A[219] and all the rest, and believe me, my dear Miss C. as ever

Yours most aff'y
Emily

Source: Hanna family files.

---

[213] On August 26, 1844, Cynthia Sheldon wrote Emily asking if she knew of someone who could come to Utica and work with a young student who needed a caregiver. The young student was seven years old, the daughter of Cephas and Stella Bennett, missionaries to Burmah. Emily wrote back on August 28 to speak of a Miss Gilman, a teacher she had known, as a candidate. On August 29, Emily wrote that for family reasons Gilman felt that she could not take the position; at the end of the letter Emily added a postscript saying that Miss Gilman had changed her mind, and would in fact accept the position if it were offered to her. Emily wrote more on September 2, 1845, and on September 3, 1845 Sheldon wrote to Emily to say that she had decided in favor of Miss Gilman. Emily wrote a note to Miss Gilman on the letter she had received from Sheldon, and passed it on. In a letter written April 15, 1845, Anna Maria is talking of the girls dispersing as the term ended, and she noted that "the stage has come for Miss Gilman" and Miss Gilman was delivering a note to Emily's sister Catharine Chubbuck.

[214] In a previous letter (August 26, 1844), Sheldon had mention to Emily that Jane Dorland was to be married.

[215] Corey, the local Baptist pastor, was staying with Sheldon at the academy because his wife and children had taken a trip. See Cynthia Sheldon's letter to Emily of August 26, 1844.

[216] Charles Chubbuck, Emily's father. Though he held varying positions over the years, he failed at most of them. With the purchase of the house for them, Emily was to continue as a significant financial contributor to the support of the family.

[217] On August 7, 1844, in a letter to Anna Maria Anable, Emily had asked C. and Anna Maria to take on a "queer commission"—that of purchasing a dozen knives and forks for their common use.

[218] Deacon Asa and Isabell Low Sheldon, parents of Cynthia Sheldon, Urania Sheldon Nott, and Alma Sheldon Anable.

[219] Alma Sheldon Anable, sister of Cynthia Sheldon and Urania Sheldon Nott, mother of Anna Maria Anable.

Emily E. Chubbuck to Cynthia Sheldon, August 29, 1844[220]

I went to see Miss G.[221] this morning, and tho' she wants to go to U. very much she cannot. She feels obliged to teach this winter—her mother is a widow and her sister very much out of health. I am very much disappointed for last spring she asked me about going and I tho't you would not like to take her she is so old. I do not know of anybody that would be equal to her. She is very anxious for a friend of hers, a cousin of Mrs. Raymond, to get the place, but I do not know her, and so of course could not recommend her.

When is A. M.[222] expected home? I do wish she would show her face this way—I have just finished a long story for Willis[223] which is pretty much all I have done since I came home. Don't you think I am having plenty of relaxation?—All send love to which is added that of Emily.

Miss Gilman[224] has just been up here. She thinks she will go if you conclude to want her, tho' she can't say certainly till she sees her friends. I hope you will want her. Write soon.

Source: Hanna family files.

Cynthia Sheldon to Emil E. Chubbuck, August 31, 1844

Dear Emily

Your good long letter came yesterday[225]—many thanks for it and good wishes attend your bachelor squibs.

I have but a moment to say we are well—a letter from dear Harriet's[226] pen quite silences anxiety there—Our long gone William[227] appeared among us two

---

[220] This letter is an addendum to a letter written by Emily Chubbuck to Cynthia Sheldon, dated August 28, 1844.

[221] Miss Gilman, a teacher Emily had known who was considering being a caregiver for the seven year old daughter of Cephas and Stella Bennett.

[222] Anna Maria Anable was the niece of the Urania and Cynthia Sheldon, the daughter of Joseph and Alma Sheldon Anable; she was Emily's closest friend at the Utica Female Academy.

[223] Nathaniel Parker (N. P.) Willis was the editor of New Mirror, which catapulted Emily into literary fame. He became a friend, mentor, and eventually a suitor.

[224] On August 26, 1844, Cynthia Sheldon wrote Emily asking if she knew of someone who come to Utica and work with a young student who needed a caregiver. The young student was seven years old, the daughter of Cephas and Stella Bennett, missionaries to Burmah. Emily wrote back on August 28 to speak of a Miss Gilman, a teacher she had known, as a candidate. On August 29, Emily wrote that for family reasons Gilman felt that she could not take the position; at the end of the letter Emily added a postscript saying that Miss Gilman had changed her mind, and would in fact accept the position if it were offered to her. Emily wrote more on September 2, 1845, and on September 3, 1845 Sheldon wrote to Emily to say that she had decided in favor of Miss Gilman. Emily wrote a note to Miss Gilman on the letter she had received from Sheldon, and passed it on. In a letter written April 15, 1845, Anna Maria is talking of the girls dispersing as the term ended, and she noted that "the stage has come for Miss Gilman" and Miss Gilman was delivering a note to Emily's sister Catharine Chubbuck.

[225] See the letters of Emily Chubbuck to Cynthia Sheldon dated August 28, 1844 and August 29, 1844.

[226] Harriet ("Hatty," "Hattie," or "Hat") Anable, one of the five Anable sisters. She had been teaching in a private residence in the New Orleans area. There had been recent concern as friends had written of Hatty down with a serious fever.

[227] Born on November 6, 1816 in Albany NY, William Stewart Anable was the son of Joseph and Alma Sheldon Anable. In an August 31, 1844 letter, Cynthia Sheldon reported to Emily that William had returned home, having "doff'd his sailor garb for

days since—he is the same good boy too—doff'd his sailor garb for age—in good health—a determination to be a merchant of first stamp if fortune favors him—he has gone to the Spring[228] for Fanny[229]—Molly and Laura went with Mr. Williams yesterday to Remsen—They will all pour in the next hour probably—Caroline Reynolds[230] left here this aft'n for Waterville School—I think Anna M.[231] will come home with Sarah Bell[232] next Friday—she will want to see William so much—you had best come too I think—we shall be ready. I hardly know what to say about Miss Gilman[233]—she seems too old to study—how long would she wish to remain and what studies pursue—A very fine girl of twenty wishes the place very much—she is an educated English girl—pious—wishes to take ornamental branches—If Miss Gilman is not intending to stay two terms at least and pay for something more than English studies I should not like to engage—I will leave it with you to ascertain—do send a letter so I may have it Tuesday morn'g—as Miss Lowell is to come in on that day for an answer—

Much love to all
Yours truly

C. Sheldon

Source: American Baptist Historical Society, AJ 26, no. 1273.

---

age." He married Olivia Williams on September 24, 1846, according to a letter written September 27 by Anna Maria Anable. They moved to Sheboygan, Wisconsin, where William opened a store. William died February 9, 1863, in Virginia CA.

[228] Fanny Anable had been at Verona Springs for her health. Sheldon had written several letters to Emily to see if she could connect with a Dr. Babcock, who was from Hamilton, but who went often to the Springs.

[229] Fanny Anable, one of five Anable sisters. She was born April 12, 1828.

[230] Caroline Reynolds, one of Emily's friends at the Utica Female Academy. Caroline Reynolds was at the Utica Female Academy with Emily—on August 19, 1841 she added to a letter written by Cynthia Sheldon, stating that in Emily's absence she had taken over her room. In a September 1842 letter she was teaching school in Port Byron, with thirty-five scholars. In a June 25, 1842 letter, Emily wrote to Catharine that "Caroline is too mean and hateful to give me a minute's peace. She is decidedly the most disagreeable thing that I ever saw, but one thing you may be assured, your amiable sister is not quite a martyr for nothing, and can make the [ ] of others somewhat uncomfortable when her own is stuck full of thorns. This I imagine Car. has found out for she has not been ten minutes in the room since breakfast. Good!"

[231] Anna Maria Anable was the niece of the Urania and Cynthia Sheldon, the daughter of Joseph and Alma Sheldon Anable; she was Emily's closest friend at the Utica Female Academy.

[232] Sarah Bell Wheeler was a teacher at the Utica Female Academy, and an intimate friend of Emily Chubbuck.

[233] Gilman, a teacher Emily had known who was considering being a caregiver at the Utica Female Academy for the daughter of Cephas and Stella Bennett.

Anna Maria Anable to Emily E. Chubbuck, September 2, 1844[234]

Dear Nem[235]

I am just as busy as I can be—Mother[236] has gone off to S.[237] this morning and on the way to the cars who should come up but Mrs. Jackson and children—promised to see her this afternoon, but met Brayton on the way to find me to go out to Trenton Falls this afternoon—a regular old fashioned frolic—all the old busksters [sic] and old maids in town going—I hav'nt [sic] got a thing to wear—but n' *importe*—I heard in Cherry Valley I had a faultless figure—so if worse comes to worst I'll sport *that*.

Mary Adams[238] came back with Jimmy[239] Saturday—the day I returned—I haven't seen Jimmy but I have seen his darling brother John from New York.

I am making my intention to get Miss Eddy out to Trenton—but she don't know [sic] any of these friends and I'm afraid I shall have to give it up. She's a charming girl, and sends a great deal of love to you—I have heaps of things to say to you—and I'll come out Thursday *I guess*. Aunt C.[240] is painting and varnishing and she wants me to go—so she can have full swing—

I have a plan in my head for you to go to St. Augustine this winter. Don't say you won't till you hear. What do you hear from your papa? Is he a darling or is he a naughty man?[241] You know my test.

You can't think how I've missed you—I have been all living alone in this great hall.

There's the dinner bell. Write and tell me if you'd rather I would not come Thursday. I've an ugly swelled lip to go out to Trenton with—interesting is not it? Never mind—Jimmy told Mary Adams I had the most beautiful hands he ever saw!!! Hurrah for Jimmy!

I want to know what Isaiah said and what you have been about.

---

[234] This letter is undated. Someone has written "Aug. 26" on it. The letter itself says it was written on a Monday Morning; the only year in this time period that August 26 was on a Monday was 1844, so accordingly we place it there. However, an August 26 letter from Cynthia Sheldon has Anna Maria in Schenectady NY with Dr. and Mrs. Nott. So we have moved this ahead one week to September 2, 1844.

[235] "Nem" or "Nemmy" was a name of endearment given to Emily by a small group of her intimate friends at the Utica Female Academy. Anna Maria Anable was "Ninny."

[236] Alma Sheldon Anable, sister of Cynthia Sheldon and Urania Sheldon Nott.

[237] Schenectady NY, where Urania Sheldon Nott lived.

[238] Mary Adams, a friend of Emily's while at the Utica Female Academy. She came from New Orleans.

[239] Jimmy Williams, often mentioned in Anna Maria Anable's letters, usually just as "Jimmy."

[240] Miss Cynthia Sheldon was the administrative and finance manager of the Utica Female Academy. She was a mentor, advisor, and friend to Emily, and she was the aunt of Anna Maria Anable.

[241] The reference here is not to Emily's father, Charles Chubbuck; rather it is a play on either George Graham of *Graham's Magazine*, or N. P. Willis of the *New Mirror*, two of the literary "fathers" in Emily's life at that moment. See also the letter of Anna Maria Anable to Emily Chubbuck dated August 21, 1844; in that letter recent comments by George Graham had been called into question by Anna Maria, who thought that they were most inappropriate. In the months to come "papa" clearly referred to N. P. Willis.

Love to your Mother[242] and Kate.[243]

From this little Ninny[244]

Source: American Baptist Historical Society, AJ 23, no. 1142.

Emily E. Chubbuck to Cynthia Sheldon, September 2, 1844[245]

My dear Miss C.

Yours of Sat. eve was rec'd this morning. You seem to be having good luck too. I am rejoiced about Hatty[246] and Wm[247] both. Mr. Williams has taken to Molly then—tell Nelly Bennett[248] to look out—it is her turn next.—Miss Gilman[249] is certainly very old to study, and I only recommended her as being the best of anybody in the world with children. However, I suppose she intends to teach as long as she lives and so would like to prepare. She attended school here a year ago. She wants to take French and Drawing—what else she has not decided. Would like to stay till spring—two terms—and have her bills stand till she can pay them.[250] Now Miss C.[251] you will know how to decide the business, for you have seen one young lady and have an exact portrait of the other, but as soon as you do decide, please write me. Miss. G. is anxious to know.

C. Cobb is to be married on Thurs. and I am in a peck of botherations about it because I hav'nt [sic] got anything to wear. I understand that the wedding is to be a smasher.—Can't come back till after the Whig map meeting night Monday 'cause

---

[242] Lavinia Richards Chubbuck, Emily's mother, was born June 1, 1875, in Goffstown NH, the eldest of thirteen children. She married Charles Chubbuck on November 17. 1805. They were the parents of seven children.

[243] Sarah Catharine ("Kate," "Kit," or "Kitty") Chubbuck, Emily's older sister, born October 25, 1816.

[244] Ninny was a name of endearment for Anna Maria Anable. Emily was Nemmy.

[245] This letter is undated. It is referenced, however, to Emily's letter to Sheldon which she wrote on Thursday, August 28, 1844. Miss Sheldon replied to it on Saturday, a letter which Emily received on Monday, September 2, and this is her reply to it. Sheldon is looking for someone to take care of a child, and Emily knew a Miss Gilman who could not only do the job, but would benefit from the educational opportunity at the academy, even as Emily had benefited.

[246] Harriet ("Hatty," "Hattie," or "Hat") Anable, one of the five Anable sisters. She had been teaching in a private residence in the New Orleans area. Recently Hatty had been ill with a fever and the family had been concerned.

[247] William Stewart Anable was the son of Joseph and Alma Sheldon Anable.

[248] Nelly Bennett was the daughter of Cephas and Stella Bennett, missionaries to Burmah. She was one of seven children, five of them girls. She was often mentioned in the letters from Cynthia Sheldon and Anna Maria Anable as several of the Bennett girls were, at different times, at the Utica Female Academy, and then the Misses Anable's School in Philadelphia.

[249] Miss Gilman, a teacher Emily had known who was considering being a caregiver for the daughter of Cephas and Stella Bennett at the Utica Female Academy.

[250] This arrangement of deferred payment is exactly what was offered to Emily Chubbuck when she came to the Utica Female Academy in fall 1840.

[251] Miss Cynthia Sheldon was the administrative and finance manager of the Utica Female Academy. She was a mentor, advisor, and friend to Emily.

why Greely is to be here and I want to hear him for Jane.[252]—Love to everybody that will accept of it. In great haste

Yours most truly

E. E. Chubbuck

Source: Hanna family files.

Cynthia Sheldon to Emily E. Chubbuck, September 3, 1844—Utica[253]

Dear Emily

Yours came this aft'n,[254] and I am happy to decide in favor of Miss Gilman[255]—hoping she is just the one—did I tell you we should wish her attention to their clothes on Saturday—if not I wish you to explain to her—our object in this arrangement is to be relieved—and some expense of much of the sewing for them—I trust no unreasonable demands will be made on her—a long letter to Mr. and Mrs. Bennett[256] has taken up my time—The evening is gone—I must answer a letter received from Lydia[257] this aft'n—applications for credit—write to Urania[258] too—as I find it necessary to make Miss Cowles a call to morrow—her health is poor—and from what I can learn about it think she will not come back—cannot rest on uncertainty longer—the main meeting today has made "an impression." Mr. W has been in to *flounce*—all well—do come Tuesday

Yours truly

C. Sheldon

Written in the top margin of the letter in Emily Chubbuck's handwriting—obviously addressed to Miss Gilman: "The letter below was rec'd this morning—I

---

[252] Jane Kelly was Emily Chubbuck's friend at the Utica Female Academy. Following the deparure of Mr. and Mrs. Nichols, Jane became the literary principal in eary 1844. Then with the departure of Cynthia Sheldon to Philadelphia in fall 1848, she became "headmistress."

[253] As soon as Emily received this letter from Cynthia Sheldon, she forwarded it to Miss Gilman; her added note, written in the top margin of Miss Sheldon's letter, is to be found below.

[254] See the letter to Cynthia Sheldon from Emily E. Chubbuck, dated September 2, 1844.

[255] Miss Gilman, a teacher Emily had known who was considering being a caregiver for the daughter of Cephas and Stella Bennett at the Utica Female Academy.

[256] Cephas and Stella Bennett, missionaries to Burmah.

[257] Lydia Lillybridge was one of Emily's closest friends at the Utica Female Academy. When Emily made the decision to go to Burmah with Adoniram Judson as a missionary, Lydia offered to go with them, and with Emily speaking to Adoniram Judson and to Dr. Solomon Peck and the Board of American Baptist missionary Union of her extraordinary abilities, she was commissioned to go with them, in spite of the fact that she remained single. Always independent and outspoken, unafraid to cause ripples in the missionary community, Lydia was to serve on the mission field for twenty-eight years. She married missionary Thomas Simons in May 1851. See the timeline on the life and service of Lydia Lillybridge Simons in vol. 1.

[258] Urania Sheldon Nott—a mentor, advisor, and friend to Emily—was the literary principal at the Utica Female Academy when Emily arrived in October 1840. In late summer 1842 Urania married Eliphalet Nott, the president of Union College in Schenectady NY

had a letter of farther inquiry about you on Mond. and ventured to say (as she required it) that you would stay two terms. I could not get down to see you. I also told her that you would take French and Drawing. What do you conclude? E. E. C."

Source: American Baptist Historical Society, AJ 26, no. 1272.

Nathaniel Parker Willis to Emily E. Chubbuck, September 7, 1844—New York City[259]

Your beautiful story, kindest of Fannies,[260] is already in type, and it is time my thanks were on the way to you. The *Mirror* reflects most pleasurably from and about you, and "we" plume ourselves not a little on having been selected by you as your literary god-father. As to *my* "making a world," I could never have made it except out of your genius, and, to that same fire within you I beg to acknowledge no inconsiderable debt. I think, by the way, that you had better be looking forward to enlarged reputation, and while you put an extra drop of Macassar [sic] on your organ of *hope*, put two on your organ of painstaking and caution. The time is not very far off when you will "have a call" to collect these tales into a volume, and it will save trouble to polish while the iron is hot. You are very much more gifted than you think, dear Fanny, (I may "dear" your *nom de guerre*) and pray, bind yourself to nothing, not even to a husband, if there be hindrance in it. I was talking to Mrs. Ellett about you a day or two ago, and she quite glorifies you.

Give my kindest remembrance to our common friend, Mrs. Kirkland,[261] when you return to Utica, and believe me,

Yours as faithfully as admiringly,

N. P. Willis

I enclose you the letter of a lady (probably a fictitious signature) who has a great deal to say about you. I have another, just received, written mostly to speculate about Fanny. F.

Source: A. C. Kendrick, *The Life and Letters of Mrs. Emily C. Judson*, 104–105; Hanna family files.

---

[259] This letter is undated. Emily has recorded on the address page that this was the third letter from N. P. Willis, so we have placed it approximately in the middle of his August 20, 1844 letter, and his September 27, 1844 letter.
[260] Fanny Forester, Emily Chubbuck's *nom de plume*.
[261] Mrs. Charles Kirkland, friend of Anna Maria Anable, N. P. Willis, and Emily Chubbuck.

Anna Maria Anable to Emily E. Chubbuck, September 11, 1844[262]

Dear Nemmy[263]

I have been thinking of you all the day long and tho' I know you were riding off grandely [sic] with your little [ ] I could not get your weeping image out of my mind. I have lost all my self-complacency. I shall never again flatter myself that my presence will cure an invalid or drive away the "blues." The truth is that I felt savagely blue myself this morning and would not be content till I had infected someone else, and who should I light upon as a fit subject for contagion but you, poor little innocent who have not enough real trouble of your own but should have all sorts of imaginary nonsense stuck in your eye. O, how I hated to come away this morning. Hamilton looked to me like a perfect paradise—and now that I have got home and every thing [sic] looks so lonesome—it seems still more so. You don't know how forlorn the room seems without any Nemmy in it; and I can't bear to go to bed—come back just as soon as ever you can won't you? There's a darling!

Jimmy[264] made me a short-call this morning.

Written along the left margin of the page: "Did you have a nice time at the wedding?"   Source: American Baptist Historical Society, AJ 23, no. 1141.

Urania Sheldon Nott to Emily E. Chubbuck and Anna Maria Anable, September 18, 1844[265]

Dear Anna M. and Emily,

I am very glad to hear that you are joint occupants of my old home, and hope that your contiguity will prove a benefit to both of you. Take care that you don't make fools of each other. The latest romance in both of you has been rapidly developed under the rays of popular admiration. You [Note: "Anna M" is inserted above the line.] perhaps will wonder how you could be affected by what you hear so indirectly [ ], but I will tell you when I see you. What I never wanted more than now. So be serious dear girls—you are not aware perhaps so much as I am, how watchful the world is, that is the Magazine readers, *and your friends*, of the changes that pop-

---

[262] This letter is undated. Anna Maria spoke in a September 2, 1844 letter, that she would be coming to visit Emily. By September 18, 1844, Emily was back in Utica at the academy. September 11 is the Wednesday (written on the letter) between those dates.

[263] "Nem" or "Nemmy" was a name of endearment given to Emily by a small group of her intimate friends at the Utica Female Academy. Anna Maria Anable was "Ninny."

[264] Jimmy Williams, often mentioned in Anna Maria Anable's letters, usually just as "Jimmy."

[265] Knowing the high spirits of Emily E. Chubbuck and Anna Maria Anable, especially at this time in their lives—Fanny Forester and Cousin 'Bel'—we wonder how their conversation might have turned as they sat together in their rooms at the Utica Female Academy and read this very stern letter from Emily's mentor and Anna Maria's Aunt.

ularity may make in you—and I want you to be still more watchful yourselves. I want to have a long talk with you both, alone in your own room, and think that I shall before very long be with you, in the mean time be very prudent. Talk very little about Willis[266] and Graham[267] and other writers of the day [Note: "To others, or even to each other" is inserted above the line.] or about your own affairs to others,

You dear Emily are in great danger of thinking too highly of the adulation that you have rece'd—Do not be offended with me—I am as sensitive to your reputation as a writer and authoress as if it were my own—and I do not want to see you spoiled by flattery—I do not know as I shall dare send this but you are both too dear to me, and girls of too much good sense to allow me to hesitate to give you a word of caution which perhaps may be unneeded.

With much affection

I am your Aunt Urania

Source: American Baptist Historical Society, AJ 25, no. 1234.

The Reverend Elon B. Galusha[268] to Emily E. Chubbuck, September 22, 1844[269]

Dear Fanny[270]

What else can I call you?—for you are one of those of whom somebody has said,

> None know thee but to love thee

---

[266] Nathaniel Parker (N. P.) Willis, along with George "General" Morris, was the editor of the *New Mirror*, a prominent literary magazine in New York. His "discovery" of Emily in the June 8, 1844 edition of the *New Mirror* catapulted her into literary fame and enabled her to command the highest prices for her articles and stories from the major magazines of that period. It was to begin a new and glorious chapter in her life. He was to become over the next two years her friend—her mentor—her confidant. His black-bordered letter of March 21, 1846, made it abundantly clear that her engagement to Adoniram Judson had come as a "death blow," and that he had expected to marry Emily upon his return that month from England. He later returned several of her letters to Emily to demonstrate to her, lest she had forgotten, why he had felt right in that expectation. In vol. 1 there is a timeline which presents in some detail the substance of their developing relationship, all from the letters which Willis had written to Emily. When she received her letters back from Willis, she had destroyed them, feeling that they would cast a negative shadow on her life, and because of that, the life and ministry of Adoniram Judson.

[267] George Graham, editor of *Graham's Magazine*, took an interest in Emily Chubbuck as Fanny Forester and paid her with the unheard of sum of five dollars a page.

[268] Elon B. Galusha, son of Governor Jonas Galusha of Vermont, was ordained to the Christian ministry at a young age and spent many years at the town of Whitesborough, which was near Utica. Afterwards Galusha served in Utica, which would have put him in the social circles of the Utica Female Academy and Emily E. Chubbuck. According to the *Baptist Encyclopaedia*, "He was one of the most unselfish and devout of Christians. He was a father and a leader in Israel, whose memory has a blessed fragrance." In a short letter written to Fanny Forester in September 1844, he quoted Hallock, "None know thee but to love thee/ Nor named thee but to praise."

[269] This letter is undated. Because he addresses Emily as "Fanny," we place it in September 1844, several months after her "Fanny Forester" piece appeared in the *New Mirror*.

[270] Fanny Forester, Emily Chubbuck's *nom de plume*. In the publication of the *Memoir of Sarah Judson*, it is spelled "Forrester."

Nor named thee but to praise.[271]

I have stolen this little sheet from my sisters [sic] portfolio to tell you that a protracted "cabinet council" deprives me of the pleasure of seeing you again before I leave town.

Allow me to assure you that if I can serve you in any way, at any time, it will afford me infinite pleasure. Call upon me without the least hesitation and count me one of your best friends. I never knew your worth till yesterday, much as I have loved the children of your fancy.

Yours truly,

E. B. Galusha   Source: American Baptist Historical Society, AJ 24, no. 1202.

George R. Graham to Emily E. Chubbuck, September 23, 1844—Philadelphia

Fanny Forester[272] *won't let me print* a word at three dollars a page[273] and will make a *fortune* by her pen and all because she has been spoiled by praise!

Shall I at the risk of being ungallant tell her that praise is a very *cheap* sort of pay and not half as jingling as a little money?[274] Why I would praise her to the end of the chapter and think her the most available of all contributors. But *Emily Chubbuck* won't do—"Fanny Forester" must write for *fame* [ ], before she cheapens her literature, under fictitious names—the first perhaps of her pen, must be given to that *name* if she would win praise from *a wide world of readers*. Therefore she cannot write for "Graham" under any other name

Now for "business." If I loved "Fanny Forester" as a writer, and she would listen to me as one, I would tell her that a *"happy hearted [ ] loving"* woman commits a sort of suicide when she adopts literature as *a profession*, unless driven to it by circumstances, which I am happy to know from Fanny Forester's pen she does not feel.

---

[271] The quote is lines from "On The Death of Joseph Rodman Drake," written by Fritz-Green Hallock (1790–1867).

[272] Fanny Forester, Emily Chubbuck's *nom de plume*.

[273] On August 28, 1844, Emily had written to Cynthia Sheldon, to say that she had recently received a letter from George Graham. In the letter Mr. Graham had stated that he would pay her no more than three dollars a page, at least "until he gets to know me better." Apparently Emily had responded quickly and forthrightly.

[274] This statement is a direct shot at the arrangement that Fanny Forester had with the *New Mirror* and its editor N. P. Willis. Willis was promoting Emily very strongly on the pages of the *New Mirror* and said that his publication would make her "coinable," that is, able to command higher prices from other magazines because of her fame. At the same time, the *New Mirror* was not able to pay for any articles, and Emily was writing them gratis. John Inman of the *Columbian* also told Emily very directly, in his letter of November 19, 1844, that while they would meet her expectations at five dollars a page, they felt it most inconsiderate that she would write for Willis for nothing.

No true and lovable woman should feel the cold criticism of the world—it chills and darkens both heart and brain. If any body [sic] talks to you about fortunes, in America from authorship, respect their *intentions* but doubt their judgment.

Of the magazine writers Willis[275] and Miss Leslie[276] have been and are the best paid. Yet where is the fortune of either? It is so easy to advise yet so hard to advise right.

I think I know as much about literature—its ups and downs—as any one in this country, and I do not know an instance in which a periodical writer has made more than a competence and yet some. T. S. H. [ ] and W. W. Herbert and others—have written their half dozen articles per month. Even in England the guinea per page was *Scots pay*, and is now Baldwin's, and [ ] "Young American" $5 per page is the *outside* price for most magazines. I committed the "indiscretion" common to young publishers as of paying more to Willis and others, but in my wildest dreams of liberality I never did adopt—I never *could* have adopted—the price as a system.

To the point however I will give you the five dollars per page and if we cannot agree you have all my advice *gratis* none the worse for being candid through it. Why be less agreeable.

Respectfully

George R. Graham.

Source: American Baptist Historical Society, AJ 24, no. 1193.

Emily E. Chubbuck to J. Walker Chubbuck, September 24, 1844—Utica

A letter you shall have my very dear brother[277] and that as fast as I can write it. It is shameful that I have not answered you before (I have rec'd only one) but if you could know how busy my pen is from morning till night you never would blame me for negligence. I have been home spending my vacation—returned last week—had a nice time and left the people as well as usual. Katie[278] teaches drawing and guitar

---

[275] Nathaniel Parker (N. P.) Willis was the editor of *New Mirror*, which catapulted Emily into literary fame. He became a friend, mentor, and eventually a suitor.

[276] In 1843, *Leslie's Magazine* was published. Named for the sister-in-law of one of the publishers, it featured literature and fashion for women. It would include contributions by Lydia Huntley Sigourney, Park Benjamin, and Henry Wadsworth Longfellow. The name changed to *Ladies' Magazine* (1844) and *Arthur's Ladies' Magazine* (1845) before the magazine merged with *Godey's Lady's Book* (1846).

[277] John Walker Chubbuck, Emily's older brother who ran a newspaper in the Wisconsin Territory. Though he regularly sent copies of the paper to Emily, she often reminded him that a paper was not a substitute for a real letter and that his family longed to hear a personal word from him.

[278] Sarah Catharine ("Kate," "Kit," or "Kitty") Chubbuck, Emily's older sister, born October 25, 1816.

music a little—not enough to amount to much. As for Wallace[279]—he's a *quiet genius*. I don't know whether he will ever amount to anything or not. He has a deal of talent but he is almost as lazy as Sin. He lives at home, takes care of the garden, and goes to school some—in the spring he intends entering a law-office. He is a great stump orator about these days and hurrahs for Polk in his sleep. They had all got it into their heads that you will come home this fall—why don't you come?

Have you seen any of the *Columbian Magazines*? I have written three stories for it at four dollars per page. I went to New York last spring and spent a most delightful fortnight. Mr. Inman,[280] the editor, a very pleasant, whole-souled man, by the way, called upon me. Do you get the weekly *New Mirror*? Lest you do not I will send you the last to let you know *what fun I am having with N. P. Willis.*[281] The letter signed "a nameless one" is written by a gentleman I am sure—C. Fenno Hoffman,[282] a poet and novelist. He saw me last spring with a blue balzarine on, and I suspect he wants to let me know that he sees through my mask. I commenced writing for Willis as Fanny Forester[283] last June about the tenth No. of the *Mirror* I think—the first letter is signed only Fanny. Since then there had been scarcely a *Mirror* without something about me in it. Get the back numbers and then tell me if you don't think I am having fun.

As for money, I get none of that from Willis, but thro' his influence I expect to get with Graham[284] and Godey[285] and then I hope to make something. I shall not write any more books—it is unprofitable.[286] My place is about half paid for but I am terribly in debt[287]—all of three hundred dollars I dare say. Kate came out here and spent five or six weeks with me last summer. Do you know that father[288] has got to be an abolitionist? He will go the Birney ticket this fall.

[279] William Wallace Chubbuck, Emily's younger brother, born January 1, 1824.

[280] John Inman was the editor of the *Commercial Advertiser* and the *Columbian Magazine*.

[281] Nathaniel Parker (N. P.) Willis was the editor of *New Mirror*, the magazine that catapulted Emily into literary fame. He became a friend, mentor, and eventually a suitor.

[282] Charles Fenno Hoffman, a prominent literary figure in Philadelphia and New York, well known in literary circles as an exceptionally talented editor, poet, and writer. Emily had started a correspondence with him as Laura Linden before he discovered that she was Fanny Forester.

[283] Fanny Forester, Emily Chubbuck's *nom de plume*.

[284] George Graham, editor of *Graham's Magazine*, took an interest in Emily Chubbuck as Fanny Forester and paid her with the unheard of sum of five dollars a page.

[285] Louis A. Godey, the founder and publisher of *Godey's Lady's Book*. This was a publication combining poetry, articles or stories, and engravings (often of elegant fashions).

[286] For *John Frink*, Emily earned $26.50 for seventy-three pages. For the same amount of magazine writing at five dollars a page, she would have earned $365.

[287] In a September 16, 1841 letter to her brother Walker, Emily had told him that she had purchased a home for her parents on Broad Street in Hamilton Village. She was able to do this from the proceeds of her writing. Emily had paid four hundred dollars for the home, payable in four payments over four years, and she was to often mention this debt, and the pressure it put upon her for continued writing, and the income derived from it. She also was paying for some tuition debt as Catharine spent another term at the Utica Female Academy that summer. She also had been there for two terms beginning in fall 1841.

[288] Charles Chubbuck, Emily's father. Though he held varying positions over the years, he failed at most of them. With the purchase of the house for them, Emily was to continue as a significant financial contributor to the support of the family.

Walker, do you want me to tell you anything of Ben?[289] He is a living *canker-worm* to all of us. What do you think he has been about now? Why stealing a cow, for which he is confined in jail—there to remain till January next. He is somewhere in the western part of the state. Ann has returned to Morrisville with her two children. It is too mortifying for anything—and I do pity Katie. Where he will go when he gets clear again I don't know—hope he won't come home, nor make tracks your way.

Do write me as soon as you can. You ought not to ask an answer to all of your letters for you have more leisure than I and might write every month. Tell me all about your affairs the people you live with etc. and give my love to every body [sic] that you love. Be a good boy and don't forget your very loving sister,

Emily E. Chubbuck

Source: Jerome Walker Chubbuck Collection, Wisconsin Historical Society Archives, Madison, WI.

Nathaniel Parker Willis to Emily E. Chubbuck, September 26, 1844—New York City[290]

Your womanly and natural letter is full of charm for me, my friend, and I assure you, I see, through its simple earnestness and modesty, a heart worth treating with respect and delicacy. I wish I could talk with you an hour, instead of writing; for writing letters to *me* is like the postman's walking for pleasure. It is the drop too much. Briefly let me offer you my friendship, and a vow [Note: In the original there is a space here equal to about four lines, and in the middle of that space Mr. Willis has drawn a cross.] to serve you and your reputation to the best of my means and ability. Mrs. Willis, who sits by me, offers you her admiring friendship also, and now to business. The *Mirror* of this week will explain to you why, with all our success, we are under the necessity of starting a new paper, requiring great outlay, and impoverishing us, for a year at least, most uncomfortably. Therefore, and *therefore only*, we do not employ you at once, and give you more than any other writer could get from us; for you are more readable than any female writer in this country. We consider ourselves your debtor, however, and shall, with our first emergence from

---

[289] Emily's older brother Benjamin or "Ben," was born March 25, 1809. In the biography she wrote for Adoniram Judson in 1846, Emily wrote that as a young boy, Ben sustained some kind of brain inflammation, which seemed to seriously impair his judgment and behavior. See Emily's letter of February 18, 1838, for some very sharp comments on Ben. Then, on April 2, 1839, Emily wrote to her brother Walker that Ben had been sent to state prison for stealing a horse, blanket, and saddle. Later correspondence had litanies of such problems—stealing a cow, difficulties holding jobs, problems with his marriage, situations exacerbated by character flaws. He died in September 1846, shortly after Emily had left for Burmah.

[290] On the address page, in Emily Chubbuck's handwriting: "N. P. Willis Esq. Sept. 27. 1844. No. 4." September 27 was the date that Willis mailed the letter (that is the postmark)—but Thursday evening would have been September 26.

this new plunge, give some signs to that effect. Thus much, though you claim no money, it was necessary for me to say.[291]

As to your *one vein* of writing, you are under a very natural delusion. The fog clears up as you go along, and you will go on writing charmingly for twenty years. Mrs. Lyman writes that you are "twenty three[292]—black eyed, and very pretty." No need either of painting the dark side. The world is full of beauty. Dismiss the attempt to weigh your to-morrows, and believe this, *with me*, that you have a fame before you. If I were "in the market," I would marry you on speculation to-morrow, as a girl with an unquestionable dowry—let alone your "black eyes."

I shall go on glorifying you in our new daily paper, until the magazine people give you fifty dollars an article, and meantime if you have any thing [sic] you can not sell (particularly a short story, or essay, or sketch of character), let us have it for the *Evening Mirror*, and we will give you its value in some shape. Do not waste time or labor, however, even upon us, but write a novel little by little. You *can*!

I do not know who the "nameless one" is, but I will send you the MS and that of "Rosalie." The women all love you.

I shall be able to write to you more comprehensibly as to what we want from you, in a month or more—when our daily paper gets under way.

I have no more time (for less than twelve thousand pair of eyes), and must stop writing to one pair only-black though they be.

Yours, with very sincere, friendship,

N. P. Willis

Source: A. C. Kendrick, *The Life and Letters of Mrs. Emily C. Judson*, 105–106; Hanna family files.

B. R. Loxley to Emily E. Chubbuck, September 30, 1844—Philadelphia

Dear Sister,

Yours of 17th was duly received and as our Cor. Secy is absent I will have to reply. *John Frink* was published as I stated in my last; it came from the Press in March and it has been forgotten by Br Peck.[293] I have made the calculation as per letter of Br Rhees to you in regard to Ms. S. S. Book, there are 26 lines in solid page, 39 letters in line, and 73 pp in book (solid) which make $26.50 at 50 cents per page solid.

---

[291] Emily would continue to write for the *New Mirror* without compensation, though later she would be asked by the other magazines about the fairness of asking five dollars a page from them while asking Willis for nothing at all.

[292] Emily would have celebrated her 27th birthday.

[293] John Mason Peck, of American Baptist Publication Society.

By this mail I will send to Bennett, Backus, and Hawley[294] and perhaps in adjusting their deed I can draw on them for the amount. I would send you a check on N. Y. by this; but I am short of funds and have 500 Dollars to make up in a few days. I will request them to pay you; if there is a balance due us there. If not you shall have it soon.[295]

The other book *Anna Bailey* has been approved, and is now in the Printer's hands—it will be out in a few weeks. If I had any way to send I would send you a few copies of *John Frink* but know of no way by by [sic] Express. If any person is coming to our city from your region let me know and I will send.

Yours truly

B. R. Loxley, Dep. Agent

Source: American Baptist Historical Society, AJ 22, no. 1077.

Emily E, Chubbuck to Anna Maria Anable, October 1844[296]

Can't you come this way and see me?
Oh! Oh! Oh!
Can't you come this way and see me?
Don't say no.
Here upon the bed I'm lying,
Kicking, sneezing, snuffing, sighing,
Sometimes e'en amost a-crying,
All alone.

Source: Hanna family files.

George R. Graham to Emily E. Chubbuck, October 4, 1844

Fanny Forester[297] must not think so meanly of me as to suppose that in giving her my *worldly* advice, I had the most distant intention of giving her pain. I spoke of the "cold criticism," only as a caution, because I thought I saw an exuberance of high hope, raised by the praises of her friend Willis[298]—than whom a more gen-

---

[294] Horace H. Hawley was enormously helpful to Emily as she published her early stories and books.

[295] We are reminded of the letters to Emily from Eliza Allen of the *Mother's Journal*, who also was having difficulty paying Emily for her work. We note that she was to ask five dollars a page from Inman and Graham; obviously secular publishing was far more profitable than religious publishing.

[296] This little note-poem is undated.

[297] Fanny Forester, Emily Chubbuck's *nom de plume*.

[298] Nathaniel Parker (N. P.) Willis was the editor of *New Mirror*, the magazine that catapulted Emily into literary fame. He became a friend, mentor, and eventually a suitor.

erous hearted man does not exist among our American literati—which ultimately might do her harm.

It is all unsaid, however, if Fanny Forester, has allowed it to darken an hour of her life.

Now you will scarcely believe me,—yet I have had from any person, the most distant *hint* that Fanny and Emily were one and the same. I detected in the article in the *Columbian*[299] at the time it was written, a pen of more than ordinary merit, with a power of description, and a freshness, which with [ ] [ ] a *love* of writing can impart to any pen, and which I did not before believe belonged to more than *one* lady—I wrote to her instantly, and as the charge of authorship involved a sort of breech of honor we had a pleasant little correspondence before I got out of it. In a word I thought the article had been written by Mrs. *Ann L. Stephens* who is under contract with me to write for no other magazine, although by courtesy I gave her liberty to write for Mr. Peterson.

On the appearance of *Fanny Forester* I suspected *her*, and when I received her letter *post marked* Utica I *knew* that no *two* pens of the same grace and liveliness could have been long buried in one little town. So Fanny Forester, there has been no betrayal of *secrets* to *me*. I give you my word of *honor* that I have never corresponded, in relation, to either name with any but yourself. Mr. Willis—if he *knows your real* name—must have detected it in some such way—or perhaps his intimacy with Mr. Inman[300] may have led to a disclosure in a free conversation upon writers.

One word more. Let your name to me be *Fanny Forester* for I detected you merely by a little critical capacity. I have no right—and I *won't*—intrude behind the veil which shrouds you from the public eye. A caution to Mr. Willis I am *sure* will be all that is [ ] to keep you secure.

Cousin 'Bel's'[301] visit is in the November number of "*Graham*"[302] and really being delightfully there—the "Chief's Daughter,"[303] as I have christened the other

---

[299] The *Columbian Magazine*, edited and published by John Inman.

[300] John Inman was the editor of the *Commercial Advertiser* and the *Columbian Magazine*.

[301] Emily's original letter to N. P. Willis in June concerned Emily and her "Cousin 'Bel'" going to New York, and having empty pocketbooks, not able to afford any of the finery they saw in the store windows. "Cousin 'Bel'" was Anna Maria Anable, Emily's best friend.

[302] *Graham's Magazine*, one of the finer literary magazines of its time.

[303] The first paragraph of "The Chief's Daughter":

Strange that powerful states should sometimes direct all their might enginery against a simple individual, whose weakness should be a protection! Strange that civilized men raise a Juggernaut to crush a butterfly! Strange that the shrinking wild flower of its own native green-wood, the timid bud unfolding by the hearth-stone of an American savage, striking its roots down into his strong heart, and caring for no other soil, could not escape the calculating eye of a great and a refined nation! Thurensera, the beautiful Day-Dawn, the daughter of the noblest sachem among all the Iroquois, the proud, peerless princess of the wilderness, whom the chivalry of the United Nations delighted to honour, to be duped at last! Ay, such is the fate of beauty and royalty; and the Indian maiden was far from being an isolated victim. In the glittering suit of Queen Anne, in the luxurious palaces of Louis, in the courts of Spain and Italy, and among the republican aristocracy of Germany, wherever power dwelt, wherever a field for intrigue existed, hardened men, and may be hardened women, too, were making throbbing hearts the stepping-stones to their projects (*Trippings in Author-land*, 273).

will appear with an engraving of the same name, from a design by Chapman in Jan or Feb'y. If you have short articles let me have them *on hand*, so as to use as often as possible. I *will* help out your *Money Making*. Below I send draft on *My Brother in N. Y.* which you can get collected through the express.

Yours truly

Geo. R. Graham

Written in the left margin of page 3: "Fanny Forester will please put her name upon the back of draft." Source: American Baptist Historical Society, AJ 24, no. 1192.

Nathaniel Parker Willis to Emily E. Chubbuck, October 30, 1844[304]

My dear friend

The letter "to Fanny Forester"[305] in the *Mirror* was not addressed to you originally, and you were not thought of while it was done. I must state this head-foremost, for I cannot wait to come to it in order—so annoyed was I at its *quality*, as a letter to *you*. You will forgive me when I tell you how it came about. The Weekly was just going to press when Mist. Morris[306] discovered that it had nothing new of *mine*. There was no time to write and I was mopey. A letter lay on my table addressed to a dashing *married friend* of mine—a lady who is *good*, but a dare-devil on paper—and the thought struck me that I could turn the Substance of it to account by writing an introduction and addressing it to Fanny Forester! *It went to press in twenty minutes*. I read it the next morning and was horrified at what I had done. My wife scolded me and said you would never write to me again and I have been repenting ever since. Now do you see! And will you forgive me, dear, forbearing Fanny!

The letter you sent me is capital. A thousand thanks. I am crazy with pen and ink and must stop and go to bed.

Ever yours admiringly & faithfully,

N. P. Willis

Please make my respects agreeable to Cousin 'Bel'.[307]

Source: Hanna family files.

---

[304] On the letter, in the handwriting of Emily Chubbuck: "N. P. Willis, October 30, 1844, No. 5."

[305] Fanny Forester, Emily Chubbuck's *nom de plume*.

[306] George P. "General" Morris, was N. P. Willis's partner at the *New Mirror* and a prominent literary figure in New York and Philadelphia.

[307] "Cousin 'Bel'" was a reference to Anna Maria Anable. The name came from the original letter that Emily wrote to Willis in June 1844 when she spoke of visiting New York with her "Cousin 'Bel.'"

B. R. Loxley to Emily E. Chubbuck, October 30, 1844—Philadelphia

Dear Sister

Above you have check on Merchants bank New York for Twenty Six 50/100 Dollars drawn to your order which will be in full for the Copy Right [sic] of *John Frink*. I have sent a dozen copies as you directed to the Astor House, New York Care of Mr. Port. Be pleased to send by mail a receipt for the above and also one for the Payment of *Effie Maurice* as I want the voucher for our committee—*Anna Baily*[308] is not yet out, but is in the Bindery and will be soon in the Depository.

Yours truly

B. R. Loxley Ass[istant] Treas[urer]
Am Bap Pub Society

Source: American Baptist Historical Society, AJ 22, no. 1076.

George Graham to Emily E, Chubbuck, November 1, 1844

Dear Fanny[309]

I cannot vote for "Birney" [sic] because I love Henry Clay too much, to please my own party. My vote is the tribute I pay to the *genius* of the man.

You and I appear to be playing at "*Cross purposes*." You entirely misinterpret me, in your paraphrase upon what I said in my last relative to justice to Mr. W.[310] I

---

[308] *Anna Bailey* was a book on the Second Commandment. On July 23, 1842, Rhees of American Baptist Publication Society had written to Emily regarding a series on the Ten Commandments. In that he had said: "In regards to the remaining commandments, we should be glad to have them all contained in the series, and tho' as you suggest the 2nd might not be so practical, still I think it would be better to have a complete series, and it has appeared to me, that the image worship of Popery might be well rebuked, and its evils exposed in such a work as you could propose." Apparently Emily took this advice to heart, for in this small book, there is significant dialogue between Anna Bailey and her mother, in which her mother explains to her the evils of Roman Catholicism, and Anna, among other things, says: "I wish these poor Irish people were not Catholics. Do they really pray to dead men instead of the living God, and go to their priests to get their sins pardoned?"

The first page of *Anna Bailey* reads:

> "Mother," said little Anna Bailey, almost breathless with the haste she had made to reach home and tell the news,—"Mother, there is another Irish shantee up to-day: this makes six—and Charley Whipple says his father says, he shouldn't wonder if there should be twenty of them yet. The neighborhood will be completely overrun."
>
> "With shantees" inquired Mrs. Bailey, without raising her eyes from her work.
>
> "With Irishmen. Why, mother, you have no idea of what ragamuffins they are; there was a troop of them rolling up logs to-day, and I didn't see a single whole coat among them all. O, they are just the queerest people!"
>
> "Queer?" said Mrs. Bailey, still sewing on.
>
> "Yes, mother. The women look so much alike that I don't believe I should ever be able to tell them apart—"

[309] Fanny Forester, Emily Chubbuck's *nom de plume*.

[310] Nathaniel Parker (N. P.) Willis was the editor of *New Mirror*, the magazine that catapulted Emily into literary fame. He became a friend, mentor, and eventually a suitor.

meant *simply this*, and should have said it[311]—that Mr. W. and I were old friends, and that his position as your fair friend and [ ] in the [ ] of letters was such, that I could not in a letter to *you*, whatever I might say *to him*, act as his critic or judge.

I say again I am glad that I wrote "*that letter*," although I got a scolding—which I half anticipated because I have read another leaf of Fanny's Character.

I find that warm hearted and impulsive as she may be, she is not a coquette *in heart or literature* and will not take from a flattering admirer, any [ ] he may be pleased to offer—in other words, she is a *girl* no longer, but a discerning *woman*, even though she may be but "gentle sixteen."

One more, and then we are done—*both of us I hope*—with explanations forever. Do not think that I intended to censure anything more than the *discretion* of Mr. W. He is more a man of the world than I am but it struck me that such a paragraph in *print* was calculated to do you harm with the public and so I find *you* thought also.[312] Now you must not argue your case, like a lawyer who has previously presented all his *facts* to the jury. How shall I know?—how do I know—*how* except what her letter last sent me *teaches* me, that Fanny Forester did not think too well of her friends to think they could not err. I love Mr. Willis, for his high genius and warm heart—I like his perseverance and energy, his past appreciation of the talents of *young writers*, and of *his own*—I esteem it a mark of genius to know its own worth—yet I do think and to you *now* I will *say* that in *many* of his published letters there has been a want of discretion, an overlooking of the *effect* of his impulsive writings upon the feelings and relation of others. That made him to Fanny Forester, *a dangerous admirer in print*.

One word as to my own letter, I do not know what it contained, but I remember something about jealousy and the [ ] privilege of facts—if there was one word that ought not to have been written forgive and forget it.

Mr. Peterson has just handed me the story. I will look it over as soon as possible and will turn it into money for you, if I can. After to-night, I will be more at leisure and will read the mss of yours I have. You shall then have a long letter full of business.

Write me as you always have done. If I see a shade more of boldness or caution in them, I shall think you have but half overlooked my own *indiscretions* and *silly* letter to you.

---

[311] In his letter of October 4, 1844, Graham had said: "'Fanny Forester' must not think so meanly of me as to suppose that in giving her my *worldly* advice, I had the most distant intention of giving her pain. I spoke of the 'cold criticism', only as a caution, because I thought I saw an exuberance of high hope, raised by the praises of her friend Willis—than whom a more generous hearted man does not exist among our American literati—which ultimately might do her harm."

[312] See the letter from N. P. Willis to Emily E. Chubbuck dated October 30, 1844, in which he apologized for a recent letter which he had published in the *New Mirror* that was directed to her, and which the next morning reading his paper he felt to be inappropriate. We wonder if Graham is referencing this letter in his remarks, or other material that might have appeared in the *New Mirror*.

This letter is longer than I thought it would be when I sat down. It is as stupid I doubt not, as you would expect.

Much yours

GRG

Source: American Baptist Historical Society, AJ 24, no. 1191.

Urania E. Nott to Emily E. Chubbuck, November 4, 1844[313]

My dear Emily,

Your letter from N. P. W.[314] I read to my good Doct.[315] who shed tears of joy at your good prospects and the generous sentiments expressed by the man.[316]

Willis must have a heart—as well as a head—and I think his great mistakes have arisen from some bad habits into which he at one time had fallen—he must be a better man now—at least I hope so—at any rate he has done you a great favor—for which we will all like him.[317] I hope you will get your pay from Inman's publisher[318]—don't depend upon Mr. Writer himself. Your little book is very good—just the thing for children—tho' I think the arguments of James Knowles[319] rather too sound and mature for a boy of his age—and not quite simple enough for children to fully comprehend. They will be likely to skip over them at any rate—still the book is excellent.

My time is gone and I can only subscribe myself

Yours very sincerely

Urania E. Nott

Source: American Baptist Historical Society, AJ 25, no. 1238.

---

[313] This letter is undated. Because it was quoted by N. P. Willis in a letter that he wrote on November 16, 1844, obviously Emily had sent it to him or quoted it to him. We place it on November 4, 1844. This would have given Emily time to have received it and sent it on.

[314] Nathaniel Parker (N. P.) Willis was the editor of *New Mirror*, the magazine that catapulted Emily into literary fame. He became a friend, mentor, and eventually a suitor.

[315] Eliphalet Nott, president of Union College, married to Urania Sheldon Nott.

[316] By this date, N. P. Willis had sent Emily letters dated June, August 20, September 7 and 26, and October 30.

[317] In his letter of November 16, 1844, N. P. Willis responded to this comment of Nott, Emily having sent it to him. He said that he "was pleased and displeased at Nott's changing her opinion of me" and went on to elaborate.

[318] John Inman was the editor of the *Commercial Advertiser* and the *Columbian Magazine*.

[319] We must assume that "James Knowles" was either a story written by Emily, or a character in a story.

Mary Gregory to Emily E. Chubbuck, November 11, 1844—Sand Lake

My dear friend,

I have a sort of fancy that I have written you one note, sometime or other, I should not like to say when, but I thought perhaps I might be mistaken, and if I am not it will do no harm to write again. I have nothing of interest to communicate in the shape of news, excepting that every week or two our ears are saluted with the sound of the Indian horn—they make a very fanciful appearance, Aunt Mary can have little idea of them from what she saw when here. Every color and shade they can find they put on, and such times as they do have, people generally are afraid of them, and they do as they please without fear of molestation. Miss Chubbuck are you not coming to see us, we should be very happy after the girls come home to receive a visit from you. I always think of you when I think of being in Utica, for I always felt that you were one of the best friends I had there. I hope my sisters will endeavor to merit your esteem and improve their lives and abilities to the best advantage. They had not been in the habit of writing compositions for two years before they went to Utica and dreaded it very much. Pa is very anxious that they should improve in writing. He thinks composition the most important study they have, connected with their Grammar. I hope if I visit Utica this winter that I shall see you. Somewhat doubtful however. Please accept much love from

your aff. friend

Mary G.   Source: American Baptist Historical Society, AJ 24, no. 1188.

Nathaniel Parker Willis to Emily E. Chubbuck, November 16, 1844—Mirror Printing Office[320]

I have just read the proof of your exquisitely beautiful outline story,[321] my dear Miss Chubbuck, and my heart is in my throat with its pathos and with my interest in your genius. I see the *inner iris* of the story, of course. I could talk, talk to you *days* of what is in your brain and heart at this moment; for I read it with my own recollections of first fame, and with the eye God has given me to see hearts with. You are gifted far beyond your own belief, but your heart is more gifted than your head. Your affections are in more need of room and wings than your imagination. I should bless God for your sake to hear that a poet and man-angel had taken you to a dell in the wilderness, never to be heard of more.

With nothing but your writings to guide me, I have begun with gaily rejoicing over a new found star, and ended with a tearful interest in your destiny, and a

---

[320] Written on the address page in the handwriting of Emily Chubbuck: "N. P. Willis, Esq. Nov. 16. 1844. No. 6."

[321] Willis is referring to the story "Dora'."

respect for your truthfulness and purity which makes me repent of ever having spoken of you triflingly. You will forgive this. Hereafter you will see no word touching yourself that does not pass through the fountain of reverence you have called up in my heart.

I am writing while "proofs" are coming—interruptedly and carelessly of course. I was pleased and displeased at Mrs. Nott's[322] changing her opinion of me; displeased at the *suspicion* that my *inner-self* had ever committed its purity to the world, or had ever been on trial in a pure mind. My dear friend, you know, though you have never perill'd [sic] your *outer* mind by laying it open to all comers, that there is an inner sanctuary of God's lighting which brightens as the world is shut out, and which would never suffer profanation. It is in this chamber of my better nature that *you* are thought of—but I have no time to explain.

The pain that you are suffering from the *exposure of fame* is a chrysalis of thought. You will be brighter for it, though the accustomed shroud of seclusion comes off painfully. The opinion of the "Uticanians" as to any thing but your amiableness and respectability, is not worth one straw—though a straw stuck in your eye is as formidable as a house-beam. By an effort of mind you can throw Utica to the distance of Rochester or Buffalo, and then every thing [sic] you hear will have just the value which the same thing would have, if said in Buffalo. Still, perhaps you have yet to learn that genius burns darkest nearest the wick, *never, never* appreciated by those who eat, drink, and walk with it. You are a hundred times more admired in New York than you ever could be in Utica, and it is the charm of city life that the "solitude of a crowd" throws even your nearest neighbor to the proper perspective distance. *Keep making* an effort to shed *neighborhood*.

Upon my word this is getting to be quite a letter, and all this work *ought* to be in a column of the *Mirror*. I would propose an intimate friendship on paper to you, if I had time to carry it on—but I *may* ask you to write to me freely, and for my eye only. Let your *genius* adopt me as a brother—at any rate till some rich possessor of your sweet and strong woman's *heart* craves a monopoly of you all.

Yours with sincere respect and affection,

N. P. Willis

Written in the right margin of the address page: "A*propos* one of our correspondents says, "Fanny Forester's[323] mind seems of the same genius as your own. Did you write those articles yourself?"

Source: A. C. Kendrick, *The Life and Letters of Mrs. Emily C. Judson*, 106–107; Hanna family files.

---

[322] For Urania Sheldon Nott's comments on N. P. Willis, which Emily had sent to him, see her letter to Emily Chubbuck of November 4, 1844.

[323] Fanny Forester, Emily Chubbuck's *nom de plume*.

John Inman to Emily E. Chubbuck, November 19, 1844—New York City

My dear Miss Fanny[324]

I can imagine how you have wondered, conjectured, grown indignant and finally downright angry at my long and apparently most rude neglect of your letters. But there was a cause, friend Fanny Forester.

Early in October it was my misfortune to fall into the category of the sick, though happily not of the dying. My brain got out of order, with some persistent inflammation, or congestion, the doctors called it, and for three weeks I lay helpless and unresisting, the victim of the most savage medical cruelties. Bled was I, over and over again; leeched, cupped, blistered, starved, shut up in darkness, debarred from society—conversation, reading and even being read to. Pleasant was it not? At length I was discharged cured, as they say at the hospital; but the severity of my curing had so reduced me that I was unable to walk, hardly able even to stand, and overborne by the slightest effort, bodily or mental. Heretofore I have been remarkable for the rapidity with which I have "got up" after severe illness, but this time has shown me that I am forty years old—coming or come to the down-hill part of life—and sick no longer in the recuperative vigor of youth. Although I have been up and about two weeks, until within a day or two I have been obliged to ride to and from the office; and the performance of my very lowest minimum of [ ] there has so exhausted my bodily strength—left me so listless and devoid of energy—that in getting home I have been able to do no more than stretch myself upon a sofa and be still for the remainder of the day.

All this to account for my not writing to you before; and now to business. You do not tell me what improvement of terms you require, but entertaining a just sense of your claims and [ ], and perceiving, moreover, that you are fast writing Fanny Forester into a position where she can have her own way, I say at once that the publisher of the *Columbian* will pay you the highest price he pays to any body [sic]—five dollars the printed page; and that, let me tell you, Miss Fanny, is good honest pay—as much as any magazine can afford, and fairly as much as a magazine article is worth to the publisher. Moreover it is a rate of pay at which clever, practical and rapid writers, like yourself, can make a very pretty thing of it by the end of the year.

I think, however, for your own sake as well as in justice to those who pay you, that you ought not to write "free, gratis for nothing" for any body; the *Mirror* folks, for example, who proclaim aloud that they do not pay a copper. You know there is competition between all periodical publications; and it is hardly fair for a clever and popular writer to receive liberal pay from one, while gratuitously helping to

---

[324] Fanny Forester, Emily Chubbuck's *nom de plume*.

build up and sustain another. We must think of each other's interests somewhat, Miss Fanny, as well as our own.

"The Bank Note"[325] will appear in the January number; and you will have five dollars the page for it.

I have not sent back, nor do I send, "Grace Linden;"[326] because, what with the death of Col. Stone, my succession to the editorial chair of the *Commercial* as his acknowledged successor, and then my illness, I have not yet been able to read it; and because the conductor of the *Columbian Magazine* has concluded, in the second year, to change the rule adopted in the first and continue articles from one number to another; whereby, as you perceive, Miss Linden will come into service at once, and bring moneys to her owner.

You may observe that I say "the conductor of the *Columbian Magazine*"; whence you may infer that I speak not of myself. It is so; with the first year my part in the editing of the magazine terminates, although my name will remain. Nominally I shall still be the editor, but the work will all be done by deputy; at least I shall exercise but a very general supervision. The doctors tell me, and the [ ] shock given to my health and energies by that brain business of which I have spoken gives confirmation of their words, that I must keep my head on less severe and continued employment; and the magazine is positively prohibited. My medical friends say that the conduct of the *Commercial Advertiser* is quite enough for me to look after.

My wish and inclination were to withdraw wholly and avowedly from the magazine, but the proprietor urged me so strongly to let him have my name for another year that I could hardly help consenting. He said that an avowed change of editor at the close of the first year, would be very injurious to the work.

This, however, is not for the public ear; only for you. People may still think me the editor if they like, but I shall be freed from the intolerable burden of the office.

I ought not to scandalize the post, however, for it has given me the acquaintance of some few people whom I should be sorry not to know—for instance, one Fanny Forester.

Pray write to me immediately, if but a line, to let me know that the wonder, indignation and anger are dispelled. And believe me,

---

[325] The first two paragraphs of "The Bank Note," as they appeared in *Alderbrook*, vol. 1, page 208:

"A pink barege, with tucks—or a flounce—no! I like tucks better; let me think—how many? Half a dozen little ones look fixed up; one deep one, doubling the whole skirt, is very suitable for mamma, but it would be rather too heavy, too dignified for me; then two of moderate size—oh! they are so common! Never mind! Madam Dufraneau shall decide that matter. But I will have the dress, at any rate, and it shall be pink—just the palest and most delicate in the world—but pink it shall be, because of my dark eyes and hair, and fair complexion."

So soliloquized pretty Rosa Warner, a good-natured, thoughtless, of some thirteen summers, whose only troublous reflection was occasioned by the distance of bright sixteen, when her mother had promised she should be allowed to abolish short dresses, and gather up her jetty curls into a comb. And this would, indeed, be quite an era in the life of the little lady;—for she had no small pretensions to beauty, and was, moreover, the only child of a very wealthy father and a very fashionable mother. Oh! what visions she had of the future!

Yours very truly and faithfully,

John Inman

Source: American Baptist Historical Society, AJ 24, no. 1177.

Nathaniel Parker Willis to Emily E. Chubbuck,[327] November 24, 1844 —New York City[328]

My Dear Friend,—

At the close of five hours of mental labor, I can scarce undertake to do more than make *mems.* of what I would say to you, and you must write me long letters for these scraps of sentences. Your last was delightful, because it was frank and sisterly.[329] Your bump of caution must be very large, however, since you supposed that the public might see the "inner bow" as I did, and dreaded the interpretation, "parading

---

[326] The first several paragraphs of "Grace Linden" as they appeared in *Alderbrook*, vol. 1, page 7:

"This will be quite pleasant, after all, mother—quite pleasant. This nice little room is just the place for me. We will train a vine over the window, and my books shall be upon the table close by—"

"We shall need the table now, my daughter. Your father thinks we can take two boarders, though for my part I see no place to put them," and the mother cast an anxious, troubled glance about the apartment.

"Two boarders! It will come hard upon you, mother."

"Oh no, dear, no! Not so hard, Abby, as upon the poor children. I cannot bear the idea of their being shut up the livelong day—stifled for the want of pure air—work, work, working every moment, till their little limbs are ready to drop off with pain. It is horrible to me, Abby!"

The poor woman, as she spoke, shuddered at the sad picture which needed not the coloring of a mother's imagination. For a moment the pale lips of the girl trembled, and a tear quivered in her eye; but, with a strong effort she suppressed the emotion, and replied cheerfully. It was certainly, so said the sympathizing Abby, a hard thing for the poor children to be shut away from the sunshine; but she was sure the labor would be light. Russel promised that, and if it was found in any way injurious to health, or even spirits, a change of some kind must of course be made. "It is only a trial, dear mother," she added, smiling.

[327] In Emily Chubbuck's handwriting on the address page: "N. P. Willis Esq., Nov. 24, 1844, No. 7."

[328] We have two versions of this letter—the original as written by N. P. Willis, and the edited version published by A. C. Kendrick in his biography, *The Life and Letters of Mrs. Emily C. Judson*. Additions made by Kendrick we have placed in parentheses (), and words in the original left out by Kendrick we have added in bold.

[329] It is a great loss that we have none of Emily's correspondence with N. P. Willis. In some letters, we have only a glimpse of what she might have said, as we have his quotes from her letters and his response. At the time of her engagement to Adoniram Judson, Emily suffered enormous pangs of guilt and anxiety, and she asked Willis to return all of her letters believing that there would be material in them that, if it ever saw the public light, would be an embarrassment to the great missionary and his new wife. Writing to Judson she said:

Why sh'd I wish the letters returned if they were not inconsistent with my new relations? Did I not tell you that it was jealousy for your honour which induced me? What has your honor to do with a common friendship? I tell you "honestly" (not for the first time I believe) that I have given W. cause to believe that I loved him, and quite honestly that *I never gave a thought to the construction that might be put upon my letters till I examined the subject with the eyes which love for you had given me.*

At first Willis refused, but apparently relented, for Emily sends Adoniram a letter not long before their departure for Burmah that Willis had, in fact, returned the correspondence. We note further, that in 1860 when A. C. Kendrick asked N. P. Willis for it as he wrote *The Life and Letters of Mrs. Emily C. Judson*, Willis wrote back and simply said that he could not locate it. Emily obviously destroyed those letters—and we suspect that they would have told us much more about her than we have come to know.

your feelings," etc.[330] Nobody could ever read a line of yours and see anything **there** but merit over-modest, as far as that goes; and there is no writing well without coloring from one's own heart—particularly in first beginnings. I was exceedingly interested in the fact that there *was* a touch of Dora in your own history, **tho'** (though) I did not and *do not* seek the least intrusion upon your confidence in such matters. My interest in you is a shadow of your *intellect*, and followed, of course, when your intellect went into your heart as a comforter. There are two worlds, my dear Dora—one imaginative and the other real life-and people of genius have separate existences in both. **In my imaginative world I always found it inevitable to have some merely intellectual idol.** Your deliciously fresh and glowing mind has possess'd me in that world, and you might marry and adore any one of ninety-nine men in a hundred, without in the least degree impoverishing my empire—(Supposing that empire mine in return). I have a wife, the model of womanly qualities, but she would as lief I were a Utica shop-keeper, with the same income, as the first poet, or statesman, or General of my time. She has not the least interest in anything about me that is ideal. Of course, my other world, of imagination is without a mistress, and its throne is usurpable—was usurp'd for years by Mrs. Norton, and is very near coming a-begging to you. I never had five months *tete a tete* with Mrs. N. in my life, and I may very well never personally know you. *Mais cela n'enipeche pas!* So on with your brilliant career, dear Emily, love your friends and listen to your lover—but there are hours when your affections will be folded like your hands when you are dreaming, and when your mind will need a companion on the wing—Now, if you do not comprehend this—if I have not explained something hitherto uninterpreted in your heart— **burn the letter and never think more of it till you marry.**

I had a call, a few days ago, from a very able artist, a friend of mine, who was so struck with a descriptive passage in your story of Dora that he wished to paint it. I commissioned him to do it, and shall send you the picture **to hang up in your room.**

The Boston lady who enquired so much about you, by the way, (did I tell you?) is a cousin of mine—Mrs. Hooper. The exchange papers are full of compliments to you. The very handsome editor of the Spirit of the Times, Mssr Porter, sat by me at the Historical Dinner and talked of your "Dora" with great praise. He is to copy it this week.

God bless you, dear Queen Dora of Spirit land!
Ever yours,

Bodiless Poetry

---

[330] See the November 16, 1844 letter of N. P Willis to Emily E. Chubbuck.

Nothing has much romance for me that any 3rd person shares—so, if you can do so easily, keep this from all eyes but your own.

Seal your letters with red wafers. Those wax seals come open and they may be read in the office, where all my letters invariably go.

Source: Hanna Family files; A. C. Kendrick, *The Life and Letters of Mrs. Emily C. Judson*, 108.

Fanny Forester to the *New Mirror*,[331] November 1844

Introduction by George Tooze

Dora' was a fictional character in this story by Fanny Forester that was released in fall 1844. A letter from N. P. Willis to Emily Chubbuck dated November 16, 1844, conveys his strong impression. Then on November 24, N. P. Willis wrote to say that his artist friend was so moved by the story that he wanted to paint the character. Without hesitation Willis said he commissioned the artist Flagg[332] to do a portrait of Dora', which he would give as a gift to Emily.

Slowly in the month that followed the details of the painting emerged. In one letter Dora' is described as sitting in a window while someone is asking her a question. In another letter the man asking the question, with his back turned to the viewer, is none other than N. P. Willis; he posed for the painter. In addition, "[the artist's] mother [is to be] the motherly guardian of Dora', and Dora' imaginative. If you [Emily] were here, he should paint your head for Dora'. The subject is the putting the question to Dora' as she sits in the window." The painting was shipped in the Christmas season and Anna Maria Anable wrote to Emily on December 30, 1844 that they had retrieved the painting from the express office. Apparently, between the time he had received the painting and brought it to the express office, it had been on display, and he told Emily that thousands had seen and admired it. Emily was to write that she was sitting in her room enjoying the picture of Dora'.

Because this became such an important event, and because the story of "Dora'" is beautifully characteristic of Fanny Forester's writing, it is included in its entirety.

Dora'

---

[331] We assume that "Dora'" was written for the *New Mirror*. N. P. Willis wrote on November 16, 1844, that he had read the proofs—and he would not have had access to proofs from the other magazines for which Emily wrote.

[332] Mr. Flagg was the artist commissioned by N. P. Willis to paint the portrait of Dora', a fictional character in a story by Fanny Forester. One of the characters in the painting was modeled on N. P. Willis. Though never identified as other than "Flagg," this may be Jared Bradley Flagg, on of a well-known family of artists. Mr. Flagg was born in 1820 and died in 1899; he painted in Hartford CT and the New York City area.

Eyes, like a wet violet, nestled among a profusion of the softest-hued Persian fringes, and hair, gathered from the elfin fields of Erin, and combed and twisted into waves by fairy fingers—such had Dora'! Then those lips, with their sad sweetness, and the love-thought in each corner! and the pale, polished cheek, and vein-crossed forehead! Hast ever seen her?

Sweet, delicate Dora'!—much I fear me, that such a vision of loveliness will never again appear at Alder-Brook.

It was years and years ago that Dora' moved among our mothers here, with a step like a fawn's, a head erect and earnest, like a wild deer on the look-out for the huntsman, and a face full of half-joyous, half-solemn surprise, such as Eve must have worn when her foot first crushed the dews and flowers of Eden. Beautiful was Dora', as a dream which turns from the daylight, to nestle in some young heart, or a thought that refuses to syllable itself in clumsy words; and yet, beautiful was she never called; but all paused and looked upon her as she passed by, and smiled, and owned a stronger power, though they knew not what it was, than that of beauty.

Stand by me, reader, and follow the direction of my finger, over the bend in the brook, and along the white clover-field to the foot of that little knoll with the two elm-trees on its crown. Do you perceive the top of a chimney-peeping from the green things piled up there, like a monument to Sylvan? You may not discover it, but I, who have looked so many times, know that little speck of reddish brown to be a chimney. Well, beneath is the smallest pattern of a human shelter that your eyes ever lighted on, now pretty much gone to decay, and grown entirely over with moss and hop-vines. I have heard that a white rose-bush once quite over-topped the front corner, and sunflowers innumerable peeped their yellow heads above the eaves at the back; and I have myself a distinct remembrance of stopping to admire the trumpet-honeysuckle that years ago graced the door-way; but not a flowering thing opens in that vicinity now. There, all alone, once lived Aunty Evans; a good, gentle old woman, who, for the want of better things to love, kept always about her a family of kittens, chickens, rabbits, and tame pigeons. Besides this, she used to make gingerbread for the little people that always looked in, upon their way from school, and supply the whole village with sage, rue, and chamomile, from a garden that would have been no wonder in Lilliput. Aunty Evans could not have been said to be without the means of living, for she fed herself, and not unfrequently her less industrious neighbours, with the proceeds of her busiest of all busy needles. One day, a letter, marked on the outside "in haste," was sent her from the village post-office; and, in an hour after, the fire was extinguished upon the hearth, the latch-string drawn, and Aunty Evans, for the first time in her life, found herself in the stage-coach. In a few days she returned with a pale, sad little girl, all in black, and was invited at once to a grand tea-party, for curiosity's sake. But the old lady had only a short story. A friend had died, and bequeathed her an only child.

"Has she money?" asked the gossips.

Aunty Evans said no; and then they all shook their heads and looked mysterious; and somehow, in a few minutes, though there could be no connection between it and the other subject, they were all talking about the new and excellent regulations which had been made at the almshouse. Aunty Evans expressed herself very glad that the poor children were to be better cared for, and thereupon sipped her tea without further concern. That subject was immediately abandoned, and the conversation took an unaccountable turn, calculated to overthrow entirely the doctrine of association, for somebody began talking about the price of plain needlework. Most of the ladies were of the opinion, that a seamstress could no more than support herself comfortably; and if by chance she did accomplish more than that, it was her bounden duty to lay by her surplus for a "rainy day." Aunty Evans appeared to listen to all this very composedly; but, in reality, her thoughts were a little absent. She was planning the number of shirts she should be obliged to make, in order to send the little orphan, Dora', to the best school in the village.

Dora' was sent to school, and forthwith, the pale child became as great a favourite as Aunty Evans herself. Dora's voice had a tone to it, like the stroke of a silver bell, reaching us through a medium of tears; and she might always be found, whether under the cherry-tree, at the back of the school-house, or nestled in a rich clover-bed, or seated on the spotted alders by the brook-side, with a group of children about her, singing the little songs that she learned of Aunty Evans. How deliciously sweet was that voice! And though the words could claim to be of no higher order than

> "Little bird, with bosom red,
> Welcome to my humble <u>shed</u>:" [sic]
> or,
> "Pretty bee, busy bee,
> If you'd but sing to me."

Many a stern old man paused to listen, and many a *business* woman raised her red bandana to her eyes, as those clear, touching tones fell, despite the crust above it, on her heart. The women did not know why they were thus affected, but Aunty Evans would have told them there was a shadow within, from which that voice stole its touch of sorrow, and which, later in the day of her life, would fall back upon her heart.

Aunty Evans might, quite unknown to those about her, have been a prophetess; but Dora' went on year after year, singing all the time more and more sweetly, and with more touching pathos, while the shadow, if any there was, must have been nearly melted by the neighbouring sunshine. One individual, considering himself somewhat wiser than his neighbours, whispered at length to some others, that the peculiarity in Dora' Evans's [sic] voice was the despairing plaint of prisoned genius; but Alder-Brook had no citizen mad enough, even though all had credited the suggestion, to bind the child for this to a lot of splendid misery. Dora's neighbors knew little of raising a God-given power to that point of famous infamy, where even its admirers are privileged to jest about it—they were common men, and had never learned that it is the misfortune of genius to consume itself in a bonfire, that others may be amused by its coruscations. So Dora' went on singing every Sabbath in the village choir, singing at the fire-side of Aunty Evans, and singing at the social gatherings in the village; always thankful, and rejoicing that she had a power which could make herself and everybody else so happy. So passed year after year, until Dora' was fifteen, and the shadow had settled on neither heart nor brow.

Dora' sat upon the knoll that I have pointed out under the two elm-trees, circled by a row of young faces, all turned earnestly loving to hers.

"Sing it again, Dora'! do! do! just once again, dear! it is *so* pretty!" went the pleading round, and Dora' smiled, and began to sing.

That morning a stranger had reached Alder-Brook by the stage-coach. He was a small man, slightly moulded, with eager piercing eyes, two wrinkles passing from their inner corners half way up the forehead; an aquiline nose, sallow cheek, and thin lips, always pressed closely together. Though he could scarcely have attained the middle age, he was slightly bald; frequent threads of silver mingled in his black hair and beard; and upon his face there was many a line, the work of a more hasty pencil than time carries. Just as Dora' commenced her song, this man was hurrying along with his usual quick step close beside the fence. As the first strain fell on his ear, he raised his eyes, and cast up to the clouds, and away into the tree tops, a glance of eager inquiry. Again it came, and again; and a smile full of beautiful delight broke over the listener's compressed lips, and a fire was kindled in the centre of his now dilated eye, which seemed burning back into his very soul.

"Ha!" he exclaimed, as his glance fell upon the pretty group cresting the green knoll; and then he crossed his arms upon his breast, lowered his earnest brows, and bent his ear to listen.

The stranger did not leave Alder-Brook that day; neither did he then continue his walk; but returning to the "Sheaf and Sickle," as soon as the little party beneath the elms was broken up, he possessed himself of all his land-lady knew concerning the rustic songstress.

"Such a voice," he muttered, as he strode up and down the piazza, "such compass! such delicacy! such pathos! she would madden them. It would be a generous deed, too—poor orphan!"

He passed on, his steps grew every moment quicker and his eyes more eagerly bright. "Ay, ay! I will do it! I cannot leave such a diamond in this desert!"

That night the artist tapped at the humble door of Aunty Evans; and drawing his chair alongside the old lady, unfolded his plans. She listened coldly.

"The child is well with her mother—she cannot go."

"But such a gift, madam!"

"A gift from God! it is a sin to tamper with it."

"Ay, from God!" answered the artist solemnly; "it was a sin to leave it unimproved."

An hour was spent in fruitless argument, when the composer suddenly inquired, "But what says the young lady herself? let her speak."

"Yes, let Dora' answer," returned Aunty Evans, triumphantly. "Thank God! I may trust her! what say you, my child?"

Dora's face was buried in the folds of muslin that hung about the little window, and at first she did not raise it.

"Speak as you would have it, darling," said the old lady, softly, drawing nearer, and bending over her idol.

Such dreams as had been swimming in the child's fancy! Such a consciousness that every word the composer had said of her wondrous power was true! Such an irresistible longing to give utterance to an undefinable something that she had always felt struggling within her! How could she resist it? Dora' loved her kind foster-mother; but now there was a fever at her heart and her brain was in a whirl. She raised her eyes. How changed were they! the soft, meek dewiness had passed—they had grown larger and darker, and wore an intensity of meaning, a depth of feeling and purpose, that made them strange to Aunty Evans. The love-thought had almost vanished from the corners of the mouth; the lips lay apart like two lines of burning crimson, the upper drawn up and knotted in the middle, and a spot of bright red glowed in the centre of each pale cheek. Dora' did not speak, it needed not that she should.

"The shadow is falling!" murmured Aunty Evans. My poor, poor Dora'! O, I have had a fearful watch!"

She folded the child in her arms, kissed her hot cheek, placed her hands upon her throbbing temples; and, saying to the composer, "She will go with you," motioned him to leave them alone.

Aunty Evans was not so ignorant of worldly matters, as to trust her precious charge, without due precaution, to the keeping of a stranger. She possessed herself of ample knowledge concerning the character and standing of the composer; and was very exacting in all her arrangements for the child's welfare, evincing a lynx-eyed policy that she had never been supposed to possess. Above all, she insisted on her being allowed to return to her humble home at any moment she should express the wish. So Dora' went away from Alder-Brook, and Aunty Evans was left alone.

Bright Summer passed in her glory—melancholy Autumn laid a worn head upon the bosom of Winter; and with sighs yielded up the spirit—and Winter came on with his cold breath and blazonry of jewels. Six months had passed away since Dora' sang to her companions on the knoll beneath the two elm-trees. Now she stood in a luxuriously furnished apartment, the soft flaxen ringlets shading her delicate throat as of yore, but with little else to mark her identity with the violet eyed child that had sung in the fields at Alder-Brook. The pale, earnest face of the composer looked out upon her admiringly from a pile of cushions at the other end of the apartment; and she was aware of the gaze, and seemed bent on gratifying him, for her small hands were clasped with unwonted energy, and determination was buried in her cheek and flashed from her eye. She stood near a piano at which a stranger was seated; and after his fingers had passed over the keys, her voice broke forth in all its olden melody. But now it was subject to her control—now she *knew* the feeling that she would express, and her voice became but the wings to bear it out—the prisoned genius had found utterance. Was Dora' happy now? Out upon such simplicity! How could it be otherwise? Was she not about to entrance a world? What blissful emotions would creep into a thousand hearts at listing! And would not the enchantress find an all-sufficient reward in the adulation of millions! Ah! Dora', Dora'! bend thy brow to the halo—tread upon the roses! Never think how the first may darken—how the last may shrivel and fall away from the sharp thorns beneath them! The path has been well trodden and watered—pass on!

The good composer, Dora's friend, was dead.

It had been published far and wide—told in the drawing-room and in the coffee-house; in the private parlour, and in the public saloon; in hall, alley and shop; lisped in the boudoir, and cried in the street—everywhere, in all the places where the virtuous dwell and vicious hide themselves—it had been told that a new star had arisen in the musical horizon; and those who would never care for the artist on account of her art, were told that she was young and beautiful. What a crowd came out to greet the first appearance of our star! Should she not have felt honoured? Lights flashed, jewels blazed, plumes waved and nodded, smiles sped to their destination, or lost themselves upon the air, and all—for her! Not one—not one! Poor Dora', even in her triumph, how desolate!

A burst of applause greeted her appearance, and for a moment her heart bounded, and her eye flashed with gratified ambition. Then rows of faces gaped upon her from the pit, box, and gallery; eyes were strained, and glasses leveled, and the young songstress felt the warm blood mounting hastily to her forehead. Poor Dora'! even in her triumphs how humiliated!

She sang as she had ever sung! for genius is always conscious of its own sacredness, and will not be stared down by bold impudence, nor raised up by admiring plaudits. She sang, and garlands fell at her feet, and all night long, the applauses of the multitude rang, like the idle mockeries that they were in her ear. Was it for that she had toiled, and hoped, and given her better nature up to a withering ambition? Was that her temple in the clouds, now dissolving into its own nothingness—a thing of vapour, bound together by a chain of gilded water-drops? The wings were melted, and Icarus was fast approaching the Aegean. What a blessing that mankind so seldom reach the goal of hope! The chase is glorious—in empty, unsatisfying *success* lies the curse.

It was the anniversary of the evening on which Dora' had resolved to turn from the bosom of her foster-mother to the world which was beckoning her. A light was burning on the white pine table, and beside it sat Aunty Evans, her Bible on her knees. She appeared older, much older, than on that night twelve-month. Thought had cut strange lines upon her face, and deepened the look of simple good nature, once so conspicuous there, to one of earnest, almost painful solicitude. The door was open, and the fragrance from the honey-suckles and roses stole into the apartment; but Aunty Evans thought not a word of the honey-suckles and roses. She was indulging most painful reflections. A passing figure rustled the vines, a shadow fell across the door-way, and a light foot pressed the threshold, yet Aunty Evans looked not up.

"Mother! Mother!—I have come home to you—I am sick, I am weary! Give me a place, mother—a place to die!"

There were sobbings and tears, half joyous, half heart-broken, in the little cottage that night; and in the morning all the village gathered to look upon the returned idol. How changed! Poor Dora'! it is needless to follow thee to the grave. The spirit that, finding food nowhere on earth, turns and eats into itself, can endure but a little time; and we will be more thankful for the natural light that again beamed in thine eye, and the natural feeling that slumbered about thy lips, than sorry for thine early loss. Thy rest is among the flowers where the bees steal their sweets, and the birds spread their winds to the sunlight.

Sleepest thou not passing well, young Dora'?

Source: Emily Judson, *Alderbrook*, 2:247–255

C. W. Dexter to Emily E. Chubbuck, November 27, 1844—Eastville

Miss Chubbuck

The object of my communication is to ascertain if you will receive in your school, Miss Richards and myself—how you can take us. From the recommend [sic] you have given us *of* the school, we think by remining [sic] there one term, we could get just such a situation to teach as we want. She will probably come if you will engage to find her a school. I can not [sic] come unless I can pay afterward. I have succeeded so well in teaching since I left school, that I flatter myself I could get a school and pay in a few months. But I don't wish you to mention it to the teachers unless you think there is some probability of their receiving me on such conditions and you think it best for me to come. Perhaps you can recommend me somewhere, a place where I can have a native French teacher and a good advantage for drawing and painting, as these are less expensive. We have talked some of the Binghampton school as they teach Spanish and Italian there. It would suit us in that respect, but it is a Catholic school you know, and I presume we shall not go there. We are both engaged for the winter and can not [sic] come before Spring if we come at all. Miss Richards wishes you to speak to the teachers, or you know who to and let her know if they will obtain her a school if she comes. You can do as you think best with regard to myself, as I don't feel particularly anxious to run in debt. Should we come, I think we can persuade another young lady to go, a graduate from Cazenovia. I am teaching in Earlville now. Have had nearly forty different scholars, but a case of small pox frightens quite a number away. Engaged last summer to return to Clarkville next month. They are building a new Academy there, and I think we shall have a very fine school, perhaps as long as I wish to remain, but I should prefer to go where I can have a stated salary. Will you have the goodness to write me as soon as possible all the particulars, and give us some advice. Do not think I adhere to Mary's old notion that good scholars are always poor writers. I was obliged to write with all sorts of noises around me etc. Please write when you will be at home and we will come and see you if we can.

Yours etc.

C. W. Dexter

Miss E. E. Chubbuck

Source: American Baptist Historical Society, AJ 24, no. 1206.

Fanny Forester, 1844

Thanksgiving Hymn.

We come with thanks to Thee, O God!
Our Father and our King;
With swelling hearts, and grateful voice,
Our humble praises bring.

We thank thee for the gentle dews,
The sunlight and the rain;
For the rich-tinted, ripened fruit,
And for the amber grain.

We thank Thee, that beneath this roof,
In health and peace we come;
And doubly thank Thee for the smiles,
That cheer the lowliest home.

We thank Thee, that, above us waves
The banner of the free,
And for that dearest gift of all,
Freedom to worship Thee.

Source: Emily Judson, *An Olio of Domestic Verses*, 110-111.

Nathaniel Parker Willis to Emily E. Chubbuck,[333] November 30, 1844[334]

You are uneasy, wholly without reason, my dear friend. I did not even suspect who the lady could be, in whose light you stood, and I called on Mrs. Mary Clavers, (Mrs. Wm Kirkland)[335] to enquire. She doubted whether she had ever named her to me—(Miss Gold.) *I had never even heard she was a writer.* I asked Mrs. K what sort of a writer she was. I give you her answer, word for word. "Nothing like your

---

[333] We have two versions of this letter—the original as written by N. P. Willis, and the edited version published by A. C. Kendrick in his biography, *The Life and Letters of Mrs. Emily C. Judson*. Additions made by Kendrick we have placed in parentheses (), and words in the original left out by Kendrick we have added in bold.

[334] On the address page, written in Chubbuck's handwriting is "N. P. Willis Esq. December 3, 1844. No. 8." We assume that this is the day that she received the letter. The preceding Saturday would have been November 30.

[335] Mr. and Mrs. William Kirkland lived in New York. Of her Willis said in another letter: "she was "my oldest female friend Mrs. Wm. Kirkland (who has been a sister to me for 16 years)."

friend Fanny Forester,[336] of course—not near so much genius—but a very smart girl for all that." If I had seen any thing of hers, by the way, and known who was the authoress, I should have noticed it favorably—very—for I almost lived at old Kip's house (her grandfather) when I was in college. The old man was very fond of me, and Mary Kip, Mrs. C. Kirkland,[337] was a kind of good-natured aunt to us. "Miss Mary Clavers" lived at New Haven at the same time, however, and *she* was my goddess. She was about four years older than I was, and that you know, is ten years in female maturity. She thought much more of my talents than I did of myself, saw exactly what was in the picture for me in the way of celebrity, acted accordingly, and of course treats me now just as she did then. In short, she stood exactly in the relation to me, *then*, that I do *now* to *you*—the one prophet of the future. Oh how wise she was of the world—how elevating—how heart-swelling with every thought she expressed to me! She was, besides, exceedingly handsome, and thus was a *little* love for her dark eyes and Spanish complexion mixed up in my feeling of spirit-worship. I used to kiss her hand, in parting from her, with a passionate idolatry that, (without my dreaming of any return of the devotion) would have made death in her service romantically welcome. She treated me invariably as a *boy* genius, however, and married her deaf old Professor. She writes, (by the way, and *entre nous*) our literary criticisms in the *Mirror*,[338] and her husband writes some of the graver articles about statistics. So we pull in one harness after all. Isn't that a round slice of "Biographia-Literarea?"—And apropos—get that same book of Coleridge's and find all the *chemistry* of celebrity explained to your hand. You will easily adopt what he says to your own case and I could write you volumes on the subject *had I time*. If you were sitting on the sofa opposite my desk, I would read your heart to you, till morning—on that subject.

It would be an exquisite luxury to me to correspond with you, mail by mail—your mind so fresh, your genius so overflowing with un-appreciated wealth—but my time is—I will tell you how, occupied. I rise at six and breakfast at seven, go to the printing office and labor till two—dine at 3—potter about from 4 to 6, and either write from six to ten, or go to the play, and write from ten to one. I have no leisure—do not visit at all—write no letters except on business or to Fanny Forester. I say it would be a luxury—but I cannot afford it. I must write you *brief* letters and receive *long* ones in return. You will not refuse me this over-pay of obligation. Your long, open-hearted letter of today charmed me.[339] I agree to your advice. In the Spirit-world there are no chains nor reluctance. *Common friend be it!*

---

[336] Fanny Forester, Emily Chubbuck's *nom de plume*.

[337] At this time Mrs. Charles Kirkland was living in Utica, and had two daughters, Julia and Amelia.

[338] The *New Mirror*, a literary magazine published in New York by N. P. Willis and General Morris.

[339] This is Willis's response to Emily's letter. Since her letters to Willis were most likely destroyed following Emily's engagement to Judson, we can gather from his response what she had written.

You have this capacity for imagination-tie, but perhaps, five years hence, *you* will propose it to *me*. You are too young to the world to be ready for abstractions now, and I bide your time. The only chance of spoiling it first is by seeing each other, when we shall of course fall into flesh and blood acquaintances. I will keep out of your way five years in the hope of a proposal of a spirit-passion—your *spirit* being as old as mine.

I am glad the idea of a picture pleases you. It is likely to be an interesting matter, for the artist, Flagg, whose mother relies on me as her son's guardian angel, told me today that he should take the opportunity to put his mother's head and mine on the same canvass! I am to be the "stranger," his mother the motherly guardian of Dora, and Dora imaginative. If you were here, he should paint your head for Dora. The subject is the putting the question to Dora as she sits in the window. Your imagination will easily see how it will look, but you must prepare to be disappointed and it will show you one very curious thing—how other people conceive of the scenes you describe. Mr. Flagg's mother, by the way, was the sister of Washington Allston and is a woman of admirable qualities. Flagg himself is the most beautiful youth I know and of an eccentric character that I love, but he is so woefully dissipated that ladies can hardly know him. I do my best to cultivate his virtuous side. He is about 25 and a capital artist. He has promised the picture for next Saturday, and I will send it to you the week following.[340]

Written in the right margin of the address page: "You are a little *disclaim-ish* I observe, on the subject of birth and station.[341] Don't think of it again—for, from where I am, there is not a hair's breadth of difference between you and any-body in Utica, and if you were to come to New York and pass a winter as Fanny Forester, you would move in circles wholly unattainable by the village grandees about you. Act, think and feel, as if 'Hon.' was before your name for exactly what that monosyllable does for Hon. Lady Augusta in England, your fame will do for you—make you an aristocrat, spite of your own modesty other people's envy. It has been drum'd into me by experience…."

Written in the left margin of the address page: "Till I have forgotten all about distinctions in society, and never think where I am above or below people—no more than a prince. If any gifted people don't wish to know me, it's *their* loss, and it's *my* loss if they do wish it, as there are hundreds more wishing to know me than I can possibly remember. It would be so with you if you were once out in the world. Good night, my dear Fanny. Yours very affectionately, N. P. W."

---

[340] See the N. P. Willis letters of November 16 and 24, 1844, and then the letters between the December 20 and December 30, 1844. This paragraph highlighted in bold was published in A. C. Kendrick, *The Life and Letters of Mrs. Emily C. Judson*, 108-109.

[341] This seems to be a theme for Emily—see the letter N. P. Willis wrote to her on November 16, 1844. In a sense he is talking to Emily about an aristocracy of elegance and talent, which would put her at the very top of the social order.

Source: Hanna Family files; A. C. Kendrick, *The Life and Letters of Mrs. Emily C. Judson*, 108–109.

Urania Sheldon Nott to Emily E. Chubbuck, December 5, 1844—Union College

Dear Emily

I saw on my way from Phil. Rev. Doct. Eddy of Newark, New Jersey—who is a very fine writer of stories and books for children, as well as books of a higher order—he said that he had been requested to take the life of Felix Neff—and rewrite it—very much in the form of "The Martyred Missionary" I think it is, an abridgment of the life of the missionary Williams by one of the Editors of the *Observer*—the object is to prepare an interesting little Sabbath School book about the size of *Charles Linn*[342] or a little larger.

Doct. Eddy's engagements are such that he cannot attempt the work—and when I mentioned you to him—he said that Mr. Lord would pay you handsomely for it—if you did it well—He had not seen any of your books—and I told him that you would send him some of them by the Express—to be delivered to Rev. Doct. A. Eddy, Newark, N.J. in care of—Dod Publishers. Mr. Hawley[343] can give you his direction—it is in the *Mirror*[344] rooms I believe near Doct. Sperry's church, New York. Doct. Eddy says that he will warrant you good pay for anything you will write—if those publishers get it out—or the Sabbath School Union employ you, and after reading your works he will speak for you himself—his influence in that quarter is very great—as he is a popular writer—You may recollect the story of old S[ ] of Canandigsia [sic] the colored man who was in the States Prison in Auburn several years—a most hardened wretch, but whose conversion was so very wonderful. Abbott in his [ ] Christian mentions him—Doct Eddy knew him well—he was a member of his church in Canandigsia [sic] and he wrote his life.

If you think best to send the books to him—I think you will not regret it—and you will hear from him as soon as convenient—if you send him your direction.

I went to several of the large *book stores* in New York to find *Charles Linn* (and) *Life as It Is*[345]—to give away, but found only *one copy* of *Charles Linn* at Newman's—the other I could not find—Do you know that Miss Leslie[346] *has written* a book about as large as yours—called "Life as it is"?

---

[342] *Charles Linn or How to Observe the Golden Rule*, Emily's first book, published in July 1841. Emily received $51 for the sold out edition.

[343] Horace H. Hawley was enormously helpful to Emily as she published her early stories and books.

[344] The *New Mirror*, the literary magazine edited by N. P. Willis and General Morris.

[345] *Life as It Is* was published in September 1842.

[346] *Leslie's Magazine* featured literature and fashion for women.

That is a sweet little piece in *The Gazette* and I am very glad you are getting on to Philadelphia—as well as growing in the affection of Mr. Graham[347]—I looked for you in the last No[348] of *Graham*—but did not see you.

I hope you will send the books, to Doct. E. I should have left them myself, but could not find them—Send me by [ ] P. anything of yours that I haven't seen.

In great haste I am yours affectionately and with love to all,

Urania E. Nott

I write this in great haste, expecting to send it by Mury [sic] for whom I have looked all day. We are obliged to go to Troy and Albany tomorrow, to return Saturday eve'g, and fear we shall miss him—but as it seems desirable that you should know of this opening as soon as possible, I send it by mail—Tell Mrs. Pierson that Mrs. Jackson is in mourning for her, indeed Schenectady looks quite desolate.

I want you to go down to Dear Mothers[349] soon and give her and father both a kiss for me[350]—that is if fathers beard is not too long—Indeed I should like to be there to kiss all the dear ones whom I so much love good night—I hope to hear from you all by Mary P. Courtland in the bargain. Say to Anna M.[351] that the hats and feathers work altogether in New York—even such as Mrs. Pearson saw at Menhills before we went up. Black velvet hats are trimmed very much with silk satin ribbon.

Source: American Baptist Historical Society, AJ 25, no. 1237.

Eugenia Damaux to Emily E. Chubbuck, December 10, 1844—New York City

My dear Emily

Have you thought that I never was going to answer your very kind letter, or have you had too much to do to think anything about it—You may have forgotten what you wrote in it—but I can assure you that I have not—Although it is some time ago. I don't think that I have many times in my life felt in lower spirits than I

---

[347] George Graham, editor of *Graham's Magazine*, took an interest in Emily Chubbuck as Fanny Forester and paid her with the unheard of sum of five dollars a page.

[348] Number, or edition

[349] Mrs. Isabell Low Sheldon

[350] Deacon Asa Sheldon, father of Cynthia Sheldon, Urania Sheldon Nott, and Alma Sheldon Anable.

[351] Anna Maria Anable was the niece of the Urania and Cynthia Sheldon, the daughter of Joseph and Alma Sheldon Anable; she was Emily's closest friend at the Utica Female Academy.

did the day that I got your letters—and yours was on the outside so I read it first—*tears* are very bad for my eyes[352] but I could not help them coming. Now My friend what will you say—here it is two days since I begin [sic] this letter—send it and is not half finished—You must be having fine times to day [sic] Thanksgiving day—I should like to be with you this evening so as to buy some of your pretty things. I might buy many as I am so *very rich*! Never the less I have just bought a beautiful silk dress—Mrs. Brown advised me to get one. You cannot imagine of the change that I have made—the difference between Mrs. B. and Mrs. E. is too great to be told. Mrs. B. is a very *kind* and fine woman. And the best of all she seems to take much interest in me—My salary is very small—only $20 a yr.—but Mrs. B. allows me to have some scholars in the morning. My eyes will not let me have many but a few will help me on if I can get them—From what Henry[353] said when I last saw him—I should suppose [sic] that Miss Cyntia[354] [sic] expected me back in the spring—Please to tell her for me, not to expect me. I *wish* that I could come back, but it is *so very uncertain* when I shall be able—that she must make every arrangement for the French Class—that will be the *most* convenient for her, and not think of poor me at all—Mrs. Brown has only engaged to keep me this quarter—but I can assure you that I feel very grateful to be here even if it only for a short time—for it [sic] so much better than—I know—Dr. Elliott is still *very kind* to me—he did not want me to go from his house—but if it was to be for my best to go he said that he would not keep me—And now he seems to be as happy as I am at my good place. There cannot be kinder hearted men than he is. I don't suppose [sic] that you will care one snap for my poor letter if I don't say some thing [sic] about your *dear friend* Hoffman[355]—Is that the way to spell it? No [ ] I have not yet seen him—but will it not be a comfort to—when I tell you that I am staying in the same city—and that some times [sic] I *do* think of, and wish that I might see *him*!![356] Emilie [sic] you must come this way again, and show your self [sic] to him. Will you my dear friend excuse this very poorly written letter, and write me some more of your good ones—How are your folks at home, and what are you writing? Now do be a good girl and write a good long letter to your

---

[352] Eugenia Damaux suffered from an eye problem that was problematic to her. Emily knew Eugenia at the Utica Female Academy.

[353] Henry Sheldon Anable, Joseph and Alma Sheldon Anable oldest child. In August 1846, Henry was in the Milwaukee WI area. In a September 27 letter, he said he might leave Utica to join William and Olivia in Sheboygan WI. He married Rosanna Frick in Sheboygan WI on February 13, 1855, and died September 3, 1887, in Flushing NY.

[354] Miss Cynthia Sheldon was the administrative and finance manager of the Utica Female Academy. She was a mentor, advisor, and friend to Emily.

[355] Charles Fenno Hoffman, a prominent literary figure in Philadelphia and New York, well known in literary circles as an exceptionally talented editor, poet, and writer. Emily had started a correspondence with him as Laura Linden before he discovered that she was Fanny Forester.

[356] It appears that Emily had shared openly with her friends the relationship with Charles Fenno Hoffman through the Laura Linden letters. Through this date there had been three of them. We know that she had sent the actual letters to Dr. and Mrs. Nott, and that Anna Maria Anable had read them as well.

Much attached friend

Eugenia

Source: American Baptist Historical Society, AJ 24, no. 1207

Anna Maria Anable to Emily E. Chubbuck, December 15, 1844[357]

Written in the left margin of the address page by Anna Maria: "Dear Nem[358] You are just as busy as bees in writing and sending out invitations—went to the concert last night with G. Spencer and sister—I have drowned my plan at your departure by gulping down. Sat up last night till the house began to grow big again trying to make something out of Revelation. This morning enraged at my folly of answers."

Written in the right margin of the address page by Anna Maria Anable: "Jane[359] opened this letter—I didn't.

"Court[360] went off yesterday—a letter came from Hat[361] last night which has been stolen by some one. When I find it you shall have it."

Written upside down in the top margin of the address page by Anna Maria: "I'll send the paper."

---

[357] These marginal notes written on the address page from Anna Marie Anable to Emily E. Chubbuck were added to a letter that Eugenia Damaux had written to Sarah Bell Wheeler at the Utica Female Academy. That letter is not included in this volume.

[358] "Nem" or "Nemmy" was a name of endearment given to Emily by a small group of her intimate friends at the Utica Female Academy. Anna Maria Anable was "Ninny."

[359] Miss Jane Kelly was the literary principal at the Utica Female Academy.

[360] Courtland Anable, younger brother to Anna Maria Anable and ordained minister. His life can be followed through the correspondence. He held several positions over the years, and he studied at Hamilton College while he boarded for a time with Emily's parents. In 1853, he returned to Philadelphia where he preached his first sermon at the Eleventh Baptist Church. He was "Uncle Court" to Emily Frances Judson. In 1880, Courtland Anable was listed in the Massachusetts census as an ordained minister serving in a church.

[361] Harriet ("Hatty," "Hattie," or "Hat") Anable, one of the five Anable sisters. She had been teaching in a private residence in the New Orleans area.

[362] Lavinia Richards Chubbuck, Emily's mother, was born June 1, 1875, in Goffstown NH, the eldest of thirteen children. She married Charles Chubbuck on November 17. 1805. They were the parents of seven children.

[363] Sarah Catharine ("Kate," "Kit," or "Kitty") Chubbuck, Emily's older sister, born October 25, 1816.

[364] Nathaniel Parker (N. P.) Willis was the editor, with General George Morris, of the *New Mirror*, a prominent literary magazine in New York. His "discovery" of Emily in the June 8, 1844 edition of the *New Mirror* catapulted her into literary fame and enabled her to command the highest prices for her articles and stories from the major magazines of that period. It was to begin a new and glorious chapter in her life. He was to become over the next two years her friend—her mentor—her confidant. His black-bordered letter of March 21, 1846, made it abundantly clear that her engagement to Adoniram Judson had come as a "death blow," and that he had expected to marry Emily upon his return that month from England. He later returned several of her letters to Emily to demonstrate to her, lest she had forgotten, why he had felt right in that expectation. In vol. 1 there is a timeline which presents in some detail the substance of their developing relationship, all from the letters which Willis had written to Emily. When she received her letters back from Willis, she had destroyed them, feeling that they would cast a negative shadow on her life, and because of that, the life and ministry of Adoniram Judson.

Written upside down in the bottom margin of the address page by Anna Maria: "Have you [ ] any my dear Pithy in consequence of your ride? Love to your mother,³⁶² Kate³⁶³ and all of the other [ ].

"They call Willis"³⁶⁴

Miss N³⁶⁵

Source: American Baptist Historical Society, AJ 24, no. 1208.

Nathaniel Parker Willis to Emily E. Chubbuck, December 16, 1844—Framer's Shop³⁶⁶

I have been here overlooking the boxing up of my friend's picture,³⁶⁷ and as it will probably reach you on Christmas Eve, this is to wish you Christmas greetings—"*meery*" if you prefer them.

Be so kind as when you write to me acknowledging the receipt of this picture to write a separate note, for *any body* [sic] *to see*—as my partners will expect to read your expression of pleasure at the transfer of your picture to canvass, and I should not like to shew [sic] them, or *any one* [sic], a letter in which you had made me your *spiritual* confidant.

Yours in haste—

N. P. W.

Source: Hanna family files.

---

³⁶⁵ "Miss Ninny." "Ninny" was an affectionate name used by Anna Maria. Emily Chubbuck was "Nemmy."

³⁶⁶ Written on the address page in Emily's handwriting, is "N. P. Willis. Dec., 1844, No. 11" (We note that this numbering is out of sequence.). Since the painting is to arrive by Christmas, and it would take about a week by Express, this would put this letter on December 16.

³⁶⁷ Dora' was a fictional character in one of Emily's stories that was released in fall 1844. The artist Flagg was very moved by the story, and N. P. Willis commissioned Flagg to do a portrait of her; details of the painting slowly came out. In a letter dated November 30, 1844, he said: "I am glad the idea of a picture pleases you. It is likely to be an interesting matter, for the artist, Flagg, whose mother relies on me as her son's guardian angel, told me today that he should take the opportunity to put his mother's head and mine on the same canvass! I am to be the "stranger," his mother the motherly guardian of Dora', and Dora' imaginative. If you were here, he should paint your head for Dora'. The subject is the putting the question to Dora' as she sits in the window. Your imagination will easily see how it will look, but you must prepare to be disappointed and it will show you one very curious thing—how other people conceive of the scenes you describe." The painting was shipped in the Christmas season and Anna Maria Anable wrote to Emily on December 30, 1844, that they had retrieved the painting from the express office. Apparently between the time he had received the painting and brought it to the express office, it had been on display, and he told Emily that thousands had seen and admired it.

Emily E. Chubbuck to N. P. Willis, Editor of the New Mirror,[368] December 17, 1844[369]

~~From the pages of New Mirror~~
Underhill Cottage, Alder-Brook.

Most Gracious "We"—That last letter of yours has a discordant tone to it, to-day; for, by my troth, my little body is a-weary of this great world. The wind is wheeling around the corner of our cottage, with a roar, a screech, and a die-away sob, which makes me feel very much like sobbing, too; and the dead leaves lie piled up in great ugly heaps, beneath my window. Ugh! what care I for a Polka this, or Polka that? Give me my volume of the *New Mirror Library*, (I have got it bound elegantly,) a woollen net-shawl, and a rocking-chair; then close the door, and fasten the shutters—your whole city for my little lease of comfort! Now, that confession pleases you, I dare say, it has such a decidedly literary sound to it. Two important qualities have I gained since joining Bluedom, fault-finding and selfishness. And this is the very day for the "come out," of both. I wonder how I *should* look in your *Mirror* with this fix on my face! Your public would not only name me sober, but sour and sixty. As I told you before,

"The day is cold, and dark and dreary."

There is a whole cloud of ghostly vapor between my window and Deacon Palmer's house; and the brook is as blue with the cold as my new *bas*. Dear! dear! what think you of wasting the flush of summer on your pavements, and then being called home to see the year in its winding-sheet? I hear that cousin 'Bel'[370] is very gay. In the summer, gaiety is a country maiden; in the winter, a city belle. Heigho!

But most of all am I vexed with you, your own proper, editorial garret self. Pray, what right had you to break the seal of that letter, even if it was your own? I contend that the moment "yours" is affixed to a letter, it is no longer the property of the writer; and I mean to consult the books about it. But, waiving the subject of right, what need to let the sovereign eighteen-millions into the secret of my inquisitiveness, and world-loving-ness, and all that sort of thing? Why, I was just on the point of setting up as a Mrs. Hannah More, or something as wise and dignified. Now, my letter, number four, seems to have been Grahamized. I have an uncomfortable impression that the post-master, postmaster's wife, and postmaster's wife's dear

---

[368] This appeared as an article in the pages of the *New Mirror*. Its title was "Reply to a Letter from the Editor of the New York Mirror."

[369] In his letter of December 24, 1844, Willis had said: "Your *cottage* article was published a week ago in our daily paper. I will send it to you."

[370] Cousin 'Bel' was Anna Maria Anable. It was Emily and Cousin 'Bel' who had gone to New York, and Emily's letter of their adventure, written to the editor of the *New Mirror* and published on June 8, 1844, that had started Emily solidly on the road to literary fame, helped a great deal in that start by the support of N. P. Willis of the *New Mirror*.

friends and confidents have all possessed themselves of the contents, and are as well versed in my affairs as I am myself. They have the same intimation about the Polka hat (do you believe it will be pretty?) and if they cannot get it themselves, will be sure to say, "silly thing! how much she *does* think of her dress!" Oh! it is excessively awkward to have every body [sic] at the rehearsal! If you *must* print your letters, just make believe that you have no idea I care a red maple leaf for knowing; and I will make my inquiries "under the rose"—put them in a postscript, to be torn off.

I have never told you anything about Alder-Brook, and my charming, funny little home. Oh! such a brook as that at the foot of our hill—when it is a brook, I mean, for now it is nothing but a palpable line of chilliness—living, "I take it," by the blue breath and ague, that shakes it into wrinkles. But I never saw it so ugly before never. You should be here in the season of cowslips and spring-violets, and let me guide you along among the budding things, all leaning forward to see their young faces in it. Oh! that stream which every body knows, with *the bridge* across it, is nothing to this! And this has a bridge, too; a low one, level with the footpath, made of logs tied together with strong wythes of beech. I laughed and crowed about this water, when I was a baby, and, therefore, I love it. I played beside it, when the days were years of summer-time, and the summers were young eternities of brightness, and therefore, I love it. It was the scene of my first grief, too. Shall I tell you? There is not much to tell, but I have a notion that there are people above us, up in the air, and behind the clouds, that consider little girls' doings about as important as those of men and women. The birds and the angels are great levellers.

It was a dry season the brook was low, and a gay trout, in a coat of golden brown, dotted over with crimson, and a silver pinafore, lay, weather-bound, on the half-dry stones, all heated and panting, with about a tea-spoonful [sic] of lukewarm water turning lazily from its head, and creeping down its back at too slow a pace to afford the sufferer hope of emancipation. My Sympathies—little girls, you must know, are made up of love, and sympathy, and such like follies, which afterwards contract into—*n'importe*! I was saying, my sympathies were aroused; and, quite forgetting that water would take the gloss from my new red morocco shoes, I picked my way along, and laying hold of my fine gentleman in limbo, succeeded in burying him in the folds of my white apron, wet face and all! But such an uneasy prisoner! More than one frightened toss did he get into the grass, and then I had an infinite deal of trouble to secure him again. His gratitude was very like that of human's, when you do them unasked service.

When I had reached a cool, shaded, deep spot, far adown, where the spotted alders lean, like so many self-enamored Narcissus's, over the ripple-faced mirror, I dropped my apron, and let go my prize. Ah! he was grateful *then*! He must have been! How he dived, and sprang to the surface, and spread out his little wings of dark-ribbed gossamer, and frisked about, keeping all the time a cool, thin sheet of silver, between his back and the sun-sick air! I loved that pretty fish, for I had been kind to it! and I thought it would love me, too, and stay there, and be a play-fellow for me; so I went every day and watched for it, and watched until my little eyes ached, but I never saw it again. That was my first grief; what is there in years to make a heart ache [sic] heavier? That first will be longer remembered than the last, I dare say.

Now I have no room to describe to you our village, and the old homestead, and the people about here, without cheating my postscript; but I will take another opportunity. In the meantime, tell all you hear, see, do, and guess, that other people are doing or expecting to do, there in your wilderness of wonders ; and make your news as fresh as possible, and be very attentive to particulars, and—and—glance your eye down the page while I am signing myself,

Yours, till the weather changes,

Fanny Forester

N. B. (Not the postscript.) I have been careful not to introduce the words *knot*, *heart*, and *Laban* into this letter, because you let them be printed in my last story, *rush*, *breast*, *labour* [sic]—to say nothing of such minor mistakes as putting *nunc.* for *mem.*, and *bones* for *shoes*. What a Cupid your proof-reader must be!

Source: Fanny Forester, *Trippings in Author-land*, 173–77

J. Post to Emily E. Chubbuck, December 19, 1844—New York City

Miss Emily E. Chubbuck

Dear Madam

Yours a long time since with the "Bank Note," were rec'd—and would have rec'd earlier attention, but for the illness of the Editor.[371] The "Bk note" was too long for our No,[372] and too good to refuse, so we broke for the first time our one rule, which we might do again for the same reason, and inserted "to be continued" etc.

We regret that you have imitated those naughty "Factory girls" and struck for higher wages[373]—It may be sport to you, but a few such strikes may be death to us.

---

[371] In his letter of November 19, 1844, John Inman had spoken of having to cut back his work, and assigning the work at the *Columbian* to someone else.

[372] Number or edition.

[373] We find Emily being compared to a "Naughty Factory Girl" an extremely interesting comparison. Post is an obvious capitalist. Post is obviously aware that on November 19, 1844, John Inman, the editor of the *Columbian Magazine*, had agreed to Emily's request of receiving the unheard sum of five dollars a page for her work.

If authors will not encourage a magazine in New York, who will? They have contributed to kill all that have started hitherto. There's Bryant[374]—Paulding, Hoffman,[375] and others among the Males, and more among the Ladies, who will not write you any *thing reasonable*—they can't be reached by magazine publishers, at living prices, and especially by those just starting, and struggling into favor. They very seldom appear in *Graham's*[376] or *Godey's*[377]—Even they can't afford to deal with them. Is this right, especially toward a New York magazine? If we mistake not—It is for the interest of our literary friends to come to our aid, for in what other form can our writers in these days of cheap and trashy literature do so well as in writing for such works as ours.[378]

We leave the matter with you however, hoping that whether you have any tender mercies or not, that you will polish for us the finest jewels in your fine collection—Give up apples or gold in pictures of silver

Very respectfully and truly Yr Obt [ ]

J Post

Source: American Baptist Historical Society, AJ 25, no. 1218.

Anna Maria Anable to Emily E. Chubbuck, December 21, 1844

There's no letter for you yet Nem[379] and I hope there won't be one till tomorrow for mine would stand but a poor chance along with Graham[380] or Willis[381]—Sunday is your news day so I shall expect heaps of things, to morrow [sic] night.

The morning after the *Swarry!* [sic] can you imagine how we feel? I got up as early as I conveniently could and just got a swallow of hot coffee—dawdled about

---

[374] William Cullen Bryant was a contributor to the *Columbian Magazine*, and to the other major magazines of the time.

[375] Charles Fenno Hoffman, a prominent literary figure in Philadelphia and New York, well known in literary circles as an exceptionally talented editor, poet, and writer. Emily had started a correspondence with him as Laura Linden before he discovered that she was Fanny Forester.

[376] George Graham, editor of *Graham's Magazine*, took an interest in Emily Chubbuck as Fanny Forester and paid her with the unheard of sum of five dollars a page.

[377] *Godey's Ladies Book* was a magazine that combined poetry, prose, and beautiful engravings, many of them about fashion.

[378] Emily, in fact, had been writing for N. P. Willis and the *New Mirror* for free because of their precarious financial state, though moving on to fame and great publicity in the process. In his letter of November 19, 1844, Inman, in agreeing to pay Emily five dollars a page for her work, had said that, fair being fair, she would have to stop writing gratis for the *New Mirror* and create equal opportunities for her work.

[379] "Nem" or "Nemmy" was a name of endearment given to Emily by a small group of her intimate friends at the Utica Female Academy. Anna Maria Anable was "Ninny."

[380] George Graham, editor of *Graham's Magazine*, took an interest in Emily Chubbuck as Fanny Forester and paid her with the unheard of sum of five dollars a page.

[381] Nathaniel Parker (N. P.) Willis was the editor of *New Mirror*, the magazine that catapulted Emily into literary fame. He became a friend, mentor, and eventually a suitor.

in Aunt C.'s[382] room until ten—went up to your room and checkmated Jane[383] till she grew desperate and vowed total abstinence from chess and the *associated*. Rushed out in the hall on the information that there was a box for Aunt Cynthia in the vain hope of getting a sight of your picture[384]—Alas! it was a box of dried fruit—sent by order.

Do you want to know how the Swarry [sic] went off? It went off in a blaze! None of your newspaper blazes like Fanny Forester's[385]—but a regular bona fide blaze. Mr. Williams had just read a verse of Home—when the whole side of the house was illuminated. The men rushed to the door—the girls screamed—every body seemed demented. It passed off however—'twas a carpenters shop down Washington Street—Miss Anable called the audience to order by an impromptu piece of music—and Mr. W. commenced anew the reading of Home—am [ ] the girls did better than I expected—Had a good audience and congratulations from the "powers that be"—i.e. trustees.

I suppose you are crazy to know why I don't send the *New World*—It's not owing to neglect Pettey[386]—[ ] [ ]!—I went down to Mr. Soaks [sic] and looked at his four last numbers—but could see nothing about you but that number we had—So it must refer to that—and the insinuation that you are Willis is the meaning of Miss Nancy—so rest your dear heart darling.

Helen Munson[387] just called and I learned accidentally that Aunt C. had a letter from you—Your package went safely to Willis as you will see by the last *Mirror*—I think that letter is about as pretty a thing as you have written for him—always excepting my pet "Dora."

Fan[388] and Jonas haven't come yet—and we haven't heard from Hat[389]—but there's a troop of country cousins from Remsen down stairs—how provoking! It's cold as Greenland to day—but nonetheless, if I had a cutter and horse I would drive out and stay till Tuesday—Wish I could—I want to get away to day [sic] to

---

[382] Miss Cynthia Sheldon was the administrative and finance manager of the Utica Female Academy. She was a mentor, advisor, and friend to Emily.

[383] Jane Kelly was Emily Chubbuck's friend at the Utica Female Academy. Following the deparure of Mr. and Mrs. Nichols, Jane became the literary principal in eary 1844. Then with the departure of Cynthia Sheldon to Philadelphia in fall 1848, she became "headmistress."

[384] N. P. Willis commissioned an artist named Flagg to do a portrait of "Dora'," one of Emily's fictional characters.

[385] Fanny Forester, Emily Chubbuck's *nom de plume*

[386] "Petty" or "Pettie" or "Nemmy Pettie" was another name of endearment used by Anna Maria Anable with Emily.

[387] Helen Munson was to marry Jimmy Williams. Jimmy was often mentioned in Anna Maria Anable's letters, usually just as "Jimmy."

[388] We thought this might be Fanny Anable, Anna Maria Anable's sister—but in a December 27, 1844 letter Anna Maria says "here are Fan and Jonas—as comfortable and natural in their *behavior* as two-year-old married folks—Fan *has* an easy way of taking things." Obviously it is another "Fan."

[389] Harriet ("Hatty," "Hattie," or "Hat") Anable, one of the five Anable sisters. She had been teaching in a private residence in the New Orleans area.

some quiet little *home*—Tell Kate[390] if she was here she should have the other blacky—Thank her for her offer about the petticoat. There! That makes me want to go—a great deal more—I won't think another word about it. Love to your Mother[391]

from Ninny[392]

Source: American Baptist Historical Society, AJ 23, no. 1128.

Nathaniel Parker Willis to Emily E. Chubbuck,[393] December 23, 1844[394]

My dear friend,

I have been intending to write you a long letter, and have wasted odds and ends of time in the hope of an hour of leisure. But I must now simply advise you of the boxing up of the picture of Dora,[395] and assure you how large a slice of the kindest side of my heart goes with it. I do not know when I shall be able to write to you, for I am so overdone with cares and work that my doctor has ordered me out of town, and I must confine myself to the most needful pen-work. **Will you comfort me in my hours of platitude with a long letter**. The picture has been visited by thousands, and is much admired. Hang it with a *side light*, and be careful in having it unpacked. **It will go from here on Tuesday. God bless you, dear Fanny**.

Your "bald composer,"

N. P. W.

Source: Hanna family files; A. C. Kendrick, *The Life and Letters of Mrs. Emily C. Judson*, 110.

---

[390] Sarah Catharine ("Kate," "Kit," or "Kitty") Chubbuck, Emily's older sister, born October 25, 1816.

[391] Lavinia Richards Chubbuck, Emily's mother, was born June 1, 1875, in Goffstown NH, the eldest of thirteen children. She married Charles Chubbuck on November 17. 1805. They were the parents of seven children.

[392] "Ninny" was a name of endearment given to Anna Maria Anable by her most intimate friends at the Utica Female Academy. Emily was "Nemmy."

[393] We have two versions of this letter—the original as written by N. P. Willis, and the edited version published by A. C. Kendrick in his biography, *The Life and Letters of Mrs. Emily C. Judson*. Additions made by Kendrick we have placed in parentheses (), and words in the original left out by Kendrick we have added in bold.

[394] In Emily's handwriting on the address page is "N. P. Willis. Dec. 26, 1844 No. 9" (for a section of letters in December, these numbers are out of sequence). In actuality it was sent from New York on December 23, and forwarded from Utica on December 26. We date it December 23.

[395] N. P. Willis commissioned an artist named Flagg to do a portrait of "Dora'," one of Emily's fictional characters.

Nathaniel Parker Willis to Emily E. Chubbuck,[396] December 24, 1844[397]

Your exquisitely truthful and womanly letter, dear Emily, would be best appreciated and most loved by angels. It has heightened the ceiling of the upper chamber in which my interest in you has been carefully prisoned. I do not suffer myself to visit you in a mental apartment—where even the furniture of common compliment would diminish the kind of reverence your purity has inspired me with—*not* purity of mind, for that would be a common quality, but purity of tenderness,—passionate purity of warm affection. I knew long ago that your heart and mind were "braided together, thread for thread." You told me nothing new in that. I have given ten or fifteen years to study of *women* as men study a science, and I know *you* better than your mother could ever know you. I see that your mind would *all be swept under* by a passionate affection for a worthy husband—singularly forcible and peculiar as that mind is. You are one of those women whose tenderness makes them sob in the throat when they speak of those they love with any sudden impulse. You think your kind of heart common *however* —and it is rare as a double diamond or a "*perfect* chrysolite." I will not go on with my portrait of you, but I will say something that will make you smile, viz:—that I have coolly estimated by my "science" of women, that as a wife, you would be of twice the value of any woman I ever knew—to a man like me.

The startling truth I have told you on the other page, I arrived at some time since, and every subsequent letter and production of yours has confirmed it, particularly this last. I can afford to tell it you, because I am married, and because you will understand that I dare write you things that might be perverted. But now let me tell you another failing toward you which I have hitherto left to your powers of divining. I have a desire to try whether I can separate love (for such a woman as I could adore under proper circumstances) from all possible selfishness—from every aim at enlisting a return—from every feeling except living beside the knowledge of her sweetness as one lives beside a beautiful river. I want to join *one* spirit in the next existence with a clasping of hands in which there shall be nothing to forget—*tho' we have loved*. You will recall, *now*, all my treatment of you since I have understood you, soberly and with a view to the spirit-future, that I love you—that had I no other chain, I should be lost unless I could link my existence with yours—that you are mingled by nature in proportions to be a *philtre* to me—but that I shall cultivate circumstances and correspondence, and alliance with your fame,—all with one tender but hallowed devotion, such as you will touch my forehead for hereafter with your spirit lips, with the approbation of a standard purer than this

---

[396] Written on the address page in the handwriting of Emily Chubbuck: "N. P. Willis Dec. 27, 1844 [the date that she received it] No. 10."

[397] This letter says that it is being written on Christmas Eve. It was post-marked as mailed on December 25, 1844.

world. Do you understand me, dear Emily? Do you see why I would not trust this delicious dream to the risk of meeting you and loving you *selfishly*?

I will not begin another page with my *visions*—but to something that will be more agreeable to you. Your picture[398] by this time is at Albany and I had hoped that you would receive it on Christmas Eve. Your friends will open it at the Academy and write you about it,—I trust they will like it. The portrait of my back (!!) is true to the life, what there is of it, every one [sic] recognizing it immediately.[399] The remark that the malicious will make, will be an injustice to both of us, for they will say that it is *Willis and one of his admirations*—etc.—but I should counsel you not to let it hang any where [sic] out of your private room. Make it a great favor to let anyone see it. By the way, I shall send Flagg to Utica to sketch you for me, and Gen. Lyman has promised to arrange the sitting in his father-in-law's house or somewhere else to avoid publicity. *You must not refuse me this*.

There seems a sympathy in our illness—for tho' perfectly well in body, I have so overworked myself of late that I have had something like swoons which my doctor tells me are precursors of *palsy of the brain*! He has ordered me out of town, to the woods, and a cessation of all work—which I cannot afford. But! shall be more *soigné* of myself, amid my myriad cares. Be careful, *you*, of Dora. By the way, your speculations as to my *looks* amuse me. Were you to see me, you would be too much surprised at one quality of mine to think of my looks. The perfection of manners is to end where we began—with nature—and you have probably seen only men *in transition*. My life at courts abroad, and in all countries, has put me *through*, and you would perhaps see in me what you would wonder at—a child who might....

Written along the left margin of the address page: "...be a gentleman if he chose. This, at least, was the compliment paid me by a very sagacious Duchess whom I visited in Scotland. People in this country compliment my personal elegance very often, but they do not know enough to understand my want of *manners*. With genius, you will *see me*, after this explanation. I am using Christmas Eve to write to you, as we have no paper tomorrow—but I dread to know how seldom I can write to you. Your *cottage* article[400] was published a week ago in our daily paper. I will send it to you."

Written in the right margin of the address page: "I am not surprised at your being so well-treated on the road, for the magnetism of a heart like yours is universal—'spectacles'"[401] notwithstanding.—Write me very long letters without

---

[398] N. P. Willis commissioned an artist named Flagg to do a portrait of "Dora'," one of Emily's fictional characters.
[399] Earlier N. P. Willis had said that he was the model for the man in the picture.
[400] See a copy of this dated December 17, 1844. It was stated as coming from "Underhill Cottage, Alder-Brook."
[401] When Emily had first written to Willis, in the letter that appeared in the *New Mirror* June 8, 1844, Willis had suggested that he first thought the letter had come from "some sharp old maid in spectacles."

waiting for answers, and when you send me a communication, send an enclosed note for *any body* [sic] to see. Direct always simply New York, and *not Mirror* office nor Astor House. They go then into my private box. God bless you, dear Emily. Ever yours."

Source: Hanna family files.

Anna Maria Anable to Emily E. Chubbuck, December 27, 1844

Only think dear Pithy[402] almost a week of the vacation has already passed! A week to day [sic] weren't we in fear and trembling for the Swarry [sic]. I reckon. Now—here are Fan and Jonas—as comfortable and natural in their *behavior* as two-year-old married folks—Fan *has* an easy way of taking things. We have chessed and checkered and back-gammoned and "Dr. Busby'd" to our hearts content—girls and all—Every evening we go down in the parlor and between lamp mats (you'd laugh to see the number working) and games and dancing—we contrive to have right royal times—Fortunately Jimmy[403] has been prevented paying his usual devotions—this week—and another fortunately Hank has been ailing just enough to confine him to the house, and give him a chance to flirt with the girls. Now—don't you wish you were here? I haven't the faintest idea of what you are about—but I imagine you with the sick head-ache all the time—Mrs. Kirkland came over to have a nice talk with me the other day—It was all about Willis[404]—she likes him very much, and told me some things about him that were quite inter*est*ing. She likes you too—when you come back you must go over and see her. There's nothing from New York. There has not been even a *Mirror*[405] this week—I expect the mail will come with a rush when it does come.

I hope it will bring Fan and Sarah. Did I tell you Mrs. Barker and Mary Gregory[406] came with Fan—

I must break off now—and pay Dr. Blakesly a visit—don't you envy me? Aunt C.[407] says Platt is going out home this week and will arrange all that matter with his sister.

[402] "Pithy" was another term of endearment for Emily Judson—others included "Nemmy"—"Petty"—"Sister Peakedchin"—"Nemmy Petty."

[403] Jimmy Williams, often mentioned in Anna Maria Anable's letters, usually just as "Jimmy."

[404] Nathaniel Parker (N. P.) Willis was the editor of *New Mirror*, the magazine that catapulted Emily into literary fame. He became a friend, mentor, and eventually a suitor.

[405] The *New Mirror* was a literary magazine published by N. P. Willis and General Morris.

[406] See the letter of Mary Gregory to Emily Chubbuck dated November 11, 1844 This letter suggested that she was formerly of the Utica Female Seminary where Emily attended and then taught.

[407] Miss Cynthia Sheldon was the administrative and finance manager of the Utica Female Academy. She was a mentor, advisor, and friend to Emily. By this time, she had become "Aunt Cynthia."

All send love. Write tomorrow—or I shall think you are sick. Love to all—ever yours

Ninny[408]   Source: American Baptist Historical Society, AJ 23, no. 1127.

Anna Maria Anable to Emily E. Chubbuck, December 30, 1844

Dear Nem[409]

After a great holler we have succeeded in getting your picture[410] from the express office in time for Fan B.[411] to see it before she left. They have just gone. Sarah Bell[412] has gone to spend a fortnight with them—the picture we intended to send by stage this afternoon but the express people say they have notes from you to have it come with them tomorrow—It will be the safest way perhaps—'Tis a beautiful thing—but you want a distant view—so you must put it in one room and look at it in another. [Note: Here a line and a half of written text are crossed out.]

You must be enjoying your vacation with your cachehinations [sic] and crazy fits.—You had better come home. You must ask Willis[413] to come and see you—you can condole with each other—Mind you keep a copy of your letters—I want to know what you have been doing to him—We expect a house full tomorrow—Giles and all his family are coming up to spend New Years—and Sam[414] and wife we don't know when to expect—We keep open house this vacation in good earnest—but the more the merrier when you are family in for hospitality—What do you mean to do to Hoffman?[415] You can tell me safely—for I don't read your letters aloud until I have first read them myself—Do you suppose he knows yet that you are F. F.?[416]

---

[408] "Ninny" was a name of endearment given to Anna Maria Anable by her most intimate friends at the Utica Female Academy. Emily was "Nemmy."

[409] "Nem" or "Nemmy" was a name of endearment given to Emily by a small group of her intimate friends at the Utica Female Academy. Anna Maria Anable was "Ninny."

[410] N. P. Willis commissioned an artist named Flagg to do a portrait of "Dora'," one of Emily's fictional characters.

[411] We believe this to be Fanny Buckingham, a neice of the Sheldon sisters, a cousin to Anna Maria. Her husband was an officer on the Swallow, which would sink on the river in April of 1845 with many lives lost. See Emily's letter of April 15, 1845.

[412] Sarah Bell Wheeler was a teacher at the Utica Female Academy, and an intimate friend of Emily Chubbuck.

[413] Nathaniel Parker (N. P.) Willis was the editor of New Mirror, the magazine that catapulted Emily into literary fame. He became a friend, mentor, and eventually a suitor.

[414] Samuel Low Anable was the fifth of the nine children born to Alma and Joseph Anable.

[415] Charles Fenno Hoffman, a prominent literary figure in Philadelphia and New York, well known in literary circles as an exceptionally talented editor, poet, and writer. Emily had started a correspondence with him as Laura Linden before he discovered that she was Fanny Forester.

[416] F. F., or Fanny Forester, was Emily Chubbuck's nom de plume. In fall 1843, Emily Chubbuck and Charles Fenno Hoffman had exchanged three letters; Emily had written to him under the nom de plume of Laura Linden. In some April, 1845 letters, Hoffman states that he still did not know who Laura Linden was in summer 1844. By April 1845 Hoffman is able to say in one of his letters that now that Laura has revealed herself—they can continue or renew their relationship. One of Hoffman's 1845 Laura Letters was mailed to Fanny Forester, care of Emily Chubbuck; another was simply sent to Emily Chubbuck.

I think he is a goat[ ] if he don't [sic]—but I strongly suspect he is of the [ ] [ ] [ ]—I feel possessed to have you do *something* to that man and yet I should not want him to feel persecution—All are well—Come back the first of the week can't you? do! Time to see the folks—Good bye—Ninny[417]

Source: American Baptist Historical Society, AJ 23, no. 1126.

Anna Maria Anable to Emily E. Chubbuck, December 31, 1844

Dear Nemmy[418]

They are draping the picture open for me to write just one little word. I can't bear to have the "pretty picture" go—I have become quite attached to her! We have got a beautiful light for her.[419]

So Missy you've been a-writing for Willy[420] again—and a-pretending for to be sick; and a-working upon the sympathies of your unsuspecting Demon at the same time. Oh!!

What do you suppose Mr. Look will say to your description of her company? She was here yesterday to see the picture. Jimmy[421] thinks it a fine picture, so *of course it is*. Come back do, for I am getting lonesome—and am crazy to know what you are doing to the fellows—we had about the grandest….

Written across the right margin and text of page 1: "…ride yesterday you ever saw. There was a little fine drissling [sic] snow all the afternoon that the girls were possessed to ride—so Henry[422] got a big concord sleigh with Jim Lorsso [sic] and

---

[417] Ninny was a name of endearment given to Anna Maria Anable by her most intimate friends at the Utica Female Academy. Emily was "Nemmy."

[418] "Nem" or "Nemmy" was a name of endearment given to Emily by a small group of her intimate friends at the Utica Female Academy. Anna Maria Anable was "Ninny."

[419] N. P. Willis commissioned an artist named Flagg to do a portrait of "Dora'," one of Emily's fictional characters.

[420] Nathaniel Parker (N. P.) Willis was the editor of *New Mirror*, the magazine that catapulted Emily into literary fame. He became a friend, mentor, and eventually a suitor.

[421] Jimmy Williams, often mentioned in Anna Maria Anable's letters, usually just as "Jimmy."

[422] Henry Sheldon Anable, Joseph and Alma Sheldon Anable oldest child.

we all piled in—and had a most uproariously fine ride.[423] Our girls are having grand times—they sit in my room and sew and carry on from morning till night. What wonder the sun am I writing so much for."

Good bye

Ninny[424]   Source: American Baptist Historical Society, AJ 23, no. 1139D.

---

[423] Sleigh riding was a popular pastime for Emily and for her friends at the Utica Female Academy. At some point Emily had written this poem to express her feelings about it. This is found in *An Olio of Domestic Verse*, 99–100. Its title is "The Bonny Sleigh."

    Come, come away, in my bonny sleigh,
    Away o'er the wintry sea, Love,
    Like a fairy boat on the foam afloat,
    It will skim with thee and me, Love;
    Gay, gayly O, through the spangled snow,
    As our bounding pulses light, Love,
    While thy dear eyes beam, as in my dream
    I saw them yesternight, Love.

    Away, away in my bonny sleigh,
    The warm furs spreading over,
    And thy timid ear, half bent to hear
    The whispers of thy lover!
    Let poets woo, when the summer dew
    With the moon-beam comes to play, Love,
    But for me the bliss of the stolen kiss,
    That hallows my bonny sleigh, Love.

[424] "Ninny" was a name of endearment given to Anna Maria Anable by her most intimate friends at the Utica Female Academy. Emily was "Nemmy."

Letters

January - June 1845

Emily E. Chubbuck to Anna Maria Anable, January 1, 1845

I have been gazing and gazing at my darling Dora[1] every minute since she came this morning[2] till I have just bethought me (now the bell is ringing for twelve o'clock) that I have two letters to write. Don't feel too grand to think you are served first for the fact is, it is so long since I have written anything that I think it best to get my hand in before writing "thank you" to Willis.[3] So Mrs. Mother-in-law,[4] you feel called upon to scold a little do you? It's no use. The first Sat. after I got home I "felt called upon" to write and inquire of W. if he got my package, which I was afraid had been lost. (If you recollect the letter in it, you will understand my anxiety.)[5] That is every word I have written him. He had no business to make the quotation he did from my letter, but Mr. Look never will recognize it—he will think it referred to another company as indeed it did. Perhaps you will

---

[1] Dora' was a fictional character in one of Emily's stories that was released in fall 1844. The artist Flagg was very moved by the story, and N. P. Willis commissioned Flagg to do a portrait of her; details of the painting slowly came out. In a letter dated November 30, 1844, he said: "I am glad the idea of a picture pleases you. It is likely to be an interesting matter, for the artist, Flagg, whose mother relies on me as her son's guardian angel, told me today that he should take the opportunity to put his mother's head and mine on the same canvass! I am to be the "stranger," his mother the motherly guardian of Dora', and Dora' imaginative. If you were here, he should paint your head for Dora'. The subject is the putting the question to Dora' as she sits in the window. Your imagination will easily see how it will look, but you must prepare to be disappointed and it will show you one very curious thing—how other people conceive of the scenes you describe." The painting was shipped in the Christmas Season and Anna Maria Anable wrote to Emily on December 30, 1844, that they had retrieved the painting from the express office. Apparently between the time he had received the painting and brought it to the express office, it had been on display, and he told Emily that thousands had seen and admired it.

[2] The painting had been sent by N. P. Willis to the Utica Female Academy, arriving on December 30, according to a letter from Anna Maria Anable. A December 31 letter said that they were forwarding it to Emily in Hamilton.

[3] Nathaniel Parker (N. P.) Willis, along with George "General" Morris, was the editor of the *New Mirror*, a prominent literary magazine in New York. His "discovery" of Emily in the June 8, 1844 edition of the *New Mirror* catapulted her into literary fame and enabled her to command the highest prices for her articles and stories from the major magazines of that period. It was to begin a new and glorious chapter in her life. He was to become over the next two years her friend—her mentor—her confidant. His black-bordered letter of March 21, 1846, made it abundantly clear that her engagement to Adoniram Judson had come as a "death blow," and that he had expected to marry Emily upon his return that month from England. He later returned several of her letters to Emily to demonstrate to her, lest she had forgotten, why he had felt right in that expectation. In vol. 1 there is a timeline which presents in some detail the substance of their developing relationship, all from the letters which Willis had written to Emily. When she received her letters back from Willis, she had destroyed them, feeling that they would cast a negative shadow on her life, and because of that, the life and ministry of Adoniram Judson.

[4] Anna Maria Anable often referred to herself in her letters to Emily as "Mother-in-law." Now the reference is by Emily Chubbuck.

[5] It is a great loss that we have none of Emily's correspondence with N. P. Willis. In some letters, we have only a glimpse of what she might have said, as we have his quotes from her letters and his response. At the time of her engagement to Adoniram Judson, Emily suffered enormous pangs of guilt and anxiety, and she asked Willis to return all of her letters believing that there would be material in them that, if it ever saw the public light, would be an embarrassment to the great missionary and his new wife. Writing to Judson she said: "Why sh'd I wish the letters returned if they were not inconsistent with my new relations? Did I not tell you that it was jealousy for your honour which induced me? What has your honor to do with a common friendship? I tell you "honestly" (not for the first time I believe) that I have given W. cause to believe that I loved him, and quite honestly that *I never gave a thought to the construction that might be put upon my letters till I examined the subject with the eyes which love for you had given me.* "At first Willis refused, but apparently relented, for Emily sends Adoniram a letter not long before their departure for Burmah that Willis had, in fact, returned the correspondence. We note further, that in 1860 when A. C. Kendrick asked N. P. Willis for it as he wrote *The Life and Letters of Mrs. Emily C. Judson*, Willis wrote back and simply said that he could not locate it. Emily obviously destroyed those letters—and we suspect that they would have told us much more about her than we have come to know.

recollect a description I once gave you of a ride home when the westerner pulled off his buffalo robe etc. The passengers were so good-natured and attentive this time that it reminded me of that, and I told it as just occurring, because I thought it would be a grand subject for Willis. I am a little vexed at the way it has turned out. I rec'd a long letter from W. last Sat. written on Christmas eve. but he says he don't [sic] know when he shall ever write me again. The poor fellow is threatened with *palsy on the brain*. He seems to think that he and Ole Bull and I are in about the same condition. I hope he don't [sic] allude to Ole Bull's *condition* a few weeks ago.

He says I must keep Dora in my own private room—what think you of that, eh? Moreover, he says he has made his arrangements to send Flagg to Utica to sketch me for him, and says I *must consent*.[6] Now I shall do no such thing—would you? I want to be painted by a good artist, but it would make a tremendous talk and I won't be talked about if I can conveniently help it.—Hav'nt [sic] heard a word from Graham[7] since I have been home.

Please thank dear Miss C.[8] for the medicine—tell her it is the very thing I need, for though I am well enough now to sit up three or four hours at a time the fever clings to me like a stick-tight. We are having rare times for father[9] is just about as sick as I, and—do you know what a sick *man* is? He was taken the day after I got home, and poor mother[10] and Kate[11] have been obliged always to run their feet off. He has'nt [sic] been any of this time so bad as I *was*, they say, but we are about on a par now. He has the real hypochondria, and he makes me so blue sometimes that mother won't let him come into the room to say good-morning. Poor father! He don't [sic] know how to be sick, and I would take his and mine

---

[6] This, and the above, was in the December 24, 1844 letter from N. P. Willis.

[7] George Graham was the editor of *Graham's Magazine*, one of the pre-eminent literary magazines of Emily's time. He took an interest in Emily Chubbuck as Fanny Forester; he mentored her, he published every piece of writing that she could submit to him, and for it all he remunerated her with the unheard of sum of five dollars a page. When, in April 1845, Emily was staying in Philadelphia with the Reverend and Mrs. A. D. Gillette, Mr. and Mrs. Graham were frequent visitors, often inviting Emily to tour parts of the city with them in their elegant carriage. That relationship picked up again when Emily returned to Philadelphia in fall 1845.

[8] Cynthia Sheldon was in charge of the administrative and financial departments of the Utica Female Academy. After Cynthia's sister married and moved away, Cynthia assumed a larger leadership role at the academy. Active and well-known in Baptist circles, Cynthia became an important mentor, advisor, and friend to Emily until the time of Emily's death in 1854. Cynthia was the aunt of Emily's best friend, Anna Maria Anable, and addressed by most as "Aunt Cynthia." In 1848, Sheldon would move to Philadelphia to help Anable with the startup of the Misses Anable's School.

[9] Charles Chubbuck, Emily's father. Though he held varying positions over the years, he failed at most of them. With the purchase of the house for them, Emily was to continue as a significant financial contributor to the support of the family.

[10] Lavinia Richards Chubbuck, Emily's mother, was born June 1, 1875, in Goffstown NH, the eldest of thirteen children. She married Charles Chubbuck on November 17. 1805. They were the parents of seven children.

[11] Sarah Catharine ("Kate," "Kit," or "Kitty") Chubbuck, Emily's older sister. Outside of the two terms at the Utica Female Academy that Emily arranged for her, Catharine always lived with her parents in Hamilton NY. The letters indicate opportunities for marriage, but Catharine remained single. She later helped care for Henry and Edward Judson when, after their return from Burmah in fall 1851, they moved in with their "aunt" and "grandparents." She was remembered by her nephews as "a dear friend."

both if I could. I don't know when I shall come back—as soon as I get well enough to ride so far I think.

What shall I do to Hoffy?[12] Just nothing at all. I don't thank him for his old paper—if he can't send something of more consequence than that he may "go to grass." I don't like him half so well as I do Willis.

The picture is much finer than I expected—how does Mary B.[13] like it? Is she so much taken up with her mother that she couldn't write one little word? I hope she and M. Gregory[14] haven't gone yet, nor won't go till I come back. You seem to be well by the high times that you are having. Give my love to everybody and tell them (I know *you* will do it without telling) to give a thought now and then to poor

Nem[15]
Source: Hanna family files.

Anna Maria Anable to Emily E. Chubbuck, January 6, 1845

My dear Nem[16]

I have just come up from the school-room where I have been looking after my girls—and if I don't embrace this hour while they are classing the girls I shall not have another opportunity this week for with Sarah's[17] and my own pupils to take

---

[12] Anna Maria Anable had asked this question in her December 30, 1844 letter. Charles Fenno Hoffman was a prominent literary figure in Philadelphia and New York, who was well known in those literary circles as an adventurer, an editor, a poet, and a writer of exceptional talent. In fall 1843 he had written three letters to Emily Chubbuck addressed to "Laura Linden," for Emily had written to him under that name, asking his advice about love, fame and fortune. Only one of these letters is in the correspondence. Hoffman was not to learn of Emily's identity until spring 1845; in a letter we have dated April 7, 1845, he spoke of Laura having taken off her mask and revealing herself to him. There were four letters from Hoffman in this April period when Emily was in Philadelphia. There were another three in December 1845 when Emily again was in Philadelphia. See vol. 1, "Cast of Characters," s.v. "Hoffman, Charles Fenno"; and vol. 1, "Places, Events, Organizations, and Magazines," s.v. "Laura Letters." Anna Maria Anable frequently intimated in her letters that Emily was interested in "Hoffy" as a beau.

[13] Mary Barber, mentioned frequently in the Emily Chubbuck Judson letters, was a student and then the art teacher at the Utica Female Academy. There were ups and downs to that relationship; in fall 1845, apparently Mary had written to someone expressing what Anna Maria Anable called "ingratitude," and Mary had been banned from the academy until she made proper apologies to Sheldon. In a September 7, 1845 letter from Anna Maria, we learn that her remarks had been about Cynthia Sheldon. In November 1847, Jane Kelly remarked that they had not heard from Mary in over a year. In 1848, Mary was back at the Utica Female Seminary teaching with Jane Kelly. Though at this time Sheldon had moved to Philadelphia, Mary had been able to reconcile with her, and in later years we find Mary very close to the Sheldon-Anable families; later, there was considerable consternation on Cynthia Sheldon's part in her correspondence with Emily about Mary's health, the seriousness of it, and Mary's impending death. These letters were written in April 1852. Sheldon went to help transfer Mary to Albany in June 1852, where she would be better situated and perhaps have access to better doctors. On September 9, 1852, Anna Maria Anable wrote to Emily of Mary's death.

[14] See the letter written by Mary Gregory to Emily E. Chubbuck on November 11, 1844. This letter suggested that she was formerly a part of the Utica Female Seminary where Emily attended and then taught.

[15] "Nem" or "Nemmy" was a name of endearment given to Emily by a small group of her intimate friends at the Utica Female Academy. Anna Maria Anable was "Ninny."

[16] "Nem" or "Nemmy" was a name of endearment given to Emily by a small group of her intimate friends at the Utica Female Academy. Anna Maria Anable was "Ninny."

[17] Sarah Bell Wheeler was a teacher at the Utica Female Academy, and an intimate of Emily Chubbuck, one of the few who addressed Emily as "Nemmy." In a September, 1847 letter, she was listed as one of the teachers at the Utica Female Academy.

care of I shall be pretty busy—the school is quite full for the first day—[ ] compositions there is no hurry about Jane[18] says—but she wants you to come back as she is very lonesome—the little bed-room looks [ ] forlorn—but she has got an elegant rocking chair—and some pictures—and clean curtains—so when *you* come back you'll look quite smash.

Now Nem I want you to come back on Thursday—I have a plan for curing you up. You mustn't write any more this winter—but you may read as much as is good for you—and we will take a little bit of a walk every fine day—or go out sleigh-riding in our little "express"—and you shall get well right off, that you shall Nemmy.

Don't be scared at the idea that you cannot write—you may write just as many letters to Willis[19] and Graham[20] and any body else as you please. Now aren't I indulgent? You may come with some little stories when you feel very much like it—But come back do! for I know you'll get well if you get back here—I don't know what to say about Flagg's painting your picture[21]—can't he come up here and take *every body's* [sic] portrait and yours among the rest? I wish he could—for I want your picture taken and Mary[22] don't [sic] seem disposed to do it. Don't be wrathy at Hoffy[23]—I don't think he knows yet that you are F. F. He's somewhat stupid.

Have you been out any in Hamilton? Has Mrs. Conant[24] honored you with a call? Ahem! What shall I say next? Oh you must *not* have the picture in your own

---

There are a number of letters from Sarah Bell before and after her marriage to Charles Gould of Boston. They were married in October 1850. There are several letters clustered in the year or two after Emily left for Burmah, and a number of letters at the time of her return to America. Emily stayed with Charles and Sarah Bell Gould in October 1851 when she arrived in Boston, after the long sea voyage from Burmah, and then England. She was to stay there a number of times following that. In 1851, Anna Maria Anable had written of Sarah Bell: "Sarah is grown so lovely in person as well as character that she must assert a blessed influence on all with whom she comes in contact."

[18] Jane Kelly was Emily Chubbuck's friend at the Utica Female Academy. Jane later became a teacher with Emily at the academy. Kelly became the literary principal in 1844 with the retirement of James Nichols and his wife from that position. During a period of Kelly's illness in 1844, Emily filled in the position for her. Then, in 1848, when Cynthia Sheldon moved to Philadelphia to help start the Misses Anable's School, Kelly became the "headmistress" of the academy and successfully brought the academy into the future, though not without some initial disparagement from the Sheldon-Anable families.

[19] Nathaniel Parker (N. P.) Willis was the editor of *New Mirror*, the magazine that catapulted Emily into literary fame. He became a friend, mentor, and eventually a suitor.

[20] George Graham, editor of *Graham's Magazine*, took an interest in Emily Chubbuck as Fanny Forester and paid her with the unheard of sum of five dollars a page.

[21] After commissioning the portrait of "Dora'," one of the Emily's characters in a story had written, N. P. Willis sent it to her after exhibiting it in New York. Writing to Emily on December 24, 1844, he said that he was going to send the artist, Flagg, to Utica to paint Emily's portrait. See also Emily's letter to Anna Maria Anable dated January 1, 1845.

[22] Mary Barber, the art teacher at the Utica Female Academy.

[23] Emily E. Chubbuck had written to Charles Fenno Hoffman as Laura Linden. There are eight responses from Hoffman, and we have labeled these the "Laura Letters." For more complete information and analysis, see vol. 1, "Cast of Characters," s.v. "Hoffman, Charles Fenno"; and vol. 1, "Places, Events, Organizations, and Magazines," s.v. "Laura Letters."

[24] Hannah Chaplin Conant, an accomplished biblical scholar, wrote a number of articles and books and was considered very competent in the biblical field.

room of course[25]—What streak is it in Willis to be now so private about it after it has been exhibiting in New York to thousands?[26]

I had a letter from Eugenia[27] last and she was making preparations to receive calls on New Years—Mrs. Brown is very kind to her. Hat[28] has also written a good long letter—she wants to stay South another year—and I rather think if she returns in the spring—she can go on again in the fall. She and Mr. B. appear to be getting up a very great friendship—she studies French with him—and he professes to be….

Written in the right margin of the address page: "…as much entertained and benefited as she—she is spending the holidays with Moll Adams who is very low spirited—she begs me to send her anything of Fanny Forester's[29] so I have sent 'Dora' and your letters from 'Underhill.'"[30]

Written in the left margin of the address page: "Give much love to your dear Mother[31] and Kate[32]—and tell your Father[33] not to let Wallace[34] crow too much over him and me in consequence of the election returns—sincerely Anna M."

---

[25] N. P. Willis commissioned an artist named Flagg to do a portrait of "Dora'," one of Emily's fictional characters.

[26] See the letter of N. P. Willis to Emily Chubbuck dated December 23, 1844, in which he spoke of displaying the picture, and of the thousands who had seen it.

[27] Eugenia Damaux, part of Emily's intimate circle of friends at the Utica Female Academy. Living in New York City, Eugenia suffered from some kind of eye problem that at times made life very difficult for her; this was a matter of comment in many of the letters exchanged between the girls themselves, and with Cynthia Sheldon. In 1848, Eugenia was in New York living "at Mrs. Brown's—the same warm-hearted French girl as ever." In 1849 she married Johnny Edmonds, described as rich and pious, and they were to live in Utica.

[28] Harriet ("Hatty," "Hattie," or "Hat") Anable, daughter to Joseph and Alma Anable and niece of Cynthia Sheldon and Urania Sheldon Nott. In 1841, she had added a note to a letter written by Cynthia Sheldon to Emily. As early as November 1842 she was away, and a letter from Emily to Catharine Chubbuck said that "she (Sheldon) expected that Hat would return as accomplished as Anna Maria." Her trips away were both educational and employment, as she worked as a private tutor in families that would bring her into their homes. In August 1843, she had just returned from Beonsen, in the vicinity of New Orleans, and was engaged to go again. A letter from Anna Maria on January 6, 1845 said that she would stay south for another year. About this time Cynthia Sheldon mentioned her concern for Hatty's spiritual health. In May 1845 she was in New Orleans. She was home again in summer 1846, but a September 27 letter from Anna Maria said she had been asked by Roman with some urgency to return and she thought that she should. She was to return home from New Orleans in January 1849 after Anna Maria Anable had started the Misses Anable's School in Philadelphia in fall 1848. Harriet was fluent in French, having placed herself earlier in a French environment in New Orleans. Hatty died in 1858.

[29] Fanny Forester, Emily Chubbuck's *nom de plume*.

[30] See the story which is in this volume under the date December 17, 1844. This is a story that Emily had written, and it had appeared on the pages of the *New Mirror*.

[31] Lavinia Richards Chubbuck, Emily's mother, was born June 1, 1875, in Goffstown NH, the eldest of thirteen children. She married Charles Chubbuck on November 17. 1805. They were the parents of seven children.

[32] Sarah Catharine ("Kate," "Kit," or "Kitty") Chubbuck, Emily's older sister, born October 25, 1816.

[33] Charles Chubbuck, Emily's father. Though he held varying positions over the years, he failed at most of them. With the purchase of the house for them, Emily was to continue as a significant financial contributor to the support of the family.

[34] William Wallace Chubbuck, Emily's younger brother. During these years of Emily's correspondence, Wallace was living at home, or near home, working at different occupations including printing, office work, and teaching. Emily wrote of him as very capable in many areas but seeming to lack ambition at times. He proved to be a strong support for the Chubbuck family over these years, and, at the time of her death in 1854, Wallace had become one of Emily's primary caregivers. After February 1854, he wrote, at her dictation, all of her letters because of her failing strength. In recent elections he had been an ardent Polk supporter, while his father had supported the abolitionist candidate Birney. See Emily's letter to Walker Chubbuck dated September 24, 1844.

Written in the right margin of page one perpendicular to the original text: "I forgot to tell you all about a grand party at Mary Adam's[35] to which you were invited and to which I was the sole representation from the Fem. Acad. and of several calls you have had—and of New Year's day—I shall keep all these things, to talk about when you get back."

Source: American Baptist Historical Society, AJ 23, no. 1124.

H. C. Conant to Emily E. Chubbuck, January 10, 1845[36]

My dear Miss Chubbuck

An evil star seems to watch over our acquaintance—nothing could be dearer to my mind than that I was to call on you yesterday afternoon—but my husband failed (as husbands will,—take heed!) to fulfill his promise of being home in season to accompany me and so it was deferred till today, when the okies, as you have yourself seen, put their rects [sic] upon it. And now I am going to put to the test your superiority to form and ceremony, by inviting you to drink tea socially with me tomorrow evening, in company with a few select friends.—Dr. Woods, whom we met this evening at his brothers [sic], has engaged to be with us, and as he dislikes to be out after nightfall, I promised that he should have an old fashioned country tea, before dark—So please to come early and bring your knitting.—that essential to an afternoon country visit,—when neighbors come together for a pleasant gossip.

Your sister[37] will I trust, in consideration of my weariness, excuse a separate note, and gratify us by accompanying you.

Yrs,

H. C. Conant

Source: American Baptist Historical Society, AJ 24, no. 1210.

---

[35] Mary Adams, a friend of Emily's while at the Utica Female Academy. Her letter to Emily in October 1845 was almost a whimsical piece of fantasy with literary pretensions. It would reflect a fairly close and whimsical relationship. A second letter in December 1845 was similar. The letters were written from New Orleans, and she spoke of Hatty Anable as being near to her. On January 29, 1849, Anna Maria Anable wrote: "Hatty says Mary Adams is going to marry Gardner Green of Norwich,—a very fine young man, of invention, fortune, piety and all that Mary's heart was sighed for." On July 8, 1850, Urania Sheldon Nott spoke of attending this wedding in New York.

[36] This letter is undated. We will place it on January 10, 1845. Emily was in Hamilton at this time, and we have a letter from Anna Maria Anable dated January 6, 1845 asking Emily if Mrs. Conant has come by for tea yet—she seems to say it with a bit of edge to the words. This letter is about inviting Emily and her sister Kate for tea; it was written on a Friday evening. January 10 was the second Friday evening in January that year.

[37] Sarah Catharine ("Kate," "Kit," or "Kitty") Chubbuck, Emily's older sister, born October 25, 1816.

Marie Dawson Bates to Emily E. Chubbuck, January 10, 1845—Cazenovia

Dearest Emily

You will see by the date that we are at home, but you cannot imagine how disappointed we are to find ourselves here *without you*, whose society for a few days or weeks, we had anticipated with so much pleasure. We intended when at your house, to make our visit at Chenango Forks and return by way of Hamilton on Thursday of last week, then bring dear "Fanny Forester"[38] home with us on Friday—but to our inexpressible regret the snow all left us, and we were detained day after day weather bound. I was really homesick for a few days—at length the long wished for *snow* made its appearance, looking as fine and innocent as if it had never disappointed anybody in the least. It fell to the enormous depth of 4 inches, but we were glad to avail ourselves of even this small quantity and started for home in double quick time, took the nearest route (through Cineindus [sic]) and reached home Wednesday 8th inst—But my dearest E. we do not like to give up so, therefore hoping for sleighing soon, if you will have the goodness to write and whether you are able to ride, and when you can come. Mr. Bates will be happy to call for you. *Will you come?* And when? I have thought of you dear friend, many many times as we last saw you, but ardently hope you were not compelled to keep your bed long—and how is your dear father now, and your *best mother*[39] and dear Kate?[40] They were all so near sick or quite, that it has made me sad to think of them, hope they are all well ere this—We found Sister Mary Anne quite well and happy—she admires you (excuse me) Fanny Forester, enthusiastically, solicits your acquaintance and—a letter! Can you find time to write her? She is young, but talented, and very *very* warm hearted, and is withal quite a favorite with our good friend Dwinella. Oh by the way, Emilius[41] saw him yesterday, and as usual he made a great many enquiries about you; said had he known you were at Hamilton he should have gone to see you—would rather have given $20 dollars than missed seeing you, etc.—Mr. W. Baker from New York was in the office also, and he said Miss Forester was making a great sensation there. So look out dear E. you are destined to receive golden honors in spite of yourself. Write us soon, will you not? And I will answer you, if possible when I am not as much hurried as I now am.

Now if the snow visits us, say will not you? Emilius wishes to be affectionately remembered to you—yes the affection of a brother.

Yours ever and truly

---

[38] Fanny Forester, Emily Chubbuck's *nom de plume*.

[39] Charles and Lavina Richards Chubbuck.

[40] Sarah Catharine ("Kate," "Kit," or "Kitty") Chubbuck, Emily's older sister, born October 25, 1816.

[41] Emilius Bates, husband of Marie Dawson Bates.

Marie L. D. Bates.

Written in the right margin of page 3: "My best love to your mother and all your family. M."

Source: American Baptist Historical Society, AJ 23, no. 1148.

Urania Sheldon Nott to Emily E. Chubbuck, January 11, 1845—Union College[42]

My dear Emily,

I found the other day your beautiful little story of the "Bank Note"—in Inman's[43] last. If the conclusion equals the beginning it is a sweet thing.[44] "Anna Bailey"[45] I read to the Doct.[46] and our little circle last Sabbath eve'g—*till* we all cried *like children*. It is very touching—and truthfulful. I think you know how to throw a charm around miserable life—that very few do, and that your success is greater there than in descriptions of luxurious scenes, or fanciful young ladies. I do think it is the practical, rather than the fanciful in writing that is your forte. I hope you will be able to command more time than you have lately had to write without being so much hurried—it appears to me that you must find story writing more laborious, particularly as you write so much.

---

[42] This letter is a fragment—we have only its first page.

[43] John Inman was the editor of the *Commercial Advertiser* and the *Columbian Magazine*—responsibilities which failing health forced him to give up early in 1845. He was Emily Chubbuck's initial contact with the *Columbian Magazine*, which began to publish some of her stories early in 1844. He strongly encouraged Emily in her writing, said that they would publish everything they could get from her, hoped that she would consider writing exclusively for them, and when she asked for it, gave her the unheard of rate of five dollars a page for her articles. When he did that, he very candidly stated that with this, they would not consider it fair if she continued to write for N. P. Willis and the *New Mirror* without charge.

[44] See John Inman's letter of November 19, 1844, and J. Post's letter of December 19, 1844. The idea of serializing a story was new, and this was the first time they had tried it. "The Bank Note" was later to appear in *Trippings in Authorland* as well as the second edition of *Alderbrook*, vol. 1.

[45] Loxley of American Baptist Publication Society had written Emily on October 30, 1844, saying that *Anna Bailey* had been sent to the bindery.

[46] Reverend Doctor Eliphalet Nott, was the president of Union College in Schenectady NY. An ordained Presbyterian minister, he was married to Urania Sheldon Nott, the sister of Cynthia Sheldon and Alma Anable, and the aunt of Anna Maria Anable.

Anna M.[47] wrote me that you had gone home worn out—now my dear girl that will ruin you—you must not forget yourself in your efforts for others—do not forget that you have a very frail[48]

Source: American Baptist Historical Society, AJ 25, no. 1236.

Nathaniel Parker Willis to Emily E. Chubbuck,[49] January 11, 1845

My dear friend

You will see by my paper that I am too hard at work to have much time to write letters. I go to the Post office daily, however, in the hope of finding something from you, and fear a relapse of your fever. I feel as if my paper (sent to Hamilton since you have been there) was a daily letter to you, for I think of your seeing it as I read proofs. So answer my daily letters, if you please. I am much better myself, but, this week, more fagg'd than usual. Write to me.

I enclose, to amuse you, one of the many letters I get to which I never reply—for it mentioned your picture.[50] Return it to me by mail, and never hesitate about postage for any thing

Yours too tired to say more

N. P. W.

Source: Hanna Family files.

---

[47] Anna Maria Anable was the niece of the Urania and Cynthia Sheldon, the daughter of Joseph and Alma Sheldon Anable. Emily first met Anna Maria in fall 1840 when she went as a student to the Utica Female Academy; both Emily and Anna Maria were to become members of the faculty there. In these years Anna Maria became Emily's dearest friend, and the extensive correspondence between the two reflects sensitive, flirtatious spirits, and a deep intimacy. Emily was "Nemmy" to Anna Maria's "Ninny." In 1848, Anna Maria Anable, with the help of her extended family, moved to Philadelphia and started the Anable's School in Philadelphia. At Emily's death in 1854, Anna Maria was given guardianship of Emily Frances Judson, daughter of Emily and Adoniram Judson.

[48] The letter ends here—obviously this is a fragment, with more that followed.

[49] Written on the address page in the handwriting of Emily Chubbuck: "N. P. Willis. Jan. 11, 1845. No. 12."

[50] N. P. Willis commissioned an artist named Flagg to do a portrait of "Dora," one of Emily's fictional characters.

Cynthia Sheldon to Emily E. Chubbuck, January 14, 1845

Dear Emily

Could you believe that I had really forgotten your request for money—

When A. M.[51] wrote last I could not do it—thought Monday would do—and now I am greatly afraid the mail will close before this reaches the office—The Regents report—sprained ankle etc. is my excuse—I hope you are getting better so we may see you tomorrow or Thursday. I am heartily sorry this sheet cannot [sic] be filled—no papers for you today—we are doing as well as possible—love from all—A. M. has this moment gone from my room. Sarah B.[52] came yesterday.

Five Dolls enclosed from yours truly

C. Sheldon

Source: American Baptist Historical Society, AJ 26, no. 1268.

Emily E. Chubbuck to Marie Dawson Bates, January 14, 1845—Hamilton

My Dear Marie,—

I was much disappointed at not seeing you here; but I could not have gone with you if you had come, for I have not yet stepped my foot upon the ground.[53] I thank you for your kind offer of sending for me; but I am now needed at Utica every day, and must return as soon as I am able to ride at all. I shall hide myself in a cloak and hood, on Saturday or Monday I think, if it is pleasant, and put myself into Wallace's[54] hands to take back as he would any other baggage. This is absolutely necessary, and, mother[55] consents to it with a better grace that I promise her that I will do nothing more than oversee my affairs until I am quite well. I am very sorry that I could not have made the visit at your house—it would have been charming—but I promise myself the pleasure at some future time.—Really, you ought to have been here and seen my picture; it is exquisitely beautiful, and charms everybody.[56] There is an artist in town who spent the last winter in New York; he says he never saw so fine a painting of the kind. It came to hand on the 1st; so my Christmas gift was turned into a New Year's one. They were intending to

---

[51] Anna Maria Anable was the niece of the Urania and Cynthia Sheldon, the daughter of Joseph and Alma Sheldon Anable; she was Emily's closest friend at the Utica Female Academy.

[52] Sarah Bell Wheeler was a teacher at the Utica Female Academy, and an intimate friend of Emily Chubbuck.

[53] See the letter from Marie Dawson Bates to Emily E. Chubbuck dated January 10, 1845.

[54] William Wallace Chubbuck, Emily's younger brother, born January 1, 1824.

[55] Lavinia Richards Chubbuck, Emily's mother, was born June 1, 1875, in Goffstown NH, the eldest of thirteen children. She married Charles Chubbuck on November 17. 1805. They were the parents of seven children.

[56] N. P. Willis commissioned an artist named Flagg to do a portrait of "Dora,'" one of Emily's fictional characters.

notice it in the paper; but I begged them not—(it would be telling everybody who Fanny Forester is,[57] you know)—and the article was suppressed. They, however, copy the notice from the *Mirror*.[58]

I received last night a letter from Graham,[59] asking for stories which I can not [sic] write—is it not provoking? "The Chief's Daughter"[60] and "Katie Holland" in the February number are mine.

I am glad your sister is so well, and above all happy. I should like exceedingly to know her, and will write if I can.[61] But pen-work is no play with me, you know. I shall try to make a compromise with my friends, and write them one poor letter for half a dozen good ones. Will *you* accede to such terms? Here begin I—

Shall I say to you, Maria dear, that I am more annoyed than pleased with the sensation I am making just now? If people talk of me, I, of course, prefer good to ill; but I would much rather they would not talk at all. There has been a New York "lion" to Utica, on purpose to see me; he would have followed me out here, but they told him I was too ill to see company. Now I do not like to be an object of curiosity like the Siamese Twins or Tom Thumb. You appreciate the matter.

It is getting quite dark, and they will not allow me to write by candle-light; so I must close my shabby apology for a letter while I can see to sign my name. My very kindest regards to your dear, good husband, and every body [sic] else that you love, and believe me,

Your warmly attached friend,

Emily E. Chubbuck

Source: A. C. Kendrick, *The Life and Letters of Mrs. Emily C. Judson*, 117–19.

---

[57] Fanny Forester, Emily Chubbuck's *nom de plume*.

[58] The *New Mirror* was a literary magazine published by N. P. Willis and General Morris.

[59] George Graham, editor of *Graham's Magazine*, took an interest in Emily Chubbuck as Fanny Forester and paid her with the unheard of sum of five dollars a page.

[60] "The Chief's Daughter" was also later published in "Trippings in Author-land."

[61] In her letter of January 10, 1844, Marie Bates had asked if Emily would be willing to write a letter to Marie's sister. "She admires you (excuse me) Fanny Forester, enthusiastically, solicits your acquaintance and—a letter! Can you find time to write her?"

Nathaniel Parker Willis to Emily E. Chubbuck,[62] January 21, 1845—Mirror Office

My dear friend,

I showed you my confidence in the entire spirituality of our friendship by supposing that you could not apply to yourself any estimate put upon others. Besides, I wished to (*arrière pensée*) to show you that I had rejected a kind of temptation to which the world thinks I would yield. I expected to stand *better* with you—I stand *worse*.[63] Well—we should not pull up roses to see if they have taken root. I calculated too fast on your belief in my spirituality of feeling towards you, and will not subject you for a while to another test. The possibility of naming yourself, in any relation of category, to the writer of that letter, shows a lack of vanity and self-esteem which amounts almost to suspiciousness of nature. *Are* you very suspicious, dear Fanny?[64] Write me a long letter about yourself only.

I am rejoiced that yesterday, you probably went back to Utica[65]—I can hear from you by so much quicker. You are very likely to overwork yourself, and a friend tells me you are very delicately structured. Take care if you love me! Now, God bless you. I must read proof.

Adieu N. P. W.

Mr. Lyn tells me Miss Anable[66] is one of the loveliest girls he ever saw—positively beautiful. I enclose you a hand-writing very like yours—and by something such a Fanny Forester, I should think. She writes beautiful poetry. You'll see it in the *Mirror*.

Source: Hanna family files.

---

[62] Written on the address page in the handwriting of Emily E. Chubbuck: "N. P. Willis. Jan. 23, 1845. No. 13."

[63] On January 1, 1845, Emily had written to Anna Maria Anable: "The first Sat. after I got home I 'felt called upon' to write and inquire of W. if he got my package, which I was afraid had been lost. (If you recollect the letter in it, you will understand my anxiety). That is every word I have written him. He had no business to make the quotation he did from my letter—."

[64] Fanny Forester, Emily Chubbuck's *nom de plume*.

[65] Emily wrote to Marie Dawson Bates on January 14, 1845, that the following Saturday she would have her brother Wallace bring her back to her work at the Utica Female Academy.

[66] Anna Maria Anable was the niece of the Urania and Cynthia Sheldon, the daughter of Joseph and Alma Sheldon Anable; she was Emily's closest friend at the Utica Female Academy.

George R. Graham to Emily E. Chubbuck, January 26, 1845—Philadelphia

My dear Fanny,[67]

I received your letter and story by this morning mail, and I was sorry, too late for March.[68] Then I have "The Funeral" which I altered in *title* to "Lucy *Dutton*."[69] I *know* more about "*taking*" title than you, and will exercise the privilege—*if you will permit*—once in a while. As you are now a "regular contributor" I must tell you, that in order to be "in *time*," it is necessary always to have articles sixty days in advance of publication in large cities. This you will understand, when I tell you that part of April No. is now printed. And then the March Number by *contract* must be in the hands of agents in St. Louis and New Orleans by 25th February. You will begin to be quite a *business woman* after a while and I write you all my business *secrets*—they *are* secrets tho' minor ones.

The draft for $50 was paid by me yesterday, and if you [ ] [ ] the *returns* a day or two later, the accounts for N. It was sent to Philadelphia for collection.

When you are again in Utica write me or *soon* whether or [ ]. I want you to write with your accustomed freedom whenever you do write because one does not always know what is really written, after reading a studied letter. When you want $50 again—draw as before.

---

[67] Fanny Forester, Emily Chubbuck's *nom de plume*.

[68] We later learn that this was "Nickie Ben."

[69] "Lucy Dutton" also appeared in vol. 2 of *Alderbrook*, page 121. The first two paragraphs read:

> It was an October morning, warm and sunny, but with even its sunshine subdued into a mournful softness, and its gorgeous drapery chastened by a touch of the dreamy atmosphere into a sympathy with sorrow. And there was a sorrowing one who needed sympathy on that still, holy morning—the sympathy of the great Heart which beats in Nature's bosom—for she could hope no other. Poor Lucy Dutton!
>
> There was a funeral that morning—a stranger would have judged by the gathering that the great man of the village was dead, and all that crowd had come out to do his ashes honor—but it was not so. Yet the little, old-fashioned church was filled to overflowing. Some there were that turned their eyes devoutly to the holy man that occupied the sacred desk, receiving from his lips the words of life; some looked upon the little coffin that stood, covered with its black pall, upon a table directly below him, and perhaps thought of their own mortality, or that of their bright little ones; while many, very many, gazed with cold curiosity at the solitary mourner occupying the front pew. This was a young creature, in the very springtime of life,—a frail, erring being, whose only hope was in Him who said, "Neither do I condemn thee—go, and sin no more." There was a weight of shame upon her head, and woe upon her heart, that together made the bereaved young mother cower almost to the earth before the prying eyes that came to look upon her in her distressing humiliation. Oh! it was a pitiful sight! that crushed, helpless creature's agony.

I got a letter from Frances Osgood[70] who says she is *quite jealous* of you for you must monopolize all my letters, and do write to her often. So you see you are making mischief already with your pen. She adds however, that if I treat you to the *villianous scratches* I send her, which take a day to decipher "*she is partly consoled.*"

I do don't I?

Yours truly

Geo R. Graham

This is very short but is written with a press of business on hand.

Source: American Baptist Historical Society, AJ 24, no. 1190.

Nathaniel Parker Willis to Emily E. Chubbuck,[71] January 27, 1845

My dear friend

Your letter surprised me[72]—for I wrote to you four or five days,[73] or a week ago, and was looking eagerly for an answer. I sent it by the "American Mail Company" who sell their *postage—paid-seals* by the 100—enabling us to pre-pay letters without going personally to the post office. Possibly it was only retarded and you have it now. I shall wait till I hear.

The poetry you sent is *wonderful!* I am afraid it is one *felicitous* hit by a mind that would not do so well again—but I shall publish it with a grand *éloge*.

See today's *Mirror* for a notice to *Cornelia*. I let the daily *Mirror* still go to Hamilton for your friends there.

---

[70] Frances or "Fanny" Osgood presents us with a very interesting counterpoint to Fanny Forester or Emily Chubbuck, with both of them achieving fame in the same period of time. Fanny Osgood was both a writer and poet, and in 1845 she was one of the regulars who were writing for *Graham's Magazine*. Estranged from her husband, famed portrait painter Samuel S. Osgood, she began a relationship with Edgar Allen Poe, who in March 1845 had become the editor and part owner of the *Broadway Journal*. Poe, by the way, had been helped to fame by N. P. Willis when in January the *New York Daily Mirror*, the paper which preceded the *New Mirror* and made Fanny Forester famous, had published his poem "The Raven." Fanny Osgood presented a poem to the *Broadway Journal* for publication, and Poe printed a poem in reply. This went back and forth over a number of months, and the two were soon involved in a relationship; it was commonly thought that Fanny Osgood's third child was fathered by Poe. All of this was being played out in the press in September 1845 when William Gillespie wrote his letter to Emily Chubbuck about the "other" Fanny. The relationship with Fanny Osgood was to, within the year, make Poe a pariah in the literary circles of New York. In January 1845, Osgood had accused George Graham of not writing to her because of all of his correspondence with Fanny Forester. In June, just before sailing to Burmah, Emily mentioned in a letter that while in New York she had stopped at Osgood's studio, hoping to make arrangements to see Fanny Osgood, but the meeting did not take place as Osgood was out of town.

[71] Written on the address page in the handwriting of Emily E. Chubbuck: "N. P. Willis. Jan. 27, 1845. No. 14."

[72] After her engagement to Judson, Emily asked Willis to return all of her letters then most likely destroyed them.

[73] See the letter of N. P. Willis to Emily E. Chubbuck dated January 21, 1845.

Write me a long—long letter, dearest Fanny,[74] and believe me
Yours most surely

N. P. W.
(great haste)

Source: Hanna family files.

Nathaniel Parker Willis to Emily E. Chubbuck,[75] January 29, 1845—"Publishing Office"

My dear friend,

Robbed of my pen, I sit down with my aversion, (a steel pen) to say that *my arrow went farther than its aim*, and that you have no occasion to be annoyed at the effect of anything you ever said or did. I correspond with you in all respects as I would with an angel of light. I love your genius as I do my sisters, and I feel as brotherly to you as to them. Nothing would make me happier than to contribute in any way to your happiness—*but* I am trying an experiment—that of an *ethereal passion*, and I take in exchange for my homage and devotion, any interest you can feel for me. Is this clear?

I have no time now to write all I feel, and wish to say, but, dear Fanny,[76] write to me as much as you can, for I am made happy, and "taken out of my cage" by your letters.

Yours most sincerely,

N. P. Willis

I will send you a daguerreotype—tho, my countenance depends so much on color, and my likeness so much on movement (so Flagg[77] says) that no daguerreotype gives you any idea of me.

Source: Hanna family files.

---

[74] Fanny Forester, Emily Chubbuck's *nom de plume*.
[75] Written on the address page in the handwriting of Emily E. Chubbuck: "N. P. Willis. Jan. 30, 1845. No. 15."
[76] Fanny Forester, Emily Chubbuck's *nom de plume*.
[77] Flagg was the artist commissioned by N. P. Willis to paint the portrait of Dora', a character in one of Emily's stories. Willis also said, in his December 24, 1844 letter, that he was going to send Flagg to Utica to paint a portrait of Emily.

Nathaniel Parker Willis to Emily E. Chubbuck, February 6, 1845[78]

Dear Fanny,[79]

A spider hanging close before your eye is as large as a mountain—*till you walk three steps backward*. Just walk three steps backward, and then wonder how such a trifle as you write about had power to make you "cry your eyes out." However, the black line I drew through my horoscope when I heard that Miss Spencer had set her mischievous foot within your charmed circle, is beginning to come round with the wheel. I was satisfied that your *very next* letter would bring some taint of her—and here it is! When I assure you that, with General Lyman and his angel wife for my most intimate friends, I have not *even bow'd* to that young lady for a year, and that she never gave me designedly any particular offence, but only awoke my particular aversion—you will see, that with all my commonplaceness of qualities, I have unaccountably *wilful* [sic] *sensitiveness*. Now it seems to me that my correspondence with you is suddenly about to stop, and that our friendship is to be so jarr'd with doubts and explanations that it will stay like a cloud after sunset. It will be so if you and Miss Anable[80] allow yourselves to talk *at all* to that spirit of Evil, for she would poison the pillow of a seraph.[81] Lies require explaining away, and I cannot stand more explaining than I have to submit to for the public.

I can not [sic] see why "Cornelia" should be unwilling to be known as the author of her communications. They shew'd great strength of mind and style, and she has suffer'd by two causes—writing at too great length, and exacting replies to her letters *in print*. I should have put her on velvet with herself if she had allowed me to give her my whys and wherefores without the world for an audience. She is exactly the person to write for periodicals of stiffer drapery—the *Knickerbocker*,[82] North-American or Southern Lit. Rev. I wanted playfulness and sentiment—the strength of my paper being supplied by politics and news. Her mind is masculine and of a kind much admired, but not what I *wanted*.

As to *enquiring* about her—I sit with the Lymans every day at dinner, and amuse them with all my riddles of correspondence. If she had lived at the North Pole, they would have given me their judgment on her productions all the same. If she is troubled at my knowing her to be one of a population of 5000, she is easily

---

[78] This letter is undated—looking at the dates on which Willis wrote, February 6 is a reasonable time for a longer letter like this. He wrote them infrequently—most were very short—and this fits here well.

[79] Fanny Forester, Emily Chubbuck's *nom de plume*.

[80] Anna Maria Anable was the niece of the Urania and Cynthia Sheldon, the daughter of Joseph and Alma Sheldon Anable, she was Emily's closest friend at the Utica Female Academy.

[81] This is a most interesting paragraph, and it is an occasion when we would wish that we could have seen what Emily wrote. We are also intrigued with the reference here. After her engagement to Judson, Emily asked Willis to return all of her letters then most likely destroyed them all.

[82] The *Knickerbocker* was one of the prominent literary magazines of the time, and it had featured a number of pieces from the pen of Fanny Forester.

annoyed. But *here* was the *pourquoi* of my curiosity;—I fear'd I was slighting some friend of my oldest female friend Mrs. Wm. Kirkland (who has been a sister to me for 16 years) and *therefore* I tried to identify the writer. It is a very trifling matter, and I can ill afford to say so much about it.[83]

Source: Hanna Family files.

Emily E. Chubbuck to Catharine Chubbuck, February 8, 1845[84]

Dear Kitty,

I have been looking and looking for a letter from home but as I don't get it I suppose I may as well write myself. I do not think that I am any better than I was when I left home, though I am a good deal better than **on the week following** (I was that next week), for it **put** (threw) me back wonderfully. The teachers help me correct compositions and I **don't do anything** (do nothing) else—**shan't write any I am afraid** (fear that I shall not write any) this winter. As for eating, I **don't** (do not) go to the table (yet) and **don't** (do not) make a glutton of myself exactly. I have lived **pretty much** (nearly) all the time on the beef and it is not more than half gone. I am expecting my breakfast of gruel **now to be bro't** (to be brought) up any minute. I have four kinds of pills to take—three kinds the largest size imaginable, **and** the others I have to take after dinner to sweeten the meal. Then I have other doses besides. **Old** doct. James[85] is in for it, and **I suppose he thinks** (he seems to think that) if he cures Fanny Forester[86] it will be the making of him. Anna Maria[87] went to Schen. yesterday[88] to spend a week and I miss her (sadly) **I can tell**

---

[83] The remainder of the letter is missing.

[84] We have two versions of this letter—the original as written by Emily E. Chubbuck, and the edited version published by A. C. Kendrick in his biography, *The Life and Letters of Mrs. Emily C. Judson*. Additions made by Kendrick we have placed in parentheses ( ), and words in the original left out by Kendrick we have added in bold. One will note significant changes and omissions. In a note in his book, Kendrick explained that interest, purpose and propriety sometimes led to these changes and exclusions. "I remark here that in giving Chubbuck's letters, I do not always indicate unimportant omissions. Real letters must always contain much which should not meet the public eye; and Emily's were real letters, dashed off hastily amidst pressing cares and duties. Written also after the exhausting labors of the day, they by no means do uniform justice to her epistolary powers." He later was to add, "In giving a few extracts from his and Chubbuck's correspondence at this time, I have no wish to minister to a prurient curiosity, not to violate that principle which would generally place letters written during the period of an 'engagement' under the shelter of inviolate secrecy."

[85] Dr. James was a trusted physician in Utica, who attended the students and faculty of the Utica Female Academy. He is mentioned frequently in the correspondence as having been consulted for varying medical complaints and his advice was always welcomed and highly regarded.

[86] Emily Chubbuck wrote under the *nom de plume* of Fanny Forester. Asked about it once, she said "Would anyone buy a book written by Emily E. Chubbuck?"

[87] Anna Maria Anable was the niece of the Urania and Cynthia Sheldon, the daughter of Joseph and Alma Sheldon Anable; she was Emily's closest friend at the Utica Female Academy.

[88] Schenectady NY was the location of Union College. The president of Union College, the Reverend Doctor Eliphalet Nott, had married Urania Sheldon in late summer 1842. Urania Sheldon Nott was the aunt of Anna Maria Anable.

you, for I can't have anything cooked nicely when she is gone—the servants don't know how.

Mary Barber[89] is taking my miniature and (don't tell it out of the family not even to the Chadwicks) I am going to send it to Willis[90]—lend it. So far it is very like [sic] and a very pretty picture. I have it taken with my spectacles off. I had a letter from (Mr. Willis) W. yesterday week **promising me his Daguerreotype**[91] but it has'nt come yet. We hav'nt had any N. Y. mail since Tues.—they must be terribly backed up below there. **Willis** (he) says he lets the Daily go to Hamilton still for you people.[92] **Now I doubted very much whether you would be pleased with the notion, but I didn't like to tell him so. If you don't want to pay the postage for it you may let Frank Chapin have it. I hav'nt** [sic] **any news.** Have **rec'd** (received) a letter from Graham,[93] but there was no particular news in it except that "Nickie Ben"[94] was too late for the March No.[95] but he has got a little tit-bit [sic] of a story about two pages that he intends to **put into the March.** (insert in it). Do write. I have no news as I told you and don't feel well enough to stretch out a long letter.

    E.

Source: A. C. Kendrick, *The Life and Letters of Mrs. Emily C. Judson*, 119–20; Hanna family files.

[89] Mary Barber, mentioned frequently in the Emily Chubbuck Judson letters, was a student and then the art teacher at the Utica Female Academy.

[90] Nathaniel Parker (N. P.) Willis was the editor of *New Mirror*, the magazine that catapulted Emily into literary fame. He became a friend, mentor, and eventually a suitor.

[91] See the letter of N. P Willis to Emily E. Chubbuck dated January 29, 1845.

[92] See his letter of January 27, 1845.

[93] George Graham, editor of *Graham's Magazine*, took an interest in Emily Chubbuck as Fanny Forester and paid her with the unheard of sum of five dollars a page. See his letter of January 26, 1845.

[94] "Nickie Ben" also appeared in vol. 1 of *Alderbrook*, page 170. The first several paragraphs read:

We have a lawyer at Alderbrook—three of them, indeed—but one we have worth talking about, one who has been talked about—one who has been blown upon, if not by "the breath of fame," by that gossiping approach to it which is fame's stage-coach—one, in short, who deserves a historian. Now, do not "think you see him," dear reader, before I begin; and so place before your mind's eye a little, spare, cunning, smooth-tongued fox of an attorney, whom it will be my bounden duty to demolish.

"A face like a wedge, made to force its way through the world, eyes like black beans a-boiling in milk, and a step like a cat's—"

Not a bit of it. Oh, no! you do *not* see *our* lawyer.

Benjamin Nichols, or "Nickie Ben," as he has been irreverently re-christened by some wag, with the consent, of everybody, has a voice—oh, *such* a voice! the north wind is an infant's whisper to it—stands very nearly six feet in his stockings, and is of dimensions never scoffed at. In good sooth, that brawny arm might have wielded the genuine old Scottish claymore by the side of Robert Bruce, and other worthies of the times that were, and never have been ashamed of the muscles in it. Nickie Ben, however, was reserved for more elegant diversions than hewing off men's heads, and slicing down their shoulders; and he rewarded fate for her flattering favors to himself by entering with great zest into the spirit which governs the modern world. In place of such boisterous cries as "A Bruce! A Bruce!" "A Richard! A Richard!" or "Beau-seant!" he slipped his fingers quietly to the bottom of his eel-skin purse, laid his thumb against the pillars, and his forefinger against the kingly head upon the sixpences there; while his eye twinkled, and his features worked in a way fully to prove his loyalty to that little piece of coin, and his determination to die, if need be, in the service *of the family*.

[95] Number or edition.

Nathaniel Parker Willis to Emily E. Chubbuck,[96] February 11, 1845[97]

My sweet friend

I am just thro' with a very trying business which you will understand by my Monday's paper. It has *crucified* me to be obliged to *prove* that I was gentleman—of course! My God! What a country to live in! But, it is done and now that the world have [sic] seen my lining, I trust to be left alone. *You* know a purer chamber of my heart than the world believes was in me. From that chamber take a pure prayer for your happiness with thanks for what you are adding to mine.

I have no time to write now. This is to throw a plank over a chasm—that is all. Your letters are delicious to me—truly delicious. Write *long* letters, and now and then I will write a long one to you.

Yours most faithfully

N. P. W.

Your heaven is a pure and perfect chrysolite of a *thought*—lacking finish. I shall finish it, but let the secret be between *us only* that I have touched it.

Source: Hanna Family file.

John Inman to Emily E. Chubbuck, February 15, 1845—New York City

Miss Emily E. Chubbuck,

Or, "Dear Fanny,"[98] if we may be permitted to imitate our friend of the *Mirror*[99]—We are looking for more of your delightful compositions.[100] We hope you will smile on us as often as possible, for you know it has always made us happy. We have heard with much anxiety, that you have been very ill, and nothing would give us more pleasure, than an [ ] account from your own pen that health and happiness are yours.

Very respectfully and truly

[ ]

J. Inman

By Company Clerk   Source: American Baptist Historical Society, AJ 24, no. 1176.

---

[96] Written on the address page in the handwriting of Emily E. Chubbuck: "N. P. Willis. Feb. 12, 1845. No. 16."

[97] This letter is undated. It is postmarked February 12, 1845, but it was written on Tuesday, February 11.

[98] Fanny Forester, Emily Chubbuck's *nom de plume*.

[99] Nathaniel Parker (N. P.) Willis was the editor of *New Mirror*, the magazine that catapulted Emily into literary fame. He became a friend, mentor, and eventually a suitor.

[100] John Inman was the editor of the *Commercial Advertiser* and the *Columbian Magazine*.

Nathaniel Parker Willis to Emily E. Chubbuck,[101] February 19, 1845

Dear Emily

You probably have no idea how wonderfully better than other people you write letters, and before telling you how *balmy* your last was to *me*, I must beg you to try something in the epistolary style for publication. It will give scope to your *playfulness of mind* which is ramp'd in a regular story.

But—what a pure and yet warm and loving spirit is in you! Your letter made me "cloud over" for a tear—so true to the truth of what you wrote about and so tender and appreciative of mental suffering. I wish to God I had been there to press in your out-spread hands. We gain by not knowing each other, my dear girl. You see only my inner nature, which is a brother to your own,—as warm but as pure too, and I see *you* without the reserve of outer womanhood. The consequence is we have no concealments and we need none. We are like two Spirits, waiting, for the withdrawing of a curtain of life between them, to *rush* into each other's arms for a spiritual companionship in eternity. I love you dear Emily—think of you often,—look eagerly for your letters—but let us first meet not far this side of a better world.

I am making time to write this—for I have no sub-editor just now. In reading over this page (which I have now turn'd over) I find I was somewhat swayed by a dread I feel that you would not like me if you knew me—would not confide in me so frankly, that is to say. I have in my face marks of the eternal defiance in which my life is pass'd and if you were to pass me in the street you would think me supercilious looking or ill-temper'd, or cold. I was surprised at the remark of an intimate friend a day or two since who was in my dressing room while I was dressing for the day. "Good heavens! Said he, you have been only 15 minutes—" I thought it took you two hours to dress at least!" This said with perfect sincerity, so that probably I look coxcombical. Don't believe such comments on me, however, if you hear them, for they describe nothing which you have any occasion to know.

I must stop. My proofs call me. I thought so much of you last night that I could not help addressing my "leader" to you in today's paper. God bless you. Take a kiss from my spirit lips.

Every yours.

W

Source: Hanna family files.

---

[101] Written on the address page in the handwriting of Emily E. Chubbuck: "N. P. Willis. Feb. 20. 1845. 17." (She would have received this letter on February 20.)

J. Post to Emily E. Chubbuck, February 21, 1845—New York City

Dr. Madam

Your two articles "Two Nights etc,"[102] and "Nancy," are in hand, and as usual please us much. "Grace Linden," if it has been here long, has been slyly nesting in Mr. Inman's[103] brain or pocket, or both; and we half suspect he has been prying deeply into it, and perhaps committing it to memory, for we know he is a great admirer of your articles. It was but yesterday that he handed it into the publishing office. It is accepted,—it is too good to reject,—and yet it is too long, is it not? By the way, what is your *real* opinion of continuing articles from month to month? You know better than we do, what the public say and think of the practice. Mr. Inman you know, set his face agt it, and may only lured [sic] from his purpose by your charming "Bank Note." We should like your candid opinion on the point, and will be governed by it.

How many Numbers of The Magazine would you think it best to give the world "Grace Linden" in? We have decided upon continuing it from age to age, unless you decide that to be too long. We think it the most natural division of the story, and least justly done to so sweet a Variature's history.

Pray let us hear no more about "*strikes*";[104] so as you continue to *strike* us to improve monthly in the fine, pure taste, exquisite thought and finish of your compositions. We have hearts big enough to make you independent for life (though we hope you are so already) but you can't know, and we can't tell you of half the difficulties thro' which we have been forced to struggle. N. York ought to have a good magazine and we resolved to give her one. And we think you misunderstood our

---

[102] "Two nights in the 'Nieuw Nederlandts'" was also published in vol. 2 of Alderbrook, page 109. The first several paragraphs are as follows:

> It was on the night of the 25th of February, 1643, that a middle-aged man, with an honest, frank, sun-browned face and a powerful frame, sat and warmed himself by the kitchen fire in the Governor's house at Fort Amsterdam. He was singularly uneasy; every now and then clenching his fist and moving his nervous arm as in angry gesticulation; while his fine eye turned from one object to another with a kind of eager dread, and his naturally clear, open countenance was drawn into a scowl compounded of various strong emotions. He was alone, and bore himself much as though belonging to the household; for he certainly could not have been greatly inferior to its master in point of dignity. All within doors was perfectly silent—painfully so, it seemed to the stern watcher—and within, the heavy, monotonous tread of a sentinel, at a little distance, gave the only evidence that the pulse of the young city had not ceased its breathings. At last the man drew from his pocket a massive "*Nuremburg egg*," and held it up to the light.
>
> "Twelve o'clock—five—almost ten minutes past! Thank God, if their hellish plan has miscarried!"
>
> A long, loud, terrible shriek, as of a multitude of voices combining their agony, came up from the distance even as he spoke; and dropping the watch upon the stone hearth, the listener sprang with an exclamation of horror to his feet.
>
> "God forgive me, if I curse my race and nation! It is a deed worthy of the devil—and they call themselves men and Christians!"

[103] John Inman was the editor of the *Commercial Advertiser* and the *Columbian Magazine*.

[104] In his December 19, 1844 letter, Mr. Post had compared Emily to "naughty factory girls" striking for higher wages.

complaint of "Bryant etc,"[105]—It was not that they were "chary" of their good things, but that they absolutely denied them to us on *livings* terms—indeed on any terms. We hoped for better things,—We looked for a little literary pride of State and City, among our literary friends. Perhaps we were wrong—admit that we were—still, when we paid better, as we know than any periodical published in this state ever paid before, and so much that *they knew* we could not live, but *must* die under it, what taste, or wish could they have had for a Magazine *this side of Philadelphia* when they refused to contribute, *at any price?*

With all this we have struggled on, and intend to struggle on, and we beg leave to note a private opinion just here for your private ear, that the time may come when some of those named will be glad to appear in the *Columbian*, at less than we most cheerfully pay you—for none of them now a days merit so much. There is but one paper in the U. S. that pays more than we do to any Writer, and the proprietor of that has informed us that he has done so to but a very few,—warning them, and that after present engagements, terminating with this year, he should not pay more than $5 the printed page to any one, as *he* could not afford it.[106] But no more of this—we should not have bored you with any of it, but that we feared we had been a little misapprehended. We hope to be *able* to take your beautiful wares, and that you can afford them on such terms as not to be under any necessity of carrying them to any other market. Unless you write more than is suitable to appear in one work like ours, we would like to have all you can spare for magazines. You take the idea—We should like to monopolize—that's plain.

But what do you think about continuing articles? Now be as frank as Frank Linden.

We are glad to hear you say *The Columbian* is spoken well of—you have an opportunity of kindness.

Mr. Child is truly enlisted, and is a jewel. If we could find half a dozen more jewels, we would make the eyes of our readers sparkle, and their hearts leap with admiration. Excuse us for this long letter.

Very respectfully and truly yours,

J. Post

Source: American Baptist Historical Society, AJ 25, no. 1223.

---

[105] In his December 19, 1844 letter, Mr. Post had spoken of Bryant and other writers like Hoffman who had priced their work so high that it was financially impossible for the magazines to use the material.

[106] George Graham discusses this with Emily in his letter of September 23, 1844.

Nathaniel Parker Willis to Emily E. Chubbuck,[107] March 4, 1845[108]

My dear Fanny[109]

You owe this letter to the excessive beauty of the morning, for with a hundred claims on my attention, I *must* tell you it is delicious weather. Does it kiss your lips? Does it lift your curls? Does it whisper "God bless you," and I would if I were there. Take one of these Spring mornings as a specimen of the climate of Italy *all the time*. How I wish we were there—but heigho! This kind of weather makes me as unhappy as a bird in prison. I want to go *away* with those I love. I want—Heaven, probably.

O how you grieve me with your tone of despondency as to your own health, dear Fanny! Take care of yourself[110]—or, if you find health going, begin early to fix your *will* on coming back to *live* near me in spirit. I *do believe* that by strong will that can be done. My "proofs" call me. Adieu, sweet and treasured friend. Write to me and excuse this brief letter

Yours faithfully N. P. Wills

Source: Hanna family files.

Nathaniel Parker Willis to Emily E. Chubbuck,[111] March 11, 1845— "Office"[112]

My dear Fanny[113]

I wish you would ask Miss Annable[114] [sic] to write me a true account of you—your health and your duties—what care you take of yourself, and whether you are to be permitted to suffer for lack of any thing—even a voyage to the West Indies. I do not like what I know of your self-*soin*, (?) and I wish to be better informed. She will oblige me so far.

The last I heard of you was thro a channel I detest—in a letter to my excellent friend Mrs. Lyman from her mischievous and poison-tongued niece, Miss Spencer.

---

[107] Written on the address page in the handwriting of Emily E. Chubbuck: "N. P. Willis. March 6, 1845. 18." (The 18 means it was the eighteenth letter she had received from him.)

[108] This letter is undated. Tuesday morning would have been March 4. It is postmarked March 6.

[109] Fanny Forester, Emily Chubbuck's *nom de plume*.

[110] We take note here the reoccurring themes of Emily's chronic illness, and this is turning up in many of the letters of this period. It was to bring her to Philadelphia the end of March hoping the change in environment would be helpful. Earlier letters have Emily saying that she will do very little writing because of her health.

[111] Written on the address page in the handwriting of Emily E. Chubbuck: "N. P. Willis esq. March 11, 1845. 19" (19 meant it was the nineteenth letter she had received from him.)

[112] This letter is undated. We have the notation of Emily Chubbuck that it was March 11, and March 11 was a Tuesday.

[113] Fanny Forester, Emily Chubbuck's *nom de plume*.

[114] Anna Maria Anable was the niece of the Urania and Cynthia Sheldon, the daughter of Joseph and Alma Sheldon Anable; she was Emily's closest friend at the Utica Female Academy.

I was really vexed to know that this little evil spirit had been to see you at the Seminary,[115] and had *busied* herself in enquiring out the matters we are all interested in. Pray be cautious with that young lady, dear Fanny. Her entire acquaintance in New York look upon her as a lump of plausible malice and treachery, and the Astor-house is not a little relieved when she is gone. I formally renounced her acquaintance a year ago, and have not even exchanged a bow with her since. The Lymans I am very much attached to, and when Mrs. L. comes up there, pray look lovingly on her—pure, sweet, kind-hearted woman that she is.

I am waiting for a moment of *fresh-minded* leisure, (the other I could easier find) to take a sunny impression of your poem and see just where the blemish was that first struck me.[116] I am determined you shall not slight anything you write simply from over-toil in your other duties. You are too precious a commodity, dear Fanny, and as your trumpeter, I will not blow my blast till I know you are ready for the attention it draws to you.

It is snowing, and a most uncomfortable day. I wish you *sat* in this other armchair in my office—for here I pass the day alone, except the interruption of errand boys, and called to my outer room for "words in my ear." I would give you a paragraph to condense—a puff to write—a young author's letter to answer—a new thought as it came into my head. Alas that you must be a *Spirit* to do this with "propriety"!

There was a misprint or two in the poem addressed to you in yesterday's paper. Write me whether "Noble" is a fictitious name. Write me, if permitted, the true name of "Cornelia." Is it Mrs. Tracy?[117]

I send you a French paper for no particular reason, except that I like the news in French for myself. Can I send you any thing else? Do you want books? What do you want? I wish I knew how I could do something for you, if it were only to brush a fly from your forehead—If you are ill again, I shall run up to Utica to see you. Make my "looks that way" acceptable to Cousin 'Bel'.[118]

Ever yours, dear Fanny

N. P. W.

Source: Hanna family files.

---

[115] The Utica Female Academy, where Emily was the composition teacher.

[116] The poem in question was "The Weaver." A commentary on, and a copy of, this poem follows this letter.

[117] For full information on this poem, see the letter of Emily Chubbuck to her sister Catharine Chubbuck, dated March 17, 1845. The poem was "Lines to Fanny Forester" By Mary Frances Noble.

[118] "Cousin 'Bel'" was Anna Maria Anable—the "character" came from Emily's letter to the *New Mirror* which was published on June 8, 1844, a letter which catapulted Emily to literary fame. The letter concerned a visit that Emily and Cousin 'Bel' had made to New York, and their lack of money to enjoy the wares of the many shops they passed by. She asked if the editor of the *New Mirror* would like to help them out.

Emily E. Chubbuck as Fanny Forester, March 1845

A. C. Kendrick, in *The Life and Letters of Mrs. Emily C. Judson*, quoted N. P. Willis on a poem that had just been received from Fanny Forester. His quote was from a letter that N. P. Willis had written to Emily E. Chubbuck on March 11, 1845:

> "Your 'Weaver' is a pure and perfect chrysalis of a thought lacking finish," and in a subsequent letters recurs thus to the subject: "I am waiting for a moment of *fresh-minded* leisure (the other I could more easily find) to take a sunny impression of your poem, and see just where the blemish was that first struck me. I am determined you shall not slight any thing [sic] you write simply from over-toil in your other duties. You are too precious a commodity and as your trumpeter, I will not blow my blast till I know you are ready for the attention it draws to you" (122).

Then, on March 17, 1845, Emily wrote to her sister Catharine, "You will find my "Weaver" in Friday's paper (The *Mirror*)."

Commenting on the poem, Kendrick said: "It is a beautifully imaginative piece, but much less finely finished than as it subsequently appeared in *Alderbrook*. This copy of "The Weaver" is the earlier version.[119]

The Weaver

A weaver sat before his loom
The shuttle flinging fast,
And to his web a thread of doom
Was added at each cast.

His warp had been by angels spun;
Bright was his weft and new,
Unbraided from life's morning sun,
Gemmed with life's morning dew.

And fresh-lipped, beautiful young flowers
In tissue rich were spread,
While the weaver told the joy-sped hours
By his pulse's bounding tread.

But o'er his brow a shadow crept,
And on the fabric lay;
The shuttle faltered as it swept

---

[119] A later version can be found in *Alderbrook: A Collectin of Fanny Forester's Village Sketches, Poems, etc.* 10th ed. (Boston: Ticknor, Reed, and Fields, 1851) 1:125–30.

Along its darkened way.

Gray was the faded thread it bore,
Dimmed by the touch of thought;
And tear-like stains were sprinkled o'er
The richest broideries wrought.

Still kept the weaver weaving on,
Though he wove a texture gray,
Its tissued brilliance all had gone,
The gold threads cankered lay.

And still, with gathering mildew, grew
Yet duller every thread,
And mingled some of coal-black hue,
And some of bloody red.

For things most strange were woven in,
Corroding griefs and fears,—
And broken was the web and thin,
And it dripped with briny tears.

He longed to fling his toil aside,
But knew 't would [sic] be a sin;
So the ceaseless shuttle still he plied,
Those life-cords weaving in.

And as he wove, and wept, and wove,
Fair tempters, stealing nigh,
With glozing words, to win him strove,
But he turned away his eye;

He turned his aching eye to heaven,
And wearily wove on,
Till life's last faltering cast was given,
The fabric strange was done.

He flung it round his shoulders bowed,
And o'er his grizzled head,
And gathering close his trailing shroud,
Lay down among the dead.

And next I marked his robe's wide folds,

As they swept the fields of air,
Bright as the arc the sunlight moulds,
As angel pinions fair.

And there inwrought was each bright flower,
As when at first it sprung:
The fairy work of morning's hour
In morning freshness hung.

And where a tear had left its stain
A snow-white lily lay,
And the leaden tracery of pain
Linked many a jewel's ray.

Wherever Grief's meek breath had swept
There dwelt a rich perfume,
And bathed in silvery moonlight slept
The sable work of gloom.

And then I prayed:—the strange web done,
To my frail fingers given,
Be Sorrow's stain the deepest one
To mar my robe in heaven.

Nathaniel Parker Willis to Emily E. Chubbuck[120] March 12, 1845

I have filled that side, dear Fanny,[121] so that you could show it to your friend—and thus let me leave *this* world's hateful coil.

I wish I had time and room (in reply to the latter part of your letter)[121] to tell you what I conceive to be around me in an atmosphere of *spirit-instinct*. I believe that "no man hath ascended into Heaven except Him who hath descended"—that spirits have in their own consciousness, the *place* of their abode till the Last Day, (or as Milton expresses it,

> (The mind is its own place, and in itself
> can make a hell of Heaven, a heaven of hell)

---

[120] Written on the address page in the handwriting of Emily E. Chubbuck: "N. P. Willis Esq. March 12, 1845. 20." (20 means that this was the twentieth letter which Emily Chubbuck had received from N. P. Willis.)

[121] Fanny Forester, Emily Chubbuck's *nom de plume*.

[122] After her engagement to Judson, Emily asked Willis to return all of her letters, at which time, and to history's great loss, she destroyed them all, fearing how they would reflect on her, on Adoniram Judson, and on the missionary cause.

and that meantime—during this intermediate abode it follows impulse and memory to scenes it is permitted to watch or loves to return to! The difficulty is in persuading oneself that Heaven is not a *place* geographically. Consciousness is the Universe, and God is in this world as much as in Heaven, and Heaven and Hell lie about us, within us, and we in either, as we do God's pleasure or not. Briefly that is my creed. I pray. I revere. I strive to do my duty, and I have my share of Heaven, and part of it is in *your bosom*—a gift from God of a love stream of which he is the fountain. Don't let us lose ourselves in speculations, however. I am content to kneel and refresh my lips at a stream from Heaven without more analysis than the taste by which I recognize it. If we should ever cease to correspond, you may always be sure that I look'd upon you as a current I would fain have kept in holy shadow for sacred visitation

Written in the right margin of the address page: "N.B. You should know, perhaps, that I was so disgusted with the religion cramm'd down at school and college that I write, or confess, on the subject, with the greatest reluctance. I *believe* with professing Trinitarian Christians—but I *feel* and *speculate alone*. It is a wonderful proof of confidingness in you, that I have spoken at all on the subject. I wish to go to the grave as the *worldly struggler with the world*, but to be known to God for something better.

"What an unpleasant letter this is! God bless you dear Fanny,

"Ever yours W."

Written in the left margin of the address page: "Your admissions with regard to your health distress me. *Take care* for *many* sakes. My brain is busy contriving a way to send you to Italy for a year. I can find you all or any of the periodicals—so don't "subscribe" for any thing. [sic]"

Source: Hanna family files, N. P. Willis to Emily, letter 20.

Emily E. Chubbuck to Catharine Chubbuck, March 17, 1845

I was sorry to hear that you were ill; I believe it is the fate of the family, for I am not quite so well as I should like to be—Dr. James[123] and Miss C.[124] think it best for me to go to a warmer place until summer comes, and so Miss C. has concluded to

---

[123] Dr. James was a trusted physician in Utica, who attended the students and faculty of the Utica Female Academy. He is mentioned frequently in the correspondence as having been consulted for varying medical complaints and his advice was always welcomed and highly regarded.

[124] Cynthia Sheldon was in charge of the administrative and financial departments of the Utica Female Academy and an important mentor, advisor, and friend to Emily.

go next week with me to Philadelphia.[125] She will put me under the care of the Rev. Mr. Gillette, a Baptist clergyman,[126] find me a nice boarding-house and then leave me for four, five, or six weeks as I think best. It will cost some money, but it seems absolutely necessary. This spring weather almost kills me, I shall get the money for my payment, and send it home before I go[127]…Did you read the poetry[128] addressed to Fanny Forester[129] in the *Mirror*?[130] And do you not think it beautiful? It is by Jane Wright.[131] You will find my "Weaver"[132] in Friday's paper…"Nickie Ben" is in the April number of Graham,[133] but I have not seen it yet. I have written another story entitled "Blanche de Monville," and that is all I have done this winter. *The Columbian*[134] people pretend to think all the world of me; Graham is as good as the bank, and Willis[135] fifty times better….

Source: A. C. Kendrick, *The Life and Letters of Mrs. Emily C. Judson*, 120.

[125] This is the first reference in the correspondence that Emily will be going to Philadelphia, hoping for an improvement in her health. Emily, with Cynthia Sheldon traveling with her, would leave Utica on March 26, spend two days in New York, and arrive in Philadelphia on March 29. She would begin her trip home around May 9, though she would stay for about two weeks in New York visiting with N. P. Willis, whom she would see almost every day that she was there.

[126] Rev. A. D. Gillette was the founding minister of the Eleventh Baptist Church in Philadelphia. He had a distinguished career there for another decade, when he left to take another pulpit in New York. Prominent in Baptist circles, he served on the Board of American Baptist Publication Society. Gillette was educated at Hamilton College, and he was known to Cynthia Sheldon. We can be sure that it was at her suggestion that Emily, in 1842, asked the Reverend Gillette to submit her book to the society for approval. In April and early May 1845, Emily stayed in Philadelphia at the home of this same Rev. Gillette, and she returned again that fall for winter 1845–1846. On Christmas Day 1845 Gillette had introduced Emily Chubbuck to Adoniram Judson in the parlor of his home. He had a short time before traveled to Boston to bring the revered missionary to Philadelphia for meetings with the churches. Gillette was to be a stalwart friend and supporter throughout it all, not only to Emily, but to the Sheldon and Anable families.

[127] In a September 16, 1842 letter to her brother Walker, Emily told him that she had purchased a home for her parents on Broad Street in Hamilton Village. She was able to do this from the proceeds of her writing. Emily had paid four hundred dollars for the home, payable in four payments over four years, and she was to often mention this debt, and the pressure it put upon her for continued writing, and the income derived from it. She had also accumulated some debt at the Utica Female Academy for some terms that her sister Catharine Chubbuck had taken.

[128] See this poem, "Lines to Fanny Forester," and a companion poem "The Convalescent" in the piece that follows this letter.

[129] Fanny Forester, Emily Chubbuck's *nom de plume*.

[130] The *New Mirror* was a literary magazine published by N. P. Willis and General Morris.

[131] On March 11, 1845, N. P. Willis had written: "There was a misprint or two in the poem addressed to you in yesterday's paper. Write me whether "Noble" is a fictitious name. " In the *New Mirror*, the poem was ascribed to Mary Frances Noble; we learn that this was a *nom de plume*, and that the writer's name was Jane Wright. On page 120 of *The Life and Letters of Mrs. Emily C. Judson*, A. C. Kendrick relates that " Wright was a member of the Seminary (the Utica Female Academy)."

[132] According to A. C. Kendrick in *The Life and Letters of Mrs. Emily C. Judson* (page 122), "Emily had sent (this) to the *Mirror* in February. It is a beautifully imaginative piece, but much less finely finished than as it subsequently appeared in *Alderbrook*. Willis writes to her: 'Your 'Weaver' is a pure and perfect chrysalis of a thought lacking finish.'" "The Weaver" appears in this volume under the date March, 1845.

[133] George Graham, editor of *Graham's Magazine*, took an interest in Emily Chubbuck as Fanny Forester and paid her with the unheard of sum of five dollars a page.

[134] John Inman had been Emily's contact at the *Columbian Magazine*, and he had agreed to pay her the unheard of price of five dollars a page for her work. He had written recently that illness was forcing him to slow down, and J. Post had begun to work with Emily. Then the responsibility had passed to Robert West, who wrote Emily a number of letters on behalf of the *Columbian Magazine*.

[135] Nathaniel Parker (N. P.) Willis was the editor of *New Mirror*, the magazine that catapulted Emily into literary fame. He became a friend, mentor, and eventually a suitor.

Mary Florence Noble to Fanny Forester, Printed in the *New Mirror*, March 1845

Introduction by George Tooze

On March 11, 1845, N. P. Willis had written to Emily Chubbuck: "There was a misprint or two in the poem addressed to you in yesterday's paper. Write me whether "Noble" is a fictitious name." As it was printed in the *New Mirror*, the poem was ascribed to Miss Mary Florence Noble; Noble, though was a *nom de plume*. The writer's name was Jane Wright. On page 120 of *The Life and Letters of Mrs. Emily C. Judson*, A. C. Kendrick relates that "Miss Wright was a member of the Seminary (the Utica Female Academy)."

Lines to Fanny Forester

By Miss Mary Frances Noble

Saw you ever a purer light
More still and fair than the harvest moon
When day has died in a shadowless night,
And the air is still as a summer noon?
No? Ah, sweet one, your eyelids shrine
A light far purer and more divine.

Heard you ever the silvery gush
Of a brook far down in its rocky dell,
And stilled your breath with a trembling hush,
As its mystic murmurs rose and fell?
'Tis thus I list to the liquid flow
Of your silvery accents soft and low.

Yes, sweet Fanny, the light that gleams
'Neath the sweeping fringe of your radiant eyes
Too purely chaste and too heavenly seems
To dwell in the glare of our earthly skies;
And too soft and low your tones have birth
To linger long 'mid the din of earth.

The sweet brow shrined is your clustering hair
Has gathered a shadow wan and deep;
And the veins a darker violet wear,
Which over your hollow temples creep;
And your fairy foot falls faint and low

As the feathery flakes of the drifting snow.

'Tis said the gods send swift decay
To the bright ones they love of mortal birth;
And your angel Dora[136] passed away,
In her youth's sweet spring time, from the earth;
Yet stay, sweet Fanny, your pinions fold,
Till the hearts that love you now are cold.

[136] "Dora'" was a character in a Fanny Forester story of the same name. Willis had commissioned the artist Flagg to paint a portrait of the story and its theme.

Sarah J. Clark to Mary Florence Noble, Printed in the *New Mirror*

Introduction by George Tooze

In the next edition of the *New Mirror* there was a response written to "Lines to Fanny Forester" by Mrs. Sarah J. Clark, titled "The Convalescent."

The Convalescent

"A thousand sweet ties bind her here;
Oh, friend, thy fears are vain!
The blessed angels will not break
So soon the golden chain;
And God, our God, who loveth her,
Shall breathe on her again.

The languor of her step shall yet
With winter snows depart;
Her foot shall spring on carpets wrought
By Flora's loving art,
And keep time to the joyous beat
Of her exulting heart!

Our souls' arms are around her thrown,
She *must not* pass away
Now, when too humble for the proud,
Too lovely for the gay,
The altar of sweet poesy
Is falling to decay.

O, there we may behold her yet
In her young beauty bow;
There may we hear her glad lip breathe

Her consecration vow;
Earth's warm life lighting up her eye—
Its glory on her brow!

There, there a priestess may she serve,
With vestments pure and fair;
There offer up her winged dreams,
Young doves from heaven's own air,
And pour the rich wine of her soul
As a libation there!

Nathaniel Parker Willis to Emily E. Chubbuck,[137] March 17, 1845

My dear friend

I have just given to the printer for tomorrow some exquisite lines addressed to Fanny Forester[138] in reply to Miss "Noble's" poetry, by Miss S. L Clarke.[139] How the women all love you, to be sure!

I am, trebly more than usual, full of cares, and have not a minute to write—but I rejoice that you are going to Philadelphia, and your illness makes it *of course* that I must see you as you pass thro. Write me word the day and hour you come to New York, and where you stay while here. God bless you, dear Emily

Ever yours

N. P. W.

Source: Hanna family files.

George R. Graham to Emily E. Chubbuck, March 19, 1845

My dear Fanny Forester[140]

I recd by last express, your letter with the Ms. It is already in the hands of the greedy printer—that is the story—and he promises to devour it at one meal. So look for it *entire* in the May number. You asked me in a recent letter whether my brother lost his *all* in a late fire in July—he *did*, but was fortunate enough to recover a payment of it, and he has so much energy of character, that he has

---

[137] Written on the address page in the handwriting of Emily E. Chubbuck: "A. P. Willis. March, 1845. No. 21" (The twenty-first letter from Willis.).

[138] Fanny Forester, Emily Chubbuck's *nom de plume*.

[139] These two poems—"Lines to Fanny Forester" and "The Convalescent" appear just prior to this letter.

[140] Fanny Forester, Emily Chubbuck's *nom de plume*.

already made part of it up, and says that "the fire will be the basis of his fortune." I have no doubt that the increased energy he expends in his business in consequence of his loss and the *notoriety*—is that the word—gained by the newspaper accounts of the loss, will enable him partly to make good his words.

But do you know that I never feel for the losses and troubles of men, as I do for the struggles of the other sex? I cannot agree with the "new lights" of the "humanity and transcendental set" who proclaim that woman is man *equal* [sic], and should meet the rough rebuffs of the world in the world context—stand side by side with him at the hastings [sic], and proclaim from the stump for rights real or imagined. I love woman too well to make her a course thing—more of a piece of granite with iron nerves—No! Woman has her fitting place. Intellectually no doubt his equal—for patient endurance in physical suffering his superior—in deep affection for the caring his [ ] and with a physical organization so blended with her hunch, that in wrong, what is reason with man is *instinct* in her. She *feels* before man *sees* the approach of evil—but I go dashing along with an essay, while Fanny is waiting for an agreeable letter.

Do I read aright, in the kind notices of your friends in the *Mirror*, that your health is really critical? Do you know that I have taken so deep an interest in your welfare that I cannot think that it is so, and I must attribute to their kind [ ] and fear, all that I read about you. Your own letters have lost a little of their joy tone, but then you have been long ill, and while I have watched the *tone* of your letters as I would the countenance of a dear friend, I have not been in *fear* for you. So tell me now frankly: is there any thing in regard to *pecuniary* matters, that at all disturbs your mind? I have written you so fully and *earnestly* on this head, that I should feel *almost* angry if you have neglected to let me know it.

Now there is a "little scolding," so if you think I am [ ] towards "agreeable people" let us get up a little warfare on our own account in opposition to Mr. Poe's "Longfellow War," which is for the public eye.

I shall come up to Utica to see you in June. God hand you his blessing, and good health and keep with you those you love and you with those who love you.

Truly yours

Geo R. Graham

Source: American Baptist Historical Society, AJ 24, no. 1189.

Eliza C. Allen to Emily E. Chubbuck, March 21, 1845—New York City

Dear Miss Chubbuck,

I have for some time intended to write to you for a double purpose. First, to ascertain whether B. B. & H.[141] have paid you the amt for which I am indebted to you for last year. I fear they have neglected it, as well as other items of business for which I have trusted to them. If you have not rec'd the money, please present the accompanying order. The matter contributed by you last year for the *Journal*[142] amounted, I believe to 7 1/4 [ ] which, after deducting $1 for the work, would leave $6.29 due you.[143] I hope the firm have [sic] paid what became your due while they owned the Jour. If you did not receive the work from them last year, please inform me.

And now permit me to urge you to write for me, and that as soon as may be convenient. I now expect to leave home in a few weeks, to be absent two or three months, on a visit to my mother and brothers at the west, and am desirous of leaving as much matter prepared for the *Journal* as I can command. Will you not send me something soon?

Do let me know if you have any trouble in getting the Jour. from B. B. & H. I will send it by mail if you prefer it, but wish to save you the postage.

Affectionately Yours

Eliza C. Allen

Source: American Baptist Historical Society, AJ 22, no. 1088.

George R. Graham to Emily E. Chubbuck, March 22, 1845

My dear Fanny[144]

I send the draft as above without counting the pages sent as your letter reached me on Saturday Morning the most busy of the week.

---

[141] Publishing firm of Bennett, Backus, and Hawley.

[142] The *Mother's Journal*, a Baptist publication ministering to mothers and children, included Emily's material as early as 1843 and continued periodically until 1849. Eliza C. Allen was the editor until her death in 1848. Mary Clarke became the editor upon Allen's death, and in 1851 would request additional material from Emily.

[143] The issue of remuneration by the *Mother's Journal* was a reoccurring one for Emily. At this time, Emily was one of the highest paid woman writers in the United States, receiving from the magazines the unprecedented sum of five dollars a page. Emily was very conscious of this, especially as she constantly dealt with the debt that she had incurred in purchasing a home for her parents, a theme which we find again and again in the correspondence. Mrs. Allen felt, and communicated to Emily, that Emily had a greater responsibility and that financial reward should be less important than her service.

[144] Fanny Forester, Emily Chubbuck's *nom de plume*.

We can talk it over when you get here. We shall try hard in Philad'a to cure you and with good wishes, well seconded, with food—efforts we *must succeed*.[145] My own family physician Proff J. K. Mitchell *has much* experience in the class of diseases which your friend fears and he shall do his utmost.

Drop me a line and let me know when you are coming.

Yours truly

Geo R. Graham

Written in the left margin: "If you have any [ ] [ ] to Utica by April 1st—make the arrangement, and rely on me for [ ]."

Source: American Baptist Historical Society, AJ 23, no. 1123.

Anna Maria Anable to Emily E. Chubbuck, March 26, 1845[146]

Dear Nemmy[147]

Do you care enough to hear from me to allow me to scribble on good old Graham's[148] letter?[149] Judging you by myself I shall take the liberty. I won't scold any more [sic] about Graham—He is a good generous honest old fellow I know—and he will be kind to you. I prognosticate all sorts of pleasant time for you. I thought of you almost every inch of the way to day—From Henry's[150] account I grew quite easy about you—thinking you would be able to go through to Troy—When you left this morning I watched for an hour thinking very probably you would come back in one of those—cachinnating [sic] fits—

What do you think I did in that hour? I went to your bed-room, and there lay on your table so meekly and uncomplainingly the little injured sun-shade [ ] that my heart was smitten—inasmuch as was in my power I repaired its injuries and—it

---

[145] George Graham and his wife were very attentive of Emily while she was in Philadelphia. They would call on her regularly and often she would ride with them in their carriage. When Emily traveled to New York on her way back to Utica, the Grahams accompanied her to the city to ensure her well-being.

[146] This letter is undated. We know, however, that it was written on the day that Emily Chubbuck left Utica, traveling first to New York City, and then on to Philadelphia, where she was to spend four to six weeks. She was accompanied on this trip by Cynthia Sheldon. Emily left for Philadelphia on March 26, 1845.

[147] "Nem" or "Nemmy" was a name of endearment given to Emily by a small group of her intimate friends at the Utica Female Academy. Anna Maria Anable was "Ninny."

[148] George Graham, editor of *Graham's Magazine*, took an interest in Emily Chubbuck as Fanny Forester and paid her with the unheard of sum of five dollars a page. He and his wife gave her special attention while she was in Philadelphia.

[149] Graham had written to Emily on March 19 and 22, 1845; these would be the letters to which Anna Maria was referring. Graham and his wife were to call on Emily shortly after her arrival; see the letter of Emily Chubbuck to her sister Catharine Chubbuck dated March 31.

[150] Henry Sheldon Anable, Joseph and Alma Sheldon Anable oldest child. In August 1846, Henry was in the Milwaukee WI area. In a September 27 letter, he said he might leave Utica to join William and Olivia in Sheboygan WI. He married Rosanna Frick in Sheboygan WI on February 13, 1855, and died September 3, 1887, in Flushing NY.

makes quite an appearance. Did you see Court[151] to day? He came in the train—and caught a glimpse of you—He has had a nice school and has come home in good spirits.

I have just been down stairs and made a nice pitcher of ginger pop—now I have undressed me and I want Nemmy to go to bed with me. I can't bear to sleep on my hard mattress now and I don't believe Nemmy will sleep *very* nicely to-night. Only think! by the time you get this you will have seen Willis![152] You must write immediately and tell me all about it—for I am dying of curiosity—and then don't you think Ninny[153] wants to know how Nemmy gets along? You must not forget to ask Willis how he likes you—so as to tell me—Blessed fellow! I know he will be good to you—and if he don't [sic] think you are beautiful tell him *I* think (on bleak days) that he is sadly deficient in taste. There, I think I have romanced enough. so well to business—

The draft Hank says wants your name—He says he don't [sic] want any money before Aunt C.[154] comes back—so there will be no use in your sending it back again—before she comes.

We had a nice French class to night but Mary[155] spent the evening in the parlor with Jimmy! She was rather too much out of sorts to recite French—but Jimmy[156] righted her.

---

[151] Courtland Anable, younger brother to Anna Maria Anable. He held several positions over the years and eventually studied at Hamilton College and boarded for a time with Emily's parents. In 1853, he returned to Philadelphia where he preached his first sermon at the Eleventh Baptist Church. He was "Uncle Court" to Emily Frances Judson. In 1880, Anable was listed in the Massachusetts census as an ordained minister serving in a church.

[152] Emily's plan had been to meet with N. P. Willis in New York; the editor of the *New Mirror*, Willis had catapulted Emily to fame with his publishing of her letters to the editor in the June editions of the magazine. Upon her arrival in New York, Emily discovered that Mrs. Willis had just died in childbirth, with complications caused by scarlet fever. Mr. Willis was in Boston where the burial was to be.

[153] "Ninny" was a name of endearment given to Anna Maria Anable by her most intimate friends at the Utica Female Academy. Emily was "Nemmy."

[154] Miss Cynthia Sheldon was the administrative and finance manager of the Utica Female Academy. She was a mentor, advisor, and friend to Emily. By this time, she had become "Aunt Cynthia."

[155] From other letters we believe that this was Mary Barber, the art teacher at the Utica Female Academy, who seemed to be a confident of Jimmy Williams.

[156] Jimmy Williams was often mentioned in Anna Maria Anable's letters, mostly simply as "Jimmy." He was around the Utica Female Academy, and she spoke of their conversations, what he was doing, his interests. She often referenced him as being with "Helen." Writing to Emily on April 29, 1845 Anna Maria had some interesting comments to make. In a paragraph of gossip she said, "[and now] I'll turn to Jimmy and Helen." She went on to talk about a party:

> It was one of the most elegant parties that has been given in a long time. Jimmy's three sisters were there—all elegant women. (Also) all the flowers of Utica Society—and among them—no not among *them* but in the rooms was [sic] poor dowdy looking little Helen giggling when she showed any animation with [ ] and girls of that class and stamp. Jimmy tried to bring her forward as much as he could—but it would not do. She will never shine in society, and what is worse Jimmy will feel her deficiency in that respect very much. He would like very much to have a wife but would entertain his guests handsomely—and yet—he loves Helen very much I have no doubt and the one hundred thousand will make up for some deficiencies or ought to. I may abuse my pity I dare say.

Then on November 14, 1845, Anna Maria said to Emily: "Do you know Jimmy is really engaged to Helen M? He hasn't been to see me yet, and he came home last Sat. Oh, love! love! Even a seven-year friendship must fade before thy potent spell. Little did I think tho' that Jimmy would be faithless."

Tell Aunt C. the girls are getting along well. The sick ones are quite comfortable, and now the house is so still—I can hear nothing but the crickets. Tell her Grand-pa and Grand-ma[157] have taken so to Court that they won't miss her half as much as they would if he had not come.

Good night Nemmy darling—don't forget to write to Ninny.

Wednesday night.[158]

Written in the left margin and across the text of page 1: "Old Jade Bacon came up to see Jane[159] this morning—he likes your 'Heaven'[160] very much—He says he hopes you will keep your loom going in P. Whatever he meant by it, he meant to say something pretty."[161]

Source: American Baptist Historical Society. No reference numbers.

Anna Maria Anable to Emily E. Chubbuck, March 29, 1845[162]

Dear Nemmy[163]

I have only this minute received your letter as the naughty folks at the office kept it last night. By this time you are nicely fixed in P. and have got good old Graham's[164] letter,[165] and he has been to see you a dozen times I suppose—if you have had such pleasant weather as we have you have got over the blues and are looking with quite a different from last Thursday's [sic] on your "prospects." I can well imagine dear Nemmy how you felt when you first heard the sad news[166]—I

---

[157] Deacon Asa and Isabell Low Sheldon, parents of Cynthia Sheldon, Urania Sheldon Nott, and Alma Sheldon Anable. Mr. and Mrs. Sheldon lived with their daughters and grandchildren as a part of the Utica Female Academy community. For many years, Mr. Sheldon led mealtime prayers for the academy family. Mr. and Mrs. Sheldon were very popular with the students. When Mrs. Sheldon died January 29, 1847, Mr. Sheldon continued to have a room at the Utica Female Academy until he died in March 1848.

[158] March 26, 1845 was a Wednesday. Anna Maria Anable apparently started this letter early in the evening, and added this postscript much later.

[159] Jane Kelly was Emily Chubbuck's friend at the Utica Female Academy. Jane later became a teacher with Emily at the academy. Kelly became the literary principal in 1844 with the retirement of James Nichols and his wife from that position. During a period of Kelly's illness in 1844, Emily filled in the position for her. Then, in 1848, when Cynthia Sheldon moved to Philadelphia to help start the Misses Anable's School, Kelly became the "headmistress" of the academy and successfully brought the academy into the future, though not without some initial disparagement from the Sheldon-Anable families.

[160] "Heaven" was one of Emily's stories recently published.

[161] This is probably an allusion to the recently published poem by Fanny Forester titled "The Weaver."

[162] An addendum to this letter, written by "J," is the next letter in the correspondence.

[163] "Nem" or "Nemmy" was a name of endearment given to Emily by a small group of her intimate friends at the Utica Female Academy. Anna Maria Anable was "Ninny."

[164] George Graham, editor of Graham's Magazine, took an interest in Emily Chubbuck as Fanny Forester and paid her with the unheard of sum of five dollars a page. He and his wife were very hospitable to Emily while she was in Philadelphia.

[165] Graham had sent letters to Emily Chubbuck dated March 19 and March 22. On March 26 Anna Maria Anable had written on one or both of them, and forwarded them to Emily in Philadelphia with her added letter.

[166] This would be the news of the death of Mary Willis, the wife of N. P. Willis, one of the editors of the New Mirror, and Emily's mentor and friend.

was almost stunned. I could hardly believe it. Poor Willis![167] My heart aches for him. With his [ ] he will doubtly reproach himself for some things—and then it seems so forlorn her being away from all family friends sick and dying in a hotel[168]—Oh, he must feel horrible—you don't know how much I got at some of the folks who laugh at the idea of his feeling much. I went over to see Mrs. Kirkland[169] yesterday. She seems to know him—She says he is so warm hearted—he cannot but feel this deeply. You know she does not think him a very *good* man. She looks upon this as a sort of providential thing—to break up his attachment to the world—You must write to him of course. Won't he want one of your dear, sweet sympathizing consoling letters? I guess he will—and he shall have every thing he wants just now from folk. Oh! how I wish I could jump down to P. and talk with you this afternoon—I gloat over every ray of sunshine for you—It has been so pleasant here we have had one window up all day and every day since you left. The girls are asking me if I don't feel lonesome without you, but as long as this pleasant weather looks—I think of you as getting health[170] and strength [ ]—and I feel invigorated and happy for you'll come back with Aunt C?[171] By no means. We shall not advise you at all. You must stay there and get well, and then by the first or middle of May—you may come back to New York—and there you must see poor Willis—for I don't know as it would be quite proper from him *now* to go to P. and see you. Oh! Nemmy. Write to me and tell me all what you are doing—and what the people say to you—and who you see—and what Willis says to you—for Ninny[172] feels this afternoon as she was going to the lonesome indeed. If you were here we would go and take a nice ride all alone for the roads are so good I would not be afraid, and we would get some little spring violets all so pretty would not we?

---

[167] Nathaniel Parker (N. P.) Willis was the editor of *New Mirror*, the magazine that catapulted Emily into literary fame. He became a friend, mentor, and eventually a suitor.

[168] Our best information is that Mary Willis died in premature childbirth. N. P. and Mary Willis kept an apartment at the Astor.

[169] Mrs. Charles Kirkland lived in Utica NY. She and her husband had at least two daughters, Julia and Amelia, who are mentioned in a letter from Anna Maria Anable to Emily dated April 21, 1845. On September 7, 1844, N. P. Willis had written: "Give my kindest remembrance to our common friend, Mrs. Kirkland, when you return to Utica." On November 30, 1844, he said, speaking of his college days: "Mrs. C. Kirkland, was a kind of good-natured aunt to us."

[170] Emily, who had been sick most of the winter, had traveled to Philadelphia planning to spend four to six weeks, with the hope that the more refreshing climate would give her a significant improvement in her health.

[171] Miss Cynthia Sheldon was the administrative and finance manager of the Utica Female Academy. She was a mentor, advisor, and friend to Emily. By this time, she had become "Aunt Cynthia."

[172] "Ninny" was a name of endearment given to Anna Maria Anable by her most intimate friends at the Utica Female Academy. Emily was "Nemmy."

Tell Aunt C. that the sick ones are all getting along finally—Miss R. is visiting around in the rooms today—and Augusta[173] has been sitting up all the morning. Grand pa and Grand ma[174] are sick—and Mother[175] matronizes [sic] admirably—Court[176] has been copying bills ever since he came home—and I guess has finished them by this time—next week he is going into the store to be cashier for Henry[177]—Jimmy[178] and Mary[179] are "going it strong"[180]—I have been out every evening since you left and she has got to blushing and squaring about him worse than ever—Jane Look made quite an impression on Mrs. F[ ] Martin yesterday—she came up to see us all—and we were all out but Jul and Mary—Jane did the honors of the house handsomely—and Mrs. M. is going to invite her down there next week—I must stop and do up your papers[181]—do have compassion on me and with your own Ninny.

I went into Beth's to buy a pair of combs yesterday and he made a *very* handsome and modest apology for what he had done—said he was thoughtless etc.

Source: American Baptist Historical Society, AJ 23, no. 1122.

---

[173] Augusta Crafts is mentioned frequently in the letters written from the Utica Female Academy. A number of references chronicle her very strong opinions; many of these were spoken against N. P. Willis and Emily's relationship to him (Mrs. Crafts did not approve of either). In an April 30, 1845 letter Anna Maria Anable said: "The Dr. is not engaged nor isn't going to be to Mary Spencer I imagine, and tho' Mrs. Crafts intimated very strongly that there was *some one* he had his eye upon, he denied it to me strongly and scolded about Mrs. Crafts gossiping tongue."

[174] Deacon Asa and Isabell Low Sheldon, parents of Cynthia Sheldon, Urania Sheldon Nott, and Alma Sheldon Anable.

[175] Alma Sheldon Anable, sister of Cynthia Sheldon and Urania Sheldon Nott. On July 28, 1814, Alma married Joseph Hubbell Anable in Troy NY (Anable's second marriage). Joseph and Alma Anable had nine children: Henry Sheldon Anable, b. June 21, 1815; William Stewart Anable, b. November 6, 1816; Anna Maria Stafford Anable, b. September 30, 1818, Cynthia Jane Anable, January 28, 1820; Samuel Low Anable, b. November 28, 1821; Harriet Isabella Anable, also known as Hatty or Hattie, was born December 18, 1823; Courtland Wilcox Anable, b. July 28, 1825; Frances Alma Anable, or Fanny, b. April 12, 1828, and Mary Juliet Anable, b. February 18, 1830.

[176] Courtland Anable, younger brother to Anna Maria Anable. He held several positions over the years and eventually studied at Hamilton College and boarded for a time with Emily's parents. In 1880, he was listed in the Massachusetts census as an ordained minister. He was "Uncle Court" to Emily Frances Judson.

[177] Henry Sheldon Anable, Joseph and Alma Sheldon Anable oldest child.

[178] Jimmy Williams, often mentioned in Anna Maria Anable's letters, usually just as "Jimmy."

[179] From other letters we believe that this was Mary Barber, the art teacher at the Utica Female Academy, who seemed to be a confident of Jimmy Williams.

[180] In her letter of March 26, 1845, Anna Maria Anable had said of Jimmy and Mary: "We had a nice French class to night but Mary spent the evening in the parlor with Jimmy! She was rather too much out of sorts to recite French—but Jimmy righted her." We believe this to be Mary Barber.

[181] In Emily's absence at the Utica Female Academy, Anna Maria Anable was helping to teach her class on composition.

"J" to Emily E. Chubbuck, March 29, 1845[182]

My dear Emily, I have just returned from down street [sic] and have had a most charming walk. Thought of you several times while I was out. This delightful weather must be doing wonders for you. We shall look for you in three or four weeks (not days as you threaten) as fair and rosy as sweet sixteen.[183] Write soon very soon and tell us that you feel differently from what you did in New York.[184] Tell us more of the particulars of Mrs. W's death.[185] Poor Mr. W.[186] My heart aches for him. Say a word of comfort to him in your own kind way. Do tell us all about yourself. You have been living months since you left us and I want to know all, that is all you are willing to tell. The Buchers drop in occasionally and all in the bedroom looks right, but the *empty* chair, and the "made" bed. Just strain your eyes a little, can't you see just how things look? I ain't [sic] going to tell you how much I miss you, or what a great empty place you've left behind!! All are well and send much love. When is Dear Miss C.[187] coming back to us? All in her line goes on well. As ever your devoted J.

Source: American Baptist Historical Society, AJ 23, no. 1122.

Emily E. Chubbuck to Catharine Chubbuck, March 31, 1845—Philadelphia[188]

Well, Miss Katy,[189] I'm in Philunydelphy [sic] at last, but I'm so shockingly tired that I can't tell you anything. However, Miss C.[190] goes back tomorrow, and as she will mail my letter in Utica you can afford to be satisfied with a short one. We left Utica Wed. morning and came down the river the same night. The weather was very fine. The first thing when I reached N. Y. Thurs. morning, I heard of the

---

[182] This letter from "J" was an addendum to Anna Maria Anable's letter of March 29, 1845.

[183] Because of health problems which had incapacitated her for the winter, Emily had traveled to Philadelphia, hoping that a stay of four to six weeks would bring improvement to her health.

[184] Emily had left Utica on March 26, arrived in New York on March 27, and was there until March 29, when they left for Philadelphia.

[185] Mary Willis, the wife of N. P. Willis, Emily's mentor and friend. Emily had planned to stop in New York on her way from Utica to Philadelphia to meet N. P. Willis for the first time. She learned of the unexpected and tragic death of Mrs. Willis when she arrived in New York.

[186] Nathaniel Parker (N. P.) Willis was the editor of *New Mirror*, the magazine that catapulted Emily into literary fame. He became a friend, mentor, and eventually a suitor.

[187] Miss Cynthia Sheldon was the administrative and finance manager of the Utica Female Academy. She was a mentor, advisor, and friend to Emily. She accompanied Emily on the journey to Philadelphia.

[188] This letter has an addendum which is dated April 2, 1845.

[189] Sarah Catharine ("Kate," "Kit," or "Kitty") Chubbuck, Emily's older sister, born October 25, 1816.

[190] Miss Cynthia Sheldon was the administrative and finance manager of the Utica Female Academy. She was a mentor, advisor, and friend to Emily. She accompanied Emily on the journey to Philadelphia.

death of Mrs. Willis. He was gone to Boston to attend the funeral and I believe has not returned yet. We spent two days in N. Y. and came here on Saturday. Mr. Gillette's[191] family *is just* the pleasantest in the world. His wife is a darling—his mother, a dear lady, is here, and he has three beautiful little boys. The eldest however is now sick—I am afraid dangerously so. Mr. & Mrs.[192] Graham[193] called to-day when I was out (we visited the Fairmount Water works) and this afternoon he called again.[194] He is the handsomest man that I ever set eyes on, and just as good as good can be. He offers me his carriage to go any time any where [sic] I choose and says he will do all he can to make it pleasant for us. Is'nt [sic] he a blessing to human nature? I anticipate rare times. Then when I go away from here I have an invitation to spend a week with Sophie Taylor[195] in Brooklyn, which I shall of course accept.

Source: Hanna family files.

Anna Maria Anable to Emily E. Chubbuck, March 31, 1845[196]

Didn't I tell you so Dear Nemmy?[197] I *knew* you would have a nice time notwithstanding the numerous petty annoyances that have poked themselves in your way for a week or more. That was a great joke of Post's and very smart of John[198] to tell you of it! It is so comfortable to go about feeling that every body is shocked at one's phiz[199] [sic]. O! I am mad at them all. The next time you write tell me who thinks you are beautiful as Ninny[200] does—Do you want "Mother-in-law"[201] to give you a role to perform in P? As it is impossible for poor Anna B[ ]ly to do it just now, she will hint *just a little*.

---

[191] A Philadelphia minister, Rev. A. D. Gillette was a stalwart friend and supporter of the Judson, Sheldon, and Anable families. Emily met Adoniram Judson in the parlor of the Gillette home in Philadelphia. She stayed with the Gillettes while she was in Philadelphia.

[192] This is the first mention that George Graham was married.

[193] George Graham, editor of *Graham's Magazine*, took an interest in Emily Chubbuck as Fanny Forester and paid her with the unheard of sum of five dollars a page. He and his wife were very hospitable to Emily while she was in Philadelphia.

[194] For a description of this visit, see Emily Chubbuck's letter to Anna Maria Anable dated April 1, 1845

[195] See the letters of Alfred Taylor, April 6, 1845, and Sophia Taylor, May 7, 1845.

[196] There is an addendum to this letter dated April 1, 1845.

[197] "Nem" or "Nemmy" was a name of endearment given to Emily by a small group of her intimate friends at the Utica Female Academy. Anna Maria Anable was "Ninny."

[198] We believe that this is a reference to John Inman, publisher of the *Columbian Magazine*, and J. Post, who handled financial matters for the magazine. Emily had become a regular contributor to the magazine.

[199] This is a reference to Emily's face.

[200] "Ninny" was a name of endearment given to Anna Maria Anable by her most intimate friends at the Utica Female Academy. Emily was "Nemmy."

[201] Anna Maria Anable frequently referenced of herself to Emily as "Mother-in-law."

Impressions. Don't allow yourself to be seen in the street except in a carriage. Be *chary* of your charms. [ ]sounders [sic]. In a drawing room monopolize the sofa, or at least look out for a seat which will give a *side light* to your face—you know the value of your *three quarter* face. Remember who said "nothing is prettier in woman than a beaming head." It is particularly becoming to *your style*. Remember also who admires above all things *repose* in a woman. Mrs. Walker who met Willis[202] in Washington soon after his return to this country—says his wife's gayety and frank enjoyment of every pleasure was annoying to him—a fib of course, but Nem that quiet manner is your *forte*—and besides it takes people all by surprize [sic] in Fanny Forester.[203] It's a great deal to get people *surprized* [sic] into looking at you. When they have once fairly got their curiosity aroused to see if there *is* any thing [sic] in you, never fear but they will find it. It's only the *non-appreciators* who see nothing in a face like yours. Doct. James[204] was here last night and I read him your joke—with a very solemn and important manner he says, "Tell your Miss Chubbuck for me *not to sell herself too cheap.*" Adieu from the French.

Source: American Baptist Historical Society, AJ 23, no. 1171.

Anna Maria Anable to Emily E. Chubbuck, April 1, 1845[205]

I have been dawdling about all day—reading the *Journal*. Then Mrs. Shield's story (beautiful isn't it), gossiping for the last half hour with Mary[206] who is laid up with a head-ache—and having made her "squirm" so that there is no probability of her getting composed again in a week, I believe I'll wind up with relating some gossip to you. Have you heard that there is a funny picture of F. F.[207] in New York? Well, there is!! There is something about you in the New World which I will send you—haven't seen it yet. Augusta Crafts[208] knows that [ ] is Mrs. D. and I suppose very body else does. Every body [sic] is talking about Willis.[209] Poor sea[ ] he has to

---

[202] Nathaniel Parker (N. P.) Willis was the editor of *New Mirror*, the magazine that catapulted Emily into literary fame. He became a friend, mentor, and eventually a suitor.

[203] Fanny Forester, Emily Chubbuck's *nom de plume*.

[204] Dr. James was a trusted physician in Utica, who attended the students and faculty of the Utica Female Academy. He is mentioned frequently in the correspondence as having been consulted for varying medical complaints and his advice was always welcomed and highly regarded.

[205] This is an addendum to a letter from Anna Maria Anable dated March 31, 1845.

[206] Mary Anable, Anna Maria Anable's sister, or Mary Barber.

[207] Fanny Forester, Emily Chubbuck's *nom de plume*.

[208] Augusta Crafts and her strong opinions are mentioned frequently in the letters written from the Utica Female Academy

[209] Nathaniel Parker (N. P.) Willis was the editor of *New Mirror*, the magazine that catapulted Emily into literary fame. He became a friend, mentor, and eventually a suitor.

take it. It's well there are a few who believe *every thing* [sic] *he says*. As a general thing he don't [sic] get the credit of having much *heart*. We are invited to Mrs. [ ]man's this evening—but I suppose Mary will stay home—and entertain Jimmy[210] if he comes! O they are having rare times! This is the first unpleasant day we have had since you left. I hope it's pleasant with you—Thermometer was 70 yesterday.

We are suffocating under our winter hats and Miss R. has not gone down yet. Tell us what you see or hear is worn. Do they have dresses low or high in the neck or just as we do in P? Fan just came home from the party 12 o'clock. Why do you suppose I sit down now to write you instead of burning up this silly letter? Well, because I imagine that Thursday will be your *bluish* day and you will be glad to get any thing [sic] however stupid from home. As usual—I had a chat with Leonard tonight about you—He thinks "Nickie Ben"[211] is the best thing you have written—but that its rather a bold flight—wonders who'll come next—etc—He says every body [sic] recognizes it—but that if old [ ] should see it—he would feel flattered—or at least he ought to. There was a young New Yorker—a cousin of Mr. Dev[ ]'s there who had a great deal of curiosity about you. By the way you must manage to make Willis call on you when you come back—for I suspect the general impression in N. Y. is that you are plain—which if he sees you—you know will be of great advantage to you—Do write and tell me every thing—who you see and what you see and what you think—you don't know how lonesome I am getting to be.

Good night Ninny[212]

Source: American Baptist Historical Society, AJ 23, no. 1171.

---

[210] Jimmy Williams, often mentioned in Anna Maria Anable's letters, usually just as "Jimmy." Several recent letters mention Jimmy and Mary together. See Anna Maria Anable's letter of March 26, 1845.

[211] "Nickie Ben" was one of Emily's published stories. We note that there are two letters received after this which make it obvious that "Nickie Ben" was a portrayal of someone real—Urania Nott was to say (April 25, 1845) that she would have been too embarrassed to have written it, it was so close to the person and she felt it so recognizable.

[212] "Ninny" was a name of endearment given to Anna Maria Anable by her most intimate friends at the Utica Female Academy. Emily was "Nemmy."

Emily E. Chubbuck to Anna Maria Anable, April 1, 1845[213]

Letter Fragment 1

Then (Mr. and Mrs. Gillette)[214] received me as if they had known me always, Mrs. Gillette[215] not even waiting for an introduction. It will not be particularly convenient to them to have me here, but they will not listen to my going away. I am growing better and better every day, and promise myself a delightful time. I think I shall like the city better than I do New York—all but the white blinds; them I can not [sic] endure. It seems all the time as though somebody was poking white sticks in my eyes. When I am in walkable order, and little Jemmy Gillette gets well, Mrs. G. and I will measure the pavements at a great rate. The weather yesterday and to-day is like June. You will be able to judge something about it, when I tell you that (such a cold body as I am) I sit all the time at the open window.

Letter Fragment 2

The meeting was very stiff. He[216] was surrounded by little boys (he brought one with him—a nephew; he has no children). I walked in shaking from head to foot. He inquired if I was Miss Chubbuck, and gave me the tips of his fingers. I expressed regret for being out this morning -then a long pause. Afterwards we talked about the *Columbian*,[217] Mr. Willis,[218] and finally about our last quarrel and money matters.[219] Sometimes I trembled, and blundered, and stumbled against big words, and then I talked on for a few minutes quite straight. On the whole, I guess he thinks I

---

[213] We have here two separate fragments from the same letter. These two fragments inform the events of the letter Emily Chubbuck wrote to her sister Catharine Chubbuck which was written on March 31, 1845, with an April 2, 1845 addendum. Though A. C. Kendrick, in *The Life and Letters of Mrs. Emily C. Judson* clearly has this dated April 1, 1845, this second fragment describes in detail the events found in the March 31 letter to her sister Catharine. Mr. and Mrs. Graham had called on Emily in the morning while she had been out; Mr. Graham came back that same afternoon.

[214] Rev. A. D. Gillette was a stalwart friend and supporter of the Judson, Sheldon, and Anable families. Emily met Adoniram Judson in the parlor of the Gillette home in Philadelphia. Emily was staying with the Gillettes while in Philadelphia.

[215] Hannah Gillette was the wife of the A. D. Gillette. Emily stayed with the Gillettes in spring 1845 and again that year in November. Emily met Adoniram Judson on Christmas Day 1845, in their parlor. Hannah would play an important part in preparing Emily for life in Burmah.

[216] George Graham, editor of *Graham's Magazine*, took an interest in Emily Chubbuck as Fanny Forester and paid her with the unheard of sum of five dollars a page. He and his wife were very hospitable to Emily while she was in Philadelphia.

[217] The major sources of Emily's writings were the *New Mirror* under the leadership of N. P. Willis, the *Columbian Magazine* under the leadership of John Inman and J Post, and *Graham's Magazine*, under the leadership of George R. Graham. She wrote as well for the *Knickerbocker* and the *Mother's Journal*. There was also what seemed to be a secondary market for Emily's pieces. This Editor has found several newspapers of the period with Fanny Forester stories in them. One example, the Hartford (CT) *Courant* put out a literary supplement on January 23 of 1845 which had a story ("A Peep Withini Doors") taken from a recent issue of *Graham's Magazine*.

[218] Nathaniel Parker (N. P.) Willis was the editor of *New Mirror*, the magazine that catapulted Emily into literary fame. He became a friend, mentor, and eventually a suitor.

[219] See George Graham's letters to Emily: September 23, 1844, October 4, 1844, November 11, 1844, January 26, 1845, March 19 and 22, 1845. The money issue is found in the September 23, 1844 letter; Emily was asking for, and eventually received, five dollars a page for her writing, an unprecedented figure at that time. Other letters revolve around something he had said and Emily had taken him to task, especially with some references Graham had made about N. P. Willis.

am very sensible girl, though not quite so pretty, and poetical, and easy, etc., as he expected. He has a mighty positive way of saying things, but you can not help believing every thing he says. He talks beautifully, and with perfect ease, when he gets a-going; but he makes very long pauses.

Source: A. C. Kendrick, *The Life and Letters of Mrs. Emily C. Judson*, 124–25.

Emily E. Chubbuck to Catharine Chubbuck, April 2, 1845[220]

Miss C.[221] did'nt [sic] go yesterday because poor little Jemmy[222] is so sick. Last night they tho't he was dying. She thinks now of starting tomorrow morning, but it is doubtful to me if she does. Graham[223] called this afternoon, but I did'nt [sic] see him for I was undressed, and he was in great haste—he is to come again tomorrow morning, and I hope he will get here before Aunt C. starts. I saw the Rev. Rufus M. Griswold[224] this morning. He don't [sic] know that I am Fanny Forester[225] but he whispered Mr. G. when he went out that "Miss Chubbuck was one of the first ladies in the country." He is a widower[226] what's more and crazy to get married. Don't you think I shall accomplish something?

I guess Graham thinks I am *pretty*; for he seems to be very anxious to say something about it. Mrs. Osgood[227] made him believe when he was in N. Y. that I was perfectly hideous. I guess Mrs. O. is jealous of me, for she has been a sort of a pet with these men, and she is afraid I will cut her out. Never mind: "every dog must have his day," and somebody will be cutting me out pretty quick. Mr. Post[228] told John Wilmarth[229] that one of the richest men in N. Y. fell desperately in love with

---

[220] This letter is an addendum to a letter from Emily E. Chubbuck to Catharine Chubbuck dated March 31, 1845.

[221] Miss Cynthia Sheldon was the administrative and finance manager of the Utica Female Academy. She was a mentor, advisor, and friend to Emily. Miss Sheldon accompanied Emily on the trip to Philadelphia.

[222] We assume this to be a nickname. A. D. and Hannah had six children between 1836 and 1849: Susan, James, Walter, Daniel, William, and Grace.

[223] George Graham, editor of *Graham's Magazine*, took an interest in Emily Chubbuck as Fanny Forester and paid her with the unheard of sum of five dollars a page. He and his wife were very hospitable to Emily while she was in Philadelphia.

[224] Reverend Rufus W. Griswold, an ordained clergyman and distinguished literary figure, had been one of Emily's "widowers."

[225] Emily Chubbuck wrote under the *nom de plume* of Fanny Forester. Asked about it once, she said "Would anyone buy a book written by Emily E. Chubbuck?"

[226] "Widower" refers to widowed older men and usually suggested availability and interest in marriage. The academy girls and their teachers were always referring to "the widower" or to "widowers" in their conversations and correspondence.

[227] Frances or "Fanny" Osgood, a contemporary writer with Emily, was one of the regulars writing for *Graham's Magazine*.

[228] J. Post was associated with the *Columbian Magazine*.

[229] Emily had visited Wilmarths when she visited New York. In a September 1845 letter, Mrs. Wilmarth chided Emily for something Emily had said that deeply wounded her, but offers to "bury the tomahawk." There are frequent mentions of the Wilmarths, their home and hospitality.

Fanny Forester, and resolved to offer her his precious person and fortune together. He was just about crazy until a place was suggested for forming the lady's acquaintance. Mr. Post gave him a letter of introduction to Mr. Hawley[230] and he set out for Utica in great glee, but he came back oh! so crest-fallen! He had seen Fanny Forester, and she was so *excessively ugly* that the sight fairly schocked [sic] him. Mr. Post said the poor fellow was really almost heart-broken. The cream of the joke is, Mr. Hawley has not introduced me to a gentleman since I was F. F.

Miss C. has just decided on starting tomorrow morning, and I must hurry to finish my letter. I have rec'd the money of both Post and Graham. Graham is a blessed man. He won't get here in the morning till after she is gone. Write *immediately* and address "Care of Rev. A. D. Gillette, 69. North 12. St., Philadelphia"—*immediately*, remember. Tell mother[231] I am getting better; and, if this nice warm weather continues, shall come back in a few weeks as strong as a bear. Tell me all the news, and if there is none say so.—I could'nt [sic] send the bonnet before I came away and I have bro't the dress with me, but you shall have all the things when I come back, if you are a pretty good girl. Don't neglect to write, a single minute.

Nem[232]

Source: Hanna family files.

Anna Maria Anable to Emily E. Chubbuck, April 4, 1845[233]

Dear Nem[234]

That last letter of mine was a horribly disagreeable one I know—this shall be more amiable that is if this *nice* has any influence, for I feel in a particularly amiable mood to day. Blessings on you for your letter of yesterday! I was feeling horribly

---

[230] Horace H. Hawley married Jane Sheldon, the niece of Cynthia and Urania Sheldon, Hawley was a member of a publishing firm and also worked with Alexander Beebee in publishing the *Baptist Register*. Hawley was enormously helpful to Emily as she published her early stories and books. There are numerous references to his help and his generosity.

[231] Lavinia Richards Chubbuck, Emily's mother, was born June 1, 1875, in Goffstown NH, the eldest of thirteen children. She married Charles Chubbuck on November 17. 1805. They were the parents of seven children.

[232] "Nem" or "Nemmy" was a name of endearment given to Emily by a small group of her intimate friends at the Utica Female Academy. Anna Maria Anable was "Ninny."

[233] Anna Maria has dated this letter in her writing as March 4–44—and someone has written above that "March 4, 1844." The content of the letter, however, is not consistent with that date; the content demands that it be April 1845. Anna Maria mentions that Emily is in Philadelphia because of her health—she mentions Willis (N. P. Willis) who was not a part of Emily's life until at least May/June 1844, well after the letter was supposedly written, and most tellingly, she speaks of the death of Willis's wife, which did not take place until late March of 1845. Further, Cynthia Sheldon, who accompanied Emily to Philadelphia, has just returned home to Utica. For all of these reasons we date it as April 4, 1845. The April 5 addendum is the next letter in the correspondence.

[234] "Nem" or "Nemmy" was a name of endearment given to Emily by a small group of her intimate friends at the Utica Female Academy. Anna Maria Anable was "Ninny."

blue—it had snowed in the morning so that it was impossible to get out—Mary[235] was sick yet—The wind whistled like the ghosts of eats (ain't [sic] that a simile) round my corner room—and to cap the canary the *chimney smoked*—Nothing was in good humour [sic] but Jane[236]—whose everlasting grinning provoked me beyond endurance. (Wouldn't she be flattered if she knew I had called the Principal "a *thing?*")

This morning the sun shines brightly—my tea rose and violets and J[ ] are all in bloom scenting the room with their fragrance—and little Fanny is chirping away so sweetly among the flowers it would be a downright shame if I should grumble—so I will not.

Lo "old Graham"[237] is young and handsome, and you have fallen "dead in love" with him—Well, look—[ ] you keep on the right side of his wife. I think she will have cause to be jealous. Tell me when you have seen her what sort of a woman she is—I feel desirous that you should fascinate her. I'd give all my *new* shoes if I could only be there with you.

The long looked for package from Hat[238] came Wednesday, by Mrs. Patton. She is homesick poor child, and I have a great mind to write to her to come on. The barrage is the most beautiful thing I ever saw. White, with a narrow blue silk stripe—very fine quality.

'Twill make a lovely evening dress. I wish you could find one like it for it is just the thing for you. Augusta Crafts[239] was here last evening—more agreeable than some—though she despises Willis[240]—she told us all about that Blidgon[241] affair and promised to send the story down for us to read. She has not decided whether to go to P. or not—is waiting an answer from Mrs. Gardold. I suppose you have heard from Willis as The *Mirror* don't come here any more [sic]. Tell me Nemmy, would anything you should hear about him—the truth of which you could not doubt—shake your confidence in him? I don't mean in his goodness of heart—but in his *honour* [sic]? I can't help having mine shaken a little—though you don't know how I hate to hear any thing [sic] against him. I do hope he will succeed in his *Mirror* undertaking. By the way, have you thought a word of Read since you

---

[235] Mary Barber, mentioned frequently in the Emily Chubbuck Judson letters, was a student and then the art teacher at the Utica Female Academy.

[236] Jane Kelly was Emily Chubbuck's friend at the Utica Female Academy. Jane was the literary principal at the Utica Female Academy.

[237] George Graham, editor of *Graham's Magazine*, took an interest in Emily Chubbuck as Fanny Forester and paid her with the unheard of sum of five dollars a page.

[238] Harriet ("Hatty," "Hattie," or "Hat") Anable, one of the five Anable sisters. She had been teaching in a private residence in the New Orleans area.

[239] Augusta Crafts and her strong opinions are mentioned frequently in the letters written from the Utica Female Academy.

[240] Nathaniel Parker (N. P.) Willis was the editor of *New Mirror*, the magazine that catapulted Emily into literary fame. He became a friend, mentor, and eventually a suitor.

[241] This is also spelled "Blidgims." See volume 1, Cast of Characters, and A Timeline for Blidgims References.

have been there? I expect you to do execution on that man, and you must not disappoint me. There was a note came for you, this morning, which Jane supposing it was from a young lady you some expected on [ ] school—has taken the liberty to open it. It was from Mrs. Allen,[242] begging you to write something for them, and giving you an order on Hawley[243] for $6.25. for what you had written. I suppose you don't care about having it sent on to you as it is in a note form—so I have put it in my port-folio to keep for you.

Source: American Baptist Historical Society, AJ 23, no. 1135.

Anna Maria Anable to Emily E. Chubbuck, April 5, 1845[244]

Sat—there Nem![245] I have had a mind not to write another word to you—You could not scare up but one letter half page could you? E! I wish I had some of Graham's[246] *spunk*! I'd make you wait a week before you heard another word from us.

Aunt C.[247] has just come at 3 o'clock, after keeping us in the greatest suspense for three hours. The cars ran off the track this side of S. and they were obliged to put back for three hours—Aunt Martha[248] and little Harriet have come on with her to make us a visit. I have just run out of Aunt C's room where they are all jabbering to finish this and send it off to-night you undeserving—No, Nem—I have thought better of it since I have had my tea. I'll put it in the package. The *Courier*?

---

[242] Eliza C. Allen was the editor of the *Mother's Journal*, which included Emily's material as early as 1843. In a letter to Emily during their courtship, Adoniram mentioned that he had met Eliza Allen and had written: "I am afraid I shall get to dislike her. She is a woman that I could make some use of. She has a sharp, strong intellect—is a good critic in the rough, but not in the nice. No heart—no amiability—very severe and what is worse, glaringly envious." Judson went on to say that the *Mothers' Journal* was considered to be a very prestigious publication for the church. After June 1844, Emily seemed to turn her literary attention to commercial publications such as the *New Mirror*, *The Columbian*, and *Graham's Magazine*, which would pay Emily five dollars a page, an unheard of sum at the time. There are six letters in the correspondence from Allen; they begin in August 1843, there are two in 1844 (January and February), one in March 1845, and two in 1846 (February and April). Later letters reflect a dialogue between Emily and Allen with Allen's expectation that Emily should write for her magazine and find her reward not in lucrative financial reward, but in the ministry of *Mother's Journal* to mothers and children. Emily replied frankly that she had financial burdens needing to be met. In December 1848, Emily received a letter from Eliza Allen's husband, the Rev. Ira Allen, describing in some detail the death of Eliza Allen.

[243] Bennett, Backus and Hawley. Hawley was a member of this publishing firm. In earlier years, he had been very helpful in the publication of Emily's first books. They were also publishers for the *Mothers' Journal*.

[244] This letter is an addendum to a letter written by Anna Maria Anable to Emily E. Chubbuck dated April 4, 1845.

[245] "Nem" or "Nemmy" was a name of endearment given to Emily by a small group of her intimate friends at the Utica Female Academy. Anna Maria Anable was "Ninny."

[246] George Graham, editor of *Graham's Magazine*, took an interest in Emily Chubbuck as Fanny Forester and paid her with the unheard of sum of five dollars a page. He and his wife were very hospitable to Emily while she was in Philadelphia.

[247] Miss Cynthia Sheldon was the administrative and finance manager of the Utica Female Academy. She was a mentor, advisor, and friend to Emily. She was returning from Philadelphia, having accompanied Emily on her trip there.

[248] Martha Sheldon, the wife of Fred Sheldon. Fred was a brother to Cynthia Sheldon, Urania Sheldon Nott, and Alma Sheldon Anable. Fred and Martha Sheldon lived in Troy NY where Fred was a shopkeeper.

I suppose Willis[249] told them to send it. It came the day you left—before the death of his wife. By the way *Mirrors* come again regularly—Do you think W. will give it up and go to Europe?[250] Aunt C. said Graham thought he had better—Poor fellow! Well—I think you and "old Graham" are having interesting times—I hope they are not such "stylish" folk that they can't pay you a good deal of attention—I mean his wife more particularly. I *do* want you to enjoy yourself in P. How will you manage to return Mrs. G's call? You must make Mr. Gillette[251] go with you. There now!—didn't you want Ninny?[252] The spare bedroom is occupied to night for the first time since you left. I feel as if *our* rights have invaded. Nem if you want to read something horrible—something that will make you look round after your own ghost and make you lie trembling and shivering all night—read "Frankenstein." It scared me most to death when I was a child—and I have been reading it again to day, so you…

Written in the right margin of the address page: "…may imagine with composure I sit here at eleven at night writing you—I am glad you are going to finish the "Exiles"[253]—I know it will be beautiful but you must not write much. We don't send you off to Philadelphia to make yourself sick a writing—Now I wish I could just hop into your bed to night [sic]. I must go to mine *any way* [sic] for I am tired most to death. AM"

Source: American Baptist Historical Society, AJ 23, no. 1135.

Alfred Taylor to Emily E. Chubbuck, April 6, 1845—Brooklyn

My Dear Miss Chubbuck

My wife has just returned from Mr. Wilmarths[254] [sic] when she saw Elizabeth, who told her she had received a letter from you, enquiring our address. It is 251 Washington Street, Brooklyn.

---

[249] Nathaniel Parker (N. P.) Willis was the editor of *New Mirror*, the magazine that catapulted Emily into literary fame. He became a friend, mentor, and eventually a suitor.

[250] N. P. Willis sailed for England with his daughter Imogene on June 1, 1845, and was out of the country until March 1846.

[251] A Philadelphia minister, Rev. A. D. Gillette was a stalwart friend and supporter of the Judson, Sheldon, and Anable families. Emily met Adoniram Judson in the parlor of the Gillette home in Philadelphia. She was staying with the Gillettes while in Philadelphia.

[252] "Ninny" was a name of endearment given to Anna Maria Anable by her most intimate friends at the Utica Female Academy. Emily was "Nemmy."

[253] One of Emily's stories written for publication. In vol. 1 of *Alderbrook*, there is a story titled "The Dying Exile." We do not know if the two are the same. Sometimes, however, we do know that the magazine publishers completely changed the names of Emily's stories.

[254] John Wilmarth. There are frequent mentions of the Wilmarths' home and hospitality.

I am very glad that I have an opportunity of repeating my wife's invitation to you to spend some days with us on your return. We shall be most happy to see you and hope it will be convenient for you to make us a long visit.

I am happy to hear that you have in some measure recovered from your indisposition, and I am sure you will hardly think of returning to your former scenes of labor and writing, until you are fully restored to health, and do allow me, since I have so good an excuse for doing it—the excuse is that I am writing you at all—to urge upon you the importance of avoiding every thing [sic] that can in any way affect your health. This seems a needless caution, as I presume you feel its importance, quite as much as I do. Still the thing is often more untried by others than by our self [sic]. Health is at the [ ] consequence and without it life is but a tedious pilgrimage!

Do if you please drop me a line a day or two before leaving Philadelphia and say when I may meet you at the cars—this will [ ] all necessity for your knowing our place in Brooklyn, please address me at no. 18 West St., New York. With sincere wishes for your prosperity, and happiness I am very truly yours

Alfred Taylor

Source: American Baptist Historical Society, AJ 26, no. 1257.

Cynthia Sheldon to Emily E. Chubbuck, April 7, 1845—Utica[255]

Dear Emily,

You cannot begin to think how constantly my mind has centered in your room, and the sick room too, notwithstanding the various scenes passing before me.

Our jaunt to N. Y. was very pleasant, I beg you will seek the same change from cars to steam boat—in N. Y. I had some two hours with the Wilmarths.[256] All well. Many kind enquiries after you—the fates seemed against my meeting Urania[257]—she had been on the watch two days for me—and appointed three o'clock Thursday—Eugenia[258] the same—but whether they concluded I was not worth to more trouble or not—is a matter of conjecture.

---

[255] This letter was part of a packet of letters written by Cynthia Sheldon, Anna Maria Anable, Sarah Bell Wheeler, Jane Kelly, and Mary Barber.

[256] There are frequent mentions of the Wilmarths' home and hospitality.

[257] Urania Sheldon Nott—a mentor, advisor, and friend to Emily—was the literary principal at the Utica Female Academy when Emily arrived in October 1840. In late summer 1842, Urania married to Eliphalet Nott, the president of Union College in Schenectady NY.

[258] Eugenia Damaux, part of Emily's intimate circle of friends at the Utica Female Academy.

My trip up the river was exceedingly comfortable. Fred[259] met me first thing as landed—concluding no news from home was good news—I spent a very pleasant day in Troy—found brothers [sic] wife in just the weak state that induced me to say she must come on with me—she entered into it with spirit but brother thought it a rash experiment. The Doct. was on my side, and we started in good spirits—at Schenectady were met by Mr. Kelly—A letter from Fan[260] the day before said they were all well—another start. When half a mile out of the city, the track gave way—a concussion of the baggage and wood cars gave us a little shock.[261] Then a stand still—the engine from the city took us back—where Mr. Kelly met us again—then a two hour visit followed at his house—Mr. and Mrs. Pearson refreshments etc.—made it to us a very comfortable breakdown—next thing the jumping at home—

Written in the left margin of the address page: "Do say to the dear friends it was in my heart to write them, but have been interrupted until a late hour—my tender sympathies are with them in this last deep affliction—I heard the sad tidings on my return sat'y e-g. May sustaining grace be their portion in great measure. Make my kind regards to Mr. Robarts[262]—with the other friends I met there—and shall love to remember—how I wish to know your prospect for sleep tonight—may guardian angels keep vigils and hold your eyelids in slumber.

"Kind regards to Mr. Graham[263]—say to him I have many regrets—[ ] many regrets at not seeing him."

Ever yours

C. S.

---

[259] Fred Sheldon and his wife Martha lived in Troy NY. An April 11, 1845 letter from Cynthia Sheldon says that Fred was a shopkeeper and that his store had recently been heavily damaged in a fire that burned a number of buildings. They had two daughters, Fanny and Harriet.

[260] Fanny Anable (who was in Philadelphia at this time) the daughter of Joseph and Alma Sheldon Anable and the niece of Cynthia Sheldon, or it could be Fanny Buckingham, the daughter of Fred and Martha Sheldon, who also was a niece of Sheldon. This also could be yet a third Fan from the Utica Female Academy.

[261] In the letters of Anna Maria Anable to Emily Chubbuck dated April 4 and April 5, Anna Maria Anable had a review of all of these events.

[262] Mr. and Mrs. W. S. Robarts lived in Philadelphia and were active in Baptist circles. They were friends of Reverend and Mrs. A. D. Gillette and in December 1845, the Robarts welcomed Adoniram Judson to stay in their home. A. C. Kendrick said, "(Gillette and Dr. Judson) arrived in (or out of) due time in Philadelphia, and Dr. Judson was welcomed to the house of and Mrs. W. S. Robarts, who became warm personal friends, as they were already active friends of the mission cause." There is a letter that indicated some hard feelings towards Mrs. Robarts for her disparaging comments about Emily's upcoming marriage and missionary service. Emily mentions this in a February 6, 1846 letter to Adoniram. Mrs. Robarts seemed to be accusing Emily of worldliness—when all the time, Emily was quick to say, Mrs. Robarts was engaging in the same activity of which Emily was accused. The correspondence also indicates a satisfactory healing of the relationship. Mrs. Robarts proved to be helpful to Emily in gathering together in a short time all that she would need to take with her to Burmah. In January 1849, Miss Sheldon told Emily that Mrs. Robarts had placed their daughter Mary in the Misses Anable's School. There also is continued mention of the social relations maintained by the Robarts and the Sheldon-Anable families.

[263] George Graham, editor of *Graham's Magazine*, took an interest in Emily Chubbuck as Fanny Forester and paid her with the unheard of sum of five dollars a page. He and his wife were very hospitable to Emily while she was in Philadelphia.

Written in the right margin of the address page: "When I began to write this, the want of letter paper was a mile of trouble—you see how nicely it was got along with—Fan is closeted with Mr. Williams I shall report when he goes—

"Well ten o'clock is here—Mr. W. only wanted to gather some particulars about the number of classes etc. that his minutes might be very correct—do you believe the report will ever come."[264]

Source: American Baptist Historical Society, AJ 26, no. 1278.

Anna Maria Anable to Emily E. Chubbuck, April 7, 1845[265]

Monday night. What a blessed good child you are Nemmy[266] to send me back a good long letter—and to tell me just every thing [sic] that I want to know. I take back every thing [sic] haughty I said in the beginning of this letter.[267] I can now form quite an idea of the society by which you are surrounded—and indeed it seems quite fascinating to me—I am glad you like the Grahams[268]—Tell me some more about them—And so you make a feint of *giving me* the widower![269] Pretty well! It's well Aunt C.[270] persisted in calling him Wilcox (who could get up any romance about *such* a man?) or I might have felt disappointed at your threat of taking him back—But I'll leave the widowers to you and Jane[271]—I believe you both have a particular fancy for them.

Willis![272] I am getting in a perfect quandary about him. We hear very naughty stories about him—which stagger very much the rest of the folks here, but I *won't* believe them. I think it's only folks that don't know anything about him who talk so—or those who like A. Crafts[273] have some private pique against him—I *know* he's a good-hearted fellow. I shall be crazy to know if he answers your letter and

---

[264] The report was an evaluation of the Utica Female Academy published by the *Baptist Register*. A lot of the academy's reputation rested on this report.

[265] This letter was part of a packet of letters written by Cynthia Sheldon, Anna Maria Anable, Sarah Bell Wheeler, Jane Kelly, and Mary Barber.

[266] "Nem" or "Nemmy" was a name of endearment given to Emily by a small group of her intimate friends at the Utica Female Academy. Anna Maria Anable was "Ninny."

[267] Apparently there was a former part of this letter which we do not have, and this was an addendum to it.

[268] George Graham, editor of *Graham's Magazine*, took an interest in Emily Chubbuck as Fanny Forester and paid her with the unheard of sum of five dollars a page. He and his wife befriended Emily while she was in Philadelphia.

[269] "Widower" refers to widowed older men and usually suggested availability and interest in marriage. The academy girls and their teachers were always referring to "the widower" or to "widowers" in their conversations and correspondence. The reference here may be to Rufus Wilmot Griswold mentioned in Emily's April 2 letter as a widower "crazy to get married."

[270] Miss Cynthia Sheldon was the administrative and finance manager of the Utica Female Academy. She was a mentor, advisor, and friend to Emily. By this time, she had become "Aunt Cynthia."

[271] Jane Kelly was Emily Chubbuck's friend at the Utica Female Academy. Jane was the current literary principal at the Utica Female Academy. In fall 1848, she followed Miss Cynthia Sheldon as the the headmistress.

[272] Nathaniel Parker (N. P.) Willis was the editor of *New Mirror*, the magazine that catapulted Emily into literary fame. He became a friend, mentor, and eventually a suitor.

[273] Augusta Crafts and her strong opinions are mentioned frequently in the letters written from the Utica Female Academy.

what he says—I form my opinion entirely upon the manner in which he *treats you*—for that is all that I know of him—Beautiful notice, those were of Mrs. W.[274] but I think the best thing that has been written was in the *Mirror*.

Fan[275] and Mary[276] have been having quite a discussion here at my side about literary people—Fan as usual blasting them all en masse—excepting Cousin Nemmy. What attracted my attention was Fan's climax—"If I were a man I would marry cousin Nemmy, but there ain't [sic] another authoress I would marry." I like Mr. Hall's sentiments extremely—only *he must look a little longer.*

I have been down to Aunt C.'s room for a minute before going to bed—Mr. Corey[277] wants to know how you like the people etc. Mary[278] after hunting in vain for an apple or a remnant of one to take her pills in—is going to retire on quince— Wouldn't I like to be witness to night [sic] of one of the *old scenes* by the stove-pipe in Jane's room? Jane and Jimmy[279] have been *consulting* about the report.[280] I am afraid that will be only a "flash in the pan" after all—I declare I have half a mind to go South next fall in spite of fate—Mary A.[281] tells me of a nice situation—I am going to write to Hat[282] to come home this Summer—and then I guess I'll go back with her. Don't be worried about the report. I have no doubt they'll do it—*in their own time.* Now Nemmy do write again *right off* such another good long letter—I thought the "Exiles"[283] was that little angel story you began till I looked at it—

---

[274] Mary Willis, the wife of N. P. Willis, had died unexpectedly the end of March; Emily was to first hear of it when she arrived in New York City on March 27.

[275] Fanny Anable was living, working, and studying in Philadelphia at this time, so this is another "Fan" or "Fanny" within the Utica Female Academy household.

[276] Without further identification, we cannot know if this "Mary" was Anna Maria Anable's sister Mary Anable, or Mary Barber, who included a letter in this packet of academy friends.

[277] Corey was the pastor of a Baptist church near the Utica Female Academy, and Sheldon and many of the girls from the academy worshiped there. In April 1844, he wrote to Emily expressing dismay that at a school program one of the girls had read a composition justifying dancing as exercise; he spoke of this as a roadblock to the salvation of many. Then on March 10, 1846, Emily indicated in a letter to Anna Maria that Corey had been very critical of her relationship and impending marriage to Adoniram Judson. Cynthia Sheldon wrote a number of times expressing Corey's regret and support, and in 1847 there were letters of reconciliation between Emily and Corey. In spring 1848, we learn that Corey's wife had died of consumption, her condition exacerbated by recent childbirth. She had left behind four children, the youngest a baby. Then in July 1849, Anna Maria Anable wrote of his impending marriage to Jane Backus, a good choice for this "rising man." Corey remained popular with the Sheldon-Anable families even after their move to Philadelphia in 1848. A March 2, 1852 letter from Charles B. Stout told of Corey's call to the Stanton Street Church in New York City, a call that Corey did not accept. Finally, in 1854, there was a pastoral letter from Corey to Emily on her illness and her possible death.

[278] We would assume that this is Mary Barber, for Mary A. is mentioned next. Mary Barber, mentioned frequently in the Emily Chubbuck Judson letters, was a student and then the art teacher at the Utica Female Academy.

[279] Jimmy Williams, often mentioned in Anna Maria Anable's letters, usually just as "Jimmy."

[280] The report was an evaluation of the Utica Female Academy published by the *Baptist Register*.

[281] Mary Juliet Anable, daughter of Alma and Joseph Anable. For about a year, from late 1846 to early 1848, she taught with her sister Hatty in New Orleans, and in 1849 she joined the staff of the Misses Anable's School in Philadelphia.

[282] Harriet ("Hatty," "Hattie," or "Hat") Anable, one of the five Anable sisters. She had been teaching in a private residence in the New Orleans area.

[283] "The Exiles" was a recent story written by Fanny Forester for the magazines.

Eugenia's[284] direction in Care of James Brown 80 Leonard St. Give much love to Mr. and Mrs. Gillette[285] and tell them how I *should* like to go down and see them—but I don't think I shall. Do you only get strong and well Nemmy—and you must not like the Philadelphians so much that you won't want to come back to your own loving Ninny.[286]

Source: American Baptist Historical Society, AJ 23, no. 1134.

Sarah Bell Wheeler to Emily E. Chubbuck, April 7, 1845[287]

My dear Nemmy[288]

I must say that I am selfish enough to wish you now sitting in your own room down stairs [sic]so that I might talk with instead of writing to you, but you must be having such nice times I'll not complain. Oh! Nemmy! I did not think you would fall in love with Graham[289] so soon. You'd better be careful or his wife will be pulling your ears before you come home. Aunt Cynthia[290] tells us Mr. Gillette's[291] family are [sic] so kind to you—didn't I say they would be? All we fear is that you will get to liking the Philadelphians so well you'll be for staying there always—Ninny[292] gives us work as she can without you.[293] We took a walk this morning and I wish you could have seen the gracious bow I gave her, and heard the "good morning Miss Anable!" Fanny Shield and mother came home with Aunt Cynthia and we expect to have a pleasant visit with her. She says there isn't anything the matter with Fan—so I feel quite relieved. Now what do you think of Miss

---

[284] Eugenia Damaux, part of Emily's intimate circle of friends at the Utica Female Academy.

[285] Rev. A. D. Gillette was a stalwart friend and supporter of the Judson, Sheldon, and Anable families. Emily met Adoniram Judson in the parlor of the Gillette home in Philadelphia. Emily was living with the Gillettes while in Philadelphia.

[286] "Ninny" was a name of endearment given to Anna Maria Anable by her most intimate friends at the Utica Female Academy. Emily was "Nemmy."

[287] This letter is undated. In it, as Sarah Bell referenced the return of Sheldon, she was speaking of Miss Sheldon's visit to Philadelphia to accompany Emily when she went there for her health in spring 1845. The "Monday morning" would place this at April 7. This letter was part of a packet of letters written by Cynthia Sheldon, Anna Maria Anable, Sarah Bell Wheeler, Jane Kelly, and Mary Barber.

[288] "Nem" or "Nemmy" was a name of endearment given to Emily by a small group of her intimate friends at the Utica Female Academy. Anna Maria Anable was "Ninny."

[289] George Graham, editor of *Graham's Magazine*, took an interest in Emily Chubbuck as Fanny Forester and paid her with the unheard of sum of five dollars a page. He and his wife were very hospitable to Emily while she was in Philadelphia.

[290] Miss Cynthia Sheldon was the administrative and finance manager of the Utica Female Academy. She was a mentor, advisor, and friend to Emily.

[291] A Philadelphia minister, Rev. A. D. Gillette was a stalwart friend and supporter of the Judson, Sheldon, and Anable families. Emily met Adoniram Judson in the parlor of the Gillette home in Philadelphia. Emily was staying in the Gillette home while in Philadelphia.

[292] "Ninny" was a name of endearment given to Anna Maria Anable by her most intimate friends at the Utica Female Academy. Emily was "Nemmy."

[293] Anna Maria Anable was taking some responsibility for Emily's composition class while Emily was in Philadelphia.

Barber?[294] She has been sick almost a week with cold and fever. She is now taking a snooze on the settee. I don't know what Jimmy[295] will do if she does not recover soon. How good you were to send Ninny such a long letter this afternoon. I hope they will come often. It is too bad that you have had such a time with your barege [sic] dress. Do make an impression in it if possible for my sake. They are all reciting French this evening and all laughing as much as ever I suppose.

I presume Ninny has told you of the long letter she had from Katy[296] by Miss Patton and about her pretty dress. I wish she could go to Philadelphia this spring vacation. You would have such times together. Do write me a little word when you can, and believe we talk of you every day (not a little).

Much love to Nemmy

From Sarah Bell

Source: American Baptist Historical Society, AJ 27, no. 1296.

Jane Kelly to Emily E. Chubbuck, April 7, 1845[297]

My *dear* "Small Servant"

I promised myself a long letter from your ladyship when Miss C.[298] returned. When lo! a little, very little note of only six lines presented itself to my astonished vision. Where is that interesting, bewitching, fascinating communication you promised me. You'd better set yourself about producing it forthwith, or you [ ]— Why you will never get another line from me as long as you live. Don't the threat [sic] horrify you?—

You are having grand times I hear—are actually the "*lion*" of the city, a living "nine days wonder." Don't I pray, get your head turned, or your heart softened by the scores of *widowers*,[299] and bachelors, that by this time must be trooping after you.

My Latin class calls me and I must tear myself away from this interesting subject.

What in the world have you to do with widowers! I feel aggrieved you are infringing on my rights. Why the whole "posse con[ ]" has been made over to me

---

[294] Mary Barber, mentioned frequently in the Emily Chubbuck Judson letters, was a student and then the art teacher at the Utica Female Academy.

[295] Jimmy Williams, often mentioned in Anna Maria Anable's letters, usually just as "Jimmy." See letters from Anna Maria Anable dated March 26, 1845 about Jimmy and Mary.

[296] Sarah Catharine ("Kate," "Kit," or "Kitty") Chubbuck, Emily's older sister, born October 25, 1816.

[297] This letter was part of a packet of letters written by Cynthia Sheldon, Anna Maria Anable, Sarah Bell Wheeler, Jane Kelly, and Mary Barber. The letter from Mary Barber was written as an addendum to this letter.

[298] Miss Cynthia Sheldon was the administrative and finance manager of the Utica Female Academy. She was a mentor, advisor, and friend to Emily.

[299] "Widower" refers to widowed older men and usually suggested availability and interest in marriage. The academy girls and their teachers were always referring to "the widower" or to "widowers" in their conversations and correspondence.

by the prop authorities as you very well know. Now whatever else you may do away off there in P. don't let me hear of your appropriating one of them to yourself. Then my Physiology class comes and I must go. It's a provoking thing to be a teacher. Before I go I must have a word of explanation. I've used this pen since the year one, it is not strange that it makes such a grand mark. If I can lay my hand on a knife at the end of the hour it shall be mended.

There was a certain person here last Thursday acting as Trustee who made some very touching and tender inquiries about you. Don't you want to know who it was?

Is there anything new in the dress line in P. I don't know how to have my silk made.

Do keep a sort of journal, let us know all about yourself and doings, also the sayings and doings of Graham.[300] *Neal.*[301] Etc. etc.

Your composition class went off tolerably.[302] I did not find it quite such a bug bear as I thought it would be. When are you coming back. [sic] What do you think of returning when I do. [sic] "It is to [sic] early" I hear you say; well, just as you like. I am all impatient for next week. Don't imagine you are the only one that is going to have fun times this Spring.

E. Hinckley will be here this afternoon. H. will leave in a few days. All things go on smoothly but the *report*[303] has not yet made its appearance. Where is it. [sic] Echo etc—

I am half provoked at myself for writing such a long letter and so good too you don't deserve it. Oh, I am too *amiable*. It's the fault of my character and I must correct it. There—I'll begin by subscribing myself forthwith.

Your devoted and forgiving

"Mistress"

Just *poke* this scratch into the stove as soon (as I) have spelled it out Sil vous plas [sic].

Source: American Baptist Historical Society, AJ 25, no. 1253.

---

[300] George Graham, editor of *Graham's Magazine*, took an interest in Emily Chubbuck as Fanny Forester and paid her with the unheard of sum of five dollars a page. He and his wife were very hospitable to Emily while she was in Philadelphia.

[301] Joseph Neal was part of Emily Chubbuck's circle of literary friends when she was in Philadelphia.

[302] While Emily was in Philadelphia, several of the Utica Female Academy staff were covering the composition class that Emily usually taught.

[303] In her letter of April 7, Cynthia Sheldon mentioned that Fan was closeted with Williams. She later said that Williams was looking for information for "the report"—and Sheldon also was skeptical that it would ever be issued. The report was an evaluation of the Utica Female Academy published by the *Baptist Register*.

Mary E. Barber to Emily E. Chubbuck, April 7, 1845[304]

Your letter is here and you are so flattering. Can't you bring me up before your mind's eye under any other association than that of a "made bed." In that literary land can't—Oh can't you possibly associate with something "Polite"?

Oh Em. why did you drop your mantle on poor me—for one whole week have I been *a pining* under it—while you were about it why didn't you bestow on me that ghost of an apple, anything but taking pills in quince—but one fever two colds and rheumatisms for every bone in your body, demand a pill, and a pill they shall have—I could wrap up Dr. James[305] himself in that cart-load of quince—do excuse me for hinting of nothing but such nauseous subject as—the above—Good night—give my best love to Mr. and Mrs. Gillette[306]—and Mrs. ME

Source: American Baptist Historical Society, AJ 25, no. 1253.

Charles Fenno "Hoffy" Hoffman[307] to Emily E. Chubbuck,[308] April 7, 1845[309]

You are pained my dear friend at my speaking of you as the "popular Fanny."[310] Really, you must not allow yourself to be worried by such associations as your fancy has conjured up around "the professional position of an Author." Write invariably—publish rather always under your *Nomme de plume*—and though the whole world may be able to identify you, your right of impersonality will never be invaded by people whose intercourse is at all desirable. I would so publish if I were you and at some festive day, select the writings with which you meet your more experienced [ ] and make a Fanny Forester Book "edited by Miss or Mrs.—" giving your own name at the time being. You have already I know appeared under your own name in the magazine. But not often enough to be at all identified with the miscella-

---

[304] This letter was part of a packet of letters written by Cynthia Sheldon, Anna Maria Anable, Sarah Bell Wheeler, Jane Kelly, and Mary Barber. This letter from Mary Barber was an addendum to the letter written by Jane Kelly.

[305] Dr. James was a trusted physician in Utica, who attended the students and faculty of the Utica Female Academy. He is mentioned frequently in the correspondence as having been consulted for varying medical complaints and his advice was always welcomed and highly regarded.

[306] A Philadelphia minister, Rev. A. D. Gillette and his wife Hannah were stalwart friends and supporters of the Judson, Sheldon, and Anable families. Emily was staying with the Gillettes while in Philadelphia.

[307] Charles Fenno Hoffman, a prominent literary figure in Philadelphia and New York, well known in literary circles as an exceptionally talented editor, poet, and writer. Emily had started a correspondence with him as Laura Linden before he discovered that she was Fanny Forester.

[308] This letter is addressed to Emily E. Chubbuck at the address of the Reverend and Mrs. A. D. Gillette; he obviously had learned by this time that "Laura Linden" was both "Fanny Forester" and Emily E. Chubbuck.

[309] All of the Laura Letters are undated. Hoffman had terrible handwriting which accounts for the many gaps.

[310] Emily Chubbuck wrote under the *nom de plume* of Fanny Forester. Asked about it once, she said "Would anyone buy a book written by Emily E. Chubbuck?"

neous crowd and only showing a touch of your quality—when you chose to appear in proprin persona [sic].

And you think you would be embarrassed by "the [ ] I promised in case we meet"—that Laura was only to be while you insisted upon preserving your anonynce [sic] with me. The dearest right I think everyone has is their impersonality—or individuality or whatever we may call it. And I would not [ ] any form of it from an intimate friend even, till it was voluntarily [ ] to me. An acquaintance shouted my name aloud when saluting me in a public room the other day. "Pardon me" said your friend, "but I came here to enjoy my [ ] and not to be known specially to the company."

"I would have you to understand Mr. H. that I did not call your name aloud for the purpose of showing I was acquainted with you. I know my members of congress sir and have been familiar with heads of department at Washington besides having the honor of knowing the president."

"You don't say so? Well my dear sir as one so intimate with political life you would be aware that every man wears a mask which he likes to pull off just when; when and how he pleases. You might nod to me the other side of the room and if you choose cross over afterwards and salute me by name as you come up to shake hands and chat. But you have no right to introduce me to the whole room of lawyers save by my express desire."

"I don't see how I did that sir by only calling out your name from the other side of this room?"

"Why I—[ ] it sir you *published* me—and that without asking whether I would go to press or not."

His offensive mood now passed off in laughter and he called upon me afterwards to say he had chewed upon the suggestion as something new to him. It was good he thought but *decidedly anti-American*—But Laura, thanks to my generous friend, has taken off her mask at last to me and though unlikely to shout her name across a tea party I certainly should not be able to keep my countenance when we meet to laugh over our whimsical former acquaintance. Is it really true that you once looked into my office? How womanishly tormenting it was to tell me of it— and then to send the note by the hand of a friend. "Who is that fellow" I thought "a brother—a lover or a husband? Laura's going to be married and coming to town for her wedding purchases. She can't resist the temptation of plaguing me—perhaps she pointed me out to her Cavalier and then they laughed together etc.

Laura 'tis ten minutes after 3. I must seal up this at once and go. I won't enclose you the old note today. 'Tis too trivial and only of about 20 lines written on a piece of wrapping paper—[ ] your verses or write me at least again to tell me you are in good humor with yourself and your friend. I am myself a wretched correspondent but when I have anything to say upon papers that I think you would like to hear I will seize the excuse to remind you of the existence of [Note: The signature is cut out on this page.]

Source: Hanna family files.

Nathaniel Parker Willis to Emily E. Chubbuck, April 7, 1845[311]

My dear friend

Your kind letter was most welcome.[312] Sympathy is sweet to receive—hard to reply to. The wife I have lost was my one window of life looking into Heaven and it is dark with the closing of it. You may have remark'd that, even to you, I was reserved in speaking of her. I was, to all the world. I felt an unconquerable aversion to letting anyone know of that pure relation I held. She married a worlding, and tho married persons assimilate, the side turned towards her changed to *her* quality. Never, it seems to me, breath'd so pure and faultless a human being. I loved her, and revered her, and cherish'd her, and she seemed absolutely happy in me and in my love till she died.

I can not [sic] write more on this theme. When you come to New York let me see you, and I will talk to you about her. This is only to reply to you and ask news of your health. I am more busy than usual, for with my unavoidable dreaming and reverie, I write very slowly and painfully.

Write to me how you are, and believe me[313]

Source: Hanna family files, N. P. Willis to Emily, letter 22.

Catharine "Kate" Chubbuck to Emily E. Chubbuck, April 9, 1845—Hamilton

Dear Nemmy[314]

And so you are really in the great city of Philadelphia. Well I hope it's warmer than it is here else you'l [sic] freeze up and no mistake twas about as cold and stormy yesterday as any day we had last winter but there's one comfort, it can't last long. We were tremendously glad to get your letter Monday, for we began to be

---

[311] On the address page, in the handwriting of Emily E. Chubbuck, we have "N. P. Willis Esq. No. 22. April 12, 1845. We believe that Emily would have received this letter on April 12, and that it was written the Monday previous, April 7, 1845.

[312] Emily had learned of the death of Mary Willis when she reached New York on March 27, 1845. In an April 9 letter, Anna Maria Anable had chided Emily: "And ain't [sic] you sorry you have not written him?" Obviously, Emily had in fact written a letter of condolence, which had reached him prior to April 7.

[313] The ending of this letter is cut away—probably by someone collecting autographs.

[314] "Nem" or "Nemmy" was a name of endearment given to Emily by her most intimate friends at the Utica Female Academy. Anna Maria was "Ninny."

scared for fear you were sick for somehow I got it into my head that we should get a letter in a week, and mother was so sure that it would make you sick—the journey I mean. Did'nt [sic] you feel awfully when you heard of Mrs. Willis'[315] death? Don't you remember what I told you I should think if she should die? I didn't [sic] think then though that she would die so soon or I rather think I would'nt [sic] have said it because I don't think it now. I have no news but you said write anyhow. I'm glad you are in such a pleasant family. Won't seem like being among strangers. I'm afraid Graham's[316] carriage won't do you much good without the weather moderates. I sincerely think he's a blessing to "human nature." I thought you were so mad at him because he did not send you the money that you would'nt [sic] see him at all and there you've seen him a dozen times for what I know. You have such a forgiving spirit to the men especially, if they are handsome and play the agreeable to you. Was'nt [sic] you ashamed when you saw Graham's pretty face, of yours so "excessively ugly" that it shocks people, just one glimpse? Father[317] has bid on two mail routes and will know in about a month if he gets any, he bid only ten dollars a year less than he had before. I hope he won't get but one. I think that's enough. Hav'nt [sic] heard a word from B.[318] yet. Walker[319] sends papers and says his health is good. Has Mr. Griswold[320] proposed yet?[321] I very much doubt whether you accomplished anything with an old widower[322] or not, if he was married you'd be as likely again to like him. I suspect now he has lost his wife you'l [sic] ship him. Poor fellow how I pity him. W. H. Graham would'nt [sic] pay Griggs the money for that order. Said his brother never had said anything to

---

[315] Nathaniel Parker (N. P.) Willis was the editor of *New Mirror*, which catapulted Emily into literary fame. It had been Emily's intention to stop in New York and see Willis on her way from Utica to Philadelphia, but when she arrived, she heard the news that Mrs. Willis had died suddenly and unexpectedly.

[316] George Graham, editor of *Graham's Magazine*, took an interest in Emily Chubbuck as Fanny Forester and paid her with the unheard of sum of five dollars a page. He and his wife were very hospitable to Emily while she was in Philadelphia.

[317] Charles Chubbuck, Emily's father. Though he held varying positions over the years, he failed at most of them. Emily was soon to become the sole support of the family. With the purchase of the house for them, Emily was to continue as a significant financial contributor to the support of the family.

[318] Emily's older brother Benjamin or "Ben," was born March 25, 1809. In the family biography she wrote for Adoniram Judson, Emily wrote that as a young boy, Ben sustained some kind of brain inflammation, which seemed to seriously impair his judgment and behavior. See Emily's letter of February 18, 1838, for some very sharp comments on Ben. Then, on April 2, 1839, Emily wrote to her brother Walker that Ben had been sent to state prison for stealing a horse, blanket, and saddle. Later correspondence had litanies of such problems—stealing a cow, difficulties holding jobs, problems with his marriage, situations exacerbated by character flaws. He died in September, 1846, shortly after Emily had left for Burmah.

[319] Born September 24, 1815, John Walker Chubbuck was twenty-three months older than Emily. Trained as a printer and having worked for a newspaper, Walker established a newspaper with a partner upon arriving in the Wisconsin Territory. We know that he married and was active in his church.

[320] Reverend Rufus W. Griswold, an ordained clergyman and distinguished literary figure, had been one of Emily's "widowers."

[321] In her April 2, 1845 letter, Emily had written: "I saw the Rev. Rufus M. Griswold this morning. He don't [sic] know that I am Fanny Forester but he whispered Mr. G. when he went out that ' Chubbuck was one of the first ladies in the country.' He is a widower what's more and crazy to get married. Don't you think I shall accomplish something?"

[322] "Widower" refers to widowed older men and usually suggested availability and interest in marriage. The academy girls and their teachers were always referring to "the widower" or to "widowers" in their conversations and correspondence.

him about it and so Griggs had to send to George R. for it, he got it by paying a couple of shillings and father paid that to him so that's all strait [sic]. F[ ]ink Chapin cashed the last note you sent. I can't think of a particle of news you know we never have any. We are all jogging on after the old sort. Wallace[323] don't [sic] improve so much as would be desirable, the garden is'nt [sic] touched yet it's so awful cold that it would'nt [sic] do any good. I guess he will do that up strait [sic]. I've just got well so that I can cut round like other folks. I am going to cleaning house now and intend to make things shine. I met Mr. Roney at Society meeting last night, he inquired about you but not quite so eagerly as he did a year ago—was surprised to learn that you were in Philadelphia. Wonder if he thinks you have sufficient "decision of character"? Dayfoot was my beau home last night, so now brag of your beaux. Mother[324] ain't [sic] very well this spring but keeps around. None of the Mrs. Professors have called since you left. I hope they won't till summer comes. I don't believe you'll stay more than a month there. You must take good care of yourself and not eat around too much. You must write often and let us know all the capers you cut. Father says you must send a paper home with the announcement of Fanny Forester's[318] arrival. Sam Griggs told him that he was in Philadelphia last week and knew you were there by seeing a paper. I'm in a hurry so no more now.

Kate

Source: American Baptist Historical Society, AJ 23, no. 1169.

Anna Maria Anable to Emily E. Chubbuck, April 9, 1845

My dear Nem[326]

I have trotted down to Dr. James[327] this even'g to see what he says about staying in P. this winter. He says his advice professionally and independent of any influence is to stay in P. It is the best climate between this and Charleston and incomparably better than Utica; but he does not know what there may be to make it better for you to be here. I told Aunt C.[328] that, and she says she will write to you

---

[323] William Wallace Chubbuck, Emily's younger brother, born January 1, 1824.

[324] Lavinia Richards Chubbuck, Emily's mother, was born June 1, 1875, in Goffstown NH, the eldest of thirteen children. She married Charles Chubbuck on November 17, 1805. They were the parents of seven children.

[325] Emily Chubbuck wrote under the nom de plume of Fanny Forester. Asked about it once, she said "Would anyone buy a book written by Emily E. Chubbuck?

[326] "Nem" or "Nemmy" was a name of endearment given to Emily by a small group of her intimate friends at the Utica Female Academy. Anna Maria Anable was "Ninny."

[327] Dr. James was a trusted physician in Utica, who attended the students and faculty of the Utica Female Academy. He is mentioned frequently in the correspondence as having been consulted for varying medical complaints and his advice was always welcomed and highly regarded.

[328] Miss Cynthia Sheldon was the administrative and finance manager of the Utica Female Academy. She was a mentor, advisor, and friend to Emily. She had become "Aunt Cynthia."

all about it. Now Nemmy how do you suppose I should get along without you? Nevertheless, if I thought (as after hearing the Dr. talk I am inclined to) that you would be decidedly better off I would rather you would stay. I think Aunt C's plan for you to go there and try there awhile is excellent. If after being with them a week you think you could spend the Winter pleasantly why then stay. I think the old bach will have reason to feel encouraged if he has any game on foot. You had better keep Neal[329] for Jane[330]—he would amuse her so nicely.

So you have kicked up a dust in P. at last! Well, don't get *sick riding on it*—that's all I have to say about it. To think that Neal's friends after all should be the kindest ones! It's quite *ominous*. Now Nem, I don't believe you are going to stay any more [sic] than I believe I am, but *supposing* you do, you had better write to this child pretty often, for won't she feel lonesome, with you and Fanny[331] and Betty Hinckley all gone. We study French, and have a *swarry* [sic] and do all I can to cast you out Miss, and when your papa[332] comes home I'll make love to him. So he wrote you a good long letter—and I wish I could see it. Had he rec'd all of yours? And ain't [sic] you sorry you have not written him? I sent a letter to N. Y. this morning for you. It was about the same that I wrote to Fan's but I supposed you would miss one of them. I am afraid Fanny is having too much to do. She should not have her music come all after school hours—but between. Aunt C. thinks if she is with the children two hours in the morn'g and one in the afternoon it is enough. Have you seen anything of Augusta Crafts?[333] Send me one of your Daguerre's by her won't you? You can spare it as Mr. G. will have one.

There is nothing under the sun going on here for me to tell you but you must write me all the news, every thing [sic] you do, and what the folks say to you etc. Have you worn your light silk yet? I suppose not! Tell Fanny I should write her if it were not so late but she must take care and not get sick, and do you take care of yourself. I don't like your getting sick at all. I wish you were here to go to bed with me now, but—Oh well—

Good night—Ninny

Source: American Baptist Historical Society, A.J. 23, no. 1163.

---

[329] Joseph Neal was part of Emily Chubbuck's circle of literary friends when she was in Philadelphia.

[330] Jane Kelly was Emily Chubbuck's friend at the Utica Female Academy. Jane was the literary principal at the Utica Female Academy.

[331] Fanny Anable, one of five Anable sisters. She was born April 12, 1828. Fanny was also living—and working—with the Gillette family.

[332] "Papa" was Anna Maria Anable's name for N. P. Willis, Emily's mentor and friend.

[333] Augusta Crafts and her strong opinions are mentioned frequently in the letters written from the Utica Female Academy.

Cynthia Sheldon to Emily E. Chubbuck, April 11, 1845—Utica

My dear Emily

Your paper of Tuesday has given me great alarm. I hardly dare cast a look into that hospitil's [sic] dwelling least the coffin meet my eyes and the sobs from stricken hearts assail my ears—would that it had been possible for me to have remained.[334]

Since my return I find reasons for great solicitude for your health. Not knowing just how you are morning and evening has an effect which I did not realize while with you—May the tender mercies of our God encompass you, mete out to you blessings unlooked for, abundant and in thankfulness—even under the trying circumstances in which I fear you are now surrounded—

The dear friends. Would that I could pour in their stricken hearts the balm of consolation—My mind is constantly centering there notwithstanding the horrifying steamboat disaster of Monday night.

We were thrown into dreadful consternation by it on Tuesday aft'n—and each successive train of cars have added to the magnitude of the calamity.

It is now certain that dear Mrs. Parker fell a victim and the friends despair of obtaining her precious remains. She was in company with Mr. Mason, going down to make purchases—the wedding was appointed four weeks from yesterday—this death occasions a chasm here, which even time cannot fill—or chase away while memory lasts—Mr. Buckingham[335] we know was saved, but the horror and continued hardships which we fear he is even now enduring must have an effect on his health. We are very anxious about him—the fire in Troy Tuesday evening consumed the store adjoining Frederick, one side—and brothers very near on the other side.[336] Both stores were seriously injured, and of course exposed them to hardships—no time to write to us, or we should have received particulars about Jonas yesterday—

Only think, on Thursday night only three previous to the disaster I was sleeping on that boat in quietness—how can I be sufficiently thankful for my safe return—I fear that I cannot be—My return from the west you know was followed very soon by the sad fate of *The Price*—a boat on which I had flit across the lake in safety—

---

[334] Cynthia Sheldon had accompanied Emily on her journey from Utica to Philadelphia. Though she had planned to leave earlier, she delayed because of the serious illness of James "Jemmy" Gillette. She had finally left Philadelphia on April 3, and arrived home in Utica on the afternoon of April 5, 1845.

[335] Mr. Buckingham was married to Fanny Sheldon (the daughter of Fred and Martha Sheldon, the niece of Cynthia Sheldon), and he was the second in command of the, *Swallow*, a passenger steamboat lost in a tragic marine accident.

[336] See the letter of Cynthia Sheldon to Emily E. Chubbuck dated April 7, 1845. She spoke there of her brother Fred Sheldon, living in Troy NY. Here we learn that he was the owner of a store.

We are very glad sister Martha[337] is here during the great commotion at home—she is gaining a little, but really too weak to endure excitement. We kept the disaster from her till Wed'y.

E. Hinckly came Wed'y—Hannah and Sarah left here this morn'g for home—Friday Evening—at 2 o'clock this aft'n the remains of Mrs. Parker was borne [sic] from the cars by her four brothers. Doct. Whiting and several other friends from N. York were in carriages and proceeded to Mr. William Tracy's—the Funeral will be held in the Dutch Chh tomorrow aft'n—I cannot begin to tell you the solemnity prevailing here—Mrs. Wetmore gave me all the particulars collected, still it is impossible to know just how she escaped from the cabin—she was found some 20 feet from deep waters. The friends had bid $100 for the recovery or probably it would not have been rescued at all—I love to think of her as I have seen her in our Relief Society, and walks of charity. A shuddering untold came over me keeping the reality fixed before my inmost heart suffering my eyes with tears—It is awful indeed, a different feeling gushes out, from what would be uppermost if a gale or other elements had done the work of death. Much blame is attached to the poor pilot who stood by the wreck all day Tuesday wringing his hands and tearing his hair. Mr. B. left the wreck in the morning boat for home where he arrived before Fanny[338] heard of the disaster. She however returned with a small steamer bearing many anxious friends from Troy—which place is made sad indeed by the deaths, and weight of this calamity. The number of lives lost cannot yet be ascertained—the cabins are still under water—four of our business men are missing who were on the boat. Many others have returned to their home—females too, with loss of every thing [sic] with them, but their lives—we can feel for them, but do not know them as we did dear Mrs. Parker. Mrs. Anable[339] and the girls have come from church sometime since—Julia Look[340] stands a candidate for baptism next Sabbath—she appears strong in the Lord. We have evidence of much more feeling among the girls on the subject of religion than for a long time—heaven grant it may continue until all shall know the Lord—I will send you the *Register*[341] in the morn'g—you will see the notice of the school[342]—not the Report so long looked

---

[337] Martha Sheldon was the wife of Fred Sheldon and was Cynthia Sheldon's sister-in-law. Miss Sheldon's letter of April 7, 1845 tells of how she found Martha Sheldon ill when she reached Troy and of how she insisted that Martha return with her.

[338] Fanny Buckingham is the daughter of Fred and Martha Sheldon, niece to Cynthia Sheldon, and cousin to Anna Maria Anable. She was married to Buckingham, the second in command of the ill-fated steamship *Swallow*, which went down on the river with the loss of a significant number of passengers. Fanny Buckingham is mentioned in Anna Maria's letters of December 28 and 29, 1847. She had a young son, and she was visiting Anna Maria.

[339] Alma Sheldon Anable, sister of Cynthia Sheldon and Urania Sheldon Nott.

[340] Julia Look, a former student of Emily's at the Utica Female Academy, was later a fellow teacher.

[341] The *Baptist Register* was a local Baptist paper in central New York that grew into a paper of regional prominence.

[342] The Utica Female Academy, where Sheldon was in charge, and where Emily was the composition teacher.

for, and which Mr. W. says will appear in the daily on Monday next[343]—Anna M.[344] has begun a letter to you, but waits to receive one—you shall have Mrs. Taylor's[345] address when Henry[346] comes back. He left for N. Y. this morning—to be absent a week. It is strange I did not think of it while at Mrs. W.[347]—Our warmest sympathies and affectionate regards to each of the dear family—Much love—from all to yourself—Yours truly,

C. Sheldon

Source: American Baptist Historical Society, AJ 26, no. 1267.

Charles Fenno "Hoffy" Hoffman[348] to Emily E. Chubbuck, April 14, 1845[349]

"Do not change I beg—I beseech do not change. Whatever I may do I will still be thy fond affectionate thy most tenderly devoted Sister"—now god bless thee Laura for these words—thy wise decision has by this time changed Andenlla [sic] into a princess of Ophia [sic], but it has not one jot abated the affectionate [ ] [ ] the most tender esteem of thy brother. Haply now I [ ] see thee hereafter more often than it [ ] otherwise for, though it may be well for us to meet but once in a sweet ten minutes of forgetfulness of either his or hers [ ] that meeting as good and well beloved children who have earned a right to it we will have and go to our books afterward—For have I not kissed the spot on the paper where thy lips were pressed in token it shall be so that those lips should meet once in all this fullness and cling lingering in one kiss as those taken the blessing I would leave with thee— Laura I take pride in those I love and it pleasures for me to think that thy pride will henceforth be [ ] in this [ ] [ ] from a depressing evil that I myself have been not unfamiliar with—Of all kinds of poverty too it seems to me that that of an author is the most cruel,—to coin one's thoughts and fancies—not for tolerance—not for honor—not for the elegant superfluities of life, but for newer fields is [ ],—for, [ ]

---

[343] The report was an evaluation of the Utica Female Academy published by the *Baptist Register*. It was extremely important for student recruitment.

[344] Anna Maria Anable was the niece of the Urania and Cynthia Sheldon, the daughter of Joseph and Alma Sheldon Anable; she was Emily's closest friend at the Utica Female Academy.

[345] See the letter from Alfred Taylor to Emily E. Chubbuck dated April 6, 1845. Sheldon is unaware that Emily already has the address of the Taylor family in New York, and has made arrangements to stay with them on her return to Utica from Philadelphia.

[346] Henry Sheldon Anable, Joseph and Alma Sheldon Anable oldest child.

[347] Mrs. John Wilmarth. There are frequent mentions of the Wilmarths' home and hospitality. Sheldon had visited with them on her return to Utica fro m Philadelphia.

[348] Charles Fenno Hoffman, a prominent literary figure in Philadelphia and New York, well known in literary circles as an exceptionally talented editor, poet, and writer and sometimes mentioned as a romantic interest of Emily's.

[349] All of the Laura Letters are undated.

exigency is terrible when the Spirit of literary adventures—between the excellencies of that half gambling life for praise and gold has worn itself out. My heart has bled before now when thinking of a woman they placed. How beautiful is your gratitude to Mr. W![350] His generous [ ]tion in your behalf has en[ ]red his character to me more than anything I ever knew of him. For though personally acquainted for 20 years and a great admirer of his pieces I have been a dozen times in his company and only know him by his vivacious qualities as a brilliant table companion. I think dear Laura that you overrate entirely the random bits at [ ] through you. I have seen nothing stronger than the paragraphs of her [ ] to which you have alluded. I think you have brought her to double the quantity of praise to balance these [ ]ollnesses. While I think of it however, I desire positively that Laura will under no circumstances makes [sic] her too aware of this correspondence which I would fain believe is now and forever between ourselves only—a sacred thing—which when suspended is to be as holy as if closed in the grave, and when closed to be held as sacred as if it might any time be renewed in after years. (By the way my Sister kisses me—I know she likes this—Her kisses have so much and such [ ] blessing in them—bless thee dear)

And I will "dream" no more of that face. Hereto Laura—I ought not own Sister to have told thee of that wild dream. It was most inconsiderate—it was wrong—yet it was somehow so pleasant to write it and to think of thee half worried—yet not altogether displeased—and yet again a little angry at thyself as not being more displeased—to think of thee looking pretty in this confusion of sensibility and propriety—Laura I would have stopped my letter after it was mailed—yet I was not sorry that I could not stop it—and how when I [ ] [ ] again poured out such idle and vagabond fancies to my sister I cannot make up my mind to grieve that she has had *one* warm fresh and [ ] picture of her rush [ ] drawing thought. When I have [ ] on the gnarled root shall I not look up from the darkling pool as the [ ] of the broad acres musing these? And when those [ ] to kiss the child that is sporting leave the brink [ ] [ ] not, as her [ ] clash they [ ] think of the [ ]—Embrace that circled tree on that spot?—no we will have no [ ] of [ ] but Laura own let that sweet dream so like reality—let the poor unsubstantial thing live [ ] at least till [ ] wholly unobjectionable pool of its own [ ] [ ] kiss in ours in real [ ] bronce.

I have read thy letter again this morning—And thy suitor is "rich, honourable [sic] respectable and good" knows that thou hast no [ ] affection for him yet graciously will weave that requisite of a blissful home to have Laura embellish his. His reward the goelification! [sic] of placing the woman of his choice in the position she is fitted to adorn! My Sister it all looks brighter to me. Those friends whom thou

---

[350] Nathaniel Parker (N. P.) Willis was the editor of *New Mirror*, the magazine that catapulted Emily into literary fame. He became a friend, mentor, and eventually a suitor.

has made so happy with thy F. F. contributions ! (Laura throw out an angel of excellence) will not their gratified prior and confirmed comfort be heart sweet to thee?—[ ] then is an ever welling fount of satisfaction. Thou has [ ] pestly in betrothing thyself—wisely and yet womanishly—For here is no forbidding "Auld Bobin Gray" no troth-plighted "[ ]" to plead for playing the Heroine—no there is nothing either in fraternal or in reality calling, on thee for such sacrifice of that which is most important to a woman—a *home*—sheltered and respectable. Believe me too dear that any man who is "honorable respectable and good" must have qualities around which such a lecture as thou will at last twine itself in placid happiness. I were [sic] the basket of *selfists* [sic] if I did not pray that it would be so, and it *will*—blessed and bright souled Laura. That kiss affirms my words.

Source: Hanna family files.

Emily E. Chubbuck to Anna Maria Anable, April 14, 1845—Philadelphia[351]

Monday Evening

My beloved Demon,

I have just rec'd dear good Miss Cynthia's[352] dear good letter[353]—ten thousand thanks tell her and more too. I have good news for her in little Jemmy's case.[354] He is improving and the doctors really think he will get well. The other children have left the nursery for the first time today. It seems like a different house from last week at this time. Tell her too, to have no fears about me. Since I have gone back to Doct. James'[355] medicine my appetite is returning—it is almost as good as it was before I left Utica. And you would be surprised to know how strong I have got to be. Yesterday morning I went to church and stood it very well, and today—what do you think I have done today? Why taken *two* long rides! In the morning Mr. and Mrs. G[356] and I myself went over to the scene of last spring's riots, Penn's monument etc., stopped at a friend's, took lunch (*wine* with it) and came home. I lay

---

[351] Even though this letter is dated April 16, 1845, the second Monday of April was April 14, and we will go by this latter date. This letter has an addendum to it dated April 15, 1845.

[352] Miss Cynthia Sheldon was the administrative and finance manager of the Utica Female Academy. She was a mentor, advisor, and friend to Emily.

[353] See the letter of Cynthia Sheldon to Emily E. Chubbuck dated April 11, 1845.

[354] James "Jemmy" Gillette, son of Hannah and A. D. Gillette. Miss Sheldon delayed her departure from Philadelphia because of Jemmy's illness.

[355] Dr. James was a trusted physician in Utica, who attended the students and faculty of the Utica Female Academy. He is mentioned frequently in the correspondence as having been consulted for varying medical complaints and his advice was always welcomed and highly regarded.

[356] George Graham, editor of *Graham's Magazine*, took an interest in Emily Chubbuck as Fanny Forester and paid her with the unheard of sum of five dollars a page. He and his wife often took Emily on carriage rides and were very hospitable to her during her stay in Philadelphia.

down and rested awhile and then we uncorked a bottle of porter and took dinner. After that I laid down and didn't I snooze, though? I di'nt even wink at the shadow of a thought for two hours. At the end of that time who sh'd come but Mrs. Graham with her sister Mrs. Rockafelmar (isn't that a name?) to take me to Laurel Hill. I could'nt [sic] resist the temptation and off I went. Oh! Mrs. Graham is a darling woman—you cannot think how much I love her. She is, barring perhaps a little too much sentiment, *one of us* completely. And the sentiment don't [sic] trouble me as it would some of you—it is rather agreeable than otherwise. She thinks Mr. Graham is the *one man in the world* and for my part I am inclined to agree with her. Her sister is older and has a low mournful voice and an expression of subdued melancholy— too real to be called even by Lane Weller a *widder's* art. She looks consumptive and has a short dry cough that I sh'd think would frighten them. That is, she had today; but it might have been occasioned by the dust, which whirled about us in a cloud. Otherwise, the day was enchanting. I mean to ride again tomorrow.

I rec'd a letter from poor Willy[357] this morning. It was written some time ago but was directed 67 instead of 69 and so I wonder that I got it at all. Poor fellow! There is a kind of hopeless misery in his tone that makes my heart ache. He says "the wife I have lost was my one window of life looking into Heaven; and it is dark with the closing of it."[358] Again he writes "she married a worlding [sic], and though married persons assimilate, the side turned towards her changed to *her* quality. Never, it seems to me, breathed so pure and faultless a human being. I loved her, and revered her, and cherished her, and she seemed absolutely happy in me and in my love till she died." Again he says, "I cannot write any more on this theme. When you come to N. Y. let me see you and I will talk to you *about her.*" And again, "I am more busy than usual, for with my unavoidable dreaming and reverie I write very slowly and painfully." Now don't you feel sorry that you have disturbed your good opinion of him by reading the Blidgeons?[359] There are few persons who have not committed faults in their lives—*very few* so far tempted that have not committed greater than he, but the side of the grave is no place to rake them up. Any way [sic], at any time, the story of his misdoings would be about as agreeable to me as that of a brother's. You will not think strange of this, nor blame me for liking to shut my eyes even to true things—if *you* like him for his kindness *to me,* how much more reason have *I* to like him for the same thing.

Source: Hanna family files.

---

[357] Nathaniel Parker (N. P.) Willis was the editor of *New Mirror*, the magazine that catapulted Emily into literary fame. He became a friend, mentor, and eventually a suitor.
[358] See the letter of N. P. Willis to Emily E. Chubbuck dated April 7, 1845.
[359] This is also spelled "Bligims." See volume 1, Cast of Characters, and A Timeline of Bligims References

Emily E. Chubbuck to Anna Maria Anable, April 15, 1845[360]

Tuesday morning.—I have just put my room in beautiful order and set myself down to finish your letter. It is a brilliant sunny morning but everything is perfectly parched for want of rain, and the air is almost suffocating with its hot dryness. They say that the peach crop is probably spoiled by the frost, and everybody seems to be mourning about it. Yesterday—Mercy me! If you had seen that last caper! Dimly, without my spectacles, I saw some kind of a live animal climbing over the corner of my port-folio, and without waiting for anything but a *yell* (please make mention of *the rat* to Jane[361]) I threw folio, letter, pen and all as far as I could. It is well my ink-stand (Jane's I mean) wasn't on my lap. The animal was quite an innocent looking affair however—a little silvery fellow, half worm, half bug, that lies there on his back yet making-believe dead. I must watch him for when he comes to life he may make for this way again. I was about saying that yesterday at Laurel Hill I took hold of some magnolia blossoms that were perfectly crisp and crumbled all to pieces in my hands, ruined by the frost. So with the green rose-leaves and other things—they look as though singed all over by fire. Did I tell you that Mr. Graham[362] is having his house re-modelled [sic]? Mrs. G says it is all turned inside out and makes Mr. homesick. She is a fidgety nervous thing and he pets her as though she was a little baby. I was telling her how frightened I get sleeping alone (night before last I dreamed all night of taking the dead bodies from the *Swallow*[363]) and she said nothing on earth could tempt her to sleep alone for one night—poor G. is awakened from many a sound sleep by her bad dreams. So, you see I am not the only simpleton in the world. When I wake in a fright if I can hear Mrs. Wheldon snore I soon get over it, but when I can't hear her I hop out of bed and go and set the door ajar and then lie trembling till she gets under way. However, I get along very well—much better than I expected, because I sleep so nicely.

Little Jemmy[364] is still better this morning—rested better than any night yet, and Mrs. Gillette[365] is very happy. She and I are to take a walk into Chesnut [sic] St. today. Oh! I like her *so* much! I am disappointed in her too, for somehow I had expected to find her a little bit silly—I scarce know why. Tell *belle Sally* that she

---

[360] This letter is an addendum to a letter dated April 14, 1845.

[361] Jane Kelly was Emily Chubbuck's friend at the Utica Female Academy. At this time, she was the literary principal at the Utica Female Academy.

[362] George Graham, editor of *Graham's Magazine*, took an interest in Emily Chubbuck as Fanny Forester and paid her with the unheard of sum of five dollars a page. He and his wife were very hospitable to Emily while she was in Philadelphia.

[363] The *Swallow* was a passenger steamboat lost in tragic marine accident. It was a blow to local families for many lost a loved one or friend. See Cynthia Sheldon's April 11, 1845 letter to Emily E. Chubbuck and Anna Maria's April 14, 1845 letter for more.

[364] James "Jemmy" Gillette, son of Hannah and A. D. Gillette. He had been critically ill when Emily arrived in Philadelphia on March 29, 1845.

[365] Hannah Gillette was the wife of the A. D. Gillette. Hannah would play an important part in preparing Emily for life in Burmah.

need'nt [sic] be a bit troubled about Mrs. Graham's getting jealous,[366] for she and I are a *little* better friends than her husband and I—a little, not much. I have found out whether she likes me or not—*she says she does*. She don't know Miss Leslie very well, and says she would'nt [sic] be tempted to, for anything. She says she is a gossiping old maid, with a face the perfect personification of conceit and ill-nature. She says Mrs. Osgood[367] looks like her sister Mrs. Rockafelmar; and if so, she has a very different face from what I expected. Mrs. R's face is thin and pale with large, slow-moving black eyes that give it an expression of melancholy. She entertained me again with a long description of Mr. Peterson, who seems to be in her opinion second only to Mr. G. but not a word of *Neal*.[368] Don't expect me home this summer for I have set my heart on seeing Neal, and see him I will. I shall inquire for him before long, for is'nt [sic] he to bring me "comfort?" Mrs. Graham was mightily tickled yesterday, at the idea of my liking the men so well (I told her I did.)—she said I acted wondrously like it. I had some notion of giving her the old adage about the "still pig" but tho't there might be no use in *proving* my follies—it was sufficient to *acknowledge* them. Mrs. G. is very sorry that I don't ride on horse back for she has got the darlingest little pony in the world so small that she can hop on his back from the pavement without help and she would like to make him over to me while I stay. Mrs. Gillette has come up to say she is ready for the walk—we are to call at Mrs. Urp's.

Written in the left margin of the address page: "Tell Mary,[369] Jane and S. B.[370] to let me hear from them. I am but one—you a half-dozen; and I have been out so little so far that I don't have much to write about. I hope Mary is well by this time.[371] Love to E. Hinckly and J. Look[372] and all the rest. Do write very often. You

---

[366] See the letter of Sarah Bell Wheeler to Emily E. Chubbuck dated April 7, 1845.

[367] Frances or "Fanny" Osgood, a contemporary writer with Emily, was one of the regulars writing for *Graham's Magazine*.

[368] Joseph Neal was a prominent member of Philadelphia's literary establishment and was a part of Emily Chubbuck's circle of friends when she was in Philadelphia. Neal was well known and respected as a writer and editor; one of his best known works was the *Charcoal Sketches*. He had founded the *Saturday Gazette* in 1842, a very successful publication which contained a great deal of humorous satire. Anna Maria Anable frequently referred to "Neal" as a beau for Emily. Neal married Alice Bradley in 1846; he died in 1847.

[369] Mary Barber, mentioned frequently in the Emily Chubbuck Judson letters, was a student and then the art teacher at the Utica Female Academy. In recent letters she had been ill.

[370] Sarah Bell Wheeler was a teacher at the Utica Female Academy, and an intimate friend of Emily Chubbuck.

[371] See the letter of Mary Barber to Emily E. Chubbuck dated April 7, 1845. It was a part of a pack with letters from Anna Maria Anable, Cynthia Sheldon, and Jane Kelly.

[372] Julia Look, a former student of Emily's at the Utica Female Academy, was later a fellow teacher. A November 22, 1845 letter from Anna Maria remarked that Julia has the hardest part because she was teaching Emily's composition class, and the students kept asking for Emily. In a September 1847 letter, Julia was listed as one of the teachers at the Utica Female Academy. On September 23, 1849, Anna Maria wrote that Julia and Albert B. Casswell are married and came to visit with her. In one 1849 letter, Julia spoke of another teacher who was teaching "our composition class." On October 27, 1850, Anna Maria Anable noted that Julia had had a son. She was one of a small number of people who addressed Emily as "Emily" or "Nemmy" in her letters.

can't *think* how much good a letter does me. I heard from Katie[373] yesterday. Have'nt [sic] written Eugenia[374] yet. I shall write to Willis[375] tomorrow, but I dread it. Mr. G. told me that he rec'd a Register[376] with a notice of the school in it but I hav'nt [sic] been able to get hold of it yet. I hope the report will be forthcoming sometime.[377] Love to everybody, yourself included from your Petty."[378]

Written in the right margin of the address page: "We have just returned from our walk, and I am quite too tired to write any more [sic]. I meant to have filled the outside, but will send my letter off to put Miss. C. out of suspense about Jemmy. Mr. G[379] told me last night that he still feared his lungs were diseased, but he seemed to get strength every day.

"Is the Blidgims[380] name Ninny or Nanny or Nemmy—I could'nt [sic] make out and if it should chance to be either of ours I am inclined to discharge it."

Written in the bottom margin of the address page: "Tell Miss C. that I send you the reply to her letter out of charity to her. I did'nt [sic] like to bore her with it but for you I have no compassion. Oh! Mercy me! Do let me crawl into bed, for *such* a walk as I have taken!"

Source: Hanna family files.

---

[373] Sarah Catharine ("Kate," "Kit," or "Kitty") Chubbuck, Emily's older sister, born October 25, 1816.

[374] Eugenia Damaux, part of Emily's intimate circle of friends at the Utica Female Academy, was living in New York City.

[375] Nathaniel Parker (N. P.) Willis was the editor of *New Mirror*, the magazine that catapulted Emily into literary fame. He became a friend, mentor, and eventually a suitor.

[376] The *Baptist Register* was a local Baptist paper in central New York that grew into a paper of regional prominence. Published by Alexander Beebee, it had significant influence in Baptist circles. As a budding writer, the *Baptist Register* would have been a natural outlet for some of Emily's work. Later, in 1846 and the immediate time after her engagement and marriage to Adoniram Judson, there would be a conflict between Emily Judson and Beebee, as he was less than enthusiastic about Emily's suitability for missionary service, reflecting the attitude of many in the wider church. Emily was, after all, a popular, secular writer, and Adoniram Judson was the venerable missionary held in awesome respect. Emily and Beebee were to be eventually reconciled, and Beebee was often mentioned in letters from Cynthia Sheldon as Emily's strongest supporter.

[377] The report was an evaluation of the Utica Female Academy published by the *Baptist Register*. It provided coverage for the academy and could entice students to the school. A good report was a matter of great hope, and consequently, considerable anxiety.

[378] "Petty" is another one of the names that Emily used with her intimate circle of friends. Sometimes it was "Nemmy Petty."

[379] A Philadelphia minister, Rev. A. D. Gillette was a stalwart friend and supporter of the Judson, Sheldon, and Anable families. Emily met Adoniram Judson in the parlor of the Gillette home in Philadelphia. Emily was staying with the Gillettes while in Philadelphia.

[380] On August 4, 1845, Anna Maria Anable had said in her letter to Emily: "Augusta Crafts was here last evening—more agreeable than some—though she despises Willis—she told us all about that Blidgims affair and promised to send the story down for us to read." See the Blidgims article and timeline in volume one.

Anna Maria Anable to Emily C. Chubbuck, April 15, 1845[381]

Dear Nemmy[382]

I began a letter to you last Friday while our minds were so agitated about the fate of our Mrs. Parker[383] and was going to wait till we heard from you before finishing it. As your letter was so long coming I have laid it by for waste paper. You cannot think what a shock the death of Mrs. P., has been to us all. The circumstances are all so aggravating I cannot describe them to you, but everything we hear about it is heart-rending. It is hard for the friends to become reconciled to such a mysterious providence. If every death on that disastrous night has occasioned so much misery—it seems as if something should be done to the pilot. The people here are exasperated against him—the immediate family try to see in it the hand of God, but it is one of those providences that are inscrutable. It may be the means of doing us good here—certainly no one could have been taken whose life would have been more widely felt. I wish you and Hat[384] were safely home. I have written for Hat to come on with M. Adams[385] but shall almost dread to have her undertake the voyage. Aunt Martha,[386] Mary Barber[387] and a good many of the eastern girls left this morning. The school is to close this afternoon and it begins already to seem like vacation.[388] There, the stage has come for Miss Gilman.[389] I have written a note to Kate[390] by her. Tomorrow I am going to tear my room to pieces and fix it up beautifully for the Summer. I always go to work when I feel desperately forlorn. You don't know that school closes this afternoon, do you? Well, it does. If it was not for the girls playing this evening I should feel horribly forlorn.

---

[381] This letter has an addendum dated April 16, 1845.

[382] "Nem" or "Nemmy" was a name of endearment given to Emily by a small group of her intimate friends at the Utica Female Academy. Anna Maria Anable was "Ninny."

[383] Mrs. Parker was one of the victims of the *Swallow* passenger accident.

[384] Harriet ("Hatty," "Hattie," or "Hat") Anable, one of the five Anable sisters. She had been teaching in a private residence in the New Orleans area.

[385] Mary Adams, a friend of Emily's while at the Utica Female Academy. She lived in New Orleans.

[386] Martha Sheldon, the wife of Fred Sheldon, a sister-in-law to Cynthia Sheldon.

[387] Mary Barber, mentioned frequently in the Emily Chubbuck Judson letters, was a student and then the art teacher at the Utica Female Academy.

[388] Letters beginning April 28 indicate that the new term was just beginning.

[389] On August 26, 1844, Cynthia Sheldon wrote Emily asking if she knew of someone who come to Utica and work with a young student who needed a care-giver. The young student was seven years old, the daughter of Cephas and Stella Bennett, missionaries to Burmah. Emily wrote back on August 28 to speak of Gilman, a teacher she had known, as a candidate. On August 29, Emily wrote that for family reasons Gilman felt that she could not take the position; at the end of the letter Emily added a postscript saying that Gilman had changed her mind, and would in fact accept the position if it were offered to her. Emily wrote more on September 2, 1845, and on September 3, 1845 Sheldon wrote to Emily to say that she had decided in favor of Gilman. Emily wrote a note to Gilman on the letter she had received from Sheldon, and passed it on. In a letter written April 15, 1845, Anna Maria is talking of the girls dispersing as the term ended, and she noted that "the stage has come for Gilman" and Gilman was delivering a note to Emily's sister Catharine Chubbuck.

[390] Sarah Catharine ("Kate," "Kit," or "Kitty") Chubbuck, Emily's older sister, born October 25, 1816.

Evening—11 o'clock. There. The girls have got thro' playing and we have talked over every thing [sic] in Aunt C's[391] room, ate apples, and drank ginger pop till—well I guess I'll send this letter off to go down to you to morrow [sic] morning—It is all selfishness that makes me sit up till 12 to night [sic]. I shall want your answer Saturday—I intend to have the "blues" all vacation. Do you ever read the wrappers of any papers? Did'nt [sic] I tell you I had a joke to tell you? Well I have had a letter from [ ]. The old fellow tells me explicitly what his *intentions* are, and assures me they were of the most *honorable (!) kind*!! He "is persuaded that the interruption in our intercourse is occasioned *solely* by my belief that his attentions are insincere etc" etc. Did'nt [sic] I give him a few precious sentences in my answer tho'? What *do* you suppose started the old fellow up? Has he been reading "Nickie Ben"[392] and got to thinking more highly of himself? Or as I suspect is the case—has somebody put him up to it? The old fool! It provokes even now to think of it tho' he wrote me more than a week ago. I see your head is getting completely turned with the widowers.[393] I am all curiosity to know how you and [ ] come on. I yield (as I foresee I shall have to) all claim to him, and advise you to make the most of him. It is'nt [sic] every body [sic] that can have a chance of going to Europe just when they want to.[394] As to your plan of making me jump in to the fire with you (tho' you may thank Mr. Gillette[395] for the kindly interest he manifests in making such a "pick" for me)—I believe I shall decline the offer. Don't think my passion for lads could induce me to commit such an indiscretion. By no means Miss I guess *I'll go to Europe too*. So they have been at you about the Sunday School books.[396] Mr. Williams says you ought to have a book written to hand over to him every time they call—you only changing the title each different time. A good idea is'nt it? He says you must insist on having an erratum inserted every time they misprint a word.

---

[391] Miss Cynthia Sheldon was the administrative and finance manager of the Utica Female Academy. She was a mentor, advisor, and friend to Emily.

[392] "Nickie Ben" was a story that Emily (Fanny Forester) wrote for publication. We note that there are two letters received after this which make it obvious that "Nickie Ben" was a portrayal of someone real—Mrs. Urania Nott was to say (April 25, 1845) that she would have been too embarrassed to have written it, it was so close to the person and she felt so recognizable.

[393] "Widower" refers to widowed older men and usually suggested availability and interest in marriage. The academy girls and their teachers were always referring to "the widower" or to "widowers" in their conversations and correspondence.

[394] N. P. Willis would leave for Europe on June 1, 1845. Following the unexpected death of his wife in late March, he wanted to return his daughter Imogen to England to spend some time with her mother's family there. Emily began to think of going to Europe as well, and of bringing Anna Maria Anable with her. Emily would go so far as to get a promise from George Graham that he would make her a roving correspondent and pay her for whatever she would write and dispatch back to *Graham's Magazine*.

[395] A Philadelphia minister, Rev. A. D. Gillette was a stalwart friend and supporter of the Judson, Sheldon, and Anable families. Emily met Adoniram Judson in the parlor of the Gillette home in Philadelphia. Emily was staying with the Gillettes at this time.

[396] In January 1843, Emily had published a small Sabbath school book of about sixty pages. There was some conversation with American Baptist Publication Society about more of them, though the society was constantly strapped for funds, and had difficulty compensating Emily even for the work she had done. Apparently, however, there was still interest, though Emily had found that books were not as profitable to her as magazine stories.

Do! I am so provoked about that I could beat the printers and old Graham[397] too. The Godeys! [sic] What have you been writing? You had better write that letter to me and cut them up. I wish you would and then insist on G's publishing it.

That report![398] did you hear it? Here it goes to you. Nem you must not lay all those stories to A. Crafts,[399] tho' she has told us all sorts of shocking stories about his neglect of his wife this Winter and during her last illness. I put but little faith in the knowledge of the persons who brought the stories from N. Y. Is it not strange he should be so talked about tho'? There is one story which E. Hickley told us. Laura Savoys who knows the Inmans[400] well says there is no doubt of it. She says he tried to seduce the Inmans' daughter—was writing to her and contriving to see her continually and she got so bewitched, her father was obliged to take her to Europe. That accounts for Inman's dislike does it not? Well now. I deduct the 75 per cent and the folks here some of them think I am as much infatuated as you are for doing it. I strongly suspect he is an arrant *flirt* but I *don't believe* he would wrong an innocent girl. I should not tell you these things, but I wanted you to make allowances for Inman. It seems too bad to make up these things against him now. *I think he has reformed.* Under your influence? May be so. We'll see. I shall judge of him entirely by what he does to you.

Source: American Baptist Historical Society, AJ 23, no. 1170.

Emily E. Chubbuck to Catharine Chubbuck, April 15, 1845

Miss Cat-erpillar [sic],

I've just pulled off my pretty frock—maybe you did'nt [sic] know I'd got a spandy new purple silk frock. Well I have—one that cost sights of money; for did you suppose Fanny Forester[401] was to show her ugly phiz[402] down this way without something for an offset? I have got a new barege [sic] too—a rare pretty one, and a little shirred shawl that cost sixteen dollars. Then I have new shoes, new gloves, and some of the nicest little under sleeves and week rigs that you ever saw. Don't you think I am fitted out nicely? Well, I was saying I have just pulled off that famous

---

[397] George Graham, editor of *Graham's Magazine*, took an interest in Emily Chubbuck as Fanny Forester and paid her the unheard of sum of five dollars a page. He and his wife were very hospitable to Emily while she was in Philadelphia.

[398] The report was an evaluation of the Utica Female Academy published by the *Baptist Register*.

[399] Augusta Crafts and her strong opinions are mentioned frequently in the letters written from the Utica Female Academy. Many of her expressions were negative toward N. P. Willis.

[400] John Inman was the editor of the *Commercial Advertiser* and the *Columbian Magazine*.

[401] Fanny Forester, Emily Chubbuck's *nom de plume*.

[402] In the vernacular this meant "face" to Emily and Anna Maria.

purple silk, 'cause why, I got disa*pp*ointed. Mr. G. (Gillette,[403] not Griswold,[404] nor Graham[405]) was to take me to the Hutchinson's concert tonight; but he had to sit in council today; and, though it is half past eight he has'nt [sic] got home yet. So I guo't [sic] up peaceably. Yesterday morning Mr. and Mrs. Gillette and myself went over to the scene of last spring's riots and to see Penn's monument; and in the afternoon Mrs. Graham and her sister[406] called and took me over to Laurel Hill. So you see I am getting pretty strong.[407] However, I can't walk yet; though Mrs. Gillette and I did go over on Chesnut [sic] St. today to make a call. Tell father[408] I can't gratify him about the newspaper; as I have not seen it; but both Mr. Gillette and Graham told me about it.[409] Yesterday when we were riding Mr. Gillette had occasion to call at Graham's office while Mrs. G. and I sat in the carriage. I drew my thick green veil (for the fun of it, you know) and it plagued the clerks terribly. One of them told Mr. G he hoped Fanny Forester had'nt [sic] *taken the veil*. There are but very few here that have seen my face yet. I like to bother and the Grahams and Gillettes enter into the spirit of it and help me on.—Graham and I did come within an ace of quarreling. I wrote him a saucy letter about the money's not coming, and he answered, after I got here dignified enough I can tell you. He had sent on a draft which reached Utica the very day I came away.[410] Did I tell you that John Wilmarth[411] teazed [sic] the money due me out of Post[412] while I was in N. Y. Graham says that Post has'nt [sic] got any capital and the *Columbian* can't last a great while. Post used to be a sort of carrier for him and Godey.[413] Did I tell you? Graham is only thirty-two and very handsome? His wife is a charming little woman—I love her very much indeed. They are in mourning for her mother and sister's husband.—I had a letter

---

[403] A Philadelphia minister, Rev. A. D. Gillette was a stalwart friend and supporter of the Judson, Sheldon, and Anable families. Emily met Adoniram Judson in the parlor of the Gillette home in Philadelphia. Emily was staying with the Gillettes at this time.

[404] Reverend Rufus W. Griswold, an ordained clergyman and distinguished literary figure, had been one of Emily's suitors. Emily referred to him in a letter to Anna Maria Anable as a "widower," who was very anxious to be married.

[405] George Graham, editor of *Graham's Magazine*, took an interest in Emily Chubbuck as Fanny Forester and paid her with the unheard of sum of five dollars a page.

[406] Mrs. George Graham, and her sister, Mrs. Rockafelmar. Of the sister, Emily said in a letter dated April 14: "Her sister is older and has a low mournful voice and an expression of subdued melancholy—too real to be called even by Lane Weller a widder's art. She looks consumptive and has a short dry cough that I sh'd think would frighten them."

[407] Emily Chubbuck's letter of April 14, 1845 to Anna Maria Anable, and her letter of April 15, 1845 to her sister Catharine Chubbuck, have many similar details in them. She arrived in Philadelphia at the end of March, hoping to improve her health.

[408] Charles Chubbuck, Emily's father. Though he held varying positions over the years, he failed at most of them. Emily was soon to become the sole support of the family. Withe the purchase of the house for them, Emily was to continue as a significant financial contributor to the support of the family.

[409] On April 9, 1845, Catharine Chubbuck had written to Emily: "Father says you must send a paper home with the announcement of Fanny forester's arrival."

[410] See the letter of George Graham to Emily Chubbuck dated March 22, 1845.

[411] There are frequent mentions of the Wilmarths' home and hospitality.

[412] J. Post worked for the *Columbian Magazine*; at the end 1844 he picked up some of the responsibilities that John Inman had relinquished because of failing health and other commitments. There are two letters in the correspondence from Post.

[413] *Godey's Ladies Book* was a magazine that combined poetry, prose, and beautiful engravings, many of them about fashion.

from poor Willis[414] yesterday. He feels dreadfully. He says in it, "the wife I have lost was my one window of life, looking into Heaven and it is dark with the closing of it." In another place he says "she married a worldling; and, though married persons assimilate, the side turned towards her changed to *her* quality. Never, it seems to me, breathed so pure and faultless a human being. I loved her, and revered her, and cherished her, and she seemed absolutely happy in me and in my love till she died."[415] I never pitied anybody in my life more than I do him. He wants to see me when I go back, and I suppose I shall see him.—Did I tell you about Mr. Gillette's sick child?[416] Well, he is better, and they hope he will get well. Mr. G. has lost a brother since I came here. I suppose you know that Daniel Gillett [sic] died some weeks ago at Mobile. He had a consumption, and had gone south for his health. He left a wife and one child.—Of course you have heard all about the accident on board the *Swallow*.[417] We came down in it and only three nights before Miss Cynthia went up in it. Mr. Buckingham, Fan Sheldon's[418] husband was second captain. You may have heard me speak of Mrs. Parker, sister to the Tracys of Utica. She was to have been married to a Dr. Whiting of New York on the eighth of May; and was on her way to N. Y. to make preparatory purchases. It was several days before her body was found and then they offered a reward of $100.

Tell the Mrs. Professors to go to grass if they don't want to call,[419] but cut round like Sancho yourself. I take it when Fanny Forester appears on the scene they won't mind the little house and old fence. Maybe your new beau is'nt [sic] so *big* close to, as he appeared in the distance. Is he another Roney?[420] I have got a funny story to tell you about [Note: The next two words are blacked out.] when I come home. Mr. G and I go it strong on the Hamilton folks, I tell you.—There is a terrible outcry of fire—bells ringing, engines flying, and people racing and yelling after. The sky is almost crimson, but there is a block of five-story houses in the way. It seems that Pittsburg is nearly ruined by fire; and every day we are hearing reports of the terrible fire in the woods of New Jersey.—Mrs. Gillette has been up and we have been watching the fire till it has subsided.—Was Griggs vexed any about the

---

[414] Nathaniel Parker (N. P.) Willis was the editor of *New Mirror*, the magazine that catapulted Emily into literary fame. He became a friend, mentor, and eventually a suitor.

[415] See the letter from N. P. Willis to Emily E. Chubbuck dated April 7, 1845.

[416] When Miss Sheldon accompanied Emily to Philadelphia, arriving on March 29, she had lingered several extra days because of the precarious health of James "Jemmy" Gillette. She finally left on April 3.

[417] See the letters from Cynthia Sheldon (April 11) and Anna Maria Anable (April 15) on the boating accident and the losses which affected them and the surrounding community.

[418] Fanny Buckingham was the daughter of Fred and Martha Sheldon, niece of Cynthia Sheldon, and cousin to Anna Maria Anable.

[419] On April 9, Catharine had written: "None of the Mrs. Professors have called since you left. I hope they won't till summer comes."

[420] On April 9, Catharine had written: "I met Roney at Society meeting last night, he inquired about you but not quite so eagerly as he did a year ago—was surprised to learn that you were in Philadelphia. Wonder if he thinks you have sufficient 'decision of character'"?

draft. [sic] I suspect the mistake all rose from having *two names*.[421] G. W. G. gave the order for Fanny Forester I suppose. The weather here has been pretty cold, but nothing like what you have had. Today it is as hot as summer. The peach crop they think was destroyed by the frost. The green leaves and early flowers look as though they had been singed in a blaze. I got Wallace's[422] paper tonight. The poetry is pretty good—*very* good but there are some faults in the metre and some *commonplaces*. He must try it again—and again—and again. I wish he would write *prose*. You did'nt [sic] tell me how he is getting along in his studies. He must make a little the grandest garden you have ever had yet.—I suspect you see by the note that I have got newly into debt with Miss C.[423] I was'nt [sic] in school but half of last term (*this* term I ought to say, as it is not out yet) and, when I was in, did'nt [sic] do much, so, of course, my salary suffers. By giving the note, however, I have been able to raise money enough to pay for the entire new thing I have got and clear all my expenses. It will be rather a dear trip, but I needed it and do not grudge the money at all. I must work and make it up when I get well—that's all. But lately it hurts my head dreadfully to write. I hope I shall get over that when I get strong.

Everybody is very kind to me; and I find that even those who don't know I am F. F. are disposed to be very polite. Emily Chubbuck is of some consequence in these diggins. I had a call from Eld. J. M. Peck[424] the other day. Oh! I can't write on the fourth side! Don't think of it.

Nem

Written along the left margin of page 3: "Tell Mother[425] I saw the prettiest thing that ever was for her a frock today; but the bother is, I hav'nt [sic] got only money enough to take me home."   Source: Hanna family files.

Anna Maria Anable to Emily E. Chubbuck, April 16, 1845[426]

Wed. evening. They are tearing up the carpet in my bedroom, and I am only waiting to finish this to go to work. Do write me for Sally and I are the only ones going to be here. It's a forlorn windy morning. Jane Kelly[427] and S. Hinckley are

---

[421] Fanny Forester and Emily E. Chubbuck.

[422] Wallace Chubbuck, Emily's younger brother.

[423] Cynthia Sheldon. Sheldon was the business administrator of the Utica Female Academy and a friend and mentor to Emily.

[424] John Mason Peck was a noted Baptist leader, related to American Baptist Board of Publication.

[425] Lavinia Richards Chubbuck, Emily's mother, was born June 1, 1875, in Goffstown NH, the eldest of thirteen children. She married Charles Chubbuck on November 17. 1805. They were the parents of seven children.

[426] This letter is an addendum to a letter dated April 15, 1845.

[427] Jane Kelly was Emily Chubbuck's friend at the Utica Female Academy. Jane was the literary principal at the Utica Female Academy. In fall 1848, she followed Miss Cynthia Sheldon as headmistress.

going off this morning. They send a great deal of love—S. H. in particular. Give my love to Mr. and Mrs. G.[428] and thank them for their kind invitation. While little Jemmy[429] is so ill I should not think of visiting them—and I do not much think I can afford to come after you Miss this summer. You seem [Note: The rest of this line is lost in a tear in the letter fold.] very well. I should like amazingly to come down in May. Don't you be after getting up cachehinations [sic] or I shall have to. Do you want me to send you the *Weekly Mirror*? If I see any thing [sic] of Willis[430] in the daily's [sic] I'll send it. He doesn't write much now poor fellow. Tell me all about him when you hear. Nobody else will see your letters to me. Good bye Nemmy[431] dear. If Betsy wasn't asking me questions about this and that continually I should write better—as it is I must go to work.

Ninny[432]

Source: American Baptist Historical Society, AJ 23, no. 1170.

Jane Kelly to Emily E. Chubbuck, April 18, 1845[433]

When the old men, as well as the young are getting their heads turned by Fanny,[434] it is high time for me to put in one word of caution. This was my impression when Judge B.[435] sent me the poetry, but M. A's[436] letter on Sat. presented the thing in the light of a positive duty.

So there is *more* than *one* reason for your deserting us? The first in considered good and sufficient, [sic] but the last is perfectly overwhelming.

You have had a letter, and are to have a visit! Walk softly, and act deliberately about these day, [sic] even if by so doing we should lose you entirely. My partiality for a certain friend of yours is so strong, that it may lead me to volunteer a piece of advice rather at variance with the interests of our school. Wonderful benevolence for which you must give me credit. We were all very much disappointed that you could not return to us this winter. But as your health seems to enjoy a different

---

[428] Rev. A. D. Gillette was a stalwart friend and supporter of the Judson, Sheldon, and Anable families. Emily met Adoniram Judson in the parlor of the Gillette home in Philadelphia. Emily was staying with the Gillettes while in Philadelphia.

[429] James "Jemmy" Gillette, son of Hannah and A. D. Gillette.

[430] Nathaniel Parker (N. P.) Willis was the editor of *New Mirror*, the magazine that catapulted Emily into literary fame. He became a friend, mentor, and eventually a suitor.

[431] "Nem" or "Nemmy" was a name of endearment given to Emily by a small group of her intimate friends at the Utica Female Academy. Anna Maria Anable was "Ninny."

[432] "Ninny" was a name of endearment given to Anna Maria Anable by her most intimate friends at the Utica Female Academy. Emily was "Nemmy."

[433] This letter is undated, and though its content fits this time period, placing it here is entirely an arbitrary decision.

[434] Fanny Forester, Emily Chubbuck's *nom de plume*.

[435] Judge Bacon was active in the Baptist circles of Utica. On March 17, 1846, he sent Emily a poem he had written about her new relationship with Adoniram Judson.

[436] Mary Adams, a friend of Emily's while at the Utica Female Academy. She came from New Orleans.

climate—I will not utter a word of complaint. All the young ladies regret it, and *many* seem to thing [sic] that to miss composition while you are absent is something terrible.[437] Come back to us as soon as you can and believe that you will most cordially welcomed by

Yours sincerely

Jane

Source: American Baptist Historical Society, AJ 25, no. 1254.

Anna Maria Anable to Emily E. Chubbuck, April 19, 1845[438]

I cannot go to bed dear Nemmy[439] without talking to you a little. My room is all settled nicely with a new cover for my settee, clean walls, and a warm fire in the dear stove. It looks so comfortable and nice I wish you were here, and we would have a nice chat wouldn't we! In the first place I would tell you that I *am* sorry for the suspicion I have allowed to enter my head about W.[440] I have been reading today one of his Slingsly [sic] stories, and you know I always think well of him when I have read anything of his—and what he says to you seems so truthful that I don't believe a word of any thing [sic] I have heard against him—I believe I hate to hear any one slander him *almost* as much as you do, but I get laughed-at or censured for my incredulity; so I shall keep my own counsels hereafter.

Poor fellow! from my soul I pity him. You must write to him and comfort him,[441] and do him good—for he needs just such a friend as you are now. It seems to me Graham[442] was right when he said he could be improved upon by artful men, and that this influence of most of his associates just now would be any thing but beneficial. Look after him Nemmy.

Source: American Baptist Historical Society, AJ 23, no. 1168.

---

[437] Several of the teachers at the Utica Female Academy were covering Emily's composition class in her absence.

[438] This letter has an addendum dated Monday, April 21, and a second addendum dated Wednesday, April 23.

[439] "Nem" or "Nemmy" was a name of endearment given to Emily by a small group of her intimate friends at the Utica Female Academy. Anna Maria Anable was "Ninny."

[440] Nathaniel Parker (N. P.) Willis was the editor of *New Mirror*, the magazine that catapulted Emily into literary fame. He became a friend, mentor, and eventually a suitor.

[441] Mary Willis, the wife of N. P. Willis, had died unexpectedly; Emily had learned about it when she reached New York City on March 27, 1845.

[442] George Graham, editor of *Graham's Magazine*, took an interest in Emily Chubbuck as Fanny Forester and paid her with the unheard of sum of five dollars a page. He and his wife were very hospitable to Emily while she was in Philadelphia.

Nathaniel Parker Willis to Emily E. Chubbuck,[443] April 20, 1845[444]

My Dear Friend,

I have once or twice tried to loosen the lockjaw of my bosom, and write to you as I could talk to you—but I must abandon the idea. I am compelled to wall in my heart, so as to go on amusing the world without braiding in threads that belong only to myself, and it requires a *habit of reserve* to do this. When you come to New York we shall meet, and my tongue is not used in my trade as my pen is.

I am made happy by hearing of your brightening under the brighter weather. Continue to *idle*, and do not write one line for the *Mirror*; I *positively forbid it*.

Yours always most affectionately,

N. P. W.

Source: Hanna Family files; A. C. Kendrick, *The Life and Letters of Mrs. Emily C. Judson*, 126–27.

Anna Maria Anable to Emily E. Chubbuck, April 21, 1845[445]

Well Nemmy,[446] what do you suppose I have been about to get on so slowly with your letter? Why, house cleaning to be sure. Yesterday I thought *my* hand was needed—so I marched down into the parlor—mounted a ladder—and with soap and water—brush and cloth belabored those Griffin and half horse half alligator things about our mirrors till their faces shone as they haven't shone for five years at least, not having been washed in that time. I tell you it was a pretty hard day's work for Ninny,[447] and she felt like going straight to bed when Jimmy[448] and Mr. G. Spencer went away in the evening—the latter gentleman was in Schenectady last Friday—dined with Mr. Nott[449] in company with Miss Barber[450] and spent the evening with Miss Kelly[451]—the folks were all well according to his tell. (Ain't my poetical genius delopeing [sic]? [ ]ide last sentence).

---

[443] Written on the address page in the handwriting of Emily E. Chubbuck: "N. P. Willis. April 20, 1845. No. 23."

[444] This letter is undated. It is postmarked April 20, 1845.

[445] This letter is an addendum to a letter dated April 19, 1845. There is a second addendum dated April 23, 1845.

[446] "Nem" or "Nemmy" was a name of endearment given to Emily by a small group of her intimate friends at the Utica Female Academy. Anna Maria Anable was "Ninny."

[447] "Ninny" was a name of endearment given to Anna Maria Anable by her most intimate friends at the Utica Female Academy. Emily was "Nemmy."

[448] Jimmy Williams, often mentioned in Anna Maria Anable's letters, usually just as "Jimmy."

[449] Eliphalet Nott, president of Union College, married to Urania Sheldon Nott.

[450] Mary Barber, mentioned frequently in the Emily Chubbuck Judson letters, was a student and then a teacher at the Utica Female Academy.

[451] Jane Kelly was Emily Chubbuck's friend at the Utica Female Academy. Following the departure of Mr. and Mrs. Nichols, Jane became the literary principal in early 1844. Then with the departure of Cynthia Sheldon to Philadelphia in the fall of 1848, she became "headmistress."

After giving us the benefit of his interesting and pointed remarks for an hour or so he (G. S.) took leave in a huff—because I wouldn't play for him the music he asked me—Bon! This morning, this bright beautiful glorious morning—the only one on which the sun has shone since school closed I spent with Mrs. Wilkie. Wasn't it abominable bad policy? I made up for it this afternoon though—Have been out to see Jan Berry—Went all over Whitesboro—saw all the people—had a delightful ramble in the sunshine—and came home by the most bewitching moonlight that ever called forth a rhapsody from a poet's heart. What do you think made me come home Miss to-night all alone in the cars, instead of waiting to eat whip and jellies and come home in the morning? Why I expected a letter *from you*. "The more fool you" say you—Well I was—I begin alot [sic] to see the folly of human expectations—Do you know (now I think of it) I am almost afraid to get your next letter—It seems to me in my last[452] I said something naughty I had heard of W.[453]—I expect such a scolding for it when I get your next—as would put Mrs. Candle to the blush *all, interely* [sic]. You remember the adage about the "guilty conscience" etc.—I confess—mine *has* troubled me a little.

The Kirkland girls[454] are home. I saw them but a moment to day. Mrs. K.[455] inquired very kindly after you and your health. Good night. I shall finish in process of time but—I'm awful tired now—almost sick.

Source: American Baptist Historical Society, AJ 23, no. 1168.

Charles Fenno "Hoffy" Hoffman[456] to Emily E. Chubbuck, April 21, 1845[457]

Well Laura[458] you are just as much of a fool as your brother—you have gone past what he would do and do again however he might repent of it, but not what he would advise another to do. I may be mistaken but I regard a sober marriage as the straightjacket for people of sentiment and impulse and I wish I had been put into it long ago by someone who had influence enough over my wayward disposition to affect the whole thing. I was once engaged and very [ ] as the world would

---

[452] See the letters of Anna Maria Anable to Emily Chubbuck dated April 15 and 16, 1845.

[453] Nathaniel Parker (N. P.) Willis was the editor of *New Mirror*, the magazine that catapulted Emily into literary fame. He became a friend, mentor, and eventually a suitor.

[454] Julia and Amelia Kirkland.

[455] Mrs. Charles Kirkland, friend of Anna Maria Anable, N. P. Willis, and Emily Chubbuck.

[456] Charles Fenno Hoffman, a prominent literary figure in Philadelphia and New York, well known in literary circles as an exceptionally talented editor, poet, and writer. Emily had started a correspondence with him as Laura Linden before he discovered that she was Fanny Forester.

[457] All of the Laura Letters are undated.

[458] Emily E. Chubbuck had written to Charles Fenno Hoffman as Laura Linden.

say, but when I woke up in the morning I wisked out of the house into the woods half distracted. Crossing a gorge I met an old friend, my senior by some years—told him very straight. He was delighted. "Tis an excellent thing. Have long hoped it would come about between you—so eligible." Told him how I felt. "Well I felt just the same way," quoth he, "To a person of any religious feeling—marriage must necessarily be an awful ceremony and to a man of honor the betrothal is as solemnly appalling as the marriage itself. You'll get over the annoyance however in a day or two as fast as naturally as a newly broken pointer etc. etc. "[ ] [ ] heaven and earth" quote your friend, "I don't love the woman. That is—tis only a sort of love. I admire her pretty face and delight in her rattling vivacity—but love—love—"

"Love's a humbug" quote my elderly friend. "She's a fine dashing generous girl. Shows good appreciation of a clever fellow and [ ] and spirit by bringing you to [ ] etc. affectionly [sic] last night. You may go home and quarrel with your good fortune if you choose, but I tell you, you are better off than you deserve to be."

I have never talked with that friend about the matter in after years. I set him down then as pretty cool man of the world. I am not half-inclined to think that (as I did, in making a flourish about the "*Pron* of Ohlin"etc.) he was kindly trying to reconcile me to a state which he believed to be already finally taken. Laura I am not apt to blow hot and cold, nor is there need of it here in explaining what I meant to imply. I have suffered from two annoyances but never on [ ] from the mortification of [ ] beaus; in my own person I do not think I could be mortified on that icon, yet my heart has bled when I have had a woman that I loved, depressed by [ ] to [ ] the outward appearance of her own poverty. Her "Prior" might have been weak if not sinful. Still that prior was *part of her* and, if I had been privileged to shield it from [ ] [ ], it would have stung my own Prior to feel that it was out of my power to throw such shields around her—

Laura, I love your friend Mr. Gillette.[459] Thank God there are some such men left to "[ ] the Fight" for true sentiment in this mechanical world—Still my Laura, Laura, dear sister of my heart—still—oh in spite of what that good and true man has said, I tremble at that idea of looking for the full development of thy nature here—"*must* and *will* love sooner or later"—Laura my [ ] my [ ] friend it is from that I could have [ ] thee—to keep thee happy a [ ] life of calm affection should be thine—keeping thine ideal life for thy pen and thy prayers. The love of genius is a fearful love and most truly art thou a precious child of genius. "My nature *half* developed!" Girl there is no proposition of terms and quantity, to the development of a soul like thine, it will go on and on and on—and its perils too as it thus unfolds. As it ex[ ] beyond the sympathy of those around it, reaching even at

---

[459] A Philadelphia minister, Rev. A. D. Gillette was a stalwart friend and supporter of the Judson, Sheldon, and Anable families. Emily met Adoniram Judson in the parlor of the Gillette home in Philadelphia. Emily was staying with the Gillettes while in Philadelphia.

infinity and but too often finding the images of that infinity in change. How you had that beautiful unprincipled novel the Countess Faustina! How you thought about the recovery at the threshold of life reminded her of her [ ] the close of hers in such a refuge. How I should like to hear thee anylize [sic] that book and tell me wherein lies the subtle falsehood of its [ ] enobling sentiment. I look again to thy letter. It brings the tears to my eyes Laura, "Forgive thee"—kiss thee?—and "have no faith in thee" Sweet sweet friend never was I more proud of her—Sister [ ] my god how I would kiss thee were thy blessed lips but near. I have no doubt of it Laura—I have no doubt the angels do. I believe wings would sprout from my shoulders this moment were [ ] angel form near to follow in [ ]. Dear I should learn to take off my coat first or they would rip it in growing. Laura I will burn both those letters if you desire it dear, the first I should instantly have returned to you had it turned out an engagement. But now I should like to seal them up and I think either you or I had better keep them. They are most admirable in [ ] of striking character, jottings down of memorable points of time in the history of your heart, to which hereafter you will [ ] wish singular interest. I think [ ] myself most glorious—so really high—so utterly free from all humbug of *sentimentality* while gushing with the highest and truest sentiment—Laura there is a very ironlike vein of strong truth in thy understanding. I used to think that it was the result of different qualities combined in thee—but it is then [ ] as a quality by itself that egotistic paper as you call it dear is [ ] by it in every sentence—those [ ] a most excellent a most admirable [ ] than some sister of mine—who can wonder that all love thee. There there Laura—There is nothing now to cry about. The trial has been gone through with. It shan't be a princess of [ ] [ ] it. Shan't [ ] dear. Is not thy brothers [sic] arms around thee is nor [ ] [ ] his bosom. Kiss thee—kiss thee darling Spirit with thee—kiss.

Source: Hanna family files.

Anna Maria Anable to Emily E. Chubbuck, April 23, 1845[460]

Wed-night—Mrs. K.[461] has been over to see Dora[462] to day [sic]—she says Willis' back[463] is like him tho' flattered—He is not handsome but had when she knew him a complexion that would blush like a girls—fine teeth and figure—but

---

[460] This is an addendum to a letter dated April 19, 1845. There is a prior addendum dated April 21, 1845.

[461] Mrs. Charles Kirkland, friend of Anna Maria Anable, N. P. Willis, and Emily Chubbuck.

[462] N. P. Willis commissioned an artist named Flagg to do a portrait of "Dora'," one of Emily's fictional characters. It was hanging at the Utica Female Academy.

[463] In his December 24, 1844 letter about the painting, Willis told Emily how he had had himself painted into the picture—it was his head and back that made up the man who was asking Dora' the question.

by no means an intellectual looking man—Cornelia tells the children he was crazy to know just how you looked—every individual feature he made them describe over a dozen times. He thought you were tall and graceful—and would not believe that you were not perfectly beautiful. Julia thinks he is very silly in conversation!! Amelia[464] does not say what she thinks—but seems to like him. The girls have not altered much—Jul has improved some—they say Mrs. Claus has gone into mourning for Mrs. W. I have brought over "Forest-Life" and intend to read it and every thing [sic] else I can get hold of till you come back, and not write you any more letters (may be)—there is no letter from Hat[465]—and not even a *Mirror*[466] to night [sic]. We have been expecting Aunt U.[467] would come to morrow [sic]—but are to be disappointed—Jane[468] will come tho' and school will begin. Don't you envy us? Don't you think about coming home? When shall a body expect you? As long as you are having fine times in P. stay, and get well. I want you to enjoy yourself this Summer. Your letters are not such as I like to get. I can *see* all the folks. I like Mrs. Graham[469] very much—hope they will get their house done time enough to invite you there before you leave.[470] You don't say so much about the widower[471]—what's become of him? Pray tell Graham[472] that you have made a bet to conquer Neal.[473] Set your *will* to work and you *can*. Did you ever know what an indomitable *will* you had? I think that is the secret of your wonderful success—not intellectually—but in "coming it over folks." Have you ever failed on paper? Why not? *Have the same determination and confidence in yourself* my daughter and you will succeed as well in the drawing-room. You see I don't want your faculties to rust in

---

[464] Julia and Amelia Kirkland, daughters of the Mrs. Kirkland mentioned in the opening of the letter.

[465] Harriet ("Hatty," "Hattie," or "Hat") Anable, one of the five Anable sisters. She had been teaching in a private residence in the New Orleans area.

[466] The *New Mirror*, the literary paper published by N. P. Willis and General Morris. It often contained material written by Fanny Forester.

[467] Urania Sheldon Nott—a mentor, advisor, and friend to Emily—was the literary principal when Emily first came to the Utica Female Academy.

[468] Jane Kelly was Emily Chubbuck's friend at the Utica Female Academy. Following the departure of Mr. and Mrs. Nichols, Jane became the literary principal in early 1844. Then with the departure of Cynthia Sheldon to Philadelphia in the fall of 1848, she became "headmistress."

[469] Mrs. Graham, the wife of George Graham, publisher *Graham's Magazine*. Mrs. Graham, her husband, and her sister, were exceedingly kind to Emily during her stay in Philadelphia, and often took her on carriage rides. Often Emily would ride with Mrs. Graham and her sister.

[470] A previous letter had spoken of work being done on the Graham's home.

[471] "Widower" refers to widowed older men and usually suggested availability and interest in marriage. The academy girls and their teachers were always referring to "the widower" or "widowers" in their conversations and correspondence. This was a reference to Rufus Wilmot Griswold.

[472] George Graham, editor of *Graham's Magazine*, took an interest in Emily Chubbuck as Fanny Forester and paid her with the unheard of sum of five dollars a page.

[473] Joseph Neal was part of Emily Chubbuck's circle of literary friends when she was in Philadelphia.

P. as they have in Utica—There's nothing like getting one's hand in. Jimmy[474] and I get along quite cozily—nothing to alarm Mary[475] however—

Written in the right margin of the address page: "This morning I got up a domestic scene for him—Went down to see him with my dear bonnet on and broom in my hand etc. He said he presumed I never swept but in vacations—Give my love to Mrs. Gillette and her good husband[476] and excuse this horrid writing."

Ninny Blidgims[477]

I wish I could send that story to you—it's the most perfect thing of its kind I ever read. It makes me think of *our*…

Written in the left margin of the address page: "…prospects for trading in Europe.[478] With twenty more years over our heads we would make very respectable Crinny's and Ninny's[479] to travel—Heaven send us such a kind nurse thro' the cholera as Willis made himself out to be.—Good night."

Source: American Baptist Historical Society, AJ 23, no. 1168.

Anna Maria Anable to Emily E. Chubbuck, April 24, 1845[480]

Dear Nem[481]

I did'nt [sic] send the "pixing" [sic] for your dress—for I did'nt [sic] know how much cambric to get nor anything else about a silk dress—and I thought your dress-maker would attend to it all probably—

The round cape is for you. I said when Aunt U.[482] was here I wished I had some troubadour muslin I would make you a cape, and she said she had a cape she

---

[474] Jimmy Williams, often mentioned in Anna Maria Anable's letters, usually just as "Jimmy."

[475] Mary Barber, mentioned frequently in the Emily Chubbuck Judson letters, was a student and then the art teacher at the Utica Female Academy.

[476] A Philadelphia minister, Rev. A. D. Gillette was a stalwart friend and supporter of the Judson, Sheldon, and Anable families. Emily met Adoniram Judson in the parlor of the Gillette home in Philadelphia. Emily was staying with the Gillettes while in Philadelphia.

[477] See vol. 1, "Cast of Characters," s.v. "Blidgims." Also vol. 1: Timeline—Blidgims.

[478] With N. P. Willis traveling to Europe, Emily began to think of going as well. She even would talk with the magazine publishers to see if they would finance the trip. Health considerations eventually made the trip impossible. Anna Maria was to accompany her.

[479] See vol. 1, "Cast of Characters," s.v. "Blidgims." Also vol. 1: Timeline—Blidgims. Anny Maria Anable was "Ninny Blidgims" and Emily Chubbuck was "Crinny Blidgims."

[480] This letter is undated. We have tied it to the letter from Martha Hooker, which we have dated April 24, 1845, because the package being sent is common to both of them.

[481] "Nem" or "Nemmy" was a name of endearment given to Emily by a small group of her intimate friends at the Utica Female Academy. Anna Maria Anable was "Ninny."

[482] Urania Sheldon Nott—a mentor, advisor, and friend to Emily—was the literary principal of the Utica Female Academy when Emily arrived in October 1840. In late summer of 1842 Urania married Eliphalet Nott, the president of Union College in Schenectady NY.

would send me for you—You see it is not tarletan [sic], and I could think of nothing to make out of it but a low neck cape for your white dress—If I had your [ ] to fit I would make it for you—Rec'd this pair of corsets Mrs. M. made for me but I thought they would be small enough for you and she had not time to make another pair—Tell Fan[483] not to forget to tell Mrs. Gillette[484] what I said about them to her and give a great deal of love to Mr.[485]—Now be a good girl and don't with all your new friends forget Ninny Blidgims.[486]

I can't make room for the great dictionary any way—but I'll send it with Kate's[487] package if I can.

Source: American Baptist Historical Society, AJ 23, no. 1139C.

Martha Hooker to Emily E. Chubbuck, April 24, 1845[488]

My dear "Miss Forester,"[489]

While occupying your honorable chair this morning (which by the by I fill with much dignity) I chanced to hear Miss Anable[490] speak of sending you a package. I begged her to enclose for me a huge quantity of that valuable commodity, Love. But I suppose you know, that cousin 'Bel'[491] of yours is not remarkably obliging, particularly after a recent visit to the land of dreams. Well that being the case this morning, she bid me write and send my own messages. At first you may judge I was quite frightened at the thought of so humble an individual as myself addressing a living breathing authoress. But taking up your trippings in author land,[492] I was reminded of a *remarkable* coincidence between my situation and your own as repre-

---

[483] Fanny Anable, one of five Anable sisters. She was born April 12, 1828. At this time, she was working in the home of Hannah and A. D. Gillette.

[484] Hannah Gillette was the wife of the A. D. Gillette. Hannah would play an important part in preparing Emily for life in Burmah.

[485] Rev. A. D. Gillette was a stalwart friend and supporter of the Judson, Sheldon, and Anable families. Emily met Adoniram Judson in the parlor of the Gillette home in Philadelphia. Emily was staying with the Gillettes in Philadephia.

[486] See vol. 1, "Cast of Characters," s.v. "Blidgims." Also in vol. 1 the "Timeline: Blidgims."

[487] Sarah Catharine ("Kate," "Kit," or "Kitty") Chubbuck, Emily's older sister, born October 25, 1816.

[488] This letter is undated. We have tied it to the letter from Anna Maria Anable, and so place it on the same day it was written, April 24, 1845.

[489] Emily Chubbuck wrote under the *nom de plume* of Fanny Forester. Asked about it once, she said "Would anyone buy a book written by Emily E. Chubbuck?

[490] Anna Maria Anable was the niece of the Urania and Cynthia Sheldon, the daughter of Joseph and Alma Sheldon Anable; she was Emily's closest friend at the Utica Female Academy.

[491] "Cousin 'Bel" was Anna Maria Anable—the "character" came from Emily's letter to the *New Mirror* which had been published on June 8, 1844, a letter which catapulted Emily to literary fame. The letter concerned a visit which Emily and Cousin 'Bel' had made to New York, and their lack of money to enjoy the wares of the many shops they passed by. She asked if the editor of the *New Mirror* would like to help them out.

[492] This is a play on the title of the book Emily was about to publish. She wrote the forward to *Trippings in Author-land* in June, and it was published that fall.

sented in your first letter, to the Editors of the *Mirror*.[493] I must tell you what it is. You must know by this time, that I need a new dress—not "a balzarine"[494] but a nice warm dress for winter. As that stern old fellow Jack Frost stands, just with out the door threatening to give me battle if I venture within his horizons. I was in quite a dilemma with regard to the way in which I should reach Anable and C's dry good store. Just at that moment your veritable cousin 'Bel', that ministering spirit of yours came to my relief, dispelling all anxious thoughts upon that point, by offering to make the extensive purchase for me. Now I beg you will not be particular about the points of resemblance between the cases compared. Remember I did not say that there were any little messengers coursing through my head; or even that possessed "a copy of Johnson's Dictionary."

Nothing very wonderful has taken place during your absence, except that last week the young ladies were excused from the usual task of writing compositions. They wandered about the house all day without seeming to know where they were.

Carrie Kingsbury has gone home. Miss Holmes still remains. She is waiting to make up two music lessons which she lost by staying at home, two or three days after the term commenced. I hope she will get the worth of her money? Don't you? Mollie Brayton has become an inmate of the nunnery. She occupies the same cell with one. I fear she will not make a very good recluse; as she has not become enough of a misanthrope. She goes into extacies [sic] about Miss Kelly,[495] Miss Anable and Fanny Forester.[496] She has an uncle for the two former and wishes that her uncle Isaac was not married and could have two wives, that she might hope to call you Aunt. Nora has a little girl about Mollie's size for [ ] [ ] wrote; and we talk of "putting" on our [ ] together. Abbie Strong sends her warmest love and thinks her literary instructions are as good, as usual. Aggie Calhoun wants you should send another letter. Mollie Walker says that the leaves have not yet appeared on the tree. Lizzy Hyde fears that her buds will be nipped by the frost. The little Angell sends love.

Please tell Fan[497] not to run away, with all the admiration, for I want some when I come. Remember me to Mr. and Mrs. . . .

---

[493] June 8, 1844.

[494] "Balzarine" is mentioned in the June 8, 1844 letter, printed in the *New Mirror*. "You know the shops in Broadway are very tempting this spring. Such beautiful things! Well, you know (no, you don't know that, but you can guess) what a delightful thing it would be to appear in one of those charming, head-adorning complexion-softening, hard-feature-subduing neapolitans; with a little gossamer vail [sic] dropping daintily on the shoulder of one of those exquisite *balzarines*, to be seen any day at Stewart's and elsewhere."

[495] Jane Kelly was Emily Chubbuck's friend at the Utica Female Academy. Following the departure of Mr. and Mrs. Nichols, Jane became the literary principal in early 1844. Then with the departure of Cynthia Sheldon to Philadelphia in the fall of 1848, she became "headmistress."

[496] Fanny Forester, Emily Chubbuck's *nom de plume*.

[497] Fanny Anable, one of five Anable sisters. She was born April 12, 1828. At this time, she was working in the home of Hannah and A. D. Gillette.

Written in the top margin of the address page: "…Gillette,[498] and tell Mr. G. I would thank him for *my* sermon."

Your ever [ ]

Martha Hooker

Martha Taylor sends love. Pray don't put on your critic's mantle when you read this. Miss Anable thinks it was rather wicked for me to tell you what I did of Miss Holmes. It was rather bad I acknowledge. Please forgive my being so [ ].

Source: American Baptist Historical Society, AJ 24, no. 1181.

Urania Sheldon Nott to Emily E. Chubbuck, April 25, 1845—Union College

My dear Emily,

If your head has not been entirely turned by the sightseeing, and being seen of Philadelphia, I shall not despair of being read with at least a degree of patience on your part—tho' I have nothing new, or very interesting to write to you—Indeed I scarcely know why I have set about it—but an unaccountable inclination to have a little chat with you this afternoon has come over me—Perhaps it is because I have just laid down a letter from Cynthia,[499] in which she mentions you—be that as it may however, no apology is needed between friends who have known each other as we have, and as long.

They say you are happy in Philadelphia—that you are treated very kindly by your literary friends, as well as others—you don't know how glad I am at this—for you deserve it all.—That Mr. Gillette[500] and his sweet little wife would do all to make you happy that lay in their power, I had no doubt, for I had tested their hospitality—and know that they have a delightful circle of acquaintance—Of your new friends—the Literati of Phil.[501] I do not know so much—it is sufficient that you like them—Please—Garde [sic] that heart of thine! So not be in haste!!

---

[498] Rev. A. D. Gillette was a stalwart friend and supporter of the Judson, Sheldon, and Anable families. Emily met Adoniram Judson in the parlor of the Gillette home in Philadelphia. Emily was staying with them while in Philadelphia.

[499] Miss Cynthia Sheldon was the administrative and finance manager of the Utica Female Academy. A sister of Urania Sheldon Nott, both were important mentors and friends to Emily Chubbuck.

[500] A Philadelphia minister, Rev. A. D. Gillette was a stalwart friend and supporter of the Judson, Sheldon, and Anable families. Emily met Adoniram Judson in the parlor of the Gillette home in Philadelphia. Emily was staying with the Gillettes while in Philadelphia.

[501] Between New York and Philadelphia, these included George Graham, Joseph Neal, Charles Fenno Hoffman, General Morris, N. P. Willis, Fanny Osgood, and Rufus Griswold.

The death of poor Mrs. Willis[502] was very sad—so sudden—so entirely unexpected to herself—as well as to her husband—poor thing, it was so hard to die from her home in a land of strangers,[503] and in New York too, the last place one would wish to die in when you drop like a leaf in the forest, and are missed about as much—but if the Christian hope was her's [sic]—it was well with her.[504] She will soon be forgotten upon the earth—but God will not forget her in his silent house.

Mary Barber[505] spent a few days with Mary P[ ] and enjoyed herself much—Anna Maria[506] has not condescended to notice us during her vacation—Jane Kelly[507] went up yesterday and today the new term begins—I hope they will have something beside *hopes* to like upon this term—the Report of the Examination will do good[508]—I think without doubt—I wish you could heat up some recruits in Phil! Don't you like Mr. Robarts?[509] His wife too? How dare you write the story of *Nickie Ben*?[510] I cannot see how you dare—would not Mr. [ ] recognize himself?—As a perfect likeness it cannot be exceeded—but I should fear to go as near the truth.

Doct Sprague has written me for your autograph! Don't you feel flattered? What could I do but promise him one of your letters—so I selected one, the best, I thought of my small collection—and have laid it aside for him—You will never blush to own the relationship—should you meet it anywhere—tho' I have no sympathy for the man's taste in general's [sic]—I have in particulars certainly—

When may we look for you now again! You will do right to stay in P. as long as you can—on account of your health—but do not protract your visit so much as to oblige you to put me off—with only an apology. I wish those dreadful boats were not between us and Philadelphia—what a mercy that our lives have been spared—

---

[502] Mary Willis, the wife of N. P. Willis, the editor of the *New Mirror*, whose help had been so critical to Emily in advancing her career. Mrs. Willis had died just as Emily was coming to Philadelphia; Emily learned of it on March 27.

[503] Mary Willis was from England; after her death, Willis traveled to the continent so that their daughter Imogen could be with her mother's family in their time of grief. In a letter written on March 29, 1845, from Anna Maria Anable to Emily Chubbuck, Anable had said: "and then it seems so forlorn her being away from all family friends sick and dying in a hotel." Mr. and Mrs. Willis lived at the Astor.

[504] Willis made some statements to Emily about his religious experience and beliefs in a letter written March 12, 1845. He labeled himself as a "Trinitarian Christian." He expressed some thoughts on his wife and her faith in a letter dated April 7, 1845.

[505] Mary Barber, mentioned frequently in the Emily Chubbuck Judson letters, was a student and then the art teacher at the Utica Female Academy.

[506] Anna Maria Anable was the niece of the Urania and Cynthia Sheldon, the daughter of Joseph and Alma Sheldon Anable; she was Emily's closest friend at the Utica Female Academy.

[507] Jane Kelly was Emily Chubbuck's friend at the Utica Female Academy. Following the departure of Mr. and Mrs. Nichols, Jane became the literary principal in early 1844. Then with the departure of Cynthia Sheldon to Philadelphia in the fall of 1848, she became "headmistress."

[508] The report was an evaluation of the Utica Female Academy published by the *Baptist Register*. A good report was essential to recruitment and retention of students.

[509] Mr. and Mrs. W. S. Robarts were active Baptists who lived in Philadelphia. Adoniram Judson would later stay with them whenever he was in Philadelphia.

[510] These comments are most interesting; apparently Emily's story "Nickie Ben" was based on an actual life, and Urania Sheldon Nott was saying that it was embarrassingly obvious who that individual was.

while dangers have stood so thickly around—we were waiting in New York for the *Swallow*[511]—and *expecting* to come up the night after the awful catastrophe—I could hardly raise courage enough to come up the river on Wed'y night and do not now think I shall ever take a night boat—when a day boat can be had—I hope you will endeavor to come up in a day boat to Troy and take the cars there that will bring you to Schenectady by 1/2 8 o'clock the same eve'g—if you write me before hand—I will meet you at the cars.

My good husband[512] is very well, and would desire to be kindly remembered did he know of my writing—

Our blossoms are just ready to burst—the weather is delightful—and we feel that spring has indeed come—you can do no more in Phil.—tho' your grass be of a deeper green than ours.

Remember me affectionately to Mr. and Mrs. Gillette—and believe me ever your most affectionate friend,

Urania E. Nott

Source: American Baptist Historical Society, AJ 25, no. 1235.

Anna Maria Anable to Emily E. Chubbuck, April 26, 1845[513]

Blessings on your dear good heart Nem![514] You don't know how happy your good long letter has made me.

Well, now why *cann't* [sic] you just step in here, and *cuddle* up on the settee and talk it all over. Jimmy[515]—the heathen—has gone up to see Augusta[516] to night [sic] and I am left alone alone [sic]. Isn't it funny how our letters cross each other? Now that you have added to your list of correspondents, I presume I shall get the start of you. Now you think Nem you have fooled this child nicely in that story about Hoffy![517] Do you think I can't see thro' you tho' you didn't mean to let me? How should he know where you are and how to address you Miss unless you

---

[511] The *Swallow* was a passenger steamboat lost in tragic marine accident. See the April 11 letter of Cynthia Sheldon and the April 15 letter of Anna Maria Anable.

[512] Dr. Eliphalet Nott, president of Union College, married to Urania Sheldon Nott.

[513] This letter is undated. It is postmarked April 29, 1845, which was a Tuesday. The first part of the letter then, written on Saturday, would have been April 26, 1845. It has an addendum dated April 28, 1845.

[514] "Nem" or "Nemmy" was a name of endearment given to Emily by a small group of her intimate friends at the Utica Female Academy. Anna Maria Anable was "Ninny."

[515] Jimmy Williams, often mentioned in Anna Maria Anable's letters, usually just as "Jimmy."

[516] Augusta Crafts and her strong opinions are mentioned frequently in the letters written from the Utica Female Academy.

[517] Charles Fenno Hoffman, a prominent literary figure in Philadelphia and New York, well known in literary circles as an exceptionally talented editor, poet, and writer. Emily had started a correspondence with him as Laura Linden before he discovered that she was Fanny Forester.

have written to him first? Now you see how much I know you had best make a clean breast of it and tell me all for as you say I am dying of curiosity. You may call him a jewel and a darling and as many more endearing epithets as you please. I subscribe to anything you say about him. Mind you keep a copy of your letter to show your *Marm* when you come home. That coming home Nemmy! You know how we want you to get well etc.—but we shall have as delightful weather here as in P. in a fortnight—and we do all want to see you so. Eugenia[518] is coming here to visit us next week, or rather to visit Mary Spencer.[519] Mary has a claim upon her which we cannot well interfere with, but we shall see her about as much as if she were at our house. You ought to be home, but I suppose you will be in Brooklyn[520] about the time she will be returning. We have had a nice visit from Emily B[ ]hend Schyler. She has improved in her personal appearance very much, and by the way she talks about her husband I should think made a nice loving little wife. They are going to housekeeping this summer in Buffalo—and Mathilda[521] [sic] will spend the summer with them.

Source: American Baptist Historical Society, AJ 23, no. 1140.

Anna Maria Anable to Emily E. Chubbuck, April 28. 1845[522]

A beautiful bright warm Monday morning and the top of it (which means this morning half past-five—ain't [sic] I beginning well?) to you I have just returned from a charming walk of two miles—a regular hunt for violets, and have come home with a basket full of the *neatest* little flowers you ever saw. The spring beauty is in abundance—also the liverwort and the [ ] and trillium to say nothing of violets. I have made over my right to them till Lydia[523] has *interested* her botany class

---

[518] Eugenia Damaux, part of Emily's intimate circle of friends at the Utica Female Academy. She was living in the New York City area.

[519] On February 28, 1848, Anna Maria Anable wrote to Emily saying: "Mary Spencer has just returned from Albany. It is said she is engaged to John James, a handsome young widower with three children, and two or three hundred thousand $'s."

[520] Emily planned to stay with Sophia Taylor and her family in Brooklyn on her way from Philadelphia to Utica.

[521] Matilda Berthoud was a friend of Anna Maria Anable, and probably as well of Emily, for Anna Maria's and Sheldon's letters make reference to her. In one letter Sheldon told how Anna Maria had gone to visit Matilda, and while there, Matilda's brother had taken Anna Maria for a buggy ride. Somehow the horse got frightened, and Anna Maria and her host were taken on a wild ride, which they survived by the heroic actions of the brother, the undaunted courage of Anna Maria, and the providence of God. In a letter shortly after their move to Philadelphia, Sheldon says that Matilda was everything to them—she was perfectly happy being with them, and she adds that she is a "host in French."

[522] This letter is undated. It is postmarked April 29, so we date the first section of the letter as April 26, 1845 (Saturday) and the second as April 28 (Monday). This is an addendum to the April 26, 1845 letter.

[523] Lydia Lillybridge was one of Emily's closest friends at the Utica Female Academy. When Emily made the decision to go to Burmah with Adoniram Judson as a missionary, Lydia offered to go with them, and with Emily speaking to Adoniram Judson and to Dr. Solomon Peck and the Board of American Baptist missionary Union of her extraordinary abilities, she was commissioned to go with them, in spite of the fact that she remained single. Always independent and outspoken, unafraid to cause ripples in the missionary community, Lydia was to serve on the mission field for twenty-eight years. She married missionary Thomas Simons in May 1851. See the timeline on the life and service of Lydia Lillybridge Simons in vol. 1.

in them, and then—hurra for bouquets of wild flowers! My room is now a perfect garden with flowers from Mr. Boyes—but my passion for the pretty crest[ ] this spring grows by what it feeds on, and I'm afraid I can never get enough. There, Jane Berry has just brought me another bouquet from her garden—I told her about your renewal of the Hoffman[524] correspondence, or rather *his* renewal. She says she is going to Poughkeepsie in a week or two, and when you come to Brooklyn—you must let her know and she will come down to N. Y. and bring you up to P. to make her a visit; besides introducing that famous cousin of hers. 'Twould be pleasant for you to stop in P. a day or two—but there is no depending on Jane—she may not get there till fall. Direct to the care of Charles Potter! We have such delightful weather now I feel as if it would be almost as well for you to be here and I do want to see you so bad: but—if you don't feel like coming back to school again just follow Willis'[525] advise and *idle* the whole summer. Willis is a generous fellow I declare, and I wish he was an independent prince—anything but a poor editor of a 'daily.' Why don't some of these sick folks leave him a legacy when they die. I'm sure he wants money bad enough and he is just the fellow that ought to have it. If *I* get sick *I* will. He is a deuced cunning fellow on paper. I can't read a line of his but it goes straight to my heart. What nice times you will have in New York seeing him and Hoffman, I suppose as will want to see you too [sic]. What a belle you are getting to be! I feel as if I ought to be there too—just to enact the 'Mother in law.'[526] How does your barege [sic] fit now? Poor Mrs. Wilkie was sadly mortified that it did not fit you better. She charged you only a dollar for making it. You must look your prettiest in N. Y. Are you really getting a more healthy look? Well, Mother[527] says you ought to stay just as long as you continue to improve, and so you may. Don't be worried at all about [Note: "The school" is crossed out here.] your class. We'll take care of it. We have commenced with between eighty and ninety scholars, and the old boarders here hardly began to come back. By the way Nem,[528] the Mirrors[529] have not come for a week past neither daily nor weekly. Do you get them? If you do, send them to me after you have read them will you—I want particularly the

---

[524] Charles Fenno Hoffman, a prominent literary figure in Philadelphia and New York, well known in literary circles as an exceptionally talented editor, poet, and writer. Emily had started a correspondence with him as Laura Linden before he discovered that she was Fanny Forester.

[525] Nathaniel Parker (N. P.) Willis was the editor of *New Mirror*, the magazine that catapulted Emily into literary fame. He became a friend, mentor, and eventually a suitor.

[526] Anna Maria often referred to herself as "Mother-in-law" to Emily.

[527] Alma Sheldon Anable, sister of Cynthia Sheldon and Urania Sheldon Nott and married to Joseph Hubbell Anable. They had nine children.

[528] "Nem" or "Nemmy" was a name of endearment given to Emily by a small group of her intimate friends at the Utica Female Academy. Anna Maria Anable was "Ninny."

[529] The New York *Mirror*, published by N. P. Willis and General Morris.

one that had your story in it. Mind you. I *won't* quit while Jimmy's[530] [ ]—here he has been sitting until ten o'clock and kept me all this evening from writing to you. I am provoked at him and wish Mary[531] would come back. Why needs he to stay so long and come every night too. Mary will be here to morrow—so I'll not fret anymore at the poor fellow. G. Spencer makes nightly calls on Jane[532] too—so a stranger might think we were going it strong.

That little Mrs. Graham[533] of yours I like. Give my love to her and tell her what a pleasant place Trenton Falls is. If they travel in the summer wouldn't they like to come this way. Tell her we should like to *try* and return some of her kindness to you. Mr. and Mrs. Gillette[534] Aunt C.[535] says are intending to come on.

Who have you promised to spend the winter with? Not with Gris[536] I hope. But—really tis too bad you should let such a chance as this go by—ready to take on right to Europe and all.

Have you done anything to heal it, or has Hoffman put him out of your head. *Persevere* Nem, and get some comfort out of him yet. He is a lazy old fellow or he would write something decent for his paper. As that is the only paper that comes regularly now, I see how stupid it is. The *Journal* is not as good as it was either. Every body [sic] is stupid but Willis, and he poor fellow has most reason to be. I have been for two or three days bewitched with Forest Life[537]—Mary [ ]. Isn't it odd that I never read it before? So she comes next before you in Mr. G's opinion. Ain't [sic] you glad you came out since his 'Poets and Poetry' was published? I agree with him about Mrs. Stephens and all that class of writers tho' and on the whole considering…

Written in the right margin of the address page: "…that you never wrote a *book* as F. F.[538] I think he must have some discernment to place you so high. If he

---

[530] Jimmy Williams, often mentioned in Anna Maria Anable's letters, usually just as "Jimmy." Recent letters from Anna Maria had linked Jimmy and Mary Barber. See letters dated March 26 and April 1. He would marry Helen Munson.

[531] Mary Barber, mentioned frequently in the Emily Chubbuck Judson letters, was a student and then the art teacher at the Utica Female Academy.

[532] Jane Kelly was Emily Chubbuck's friend at the Utica Female Academy. Following the departure of Mr. and Mrs. Nichols, Jane became the literary principal in early 1844. Then with the departure of Cynthia Sheldon to Philadelphia in the fall of 1848, she became "headmistress."

[533] Mrs. Graham, the wife of George Graham, who published *Graham's Magazine*. The Grahams were exceedingly kind to Emily during her stay in Philadelphia and often took her on carriage rides.

[534] Rev. A. D. Gillette was a stalwart friend and supporter of the Judson, Sheldon, and Anable families. Emily met Adoniram Judson in the parlor of the Gillette home in Philadelphia. Emily was staying with the Gillettes while in Philadelphia.

[535] Miss Cynthia Sheldon was the administrative and finance manager of the Utica Female Academy. She was a mentor, advisor, and friend to Emily. She had become "Aunt Cynthia."

[536] Reverend Rufus W. Griswold, an ordained clergyman and distinguished literary figure, had been one of Emily's suitors. Emily referred to him in a letter to Anna Maria Anable as a "widower" who was very anxious to get married.

[537] The editor thought *Forest Life* might be a volume by N. P. Willis, but a search reveals no book by this name by him. We did find a book of this title published by Caroline Kirkland in 1842. Mrs. Kirkland lived in New York and certainly would have been a contemporary of N. P. Willis.

[538] Fanny Forester, Emily Chubbuck's *nom de plume*.

wasn't a Baptist I should think sincerely of him myself. I would give a great deal to be able to run down and see all you folks and come home with you—but alas! I am tied—hands and feet to the piano stool. I have been looking over an old catalogue and have found that it is eleven years this Spring since I began to teach. Is not that a long apprenticeship? But I won't have J. and nobody better offers. Poor me!"

Written in the left margin of the address page: "Jane was intending to fill my fourth page but was obliged to go to bed with a head ache, and poor Sally has such a sore finger that she can't use it at all.

"[ ]—Mary Jerome has just come in and sends a great deal of love to you. She is as sweet as ever. We have had a letter from Hatty.[539] She had not received mine urging her to come home and was homesick enough, as she had not heard from home in five weeks. Mary Adams[540] will leave about this time and will probably be in New York at the same time with you."

Written in the bottom margin of the address page: "Do write Nem,[541] and tell me all about the W. affairs. You don't know how I *let* in your letters. Good bye I must go and walk with the girls. Ninny."[542]

Source: American Baptist Historical Society, AJ 23, no. 1140.

Emily E. Chubbuck to Anna Maria Anable, April 28, 1845[543]

Oh! I was *so* glad to get your letter Saturday night Ninny![544] Sit down the minute you get this and write, do. I wish you were here this morning—there are fifty things I want to say to you that I can't put on paper. I have just answered the letter I got from Willis[545] a week ago[546] and shall send it in the same mail with yours. I don't want to see him in New York and I have argued the case in a simple earnest way that I think will make him fall in with my notions about it. I am going to break off the correspondence too, but that I shall do by degrees. Not that I think any less of him, but it can't last always and there never will be so good a time to

---

[539] Harriet ("Hatty," "Hattie," or "Hat") Anable, one of the five Anable sisters. She had been teaching in a private residence in the New Orleans area.

[540] Mary Adams, a friend of Emily's while at the Utica Female Academy. She lived in New Orleans.

[541] These were used as names of endearment for Emily Chubbuck. Emily sometimes used it of herself. See Adoniram Judson's letter to Anna Maria Anable dated May 14, 1846, for one example of this. Nem was short for Nemmy.

[542] "Ninny" was a name of endearment given to Anna Maria Anable by her most intimate friends at the Utica Female Academy. Emily was "Nemmy."

[543] This letter has an addendum dated April 29, 1845.

[544] "Ninny" was a name of endearment given to Anna Maria Anable by her most intimate friends at the Utica Female Academy. Emily was "Nemmy."

[545] Nathaniel Parker (N. P.) Willis was the editor of *New Mirror*, the magazine that catapulted Emily into literary fame. He became a friend, mentor, and eventually a suitor.

[546] See the letter of N. P. Willis to Emily E. Chubbuck dated April 20, 1845.

stop as now. So he imagines me tall and graceful—well, other people may undeceive him—I shall not. It would be the most awkward thing in the world to meet him; and what have I done bad that I should be so punished? Catch *me*! I conclude that Julia Kirkland[547] is quite as capable of judging of Willis as some make-believe wiser ones about him—her story about his talking silly is really the freshest, most natural, and most likely of any I have yet heard. Graham[548] agrees with Mrs. K. about his looks. He says that his face is plain—he has a poetical eye, but in nowise an intellectual face—his figure he says is magnificent, a fact of which Willis is well aware. I hav'nt [sic] heard from the Grahams since the day I called. I am afraid he is very sick. Saturday as I did'nt [sic] get any papers I went over into Chesnut St. [sic] and purchased a *Broadway Journal*,[549] *Weekly Mirror*, and a copy of Cothen. They have just commenced sending me the daily. Mr. Gillette[550] left house today to attend a convention in Providence. He will be gone a week, and I hardly know how the time will go with me. Ninny I am afraid I never shall be strong enough to walk again without losing my breath and my knees knocking together. You can't think how awkward I am at it. I went to church yesterday for the second time. Did I tell you that I had a seranade [sic] last week?—Mrs. Gillette says it was mine, for they never have been here before. And who do you think Missy was one of them? Why, your little widower,[551] the law-merchant. Now don't you feel sorry that you didn't come? It was exquisite any how [sic], and I wish they would come again. I hav'nt [sic] seen Neal[552] yet, and am really afraid I shall have to *quo't up*. I won't though. Wait till I just get a little better and then see. Why I'll parade up and down Chesnut St. till—I'll dislocate my ankle, that's what I'll do, right before his door and he can't do any less than pick me up. *Did* you know that Walter Colton had been married lately—the old bach! Why he was pretty well towards sixty and married a girl of twenty. I am afraid Hoffy[553] has *did it* [sic] by this time. You would think so by the fatherly tone of his letter. He says I must confess all my evil deeds

---

[547] Mrs. William Kirkland lived in the Utica area, and she and her girls, Julia and Amelia, are mentioned in some of the letters of Anna Maria Anable to Emily E. Chubbuck. N. P. Willis had also written of her, saying on February 5, 1845 that she was "my oldest female friend Mrs. Wm. Kirkland (who has been a sister to me for 16 years)."

[548] George Graham, editor of *Graham's Magazine*, took an interest in Emily Chubbuck as Fanny Forester and paid her with the unheard of sum of five dollars a page. He and his wife were very hospitable to Emily while she was in Philadelphia.

[549] The *Broadway Journal* was being published by Edgar Allen Poe.

[550] A Philadelphia minister, Rev. A. D. Gillette was a stalwart friend and supporter of the Judson, Sheldon, and Anable families. Emily met Adoniram Judson in the parlor of the Gillette home in Philadelphia. Emily was staying with the Gillettes while in Phialdelphia.

[551] "Widower" refers to widowed older men and usually suggested availability and interest in marriage. The academy girls and their teachers were always referring to "the widower" or to "widowers" in their conversations and correspondence.

[552] Joseph Neal was part of Emily Chubbuck's circle of friends when she was in Philadelphia.

[553] Charles Fenno Hoffman, a prominent literary figure in Philadelphia and New York, well known in literary circles as an exceptionally talented editor, poet, and writer. Emily had started a correspondence with him as Laura Linden before he discovered that she was Fanny Forester.

to my "gudeman" [sic] and adds parenthetically, "love without such understanding is humbug, Laura." I thanked him for the benefit of his *experience* in the matter.

Mrs. Jenkins is here and I like her exceedingly. She says she is going to take me in hand and make me strong. Mrs. Wheldon went on to N. Y. this morning with her son. Mrs. Gillette has not come yet from Mobile, and the expected cousin is not here. Little Jemmy[554] is gaining strength almost miraculously. He is dressed every day and tries to get about the house. He walks exactly as Rosa Pitcher did— as though his ankles were tied together. I will have my letter now and take a walk and see if I can't get my own *understanding* strengthened a little.

Evening—The true reason of my stopping writing was that I expected the package from Hoffman, and was afraid you would pull my hair all the way from Utica if I did'nt [sic] tell you the particulars of the affair.[555] It didn't come, but I was consoled by the receipt of a dear good letter from Mrs. Nott.[556] Since I wrote the last paragraph (this morning) we have had quite an alarm about Jemmy. He complained last night of its hurting him to breathe and Mrs. G was a good deal alarmed. I thought though it was only the effects of fatigue and supposed this morning it had passed off. He has lain stupid however all day (partly the effects of opium) but the doctor would'nt [sic] give him so much for a trifle) and I do not know how it will end. I shall not send my letter till I know. Mr. G's cousin arrived this afternoon.—Did you see the *Knickerbocker* advertisement on the cover of the *Broadway Journal*. There seems to be a poem of Fanny Forester's[557] in the May no. but I hav'nt [sic] sent anything there these two years. I tried to get a K.[558] when I was out today but could'nt [sic]—nor a *Columbian* either. I see that Fanny leads off the C. this month—that poor forlorn "Nancy" story!—I don't believe I shall ever write any more. I can't. It is not in me.—I will save the rest of my paper for tomorrow.

Source: Hanna family files.

---

[554] James "Jemmy" Gillette, son of Hannah and A. D. Gillette.

[555] Emily had written to Charles Fenno Hoffman and asked him to return the letters which she had sent to him. Later she did the same with N. P. Willis. Hoffman finally acceded to her request; Willis did not, until she asked again a year later after her engagement to Adoniram Judson.

[556] Urania Sheldon Nott—a mentor, advisor, and friend to Emily—was literary principal of the Utica Female Academy when Emily arrived in October of 1840. In late summer of 1842 Urania married Eliphalet Nott, the president of Union College in Schenectady NY.

[557] Fanny Forester, Emily Chubbuck's *nom de plume*.

[558] *Knickerbocker Magazine*. They published some of Emily's stories.

Charles Fenno Hoffman[559] to Emily E. Chubbuck, April 28, 1845[560]

Translated from Aesop and supposed to be the original of La Fontaine's fable of "the boy who wanted to *have* his pie and eat it too"

"A hermit who occupied a small and somewhat barren spot of ground in Bretia was surprised to find upon coming out of his cell one morning a number of willow stakes driven into a mossy spot that somewhat deformed his little heritage. "Pardon me" said his rich Athenian neighbour [sic] who was taking the air in his villa grounds thus early "I had some loose cuttings from my trees which I took the liberty of telling my gardener to set out in your unoccupied field"

"Oh indeed I am much—much obliged to you sir" [Note: "Kurios" is written here in Greek letters.] replied the hermit, in perfect sincerity.

The next morning when the hermit was [ ] and [ ] his most unexpected and well appreciated gifts, there stood the Athenian again looking over his fence. "I do hope you have pardoned the liberty I have taken said he"

"I assure you again that with me it is no liberty" replied the hermit. "I already take great delight in this shrubbery and again I thank you sir."

Many weeks now elapsed the seasons were propitious the willow stakes had taken root and germinated into shrubbery as the hermit had foreseen when one morning he looked up and there again stood the Athenian resting his chin on the fence.

"I really" said he "took a great liberty with you in planting those useless foolish things in your field."

The hermit could only repeat his customary reply in still stronger terms.

"Yes, but" rejoined the Athenian "I feel so mortified at myself. It was so very unusual a thing to do that I cannot bear the idea of these evidences of my folly being in your possession."

"Friend," replied the hermit in some surprise, "it were indeed foolish to venture thus with everyone but I thought that you knew both your man and your ground when you selected me and my lot for this kindness. That you guessed rightly these plants would be welcome to me and felt secure that any property you might still wish to claim in them would be safe under my care."

"I did think I knew you, and the ground, and myself and all" replied the Athenian "But now I am so concerned both at what I have done and at these evidences of my rashness being in your possession that I must—I must really have them back."

---

[559] Charles Fenno Hoffman, a prominent literary figure in Philadelphia and New York, well known in literary circles as an exceptionally talented editor, poet, and writer. Emily had started a correspondence with him as Laura Linden before he discovered that she was Fanny Forester.

[560] All of the Laura Letters are undated.

"What now when they have roots and leaves on them" cried the hermit in deep mortification. "Oh, I understand you—these stray cuttings were only put into the soil here to germinate and transplanted; not as a permanent gift to the proprietor of the lot."

The Athenian though a little confused nodded assent over the fence, while the hermit without more ado dug up the sprouting willows and restored the property thus claimed, to its original owner; who, not perfectly easy in his own mind as to the degree of real consideration he had shown the hermit notwithstanding the fine speeches he had made him, tossed a willow branch over the garden fence ere he went into his house and shut the door upon the latter. This according to your writing is the origin of that famous ode which is often so sonorously ascribed to Anainon but which was in fact written by this Bretian hermit. [Note: There is a line here written in Greek letters.]

"Ah the days of chivalry are over if poor Laura fail."

Laura[561] you don't know what "chivalry" is. It has nothing to do with joy my friend—and I will now let you into a secret. It was your *chivalrous* trust in me—not your genius—which come upon me. Fearless trust in another, though often most unwise, is still the surest indication of through-and-through[ ]hishness of character—of Soul-reliability .

The enigma with me from the first was this—these amazingly clever letters spring from this *mental* [ ] of some clever women or is it natural *character* thus unconsciously affecting its rights and peculiarities in simple and noble confidence that it cannot be misunderstood. From the moment I believed it to be the latter I thought it wrong to go on, not wrong in itself but exposed to distortion into wrong. Had I though it the former Laura I would have written to you nine times a week for your amusement and my own. The stopping my Laura of the correspondence was the highest compliment I could have paid you. For much of a preacher and worldly wide oracle of you count me I do not "go in" for that sort of thing. No, not at all dear Laura, save when I discover in another a trait of rom*antique* [sic] ab*and*on of Soul—a quality I [ ] so much in a woman that it would always chill me into awful respect, did not the knowledge of its unsuitableness to the world call out at the same time almost a tender anxiety for the hard nobs [sic] it may expose her to. Now Laura I turn lecturer; deeming that I recognize something of my own soul in its callous state, and mindful of its own bruises I am zealous to preach up this [ ] of feathers to fledgling natures. But a truce to egotism. Then friend Laura can now

---

[561] Emily, under the name of Laura Linden, had first corresponded with Hoffman in fall 1843. In a November 30, 1843 letter, she told Catharine that they had exchanged three letters, and she had not revealed her name to him. Here Hoffman says that in the summer 1844, he did not know of her identity. Then in what he had dated as April 7, 1845, he states that Laura has revealed herself to him.

take care of herself[562] she had all her letters back down the last line she is safe and sound spick and span all busy and guarded in her correspondence.[563] By the way, I heard it mentioned in company the other day who Fanny Forester was, and I was quoted as authority. I denied it and it was proven to me, and then I remembered having alluded to a paragraph in Mr.[ ] goods True Sun last summer at a time I had no suspicion of the identity of Fanny[564] with Laura. I mention this lest it should reach your ears in some other shape. I did not address the letter to FF through the *Mirror*—and now good by, dear Laura. Take my fable good humourously [sic] as it was intended and pause in each interval of taking a piece out of your dress when retiring, to breathe a little prayer that you have got yourself completely out of the hands of such a perilous person, such a "stubborn" "naughty?" (Laura dear that a very hard word) "ungenerous" fellow citizen as C. F. H. God Bless thee Laura

Source: Hanna family files.

Emily E. Chubbuck to Anna Maria Anable, April 29, 1845[565]

Tuesday noon.—The package from Hoffman[566] has'nt [sic] come yet, and of course I am in a tease about it—who would'nt [sic] be? It takes him a wondrous while to consider. However, I'll send off my letter. The only satisfaction I can have is to put you into a stew like myself. I had a paper from Willy[567] this morning—the first that I have rec'd from his own hand since I came here. He don't [sic] seem to make use of my story—wonder if he don't [sic] like it. I don't care whether he does or not. I am going to get a pension for services down the state in the teaching line and live on that. I don't mean to write any more [sic].

James[568] is better this morning—not able to be up at all, but well enough to silence our fears of a relapse.—I read Eothen[569] yesterday and if you want anything calmly and quietly beautiful—not exactly the thing to dream over, but something to prepare you for acting in a graceful lady-like manner during a whole evening, just read Eothen. I don't suppose this book strikes anybody else, however, as it does me—you know I can't bear to read for the knowledge, it is for the *feeling*, the influ-

[562] This was quoted by Emily in a May 18, 1845 letter to her sister Catharine.

[563] Emily had been trying to retrieve her correspondence from Hoffman for some time, and we have an indication here that he did indeed return it.

[564] Fanny Forester, Emily Chubbuck's *nom de plume*.

[565] This letter is an addendum to a letter dated April 28, 1845.

[566] Charles Fenno Hoffman, a prominent literary figure in Philadelphia and New York, well known in literary circles as an exceptionally talented editor, poet, and writer. Emily had started a correspondence with him as Laura Linden before he discovered that she was Fanny Forester. The package refers to her letters to him. She had asked that they be returned.

[567] Nathaniel Parker (N. P.) Willis was the editor of *New Mirror*, the magazine that catapulted Emily into literary fame. He became a friend, mentor, and eventually a suitor.

[568] James "Jemmy" Gillette, son of Hannah and A. D. Gillette.

[569] *Eothen*—or *Traces of Travel brought home from the East*—one edition of which was published in 1844.

ence a book has over my mood of mind that I read, and I am very glad to get anything so quietly life-like. But I laughed once, aloud. It was when he felt so particularly small after having *chunked* down from the back of the dromedary in the dark—So you are mogging away in school again! Bless me! how it makes me *lithe* to think on't—I wish so much of educating their daughters as in New York.—Is'nt [sic] it provoking about that package?

Written in the right margin of the address page: "I send this letter merely for the sake of getting an answer for I am afraid you will put off writing till you get it. Don't wait a minute, but let me hear from you immediately. Give love to all, and don't get so used to having me away, that you will not care to see me back."

Yours quite *intirely* [sic].

Pithy[570]

Written in the left margin of page one: "Did I tell you Mrs. Graham[571] thinks I am—ahem! Hem!—am handsome!!!!"

Source: Hanna family files.

Anna Maria Anable to Emily E. Chubbuck, April 29, 1845

Well Nem[572] I am home from the party and as I don't feel sleepy I'll tell you something about it.

Imprimis [sic] Sarah Bell[573] and I were the only two representatives of the Gren-Lene. [sic]

Secundus [sic] she looked very sweet and pretty in a new blue tenteton [sic], and received her much of admiration.

Tutius [sic]—this child has had her spotted muslin made long waisted and cut down in the neck and done up beautifully, *and* it makes as pretty a dress as she wants. Then she has a beautiful neck wreath of flowers with silver bows which make a chaste and somewhat distingue head-drop—and she wears now long curls in front and goes without her glasses altogether—so you see she is rather a different person from what she used to was [sic] but notwithstanding this change she did not perceive any lack of attention from the beaux. Dr. Bergy [sic] was very devoted until he thought people were beginning to observe and then I told him to

---

[570] "Pithy" is one of the many "nicknames" Emily used with her intimate friends. In vol. 1, "Cast of Characters," s.v. "Chubbuck, Emily—*Nom de plumes*."

[571] Mrs. Graham, the wife of George Graham, who published *Graham's Magazine*. The Grahams were exceedingly kind to Emily during her stay in Philadelphia and often took her on carriage rides.

[572] "Nem" or "Nemmy" was a name of endearment given to Emily by a small group of her intimate friends at the Utica Female Academy. Anna Maria Anable was "Ninny."

[573] Sarah Bell Wheeler was a teacher at the Utica Female Academy, and an intimate friend of Emily Chubbuck.

go. Then Charley Kurlburt [sic] came after me, and such an old fashioned talk as Charley and I had you never had.

It seems those fellows down at Baggs set the story a-going that Johnny Edmonds[574] and I were engaged, and I thought Charley would burst a-laughing to watch Johnny. He has only bowed to me every time I have been out since my return—and he acts scared clear off. Charley says "To tell the truth Miss Anable John Edmunds has always liked you." There, I've said enough about myself now and I'll turn to Jimmy and Helen.[575] It was one of the most elegant parties that has been given in a long time. Jimmy's three sisters were there—all elegant women. Ken Lyman, Mrs. Shannard (Jimmy's old flame), Mrs. Kirkland[576]—Liccard Hunt etc.—indeed all the flowers of Utica Society—and among them—no not among *them* but in the rooms was [sic] poor dowdy looking little Helen giggling when she showed any animation with Joe. Kurlbert [sic] and girls of that class and stamp. Jimmy tried to bring her forward as much as he could—but it would not do. She will never shine in society, and what is worse Jimmy will feel her deficiency in that respect very much. He would like very much to have a wife but would entertain his guests handsomely—and yet—he loves Helen very much I have no doubt and the one hundred thousand will make up for some deficiencies or ought to. I may abuse my pity I dare say.

Sarah Farwell has just returned from New York and she says Eugenia's[577] eyes are no better and that she is a good deal discouraged about them. Now Nem write me just such another good letter and tell me all about folks (who was the bride you wrote of? one of Mrs. G's[578] friends?) and if you hear any more from Hoffman[579] or Willis[580] or anybody.

Good night

A. M.

---

[574] Johnny Edmunds was from Utica. On July 27, 1849, Anna Maria announced that Eugenia Damaux would marry Johnny Edmonds—she said it was a good match, and she described him as rich and pious, and that they would be living in Utica. Eugenia had declared that she and Edmonds would be very happy—for they had been praying for four years about this possibility of being together.

[575] Jimmy Williams, often mentioned in Anna Maria Anable's letters, usually just as "Jimmy." Recently, Jimmy was mentioned with Mary Barber. He married Helen Munson.

[576] Mrs. Charles Kirkland, friend of Anna Maria Anable, N. P. Willis, and Emily Chubbuck.

[577] Eugenia Damaux, part of Emily's intimate circle of friends at the Utica Female Academy. She had chronic eye problems. In one letter, she wrote that even tears were hurtful. Eugenia was living with a family in New York.

[578] Hannah Gillette was the wife of the A. D. Gillette. Hannah would play an important part in preparing Emily for life in Burmah.

[579] Charles Fenno Hoffman, a prominent literary figure in Philadelphia and New York, well known in literary circles as an exceptionally talented editor, poet, and writer. Emily had started a correspondence with him as Laura Linden before he discovered that she was Fanny Forester.

[580] Nathaniel Parker (N. P.) Willis was the editor of *New Mirror*, the magazine that catapulted Emily into literary fame. He became a friend, mentor, and eventually a suitor.

The white sash I send to Fan[581]—I wore it to-night but she needs it—I think it's a beautiful ribbon. I have looked all over to get some handsome flowers for you but I can't find any that are worth sending.

Source: American Baptist Historical Society, AJ 23, no. 1139.

Nathaniel Parker Willis to Emily E. Chubbuck,[582] April 30, 1845

My dear friend

I have had two new daily tasks lately, beside a sick heart and a new trial. My child, Imogen, has been ill for several days, and it has put me in torture, leaning on her as I do with the whole burthen of a love no longer returned—I feel every day more and more unreconciled to the loss of my incomparable wife—I have had my new volume of Tales to put to press, and I have been writing (for Imogen to remember by, hereafter), all that is possible to record of the appearance, manners and character of the mother she has lost. Do you see, my sweet friend, why I have not written to you? I have had pen in hand at least ten hours this day, and I get too much of it. But you are invalid and I love you too well not to give you something when I can, to draw your thoughts out of yourself.

I should like to see you here, as you pass through, notwithstanding what you say.[583] I have a note to say that I cannot write, and my heart is too heavy for misgiving. I go abroad in a few months probably,[584] and we may scarce have another chance to meet in this world. Besides, I wish to show you my Imogen. Write and tell me where you are to stay and when you are to be here. I must drop this heavy pen tonight.

Yours ever faithfully, N. P. Willis

Source: Hanna family files.

---

[581] Fanny Anable, one of five Anable sisters. She was born April 12, 1828. At this time, she was working in the home of Hannah and A. D. Gillette.

[582] Written in the address page in the handwriting of Emily Chubbuck: "N. P. Willis. April, 1845. No. 24."

[583] See The letter of Emily E. Chubbuck to Anna Maria Anable dated April 28, 1845, in which she said that she has written to Willis that she would not see him as she passes through New York on her way home to Utica.

[584] N. P. Willis, with his daughter Imogen, would leave for England on June 1, 1845.

[585] Nora Westcott was one of the girls from the Utica Female Academy. On January 17, 1847, Anna Maria Anable noted that Nora was in Mississippi, though dying of consumption. In November 1849, Sarah Hinckley spoke of her death.

[586] This letter is undated. The content mostly supports the April 30 date. The reference to meeting someone at the Springs does not fit—but the references to Fanny and Mrs. Gillette are perfect fits to the time when Emily was in Philadelphia.

Nora Westcott[585] to Emily E. Chubbuck, April 30, 1845[586]

My Dear Miss Chubbuck

Some wery [sic] queer sensations come over me at the mere thought of writing to the "Honorah chose" [sic] of the modern age (as Mr. Prentiss has without hesitation pronounced *you*. Think of it!!) but shall endeavor to forget that you are other than the bonny lass who drank milk and ate like any one [sic] else, on the breezy hills of Springfield.

I received your dear letter and could have answered it immediately, but that I expected to meet you again so soon. I was not a little disappointed when I found you were gone. What are you doing now, that you do not shew [sic] your dear little face *here*, where you would *be so gladly* welcomed?

The house don't [sic] seem like the same place, composition writing ain't [sic] the pleasure it used to be (!!!!)—the table looks deserted,—and everything shows how badly "Fanny Forester"[587] is needed!

Won't you come? And so, *that* widower[588] whispered soft nothings, and gave you a book with little tender passages marked on it (sans doubt) and made himself *particularly agreeable*. Eh! [ ] a crafty set, those widowers! You dinna ken [sic] how amazed I was when Ned came home and said you met Mr. Townsend at the Springs. Did he go on with you, or was he so *self denying* as to remain to let *you* leave him? I have a "vast many" things to tell you, dear Miss C. but you must know that it is nearly eleven P.M., I have been monetran [sic] and am very tired—my lamp burns dim, my eyes will shut, in spite of myself—and I shall have to save all my questions and communications till I see you again, from utter inability to waste them. Mother, sisters, and Father send oceans of love, to you. Sister E. presented us a fine "Baby" the Wednesday after you left.

Both are doing "as well as can be expected!" Please give my love to Fanny Anable[589] and Mrs. Gillette[590] and accept for your dear little self the

Very best love of

Nora

Do come back *soon* dear Miss Chubbuck. We *cannot* do without you.

Please pardon this ill looking note, for my pen is to blame entirely. May not we look for you next week? Do come! Nora

---

[587] Fanny Forester, Emily Chubbuck's *nom de plume*.

[588] "Widower" refers to widowed older men and usually suggested availability and interest in marriage. The academy girls and their teachers were always referring to "the widower" or to "widowers" in their conversations and correspondence.

[589] Fanny Anable, one of five Anable sisters. She was born April 12, 1828. At this time, she was working in the home of Hannah and A. D. Gillette.

[590] Hannah Gillette was the wife of the A. D. Gillette. Hannah would play an important part in preparing Emily for life in Burmah.

Miss Anable[591] is looking so sweet—as a moss rose bead now a days.

Source: American Baptist Historical Society, AJ 27, no. 1297.

Anna Maria Anable to Emily E. Chubbuck, April 30, 1845[592]

Dear Nem[593]

Lydia[594] is fretting and scolding and teazing [sic] me to come to bed because it is after ten, and I must say that if I had not your dear papa's letter[595] here or did not know how much you want it I should be strongly tempted to yield to her. But it would be too bad of me *to keep it* any longer when you are so kind as to send it to me. Not withstanding my non-appreciation of such little tendernesses, I *did* try to steal the kiss after I had read the letter[596]—it was such a sweet letter I could not help it. Do send me Hoffman's[597]—I want to compare notes. Do you know what a vivid interest in all your affairs these little attention, keep up in me? It is next to having a good long talk. You are a good child to think of them.

We had a little sociable here last evening, that Aunt C.[598] had, but I invited two or three gentlemen. I *did n't* [sic] invite Jimmy,[599] for I thought he would rather be with his fiancée. They say they are perfectly devoted to each other. Some say they will be married in two or three weeks, but I suspect they will not until Spring. Geo Spencer is very anxious to know the gentleman to whom I am engaged. He says I have the look and manner of an appropriated young lady—a sort of freedom from anxiety expression which he always observes where young ladies are in *status quo*. Thank fortune I have at last found out what he means by that bit of Latin or Bergg [sic] and I counted up no less than seventeen engagements of marriage—fifteen to be consummated between this and Spring. Won't there be thinning in the old maids ranks tho'? I should begin to calculate on having a glorious sway if this

---

[591] Anna Maria Anable was the niece of the Urania and Cynthia Sheldon, the daughter of Joseph and Alma Sheldon Anable; she was Emily's closest friend at the Utica Female Academy.

[592] This letter has an addendum dated May 1, 1845.

[593] "Nem" or "Nemmy" was a name of endearment given to Emily by a small group of her intimate friends at the Utica Female Academy. Anna Maria Anable was "Ninny."

[594] Lydia Lillybridge, who in 1846 was to go to Burmah with Emily and Adoniram. Lillybridge served on the mission field in many capacities for twenty-eight years.

[595] This is a reference to a letter sent to Emily by N. P. Willis; Anna Maria often referred to him as "papa." Emily obviously sent his letters on to Anna Maria for her to read.

[596] Willis had closed his letter of February 19, 1845, with the words: "Take a kiss from my spirit lips."

[597] Charles Fenno Hoffman, a prominent literary figure in Philadelphia and New York, well known in literary circles as an exceptionally talented editor, poet, and writer. Emily had started a correspondence with him as Laura Linden before he discovered that she was Fanny Forester.

[598] Miss Cynthia Sheldon was the administrative and finance manager of the Utica Female Academy. She was a mentor, advisor, and friend to Emily. She had become "Aunt Cynthia."

[599] Jimmy Williams, often mentioned in Anna Maria Anable's letters, usually just as "Jimmy."

were any peace to glory in. The Dr. is not engaged nor isn't going to be to Mary Spencer[600] I imagine, and tho' Mrs. Crafts[601] intimated very strongly that there was *some one* [sic] he had his eye upon, he denied it to me strongly and scolded about Mrs. Crafts gossiping tongue. I have half a mind to set my ax for two [ ] myself—I suspect there would be no chance of success tho' and he is not worth trouble.

I should like to know how all your beaux know anything about me. Are you acting the part of my trumpeter this winter? As I shall probably never see any of them, you can make as grand a story as you please. Tell Mr. Griswold[602] I have followed his advice, and abjure Schenectady, in toto, with as much heartiness as he does—and if Mr. *Neal*[603] wants to see me, why, it's very proper for him to come and see me, and I guess you will have to bring him home with you in the Spring. I am getting up quite an interest in the old bachelor and so you needn't play the fool with him Miss Nemmy Forester.[604] How old is he? Now you see the danger of talking to your beaux about me and then writing me of it. I am for having my finger in the pie too. But—"Keep a doing it" nevertheless.

Mrs. Walker invited Jane[605] and me there to tea this evening but we could not go. You didn't know how I detest going out. I am getting to be quite a recluse. But Mr. Martin by the way was Mrs. M's husband. Did you ever know of my going into extacics [sic] over a single man?

Ain't [sic] this a slim little note from Hat.[606] She deserves a whipping—and to think of her threatening not to come back in the Spring.

I suppose by this time you will have rec'd the valise from Mrs. Perdreaseville. Fanny's[607] muslin dress was left out by mistake, and we send it to New York

---

[600] On February 28, 1848, Anna Maria Anable wrote to Emily saying: "Mary Spencer has just returned from Albany. It is said she is engaged to John James, a handsome young widower with three children, and two or three hundred thousand $'s."

[601] Augusta Crafts and her strong opinions are mentioned frequently in the letters written from the Utica Female Academy.

[602] Reverend Rufus W. Griswold, an ordained clergyman and distinguished literary figure, had been one of Emily's suitors. Emily referred to him in a letter to Anna Maria Anable as a "widower," very anxious to be married.

[603] Joseph Neal was part of Emily Chubbuck's literary circle of friends when she was in Philadelphia.

[604] This is a play on "Nemmy" Emily's name to her intimate friends, and Fanny Forester, the *nom de plume* under which she wrote.

[605] Jane Kelly was Emily Chubbuck's friend at the Utica Female Academy. Following the departure of Mr. and Mrs. Nichols, Jane became the literary principal in early 1844. Then with the departure of Cynthia Sheldon to Philadelphia in the fall of 1848, she became "headmistress."

[606] Harriet ("Hatty," "Hattie," or "Hat") Anable, one of the five Anable sisters. She had been teaching in a private residence in the New Orleans area.

[607] Fanny Anable, one of five Anable sisters. She was born April 12, 1828. At this time, she was working in the home of Hannah and A. D. Gillette.

tomorrow by express, so that Mrs. Gratiot[608] will bring it on. She has your bonnet and muff and Fan's flowers too—I suppose they will be in P. by the last of next week.

Now good night for I am too sleepy to write any more. Lib Kinehery is here and we have been having a nice snug time in my room—she goes tomorrow morning.

Source: American Baptist Historical Society, AJ 23, no. 1139A

Anna Maria Anable to Emily E. Chubbuck, May 1, 1845[609]

Lydia[610] wants me to remind you to send home her shawl—by the way you don't know how Lydia is coming out this winter. She has got a beautiful green velvet bonnet with flowers and a new cashmere dress with ever so many colors in it. She is the best French scholar in the class—and is getting up quite a taste for polite literature. She cried like a great baby over "Lucy Dutton"[611] the other day. The only thing she seems to take to heart, is my sitting up till twelve o'clock o'nights, but how can I go to bed when I haven't my little peaked chin[612] here. Nem[613] if you don't come back in the Spring—if they do entice you to stay away next summer and Willis[614] will try hard I know—why I'll never forgive you. Miss Crafts[615] had a beautiful dress sent her from Philadelphia. It is a large rich plaid cashmere—of the quality we looked for so long, when you were getting your cloak.

---

[608] Ann Sheldon was a younger cousin of Cynthia Sheldon, Alma Sheldon Anable, and Urania Sheldon Nott. She married Charles Gratiot, the son of a prominent army officer and engineer who had opened up the port of St Louis. Because Charles and Ann Gratiot often lived with the Sheldon—Anable families, both at Utica and in Philadelphia after 1848, they were very often mentioned in the correspondence. We learn of the birth and growth of their six children (one born very close to the birth of Emily Frances Judson), and of Ann coping in her husband's absence as he went west during the gold rush to seek his fortune.

[609] This letter is an addendum to Anna Maria's letter of April 30, 1845.

[610] Lydia Lillybridge, who in 1846 was to go to Burmah with Emily and Adoniram. Lillybridge served on the mission field in many capacities for twenty-eight years.

[611] "Lucy Dutton" was one of the stories written by Fanny Forester. It was later published both in *Trippings in Author-land* and vol. 2 of *Alderbrook*.

[612] Emily E. Chubbuck used a number of different names over the course of her life and career. Most obviously, of course, was the fact that she wrote often under the name "Fanny Forester," her argument being "who would buy a book authored by Emily Chubbuck?" At other times she used Amy Scribbleton (July 6, 1841); Amy S. (September 28, 1841); "Nem" or "Nemmy" (Emily was always "Nem" or "Nemmy" to Anna Maria Anable who was "Ninny"); "Pithy" to Anna Maria (April 29, 1845); "Peaked chin" (See Anna Maria Anable, November 12, 1845; Sister Peakedchin (See Emily Chubbuck, February 28, 1846.); Peakedchin (Adoniram Judson, March 7—quoting that he had a letter from her); Nemmy Petty (Adoniram Judson, March 7, 1846; also "Petty," April 13, 1846—Emily uses Nemmy Petty of herself); Pithy (Emily to Anna Maria, April 28, 1845).

[613] "Nem" or "Nemmy" was a name of endearment given to Emily by a small group of her intimate friends at the Utica Female Academy. Anna Maria Anable was "Ninny."

[614] Nathaniel Parker (N. P.) Willis was the editor of *New Mirror*, the magazine that catapulted Emily into literary fame. He became a friend, mentor, and eventually a suitor.

[615] On December 5, 1845, Anna Maria Anable wrote that Miss Crafts was a delight. "What a blessing to society it is, that she was never married. What a shame it would have been for *her* to have settled down into a mere *me* and my *husband* and my *children*!" Miss Crafts is not to be confused with Mrs. Augusta Crafts, who was noted as having a sharp disposition and a gossipy tongue.

William[616] brought up some goods of the same style—and Mary[617] has a cloak of it. The next dress I get shall be of that.

Sarah Gold writes under the signature of *Emily Ames*.

Tell Fan[602] to write immediately—I suppose she is taking two lessons a week—she must try hard to make an accomplished singer before Spring—but she must not go out in bad weather. I would not have her sick there for the world.

Write me good letter right off darling.

Adieu AM

Miss Crimmy Blidgims[619]

Cynthia Sheldon to Emily E. Chubbuck, May 2, 1845

Dear Emily

We have been chatting in Jane's[620] room about you this hour or more, past bed time for the rest, but I shall in my usual way, splice on a piece to the evening—we are exceedingly anxious about your [ ], wish you were here now for your own good—what do you think about it—the weather is fine—you could see the foliage green even by rising with the sun—our school opens very encouragingly—about one hundred now—six new boarders—an increase already over the best term—we will hope on.

My mind is often with you, and the dear family. Your letter this aft'n contains many things that I wish we could chat about—do not get the feeling that providence blasts your promised joys by the dispensations which afflict your friends, for in the right view of our relation to every thing [sic] earthly we have no promise of its continuance, consequently our chief business as marked for us, is to hold every thing [sic] as belonging to another, our selves [sic] being stewards for God. I have no doubt but the sickness in the house,[621] and out of it too has done much in

---

[616] Born on November 6, 1816 in Albany NY, William Stewart Anable was the son of Joseph and Alma Sheldon Anable. In an August 31, 1844 letter, Cynthia Sheldon reported to Emily that William had returned home, having "doff'd his sailor garb for age." He married Olivia Williams on September 24, 1846, according to a letter written September 27 by Anna Maria Anable. They moved to Sheboygan, Wisconsin, where William opened a store. William died February 9, 1863, in Virginia CA.

[617] This could be Mary Anable, Anna Maria's sister, or Mary Barber.

[618] Fanny Anable, one of five Anable sisters. She was born April 12, 1828. At this time, she was working in the home of Hannah and A. D. Gillette.

[619] "Blidgims," and the variation "Blidgy," is used quite frequently, and interchangeably, as names of endearment for Anna Maria Anable. In April 1845 Anna Maria signed several of her letters "Ninny Blidgims." On May 8, 1846, Adoniram began a letter to Anna Maria "Dearest Blidgy," and on May 14 addressed " Ninny Blidgims." See vol. 1, "Cast of Characters," s.v. "Blidgims." See also in vol. 1 the Timeline: Blidgims. Emily was Crinny Blidgims and Anna Maria was Ninny Blidgims.

[620] Jane Kelly was Emily Chubbuck's friend at the Utica Female Academy. Following the departure of Mr. and Mrs. Nichols, Jane became the literary principal in early 1844. Then with the departure of Cynthia Sheldon to Philadelphia in the fall of 1848, she became "headmistress."

[621] This is a reference to the illness of James "Jemmy" Gillette.

retarding your recovery, and I beg you not to be discouraged—but cast about to find what course is best to pursue. If as I almost believe you might gain faster here, with the absence of labors which formerly rested on you—not a word more, only come as speedily as you can without fatigue. I am sorry indeed Mr. Graham[622] is sick. Mr. Gillette[623] gone too, but he will of course be at home by the time this reaches you—and could find the right company for you to New York.[624] Eugenia[625] comes on the last of next week, she would be so kind and so glad to have you come. You know why I say all this—of course you must be judge—but do think of it—one part of your letter delighted me more than I can tell—your decision about not seeing Willis[626] in N. York—I will disclaim prejudice and declare this view of it, is the only consistent one under all circumstances—It will perplex you much to effect it and make your visit in Brooklyn—Still if you really think that could be dispensed with consistent with your object, your health not suffer by a speedy return, it would give you a real slide through. That tells difficulty—W. could not draw an inference either flattering to his vanity, nor a pique—Many tongues here would be bridled by a knowledge of having nothing to talk about.—let us know my girl if we may look for you with E.—If you write to her direct to Brown Brothers and Co.[627] requesting them to forward it—as she takes Mrs. B. and children to Ri[ ]oles for the week—she intends coming up the river on Friday I believe—Urania[628] thinks she must have a visit from you this time—If you could stand it to go to S. after leaving the boat at 7 P.M. and take the Sat'y aft'n train here—she would have a short one—I shall write to E—that you will be at Mr. Wilmarths[629] if you conclude to come on with her—now my girl your own feelings are to decide this weighty matter—May kind heaven guide you—make practible [sic] every thing which will be conducive to your health and happiness—I know you will want to dodge your

---

[622] George Graham, editor of *Graham's Magazine*, took an interest in Emily Chubbuck as Fanny Forester and paid her with the unheard of sum of five dollars a page. He and his wife were very hospitable to Emily whie she was in Philadelphia.

[623] A Philadelphia minister, Rev. A. D. Gillette was a stalwart friend and supporter of the Judson, Sheldon, and Anable families. The week prior to this Gillette had left for a convention. Emily was staying with the Gillettes while in Philadelphia.

[624] In the days to come, there will be considerable discussion in the correspondence as to Emily's return to Utica. She would travel by way of New York City, and her family and friends would feel strongly that it was not safe with her illness to travel alone.

[625] Eugenia Damaux, part of Emily's intimate circle of friends at the Utica Female Academy.

[626] Nathaniel Parker (N. P.) Willis was the editor of *New Mirror*, the magazine that catapulted Emily into literary fame. He became a friend, mentor, and eventually a suitor. Here, Miss Cynthia Sheldon makes it clear that she thinks any idea of Emily meeting with Willis in New York is not appropriate.

By this time Emily had told Sheldon, or Anna Maria had shared the information from Emily's letter to her on April 28, 1845, that she had decided not to see Willis when she passed through New York City, and Sheldon allowed her true feelings about the relationship to emerge. This was a painful time for Emily as she tried to resolve the matter of her relationship with Willis.

[627] Eugenia Damaux had a position with the Brown Family.

[628] Urania Sheldon Nott—a mentor, advisor, and friend to Emily—was the literary principal at the Utica Female Academy when Emily arrived in October of 1840. In late summer of 1842 Urania married Eliphalet Nott, the president of Union College in Schenectady NY.

[629] There are frequent mentions of the Wilmarths' home and hospitality.

renewed acquaintance notwithstanding, your mysterious package—If you do not like my plan of winding up knots and all—make the yarn straight in your own way—only give the ball which will roll on any way you fix it, a smooth surface—that will do the thing well enough—for your truly attached and interested friend C—

To tell you truth, I am almost nodding, say every thing [sic] to the family that could be added by way of love to everyone—good night—[630]

Source: American Baptist Historical Society, AJ 26, no. 1266.

Anna Maria Anable to Emily E. Chubbuck, May 2, 1845

Dear Nemmy[631]

I am going to forestall Aunt C.[632] by beginning on her third page and leaving her to write at her leisure after we have gone to bed. Well Nem, what a little teaze [sic] of a body you are! I wonder if Hoffman[633] don't [sic] think so. You think I don't know anything about that package that you intended to put me in a "stew" about, but it has just popped into my head that you have been writing to him for your letters. *Of course* he don't [sic] want to give them up and don't believe he will if he can help it;[634] nevertheless, let me know when the package comes—for I am in a "stew" enough. You don't know how badly I feel because you don't get any stronger. I almost feel as if you would be better here. We are having delightful weather now—and the Dr.[635] is going to send Grand-pa[636] one of his three wheeled carriages—Couldn't we have nice times? I wish I was a man I'd marry you and take you some where [sic] to *some* fountain health. I am afraid this journey won't improve you much. They *must* all be feeling very foolish at Mr. Willis[637] and

---

[630] Anna Maria Anable added a letter to this; it appears, with the same date, as the next letter in the correspondence.

[631] "Nem" or "Nemmy" was a name of endearment given to Emily by a small group of her intimate friends at the Utica Female Academy. Anna Maria Anable was "Ninny."

[632] Miss Cynthia Sheldon was the administrative and finance manager of the Utica Female Academy. She was a mentor, advisor, and friend to Emily. She had become "Aunt Cynthia."

[633] Charles Fenno Hoffman, a prominent literary figure in Philadelphia and New York, well known in literary circles as an exceptionally talented editor, poet, and writer. Emily had started a correspondence with him as Laura Linden before he discovered that she was Fanny Forester.

[634] Emily had asked both Charles Fenno Hoffman and N. P. Willis to return her letters. We wonder what was going through her mind at this time? Hoffman did send them back. N. P. Willis refused at this time, but acquiesced the next spring after her engagement to Adoniram Judson. Some of them Willis returned lined with red pencil, and the statement that if Emily would read the underlined passages, she would see why he would have come to the conclusion that they would be married upon his return from England. No wonder Emily wanted them back!

[635] Dr. Eliphalet Nott, husband of Urania Sheldon Nott.

[636] Deacon Asa Sheldon, father of Cynthia Sheldon, Urania Sheldon Nott, and Alma Sheldon Anable.

[637] Nathaniel Parker (N. P.) Willis was the editor of *New Mirror*, the magazine that catapulted Emily into literary fame. He became a friend, mentor, and eventually a suitor.

Graham[638] is sick and don't you think you had better make Sophia Taylor[639] her visit now and then come home? Eugenia[640] will be coming the latter part of next week—we had a letter to day [sic] from her saying she would not come this week—so if you come early enough you'll see her. I really feel distressed about you being so long away and not gaining any more strength. Do you know I'm getting to be the smartest girl in the house—up at five every morning and taking a walk of two miles! I got so many [ ] from Aunt U[641] for it that I feel quite vain. She came up yesterday and went down to day [sic]—had a delightful visit from her. She wants you to stop and visit so very much and you *must*. She will expect a letter from you to let her know when to be home. I had the pleasure of having her battle a little with Augusta Crafts[642] last night for Willis. She don't [sic] think any too well of his principles, morals etc. but she thinks he is not totally *heartless* and she believes he loved his wife. She took the Blidgims[643] down with her to read, but says it won't alter her opinion much—for she said before Jimmy[644] and Augusta, that Miss Anna was an exceedingly prejudicial (?) [Note: The question mark in parentheses is original to the text.] woman—So, you are not going to see Willis?[645] Well do your own doings. I *say* nothing but *listen*. All I know is…

Written in the right margin of the address page: "…that if you don't see him now he'll be after seeing you some way or another as soon as—If it teases [sic] him any I should sort a' like to be invisible a while longer. If you do meet him I *should* like to be a mouse in the wall. What *would* you say? I suspect *you* would drop flat on the carpet at his feet—and he—oh! he'd *fascinate* you, so some of the good folks say. There is a good deal of wonderment as to whether you'll see him or no."

Written in the left margin of the address page: "Now ain't [sic] I a good girl to do just as you told me to—and write immediately—I shall be expecting an answer to my last (another cross) to morrow [sic], in which I suppose shall be somewhat enlightened on the [ ] at present pending. Wonder if you'll go to the castone [sic]

---

[638] George Graham, editor of *Graham's Magazine*, took an interest in Emily Chubbuck as Fanny Forester and paid her with the unheard of sum of five dollars a page. He and his wife were very hospitable to Emily while she was in Philadelphia.

[639] Sophia Taylor lived in New York, and she and her husband had both written to Emily, inviting her to stay when them when she came to New York from Philadelphia. Emily did stay there beginning May 9 and was there for close to two weeks. In that time she visited friends, and saw N. P. Willis quite frequently, if not every day.

[640] Eugenia Damaux, part of Emily's intimate circle of friends at the Utica Female Academy. She was living in New York City.

[641] Urania Sheldon Nott—a mentor, advisor, and friend to Emily—was the literary principal at the Utica Female Academy when Emily arrived in October of 1840. In late summer of 1842 Urania married Eliphalet Nott, the president of Union College in Schenectady NY.

[642] Augusta Crafts and her strong opinions are mentioned frequently in the letters written from the Utica Female Academy.

[643] See vol. 1, "Cast of Characters," s.v. "Blidgims."

[644] Jimmy Williams, often mentioned in Anna Maria Anable's letters, usually just as "Jimmy."

[645] See the letter of Emily Chubbuck to Anna Maria Anable dated April 28, 1845. Since we know that Emily did in fact meet with N. P. Willis when she passed through New York—in fact she saw him almost every day of the close to two weeks she was there, we are able to see this time, these statements, and the several letters that she wrote as indicative of her state of mind—the confusion and the conflict that she felt over the relationship.

house this spring! Do! I should take this down to Aunt C. or she won't have time to write—Write often, *as soon* as you get mine, for we bet on your letters—You wouldn't think we had got used to your being…"

Written upside down to the rest of the text in the right margin of the address page: "…away if you could see how Jane[646] takes on about being lonesome."

Good night

Ninny[647]

Source: American Baptist Historical Society, AJ 26, no. 1266B. There are two letters in this file, the second being the letter from Cynthia Sheldon.

Martha Hooker to Emily E. Chubbuck, May 5, 1845[648]

My dear Miss Chubbuck

You certainly did *très bien* when you added the weight of your example to the oft repeated precept "be punctual." But what think you I am about to lay claim to as large a share of punctuality as yourself. Your note came to hand Saturday evening. Of course I would not write on the Sabbath but half past nine Monday morning finds me seated pen at hand and paper before me answering your kind little note. The girls are all very much disappointed to learn where you have taken up your abode for the winter. We had hoped to see you here last week.[649] It would be careless to tell you of the affection with which you are regarded by all here. Miss Strong says she would trouble you with a note if it were not washing day and Lord Kames did not call for time and attention. Mary Walker would write if she had two eyes. She has injured one of her eyes as much as to be obliged to wear a bandage. Miss Hyde sends love and would write if she had time, as would all the others. Frank Kirby sends you a kiss. I kissed [ ] Brayton for you, and she returns you any quantity of love. Your pet Martha Taylor is very sorry you will not come and see her. [ ] sends her love. I would write more but fear I shall be too late.

Yours ever affectionately

Martha

Source: American Baptist Historical Society, AJ 24, no. 1181B.

---

[646] Jane Kelly was Emily Chubbuck's friend at the Utica Female Academy. Jane was the literary principal at the Utica Female Academy. In fall 1848, she followed Cynthia Sheldon as headmistress.
[647] "Ninny" was a name of endearment given to Anna Maria Anable by her most intimate friends at the Utica Female Academy. Emily was "Nemmy."
[648] This letter is undated.
[649] The Utica Female Academy girls had just returned to Utica from a school break.

Anna Maria Anable to Emily E. Chubbuck, May 6, 1845[650]

Lo! Nem[651] you have worked yourself up into a great "two" about nothing. *Who* don't [sic] want you to see Willis?[652] You said you had decided not to[653] and though I was half provoked at you for deciding so of course I could say nothing against it. I don't know what notions Aunt C.[654] may have got in her head[655]—I know she thought it mighty nice in you to decide on not seeing him—she said would be so nice to *say* you had not—but I don't think so—People if they think any thing [sic] about it think you will see him *of course*.

Do say something consoling or kind to the poor fellow for I feel distressed for him.[656] Make as long a stay in Brooklyn as you like—we don't want to hurry you, but we had got a notion that you were a little homesick! Probably it was a suggestion of our own hearts. You need not hurry a bit on account of the school, for it will be looked after even if literary reparté is *not* here. William[657] is going to New York sometime between the 17th and 25th and will be he says most happy to take care of you. You will be safe in his hands—and [sic] old sailor you know. According to this arrangement you will have quite a visit in B. and I hope it will be indeed a *bonne bonehas*. Take as much comfort as you can in the warm weather—for sorry a bit of it will you find here at the rate of the last fortnight. You must stop and see Aunt U.[658] if only for a day or so—she will never forgive you if you cut her this time—Show her W's letter too if you can. I like to have her and the Dr.[659] think

---

[650] Anna Maria added an addendum to this letter which appears as a May 7 letter. Addressed to Emily in Philadelphia, the address page shows that it was forwarded to New York, where Emily was staying with her friend Sophia Taylor and her husband.

[651] "Nem" or "Nemmy" was a name of endearment given to Emily by a small group of her intimate friends at the Utica Female Academy. Anna Maria Anable was "Ninny."

[652] Nathaniel Parker (N. P.) Willis was the editor of *New Mirror*, the magazine that catapulted Emily into literary fame. He became a friend, mentor, and eventually a suitor.

[653] See the letter of Emily E. Chubbuck's to Anna Maria Anable dated April 28, 1845.

[654] Miss Cynthia Sheldon was the administrative and finance manager of the Utica Female Academy. She was a mentor, advisor, and friend to Emily. Anna Maria Anable was Miss Sheldon's niece.

[655] See the letter of Cynthia Sheldon to Emily E. Chubbuck dated May 2, 1845. In that she had said:

> One part of your letter delighted me more than I can tell—your decision about not seeing Willis in NY—I will disclaim prejudice and declare this view of it, is the only consistent one under all circumstances—It will perplex you much to effect it and make your visit in Brooklyn—Still if you really think that could be dispensed with consistent with your object, your health not suffer by a speedy return, it would give you a real slide through. That tells difficulty—W. could not draw an inference either flattering to his vanity, nor a pique—Many tongues here would be bridled by a knowledge of having nothing to talk about.

[656] N. P. Willis had lost his wife the end of March 1845. Emily had heard the news when she reached New York City on March 27. Willis had spoken personally in his letters to Emily about his utter desolation at his loss.

[657] William Stewart Anable was the son of Joseph and Alma Sheldon Anable, the brother of Anna Maria Anable. He recently had given up his life as a sailor, adn hoped to become a shopkeeper.

[658] Urania Sheldon Nott—a mentor, advisor, and friend to Emily—was the literary principal at the Utica Female Academy when Emily arrived in October of 1840. In late summer of 1842 Urania married Eliphalet Nott, the president of Union College in Schenectady NY.

[659] Eliphalet Nott, president of Union College, married to Urania Sheldon Nott.

well of him. The Dr.[660] has sent Grand Ma[661] his nice little covered buggy—and she has had a nice ride in it to day. *We'll* make a little use of it when you come. It's a little the nicest contrivance that ever was thought of for *scarey* [sic] folks.

Don't you feel provoked now that you have closed up matters with Hoffman?[662] I know you would give all your old shoes if you had not written him. I am crazy to know how you managed it see, and on what terms you are now?— won't you have "loads of things" to tell me when you do really get here. I am *real* glad you are going to see W. for it seemed to me low or *flat* to come home without seeing him or any of the folk we talk so much about. I want you at least to do as much as *dodge among the pillars*. Do you know we have been having the greatest time here having Jimmy's[663] relations to tea? Mary[664] and I got into a rare frolic last Friday about inviting old *Mrs.* Kirby (Fanny's mother and a pattern woman according to Jimmy) up here to see my girls dance. We formed various plans for entrapping her into committing some *im*propriety. We expected to disgrace ourselves with all our nonsense in our heads for the evening—but it passed off very "properly" no more serious impropriety occurring than Mary's tipping over a bouquet of flowers and sending the water a sprawling over the mahogany. They are all up to Mrs. Crafts[665] to night [sic] so I have this evening to myself—for which I am exceedingly thankful—as I have such a cold I can scarcely speak loud—I have made myself comfortable in double gown and blanket shawl to devote myself to you—but you must not be disappointed at any extra degree of dullness—for I confess about these times I have a great penchant for that good comfortable old fellows [ ]lext [sic] Morpheus. Jule—had a letter from Hannah H. yesterday—she is having nice times—receives a good deal of attention—has been out to a party of 150 etc. etc—We don't hear a word from that—I should not much wonder if she was on her way—Mary Adams[666] was to sail the 1st of May. You will probably be in N. Y. at the same time. Eugenia[667] comes up this week. Seems to me I *should* like to see you just a little to night [sic]—I want to throw aside the pen and portfolio and throw myself down on the settee and have you here to talk to me. Any way [sic] my *first* wants must be gratified and as there is an impossibility in the last—I will

---

[660] Dr. Eliphalet Nott, husband of Urania Sheldon Nott. See Anna Maria Anable's letter of May 2, 1845.

[661] Mrs. Isabell Low Sheldon, mother of Cynthia Sheldon, Urania Sheldon Nott, and Alma Sheldon Anable.

[662] Charles Fenno Hoffman, a prominent literary figure in Philadelphia and New York, well known in literary circles as an exceptionally talented editor, poet, and writer. Emily had started a correspondence with him as Laura Linden before he discovered that she was Fanny Forester.

[663] Jimmy Williams, often mentioned in Anna Maria Anable's letters, usually just as "Jimmy."

[664] This would be either Mary Barber or Mary Anable.

[665] Augusta Crafts and her strong opinions are mentioned frequently in the letters written from the Utica Female Academy.

[666] Mary Adams, a friend of Emily's while at the Utica Female Academy. She lived in New Orleans.

[667] Eugenia Damaux, part of Emily's intimate circle of friends at the Utica Female Academy. She lived in New York.

endeavor with all the decorum and dignity that is yet this side the land of Nod to "bid you good evening."

Ninny[668]

Source: American Baptist Historical Society, AJ 23, no. 1167.

Anna Maria Anable to Emily E. Chubbuck, May 7, 1845[669]

I was going to leave the rest of the page for somebody to fill up—but it's such a bright morning every body [sic] is more busy than I. Mary B.[670] says she has got a paper all done up to send you "but you are going to be so on the go." That she thinks she will leave it on your table for you to have you get here [sic]—the [ ] officer is just starting for a walk with the girls. I have promised to drive Grand ma[671] a little ways before school. Grand pa is getting to be such a *frisky* old gentlemen that Grand ma don't [sic] feel quite safe with him—Lucky for me isn't it? Now Nem[672] do write immediately there's a…

Written in the right margin of the address page: "…darling. You have been way good so far—but I am a little suspicious you will neglect me the rest of the time. Disappoint me won't you? Give my love to Mr. and Mrs. Gillette[673] and tell them we are anticipating their visit with a great deal of pleasure. I have got so accustomed to sitting up in my own room that Jane[674] and I will have to be introduced to each other when you come home."

Written in the left margin of the address page: "We had a nice visit from Prof. Raymonds—Sunday. Has any one told you that cousin John Sheldon saw your brother[675] in Milwaukee and that he said he was coming home this summer. I have

---

[668] "Ninny" was a name of endearment given to Anna Maria Anable by her most intimate friends at the Utica Female Academy. Emily was "Nemmy."

[669] This letter is an addendum to Anna Maria Anable's letter of May 6, 1845. Addressed to Emily in Philadelphia, the address page shows that it was forwarded to New York, where Emily was staying with the family of her friend Sophia Taylor.

[670] Mary Barber, mentioned frequently in the Emily Chubbuck Judson letters, was a student and then the art teacher at the Utica Female Academy.

[671] Mrs. Isabell Low Sheldon, mother of Cynthia Sheldon, Urania Sheldon Nott, and Alma Sheldon Anable. Deacon Asa and Isabell Low Sheldon lived with their daughters and grandchildren as a part of the Utica Female Academy community. Mr. and Mrs. Sheldon were very popular with the students. When Mrs. Sheldon died January 29, 1847, Mr. Sheldon continued to have a room at the Utica Female Academy until he died in March 1848.

[672] "Nem" or "Nemmy" was a name of endearment given to Emily by a small group of her intimate friends at the Utica Female Academy. Anna Maria Anable was "Ninny."

[673] Rev. A. D. Gillette was a stalwart friend and supporter of the Judson, Sheldon, and Anable families. Emily met Adoniram Judson in the parlor of the Gillette home in Philadelphia. Emily was staying with the Gillettes while in Philadelphia.

[674] Jane Kelly was Emily Chubbuck's friend at the Utica Female Academy. Jane was the literary principal at the Utica Female Academy. In fall 1848, she followed Cynthia Sheldon as headmistress.

[675] The reference is to Anna Maria's cousin John Sheldon and Emily's brother, J. Walker Chubbuck, who lived in the Wisconsin Territory, working in the newspaper business. We assume that "Cousin John Sheldon" was the son of John Sheldon, who was the brother of Cynthia Sheldon, Urania Sheldon Nott, and Alma Sheldon Anable.

got my cap 'all set'—The horse is harnessed so I must go—If you want my letters you must give us your directions in Brooklyn."

Source: American Baptist Historical Society, AJ 23, no. 1167.

Sophia C. Taylor to Emily E. Chubbuck,[676] May 7, 1845

My dear Miss Chubbuck

I have a word to say to you this morning and very likely I have a little news to tell you. Mrs. Hall has a daughter four weeks old last Monday. Yesterday Maria was out shopping, she is very well, the baby they think is just the thing of course—they call it "Margaret Wilmarth."[677] Lizzy said that I must tell you that Dan had returned from New Orleans without Hat Anable,[678] he came home night before last, and went off to bed without their knowing any thing [sic] about it, and she says they can't get a word out of him, they don't know whether Hat intends to say through the summer or not.

We have expected a letter from you every day for two weeks and I was fearful you might be quite sick. I was delighted to hear that you have had so fine a time and hope you will enjoy your visit with us as well—Do write to us very soon, No 18 West St New York—don't forget. We are all well and expect to see your dear self very soon.[679]

Yours truly and affectionately

Sophia C. T.

Source: American Baptist Historical Society. No reference numbers

---

[676] See also the letter from Alfred Taylor to Emily E. Chubbuck dated April 6, 1845.

[677] The Wilmarth family was well known to the Sheldon-Anable families. Miss Cynthia Sheldon had stopped for a visit on her way through the city as she returned to Utica in early April.

[678] Harriet ("Hatty," "Hattie," or "Hat") Anable, one of the five Anable sisters. She had been teaching in a private residence in the New Orleans area.

[679] Emily was to stay with Sophia Taylor and her husband for the time she was in New York City as she returned from Philadelphia to Utica.

Robert A. West to Emily E. Chubbuck, May 10, 1845—New York City[680]

My dear Miss C.

I beg you not to start at the appellation since Mr. Inman[681] has awakened in my mind a very strong desire for other terms of correspondence than those of mere official correspondence. Moreover though not an old man—for if "thirty-five" be the summit of life's hill, and man is to be allowed a few month's rest after the ascent, a few miles of local country before the descent commences, I suppose I may claim that intermediate spot as my whereabouts—still I have been for twelve years "the husband of one wife" next to which blessing I count four little girls and a little infantile rascal who though he visited us for the first time only three days ago, has already made considerable *noise* in the world by way of satisfying us that he intends to have his "say" as soon as he can make himself understood. With such credentials and on my own assurance, a tolerable character, may I venture beyond the editorial lines without a violation of treaties?

As you will perceive, Mr. Post's[682] corresponding clerk and myself are separate and distinct beings, though he almost passed me thus summonly to overthrow your conjecture. It is needless to enter into explanations why he addressed you. It was an inadvertence, and [ ], an invasion of *privilege*; yet though it might appear discourteous really sprang from the opposite feeling. Mr. Inman's illness and other circumstances had caused an arrearage of correspondence which it was necessary to dispose of, that *is* now disposed of and you shall have no more *anonymous* correspondence from the *Columbian*, and should have had none, with my knowledge, even under the peculiar pressure which existed.[683]

We agree to your terms—five dollars per page—and should like to have you all to ourselves—as who would not?—but far be it from us to press a point which might conflict with your interests, knowing as we do, by report, the praiseworthy object at which you aim. Your wishes as to "Grace Linden," (of the acceptance of which you have, I believe, been advised), shall be attended to. In defiance of your modest disavowal of its merits as a continuous story, I assign it a high place as such; and believe our readers will confirm my judgements [sic]. We rely upon your kind assurance of interest in our success, as a guarantee that you will continue to favor us

---

[680] Robert A. West became the editor of the *Columbian Magazine* after the illness of John Inman. In this letter Robert West ran out of paper and turned the front page ninety degrees and wrote perpendicular to the original lines three more paragraphs. Fortunately he has a very clear and distinctive handwriting style. As Emily later was heading to Burmah, West wrote to her that he was a very active layman in the Methodist Church.

[681] John Inman was the editor of the *Commercial Advertiser* and the *Columbian Magazine*.

[682] Post had filled in at the time of Inman's illness. His two letters in December 1844 and January 1845 were written by his corresponding clerk.

[683] See the letter from Mr. Post dated February 21, 1845, signed by his corresponding clerk.

with your contributions, and beg us return to assure you, that on our part your wishes shall at all times be met with the cordial courtesy to which your talents, nor less your character, are entitled. Mr. Post will attend to the important matter of remittances, and should he, which I do not anticipate, be forgetful of your convenience, do not scruple about a reminder either direct to him or through your humble scribe.

While on this subject permit me with all deference to suggest, speaking irrespective of the merits of an article, that, as a general rule, you would best suit the views of magazine makers and readers, by articles occupying from five to seven pages of a number, continuous or otherwise. Individually my views, as to "continuous articles" coincide with your own discriminating criticisms; and as the conduct of the *Columbian* now mainly devolves upon myself I shall endeavor to act upon them. I think a *rule* on the subject cannot be rigidly adhered to, and is therefore of little use; but I think I should decline admitting more than one, or at most two continuous articles at one time; if two, they should be of decidedly different character. Am I right in this?

Mr. Brougham I do not yet know personally. I believe he is connected with the stage. He has not written much, I think, and his admirable tale (of) the Blarney Stone is one of his happiest efforts. I have just been reading a manuscript of his written after the manner of Ingolesby [sic]—it displays a wonderful facility in rhyming, but his wit, racy when pure, is rather prone to descend into "slang." I have not had time to refer to the article by C. N [ ] ius Eimi [sic] and do not know him; but after your commendations I shall hunt him up. I write with freedom and in confidence, and shall always be glad of your counsels in these matters. I cannot at this moment recal [sic] any literary intelligence that you are not quite as likely to know as myself. Edgar A. Poe, recently became associated in the editorship of the "Broadway Journal," is at war with some of the city newspapers on account of a lecture delivered by him on "The Poets and Poetry of America." He denied the honesty of newspaper criticism—they retorted—and he published a rejoinder in the *Journal*, with something like a threat of carrying the war further.

If I have not already wearied you I have a word to say from Mr. Inman with whom I have the pleasure to be associated in the editorial conduct of the *New York Commercial Advertiser* as well as the *Columbian*. In November last he had a very *severe illness*, brought on I fear by excessive literary labor[684]—a hint by the way for your own good self. His complaint was congestion of the brain. He has not to this day entirely recovered and by his medical advisors is strictly prohibited from reading or writing a line beyond what is absolutely necessary from his connexion [sic] with the *Commercial*. Otherwise he commands me to assure you he would

---

[684] See the letter of John Inman to Emily E. Chubbuck dated November 19, 1844.

have written you. So soon as the weather becomes suitable he will take a health tour. He commissions me to assure you of his very kind regards and insists upon my letting "you have your own way on everything" pertaining to the *Columbian*. I will obey to the letter. Could you desire more?

I suppose you will think I ought to have known you "seven years" before writing such a letter as this—I can only say that already I know you sufficiently to induce me to take advantage of this opportunity of paying a tribute of admiration to Fanny Forester[685] and subscribing myself.

Very truly yours

Robert A. West

Source: American Baptist Historical Society, AJ 27, no. 1302.

Anna Maria Anable to Emily E. Chubbuck, May 12, 1845[686]

May 11–44

I cannot go to sleep dear Nemmy[687] without writing you tho' it is now eleven o'clock or later. Eugenia[688] the darling is here and I have just left her in M. B.'s[689] room. You don't know how good it seems to have her here again—and we have got her with *us* for the first week tho' she was engaged to Mr. Spencer. Mary was so kind as to send money for her journey and we did not how we should manage [sic] to get her here without meddling—but it has all come around right and we are all rejoicing over a little *ruse*. By the way we have postponed our French class to an indefinite period—when you come home may be [sic]! One reason I suppose will be *obvious* to you—Eugenia says she has been so busy taking care of Mrs. B[690]— sick children she has not had a moment of time to write you—They all had the chicken pox or measles and she took them over to her fathers [sic] to nurse them. She and M. B. send a great deal of love—Nemmy darling you don't know how bad your last two letters have made us feel. You write as tho' you had got the impres-

---

[685] Fanny Forester, Emily Chubbuck's *nom de plume*.

[686] Anna Maria has written May 11–44, and someone has written May 11, 1844 above her date. The content of the letter, however, clearly does not allow this, and it must be placed in May 1845. We need no more reason than the fact that it is addressed to Emily care of Alfred Taylor in New York City. Emily knew his wife Sophia, and stayed with them on her way home to Utica from Philadelphia in May 1845. May 12 would be the first Monday Emily was there. There is an addendum to this letter dated May 13, 1845.

[687] "Nem" or "Nemmy" was a name of endearment given to Emily by a small group of her intimate friends at the Utica Female Academy. Anna Maria Anable was "Ninny."

[688] Eugenia Damaux, part of Emily's intimate circle of friends at the Utica Female Academy. She had been living in New York City.

[689] Mary Barber, mentioned frequently in the Emily Chubbuck Judson letters, was a student and then the art teacher at the Utica Female Academy.

[670] Eugenia worked in New York City for the Brown family.

sion we were anxious you should return home *to teach*. Your last letters from P. gave rather a doleful account of the condition of Mr. Gillette's[691] family and Mr. Graham's[692] and your health, so we concluded that your stay in P. was not benefiting you and would probably be no longer agreeable to you; *for that reason only* we advised you to come home. I hope you know that our greatest desire with regard to you is that your health may be permanently restored. Aunt C.[693] says [Note: Inserted here is: "And have I not repeatedly written you."] you must not be worried in the least about teaching—If you think it best "to idle" away the summer in P. or Brooklyn or home or any where [sic] to do it without any further thought. If you will decide within a fortnight she will make arrangements with Sarah Gold or *somebody* to take charge of the courses for the Summer—Now do Nemmy just what you think would be for your health. If you want to go back to P. you can change your mind you know—and you may stay just as long as you please in Brooklyn—and when you come back to us you can play lady if you like and do nothing—on the whole I think the last a very good plan—for I have seen the compos have troubled you for some time, and until you get strong I should not advise you to think of touching them[694]—Do pray go and see the clairvoyant woman—I have been sending Miss Martineau's letters and have added a letter to my faith in Mesmerism, tho' I think the letters are silly enough—You must do anything that you think will benefit you—I wish I could be there to see what you need, but you must trust to Willis'[695] and Graham's and your own judgment. What plan has to—for your going to the West Indies? N. O.[696] has no more any attractions for me. Hat[697] writes such forlorn letters that I am almost sure something has happened to her, and we have sent for her to come home immediately with young Mrs. Patton. Mary A.[698] sailed the 1st of May and will probably be in N. York soon—If you direct to her—care of Mrs. Wolsay, 17 Rutgers place she may have time to come and see you.—I wish you

---

[691] Rev. A. D. Gillette was a stalwart friend and supporter of the Judson, Sheldon, and Anable families. Emily met Adoniram Judson in the parlor of the Gillette home in Philadelphia. Emily was staying with the Gillettes while in Philadelphia.

[692] George Graham, editor of *Graham's Magazine*, took an interest in Emily Chubbuck as Fanny Forester and paid her with the unheard of sum of five dollars a page. He and his wife were very hospitable to Emily while she was in Philadelphia and the Grahams had accompanied Emily on the trip from Philadelphia to New York.

[693] Miss Cynthia Sheldon was the administrative and finance manager of the Utica Female Academy. She was a mentor, advisor, and friend to Emily. Anna Maria Anable was Miss Sheldon's niece.

[694] Emily taught composition at the Utica Female Academy, and could have as many as one hundred and twenty students in her class

[695] Nathaniel Parker (N. P.) Willis was the editor of *New Mirror*, the magazine that catapulted Emily into literary fame. He became a friend, mentor, and eventually a suitor.

[696] New Orleans. Anna Maria Anable's sister Harriet or "Hat" or "Hatty" had been living in New Orleans, and in the next sentence Anna Maria went on to say how forlorn that city seems to be.

[697] Harriet ("Hatty," "Hattie," or "Hat") Anable, one of the five Anable sisters. She had been teaching in a private residence in the New Orleans area.

[698] Mary Adams, a friend of Emily's while at the Utica Female Academy. She lived in New Orleans.

would and find out all you can about Hat, but don't let Mrs. Wilmarth[699] know we are in a "teaze" [sic] for I suspect she has had some trouble with Dawn—I should go down with Will[700] to see you and her if I could leave but I have a good deal to do this term. We have 115 scholars—So you did make your *debut* in the DeLaine? *I told you so!* I hope Willis will tell you as frankly as Graham did what sort of an impression you make—I am glad he seems so kind and *motherly*—Tell him I will depict him to fill my office—but he must take care of you for of course I shall be suspicious of any innovation—I hope you have got my letter from P. by this time and I hope it will get you right again about my opinion of our seeing him—The clock struck 12 some time ago—and I must jump into bed for I am very tired. Good Night. *Nannie.*[701]

Anna Maria Anable to Emily E. Chubbuck, May 13, 1845[702]

Morn'g I can't help saying again this morning how sorry I am you have left P. This last letter of yours is the first one in which you have spoken of your stay there as being decidedly beneficial. I would not have had you come away for the world while you were improving there.

Written in the right margin of the address page: "We have had three days warm enough to keep even such cold bodies as you and me from freezing. It is clouding up for a thunder storm [sic] now. Write as soon as you get this—for we shall be very anxious to hear from you. Don't get in a 'stew' about how to spend your Summer but whatever is proposed to you that is pleasant, enjoy it as though there was no future to be looked after at all. I think it is your *duty* now first of all to take care of your health."

Written in the left margin of the address page: "Jane Berry leaves tomorrow for Poughkeepsie. She would like you to stop and visit her. Aunt U.[703] wants you to make her a visit—She's got the same impression that you were not gaining much

---

[699] Mr. and Mrs. John Wilmarth. There are frequent mentions of the Wilmarths' home and hospitality. They lived in New York City.

[700] William Stewart Anable was the son of Joseph and Alma Sheldon Anable. William was due to travel frorm Utica to New York City and the hope was that Emily would return with him.

[701] This could be "Nonnie"—the writing is difficult. Anna Maria has used a number of names—usually "Ninny." This is a new one.

[702] This letter was written as an addendum to the May 12, 1845 letter of Anna Maria Anable to Emily E. Chubbuck.

[703] Urania Sheldon Nott—a mentor, advisor, and friend to Emily—was the literary principal of the Utica Female Academy when Emily arrived in October 1840. In late summer 1842 Urania married Eliphalet Nott, the president of Union College in Schenectady NY.

in P.—We had a letter from E. Joselyn[704]—she inquires very particularly after you and intends writing you soon. Mrs. Lynde also wrote Aunt C.[705] She has been flourishing in Washington—visiting all…"

Written in the bottom margin of the address page: "…the young folk and having nice times. If you can do let her know that you are in B. I should like of all things that you should see him. Give much love to Sophia and her husband[706] and present my kind regards to Mr. Willis[707] with whom I feel already well acquainted and shall feel more…"

Written in the left margin of the address page perpendicular to and across the text: "…so the more you tell me of him. Is his little daughter there?[708] I see nothing of Mrs. Lyman and should probably not see her unless it is in church or in the street. Walter has come up for my scrawl—Write as soon as you get this do! Ninny"[709]

Source: American Baptist Historical Society, AJ 23, no. 1133.

Nathaniel Parker Willis to Emily E. Chubbuck,[710] May 15, 1845[711]

My dear friend Emily

I am not surprised at your letter—not so surprised as I should have been had a clairvoyant told me you had no such feelings as you describe. It is inevitable that you should feel how much your strong *mind* has overleaped common barriers and placed you mentally foremost, while your diffidence keeps your *person* a prisoner to common usage and progression. With one grain of vanity you would have found yourself comfortably even with any body—body and mind.

---

[704] Mrs. Josslyn was associated with Emily at the academy in Utica—her letters are filled with references to people they both knew. At the time of the second letter, she was living in Michigan—her husband had just sold their farm and they were thinking of moving into town. They were uncertain about the future, but Josslyn had a business of making buggy whips. Though this later letter was written in January, Mrs. Josslyn did not have any idea that Emily had been in Philadelphia for the previous two months for her health.

[705] Miss Cynthia Sheldon was the administrative and finance manager of the Utica Female Academy. She was a mentor, advisor, and friend to Emily. Anna Maria was Miss Sheldon's niece.

[706] See the letter from Alfred Taylor, April 6, 1845. He was the husband of Sophia Taylor. Emily would stay with them in New York.

[707] Nathaniel Parker (N. P.) Willis was the editor of *New Mirror*, the magazine that catapulted Emily into literary fame. He became a friend, mentor, and eventually a suitor. He had a daughter Imogen.

[708] N. P. Willis had a daughter Imogen.

[709] "Ninny" was a name of endearment given to Anna Maria Anable by her most intimate friends at the Utica Female Academy. Emily was "Nemmy."

[710] Written in the address page in the handwriting of Emily Chubbuck: "N. P. Willis Esq. 25. May 15, 1845." This tells us that it was the twenty-fifth letter she had received from N. P. Willis.

[711] This letter was written to Emily while she was staying in New York with Alfred and Sophia Taylor. It is undated, but Emily is recorded as having received it on May 15, 1845. It is obvious from the letter that they, N. P. Willis and Emily, have met for the first time. In a letter written on May 18, she reported to her sister Catharine that she had seen Willis five times.

No, my sweet friend—I *won't* give you your letters unless you insist upon it[712]—for they are filed away for my daughter, and I consider them most valuable data commemorative of my recognition of your genius and of your instant sympathy and friendship.[713] I see you as I saw you a fortnight ago, and I smile to see how cold your clasp of the hand is, when I know your heart is cordial, and I do not feel one bit repell'd by so thin a mask as your frigid manner. I had more than half a mind to imprint a kiss on your round forehead and tell you I knew your heart would pardon me.

Your exterior is certainly far too cold, and had I met you without first knowing you as I do, I should have set you down for an unsympathising and unapproachable ascetic. But, with a bosom full of untold riches, and a nature as passionate and lofty as that of an improvesatrice, I have no idea of letting you pass for an icicle, even tho you label yourself. So pray prepare to give me a kinder pressure of the hand when next I see you, and be assured of the sincere love, *real and ideal* of

Yours always faithfully

N. P. Willis

Source: Hanna family files.

Emily E. Chubbuck to Catharine Chubbuck, May 18, 1845—Brooklyn[714]

Dear Kitty,

Do you want to know where I am and what I am doing? Well, I am in Sophy ~~Edward~~ Taylor's[715] parlour [sic] writing you a letter. I left Philadelphia last Friday week[716] and came (here in) in company with the Grahams[717] who spent a week here at the Astor Hotel. I have had just as nice a time as one would care to have, [ ] [ ] almost as well as I was last summer, and shall start (for home) [Note: "Next"

---

[712] We note that Emily had also asked Charles Fenno Hoffman to return the letters she had sent to him, and he did return them.

[713] Emily had asked both Charles Fenno Hoffman and N. P. Willis to return the letters that she had sent to them. Hoffman complied, Willis did not, as this letter indicates. After her engagement to Adoniram Judson, Emily pressed Willis all the more, for she feared that, made public, the letters could prove an embarrassment to her, to Judson, and to the mission movement. He finally did return them and she did destroy them, an action which we greatly mourn. It is of interest that she kept in her files the letters that Willis had sent to her, beginning in June 1844.

[714] This later is undated. A letter with similar content was posted May 19, 1845 to Cynthia Sheldon, so May 18 and 19 is suitable for this letter and its addendum (See next letter in the correspondence. There is a tear with a piece missing from the letter; therefore, I have provided clarifying material in brackets.).

[715] Sophia Taylor. See her husband's letter of April 6, 1845, and her letter of May 7, 1845, both to Emily.

[716] Emily had arrived in Philadelphia on Saturday, March 29, and left on Friday, May 9, so she was there just six weeks.

[717] George Graham, editor of *Graham's Magazine*, took an interest in Emily Chubbuck as Fanny Forester and paid her with the unheard of sum of five dollars a page. The Grahams had accompanied Emily on the trip from Philadelphia to New York.

is written and crossed out.] this week sometime. I have seen Willis[718] five times [since I have] been here[719] and am dead in love with him, he is so handsome, so good.[720] He leaves for Europe in about a month[721]—is going to (take) his little daughter Imogen to her Mother's friends, and will probably spend a year abroad himself. I like him even better than I (expected); and what is *quite as* agreeable, I think he likes me. He says (he) will have me for his *other daughter*, so I call him "papa" to (his) face[722]—rather an old daughter—don't you think so? Imogen (my sister) is in Boston, so I shall not see her. Tomorrow Willis is to introduce me to "the Brigadier"[723]—I sort o' dread it, but then I am getting used to such things—I have seen oceans of big folks since I have been gone. Willis has proposed a system for *fattening* me the way they do the Circassian [sic] girls and I am going to carry it out. He has a great contempt for lean people. I went to Greenwood cemetery last week—it is the most beautiful place in the world. I visited the Academy of Design too, and went to Willis's room in the Astor where I saw among other choice things a portrait of his wife. It was exquisitely beautiful. That is all I have been about here besides making two or three calls. Tomorrow I aim to visit at the Wilmarths[724] and call on Mary Colgate[725] and Mrs. Ellen Jim. Do you get the *Mirror* yet? They say there is a fine compliment to me in last Saturday's, but I hav'nt [sic] been able to get my finger on it. I have had another flirtation with Hoffy[726] and he has found out who I am but he don't know [sic] that I am in Brooklyn. He has returned [ ]

---

[718] Nathaniel Parker (N. P.) Willis was the editor of *New Mirror*, the magazine that catapulted Emily into literary fame. He became a friend, mentor, and eventually a suitor. The relationship between Emily and Willis is deepening, and she does follow this line with an expression of love. On April 28, 1845, Emily had written that she was not going to see Willis as she passed through New York; in fact, she was to see him almost every day she was there, a period of almost two weeks.

[719] On April 28, 1845, Emily had written that she had decided not to see Willis in New York. We also find it interesting that she tells Catharine that she has seen Willis five times, but in writing to Cynthia Sheldon, she says that she has only seen him "several times."

[720] This is the first time we have had this kind of expression of feeling. After her engagement to Adoniram Judson and her great angst over expression she made in her letters to Willis, she affirmed that she had in fact told Willis that she loved him. However, referencing it through the window of her love for Adoniram Judson, she said that her feelings of love for Willis were more of friendship. They certainly did not plumb the depths of her love for Judson.

[721] N. P. Willis and Imogen would leave June 1, 1845.

[722] This had been going on with Anna Maria Anable, for in many instances Anna Maria in her letters referred to Willis as "papa."

[723] George P. "General" Morris, was N. P. Willis's partner at the *New Mirror* and a prominent literary figure in New York and Philadelphia. The original founder of the *New York Mirror* in 1823, beginning in 1843 with the *New Mirror*, he entered into a succession of publication enterprises with Willis. A writer, poet, and songwriter, he published a number of anthologies of both prose and poetry. After Willis's wife died, he went to Europe in 1845 and asked General Morris to guide Emily in her literary endeavors. Known universally as "General Morris," his title came from his rank as a brigadier-general in the New York militia.

[724] Mr. and Mrs. John Wilmarth. There are frequent mentions of the Wilmarths' home and hospitality.

[725] Mary Colgate was the name of both the wife and the daughter of William Colgate, the prominent industrialist and manufacturer. There are letters in the correspondence from Mrs. Mary Colgate, her husband William Colgate, their son James Colgate, and Mrs. Ellen Colgate, the wife of James Colgate. We believe that this is a reference to Mary, the daughter.

[726] Charles Fenno Hoffman, a prominent literary figure in Philadelphia and New York, well known in literary circles as an exceptionally talented editor, poet, and writer. Emily had started a correspondence with him as Laura Linden before he discovered that she was Fanny Forester.

[ ][727] and we have settled up accounts for good. He says, "Laura can (take) care of herself now."

Mr. Graham was sick in bed a fortnight while I was in P. but nevertheless he found time to be very good natured to me, the jewel. He urged me to stay till July and invited me to his house. Willis thinks Utica is a bad place for me and that I ought not (to) teach, but when I proposed going to Hamilton he said that would (be) worse yet. He is all agog to have me go to Italy and spend a year. (I) shouldn't wonder if I did go before long. I think if some pleasant family was going Graham would pay my traveling expenses for letters I would write him. And I am mighty anxious to go I [ ] [ ]. They say it would make me fat and rosy. If the pesky old [ ] [ ] paid for, I would be as lazy as lazy could be for one while, [ ] [ ] [ ] all the time, it does me so much good.

[ ], Kate, ah sorra! I hav'nt [sic] cotched [sic] a beau. 'Taint [sic] no (use to) look sweet and pretty—they are all shockingly sharp sighted. [ ]'s Gris.[728] I tho't him as good as mine; but it was no go. Another widower[729] gave me a seranade [sic] *but not* his—heart. Hoffy is lost—poor Willy says if he was to live his life over again he never would marry, and so I must go back again to teaching—alas! Did I tell you Anna Maria[730] had had an offer from L? Pity he did'nt [sic] offer me.—This is pretty stuff for Sunday but fact is I hav'nt [sic] been to church today it has rained so, and I can't make it seem like Sunday.

Source: Hanna family files.

Emily E. Chubbuck to Catharine Chubbuck, May 19, 1845[731]

Monday morning. I have taken up my pen this morning merely for the sake of telling you what a glorious day it is. We will have a delectable tramp in N. Y.—Did I tell you I had had an application from Godey to write for the *Lady's Book?*[732] I wish I had more hands and heads. Mr. Taylor[733] is waiting to take my letter over to N. Y. so I will close by subscribing myself

---

[727] Emily had asked Charles Fenno Hoffman to return to her the letters which she had written to him—a request which he had honored.

[728] Reverend Rufus W. Griswold, an ordained clergyman and distinguished literary figure, had been one of Emily's suitors. Emily referred to him in a letter to Anna Maria Anable as a "widower," very anxious to be married.

[729] "Widower" refers to widowed older men and usually suggested availability and interest in marriage. The academy girls and their teachers were always referring to "the widower" or to "widowers" in their conversations and correspondence.

[730] Anna Maria Anable was the niece of the Urania and Cynthia Sheldon, the daughter of Joseph and Alma Sheldon Anable; she was Emily's closest friend at the Utica Female Academy.

[731] This letter is an addendum to Emily's May 18 letter to her sister Catharine.

[732] *Godey's Ladies Book* was a magazine that combined poetry, prose, and beautiful engravings, many of them about fashion.

[733] Alfred Taylor and his wife Sophia were hosting Emily while she was in New York.

Your very loving sister

Nem

Source: Hanna family files.

Emily E. Chubbuck to Cynthia Sheldon, May 19, 1845—Brooklyn

My dear Miss C,

The rain has at last gone by and left us a day exquisitely beautiful which Sophy[734] and I are intending to improve. First, however, I will drop you a line to say that my plans have come to anchor and I have decided on coming back with William.[735] I shall look for him every day now till he comes. I wish he would let Mrs. Nott[736] know when you return for I am very anxious to make her a visit and she said I must tell her beforehand. I suspect I have got so lazy since I have been gone that I shan't be worth much, but I take it you will be a little surprised to see how well I am. I have grown quite fat upon it and fully intend to keep it up when I come back.

I have seen Mr. Willis[737] several times[738] since I wrote Anna M.[739] and have at last succeeded in convincing him that Utica is the best place for me, certainly while the warm weather lasts. Graham[740] however would'nt [sic] be convinced. He is as obstinate as I imagined. Willis has changed his mind with regard to going abroad and is to sail in four or five weeks with his little Imogen. He can't be contented till she is with her mother's friends. He will stay six months or a year now, but he will not break off his connection with the *Mirror*. I rather think he never will live in this country much more. He is not gloomy as I was afraid—is quite cheerful, indeed, particularly when there are several present, but his voice fails him

---

[734] Sophia Taylor. See the letter to Emily E. Chubbuck of Alfred Taylor dated April 6, 1845, and the letter of Sophia Taylor dated May 7, 1845.

[735] William Stewart Anable was the son of Joseph and Alma Sheldon Anable. He was traveling from Utica to New York City and it had been hoped Emily could return with him.

[736] Urania Sheldon Nott—a mentor, advisor, and friend to Emily—was the literary principal of the Utica Female Academy when Emily arrived in October 1840. In late summer of 1842 Urania married Eliphalet Nott, the president of Union College in Schenectady NY.

[737] Nathaniel Parker (N. P.) Willis was the editor of *New Mirror*, the magazine that catapulted Emily into literary fame. Within a few months of Emily's departure for Burmah, Willis was married to the ward of a United States senator; in one of the letters to Emily from her friends, it is stated that his new bride had significant wealth. The *New Mirror* went out as Willis was returning to the United States, and he established another publication with General Morris.

[738] At this same time Emily told her sister Catharine that she had seen Willis five times since arriving in New York, and later she would say that they were together almost every day that she was there.

[739] Anna Maria Anable was the niece of the Urania and Cynthia Sheldon, the daughter of Joseph and Alma Sheldon Anable; she was Emily's closest friend at the Utica Female Academy.

[740] George Graham, editor of *Graham's Magazine*, took an interest in Emily Chubbuck as Fanny Forester and paid her with the unheard of sum of five dollars a page. The Grahams had accompanied Emily on the trip from Philadelphia to New York City.

when he speaks of his wife. He says he never knew her to have a wrong feeling or express an improper tho't [sic]—as far as he could be a judge of perfection she was *perfect*. He told me a story which I dare say you have heard, about his shopping with a lady in Broadway this spring (I say I presume you have heard it because you seem to have been devoured with all the gossip tho' I first learned it from him.)[741] and spoke bitterly enough of the inquisition that men established over a poor brother man because he was "stricken of God." He said men might say of him what they chose—thrusts of that kind were all he ever felt. I got a full account Saturday of the affair of Miss Inman. *She* was anything but *artless*. She was privately married before she went to Europe to a bad worthless fellow here in N. Y. and since her return the marriage has been acknowledged and she is living with him.[742] I will give you the particulars when I come home. The "Blidgemses"[743] too we have had over the coals and it is very agreeable to have an opportunity of hearing two versions of a story. *I don't blame him one bit for writing the take off.* He is going to publish it in his new book. He had Miss Kate Bridgen [sic] (Kate I believe her name is) *in his lap* last week. It is the best joke I have heard lately. Godey[744] applied to Willis last week to engage me as contributor to his magazine—so you see I shall have work enough if I can only do it. Graham offered Willis $2500 a year if he would write him letters from abroad and give up the *Mirror*. I wish he would make me the offer. I think Anna Maria and I could both live on that and abandon the concert scheme.

I have'nt seen [sic] Mr. Wilmarth's[745] folks since I wrote, for it has rained all the time. Neither have I called on Mary Colgate,[746] but intend to do it.

---

[741] Emily and Cynthia Sheldon had a precious relationship, one that emerged out of Sheldon's recognition of Emily's ability and her interest in encouraging that genius. This statement to Cynthia has a bit of an edge to it, and its tone is extremely rare on those occasions when Emily addressed Sheldon. That she defends Willis so adamantly, and ridicules his accusers, would certainly be a statement of the depth of her feelings. The day before, on May 18, she had written to her sister Catharine that she was "dead in love with him, he is so handsome, so good."

[742] Here Emily is reciting accusations about Willis that have been written to her in the correspondence, and which have come to her in conversations. On April 15, 1845, Anna Maria Anable had written: "Laura Savoys who knows the Inmans well says there is no doubt of it. She says he tried to seduce the Inmans' daughter—was writing to her and contriving to see her continually and she got so bewitched, her father was obliged to take her to Europe."

[743] There is an interesting reference in an April 16, 1845 letter to a book that seems to have been written by N. P. Willis. Anna Maria was speaking about someone's opinion of N. P. Willis and she says that this person (Augusta Crafts) thought N. P. Willis unlikable, though "not totally heartless and she believes he loved his wife—she took the Blidgims down with her to read, but says it won't alter her opinion much." We assume that this piece about the Blidgims should show Willis in a good light. We note that a Google search does not turn up any such work, even when referenced to N. P. Willis.

In line with this, in a March 5, 1845 letter, Anna Maria said: "Augusta Crafts was here last evening—more agreeable than some—though she despises Willis—she told us all about that Blidgims affair and promised to send the story down for us to read."
See vol. 1, "Cast of Characters," s.v. "Blidgims." Also vol. 1: Timeline—Blidgims

[744] Louis A. Godey, the founder and publisher of *Godey's Lady's Book*, a magazine that combined poetry, prose, and beautiful engravings, many of them about fashion.

[745] Mr. and Mrs. John Wilmarth. There are frequent mentions of the Wilmarths' home and hospitality.

[746] This is either the wife or the daughter of William Colgate, the prominent industrialist and manufacturer, but probably the daughter.

Anna Maria's last letters have'nt [sic] been overstocked with news so I don't know exactly what you are about, but I conclude you are going on pretty much after the old sort only more pupils. I wish you could save her a paper with the report.[747] I want to send it to Graham. Mr. Robarts[748] carried off the one I reserved for the purpose, and Mr. G.[749] spoke of a niece he should like to send if she could be persuaded to go so far from home. I wish I knew what day Wm. would be here. The term will be almost half out by the time I get back. It scares me when I think how much time I have wasted—but then it has done me a deal of good.

We are to spend the day at Mrs. Wilmarth's and want to go early so (as I have a letter to write to Kate[750] this morning) I will reserve my news till I may communicate it verbally—though I have written so often and such long letters that I shall have but little to tell. Give my very best love to grandpa, grandma,[751] Mrs. Anable,[752] the "girls" and the "young ladies"—everybody that you know cares for it, for indeed I do love you all very much. I have been just as happy as I could be here, but notwithstanding all that, I shall be more delighted than I can tell to get back again.

My heart goes pit-a-pat at the thought of it. And it will be very soon now. Till then and ever believe me

Yours most affectionately,

Emily

Source: Hanna family files.

Cynthia Sheldon to Emily E. Chubbuck, May 20, 1845

Dear Emily

William[753] leaves early in the morning and unexpectedly to me too—or I might have inflicted some four pages upon you at this time—so you tell Mr. W.[754] I have the most influence over you of any one [sic]. That's a queer fancy—it could only

---

[747] The report was an evaluation of the Utica Female Academy published by the *Baptist Register*.

[748] Mr. and Mrs. W. S. Robarts of Philadelphia, friends of the Sheldon and Anable families. In 1848, their daughter would attend the Misses Anable's School. Adoniram Judson was to stay with them when he was in Philadelphia.

[749] Rev. A. D. Gillette; Emily had stayed with the Gillette family while in Philadelphia, or George Graham.

[750] Sarah Catharine ("Kate," "Kit," or "Kitty") Chubbuck, Emily's older sister, born October 25, 1816.

[751] Deacon Asa and Isabell Low Sheldon, parents of Cynthia Sheldon, Urania Sheldon Nott, and Alma Sheldon Anable.

[752] Alma Sheldon Anable, sister of Cynthia Sheldon and Urania Sheldon Nott and married to Joseph Hubbell Anable.

[753] William Stewart Anable was the son of Joseph and Alma Sheldon Anable. From previous letters we know that William will be traveling to New York City, and there was a hope that Emily would return to Utica with him. On May 19, Emily had written to Sheldon that she would return with William, but obviously Sheldon had not yet received that letter.

[754] Nathaniel Parker (N. P.) Willis was the editor of *New Mirror*, the magazine that catapulted Emily into literary fame. He became a friend, mentor, and eventually a suitor. It is obvious from this letter that Miss Cynthia Sheldon does not approve of Willis or of the fact that Emily is agreeing to see him in New York.

have been momentary—for I am quite certain my girl you have got in a whirl which carried you in a maze above terra firma—but not to the throne of grace as often as in time of less temptation; is it not so right Mr. W. to have presumed to make you a Sunday visit, or did I mistake, when Anna M. read me your letter. I have made no comment to anyone, only that was the impression I got at the time—a different visitor would give a different impression—but he is professionally a man of the world, and should know his bounds—you know Emily I am not fastidious where the requirements of Christian obligations are out of the question.[755]

Heaven grant you wisdom, and strong confidence in God, that your every step may prove for your own good and his glory—we are more anxious about Harriet[756] than you can imagine (I hope you can see Mary Adams[757]) if she has closed the business with Dan in the right way—and on the principle of right I am heartily glad of it—but the dear girl has evidently been in such a backslidden state for a long time I tremble for her earthly happiness now—nothing I now desire so much as having her home very soon—do not think hard of one for the hints in the onset. There truly is danger when we see it not—shattered health is nothing in comparison to losing sweet intercourse with our *Saviour friend*.[758]

Written in the right margin of the address page: "I hope you will conclude to come with William without something there proposes more quietude—than you have had lately—It is a question which I will not settle whether it would be best for you to resume…"

Written in the left margin of the address page: "…any school duties this summer or not—that must rest entirely with yourself—only be assured my girl that whatever is for your best good there is no one more anxious than your truly attached friend. C."

Source: American Baptist Historical Society, AJ 26, no. 1263.

---

[755] On April 28, 1845, Emily had written to Anna Maria that she did not think she would stop in New York City to visit with N. P. Willis as she had previously planned. On May 2, Cynthia Sheldon wrote to say how much this decision of Emily's pleased her. "One part of your letter delighted me more than I can tell—your decision about not seeing Willis in N. York—Many tongues here would be bridled by a knowledge of having nothing to talk about." Here again in this paragraph Sheldon makes her feelings known. Emily has been existing in a world above "terra firma"—she has been absent "the throne of grace"—and then above all, she had allowed Willis to visit with her on a Sunday. Earlier, Sheldon had said that she would have liked to have written a four page letter; it just may be that Emily was fortunate that Sheldon did not have sufficient time for such a missive!

[756] Harriet ("Hatty," "Hattie," or "Hat") Anable, one of the five Anable sisters. She had been teaching in a private residence in the New Orleans area. Hatty had periods of illness. Again, Miss Sheldon's comments about Hatty reveal a stern, judgementmental side.

[757] Mary Adams, a friend of Emily's while at the Utica Female Academy. She lived in New Orleans, but would be in New York City on her way back to Utica.

[758] This paragraph is a wonderful example of Cynthia Sheldon's deeply held religious feelings and expectations, and the judgments to arise from them.

Nathaniel Parker Willis to Emily E. Chubbuck,[759] May 30, 1845

My dear Emily

I shall surprise you with this sudden adieu, but I am off for England, setting sail in the *Britannia* from Boston on Sunday. This at least is my present design. I have ten times as much to do as is possible before being ready, but I send you this line, and will repeat my farewells from the other side of the water. I have not yet recovered from my two surprises—first your freezing of me, and then your leaving[760] me just as I had begun to feel perfectly acquainted with you—but I *exhort* you to *heighten your opinion of yourself*. Feel and act as if you were the superior creature that you are, and so brighten existence about you. Above all, don't submit to any undervaluation. I saw Mr. Cha's Kirkland[761] last evening and told him of what you could be made, and he expressed the strongest admiration of you and a determination to make his wife draw you out. So, dear Emily, be *cordial* to these people, and use them as friends.

Now God bless you—for I have not a minute more to write. Send your letters to Morris.[762]

Believe me faithfully & affectionately

Yours

N. P. W.

Source: Hanna family files.

---

[759] Written on the address page in the handwriting of Emily E. Chubbuck: "N. P. Willis Esq. 26. May 31, 1845."

[760] On May 18, 1845, Emily had written to her sister Catharine that she had been with Willis five times. On June 2, Emily wrote to Mrs. Hannah Gillette that she had been with Willis almost every day when she was in New York.

[761] There are three Kirkland families in the correspondence. First is William Kirkland of New York City; of this family N. P. Willis had said on February 5, 1845: "she was "my oldest female friend Mrs. Wm. Kirkland (who has been a sister to me for 16 years)." On January 2, 1847, Anna Maria Anable wrote that this Kirkland had drowned in a tragic accident about six week prior to her letter. In November 1846 she mentioned to Emily that Mrs. Kirkland hoped that she would visit with her when she passed through New York City on her way to Philadelphia.

Secondly, there is a mention of a Charles Kirkland family. We believe that they lived in Utica, and that they had two daughters Julia and Amelia, who are mentioned in some of the April, 1845 letters of Anna Maria Anable to Emily E. Chubbuck.

A third reference is to Mrs. Kirkland, the mother of William Kirkland; she was terribly distressed at the time of his death because he had recently accepted Unitarian principles. We believe that she lived in Utica.

[762] George P. "General" Morris, was N. P. Willis's partner at the *New Mirror* and a prominent literary figure in New York and Philadelphia.

Nathanial Parker Willis to Emily E. Chubbuck,[763] June 1, 1845—Boston

My dearest friend,

I was taken ill on getting here and instead of writing to you I had to go to bed under the care of a physician. You will forgive me. I am too ill to do aught but go on board, one hour from this. The sea will set me up. Write to me by Gen. Morris.[764]

God bless you

Ever yours faithfully

N. P. Willis

Source: Hanna family files.

Emily E. Chubbuck to Urania Sheldon Nott, June 6, 1845[765]—Utica

My Very Dear Friend,

Your note to Anna Maria[766] and myself was most gratefully received (on my part, at least), because it gives evidence of your kind interest.[767] Do you know what a strong light it throws on your opinion of myself, my weakness, etc.? I really thought that I stood higher with you; but I find it is one of the most difficult things in the world to find out precisely how "others see us." Now if I write you very frankly, and even egotistically, I know you will forgive me; because this is a subject that my friends *must* understand, if they would not make me very uncomfortable.

You are afraid that I will grow vain—or rather you think I am so; for people never caution without supposed cause. I have a great deal of pride;—more than you ever thought, because you have always been so very kind to me that it has never been called out in your presence. I have some vanity; but unless I am seriously mistaken in my estimate of my own character (and I have scrutinized it more severely than you could), I have less, rather than more, than the generality of women. Now what cause have I given you to believe that I was puffed up by

---

[763] Written on the address page in the handwriting of Emily E. Chubbuck: "N. P. Willis Esq. No. 27. June 8, 1845."

[764] George P. "General" Morris, was N. P. Willis's partner at the *New Mirror* and a prominent literary figure in New York and Philadelphia.

[765] This lengthy letter to Urania Sheldon Nott, written carefully, soberly, and thoughtfully, is an incredible letter. It shows a high degree of maturity on Emily's part, a very strong self-awareness of who she is, what she has become, and how that transition took place through will power and hard work. It gives a clear picture as to where Emily is at this time in her life. Over the years, Emily wrote several such letters, and in each instance, they define her.

[766] Anna Maria Anable was the niece of the Urania and Cynthia Sheldon, the daughter of Joseph and Alma Sheldon Anable; she was Emily's closest friend at the Utica Female Academy.

[767] One such letter from Urania Sheldon Nott is her letter of September 18, 1844 to both Anna Maria Anable and Emily. We infer from this letter of Emily's six months later that there were other letters from Urania Sheldon Nott as well. Nott responded to this letter on June 11, 1845.

praises? Do I look pleased with a compliment? I am pleased particularly when I am conscious of deserving it, and so willing to share my gratification with others that I act as I feel. This (the pleasure) is human nature, and if I pretended to rise above it I should be a hypocrite.

My life, from my cradle, has been full of changes. Without one of my own kindred to assist me, I have struggled with almost every kind of difficulty up to the present moment. Even *you can not* [sic] dream of half that I have borne. Heaven knows, enough to make me humble. Within the last year—one short year—I have gained for myself a position which others have been all their lives in attaining, and I have a right to be proud of it. You may tell me it is a small thing to be a magazine writer. So it is. But it is not a small thing for a woman, thrown upon her own resources, and standing entirely alone, to be able to command respect from every body [sic], rising by her own individual efforts above the accidents of fortune. Does all this sound like boasting? I only want to prove to you that I understand my ground, and take too comprehensive a view of it to have my heart set a fluttering by every swing of Mr. Nobody's censer. I know precisely what my reputation is worth to me, for I have measured it carefully; and I know, too, what all these silly compliments are worth. If such a man as Bryant[768] praises me (I believe he has had the bad taste to set me before Miss S—), I suppose that he thinks what he says; still it is only *the opinion of one man*. If a hundred other people echo the praise, I know that they take it on trust; so the compliment is in reality to Bryant, not to me. These newspaper puffs are accidental and ephemeral things, and while I will not despise them, because in their way they are an advantage to me, do not, I beg of you, think that I am such a simpleton as to be "spoiled" by them. As to the attentions I have received since I have been gone, they have certainly put me a little more at ease with myself, but I do not believe that you will say they have been disadvantageous. In sober truth, Heaven has blessed me (as a balance for the romance which I am not going to disclaim) with a sort of mathematical genius, a dollar-and-cent way of estimating things, which, when necessary, takes the poetry out of them in a twinkling. Will you not give me credit for some *common sense* at bottom? Think of all the things that I have to occupy my mind: the serious duties of life; the cares which nobody can share with me, and which I think about none the less for not always talking of them. Think of these, and see if I have any time to spare to vanity. Have I ever, my dear Mrs. Nott, managed my own affairs indiscreetly, that you should fear that, with more experience to guide me, I will do it now? Do I look or act like a vain woman? Do I try to make a great show and attract attention to myself? Do I put myself forward in society? I intend to take a little different position from what I have, for I see that people expect it of me, and my diffidence and disposition to keep

---

[768] William Cullen Bryant. Many of Bryant's works were in the same publications that used Emily's stories.

out of sight have obtained for me the reputation of being cold-hearted and indifferent. Indeed, I am not a little child, to go into ecstacies [sic] at every pretty thing that is said to me, and as for romance, I have not half so much as when you first knew me. It is my *trade* now, and much less in my *heart* than then. As for talking, I must talk to my room-mates of the things that I think about, and with others I will try to use all needful discretion. If you hear of any thing [sic] unwisely said or done on my part, please suspend judgment until you know the wherefore. Things always have two sides. I have been treated by some persons most generously, and it would be the height of ingratitude in me to refuse them the slight tribute of a kind word. It is not in my nature to do it, and I do not believe that even the coldest kind of policy requires it. Trust me, my dear Mrs. Nott, I can be discreet, and will…. I am governed by a sense *of right* in these things, though I seem to have lost the confidence of some of my friends to such a degree, that I should hardly get credit for any thing [sic] better than vanity—or, at least, fancy.

I should like much to have a long talk with you, for there are, of course, many things which I can not [sic] put into a letter. Indeed, it seems to me that I have said nothing as I meant to say it; but I hope to see you before long. Let me entreat you, however, once for all, never to be for a moment troubled about all this fol-de-rol stuff's turning my brain. Were you in my place, you would see it with different eyes from what you do. Things very pretty to look at become smoke when you touch them. Now, *I am touching* them, and I laugh to find what painted bits of butterflies' wings might have seemed wondrously attractive, if, half a dozen years ago, I could have foreseen that it was to be my lot to catch them. "Distance," you know, "lends enchantment." One thing more I wish to say. I beg of you not to be annoyed on my account, if you hear my literary merits spoken of lightly. It is what I ought to expect, and I am fully prepared for it. I hope those who take an interest in me will be prepared too, for, of course, I can not [sic] please every body [sic].

I more than half suspect that I have spoiled my own case by telling you so frankly my opinion of myself while disclaiming undue vanity; but, surely, a sober consciousness of one's own capabilities is the surest safeguard against all vagaries of fancy. Forgive my long, tedious letter. Forgive me, also, if I have written too seriously and earnestly, for really I could not bear to be so misunderstood by you. I do not expect to be appreciated by the multitude, and do not care to be; but if I lose the confidence of my friends, I shall be a forlorn thing indeed. Please write me a line to say that my plainness has not offended you, and believe me, my dear Mrs. Nott, your truly attached friend, now and ever,

Emily

P. S. Anna Maria and I "chum" it together beautifully, and the room is as pleasant as pleasant as can be. It lacks only its old occupant to make it as agreeable as in the palmist days. When can you come and see it? Dear Mrs. Nott, do not think, from what I have written, that I am ungrateful for your generous interest, or impatient under your advice. If you did not advise me, I should think that you did not love me any more [sic]; and what I have written has been from a sense of justice to you as well as to myself. You ought to know me, for I owe to you a great deal of care and kindness.

Source: A. C. Kendrick, *The Life and Letters of Mrs. Emily C. Judson*, 128–31.

Emily E. Chubbuck to her "Cousin 'Bel'"—Printed in the *New Mirror*, June 1845[769]

My Belle-Cousin—There are people in the world who mark the sun's cycles on a stick, counting them-selves graveward, as aunt Margery counted my cups of milk in days of yore by the chalk-marks above the shelf. You give grand birth-day parties, and have troops of friends rejoicing that a new leaf is turned over in your destiny— as though the new leaf were always sure to be brighter than the old, 'Bel'. In imitation of you and the savages, I too would fain tie a knot in my thread of life, lest it should slip through my fingers unheeded. So here is a notch in my stick—a little ink-mark to show that I have closed a paragraph, and, with almost the trembling uncertainty of a year ago, am about commencing another.

A year ago! Do you recollect it, 'Bel'? Do you remember how you urged my foot into this new path, and steadied it there, and pointed out the future, before I knew how ready the stars are to welcome the faintest glimmer that seems to have any of their own fire about it? Do you remember how you cheered and prophesied—and what a bright, long, unbroken path of light your finger traced for me; till, with the feelings of a newly-fledged bird, I lifted my wings and flew—not heavenward, true, but so near the earth as never to lose the smell of violets on it. There is less danger in flying near the sod, 'Bella, for a fall would only treat me to a bath of dew and perfume—my own tears and your pity—whereas, if I only attempt to play sky-lark, some marksman might mistake me for his target.

The children have made a crown for me to-day—wet violets with most graceful tassels of the soft-breathed tiarella—frail things enough to have an inner weight of meaning, which makes them lie more heavily against my brow than I care to have things press upon it just at this moment. I remonstrated at first, but chil-

[769] This article was published on the one year anniversary of Emily's initial letter to N. P. Willis, the editor of the *New Mirror*, a letter which, with the encouragement of Willis, catapulted Emily into literary fame. See June 8, 1844, and June 29, 1844.

dren have a Cassandra-like vision, and can discover truth, invisible to eyes dimmed by worldly wisdom, and so I have let them have their own way, and donned the emblematic wreath uncomplainingly.

To the world, I am just one year old to-day. To you—do you ever think, 'Bel', whether I am ten, or four times ten? "The heart has its changing seasons," somebody has said; but it was, I am sure, a rhymester, not a poet. Poets sing *truth*, and there is no truth in that. True, there are autumn hearts, and winter hearts, and fresh, bright, gladsome spring hearts, always swelling with young buds, and dancing to bird-music; the first wore the yellow leaves for their swaddling-clothes—the last will claim the fresh living green for a pall, and go to the grave with a circlet of dewdrops about them. My season is that of the roses—glad, warm, glorious—the season of soft indolent airs, and heavy perfumes; and do you think my roses can fade? Ah-, 'Bel'! cheek-roses are very pretty things, but a single day may take them from us—heart-roses wither never.

So many lines, 'Bel', have I wasted on an incontrovertible fact, that though you and I

> "—should live to be
> The last leaf on the tree,
> In the spring,"

being spring leaves, and not autumn ones, we would yet nod and whisper to the breezes, and flaunt in the face of the sky with all the impudence of the days that have been. Talk of hearts changing! Why, what in the wide world is there to induce change? Tears only freshen them, and trials bring out clusters of fragrant, beautiful buds, that otherwise would have waited the sun and dews of heaven. But I must put the finis to that chapter.

The truth is, brightest *cusina mia*, I write with one side of my heart so far from the other, that how the meeting point is managed, is as great a mystery as the difference in velocity between the outer and inner rim of a wheel used to be, in the days when my eyes needed to be reset, after listening to the wondrous wonders in physics. I have somehow incurred the doom of Pontheus, on this bright morning of my literary birth-day—the mystifier of a double sight. Now, you are my Thebes, as ever; now, the glorious city lies away in the far-off future, and I feast my eyes on the glitter of its spires and minarets, and snuff the perfumes of its waving censers. The flutter of a rose-leaf sends me hither, and yon, my heart, one side of it, at least, bounding forward, then turning back lovingly, and so I keep up the race between the present and the future—you and the winsome damsel, men have named Hope. It vexes me—this propensity to be constantly looking into the future, when the present has a heartfull for us; but I console myself with the knowledge that I am in the majority. Everybody hopes, and hopes, and wishes for next week, and next month, and next year—all shaking the sands out recklessly from the scantily filled glass, and wishing that the orifice were larger, that they might grasp a handful at once; until the last is ready to drop. But they make no haste to part with that last one, 'Bel'! They would beat the one grain into a thousand particles, and have them doled out, a groan tacked to each, to retard its falling. Poor, foolish humans!

But I claim no monopoly of wisdom—I, too, have a meteor in the distance. So adieu, *ma belle-cousine*, while I rest my forehead here, where June has spread out a gorgeous pillow of roses, and dream. If my dreams ever become real, I shall enjoy them twice—live two lives—if not, I shall lose only the least attractive half. So I to my dreaming, and you, dear 'Bel', to whatever makes you happiest. *Au revoir.*

Fanny Forester.

Source: Fanny Forester, *Trippings in Author-land*, 236–39.

Emily E. Chubbuck in *Trippings in Author-land*, June 17, 1845[770]

Preface

In presenting the labours of the past year, to a public which I, of all others, have a right to term *generous*, I have only to ask the same kind consideration for them collectively and alone, that they may, heretofore, have owed in part to their surroundings. A preface is usually an introduction or an apology for intrusion; and I scarce feel it necessary, since I am only sending my brain-children out among my *friends*, confident that though their faults may not pass unnoticed, they will be treated with the tenderness usually shown to the *unintentional* offender. It may not be amiss, however, to give some explanation concerning them.

About a year ago, a girl sat down in her own quiet little room, and, for very idleness, without object and without a plan, produced a letter, which the next week, found its way into the *New York Mirror*.[749] It was the first letter in this collec-

---

[770] This is the preface to *Trippings in Author-land*, a compilation of Emily Chubbuck's (Fanny Forester's) writings from the previous year. The book was published in November 1845. Towards the end of December, the Reverend Abram Dunn Gillette, pastor of the Eleventh Baptist Church of Philadelphia, representing Philadelphia Baptists, took the train to Boston to bring back Dr. Adoniram Judson, missionary to Burmah, for meetings in the Philadelphia area. As the train was delayed, the Reverend Gillette presented a copy of *Trippings in Author-land* to Dr. Judson for his amusement, to fill up the time of delays on a boring train ride. Thinking of having a Memoir written of the life of Sarah Hall Boardman Judson, Adoniram Judson's second wife, who had died on the return trip to America, Adoniram Judson asked if he could meet the author, and the Reverend Gillette set up the meeting for Christmas Day 1845. The rest, as they say, is history!

[749] See the *New Mirror* letters under the dates June 8, 1844, and June 29, 1844.

tion; and Mr. Willis,[771] one of the editors, after various speculations concerning the author, added—

"Well—we give in!—*On condition* that you are under twenty-five, and that you will wear a rose (recognizably) in your bodice the first day you appear in Broadway with the hat and 'balzarine,' we will pay the bills. Write us, thereafter, a sketch of 'Bel' and yourself, as cleverly done as this letter, and you may 'snuggle down' on the sofa, and consider us paid, and the public charmed with you."

A reply was given by way of carrying out the frolic still farther, accompanied by the sketch of "The Cousins," which appeared in the *Mirror* immediately after. These met with such a kind reception, that the pen became a more familiar thing that formerly in those fingers, and so, behold upon them an indelible ink-mark.

To the gentle courtesy and well-tried forbearance of former friends and readers, these labours, of a single happy year, are confidently entrusted, by the novice hand of the would-be artist.

Fanny Forester

Horace Binney Wallace—writing on Fanny Forester,[772] June 1845[773]

She possesses many talents; and an assemblage of lesser accomplishments, which in her seem to be so genuine and instinctive, that they might almost be mistaken for natural talents. The movements of her mind have a quiet, soft brightness that seems to shine for itself rather than for others, and to be spontaneous more than exerted; glowing, apparently without design, and almost in despite of consciousness. Her powers of reasoning are strong; her feelings prompt and abounding; her sense of humor quick and various—but these and other faculties are subordinated in their exercise to a *delicacy* of character and taste, ethereal almost in sensibility, and timorous, even painfully, of every offense against refinement,—the deepest surest fascination that can belong to a woman; beautiful in the errors it may lead to, and most enchanting perhaps when it is most in excess; whose power is as enduring as the pleasure which it imparts is pure and exquisite. But there are secondary qualities, going rather to the manner, than to the nature or degree of that capacity which we desire to define as constituting a great and splendid faculty in this gentle and modest person. We regard her as possessing talents for *narrative* of a very high and rare order—talents which place her in the front rank of writers of dramatic fiction on either side of the water....

---

[771] Nathaniel Parker (N. P.) Willis was the editor of *New Mirror*, the magazine that catapulted Emily into literary fame. He became a friend, mentor, and eventually a suitor.

[772] Fanny Forester, Emily Chubbuck's *nom de plume*.

[773] This appeared in his magazine "Literary Criticisms"—it is written about Fanny Forester.

We are desirous to see the fine and varied faculties which this lady unquestionably possesses exerted upon some extensive and sustained work of fiction upon which all her powers may be fully concentrated and tested. She lingers below her destiny in being contented with even the greatest popularity; the native and true atmosphere of her renown is in the regions of fame

Source: A. C. Kendrick, *The Life and Letters of Mrs. Emily C. Judson*, 137

Letters

—⚎—

July - December 1845

Emily E. Chubbuck to Hannah Gillette,[1] July 2, 1845—Utica

My Dear Mrs. Gillette,—

I should have written you before, but I really did not believe my letter would be worth eighteen pence; and so I have waited to "patronize" the new postage law. I hope you will follow this most laudable example far enough to write me on the day that you receive this. Will you? May I hear from you very, very soon?

I had a delightful time at Brooklyn. Spent two weeks there, and saw my good friend W——[2] nearly every day.[3] I like him even better than I anticipated; he is, however, any thing [sic] but happy.[4] He sailed for Europe just a week[5] after I left. I wish you had been along, for there were a thousand little things happening every day, very pleasant to enjoy, but scarce worth detailing, or at least writing down.

I shall claim your promise to let me come and live with you next winter, provided I do not go where it is still warmer.[6] I have some anticipation of going where the oranges grow, and they have roses in winter time [sic]. Seriously, I talk somewhat of a trip to Italy this fall.[7] Mr. L., our consul to Genoa, is now here and will return in a few months with his family, and I entertain the idea of accompanying them. Would it not be quite an expedition for me? The matter, however, is quite doubtful yet, though I certainly shall not remain in this cold climate.

The pleasant time that I spent with you I shall not soon forget. I only wish that the whole could be repeated. Is my little husband married again, or does he remain constant? Tell him that when I come back from Italy I think we shall be about big enough to commence house-keeping. Kiss all the little fellows for me, and tell

---

[1] While she was in Philadelphia, Emily had stayed with the Reverend and Mrs. Gillette and their family, from March 29 through May 9, or six weeks. As this letter is from A. C. Kendrick, *The Life and Letters of Mrs. Emily C. Judson*, we know that it is only fragments of the original.

[2] Nathaniel Parker (N. P.) Willis, along with George "General" Morris, was the editor of the *New Mirror*, a prominent literary magazine in New York. His "discovery" of Emily in the June 8, 1844 edition of the *New Mirror* catapulted her into literary fame and enabled her to command the highest prices for her articles and stories from the major magazines of that period. It was to begin a new and glorious chapter in her life. He was to become over the next two years her friend—her mentor—her confidant. His black-bordered letter of March 21, 1846, made it abundantly clear that her engagement to Adoniram Judson had come as a "death blow," and that he had expected to marry Emily upon his return that month from England. He later returned several of her letters to Emily to demonstrate to her, lest she had forgotten, why he had felt right in that expectation. In vol. 1 there is a timeline which presents in some detail the substance of their developing relationship, all from the letters which Willis had written to Emily. When she received her letters back from Willis, she had destroyed them, feeling that they would cast a negative shadow on her life, and because of that, the life and ministry of Adoniram Judson.

[3] Emily had written to Cynthia Sheldon on May 19 telling her that she had seen Willis several times. On the May 18 she told her sister Catherine that she had see Willis at least five times. Now she intimates that she had seen him perhaps as much as a dozen times—almost every day over two weeks.

[4] Willis had lost his wife unexpectedly towards the end of March, and several of his letters to Emily in April and early May were filled with the pain that such a loss will bring.

[5] N. P. Willis sailed from Boston on June 1, 1845.

[6] Emily was to arrive in Philadelphia around the first of November, and stay through February 17.

[7] This was given very serious consideration by Emily, and in the end it was her frail health that kept her home. George Graham, of *Graham's Magazine*, had offered to pay her as a correspondent if she would write letters back to be published in the Magazine.

them that Cousin Emily would cry her two eyes out if they should forget her… All unite in sending love, and please accept for yourself an extra share from

Yours very sincerely and affectionately,

E. E. C.

Source: A. C. Kendrick, *The Life and Letters of Mrs. Emily C. Judson*, 132–33.

Emily E. Chubbuck to J. Walker Chubbuck, July 2, 1845—Utica

My very dear brother,

It is a long time since I have written you, but when I come to tell you the reason why you will not scold me a bit. You will see by the magazines that, as *Fanny Forester*,[8] I have had both hands full, but that is not more than half I have done when you take my school duties into the account. But worse still, last December I was taken with an illness which made me quite useless all winter. As soon as the spring opened I took a *health tour to Philadelphia*, spent five or six weeks there, came back *to Brooklyn* and spent a fortnight[9] and then came up to Utica about six weeks ago. I have been home to Hamilton and spent a week since I came back. Mother's[10] health is miserable and father's[11] not particularly good. You would find that the years you have been away have made a great deal of difference in them—mother particularly is all broken down. Kate[12] is *pretty fat and healthy*, and perfectly crazy to see you. When *are* you coming? Mr. John Sheldon[13] wrote that you were to be here this summer. I hope you will come, for if you don't you will very likely never see me. *I think very seriously of a tour to Europe this fall*—shall spend the winter in

---

Emily was working on Anna Maria Anable to go with her. This plan coincided with the fact that N. P. Willis was also in Europe during this time.

[8] Fanny Forester, Emily Chubbuck's *nom de plume*.

[9] In Brooklyn, Emily stayed with Alfred and Sophia Taylor, and managed a number of visits and excursions with N. P. Willis—something almost every day, and then also did some calling on friends living in the city.

[10] Lavinia Richards Chubbuck, Emily's mother, was born June 1, 1875, in Goffstown NH, the eldest of thirteen children. She married Charles Chubbuck on November 17. 1805. They were the parents of seven children.

[11] Emily's father, Charles Chubbuck, was born at Bedford NH on March 3, 1780; he married Lavinia Richards in Goffstown NH on November 17, 1805, and together they had seven children. Though he held varying jobs over the years, Charles failed at many of them. Emily became a significant financial support for the family and purchased a home for them in fall 1842.

[12] Sarah Catharine ("Kate," "Kit," or "Kitty") Chubbuck, Emily's older sister by ten months. Outside of the two terms at the Utica Female Academy that Emily arranged for her, Catherine always lived with her parents in Hamilton NY. The letters indicate opportunities for marriage, but Catherine remained single. She later helped care for Henry and Edward Judson when, after their return from Burmah in fall 1851, they moved in with their "aunt" and "grandparents." She was remembered by her nephews as "a dear friend."

[13] See the May 7, 1845 letter from Anna Maria Anable to Emily E. Chubbuck about "Cousin John Sheldon" saying that Walker would be coming home for a visit. There was a John Sheldon who was a brother of Cynthia Sheldon, Urania Sheldon Nott, and Alma Sheldon Anable. Mentioned here is his son, also "John Sheldon"; he would be a cousin to Anna Maria Anable.

Italy and then travel north and return—I don't know when—perhaps never. Will you come?

If I go Mr. Graham[14] (of *Graham's magazine*) will send me and give me a salary for my letters—letters from abroad by Fanny Forester. I got to be quite a belle while I was gone—gallivanted about with Graham and R. W. Griswold[15] in Philadelphia, went to the opera with N. P. Willis,[16] and cut up all manner of shines. Willis, as you probably know, set sail for London about five weeks ago, a week after I left.[17] He is a noble fellow and the very best friend I have got. It is his present intention to spend a year abroad, when he will return to see to his *Mirror* business.

Wallace[18] was intending to write you when I left home; and I suppose he and Kate keep you informed of the proceedings of the old Morrisvillers and of things at home etc. So I shall not attempt to say anything about them. Wallace has a deal of talent but no application. He is too lazy for anything. Miss A. M. A. (my cousin 'Bel')[19] is lying on the bed beside me and she says I must tell you that she never will marry you in the world, just because you did'nt [sic] answer the letter that I wrote you while I was sick last winter. Did you get it? If you did'nt [sic] maybe you never heard what an elegant New Years' present I had. Mr. Willis sent me a magnificent

---

[14] George Graham was the editor of *Graham's Magazine*, one of the pre-eminent literary magazines of Emily's time. He took an interest in Emily Chubbuck as Fanny Forester; he mentored her, he published every piece of writing that she could submit to him, and for it all he remunerated her with the unheard of sum of five dollars a page. When, in April 1845, Emily was staying in Philadelphia with the Reverend and Mrs. A. D. Gillette, Mr. and Mrs. Graham were frequent visitors, often inviting Emily to tour parts of the city with them in their elegant carriage. That relationship picked up again when Emily returned to Philadelphia in fall 1845.

[15] Reverend Rufus W. Griswold was an ordained clergyman, noted anthropologist, editor, writer, and one of the distinguished literary figures of this period. Griswold originally showed up in an April 2, 1845 letter, in which Emily referred to him as a clergyman who had called upon her, a widower "crazy to get married."

[16] Nathaniel Parker (N. P.) Willis was the editor of *New Mirror*, the magazine that catapulted Emily into literary fame. He became a friend, mentor, and eventually a suitor.

[17] N. P. Willis sailed from Boston on June 1, 1845.

[18] Born January 1, 1824, William Wallace Chubbuck was six years younger than Emily. During these years of Emily's correspondence, Wallace was living at home, or near home, working at different occupations including printing, office work, and teaching. Emily wrote of him as very capable in many areas but seeming to lack ambition at times. He proved to be a strong support for the Chubbuck family over these years, and, at the time of her death in 1854, Wallace had become one of Emily's primary care-givers. After February 1854, he wrote, at her dictation, all of her letters because of her failing strength.

[19] Anna Maria Anable was the niece of the Urania and Cynthia Sheldon, the daughter of Joseph and Alma Sheldon Anable. Emily first met Anna Maria in fall 1840 when she went as a student to the Utica Female Academy; both Emily and Anna Maria were to become members of the faculty there. In these years Anna Maria became Emily's dearest friend, and the extensive correspondence between the two reflects sensitive, flirtatious spirits, and a deep intimacy. Emily was "Nemmy" to Anna Maria's "Ninny." In 1848, Anna Maria Anable, with the help of her extended family, moved to Philadelphia and started the Misses Anable's School in Philadelphia. At Emily's death in 1854, Anna Maria was given guardianship of Emily Frances Judson, daughter of Emily and Adoniram Judson.

painting from my story of Dora', done by Flagg.[20] It was valued in New York at two hundred dollars.

I think our folks are very comfortably situated now; and if I can manage to get the place paid for before I go away, I shall feel very contented. I owe some three hundred on it yet, and about one here on Kate's account.[21] Write immediately and tell me when you will come home. I don't know just when I shall start, for I expect go out [sic] with the consul to Genoa and I don't know when he sails. But you must come quick. My love to everybody who is kind to you there and ever and ever so much for yourself from

Your most aff. Sister

Emily

As I write under the new post office law, I don't feel bound to stuff my letter very full.

Source: Jerome Walker Chubbuck Collection, Wisconsin Historical Society Archives, Madison, WI.

Hannah Gillette to Emily E. Chubbuck,[22] July 5, 1845—Philadelphia

Dear Cousin Emily

We have just returned but a few moments from our "fourth of July" excursion this morning when we received your welcome letter—we had received a letter from Aunt Cynthia[23] a few days ago in which she had informed us of your late attack of difficulty in breathing—and although she remarked that you was better

---

[20] Dora' was a fictional character in one of Emily's stories that was released in fall 1844. The artist Flagg was very moved by the story, and N. P. Willis commissioned Flagg to do a portrait of her; details of the painting slowly came out. In a letter dated November 30, 1844, he said: "I am glad the idea of a picture pleases you. It is likely to be an interesting matter, for the artist, Flagg, whose mother relies on me as her son's guardian angel, told me today that he should take the opportunity to put his mother's head and mine on the same canvass! I am to be the "stranger," his mother the motherly guardian of Dora', and Dora' imaginative. If you were here, he should paint your head for Dora'. The subject is the putting the question to Dora' at as she sits in the window. Your imagination will easily see how it will look, but you must prepare to be disappointed and it will show you one very curious thing—how other people conceive of the scenes you describe." The painting was shipped in the Christmas Season and Anna Maria Anable wrote to Emily on December 30, 1844 that they had retrieved the painting from the express office. Apparently between the time he had received the painting and brought it to the express office, it had been on display, and he told Emily that thousands had seen and admired it.

[21] Emily had incurred two debts. The first debt was educational expense for her sister Catharine when, in fall 1841, she spent several terms taking classes at the Utica Female Academy, studying amongst other things, guitar and drawing. She was in Utica through March 1842, and then had returned a little over a year later to take a shorter course of study. Then, secondly, in the late summer 1842, Emily had purchased a home for her parents in the village of Hamilton NY, taking out a mortgage of four hundred dollars, to be paid at one hundred dollars a year.

[22] This letter has an addendum added by A. D. Gillette dated July 7, 1845.

[23] Cynthia Sheldon was in charge of the administrative and financial departments of the Utica Female Academy. After Cynthia's sister married and moved away, Cynthia assumed a larger leadership role at the academy. Active and well-known in Baptist circles, Cynthia became an important mentor, advisor, and friend to Emily until the time of Emily's death in 1854. Cynthia was the aunt of Emily's best friend, Anna Maria Anable, and addressed by most as "Aunt Cynthia." In 1848, Sheldon would move to Philadelphia to help Anable the startup of the Misses Anable's School.

[sic]—yet we feared that it might seriously retard your improvement in health. I am glad that you are able to recover your old trade of letter writing; I did not intend to wait longer for you, had not you written for I have in my hands the [ ]ful which you should have had when you were in Phi. But according to your own idea of *our sending* you the money—we as well as yourself were anxious to *patronize* the new postage law particularly as this would be a double letter; but for love! do you intend to increase your correspondence on account of this new law. Oh! [ ] poor *fingers* and *hands*, I am sure will ache—and ache again; I am sure you will have to send to Uncle Sam to put on an extra mail bag for Fanny Forester[24] letters. He will! Then I may hope to hear from you accordingly may I not! but oh dear—if you go to Italy—Italy[25]—I would be happy dear Fanny to perform my promises to you in the matter of next winter arrangements;[26] indeed I secretly or selfishly hope that you will conclude to stay a winter in this city—but—of course as to the comparison of climate there can be none; the southern clime is the one for you—and as to Italy? Who could refuse going if a good opportunity offered; of course if you go to far places we shall hear often from "Fanny Forester" or a Foreign Correspondent; I am glad you was pleased [sic] with Willis[27] for I became quite interested in him—and as to Hoffman[28] I am determined to see him. I shall go to the Custom house the first time I go to New Y. and think of you as you stealthily [ ] in [ ] from [ ] [ ] [ ].

Now dear Emily as to the great anticipated visit to Utica this summer I cannot reply; you may be sure that I am willing and anxious to go—I cannot imagine any thing [sic] so delightful as a trip of that sort but for some reason Mr. G. is not so anxious—he does not feel as though he leave a long time [sic] and he is intending

---

[24] Fanny Forester, Emily Chubbuck's *nom de plume*.

[25] George Graham of *Graham's Magazine* had offered to pay Emily's expenses for a European trip if she would send letters back to be published. In Emily's letter of July 2, 1845 she mentioned that the consul to Genoa was in Hamilton, and she could travel back to Italy with him. Her travel to Europe was also being encouraged by N. P. Willis. In the end, it was Emily's health that was to keep her from her trip.

[26] Emily had lived with the Gillettes for approximately six weeks in the spring 1845 when she had traveled to Philadelphia for her health. That fall, Emily was to stay with the Reverend and Mrs. Gillette from approximately November 1, 1845, until she left for home on February 17, 1846.

[27] Nathaniel Parker (N. P.) Willis was the editor of *New Mirror*, the magazine that catapulted Emily into literary fame. He became a friend, mentor, and eventually a suitor.

[28] Charles Fenno Hoffman was a prominent literary figure in Philadelphia and New York, who was well known in those literary circles as an adventurer, an editor, a poet, and a writer of exceptional talent. In fall 1843 he had written three letters to Emily Chubbuck addressed to "Laura Linden," for Emily had written to him under that name, asking his advice about love, fame and fortune. Only one of these letters is in the correspondence. Hoffman was not to learn of Emily's identity until spring 1845; in a letter we have dated April 7, 1845, he spoke of Laura having taken off her mask and revealing herself to him. There were four letters from Hoffman in this April period when Emily was in Philadelphia. There were another three in December 1845 when Emily again was in Philadelphia. See vol. 1, "Cast of Characters," s.v. "Hoffman, Charles Fenno"; and vol. 1, "Places, Events, Organizations, and Magazines," s.v. "Laura Letters." Anna Maria Anable frequently intimated in her letters that Emily was interested in "Hoffy" as a beau.

to visit with his brother a week or two, to get up a Memoir of his brother [ ].[29] I have said all I could in favor of Aunt Cynthia—and so do tell her for me that if we should not come she must scold *him*—should we come I could not think of bringing the "whole household" but only our little James[30]—he is quite well but looks thin.

I have enjoyed myself in Phil. thus far this summer in the way of pic-nic [sic] parties, and next week we are to have a boat-row, how I wish you were here to enjoy it; it is a club composed of the members of Dr. McDowel's choir or at least a number of them—fine young men, and by the bye those elegant [ ] [ ] to compose it [ ]! I have never had mine yet—[Note: Two thirds of this line is lost in the letter fold.] you come back.

Your little husband is constant—he talks much of you and thinks it hard that he should be separated from you.[31] Give much love to the Friends in Utica, and say to them how happy I should be to visit them this summer and as soon as Mr. G. determines he will let Cynthia know. We must blame him, for indeed I am half crazy to go; the friends here are well, and would send their love if they knew I was writing. But receive for yourself much affection and esteem from your friend

Hannah J. Gillette

Source: American Baptist Historical Society, AJ 24, no. 1199.

The Reverend Abram Dunn Gillette to Emily E. Chubbuck, July 7, 1845[32]

Dear Cousin Emily—

My pet wife has concluded to forgive you in the affair of the elopement but I think she retains a little wrath against me as she lay at my door *all* the reasons why we do not promise to visit you in Utica. I want much to come, and it is possible we may, but *reasons* exist for doubting.

I seem to hear you say, "I'll go to Hality [sic].

"Hang me if the thought don't burn me up."

---

[29] In an April 16, 1845 letter to her sister Catharine, Emily wrote: "G. has lost a brother since I came here. I suppose you know that Daniel Gillett [sic] died some weeks ago at Mobile. He had a consumption, and had gone south for his health. He left a wife and one child."

[30] James "Jemmy" Gillette, son of Hannah and A. D. Gillette. He had been critically ill when Emily arrived in Philadelphia on March 29, 1845. His recovery was precarious—improving one day—a very bad spell the next.

[31] See the letter of Emily E. Chubbuck to Mrs. Hannah Gillette dated July 2, 1845, where she asked, "Is my little husband married again, or does he remain constant? Tell him that when I come back from Italy I think we shall be about big enough to commence house-keeping."

[32] This letter was an addendum to the July 5, 1845 letter of Hannah Gillette to Emily. The "Monday" places it on July 7.

Written in the right margin of the address page: "I hope whatever is best for your health and happiness and usefulness will be done. We shall rejoice if it is the will of Providence, that you spend the winter with us—I never was more anxious to go any where than I am to visit Utica—this very summer. I want see you all and especially your Father[33] and Mother.[34] May I see them *once more?*"

Written in the left margin of the address page: "We will let you know at least a few days before if we can come. The *kiss*, I'll remember, fear not *me*. We will see Mr. Griswold[35] and make all right about the Book etc. Give my kind regards to Mr. Corey[36] and all the friends. Love to yourself and the Dear family. Miss C.[37] lays under great obligations by her urgent solicitation."

Yours truly

A. D. Gillette

Written in the bottom margin of the address page: "I enclose fifteen dollars 75 cents we will pay when we meet you."

Written in the bottom margin of the address page with the writing upside down from the writing above it: "It is now very warm here bef night yet the city is healthy. I want to attend if I go north Schenectady and Hamilton[38] commencements—I shall not be D. D. this year I fear never unless you ladies sue for me to *truth.*"

Source: American Baptist Historical Society, AJ 24, no. 1199.

---

[33] Charles Chubbuck, Emily's father. Though he held varying positions over the years, he failed at most of them. With the purchase of the house for them, Emily was to continue as a significant financial contributor to the support of the family.

[34] Lavinia Richards Chubbuck, Emily's mother, was born June 1, 1875, in Goffstown NH, the eldest of thirteen children. She married Charles Chubbuck on November 17. 1805. They were the parents of seven children.

[35] Reverend Rufus W. Griswold, an ordained clergyman and distinguished literary figure, had been one of Emily's suitors. Emily referred to him in a letter to Anna Maria Anable as a "widower," and "crazy to be married."

[36] Corey was the pastor of a Baptist church near the Utica Female Academy, and Sheldon and many of the girls from the academy worshiped there. In April 1844, he wrote to Emily expressing dismay that at a school program one of the girls had read a composition justifying dancing as exercise; he spoke of this as a roadblock to the salvation of many. Then on March 10, 1846, Emily indicated in a letter to Anna Maria that Corey had been very critical of her relationship and impending marriage to Adoniram Judson. Cynthia Sheldon wrote a number of times expressing Corey's regret and support, and in 1847 there were letters of reconciliation between Emily and Corey. In spring 1848, we learn that Corey's wife had died of consumption, her condition exacerbated by recent childbirth. She had left behind four children, the youngest a baby. Then in July 1849, Anna Maria Anable wrote of his impending marriage to Jane Backus, a good choice for this "rising man." Corey remained popular with the Sheldon-Anable families even after their move to Philadelphia in 1848. A March 2, 1852 letter from Charles B. Stout told of Corey's call to the Stanton Street Church in New York City, a call that Corey did not accept. Finally, in 1854, there was a pastoral letter from Corey to Emily on her illness and her possible death.

[37] Cynthia Sheldon was in charge of the administrative and financial departments of the Utica Female Academy and an important mentor, advisor, and friend to Emily.

[38] The Reverend Gillette had attended both the Hamilton Literary and Theological Institution in Hamilton NY, and Union College in Schenectady NY.

Emily E. Chubbuck to Catharine Chubbuck,[39] July 9, 1845—Utica

Dear Kitty,—

I was glad enough to get your letter I can assure you, for I had got almost crazy about mother.[40] **I thought you had concluded not to write any more [sic]. I am glad Mother has got Doct. Douglass for he will not do her harm if he don't [sic] good, and I think the homeopathick [sic] medicine will be good for her. The turnip stuff can't hurt her nor interfere with the other things if she don't [sic] put the gin in, and aunt C.**[41] **is anxious that she should try it. Grate up the turnip, put in loaf sugar and then pour on boiling water. I have had to use a great deal of it lately.** I am not able to write any yet, and think I shall not attempt it again until I come home in vacation. Then I intend to "put in." I have been making arrangements about getting my book published,[42] or rather have written **the General** (to Gen. Morris[43]) about **getting** (procuring) a publisher for me, and I shall want some of the stories that are in your hands as I am too stingy to buy the magazines over again. I want "The Bank Note," "The Peep within Doors,"[44] "Nickie Ben," "Two Nights in New Niederlandts," and "Grace Linden." I believe I have all the rest. I want you to cut them from the magazines and send them by the first opportunity. **You see it would cost me fourteen shillings to buy the Mags again.**

---

[39] We have two versions of this letter—the original as written by Emily E. Chubbuck, and the edited version published by Dr. A. C. Kendrick in his biography, *The Life and Letters of Mrs. Emily C. Judson*. Additions made by Dr. Kendrick we have placed in parentheses (), and words in the original left out by Dr. Kendrick we have added in bold. One will note significant changes and omissions. In a note in his book, Dr. Kendrick explained that interest, purpose and propriety sometimes led to these changes and exclusions. "I remark here that in giving Chubbuck's letters, I do not always indicate unimportant omissions. Real letters must always contain much which should not meet the public eye; and Emily's were real letters, dashed off hastily amidst pressing cares and duties. Written also after the exhausting labors of the day, they by no means do uniform justice to her epistolary powers." He later was to add, "In giving a few extracts from his and Chubbuck's correspondence at this time, I have no wish to minister to a prurient curiosity, not to violate that principle which would generally place letters written during the period of an 'engagement' under the shelter of inviolate secrecy."

[40] Lavinia Richards Chubbuck, Emily's mother, was born June 1, 1875, in Goffstown NH, the eldest of thirteen children. She married Charles Chubbuck on November 17. 1805. They were the parents of seven children.

[41] Miss Cynthia Sheldon was the administrative and finance manager of the Utica Female Academy. She was a mentor, advisor, and friend to Emily. She had become "Aunt Cynthia."

[42] This was the plan for *Trippings in Author-land*. She had written the Preface on June 17, and it would be published in November 1845.

[43] George P. "General" Morris, was N. P. Willis's partner at the *New Mirror* and a prominent literary figure in New York and Philadelphia. The original founder of the *New York Mirror* in 1823, beginning in 1843 with the *New Mirror*, he entered into a succession of publication enterprises with Willis. A writer, poet, and songwriter, he published a number of anthologies of both prose and poetry. After Willis's wife died, he went to Europe in 1845 and asked General Morris to guide Emily in her literary endeavors. Known universally as "General Morris," his title came from his rank as a brigadier-general in the New York militia.

[44] "The Peep Within Doors" did not appear in *Trippings in Author-Land*, nor did it appear in either of the two *Alderbrook* volumes. Originally it had been published in the January issue of *Graham's Magazine*, which meant that she would have written it in the early fall of 1844. The Editor found it republished in a January supplement to the Hartford (CT) *Courant* with the title "A Peep Within Doors." It is a perfectly wonderful story modeled on the Biblical story of the Prodigal Son as found in Luke's gospel.

I have an invitation from Mrs. Nott[45] to attend commencement,[46] and shall go down week after next, if I am well enough. I anticipate a rare time. **A man there has fallen in love with me—Mr. Gillespie,**[47] **author of "Rome as seen by a New Yorker." I had a letter from Mrs. and Mr. Gillette**[48] **this morning. So they are treating you handsomely—the Hamiltonians. They better—they had. But you must be very sociable—all condescension—as tho…**

Written in the right margin of the address page: "…**felt yourself of so much consequence that you could stoop to be agreeable even to them. Talk a great deal, and put yourself forward. It is right and proper for you are nearly twenty-six now—and moreover you are the great Fanny Forester's**[49] **sister. If you can't have everything nice or as you would like it—just think it don't [sic] make two-pence difference—you are of consequence enough to dispense with such accidentals. Why did'nt [sic] you tell me who was at the party and on whom you made an impression."**

Written in the left margin of the address page: "**I enclose to you a dollar to pay for doing your bonnet. If you or Mother want anything let me know.—Did you know that poor Willis**[50] **arrived in London sick of a brain-fever?**[51] **I am very much alarmed about him. I wrote to Walker**[51] **last week. Write again and tell me everything I want to know."**

Source: A. C. Kendrick, *The Life and Letters of Mrs. Emily C. Judson*, 133; Hanna family files.

---

[45] Urania Sheldon Nott—a mentor, advisor, and friend to Emily—was the literary principal when Emily entered the Utica Female Academy. In late summer 1842, Urania married Eliphalet Nott, the president of Union College in Schenectady NY.

[46] Reverend Doctor Eliphalet Nott, was the president of Union College in Schenectady NY. An ordained Presbyterian minister, he was married to Urania Sheldon Nott, the sister of Cynthia Sheldon and Alma Anable, and the aunt of Anna Maria Anable.

[47] See the letter from Mrs. Urania Nott to Emily E. Chubbuck dated June 11, 1845. She mentioned that Gillespie had brought her the latest *Columbian Magazine* with the first installment of Emily's story in it. The story would have been "Grace Linden." See also the letters from Gillespie to Emily E. Chubbuck dated August 2 and September 13, 1845.

[48] Rev. A. D. Gillette was the founding minister of the Eleventh Baptist Church in Philadelphia. He had a distinguished career there for another decade, when he left to take another pulpit in New York. Prominent in Baptist circles, he served on the Board of American Baptist Publication Society. Gillette was educated at Hamilton College, and he was known to Cynthia Sheldon. We can be sure that it was at her suggestion that in 1842 Emily asked the Reverend Gillette to submit her book to the society for approval. In April and early May 1845, Emily stayed in Philadelphia at the home of this same Rev. Gillette, and she returned again that fall for winter 1845–1846. On Christmas Day 1845 Gillette had introduced Emily Chubbuck to Adoniram Judson in the parlor of his home. He had a short time before traveled to Boston to bring the revered missionary to Philadelphia for meetings with the churches. Gillette was to be a stalwart friend and supporter throughout it all, not only to Emily, but to the Sheldon and Anable families.

[49] Fanny Forester, Emily Chubbuck's *nom de plume*.

[50] Nathaniel Parker (N. P.) Willis was the editor of *New Mirror*, the magazine that catapulted Emily into literary fame. He became a friend, mentor, and, after the two weeks Emily had spent in New York, eventually a suitor.

[51] See the letter of N. P. Willis to Emily Chubbuck dated June 1, 1845. In that letter he stated that he was very ill as he embarked for England.

[52] Born September 24, 1815, John Walker Chubbuck was twenty-three months older than Emily. Trained as a printer and having worked for a newspaper, Walker established a newspaper with a partner upon arriving in the Wisconsin Territory. We know that he married and was active in his church.

J. Watson Williams to Emily E. Chubbuck,[53] July 14, 1845—Utica

Miss Chubbuck,

I have the pleasure of sending herewith a couple of Volumes of Burke. There is a part of his "Thoughts on the Causes of the present Discontents," in the first Volume, commencing where I have placed a mark, which I commend to your perusal as a very favorable specimen of his turn of thought and style of writing.—In this same Volume, you will find his great speech on American affairs, which contains some passages of remarkable eloquence and beauty, which you will not overlook.

In the other volume, you will find his capital speeches on the Impeachment of Warren Hastings. I hope their great length will not deter you from reading them, particularly the first, which is a splendid historical picture, that will impress you as strongly as the canvass itself would. It contains masterly sketches of the manner and customs of the Gentus, and a full length portraiture of Warren Hastings, colored of course with strong partisan tints, yet laid on a ground of sober truth and gravity.

I have in reserve, provided your appetite holds good [sic], the Reflections on the French Revolution which in their day formed his most celebrate work.

Very cordially yours,

J. Watson Williams

Source: American Baptist Historical Society, AJ 27, no. 1292.

Nathaniel Parker Willis to Emily E. Chubbuck, July 17, 1845—London

Dear Emily

I was rather sadder than I should otherwise have been when the *Caledonia* came in and there was no letter from my sweet friend Fanny.[54] The packets sail but once a fortnight and you *might* write me *a line* at least by each one. I assure you there in no one in America from whom I would rather hear.

I am quite well now, and overrun with civilities and kindness. The people of high rank whom I formerly knew have been so kind to me that I hardly know how to be grateful enough for their delicate attentions, and then, you know, I have connexions [sic] here (by marriage) who would engross me entirely if I could afford the time. So that private letter-writing is a proof of very great need to express myself. I

---

[53] Williams had written to Emily on January 12 and March 1845 offering her resources for her writing and her own learning.

[54] Fanny Forester, Emily Chubbuck's *nom de plume*.

wish you were here, in my solitary room, to talk to me in the long hours when I am alone.

Write to me long letters, and believe me
Ever yours most sincerely

N. P. W.

Source: Hanna family files.

Nathaniel Parker Willis to Emily E. Chubbuck,[55] July 24, 1845—London

Dearest Fanny[56]

The packet sails tomorrow and I must send one line, tho" I have *work*—written up to the hour for closing the mail—all but just time enough to tell you that I think of you and wish you where I could talk to you. I am off in a few days to pass the winter in Vienna. I shall have there, as I have here, many lonely hours every day which you can cheer and occupy by writing to me. Write long letters, dear Fanny, and for my eye only. I feel toward you as if I had some property in you and look to you for affection.

Ever yours faithfully

W

A note has come in while I am finishing this, from Lady Georgiana Fane, daughter of the Earl of Westmoreland, and perhaps you would like to see how *legibly* noble fingers write. The translation of it is this:—Lady G. F. presents her comp's to Mr. W. and is desired by Lady Anne Beckett to say she hopes to see him at a party she gives tomorrow evening. Lady Anne is in the same house in Stratford Place that she inhabited some years ago.

5 Upper Brook St.
Would you ever have decyphered [sic] it?

Source: Hanna family files.

---

[55] Written on the address page in the handwriting of Emily E. Chubbuck: "N. P. Willis–29." This would make this letter the twenty-ninth letter Emily had received from Willis.
[56] Fanny Forester, Emily Chubbuck's *nom de plume*.

Dr. William M. Gillespie[57] to Emily E. Chubbuck, August 2, 1845—New York City

My dear Miss Fanny[58]

Enclosed you will find a lovely note from the *other* Fanny,[59] which she scribbled while the steamboat bell was ringing to summon it and me away. You are indebted for it to my having teased her about slandering you, though I knew well, as I assured you in advance, that whatever she had said had been in the most unreflecting playfulness. She would not really slander, or even tell half the real evil of Satan himself, for her heart is a lineal descendant from that fair saint who said of the Prince of Darkness "Poor fellow—how unhappy he must be—he cannot love!"

Her note is exactly "like herself" and it would need no skill in autography to decipher there from very many of her lovely traits. When you answer it, please to enclose your note to me (30 Dey St. N.Y.) that I may forward it to Mrs. Osgood, as her whereabouts is just now as un-foretell-able as a woman's will.

I have found the article which I transplanted from Utica three years ago, in the *Mirror* for October 1, 1842. It is called "Our Rose," and is credited to the "Young Ladies' Miscellany."[60] On reperusing it, it does not appear quite so characteristic as

---

[57] Dr. William Gillespie, professor of engineering at Union College in Schenectady NY. He wrote two long letters to Emily, this one of August 2, and a second dated September 3, 1845. His second letter originated from Union College where Dr. Nott (husband of Urania Sheldon Nott) was the president, and he makes note that Urania Nott was "his special friend." In his first letter he asks Emily if a certain poem appeared in the New York *Mirror*, and if it had, he had identified the writer early on as one of great promise. In a time when Emily was considering a trip to the continent, he spoke to her of weather conditions in certain of the European countries. His second letter is filled with literary allusions, a long story to prove the point that "widows are dangerous," and a reflection on some of her writings. Gillespie is mentioned in the June 11, 1845 letter of Urania Sheldon Nott to Emily; he had given Urania Sheldon Nott the latest issue of the *Columbian Magazine* with the first installment of Emily's story "Grace Linden" in it. Then on July 9, 1845, Emily mentions Gillespie in a letter to her sister Catherine. Emily is speaking of going to Schenectady for the Commencement of Union College, and she says: "A man there has fallen love with me—Gillespie, author of 'Rome as seen by a New Yorker.'"

[58] Fanny Forester, Emily Chubbuck's *nom de plume*.

[59] Frances or "Fanny" Osgood presents us with a very interesting counterpoint to Fanny Forester or Emily Chubbuck, with both of them achieving fame in the same period of time. Fanny Osgood was both a writer and poet, and in 1845 she was one of the regulars who were writing for *Graham's Magazine*. Estranged from her husband, famed portrait painter Samuel S. Osgood, she began a relationship with Edgar Allen Poe, who in March 1845 had become the editor and part owner of the *Broadway Journal*. Poe, by the way, had been helped to fame by N. P. Willis when in January the *New York Daily Mirror*, the paper which preceded the *New Mirror* and made Fanny Forester famous, had published his poem "The Raven." Fanny Osgood presented a poem to the *Broadway Journal* for publication, and Poe printed a poem in reply. This went back and forth over a number of months, and the two were soon involved in a relationship; it was commonly thought that Fanny Osgood's third child was fathered by Poe. All of this was being played out in the press in September 1845 when William Gillespie wrote his letter to Emily Chubbuck. The relationship with Fanny Osgood was to, within the year, make Poe a pariah in the literary circles of New York. In January 1845, Osgood had accused George Graham of not writing to her because of all of his correspondence with Fanny Forester. In June, just before sailing to Burmah, Emily mentioned in a letter that while in New York she had stopped at Osgood's studio, hoping to make arrangements to see Fanny Osgood, but the meeting did not take place as Osgood was out of town.

[60] *The Young Ladies' Miscellany* was a magazine started and edited by Emily in fall 1842, with the help and cooperation of the students and staff of the Utica Female Academy. Advertisements for subscriptions had been in the religious press as early as December 1841. It was to survive only through the end 1843. In *The Life and Letters of Mrs. Emily C. Judson*, A. C. Kendrick said; "While it drew forth much talent from the school, Chubbuck, of course, under every variety of disguise, figured largely in its columns. Now a Greek "maiden"—Kore—now a Latin "nobody"—Nemo—now a reluctantly accepted country contributor—now in all the dignity of the editorial "we," she played off both her heavier and lighter artillery on the public. Essays, stories,

it had seemed to me in memory, though still, if not yours, it deserves to be; and perhaps it now appears less strikingly charming than it did at first, only because you yourself have given me such a high standard to measure it by. Tell me if it be really yours. If it be, I shall be proud of my discrimination, for I told Willis,[61] when your star first broke through the clouds, that I had first discovered the comet.

The Book of which I spoke to you, is "The Sanative Influence of Climate by Sir Samuel Clark, Physician to the Queen." An American edition, of which I was not previously aware, has been published at Philadelphia by "Barrington and Haswell"; and has thus made the book easily accessible. It gives minute and practical information as to the effects of all the best climates in the world upon particular predispositions and complaints. *Nice* is described as "very dry and uniform in temperature," but "more injurious than beneficial to confirmed consumption." *Florence*, delicious as it is, is "unfavorable for invalids" from its cold piercing winds and sudden changes. *Pisa* is "favorable for consumptive patients." *Rome* has a climate "mild and soft, but rather relaxing and oppressive." It excites too powerfully the nervous system. *Naples* is bad for consumptive persons, but "well suited as a winter residence for those who are laboring under general debility and deranged health without any marked local disease." *Madeira* has a "climate mild and equable," and is "superior to the best climates on the Continent." Full details on all these points you will find in the volume. I trust you may not need them.[62]

Gen. Morris[63] tells me that he has completed an arrangement with Messes. Ferrett which he thinks very advantageous, and that he is now expecting "Copy" for you.[64]

Will you please to present my warm respects to Mrs. President Nott,[65] and tell her that I have made the enquiries which she desired, and have obtained informa-

---

songs, and sonnets, now grave, now gay, were thrown oft from her facile and fertile pen. The magazine ran gracefully through its single year of existence, and then quietly resigned its breath, having delighted its friends, edified, it is hoped, the public, contained much sound instruction, sparkled with many bright gems of genius, and contributed much to the reputation, and not a cent probably to the purse of the editor. But the dramatic genius of Fanny Forester flashes through its vivacious sketches" (77–78).

[61] Nathaniel Parker (N. P.) Willis was the editor of *New Mirror*, the magazine that catapulted Emily into literary fame. He became a friend, mentor, and, after the two weeks Emily spent in New York, a suitor.

[62] We assume that Gillespie had learned from Urania Sheldon Nott that Emily was thinking of a trip to Europe, to write for *Graham's Magazine*. Her latest thought, in her letter of July 2, 1845, had been to travel with the Consul to Genoa, who was returning to his post. There is little doubt that the presence of N. P. Willis in Europe was a strong motivating factor. In the end, her health would not allow her to make such an extensive and strenuous journey.

[63] George P. "General" Morris, was N. P. Willis's partner at the *New Mirror* and a prominent literary figure in New York and Philadelphia.

[64] At this time Emily was searching for a publisher for what was to be *Trippings in Author-land*. In her July 9, 1845 letter to her sister Kate, she had mentioned that General Morris, the partner of N. P. Willis in the *New Mirror*, was helping her in this endeavor.

[65] Urania Sheldon Nott—aa mentor, advisor, and friend to Emily—was the literary principal at the Utica Female Academy when Emily arrived in October 1840. In late summer 1842 Urania married Eliphalet Nott, president of Union College in Schenectady NY.

tion which will enable me to execute her wishes in the most approved manner upon my return. At present I am about making a series of Magnetic observations for the U. S. Government.

    Give my love to "Cousin 'Bel,'"[66] and believe me
With high respect

Yours sincerely Wm M. Gillespie

Source: American Baptist Historical Society, AJ 24, no. 1201.

Emily E. Chubbuck to Cynthia Sheldon, August 14, 1845—Springfield[67]

My dear Miss C.,

    I returned yesterday from Cooperstown where I left A. M.[68] well and very happy. She is to go to Cherry Valley on Monday next to stay I don't know how long. She will return to Utica before going to the Helderbergs. I cannot possibly get away from here till Sat. and so shall make my arrangements to go to Hamilton with Julia Look[69] and Mrs. Gillette[70] on Monday. I am having just the most delightful time that could be imagined and am getting—O *so* well! I have scarcely had even a head-ache since I have been here. I don't try to walk but I ride constantly. Doct. Westcott has just got out his horse now and I must stop writing.

    Yours very affectionately,

    Emily

Source: Hanna family files.

---

[66] "Cousin 'Bel'" was Anna Maria Anable—the "character" came from Emily's letter to the *New Mirror* which was published on June 8, 1844, a letter which catapulted Emily to literary fame. The letter concerned a visit which Emily and Cousin 'Bel' had made to New York, and their lack of money to enjoy the wares of the many shops they passed by. She asked if the editor of the *New Mirror* would like to help them out.

[67] This letter is undated. We place it at August 14, 1845, based on the two dated letters we have in the correspondence from H. Loucks (August 14 and 23, 1845).

[68] Anna Maria Anable was the niece of the Urania and Cynthia Sheldon, the daughter of Joseph and Alma Sheldon Anable; she was Emily's closest friend at the Utica Female Academy.

[69] Julia Look, a former student of Emily's at the Utica Female Academy, was later a fellow teacher. A November 22, 1845 letter from Anna Maria remarked that Julia has the hardest part because she was teaching Emily's composition class, and the students kept asking for Emily. In a September, 1847 letter, Julia was listed as one of the teachers at the Utica Female Academy. On September 23, 1849, Anna Maria wrote that Julia and Albert B. Casswell are married and came to visit with her. In one 1849 letter, Julia spoke of another teacher who was teaching "our composition class." On October 27, 1850, Anna Maria Anable noted that Julia had had a son. She was one of a small number of people who addressed Emily as "Emily" or "Nemmy" in her letters.

[70] Hannah Gillette was the wife of the A. D. Gillette. Emily stayed with the Gillettes in spring 1845 and again that year in November. Emily met Adoniram Judson on Christmas Day 1845, in their parlor. Hannah would play an important part in preparing Emily for life in Burmah.

H. Loucks to Emily E. Chubbuck, August 15, 1845

Dr Fanny[71]

The bearer for this is my son Samuel—I give him this line of introduction to you—Should you be at Sharon Springs—you can repose perfect confidence in my son as a young gentleman highly accomplished and worthy of your friendship.—

It will be very gratifying to me if it comports with your arrangements on your return to Utica, to make us a call—which should be so fortunate as to be favored by it. I trust you will find no cause to regret—

Have the goodness to drop me a line (of course) when you may be expected home.

Truly yours, etc.

H. Loucks

Source: American Baptist Historical Society, AJ 25, no. 1248.

Nathaniel Parker Willis to Emily E. Chubbuck,[72] August 16, 1845— London

My dear Fanny,[73]

A letter of yours dated July 3, lies before me, and probably as the *Great Western* arrives today, there are, I trust, at least two more for me within a mile or two, undelivered—but I have a half hour of leisure so I will reply in advance. In the first place, however, you had better usually write to me *direct* as Morris[74] waits to send by private hand and thus your letter of July 3 only arrived yesterday. Direct "London care of Saunders and Otley, Conduit St."

Touching your trip to Europe[75]—go (or rather *come*) by all means. Graham[76] will probably give you or get given to you by some editor of a weekly in Philadelphia, ten dollars each for your letters. A hundred letters will pay your way for a year, if you go with a party as of course you will. You will write them easily for the matter is abundant. It would make me perfectly happy to join you and travel with you, but I fear I am fixed between Paris and London for the time I remain

---

[71] Fanny Forester, Emily Chubbuck's *nom de plume*.

[72] Written on the address page in the handwriting of Emily E. Chubbuck: "N. P. Willis–30." This was the thirtieth letter that she had received from him.

[73] Fanny Forester, Emily Chubbuck's *nom de plume*.

[74] George P. "General" Morris, was N. P. Willis's partner at the *New Mirror* and a prominent literary figure in New York and Philadelphia.

[75] In recent letters, the idea of travel to Europe was very much on Emily Chubbuck's mind. George Graham had told her that he would pay well for any dispatches she sent for publication. In the end, Emily's health prevented any such travel.

[76] George Graham, editor of *Graham's Magazine*, took an interest in Emily Chubbuck as Fanny Forester and paid her with the unheard of sum of five dollars a page.

abroad. Your letter by the *Western* will probably throw some light on the subject, however.

I was delighted with your changes of habits—spectacles, ale, bouquets, etc. But take care not to make the women curious and jealous of your influence with "bachelors of thirty-five." They are bitter toward their own sex and they would like it better if you remained spectacled. A word to the wise!

I can talk to you about my "inner self," dear Emily, but I cannot *write*. When we meet I shall have a great deal to tell you! I hope you will not be going abroad, by the way, when I am returning. I shall sail from England probably, by the first of March next.

I will endeavor to do your preface soon and send it.[77] It will require thought and I cannot do it in a hurry.

On looking again at your letter, I find you speak of *hurrying* off to Europe and you name *Sicily*. An intimate friend of mine, Lady Franklin, has just left London for Italy and means to pass the winter at Palermo. She would be a charming friend for you, and I will write to her to expect you. If your letter of tomorrow announces your departure for any port of Sicily I shall send you thither a letter of introduction—this letter of mine following you of course.

My health is quite re-established and I am busy with seeing and writing—but dreadfully lonely at times. I wish with all my heart you were with me.

My daughter Imogen is well and happy.

Take care of your health, my dear Emily. Write me as many and as long letters as you possibly can and believe me,

Ever affectionately yours,

N. P. Willis

Source: Hanna family files, N. P. Willis to Emily, letter 30.

Reverend Abram Dunn Gillette to Emily E. Chubbuck,[78] August 21, 1845—Utica

My Dear Dear Friend,

Why was it our fate not to meet and see you in your own lovely little cottage? We did not know of your arrival, and made arrangements to leave by chartered

---

[77] The preface would have been for *Trippings in Author-land*, which was to be published in November 1845.

[78] This letter speaks of a recent visit by and Mrs. Gillette to Hamilton NY. See their letters to Emily dated July 5 (Mrs. Gillette) and July 7 (Gillette) in which they spoke of their hope to make the trip, though because of other factors, they doubted that it would be possible.

stage last eve—We repented our plans, when alas, as in the case with much repentance it was *too late*.

I did see you as I passed in the stage, and your form in white apparel appeared at the neat little cottage above, you put your glass to your eye and looked towards *me*. I waved, waved my hand—poor hand alas it would not reach you. I suppose you did not recognize me. Were *I a young man*, I might write about that passing glance, its impressions, its reality and yet its dreamlike vision. O if I were a poet, as the Will-is,[79] or a Fanny Forester,[80] I would make others feel and see what I did. O my, to be so near a friend and yet driven by in a rattling old stage, [ ] clouds of dust, thick enough to inflict the curse of being turned to dust. Really I am out of patience for leaving last eve—and so is Mrs. G. I hope she will add a line—perhaps not sentimental as this—but you know *me*—Well now my loss—that K—I dare not spell it, for I saw nothing in H.[81] that indicated the allowance of such things, *only among* the *graduates*. But if you were here I should claim my right. The debt will be a great one before next winter—I must have interest if I wait so long.

My Dear Wife and self—engaged ourselves *much very much* at H.—I am in love with the Institution four fold above what I was before—I think it *noble*—its able faculty not equaled in the world—all things considered. I regret we could not visit all who invited us—some urged—Prof. Raymond and Lady—do apologize for us. It is our loss, and then, not even to go into that neat *Cottage home*. O it looked so *homelike*. We shall never cease our regrets—no never—we are not happy now because we left and saw not *you*.

About the *book of Tales*[82] Mr. Griswold[83] will execute what you please. Write me freely—If Mr. Willis[84] does not get your letter in time about the preface—only let me know your wishes. I know such is Mr. G's nobleness, that a prompt compliance would be his pleasure—he need not know you asked W. to write it. If he should it would not alter his spirit, to serve you in any way you allow.

Make use of me—by any way by which your interests or happiness will allow in this or other matters.

---

[79] This is a play on the name of Emily's friend and mentor, the editor of the *New Mirror*, N. P. Willis.

[80] Fanny Forester, Emily Chubbuck's *nom de plume*.

[81] In his letter of July 7, Reverend Gillette had said that if he could make it to Hamilton, he wanted to get there for the graduation of the Hamilton Literary and Theological Institution, a school which he had attended.

[82] Emily was pulling together a collection of her recent stories—it was published in November 1845 as *Trippings in Author-land*.

[83] Reverend Rufus W. Griswold, an ordained clergyman and distinguished literary figure, had been one of Emily's possible suitors. From this reference we gather that Emily had also asked him to write the preface for *Trippings in Author-land* or at least entertained the idea.

[84] See the letter from N. P. Willis to Emily E. Chubbuck dated August 16, 1845. Writing to Emily from Europe, he agreed to do the Preface, though it would have to be done on his schedule. The reference would be to *Trippings in Author-land*. We note that when this was published, the Preface had been written by Fanny Forester—she had dated the Preface June 17, 1845.

I imposed myself on the attention of your sister,[85] for the best of reasons; she reminded me of you. If she knew me as you do, perhaps she would not think me rude.

I am ashamed as I reflect on what I attempted to do in preaching and speaking in H., so many to hear, who could see me *all thro*, I am now like one that has rushed into danger and survived—but I seek not Men's approval only. I tried to do something for mans spiritual good—

Mrs. G. joins me in the best of bonds,

A. D. Gillette

Source: American Baptist Historical Society, AJ 24, no. 1198.

Robert A. West to Emily E. Chubbuck, August 22, 1845—South Brooklyn

Dear Madam,

The proprietor of the *Columbian* only returned to the city today which must be my apology for not writing you at the time promised on the subject of your last letter. Presuming that it will be most agreeable to you to have them returned direct, I enclose the articles by your friend. I believe your own judgment will justify me in pronouncing them ineligible for our pages.[86]

I deeply regret that indisposition should be the cause of your proposed visit to Italy; but you should have to visit those milder, summer climes. I sincerely hope that perfect restoration to health will be vouchsafed to you. As to your proposal, to write exclusively for the *Columbian* during your projected tour, we would decidedly prefer that you would propose the terms specifically—we will then judge of the matter and apprize [sic] you whether we think the arrangement will be within our compass. Remembering your early association with the *Columbian*, we should have felt gratified had a similar proposal made by us, some time ago, met with a more favorable response from your poor good self.[87]

---

[85] Sarah Catharine ("Kate," "Kit," or "Kitty") Chubbuck, Emily's older sister by ten months. Outside of the two terms at the Utica Female Academy that Emily arranged for her, Catherine always lived with her parents in Hamilton NY. The letters indicate opportunities for marriage, but Catharine remained single. She later helped care for Henry and Edward Judson when, after their return from Burmah in fall 1851, they moved in with their "aunt" and "grandparents." She was remembered by her nephews as "a dear friend."

[86] Emily was constantly being asked by friends to help them find publishers for their books, articles, or poetry. As an example, see the letters from H. M. Dodge, dated July 4, 1842 and November, 1842. Mrs. Dodge was a rather insistent inquirer.

[87] See other letters from John Inman, J. Post, and Robert West. The editors of the *Columbian* had made Emily offers to write exclusively for their magazine, and Emily had consistently refused to do that. We do wonder here what had happened to her previously expressed option in a May 18, 1845 letter, that George Graham and *Graham's Magazine* would pay for the expenses of her trip to Europe, in exchange for letters.

However you may decide as to your voyage to Italy—we hope to be favored, on terms as heretofore, with contributions from your pen, of the same character, so far as subjects are concerned, with the welcome articles we have been accustomed to receive; pre[ ]sing however that we do not find long articles please our readers so well as those filling only from five to eight pages, however meritorious the articles may be. For though Fanny Forester's[88] pen may triumph over the difficulty, still as a rule, only now and then to be suspended, short articles serve us best.[89] We are now open for something from you and shall be glad of it whenever it suits your convenience; but, pardon my frankness, we do not quite like the title you mention—"Letter to cousin 'Bel'"[90] for one or two reasons, solely of a prudential character, and apart from the intrinsic merits which we know they would have. The principle reason perhaps would be that the title is known in a quarter whence we should feel unwilling to adopt it into the *Columbian*.

The last three numbers of the *Columbian* have brought us golden opinions from many quarters, and you will be glad to hear that our prospects are good.[91] Mr. Inman[91] thanks you for your kind remembrance and cordially reciprocates it. Hoping soon to hear from you and with sincere esteem, I am yours very respectfully,

Robert A. West

Source: American Baptist Historical Society, AJ 27, no. 1301.

---

[88] Fanny Forester, Emily Chubbuck's *nom de plume*.

[89] See the letter from Robert West to Emily E. Chubbuck dated May 10, 1845, in which he introduced this idea of running articles over several issues—which they were doing at that time with several of Emily's pieces including "Grace Linden."

[90] "Cousin 'Bel'" was Anna Maria Anable—the "character" came from Emily's letter to the *New Mirror* which was published on June 8, 1844, a letter which catapulted Emily to literary fame. The letter concerned a visit which Emily and Cousin 'Bel' had made to New York, and their lack of money to enjoy the wares of the many shops they passed by. She asked if the editor of the *New Mirror* would like to help them out.

[91] Previous letters from Emily's literary friends had indicated that the *Columbian* was on extremely shaky financial ground.

[92] John Inman was the editor of the *Commercial Advertiser* and the *Columbian Magazine*—responsibilities which failing health forced him to give up early in 1845. He was Emily Chubbuck's initial contact with the *Columbian Magazine*, which began to publish some her stories early in 1844. He strongly encouraged Emily in her writing, said that they would publish everything they could get from her, hoped that she would consider writing exclusively for them, and when she asked for it, gave her the unheard of rate of five dollars a page for her articles. When he did that, he very candidly stated that with this, they would not consider it fair if she continued to write for N. P. Willis and the *New Mirror* without charge.

H. Loucks to Emily E. Chubbuck, August 23, 1845—Palatine Bridge[93]

Dear Fanny,[94]

I received your very polite note of yesterday, apprising me of your return from Springfield without being able to make us the intended visit. Perhaps I asked too much of you. Pardon me for what I am sure you will attribute to an exuberance of feeling rather than a want of judgment or etiquette—On a moments [sic] reflection after my return home I became sensible of having perhaps drawn too largely upon you and by way of making the best and readiest reparation in my power dispatched my son Samuel (not unworthy of your friendship) on the day you was [sic] expected at Sharon Springs, with a letter of introduction to accompany you here, and if needful, to see you safe at Utica. I deemed a visit from you important as condusive [sic] to the speedy restoration of your health, besides the gratification we anticipated to derive from it—Sam'l was much pleased with the account I gave him of my very interesting and delightful interview with you at the Academy of the excellent painting "Dora'."[95] He is quite desirous of seeing the Picture itself—who can blame him? I hope he will enjoy that pleasure in due time.

How is your health! Fanny, take good care, very good care of it. Only believe it can be perfectly restored. Take the necessary relaxation from mental exertion and take sufficient bodily exercise, and it can easily be accomplished. That such may speedily be the case, and that you may enjoy a long life as happy and useful as your fame in the literary world is already brilliant, is the sincere and parental wish of your very ardent friend

And well wisher H. Loucks

P.S. Be pleased to accept of my and my son's (he joins me) warmest thanks for the specimen of your autograph. Let me again hear from you. I also forward you a late Southern newspaper just rec'd from my other son (Richard), the Baton Rouge Gazette of the 9th inst.

H. L.

Source: American Baptist Historical Society, AJ 25, no. 1247.

---

[93] See the previous letter of Loucks to Emily E. Chubbuck dated August 15, 1845.
[94] Fanny Forester, Emily Chubbuck's *nom de plume*.
[95] N. P. Willis commissioned an artist named Flagg to do a portrait of "Dora,'" one of Emily's fictional characters.

Anna Maria Anable to Emily E. Chubbuck, September 1, 1845[96]

I have been fussing around to clean up the house and make my part of it look habitable all the morning and now I am going to be better than my word and send this to you today—my conscience [ ]ing's me a little for not attending the funerals of Mrs. Bacon's and Mrs. Liffany's little girls.

Nemmy[97] Aunt C.[98] says you must come back here on Monday as you have appointed and then you can *consult* and *consider* what is best for you to do this winter. If you stay with us you may do just as little or just as much as you please and no more—and if you don't want to do anything you must not. I think under these circumstances we can manage to live quite comfortably in our little room.

Aunt C. had a very saucy and impertinent letter from Mary B.[99] which she sent down to S. for Jane[100] to attend to—she will not receive Mary again here until she makes an apology—She does not anticipate but that she will do it, and behave herself better after this fracas for she had just such a time with her once before in S. I do hope so for it is getting to be almost too much of a Nichols[101] [sic] affair to be comfortable.

---

[96] This letter is undated. It carries a September 4, 1845 postmark—the nearest Monday to that would be September 1, so we place it on that date.

[97] "Nem" or "Nemmy" was a name of endearment given to Emily by a small group of her intimate friends at the Utica Female Academy. Anna Maria Anable was "Ninny."

[98] Miss Cynthia Sheldon was the administrative and finance manager of the Utica Female Academy. She was a mentor, advisor, and friend to Emily. Anna Maria Anable was Miss Sheldon's niece.

[99] Mary Barber, mentioned frequently in the Emily Chubbuck Judson letters, was a student and then the art teacher at the Utica Female Academy. There were ups and downs to that relationship; in fall 1845, apparently Mary had written to someone expressing what Anna Maria Anable called "ingratitude," and Mary had been banned from the academy until she made proper apologies to Sheldon. In November 1847, Jane Kelly remarked that they had not heard from Mary in over a year. In 1848, Mary was back at the Utica Female Seminary teaching with Jane Kelly. Though at this time Sheldon had moved to Philadelphia, Mary had been able to reconcile with her, and in later years we find Mary very close to the Sheldon-Anable families; later, there was considerable consternation on Cynthia Sheldon's part in her correspondence with Emily about Mary's health, the seriousness of it, and Mary's impending death. These letters were written in April 1852. Sheldon went to help transfer Mary to Albany in June 1852, where she would be better situated and perhaps have access to better doctors. On September 9, 1852, Anna Maria Anable wrote to Emily of Mary's death.

[100] Jane Kelly was Emily Chubbuck's friend at the Utica Female Academy. Jane later became a teacher with Emily at the academy. Kelly became the literary principal in 1844 with the retirement of James Nichols and his wife from that position. During a period of Kelly's illness in 1844, Emily filled in the position for her. Then, in 1848, when Cynthia Sheldon moved to Philadelphia to help start the Misses Anable's School, Kelly became the "headmistress" of the academy and successfully brought the academy into the future, though not without some initial disparagement from the Sheldon-Anable families.

[101] After the marriage of Urania Sheldon to the Reverend Doctor Eliphalet Nott, and with her moving to Schenectady, James Nichols and his wife became the literary principals of the Utica Female Academy. When illness forced them to move on, the position had been taken by Jane Kelly. Letters between Anna Maria and Emily had sometimes suggested that Mr. Nichols had a personality that could be judgmental and difficult.

Mary Adams[102] is enjoying herself they say—she has now gone out to Whitesboro. What do you think? Jimmy[103] went out to Trenton *alone* that is to be escort to Augusta[104]—C—Mary and Helen Munson.[105] Isn't he a monopolizer tho'? Mary B. and I had a joint letter from Hat[106] and Lou yesterday—tho' Hatty said but a word as she was suffering from sick head-ache. She will try and find a place for you she says as soon as possible—she was then going to visit Lou. I see by the daily that the *Caledonia*[107] has arrived so maybe you will have a letter from your cher papa.[108]

Give love to all the folks at your house and write me a great letter right off.

---

[102] Mary Adams, a friend of Emily's while at the Utica Female Academy. Her letter to Emily in October 1845 was almost a whimsical piece of fantasy with literary pretensions. It would reflect a fairly close and whimsical relationship. A second letter in December 1845 was similar. The letters were written from New Orleans, and she spoke of Hatty Anable as being near to her. On January 29, 1849, Anna Maria Anable wrote: "Hatty says Mary Adams is going to marry Gardner Green of Norwich,—a very fine young man, of invention, fortune, piety and all that Mary's heart was sighed for." On July 8, 1850, Urania Sheldon Nott spoke of attending this wedding in New York.

[103] Jimmy Williams, often mentioned in Anna Maria Anable's letters, usually just as "Jimmy." He was around the Utica Female Academy, and Anna Maria spoke of their conversations, what he was doing, and his interests. She often referenced him as being with "Helen." Writing to Emily on April 29, 1845, Anna Maria wrote, "(and now) I'll turn to Jimmy and Helen." She went on to talk about a party:

> It was one of the most elegant parties that has been given in a long time. Jimmy's three sisters were there—all elegant women. (Also) all the flowers of Utica Society—and among them—no not among *them* but in the rooms was [sic] poor dowdy looking little Helen giggling when she showed any animation with [ ] and girls of that class and stamp. Jimmy tried to bring her forward as much as he could—but it would not do. She will never shine in society, and what is worse Jimmy will feel her deficiency in that respect very much. He would like very much to have a wife but would entertain his guests handsomely—and yet—he loves Helen very much I have not doubt and the one hundred thousand will make up for some deficiencies or ought to. I may abuse my pity I dare say.

Then on November 14, 1845, Anna Maria said to Emily: "Do you know Jimmy is really engaged to Helen M? He hasn't been to see me yet, and he came home last Sat. Oh, love! love! Even a seven year friendship must fade before thy potent spell. Little did I think tho' that Jimmy would be faithless."

[104] Augusta Crafts is mentioned frequently in the letters written from the Utica Female Academy. A number of references chronicle her very strong opinions; many of these were spoken against N. P. Willis and Emily's relationship to him (Mrs. Crafts did not approve of either). In an April 30, 1845 letter Anna Maria Anable said: "The Dr. is not engaged nor isn't going to be to Mary Spencer I imagine, and tho' Mrs. Crafts intimated very strongly that there was *some one* he had his eye upon, he denied it to me strongly and scolded about Mrs. Crafts gossiping tongue."

[105] Helen Munson was the fiancée of Jimmy Williams, mentioned just before in this letter.

[106] Harriet ("Hatty," "Hattie," or "Hat") Anable, one of the five Anable sisters. In 1841, she had added a note to a letter written by Cynthia Sheldon to Emily. As early as November 1842, she was away, and a letter from Emily to Catherine Chubbuck said that "she (Sheldon) expected that Hat would return as accomplished as Anna Maria." Her trips away were both educational and employment, as she worked as a private tutor in families that would bring her into their homes. In August 1843, she had just returned from Beonsen, in the vicinity of New Orleans, and was engaged to go again. A letter from Anna Maria on January 6, 1845 said that she would stay south for another year. About this time Cynthia Sheldon mentioned her concern for Hatty's spiritual health. In May 1845 she was in New Orleans. She was home again in the summer 1846, but a September 27 letter from Anna Maria said she had been asked by Roman with some urgency to return and she thought that she should. She was to return home from New Orleans in January 1849 after Anna Maria Anable had started the Misses Anable's School in Philadelphia in fall 1848. Harriet was fluent in French, having placed herself earlier in a French environment in New Orleans. Hatty died in 1858.

[107] In his letter of July 17, 1845 written from London, N. P. Willis remarked that he was disappointed because the *Caledonia* had arrived and it had not carried any mail from Emily.

[108] "Papa" was a name that Anna Maria frequently used with Emily to refer to N. P. Willis. At this time Willis was traveling in Europe.

Ninny[109]

I forgot to tell you that Mrs. Conant[110] has the most beautiful wood-bine I ever saw—it grows from the slip and very rapidly—Mrs. Eaton[111] said if Wallace[112] would come up anytime she would give him slips of hers or of Mrs. C's—so make him get it.

AM

Written along the right margin of page 3: "If he sets it out now it will be very beautiful in two or three years."

Written in the right margin of the address page: "I shall send you a basket of fruit tomorrow or next day by the stage—so Wallace must be on the look out. Shall I send on some of E. Spencers wedding cake? I wonder what she will say to P. F. H."

Written in the left margin of the address page: "I found my dear little Johnny Williams card on the table—He called Tuesday the day I said I'd be home and I suppose he's gone now. Ah! Me!"

Source: American Baptist Historical Society, AJ 23. These undated letters are found in numbers 1134, 1137, 1139, and 1163.

---

[109] "Ninny" was a name of endearment given to Anna Maria Anable by her most intimate friends at the Utica Female Academy. Emily was "Nemmy."

[110] Hannah Chaplin Conant, an accomplished biblical scholar, wrote a number of articles and books and was considered very competent in the biblical field. Earlier letters indicate that she had called on Emily a number of times when Emily was in Hamilton, and the references are always very cordial. When Emily returned to the United States, a warm letter from Conant invited Emily to stay with her should she come to Rochester. After the publication of the Judson Memoir, written by Francis Wayland in collaboration with Emily Judson, Emily planned to write an abridgement of those two volumes as a more popular offering. As Emily's health deteriorated in late 1853, and it became increasingly obvious that she would be unable to take on such a task, Mrs. Conant was asked to take the responsibility for that project and eventually it was to be published as: *The Earnest Man: A Memoir of Adoniram Judson, D.D., First missionary to Burmah*.

[111] Mrs. Eaton was the wife of the Reverend Doctor George W. Eaton, a distinguished professor and future president of Madison University, and then the Hamilton Theological Institution. From the correspondence it is obvious that the Eaton family had a warm relationship with the Sheldon—Anable families, especially while they were at the Utica Female Academy.

[112] William Wallace Chubbuck, Emily's younger brother, born January 1, 1824.

Anna Maria Anable to Emily E. Chubbuck, September 7, 1845[113]

Dear Nem,[114]

I am glad to see from your letter that you have recovered your spirits and have been having such nice times;—I really wish I could have staid [sic] for its horribly stupid here—notwithstanding I have been out every evening since I returned. Mother[115] and Molly[116] came home last evening with Henry[117]—they have had a very nice visit. Sam's[118] wife had had a miscarriage—but is now very well. It's a little more than two months since she was sick.

We are expecting Jane[119] tomorrow and Nemmy, Aunt C.[120] wants you to come if you can as well this week—on Wednesday or Thursday. Do come! For I am so lonesome and besides I think I shall have company this week.

Is'nt [sic] this a dreadful cold spell of weather? I shall have our stove first up tomorrow. I can't tell you anything about Mary B.[121] for I don't know anything yet. It seems she has written something to Jane about Aunt C. and we can't do or say anything till Jane comes—We must be as ignorant of the matter as newborn babes—Mary is finally going to visit her friends this winter.

Have you heard from your papa?[122] There's a letter on the way to you which I *guessed* was from him.

---

[113] This letter is undated. We place in on September 7, 1845. We do this because in a letter we have dated September 1, Anna Maria had written this: "Aunt C. had a very saucy and impertinent letter from Mary B. which she sent down to S. for Jane to attend to—she will not receive Mary again here until she makes an apology." There is a follow up statement to what she had said in this letter, where she says that "I can't tell you anything about Mary B. for I don't know anything yet." The earlier letter was posted on Thursday, September 4, so the following Sunday is logical for this letter.

[114] "Nem" or "Nemmy" was a name of endearment given to Emily by a small group of her intimate friends at the Utica Female Academy. Anna Maria Anable was "Ninny."

[115] Alma Sheldon Anable, sister of Cynthia Sheldon and Urania Sheldon Nott. On July 28, 1814, Alma married Joseph Hubbell Anable in Troy NY (Anable's second marriage). Joseph and Alma Anable had nine children: Henry Sheldon Anable, b. June 21, 1815; William Stewart Anable, b. November 6, 1816; Anna Maria Stafford Anable, b. September 30, 1818, Cynthia Jane Anable, January 28, 1820; Samuel Low Anable, b. November 28, 1821; Harriet Isabella Anable, also known as Hatty or Hattie, was born December 18, 1823; Courtland Wilcox Anable, b. July 28, 1825; Frances Alma Anable, or Fanny, b. April 12, 1828, and Mary Juliet Anable, b. February 18, 1830.

[116] Mary Anable.

[117] Henry Sheldon Anable, Joseph and Alma Sheldon Anable oldest child. In August 1846, Henry was in the Milwaukee WI area. In a September 27 letter, he said he might leave Utica to join William and Olivia in Sheboygan WI. He married Rosanna Frick in Sheboygan WI on February 13, 1855, and died September 3, 1887, in Flushing NY.

[118] Samuel Anable, one of the nine children of Joseph and Alma Anable.

[119] Jane Kelly was Emily Chubbuck's friend at the Utica Female Academy. Following the departure of Mr. and Mrs. Nichols, Jane became the literary principal in early 1844. Then with the departure of Cynthia Sheldon to Philadelphia in the fall of 1848, she became "headmistress."

[120] Miss Cynthia Sheldon was the administrative and finance manager of the Utica Female Academy. She was a mentor, advisor, and friend to Emily. Anna Maria Anable was Miss Sheldon's niece.

[121] Mary Barber, mentioned frequently in the Emily Chubbuck Judson letters, was a student and then the art teacher at the Utica Female Academy. See the first footnote for this letter about Mary B. and her trouble with Cynthia Sheldon.

[122] In letters to Emily, Anna Maria Anable frequently spoke of N. P. Willis, Emily's mentor and friend, as "papa." Willis was traveling in Europe at this time.

My dear Prof. Kendrick[123] has been to church with *me* this evening and is here staying all night the darling man; he preached a grand sermon this afternoon in Beecher St.

Adieu Anna M.

If I had time to get it this morning I'd send you some fruit.

Source: American Baptist Historical Society, AJ 23, no. 1139F.

Anna Maria Anable to Emily E. Chubbuck, September 10, 1845[124]

Dear Nem,[125]

You know what you promised me about coming if I had company here. I intend to give very much such a party as I had last spring on Friday evening of this week—I can't put it off till next week on account of the fair—we may have a house full next week. So *ma fille*, mind your Mama[126] and come right off—No matter if you do get tired most to death—you know you always look better then—School has begun and—with 80 scholars—and Jane[127] is in the best humour [sic] imaginable—E. Hinckley is settled in M. B's[128] room—Sarah[129] is not coming till next week. Moll Adams came last-night [sic] and we are having nice times—Give much

---

[123] When Emily Chubbuck was in her teens, Dr. Nathaniel Kendrick had been the pastor of the Baptist church in Eaton and also a theological professor in a local theological school; he eventually became the president of the Hamilton Literary and Theological Institution. At that time, Emily spoke with him about becoming a missionary. Dr. Kendrick had given her the wise counsel of discernment, patience, and waiting. It was to Dr. Kendrick that Adoniram and Emily turned to officiate at their marriage. A. C. Kendrick, in *The Life and Letters of Mrs. Emily C. Judson*, says that the marriage of Emily and Adoniram Judson was the last service for which Dr. Kendrick was able to leave his home. Other correspondents mention his continued frailty. He died on September 11, 1848.

[124] This letter is undated. There is a notation on it that it was written September 10—Wednesday, September 10 places it in 1845.

[125] "Nem" or "Nemmy" was a name of endearment given to Emily by a small group of her intimate friends at the Utica Female Academy. Anna Maria Anable was "Ninny."

[126] In letters to Emily, Anna Maria often referred to herself as "Mama" or "Mother-in-law."

[127] Jane Kelly was Emily Chubbuck's friend at the Utica Female Academy. Following the departure of Mr. and Mrs. Nichols, Jane became the literary principal in early 1844. Then with the departure of Cynthia Sheldon to Philadelphia in the fall of 1848, she became "headmistress."

[128] Mary Barber, mentioned frequently in the Emily Chubbuck Judson letters, was a student and then a teacher at the Utica Female Academy. A prior letter spoke of M.B. traveling, and of some contention with Cynthia Sheldon.

[129] Sarah Bell Wheeler was a teacher at the Utica Female Academy, and an intimate of Emily Chubbuck, one of the few who addressed Emily as "Nemmy." In a September, 1847 letter, she was listed as one of the teachers at the Utica Female Academy. There are a number of letters from Sarah Bell before and after her marriage to Charles Gould of Boston. They were married in October 1850. There are several letters clustered in the year or two after Emily left for Burmah, and a number of letters at the time of her return to America. Emily stayed with Charles and Sarah Bell Gould in October 1851 when she arrived in Boston, after the long sea voyage from Burmah, and then England. She was to stay there a number of times following that. In 1851,

love to your mother[130] and Kate,[131] and tell them it will only make a day or two difference.

A. M.

Written in the left margin of page 1: "I shall be disappointed if you don't come."

Source: American Baptist Historical Society, AJ 23, no. 1138.

Dr. William M. Gillespie to Emily E. Chubbuck, September 13, 1845—Union College

My dear friend,

Your kind answer to my hasty epistle[132] has been a great traveler since it left you in search of me. Not finding me at home in N. Y. it followed me far down East from town to town, and like Noah's dove in its first flight from the ark, it found no rest for the sole of its foot, but like that dove in its second flight, when it did at last find me, it bore an olive leaf for the *other* Fanny,[133] to whom I immediately transferred it to her great delight. She has just returned to N. Y. to pass the winter. A collection of her poems is in press by Clarke and Austin (the publishers of Willis's[134] poems) to form the first of a series of American poetesses—but this is as yet a secret I believe.

When does your first number appear? I expect to find some new friends in it, as I used utterly to eschew the magazines, and even now only read in them the pages headed by Fanny Forester[135] and Fanny Osgood—and by the way I picked up in a Connecticut village an odd number of the "Columbian" and found in it your story of "The Banknote" which touched my feelings so deeply, and made my heart so swell, that I should place it for pathos at the very head of your long line of [ ] of commissions. I *won't* like "Dora'"[136]—overmuch I mean—partly from contrariety, because everybody else does, and partly because I have seen a shocking daub by

---

Anna Maria Anable had written of Sarah Bell: "Sarah is grown so lovely in person as well as character that she must assert a blessed influence on all with whom she comes in contact."

[130] Lavinia Richards Chubbuck, Emily's mother, was born June 1, 1875, in Goffstown NH, the eldest of thirteen children. She married Charles Chubbuck on November 17. 1805. They were the parents of seven children.

[131] Sarah Catharine ("Kate," "Kit," or "Kitty") Chubbuck, Emily's older sister, born October 25, 1816.

[132] See Gillespie's first letter to Emily E. Chubbuck dated August 2, 1845.

[133] Frances or "Fanny" Osgood, a contemporary writer with Emily, was one of the regulars writing for *Graham's Magazine*.

[134] Nathaniel Parker (N. P.) Willis was the editor of *New Mirror*, the magazine that catapulted Emily into literary fame. He became a friend, mentor, and eventually a suitor.

[135] Fanny Forester, Emily Chubbuck's *nom de plume*.

[136] N. P. Willis commissioned an artist named Flagg to do a portrait of "Dora,'" one of Emily's fictional characters.

Flagg[137] (whose puffs by Willis always seemed to me interisest [sic] irony) intended to "*illustrate*" it. "Illustrate" a lily by a bushel of charcoal!

My vacation has been passed all along shore between N. Y. and Newport, with divers [ ] accidents by field and flood—and *widows*. Old Mr. Weller was a true philosopher, when he said to his distinguished son, "Samuel, beware of widders." I was escorting a young and pretty one a dark night beside the Railroad Depot at Stonington, when suddenly a mammoth baggage car loomed up in the fog, rushing down upon us like a black avalanche. I seized the widow to drag her back to a side door in the depot as our only chance of being saved, but she obstinately attempted to rush into the river alongside. This I decidedly objected to, as I should have been bound to jump in after her—but she headstrongly and woman like, was determined to drown herself—and me—and thus she frantically struggled with me, the car rushing onward, and it was only by actual violence that I succeeded in forcing her back far enough to give the car time to be stopped by the men aroused by her screams. For some moments I expected that we should both be crushed to death, as a consequence of her obstinacy, and I afterward proved to her that our imminent danger resulted entirely from her want of confidingness, and trustfulness in me—always lovely attributes in woman, but in such a predicament positively life-preservers as well as life beautifiers. To crown all, she chose to faint when the danger was over, just as all the passengers for N. Y. were passing by, and one who recognized me, told in N. Y. a long story of a beautiful woman fainting in my arms, which saluted me from all sides the moment of my return. I say then with the respected Mr. Weller, that widows *are* dangerous.

In spite—or in consequence of all these perils I have returned with such a copious supply of health that I have some to spare and would most gladly transfer to you a good portion of it, if such an exchange were possible. Alas that "transfusion" is only a glorious dream—akin to the "philosopher's stone," and the "elixir of life"—poetic fancies with which man has tried to console himself for the narrow limits of his earthly sphere of existence, by sending forth his soul in aspirations and imaginings of what *might* be—and what indeed *will* be in some place and at some time—(perhaps in the millennium)—for the capacity of dreaming such visions implies and pledges the eventual power of realizing them, when man has attained that higher state of being to which he is tending. I like such day-dreams—or rather moonlight ones; which they are just now. But since transfusion is as yet only a dream, tell me what the reality is as to your health. Our excellent friend, Mrs.

---

[137] See the preceding footnote.

Nott,[138] tells me that you have thought very seriously about New Orleans. Is it so, or what are your plans?

You speak of writing a story for an annual. Pray Miss Fanny, did it ever occur to you that it is very wicked to *tell stories* so often as you do? Fibbing is very naughty; and you tell your stories in such a truthful way, that every one forgets that they are stories, and so much the *greater* is therefore your wickedness, for you deceive doubly. Your friends will say indeed (and with good reason) that your stories all tend to make people happier and better (by the way *I* have been growing better, in obedience to your parting injunctions) but even admitting that they do, you are only *doing evil* that good may come. How can you escape this syllogism—

    1. She who tells stories is naughty
    2. Fanny tells stories
Therefore, 3. Fanny is naughty.

As to my telling you a story—in the first place, I *won't*—and in the second (query-*first*!) place, *can't*. I have not the slightest shade of invention, and therefore you may always trust the literal truth of all that I say, and especially that I remain

Most truly Yours

Wm M. Gillespie

Written in the top margin of page 1: "Be not dismayed by these double sheets, for you will escape with only four pages."

Source: American Baptist Historical Society, AJ 24, no. 1200.

M. Wilmarth to Emily E. Chubbuck,[139] September 17, 1845— New York City

Dear Miss Chubbuck,

I received your letter last week and should have answered it much sooner could I possibly have done so. I am sorry any thing [sic] should ever have occurred to mar our friendship but I must confess that my feelings were very much wounded indeed at your manner of speaking to me of your visit here. We always try so much to please our friends when they visit in that it is very mortifying to us to have such remarks made. However I am willing to "bury the tomahawk" and hope we shall in

---

[138] Urania Sheldon Nott—a mentor, advisor, and friend to Emily—was the literary principal at the Utica Female Academy when Emily arrived in October 1840. In late summer 1842 Urania married Eliphalet Nott, president of Union College in Schenectady NY.

[139] Emily had visited the Wilmarths when she visited New York in May 1845.

future be good friends. Hoping to hear from you very soon I remain your true friend,

M. Wilmarth

Source: American Baptist Historical Society, AJ 27, no. 1290.

Emily E. Chubbuck to Catherine Chubbuck, September 23, 1845—Utica

Dear Kitty,

If it will do you five cents worth of good to know that "I am well and hope these few lines will find you enjoying the same blessing." I will just stop and say it, for I have no time for anything more. We had so much botheration with the big Fair last week that I could'nt [sic] do anything and this week[140] I am trying to write a story, but I doubt whether I ever finish it. There was a party every evening last week, but I did'nt [sic] [ ] [ ] [ ] but one (at Alderman Wilson's) for I could'nt [sic] st[ ]. I came out very safely and was'nt [sic] much *sic*[ ] [ ] [ ] stage that when I started—had Eld. Knap [ ] [ ] [ ] Mr. John Sheldon[141] is here. He saw Walker[142] [ ] [ ] [ ]Madison, where he was engaged in [ ] [ ] [ ] during the session of the legislature. T[ ] [ ] [ ] that Mr. S. tho't he was [ ] [ ] [ ].

My book[143] is to be divided into two at twenty-five cents each.—Write and tell me all the news.

Give love to Mary—tell her she don't know [sic] what bad stories I am telling the Lillybridges about her.

Good-night

Source: Hanna family files.

---

[140] See the letter from Anna Maria Anable to Emily E. Chubbuck dated September 10, 1845. In that letter Anna Maria urged Emily to come to Utica earlier than she had planned as Anna Maria was planning a big party and wanted Emily to be there. She said also that the Fair would be the following week.

[141] There are two John Sheldon's in the correspondence. One we believe to be Cynthia Sheldon's brother—in May 1841 Sheldon accompanied him to the Wisconsin Territory where his daughter was to marry H. Hawley, a friend of Sheldon's who was in the publishing business. Then on May 7, 1845, Anna Maria mentioned a Cousin John Sheldon who had seen J. Walker Chubbuck in the Wisconsin Territory. This we would assume to be a son of John Sheldon—who would also be Anna Maria's cousin.

[142] John Walker Chubbuck, Emily's older brother who ran a newspaper in the Wisconsin Territory. Though he regularly sent copies of the paper to Emily, she often reminded him that a paper was not a substitute for a real letter and that his family longed to hear a personal word from him.

[143] This is no doubt a reference to *Trippings in Author-land*, which was published in November, 1845. It was published as a single volume.

Timothy Shay Arthur[144] to Emily E. Chubbuck, September 26, 1845—Philadelphia[145]

Fanny Forrester [sic][146]

In my last letter to you, I explained to you as clearly as I could, what would be the probable result of the publication of your book[147] by Fenett Co, so for [Note: The remainder of the line is lost in the letter fold.] did the same to Gen'l. Morris.[148] To day [sic] I have recd a letter from him, in which he says—

"After I rec'd your last letter I wrote to Fanny Forrester [sic], and advised her to leave every *thing* [sic] *to you*. She has done so. Since then I have had a conversation with some booksellers here, who will give the author better terms than you offer. You requested me to consult F. F.'s interest and *not* yours, in the disposal of her mhs.—I do so in making this statement. I leave the matter with you, however. If you think proper to go on with the work, do so. If you feel disposed to return the copy, do so at once."

Both Mr. Fenett, my partner, and I think alike and feel alike in this matter. We are conscious that the amt of profits we could get out of your book, if it all went to you, would not be an adequate compensation for your labors. Therefore cheerfully do we return the copy of your book to Geo. C. Morris, and we feel a sincere pleasure in the belief that you will be [Note: "More adequately compensated" is written and then crossed out.] better paid by the change of publishers.

Should you not find the new arrangement so satisfactory as it were promised, we shall be at any time ready to take hold of any new book you may think of offering the public.[149]

The new volume of "Authors Magazine" which will commence in January next, we shall greatly improve; the price will be raised to $3, and the whole work be put upon a par with Graham's[150] or any other magazine. I shall be very glad to make

---

[144] Timothy Shay Arthur was an active temperance crusader, an editor, and an author of both fiction and non-fiction works. Born in 1809, he was schooled at home by his mother because of his frail health. Around 1833 he started his career as the editor of the *Baltimore Athenaeum and Young Men's Paper*, and by 1839 he was editing the *Baltimore Merchant*. In the next decade he wrote a number of books, contributed to magazines such as *Godey's Lady's Book*, and from 1844 to 1846 he published and wrote for *Arthur's Ladies' Magazine*. In 1845 he had been contacted about publishing Emily's *Trippings in Author-land*, but the manuscript was returned to General Morris of the *New Mirror*, who was handling Emily's publishing affairs, with the statement that Emily would profit better with someone else as her publisher. T. S. Arthur continued active in publishing circles until his death in 1885.

[145] This was the first of two letters. After this one had been written, Arthur received a letter from Emily Chubbuck, and that prompted the second letter of the same date.

[146] Fanny Forester, Emily Chubbuck's *nom de plume*.

[147] This would be the publication of *Trippings in Author-land*, a compilation of her Fanny Forester stories.

[148] George P. "General" Morris, was N. P. Willis's partner at the *New Mirror* and a prominent literary figure in New York and Philadelphia.

[149] *Trippings in Author-land* was eventually published by Paine and Burgess, New York.

[150] *Graham's Magazine*, published by George Graham, was one of the preeminent literary magazines of the period. Fanny Forester's stories were published regularly in this very well known and respected publication.

you among its regular contributors. We will pay as good a price as any of the publishers. Will you not let me have an article for the January number? I shall want it in about 6 weeks—

I am exceedingly well pleased with your article for the *Snow Flake*—having read it in the proofs.

Yours very sincerely

T. S. Arthur

Source: American Baptist Historical Society, AJ 22, no. 1074.

Timothy Shay Arthur[151] to Emily E. Chubbuck, September 26, 1845—Philadelphia[152]

Fanny Forrester[153] [sic]

After sending your Ms. to Gen'l Morris,[154] and writing to you the enclosed letter, your welcome favor of 23rd inst: was rec'd.

I trust you will fully understand the motives what have governed us in deferring to a N. York Publisher.[155] We have looked to your interest and such to our own, and we sincerely hope the change may be a more advantageous one to you.

I think it very likely that if you go to St. Augustine your arrangement for letters [ ] be made with Sat. *Conner* or Neal's *Gazette*.[156] I will see the publishers as early as possible, and let you know their news

[ ] [ ] have an article for [ ] Magazine [ ]. I want particularly an article from your pen in January number, which we wish to [ ] [ ].

Very sincerely

Yours

T. S. Arthur

Source: American Baptist Historical Society, AJ 22, no. 1073.

---

[151] Timothy Shay Arthur was an active temperance crusader, an editor, and an author of both fiction and non-fiction works.

[152] This was the second of two letters. After the first had been written, Arthur received a letter from Emily Chubbuck, and that prompted the second letter of the same date. See also the letter from T. Arthur, also dated September 26, 1845.

[153] Fanny Forrester, Emily Chubbuck's *nom de plume*.

[154] George P. "General" Morris, was N. P. Willis's partner at the *New Mirror* and a prominent literary figure in New York and Philadelphia.

[155] General Morris had written Arthur that a New York publisher could offer Emily better terms for the sale of the book and that would be most advantageous to Emily.

[156] Joseph Neal was a prominent member of Philadelphia's literary establishment and was a part of Emily Chubbuck's circle of friends when she was in Philadelphia. Neal was well known and respected as a writer and editor; one of his best known works was the *Charcoal Sketches*. He had founded the *Saturday Gazette* in 1842, a very successful publication which contained a great deal of humorous satire. Anna Maria Anable frequently referred to "Neal" as a beau for Emily. Neal married Alice Bradley in 1846; he died in 1847.

Nathaniel Parker Willis to Emily E. Chubbuck,[157] September 27, 1845—Leipzig[158]

My dearest Fanny,[159]

I received a day or two since your long and kind letter dated from Hamilton. I would almost rather not reply to it at all than to touch as lightly as I must on some of its topics, but we shall have the more to put right when I return—for brief I must be. I was very indignant at your accusation of my ever having turned our first meeting into ridicule. On the contrary, I thought it a beautiful instance of a character of outer reserve giving way to a previous mental acquaintance, and whenever I spoke of it, I so described it. I give you my honor I gave no one occasion to do other than admire you by anything I ever said on the subject, but it seems you are yet to learn how easily the malicious turn the best things into plausible untruths. The sweetest pleasure to your enemies would be a separation of interest between us. Enough of this, however! I only implore you to decide upon nothing you hear without better evidence than you seem willing to confide in now.

You have no idea how much advice you need at this moment, dear Fanny. You are venturing into a wounding, cruel and bad world, with a heart newly open to the light and air, and envy is laying up misinterpretations of every word you say. You cannot believe this, but I beg of you to be careful in your confidences. Your flame is too brilliant not to make you hosts of enemies, and before long they will think it time to bring you down from your popularity. I have only time to say this much. Imagine the rest.

You ask me whether you shall marry for convenience. *Most decidedly*, *no*! What convenience would pay you for passing eighteen hours out of every twenty-four for the rest of your life, within four walls, in company with a person not to your taste? I judge of you by myself. *I would not pass one year thus for any fortune on earth*. The private hours of one single month are too precious for any price but love. **Good God!** Think how little of the day poverty can touch after all. Only the hours when you are out of your chamber. But the moment your chamber door is shut on you alone, all comparison between you and the richest is at an end. **My dear Emily**, let the majority of women marry for convenience, if they will; but *you* are brim-full of romance, and delicacy, and tenderness, and a marriage without love, *for you*, would

---

[157] We have two versions of this letter—the original as written by Emily E. Chubbuck, and the edited version published by A. C. Kendrick in his biography, *The Life and Letters of Mrs. Emily C. Judson*. Additions made by Kendrick we have placed in parentheses (), and words in the original left out by Kendrick we have added in bold.

[158] Though written on September 27, 1845, this letter was received in Utica on November 8, 1845, and forwarded to Emily in Philadelphia.

Written on the address page in the handwriting of Emily E. Chubbuck: "Willis. 31. Nov. 5, 1845. Leipzig Sept. 27."

[159] Fanny Forester, Emily Chubbuck's *nom de plume*.

be sealing up a volcano with a cobweb. You must love—you *must* and *will* love, passionately and overpoweringly. You have as yet turned but one leaf in a volume of your heart's life. Your bosom is an altar on which there is a fire newly lit—lit by the late and sudden awakening of your genius. *Your peculiarity is*, that your genius has its altar on your heart, and not like other people's, in the brain. Take care, **for heaven's sake**, how you throw away the entire music and beauty of a life for only *a home that will grow hateful to you*. I *warn* you that you *must love* sooner or later.

In reading over the last page I find that I have advised you to a course that will keep you at work for the present—but let it be so. You are lifting yourself tho' through a stratum of valuation at every struggle, and, leave off when you will, it will be better than having left off before. **Meantime take care of your health, and do not let the world see too much of you.** Jane Porter told me she never could thank her mother sufficiently for having removed her to a secluded life when she began to be famous. You are thus out of the reach of ill will and depreciation.

I shall be in New York in the course of the winter, or in the Spring at the farthest, and when I see you, I can talk more with you in five minutes than I can write in a month. When I have once torn myself from my life's blood, my child, I must pass two or three years alone in New York, and I shall need somebody to be interested for. I shall do what I can to make you famous and happy.

I am here with my brother Richard, a student, and not having seen him for four or five years, our meeting has been a great happiness. I love him very much, and just now I feel happier than I have done for a long time.

Write to me "to the care of Kelly, No 2 Tigo Street, London." She will forward to me—(my old landlady).

Well—God bless you, dear Emily. I conjure you to keep the relations between us entirely secret even from your most intimate confidant, otherwise, elevated and truthful as our feelings are, the world will endeavor to divide us.

Ever yours affectionately,

N. P. W.

Source: Hanna Family files; A. C. Kendrick, *The Life and Letters of Mrs. Emily C. Judson*, 134.

Mary Adams[160] to Emily E. Chubbuck, October 12, 1845—Sachem's Grove[161]

You are a chicken through, Em Chugup[162] [sic] to suppose that I could answer a letter I never received, so hush your scolding, and hear how this here scratches—

You "have heard several times etc" so have I, but I don't believe it yet—if the 'Ondix' of the public be trice, there am I a [ ]! Not that I should have the slightest objection to fall in with any one [sic] of the delightful arrangements my friends have been so kind as to make for me—but suppose the case stands thus—each one of my numerous so called "adorers"—seems to be particularly anxious to secure me for his friends—generously declining the pleasure of appropriating me to himself—"How can the girl"—I won't tell you a word about my going south—why? because I don't know any thing [sic] about it—when? How? With whom? I don't know and what's more I don't care—

"Fill *my* place"—the presumption of small people is astonishingly "Fill my pocket," and willingly may you fill my *place*—"This it is and nothing more"—prevents my following inclination, and remaining here this winter, oh when shall I be rich enough to rest from my labors? "Quoth the raven, Never more"—I've had a horrid cold, "Merely this, and nothing more" has kept me here in Yankee land so long—I shall make a desperate effort to get to New York Tuesday—but Jane[163] sent me last evening a package of letters and cards that have been collecting there for the last fortnight, yours was amongst them—I am sorry indeed to have lost the sight *of several* Utica friends, I hope that Mrs. Crafts[164] will remain through the week—If I had been there, I might have aided my friend Mr. Brayton in selecting the wedding ring! Efforts of riding in a close carriage–1. Getting to your destination some moments sooner than if you walked–2. Keeping dry feet on a wet morning–3. Saving your locomotive energies, for those occasions when you can't ride–4. Gives your friends food for scandal–5. Patronizes "Lucy Nobles"–6. Marries the chambermaid. 7. Goes to N.Y. to buy the wedding ring—"only this and nothing more." What was there in that carriage? "Silence then and nothing more."

The summing up of the matter is this—that my exchequer is too low to spend this winter—and I had rather return now than after another six months frolic—I sincerely wish you might make some arrangement to go out with me. Will you not

---

[160] Mary Adams, a friend of Emily's while at the Utica Female Academy. She lived in New Orleans.

[161] This is written as it reads—a flowing stream of consciousness style, with the punctuation the despair of any knowledgeable reader.

[162] Mary Adams uses this spelling of "Chubbuck" in both of her letters to Emily (the other is December 16, 1845).

[163] Jane Kelly was Emily Chubbuck's friend at the Utica Female Academy. Jane was the literary principal at the Utica Female Academy. In fall 1848, she followed Cynthia Sheldon as headmistress.

[164] Augusta Crafts and her strong opinions are mentioned frequently in the letters written from the Utica Female Academy.

be in New York this month, I hope to see you there—and now bidding you a very good night.

I with love to you will hold forth to Betsy for a moment.

In a magazine blue satin, "She looked magnificent." So I did write to Sarah and Charlotte—Oh Betsy, "I saw him but an hour" yet felt an age of pain."

Clarkson! I should certainly have stayed another day in Dor[ ], had not my too susceptible heart warned me to depart. We arrive [ ]—I won't say anything more—Mother, Eugenia[165] and myself go down on Tuesday, I shall probably be in New York some weeks—Where is Augusta[166]—tell her Jane is provoked with her for not coming back with me—I hope to see her in the city before I leave—If you should come down Betsy bring with you a book I left at Mrs. La[ ]—The Siege of Barletta—I have not read it yet.

I've been trying to console myself—by driving about, walking and such like exploits. Our forests are resplendent, I have either never seen the fall of the year so beautiful or I have just taken a "realizing sense"—of etc.

Betsy if you should, notice any thing [sic] peculiar my style—know that all the time I have been writing, Mrs. Goddard has been holding forth from, "Proverbial Philosophy"—which added to the distant sound of Bye oh bye, my baby dear, the eating of chestnuts, apples etc, may have interfered with the usual perspicacity of my ideas and marred the flowing elegance etc.—My love to all from Grandpahler [sic] to the end of the chapter.

Write me all the news, and when positive arrangements are made for my establishment in Utica, let me know, and I'll be there

I wrote to Moll Barber, the other day—I hope Charley is keeping a faithful record of passing events for my benefit—stir him up—occasionally.

Pleasant dreams Betsy, and do get up to breakfast.

Your sleepy mopsy.

Source: American Baptist Historical Society, AJ 22, no. 1093.

---

[165] Eugenia Damaux, part of Emily's intimate circle of friends at the Utica Female Academy.
[166] Mrs. Augusta Crafts and her strong opinions are mentioned frequently in the letters written from the Utica Female Academy.

Morven M. Jones to Emily E. Chubbuck,[167] October 17, 1845—Utica

Dear Madam

"Better late than never" is an old maxim, but I can't say that it furnishes an excuse for delays in matters of friendship or politeness. A "good bit since" I received from your hand per Mr. Hawley[168] a packet of valuable autographs for which even now I hope your forbearance will permit you to accept my heartiest—no, my heart's Mollys—but my most *sincere* thanks—Here I am safely over a terrible bad bridge by way of introduction—the autograph monomaniact [sic] are never more pleased than when such a treasure as the one sent is received and there's reason in the thing—It must be nought but the very quintessence of *good nature* that would prompt any one to humor the whims of we autographians—Ergo you must have a pretty considerable stock of that commodity on hand i.e. goodness.—If you were ever flattered (and who hasn't been?) you will now expect I have an axe to grind—I would like a few lines of your own writing now, say 3 or 4 verses with the signature of the author underneath—that isn't much, but after all it may [ ] [ ] will be granted, so Miss C. may suit her own convenience in the matter.

It would be bad taste to add anything like sense to the above and there's enough of that sort, so nought more should be written but

M. M. Jones

Source: American Baptist Historical Society, AJ 24, no. 1175.

---

[167] Emily was to receive a lot of letters asking her for something—her autograph—the autograph of Adoniram Judson—a poem dedicated to the memory of a loved one unknown to Emily—a story or a paper or a statement for a book to be published—a hymn for a special missionary meeting—and Emily was very compliant in responding to such requests. In terms of autograph collectors, we note that many of the original letters in the correspondence have the signature cut out of the paper, where someone had removed it for their collection.

From Utica, Morvan Jones was well known to the Utica Female Academy family. He was to write six more letters to Emily—one in 1846—three in 1848—and two in 1852. They were to contain congratulations on Emily choosing the missionary life—news of Utica and the political scene—comments on Emily's conflict with Alexander Beebee at the time of her engagement to Adoniram Judson—his health and the terrible accident that had happened to his wife—abstracts from magazines on the mission that would possibly be helpful to Emily in working on the Judson Memoir with Dr. Francis Wayland.

[168] Horace H. Hawley married Jane Sheldon, the niece of Cynthia and Urania Sheldon, Hawley was a member of a publishing firm and also worked with Alexander Beebee in publishing the *Baptist Register*. Hawley was enormously helpful to Emily as she published her early stories and books. There are numerous references to his help and his generosity.

Paine and Burgess to Emily E. Chubbuck, October 23, 1845

Charming Fanny Forester[169]

What a commencent [sic] to a letter by grave and venerable Publishers, but we can't see what other way to begin this, and after racking our brains between plain prose and any imaginings, simple Misses and respected Madam the pen has touched on the paper "Charming Fanny Forester" but to change the spirit of our tale, we send you at the suggestion of the smiling "Brigadier"[170] the proof sheets of the sketches as far as printed.[171] The Book will contain 240 pp of this size—it is all stereotyped except the first few pages containing the Title Preface etc. We should like to have some title decided upon as soon as possible that there may be no delay in getting this work printed and published.

With respect Yours Faithfully

Paine and Burgess

Source: American Baptist Historical Society, AJ 25, no. 1220.

I. M. Loomis to Emily E. Chubbuck, October 24, 1845—Hamilton Institute

My Dear Miss Forester,

Many thanks to you for the honor conferred upon me a few weeks since and also for the privilege of which I now avail myself. Who would have supposed till the memorable evening of Ms. Nichols' Wedding that I should even have the honor of being presented to address the authoress Fanny Forester?[172] Not I. And I could not now do it in so familiar a style had I not been very much disappointed upon forming an acquaintance with her. I had supposed that the combination of Scholar, Teacher and Authoress was sufficient to insure instead of a lively and familiar address sedateness and formality. In this I acknowledge my mistake.

When I presumed upon your generosity perhaps too much by proposing a correspondence it had several objects in view. I suppose it might be beneficial not only in the improvement of my style, but also in the cultivation of *the* sociable. You know we, as an illustration, are very much isolated. This, while it may contribute to the accomplishment of the main object which we have in view, leaves us in

---

[169] Fanny Forester, Emily Chubbuck's *nom de plume*.

[170] George P. "General" Morris, was N. P. Willis's partner at the *New Mirror* and a prominent literary figure in New York and Philadelphia. Willis had asked General Morris to help Emily with any literary or publishing problems she might have.

[171] These would be the proof sheets for *Trippings in Author-land*, a compilation of stories which Emily had written for the various magazines. It was to be published in November 1845.

[172] Fanny Forester, Emily Chubbuck's *nom de plume*.

many particulars quite unprepared for intercourse with the world. This I have experienced to my satisfaction, or rather to my dissatisfaction. And we are to be still more isolated. A Church is about to be organized on the Hill and arrangements are already made to have services here all day on Sabbath. In the morning students preach, in the afternoon the Faculty. In that we have now nothing to call us to town.[173] We can now mingle very little in the society of the "fairer sex" to experience their refining influences. What will become of the finer sensibilities of our nature if they (are) left without cultivation? You appreciate my motives I presume. Are they not just?

I wonder if you have recovered from the influences of that evening, the embarrassment and other bad feelings of which you complained? How unfortunate that you should be so unfavorably affected on such an occasion! Even your official station and the marked stillness and attention of all present failed to render your situation agreeable. It was supposed a change might be favorable. This also proved insufficient. The balmy zephyrs, the shady bower and charms of evening—the very soul of Romance—all failed to sooth your troubled spirit. But I trust that with the occasion the exciting causes are removed and you have since become composed.

I have often recurred to that evening's interview with a great deal of pleasure. And you will not accuse me of a design to flatter when I said that aside from all other considerations, my interview with you more than compensates for my journey there and back. Even that *great difficulty* which arose between us cannot make me feel otherwise. But I believe that was amicably settled was it not? If not, would not another such a walk on such an evening settle it?[174]

Suffer me here to digress and make an inquiry. When does your next term commence? One of my sisters thinks of attending your school and wished me to ascertain if possible and inform her. Perhaps I can obtain a circular which will give the requisite information. It is supposed however by some that an alteration has been recently made. What are the facts in the case?

And now Fanny, I hope you will excuse my familiarity for I cannot well avoid it. While writing I cease to look upon you as an Authoress or a Critic and regard you as a friend. I feel just as well acquainted with you as if I had known you for years. When do you return to Hamilton? Are you going South this winter? But you will anticipate such inquiries in your answer, which I shall expect soon. I have the honor to be

Yours most respectfully,

I. M. Loomis   Source: American Baptist Historical Society, AJ 25, no. 1249.

---

[173] This suggests that Loomis was a student at the Hamilton Literary and Theological Institution.

[174] We would be very, very curious to know what happened at the Nichols' wedding between Emily Chubbuck (Fanny Forester) and I. M. Loomis.

Nathaniel Parker Willis to Emily E. Chubbuck,[175] October 26, 1845—Berlin[176]

Dearest Emily,

I received yesterday two letters from you that had been delayed on the way, for they are a month or two old, tho their sweetness has by no means evaporated. I have quite fed upon them, for I have a large altar in my bosom whose fires sadly lack such spice-wood as your affection. If you ever mean to stop being kind to me, wait till you can first announce it to me in *words*. A cold letter would be unendurable.

But what mischief there must be at work to separate us. You say in one of your letters (a late one also just received) "I have heard that you lost all interest in me as soon as your curiosity was gratified." Who could say such a thing? My dear friend, never believe one word that comes to you with a purpose or tendency to make you doubt my interest in you. I have made up my mind for life as to your quality and value. I know that there are few women your equals, either in heart or mind, and I am satisfied "once for all" that you are worth any outlay of cherishing and caring for. The tie between us, also is a poetical and unusual one, and the only misfortune about it is that *the world* would never believe in its strength or endurance. We are doomed to walk this world coupled by a chain whose links are invisible and incredible. People will try to walk between us—but don't let the jar of their disappointment break the chain. Can you not fancy how noble a pleasure it was to me to discover such a mind as yours and be the first to interpret it to the world. I feel as if you belonged to me, as much as a star to its first discoverer or a rare flower to an admiring naturalist. You go on shining, or drinking light and dew, without changing essentially, but mine is the joy and pride of having first appreciated you and call'd you by your right name. I have been compelled to be a worldling outwardly, my dear Emily, but my chamber door never shuts a worldling in. I am as natural and poetical, when only the angels are with me, as ever I was or could be. Had I the means, I would never again step out of the inner ring which encloses me when alone—were I rich enough, that is to say, to afford to stay away from contact with the world around me. I wish it was possible to make this same world forget that so sweet a tie belongs to me and your affection. I should like to visit you only in spirit, melt my heart into yours, and be unseen by the coarse eyes of mortals. But this is sweet dreaming from which I must wake presently.

---

[175] On the address page, Emily had written "32," meaning that this had been the thirty-second letter she had received from N. P. Willis.

[176] With the time delay of sending this from Berlin to Utica NY, and then having it forwarded to Philadelphia, we are aware that this would have reached Emily not more than a week or two before her meeting with Adoniram Judson. Interestingly, we note expressions of feelings in this letter by Willis that had not been expressed previously.

Where shall you be when I return? I shall probably be in America in March—but tied to New York by business unceasing. You say you are well—thank God for that—but where shall you be? How shall I see you? There would be talk enough about my going to see you to make you very uncomfortable. Can not [sic] you live in New York and follow a literary life? I must delve there to be able to leave something to my darling Imogen, and that is now all my future. After this beautiful child, you are the nearest human being to my heart—but to ensure her happiness I would give up my life tomorrow.

To make your letters come direct to me, you will be obliged to inflict some expense upon yourself. You must mail a letter for the…

Written in the left margin of the address page: "…steamer three days before she sails, and pay the postage. Direct 'N. P .W. to the care of Mrs. Kelly No.2 Vigo St. London.' There is no other way of sending with speed and certainty.

"Well, God bless you. Take care of your health, put your rich heart into your writings, (or rather put its history there), and let no outward word or influence affect our friendship. I long to get home and once more see the casket which holds in such a treasure as the mind and affections of Fanny Forester.[177] Put a proper value on both. You will find a kiss in the corner below.

"Ever yours affectionately

"N. P. W."

Source: Hanna family files.

---

[177] Fanny Forester, Emily Chubbuck's *nom de plume*.

Anna Maria Anable to Emily E. Chubbuck, November 2, 1845[178]

Sunday Morn'g
Clifton Grove 3rd story in Eugenia's[179] room
looking out upon a rainy morning for
my amusement

Don't congratulate me on my safe arrival dear Nem[180] for if you knew my present trial you will find me no fit subject.

I had a delightful ride yesterday with Mr. Sargeant—he is a very entertaining man and he paid you some handsome compliments—I took another scolding on your account when I arrived at the Wilmarths[181] and took myself over to Brooklyn as quick as I conveniently could. They were rather surprised to see me so soon and had about concluded to have Miss T wait and go up with you—but I represented my forlorn condition in such pitiful terms that they at last consented that she should go tomorrow with me. I am to look after her winter 'rigging' a little which considering that my two other children are out of my hands for the present, will be no bother. The stages doing their utmost for me I could not get back to Crosby St. before five o'clock, but I had rec'd such an imploring note from Eugenia to come directly to her that late as it was I started for the Hoboken ferry. By the time I got there it was pitch dark, and I was a 'little skeared,' but I made known to the ferry master where I was going, and asked him to procure me a carriage. I was treated with all possible deference to be sure, but that did not sooth the fretting of my spirit at an hours' delay at the ferry house before a carriage could be procured. Then, when it was so dark I could scarcely see the horse before me, I stept [sic] into a little covered buggy with a driver I discovered by his accent to be a foreigner.

---

[178] This letter has been very difficult to date. We originally dated it to December 28, because it seemed to contain a Christmas party for children, and it was written on a Sunday which would be the 28th. However on December 23 Anna Maria writes of going to western with mary Brayton, and on the 30th she tells of that trip and is back in Utica. The contents of this letter are incongruous with this schedule. We then found a letter November 6, when Anna Maria was coming back from New York and her Aunt Urania caughter her at the cars and took her home to stay with Dr. Nott whiel Urania Nott went on to Utica to have some dresses made. The Sunday previous to this, we think, would be a good time to place Anna Maria in New York City and Hoboken, New Jersey, and so we place the letter on Sunday, November 2. We believe that when Emily left Utica for her stay in Philadelphia, Anna Maria went with her as far as New York. Emily arrived in Philadelphia on November 1, and Anna Maria went in search of Eugenia Damaux.

[179] Eugenia Damaux had been part of Emily's intimate circle of friends at the Utica Female Academy. Living in New York City, Eugenia suffered from some kind of eye problem that at times made her life very difficult; this was a matter of comment in many of the letters exchanged between the girls themselves and with Cynthia Sheldon. In 1848, Eugenia was in New York living "at Mrs. Brown's—the same warm-hearted French girl as ever." In 1849, she married Johnny Edmonds, described as rich and pious, and they lived in Utica.

[180] "Nem" or "Nemmy" was a name of endearment given to Emily by a small group of her intimate friends at the Utica Female Academy. Anna Maria Anable was "Ninny."

[181] Mr. and Mrs. John Wilmarth. There are frequent mentions of the Wilmarths' home and hospitality. In a letter earlier that year, Emily had been offended by something said during her visit, and Mrs. Wilmarth had apologized. See her letter dated September 17, 1845.

We had not gone a half mile before it began to rain in torrents! All the horrible stories I had ever heard of Hoboken flashed thro' my mind, all the newspaper outrages I have read in the morning, and my poor innocent little foreigner for a few minutes suffered not a little in my suspicions. I was fairly in the condition Scott's old woman in the turret. *N'importe* for that. He brought me safely home at last. As the [ ]all door was opened upon me a flood of light poured out from the parlors, and such a scampering of children, such a cracking of torpedo mothers, such a confusion of cakes and fruits and nuts would have delighted the heart of my little husband at least. It was a children's party. Mademoiselle Fanny was not at home! Mrs. Brown rec'd me very cordially, and has given me every possible attention, condoled with me and laughed—There! Nem imagine the rest of that sentence for I have not time to finish it. I was interrupted by a call to put my things on and get into their family carriages which that morning held twelve persons and after having deposited eleven individuals at the country church, the driver was to take me over to Jersey City (6 miles) where I found Eugenia—or rather when I found she had gone to church. We visited hard yesterday afternoon tho' and today I am most tired to death getting music. O I wish I was home! Do come home quick for I am dreadfully lonesome. Write me as soon as you get this and tell me all you are doing, how Fanny[182] is, etc. and I shall be anxious to know if you receive the money. My purse was tucked under a pair of dirty stockings in my valise. Tell Fan she must write back without fail. Give much love to Mr. and Mrs. G.[183] the children all—I must start in a few minutes and they are waiting tea for me. Good by. Do write.

Anna Maria

Source: American Baptist Historical Society, AJ 23, no. 1139B.

---

[182] Fanny Anable, one of five Anable sisters. She was born April 12, 1828. At this time, she was working and living in the home of Hannah and A. D. Gillette in Philadelphia.

[183] Rev. A. D. Gillette was a stalwart friend and supporter of the Judson, Sheldon, and Anable families. Emily met Adoniram Judson in the parlor of the Gillette home in Philadelphia. Emily was staying with the Gillettes in Philadelphia.

Horace H. Hawley[184] to Emily E. Chubbuck, November 2, 1845 —New York City[185]

Miss E. E. C.

I believe I understood from our good Miss Cynthia[186] that the letter which I mailed for you yesterday at this place, would inform you of my whereabouts, and time of leaving this city, and that I might hope for the pleasure of your company to Utica[187]—Fearing that something might occur to change my arrangements for leaving, I took the precaution to copy your address from Miss C's letter. I would now say, that I find I can accomplish my business without visiting New Haven, as I intended, and shall therefore try to leave for home in the *Thursday* afternoon boat—I shall esteem it a privilege to be of service to the "charming Fanny Forester,"[188] and would wait a day or two longer, if I could do so in justice to my business, and it would more fully meet your wishes, but as it is, if you would avail yourself of my poor beauship [sic], I think it will not be safe to delay your coming beyond Thursday—I believe the boat leaves here at six—

Very briefly,

H. H. Hawley

Source: American Baptist Historical Society, AJ 24, no. 1185.

---

[184] Horace H. Hawley was enormously helpful to Emily as she published her early stories and books.

[185] This letter is undated. In her letter of November 6, Anna Maria Anable wrote that she assumed that Emily had seen Hawley. November 2 would be the prior Sunday.

[186] Miss Cynthia Sheldon was the administrative and finance manager of the Utica Female Academy. She was a mentor, advisor, and friend to Emily.

[187] In the correspondence, there is always concern for Emily traveling alone because of her health, especially on trips long and complicated, such as Utica to Philadelphia by way of New York City. At some point late in October Emily had returned to Philadelphia; correspondence had indicated that Emily planned to return to Utica in early November. A letter written November 9 from Mary Colgate responded to a letter from Emily asking if she could stay with them on her way through New York. By November 18, Emily was talking of staying in Philadelphia for the remainder of the winter. In her letter ofn November 21, Anna Maria was becoming resigned to this fact of Emily's prolonged absence.

[188] Fanny Forester, Emily Chubbuck's *nom de plume*.

J. M. Lightbody[189] to Emily E. Chubbuck, November 3, 1845—New York City

Miss Fanny Forester[190]

I send you with this the Proofs[191]—you must excuse me for any neglect. The printer promised faithfully to send the proof, and I supposed had done so till I received your letter. These with the exception of the last signature will complete the vol. that will be printed tomorrow and make a finish of the "Trippings" as the work is so far advanced, and every arrangement made to publish it at a certain time, without the errors and very material I would advise publishing the work as it is, and in a new edition have the errors all corrected, as a delay now might injure the sale of the book. I had written so far when Gen Morris[192] came in and says "by all means let there be no delay, as the edition will be small and soon exausted [sic] it will answer just as well to have the corrections made on the second edition tell Miss Fanny that I will take care of her" and the General of course possesses a despot's sway and we must abide by his decision. "Songs and Ballads" will be ready for publication in a few days. At the Brigadiers' suggestion we will publish it at the same time with yours. He says that he will protect and support it in its rough passages and make the Protégé the bright companion of his rambles.

I told the General that his support was like the old poetic simile, the Ivy and the ruined wall. The wall gave a slight support while the Ivy covered up the cruel rents that envious time had made. Was not that unkind, but the General is steeled against jeers and praise.

Yours most Faithfully

J. M. Lightbody
not Doolittle

Source: American Baptist Historical Society, AJ 25, no. 1252.

---

[189] Lightbody was with the publishing firm of Paine and Burgess, which was the publisher of *Trippings in Author-land*.

[190] Fanny Forester, Emily Chubbuck's *nom de plume*.

[191] The proofs would be of Emily's new book, *Trippings in Author-land*.

[192] George P. "General" Morris, was N. P. Willis's partner at the *New Mirror* and a prominent literary figure in New York and Philadelphia.

Anna Maria Anable to Emily E. Chubbuck,[193] November 6, 1845—Schenectady[194]

Dear Nem

Here is your letter to Aunt U.[195] lying on the table. How I long to read it for then I sh'd feel as if I had seen you and talked with you a moment and how I am so lonesome; the only female woman in the house, the servant [ ] [ ]. I suppose from your writing so soon to Aunt U. that you have seen Mr. Hawley[196] and know why I am here. Is not it too bad? Did you ever know anything; so [ ] as all our arrangements? It seems they don't expect me home till this Saturday and [ ] Aunt U. waylaid me Tuesday at the cars and here I am keeping house for her while she has gone up to Utica to purchase and have fitted her dresses.[197] I read much and play with the Dr.[198] all day. Isn't it interesting? Your friend Mr. G.[199] has been here once or twice—but it's too much trouble to make oneself entertaining to him. It rained all day yesterday—and I have not been down [sic] town yet. I shall expect a letter from you as soon as I get home telling me all about matters and things—have you seen Gris.[200] yet? and Graham[201] or Arthur?[202] Tell me if Graham insists on his visit.

The Wilmarths[203] were just as kind as they could be [ ] [ ] from Jersey City. It seemed as if the [ ] [ ] could not do enough for me. By the way tell Mr. Gillette I think we can cousin it. Mrs. Lyons is Mrs. W's stepmother and Mrs. Young her half-sister. As he is a clergyman it would not be quite respectful enough to say Cousin Ab—but he may continue to call me Cousin Anna.

---

[193] There is an addendum to this letter dated November 11, 1845.

[194] This letter refers to some of the most prominent literary figures of the mid-nineteenth century, including General Morris, Charles Fenno Hoffman, Fanny Osgood, George Graham, Rufus W. Griswold. Others mentioned in other letters include Joseph Clay Neal and N. P. Willis. With this circle of friends, it is possible to gain an idea of Emily's gaining prominence in the literary world, a prominence which meant nothing to her after experiencing the love of Adoniram Judson, and committing herself to follow him to Burmah and to the mission field.

[195] Urania Sheldon Nott—formerly the literary principal at the Utica Female Academy—a mentor, advisor, and friend to Emily.

[196] Horace H. Hawley was enormously helpful to Emily as she published her early stories and books.

[197] See the letter of Urania Sheldon Nott to Emily Chubbuck dated November 8, 1845.

[198] Eliphalet Nott, president of Union College, married to Urania Sheldon Nott.

[199] Dr. William M. Gillespie had written to Emily. He was associated with Union College.

[200] Reverend Rufus W. Griswold, an ordained clergyman and distinguished literary figure, had been one of Emily's suitors. Emily referred to him in a letter to Anna Maria Anable as a "widower" and "crazy to get married."

[201] George Graham, editor of *Graham's Magazine*, took an interest in Emily Chubbuck as Fanny Forester and paid her with the unheard of sum of five dollars a page. He and his wife were most hospitable to Emily when she was in Philadelphia.

[202] Timothy Shay Arthur was an active temperance crusader, an editor, and an author of both fiction and non-fiction works.

[203] Mr. and Mrs. John Wilmarth. There are frequent mentions of the Wilmarths' home and hospitality. On September 17, 1845, Mrs. Wilmarth had written to Emily offering to "bury the tomahawk"; apparently Mrs. Wilmarth had felt very offended by something that Emily had said on her previous visit in May.

Tell Fanny[204] she must write and tell me all about her first lesson with Mrs. G.—I came up the river with Mrs. Denio and Mrs. Lothrop—saw James [ ] a few moments on board the boat. (Miss [ ] stopped here with me Tuesday night and went up with Aunt U. yesterday.) [Note: Written upside down between the lines of the above sentences: "Funny how [ ] [ ] will [ ] [ ] right place in my letters isn't it?"] Mrs. Lothrop said that Mrs. Kirkland[205] wanted to see you—so you must tell the Gen'l[206] to let her know when you are coming. Mrs. K. thought you were going to spend the winter in New York and she told Mrs. L. she would like you to come and board with her. Gillespie[207] was telling Aunt U. the other evening of the Sedgwick's having weekly soirees, at which all the elite of the literati of N.Y. receive standing invitations—Mrs. Kirkland has soirees also—but they are not so select. Fanny Osgood[208] and Mrs. Smith etc. attend Mrs. K's—but Hoffman,[209] Halleck and the older poets visit the Sedgwicks[210]—so says Mrs. G. If (I) hear anything more that I think will interest you I shall write—if not I shall wait till I get home to finish this—Tell me if you have rec'd my letter from N.Y. with the money in it.

Source: American Baptist Historical Society, AJ 23, no. 1164.

---

[204] Fanny Anable was one of nine children born to Joseph and Alma Anable and was a niece of Cynthia Sheldon and Urania Sheldon Nott. By 1845, Fanny had moved to Philadelphia to study and work in the home of the Reverend A. D. Gillette and his family. In fall 1848, she became a part of the teaching faculty at the Misses Anable's School in Philadelphia.

[205] There are three Kirkland families in the correspondence. This reference is to Mrs. William Kirkland of New York City; of her N. P. Willis had said on February 5, 1845: "She was my oldest female friend Mrs. Wm. Kirkland (who has been a sister to me for 16 years)." In this letter Anna Maria is telling Emily to visit with Mrs. Kirkland on her way through New York on her way to Utica. On January 2, 1847, Anna Maria Anable wrote that Mr. Kirkland had drowned in a tragic accident about six week prior, and that his mother had been concerned because he recently had adopted Unitarian principles.

[206] George P. "General" Morris, was N. P. Willis's partner at the *New Mirror* and a prominent literary figure in New York and Philadelphia.

[207] Dr. William Gillespie, professor of Engineering at Union College in Schenectady NY.

[208] Frances or "Fanny" Osgood, a contemporary writer with Emily, was one of the regulars writing for *Graham's Magazine*.

[209] Charles Fenno Hoffman, a prominent literary figure in Philadelphia and New York, well known in literary circles as an exceptionally talented editor, poet, and writer. Emily had started a correspondence with him as Laura Linden before he discovered that she was Fanny Forester.

[210] Catherine Maria Sedgwick, born in Stockbridge MA, attended Payne's Finishing School in Boston. She was a prolific writer whose works include *A New England Tale* (1822), *Hope Leslie or Early Times in Massachusetts* (1827), *Married or Single?* (1857), *Redwood, A Tale* (1824), *Clarence: or, A Tale of Our Times* (1830), *The Linwoods: or, Sixty Years Since in America* (1835), *Didactic Tales: Home: Scenes and Characters Illustrating Christian Truth* (1835), *Live and Let Live: or, Domestic Service* (1837), *Tales and Sketches, Second Series* (1844). She was featured in many of the same magazines that later featured Emily's stories.

Urania Sheldon Nott to Emily E. Chubbuck, November 8, 1845—Union College

Dear Emily—

Yesterday on my return from Utica, I found yours of the 4 on my table for which I take this early opportunity to thank you—I rejoice that you are enjoying such health and spirits in Phil. and almost regret to hear that you think of leaving it so soon—Anna Maria[211] arrived at our house on Tuesday morn'g last—on her way to Utica—and as I have made all necessary arrangements with her Aunt Cynthia[212] to have her stop with me, we way-laid her at the cars[213]—and bro't her home in triumph—on Wed'y I went to Utica, *accompanied by Miss Martha Taylor* of Brooklyn—and left A.M. to keep house for me during my absence—Yesterday I returned after a delightful visit, and this morn'g in the midst of a drissling [sic] rain storm [sic] she started for Utica.

Your letter to Mr. Cone's class had arrived, also Anna M's with other notes—By hers I ascertain that you think of leaving P. on Monday—but as there is some uncertainty about it[214]—I shall avail myself of the Rev. Mr. Backus's politeness to send this with a little package to Fanny[215]—to be forwarded to you at New York if necessary.

Anna M. will write about her peregrinations. The family are [sic] well at Utica—and my visit was very pleasant—but I missed several familiar faces. It seemed strange not to find you and A.M. there—notwithstanding there was a house full of the Western cousins.

I thank you for the sweet letter in the *North American*—with its beautiful Moral—how true it is that happiness is not to be found without the sphere for which God created us—the great thing is to know when we are in it—and to be satisfied with it—If you are still in P. I wish you would tell Augusta[216] that I shall be most happy to see her on her way home—If you come on together, you must make me a visit together—in either case you must stop—[Note: The letter ends here with the last page missing.]

Source: American Baptist Historical Society, AJ 25, no. 1232.

[211] Anna Maria Anable was the niece of the Urania and Cynthia Sheldon, the daughter of Joseph and Alma Sheldon Anable; she was Emily's closest friend at the Utica Female Academy.

[212] Miss Cynthia Sheldon was the administrative and finance manager of the Utica Female Academy. She was a mentor, advisor, and friend to Emily.

[213] See the letter of Anna Maria Anable to Emily E. Chubbuck dated November 6, 1845.

[214] A. C. Kendrick in *The Life and Letters of Mrs. Emily C. Judson* says that Emily left Utica in October—she spent several days in New York City visiting friends, and then went on to Philadelphia, probably arriving around the first of November. After her engagement to Adoniram Judson, Emily went home to make preparations for their life in Burmah. She arrived in Hamilton the first week of March.

[215] Fanny Forester, Emily Chubbuck's *nom de plume*.

[216] Augusta Crafts and her strong opinions are mentioned frequently in the letters written from the Utica Female Academy.

Mary Colgate[217] to Emily E. Chubbuck, November 9, 1845—New York City

My dear Miss Chubbuck

I rec'd your letter yesterday and was very happy to learn that you will so soon favor us with your company. I assure you your visit will not inconvenience us in the least. I promise you a hearty welcome within our family circle—and hope your visit will prove a *very pleasant* one to yourself. I am pleased to hear you are spending your time so delightfully in Philadelphia.[218] Fearing least you may have forgotten the number of our house I will give you *strait directions* to drive to Wm Colgate's forty one John St.

Hoping soon to see you I am
Yours affectionately

Mary Colgate

Source: American Baptist Historical Society, AJ 24, no. 1211.

Anna Maria Anable to Emily E. Chubbuck,[219] November 11, 1845[220]

I have been bothering my wits to know where to send your letters,[221] and finally "gave it up" 'cause my wits won't help one. Don't you know miss, that you said you might go to New York Monday? I wonder if you have gone. Jimmy Williams[222] goes down to night and I told him to bring you home but don't come if you are enjoying yourself very much. I have told the folks here all about what a

---

[217] Mary Colgate, wife of William Colgate.

[218] A. C. Kendrick in *The Life and Letters of Mrs. Emily C. Judson* says (page 135) that Emily left Utica in October and spent a few days in New York City visiting friends before going on to Philadelphia. We believe that we can make a good case that Anna Maria Anable traveled to New York with her. We know that Anna Maria wrote a letter to Emily from Clifton Grove, New Jersey on Sunday, November 2, that she had traveled over from Brooklyn the day prior, and that she was on her way back to Utica on November 4 when her Aunt Urania caught her going through and usurped her to housekeeping with Dr. Nott while Mrs. Nott went on to Utica to do some shopping. Kendrick says that Emily probably arrived in Philadelphia on Saturday, November 1.

[219] This letter is an addendum to the letter from Anna Maria Anable dated November 6, 1845.

[220] This is being written to Emily who had returned to Philadelphia, with a several day stop in New York City on her way from Utica. We note that in this letter there are references to some of the most prominent literary figures of the mid-nineteenth century, including General George Pope Morris, Charles Fenno Hoffman, Fanny Osgood, George Graham, Rufus W. Griswold. Others mentioned in other letters include Joseph Clay Neal and N. P. Willis. With this circle of friends, it is possible to gain an idea of Emily's gaining prominence in the literary world, a prominence which meant nothing to her after experiencing the love of Adoniram Judson, and committing herself to follow him—and her Savior—to Burmah.

[221] A. C. Kendrick in *The Life and Letters of Mrs. Emily C. Judson* says (page 135) that Emily left Utica in October and spent a few days in New York City visiting friends before going on to Philadelphia. We believe that we can make a good case that Anna Maria Anable traveled to New York with her. We know that Anna Maria wrote a letter to Emily from Clifton Grove, New Jersey on Sunday, November 2, that she had traveled over from Brooklyn the day prior, and that she was on her way back to Utica on November 4 when her Aunt Urania caught her going through and usurped her to housekeeping with Dr. Nott while Mrs. Nott went on to Utica to do some shopping. Kendrick says that Emily probably arrived in Philadelphia on Saturday, November 1.

[222] Jimmy Williams, often mentioned in Anna Maria Anable's letters, usually just as "Jimmy."

sensation you produced in N. York and they seem to enjoy it very much. They are all particularly pleased with your seeing Hoffman[223]—they wondered at first how it came about, but I let them think he learned it as the others did,—thro' the papers, or the Gen'l.[224] Some of those kind of hope you won't get puffed up, so that you won't want to come back again, but—they don't dare to express it. Every body [sic] is pleasant and kind, but oh, how I do want you here! You don't know how lonesome I feel—the ground is covered with snow sloppy and dreary.

What did your papa[225] say to you Nemmy?[226] Aunt C.[227] rather thought it was your preface.[228] If it was I suppose you are in N. Y. I should expect to hear from you to night. You were a good child to write me so soon, but I did not get your letter till Friday. I came home and found Mrs. McKnight here. Mr. and Mrs. Gratiot[229] and Mrs [ ] Lou Sheldon, they all left except Mrs. G. and the children yesterday and Mrs. G. is going to spend the Winter with us instead of going to England. It will be quite pleasant will it not?

---

[223] Charles Fenno Hoffman, a prominent literary figure in Philadelphia and New York, well known in literary circles as an exceptionally talented editor, poet, and writer. Emily had started a correspondence with him as Laura Linden before he discovered that she was Fanny Forester.

[224] George P. "General" Morris, was N. P. Willis's partner at the *New Mirror* and a prominent literary figure in New York and Philadelphia. Willis had asked Morris to watch over Emily in his absence.

[225] This is a reference to Emily's friend and mentor, N P. Willis. Anna Maria referred to him as "your papa" on a number of different occasions, and Emily referred to him as "papa" or "my papa."

[226] These were used as names of endearment for Emily Chubbuck. Emily sometimes used it of herself. See Adoniram Judson's letter to Anna Maria Anable dated May 14, 1846, for one example of this.

[227] Miss Cynthia Sheldon was the administrative and finance manager of the Utica Female Academy. She was a mentor, advisor, and friend to Emily. Anna Maria Anable was Miss Sheldon's niece.

[228] Letters from abroad, sent to Emily by N. P. Willis, were going to the Utica Female Academy and then being forwarded to Emily in Philadelphia. Emily had asked Willis to write the Preface to *Trippings in Author-land*, and in his letter of August 16, 1845 he said that he would do it, but it would require some thought and he could not do it in a hurry. We suspect that Anna Maria and those at the Utica Female Academy thought the letter that they were forwarding included the long-awaited Preface. In the end, it was suggested that Rufus Wilmot Griswold could write it in the absence of the one from Willis, but finally what was used was the Preface that Emily herself wrote on June 17, 1845.

[229] Ann Sheldon was a younger cousin of Cynthia Sheldon, Alma Sheldon Anable, and Urania Sheldon Nott. She married Charles Gratiot, the son of a prominent army officer and engineer who had opened up the port of St Louis. Because Charles and Ann Gratiot often lived with the Sheldon—Anable families, both at Utica and in Philadelphia after 1848, they were very often mentioned in the correspondence. We learn of the birth and growth of their six children (one born very close to the birth of Emily Frances Judson), Charles Gratiot's journeys to California in search of gold, and his religious awakening.

Sarah Hinckley[230] leaves in about a fortnight and if Mary B.[231] does not come back Miss Crafts[232] will take her room. Miss C. and Lydia[233] have got quite ahead of us in French.

Jimmy wanted to know when and what we have heard from Mary B but he hardly listened to my reply, so I concluded it was to direct my attention from Helen M.[234] about whom I was teazing [sic] him just a little. I really believe the fellow is a gone case. If you want to go to Boston there is a chance for you. He is going on direct.

The teachers and girls all send a great deal of love. They want you to come back because they want to see you—but they are real glad you are having such nice times, and Julia[235] and Sarah[236] get on beautifully with their classes.

I shall enclose this in Fan's[237] letter with a request to burn it if you have gone to N. Y.

Write me soon do! Ever and always the same old

Ninny

Miss Emily Chubbuck

Dear Nem

If you see any pretty, simple patterns for window-seats or ottomans I wish you would get one for me if you can. I intend to work this winter.

Source: American Baptist Historical Society, AJ 23, no. 1164.

---

[230] Sarah Hinckley was one of the girls from the Utica Female Seminary; there are some letters from her in the collection. Sarah Hinckley was at the Utica Female Academy as a student to Emily. In an 1849 letter Hinckley reminisced about that time and brought Emily up to date on many of those who were there with her. She also spoke of the sad farewell when Emily left for Boston and then Burmah.

[231] Mary Barber, mentioned frequently in the Emily Chubbuck Judson letters, was a student and then the art teacher at the Utica Female Academy. She had had a falling out with Cynthia Sheldon, and it would be quite some time before it was resolved.

[232] On December 5, 1845, Anna Maria wrote that Miss Crafts was a delight. "What a blessing to society it is, that she was never married. What a shame it would have been for *her* to have settled down into a mere *me* and my *husband* and my *children*!" Miss Crafts is not to be confused with Mrs. Augusta Crafts, who was noted as having a sharp disposition and a gossipy tongue.

[233] Lydia Lillybridge was one of Emily's closest friends at the Utica Female Academy. When Emily made the decision to go to Burmah with Adoniram Judson as a missionary, Lydia offered to go with them, and with Emily speaking to Adoniram Judson and to Dr. Solomon Peck and the Board of American Baptist missionary Union of her extraordinary abilities, she was commissioned to go with them, in spite of the fact that she remained single. Always independent and outspoken, unafraid to cause ripples in the missionary community, Lydia was to serve on the mission field for twenty-eight years. She married missionary Thomas Simons in May 1851. See the timeline on the life and service of Lydia Lillybridge Simons in vol. 1.

[234] In letters dated March 26 and April 1, 1845, the names of Jimmy Williams and Mary Barber were linked. Then that ceased, and Jimmy's name was linked to Helen Munson, who was currently his fiancée

[235] Julia Look was a student of Emily's at the Utica Female Academy, and then a fellow teacher.

[236] Sarah Bell Wheeler was a teacher at the Utica Female Academy, and an intimate friend of Emily Chubbuck.

[237] Fanny Anable, one of five Anable sisters. She was born April 12, 1828. At this time, she was working in the home of Hannah and A. D. Gillette in Philadelphia.

Anna Maria Anable to Emily E. Chubbuck, November 12, 1845[238]

I have received your little note to night [sic] dear Nemmy[239] and as I told Fan[240] to burn a letter I sent you this morning if you had left I hasten to be very punctual. I was waylaid as I said in Schenectady[241] and taken up on the hill willy-nilly by the Dr.[242] Aunt U[243] wanted to go up to Utica to do some shopping etc. and she had got permission from home for me to stay in S. till Saturday and keep house for her while she was gone. I had a nice quiet time, and when I got home found Mr. Gratiot[244] and Mrs. McKnight here. Mrs. G. and the children are fairly settled here for the winter. They are in the nursery and Mother[245] is coming up opposite and Mrs. Taylor and I are chumming together till you come. Liz Hinckley leaves in about a fortnight and if you come home as soon as your letter to night indicates you will see her again. Hannah too talks of coming here to make us a visit during her vacation.

I have just come up from a French recitation and Mr. [ ] is very inquisitive about you as usual. The folks all think you are having real nice times, and they are all glad of it, and hope you won't hurry home before you have made out your visit etc. We all want to see you (you can hardly tell how much I miss you) but for pity sakes if you find *tolerable* weather any where [sic] else pray enjoy it. It rained here all day Saturday and four inches of snow fell on Sunday and ever since it has been snowing and raining alternately. It is too cold for the snow to melt and yet not cold enough to freeze and make good walking. Fan says your cloak is beautiful; if you were here it would be just in time.

Sarah Hinckley[246] has just been in to help Martha and me eat some cake and she says the girls are doing nicely and your little [ ] came safe to hand and Miss

---

[238] This letter dated November 12, 1845, is sent care of "Wm Colgate, a few doors from Broadway, N.Y." See Mary Colgate's letter to Emily dated November 9, 1845. Emily had written to see if she could stay with her on her return trip through the city, so obviously she had been planning to return home before deciding to stay in Philadelphia for the winter.

This letter has an addendum dated November 13, 1845.

[239] "Nem" or "Nemmy" was a name of endearment given to Emily by a small group of her intimate friends at the Utica Female Academy. Anna Maria Anable was "Ninny."

[240] Fanny Anable, one of five Anable sisters. She was born April 12, 1828. At this time, she was working in the home of Hannah and A. D. Gillette in Philadelphia.

[241] See the letter of Anna Maria Anable to Emily E. Chubbuck dated November 6, 1845, and the letter of Urania Sheldon Nott to Emily E. Chubbuck dated November 8, 1845.

[242] Eliphalet Nott, president of Union College, married to Urania Sheldon Nott.

[243] Urania Sheldon Nott—formerly the literary principal at the Utica Female Academy—a mentor, advisor, and friend to Emily.

[244] Charles Gratiot grew up in St Louis, where his father was an Army Engineer responsible for developing the Port of St Louis. He married Ann Sheldon, who was a cousin of Cynthia Sheldon, Urania Sheldon Nott and Alma Sheldon Anable, and together Charles and Ann Gratiot had six children. Because they often lived with the Sheldon family we hear a great deal of him. Letters in 1847 speak of his religious awakening—those of 1849 speak of his leaving for the California gold fields. In 1853, Charles Gratiot was to apply for a grant of four hundred acres in Illinois, with the application telling us that he already owned 148 acres.

[245] Alma Sheldon Anable, sister of Cynthia Sheldon and Urania Sheldon Nott and married to Joseph Hubbell Anable. She was the mother of nine Anable children.

[246] Sarah Hinckley was one of the Emily's students at the Utica Female Seminary.

Look[247] read your lines to your mother last Friday and they (Martha's [ ] girls) glorify you at a great rate. Indeed—I have heard from nearly all the girls of your beautiful letter to them. Now Sally Bell[248] comes in. It's just Nem dropping in time and she says you must fall in love with Hoffman[249] and have him. What do you think of her advice? I hope you will see him. Did you get a letter from your papa[250] before leaving P.? What does he say for himself? Something I'll warrant to make you more in love with him than ever.

The folks here are all mightily pleased with your seeing Hoffman and they think it would be the nicest thing in the world for you to get him.[251]

So you have fairly whipped the Philadelphians!

Well you served them right, and I hope they will feel it. What sort of a looking chap is Neal?[252] If you quarrel so much with Graham[253] it will very soon be mere editor and correspondents. The fact is he is so taken up with money-making he can't think of any thing [sic] else. Mrs. Denio, who came up the river with me said he had made a fortune by his magazine. Jimmy Williams[254] was to have you down the river last night, but we heard from some other "callers" that he was seen sitting cozily with Miss Munson,[255] and to day [sic] I hear he is not very well, and now there is no telling when he will go down. I presume that he will be in N.Y. this week. He said he would see you if possible and be very happy to escort you home so you need not worry about an escort.

If you see the Gen'l[256] say something pretty to him for me, for I should try to if I were there. I want to make up with him for making fun before his face of his "guffaws." Has your book come out yet. [sic][257] And was that big letter I heard about a

---

[247] Julia Look was a student of Emily's at the Utica Female Academy, and then a fellow teacher.

[248] Sarah Bell Wheeler was a teacher at the Utica Female Academy, and an intimate friend of Emily Chubbuck.

[249] Charles Fenno Hoffman, a prominent literary figure in Philadelphia and New York, well known in literary circles as an exceptionally talented editor, poet, and writer. Emily had started a correspondence with him as Laura Linden before he discovered that she was Fanny Forester.

[250] Anna Maria often referred to N. P. Willis, Emily's mentor and friend, editor of the *New Mirror*, as "papa." At this time Willis was in Europe for an extended stay.

[251] When Emily passed New York City on her way to Philadelphia, she met with Hoffman. See Anna Maria Anable's letter of November 11, 1845.

[252] Joseph Neal was part of Emily Chubbuck's circle of literary friends when she was in Philadelphia.

[253] George Graham, editor of *Graham's Magazine*, took an interest in Emily Chubbuck as Fanny Forester and paid her with the unheard of sum of five dollars a page.

[254] Jimmy Williams, often mentioned in Anna Maria Anable's letters, usually just as "Jimmy."

[255] Helen Munson was the fiancée of Jimmy Williams.

[256] George P. "General" Morris, was N. P. Willis's partner at the *New Mirror* and a prominent literary figure in New York and Philadelphia.

[257] This would be a reference to *Trippings in Author-land*.

preface from Willis[258] as Aunt C.[259] conjectured. Or has he written you one great long letter for all of yours. Ain't [sic] you sorry now you have not written him? Just please to answer all these questions forthwith—and tell as much more as you have a [ ] to. I am sleepy and tired and must hop into bed. Martha says she wants to see you, but she don't [sic] care about your coming so soon for then she will have to give up her nice room, a sentiment which I do not appreciate. I want little "peaked chin."[260]

Good night.

A. M.

Source: American Baptist Historical Society, AJ 23, no. 1162.

Anna Maria Anable to Emily E. Chubbuck, November 13, 1845[261]

Written in the left margin of the address page: "Thursday morn'y

"I have just been talking a few moments with Aunt C.[262] and she says *if you want* to stay through the convention and see all the folks—at any rate don't hurry away on that account unless you have an excellent opportunity to come. I think myself you had better come with Jimmy.[263] Aunt U.[264] wants you to make her a visit and much as I want you to get back I think you would…"

---

[258] Nathaniel Parker (N. P.) Willis was the editor of *New Mirror*, the magazine that catapulted Emily into literary fame. He became a friend, mentor, and eventually a suitor.

See the letter from N. P. Willis dated August 16, 1845. In that letter he told Emily that he would be delighted to write a Preface to her new book, and he would get it to her after he had given it some thought. Apparently Anna Maria mistook a letter from Willis waiting for Emily as the Preface. In the end Emily wrote the Preface herself.

[259] Miss Cynthia Sheldon was the administrative and finance manager of the Utica Female Academy. She was a mentor, advisor, and friend to Emily. Anna Maria Anable was Miss Sheldon's niece.

[260] Emily E. Chubbuck used a number of different names over the course of her life and career. Most obviously, of course, was the fact that she wrote often under the name "Fanny Forester," her argument being "who would buy a book authored by Emily Chubbuck?" At other times she used: Amy Scribbleton (July 6, 1841); Amy S.—September 28, 1841; "Nem" or "Nemmy" (Emily was always "Nem" or "Nemmy" to Anna Maria Anable who was "Ninny"); "Pithy" to Anna Maria, (April 29, 1845); "Peaked chin" (See Anna Maria Anable, November 12, 1845); Sister Peakedchin—(See Emily Chubbuck, February 28, 1846); Peakedchin—(Adoniram Judson, March 7—quoting that he had a letter from her); Nemmy Petty (Adoniram Judson, March 7, 1846 Also "Petty"; April 13, 1846—Emily uses Nemmy Petty of herself; Pithy (April 28, 1845: Emily to Anna Maria).

[261] This letter is an addendum to the letter dated November 12, 1845.

[262] Miss Cynthia Sheldon was the administrative and finance manager of the Utica Female Academy. She was a mentor, advisor, and friend to Emily. Anna Maria Anable was Miss Sheldon's niece.

[263] Jimmy Williams, often mentioned in Anna Maria Anable's letters, usually just as "Jimmy." Recent letters indicated that Jimmy Williams would be traveling to New York City, and that if Emily were coming home, he could accompany her.

[264] Urania Sheldon Nott—formerly the literary principal at the Utica Female Academy—a mentor, advisor, and friend to Emily.

Written in the right margin of the address page: "…enjoy a visit there and it would help to make the winter shorter for you. Give my love to Mary Colgate[265] and if you go to the Wilmarths,[266] there is a package there I wish you to take charge of. In my haste I left it. It is from Eng(land) and you will see by the address where to send it. Write immediately do! for I am dying to hear from you. AM"

Source: American Baptist Historical Society, AJ 23, no. 1162.

Emily E. Chubbuck to Anna Maria Anable, November 18, 1845[267]

My dear Ninny,[268]

This is the time fixed upon for me to leave Phil. but I am so near sick that I have been obliged to alter my plans. I shall stay here now until after the convention.[269] I have just had a call from some darling new friends who are just as kind to me as they can be, but I was unable to go down and see them. The next morning after Neal[270] called with Graham,[271] he sent a Mrs. Mitchell[272] to see me—oh! I told you about that, and about my invitation to the theatre etc. etc. Well, the next day came an invitation from the Mitchells for me to take tea with them. I was pre-

---

[265] Mary Colgate, daughter of William Colgate.

[266] Mr. and Mrs. John Wilmarth. There are frequent mentions of the Wilmarths' home and hospitality.

[267] The last page of the letter is missing. This is an undated letter—we have placed it in November 1845 because Emily was writing from Philadelphia, she was wanting to leave as planned to go home, but now has decided to stay until after the convention—then in another letter on November 23 she spoke of and Mrs. Gillette being in the New York for the convention.

[268] "Nem" or "Nemmy" was a name of endearment given to Emily by her most intimate friends at the Utica Female Academy. Anna Maria was "Ninny."

[269] The Triennial Convention, held in New York. Adoniram Judson was there and received tremendous affirmation for his life and work.

[270] Joseph Neal was part of Emily Chubbuck's circle of literary friends when she was in Philadelphia.

[271] George Graham, editor of Graham's Magazine, took an interest in Emily Chubbuck as Fanny Forester and paid her with the unheard of sum of five dollars a page.

[272] Mr. and Mrs. Mitchell lived in Philadelphia; Mrs. Tyndale, Mrs. Mitchell's mother and owner of a prosperous china shop in downtown Philadelphia, lived with them. In November 1845, as Emily was thinking of prolonging her stay in the city to last through the winter, the Mitchells offered to open their home to her, promising that they would do everything in their power to take good care of her—her own room—solitude or company as desired—the ability to write—all of the comforts they could provide. Emily did express appreciation—many of her friends told her what wonderful people they were and how sensitive they were to the needs of an invalid such as Emily was at that time. Her one serious reservation was that they were Unitarians. In the end Emily decided that she would stay with the Reverend and Mrs. Gillette, knowing from her past experience that she would be more than comfortable with them.

viously engaged to Mrs. Robarts,[273] but it was a rainy day and Mrs. M. would send a carriage and so I sent a note to Mrs. R and accepted the last *invite*. Neal was there and a young Mr. Hamersley (a mighty agreeable fellow) and some half-dozen others. Mr. Sully and his daughters were invited, but they had a previous engagement. Mrs. M's mother keeps an immense China store on Chesnut[sic] St. and manages all the business herself, one of the very biggest establishments in the city.

Well, what plan do you think they had been arranging during the day? To keep me all winter. Mrs. M said I sh'd have a room by myself whenever I wished and sh'd not be disturbed even to go to my meals. When I wanted to write, and when I wished it I sh'd have just as much and just as little company as I chose. Mr. Mitchell is a nice whole-souled Virginian and he joined most heartily in the invitation and Mrs. Tyndale (Mrs. M's mother) argued all the evening to prove that nobody could take so good care of me as she could. Their interest in me was so sudden and strong that I hardly knew what to make of it and I told them I would go home and think the matter over. Last evening Mr. Neal called as he said to give me confidence in my new friends. He says they are perfectly sincere and the noblest-hearted people on earth, and he advises me by all means to stay, for as he is something of an invalid him*self* he feels a strong interest in me. And that is the secret of the whole. *He* is an invalid and they think the world and all of him (he and his mother live next door) and Mr. Read, the Boston artist I told you of, is an intimate friend of theirs and in most miserable health; and they think they know all *about* the ailings of such people and sympathize with them I suppose even in their whimseys. Moreover Mrs. Tyndale has lost several children with consumption and Mrs. Mitchell was in miserable health when they came here and she thinks the air of Philad. cured her. Mrs. M said she was afraid I would consider them officious, but I must recollect that I was no stranger to them, tho' they were to me. Now I want you to get Miss C's[274] opinion about this matter and have her talk with Doct. James;[275] and then write me immediately. I sh'd much rather come back to Utica if

---

[273] Mr. and Mrs. W. S. Robarts lived in Philadelphia and were active in Baptist circles. They were friends of Reverend and Mrs. A. D. Gillette and in December 1845, the Robarts welcomed Adoniram Judson to stay in their home. A. C. Kendrick said, "(Gillette and Dr. Judson) arrived in (or out of) due time in Philadelphia, and Dr. Judson was welcomed to the house of Mr. and Mrs. W. S. Robarts, who became warm personal friends, as they were already active friends of the mission cause." There is a letter that indicated some hard feelings towards Mrs. Robarts for her disparaging comments about Emily's upcoming marriage and missionary service. Emily mentions this in a February 6, 1846 letter to Adoniram. Mrs. Robarts seemed to be accusing Emily of worldliness—when all the time, Emily was quick to say, Mrs. Robarts was engaging in the same activity of which Emily was accused. The correspondence also indicates a satisfactory healing of the relationship. Mrs. Robarts proved to be helpful to Emily in gathering together in a short time all that she would need to take with her to Burmah. In January 1849, Miss Sheldon told Emily that Mrs. Robarts had placed their daughter Mary in the Misses Anable's School. There also is continued mention of the social relations maintained by the Roberts and the Sheldon-Anable families.

[274] Miss Cynthia Sheldon was the administrative and finance manager of the Utica Female Academy. She was a mentor, advisor, and friend to Emily.

[275] Dr. James was a trusted physician in Utica, who attended the students and faculty of the Utica Female Academy. He is mentioned frequently in the correspondence as having been consulted for varying medical complaints and his advice was always welcomed and highly regarded.

it is best or rather, it would be as well for me, for however kind new friends are they are not like the old. But since there is such an urgent request for me to stay from such an unexpected quarter and everybody here thinks it imp[ortant][276] I don't like to take upon myself the responsibility of deciding. I wish you would write me immediately. Mr. Gillette[277] don't [sic] know the Mitchells, but Mr. Neal says I can't fail of being happy with them. I have one strange objection to staying with them which I don't know whether you will appreciate or not. They are Unitarians. They are not gay people nor fashionables. (Mrs. Tyndale I have told you keeps a China store) but they are remarkably intelligent and seem to live (without being professionally literary themselves) in a little literary circle that is vastly pleasant.

I rec'd a sweet—no, not sweet, a warm earnest soulful letter from my darling of a papa[278] last week, full of advice to me and anxiety about me. It has been about six weeks on the way. He wrote from Leipsice where he was staying with his brother and he says he is happier than he has been before in a long time. He is to be home during the winter, or at the latest in the Spring. I would give the world to see his blessed face. Oh you may take Hoffy[279] and welcome for he is a jewel.

I hav'nt [sic] seen anything of any of the Grahams since Thurs. eve. Mrs. G was to have taken me to Germantown Fri. but she sent an apology. Doct. Mitchell has'nt [sic] called yet, but he sent word by Neal that he was just now thronged with students and sh'd do himself the favour in a few days. Yesterday I called on Mrs. Neal[280] who is too much of an invalid to get out, and took Fanny[281] with me. Clara Tyndale[282] and Fanny are to be great friends. She is a sweet girl about sixteen. Last evening we all took tea at Mrs. Knowles and this evening we are engaged to Mrs. Robarts, but poor I shall not be able to go. I regret it because it was for me the engagement was broken before. There was an elegant lady at Mrs. K's last evening—a Mrs. Judge Jones from Wissahicon [sic]. She lives in something like a palace there, and is particularly anxious that Mrs. Gillette sh'd take me out there. Mr. Robarts has promised to buy a book for every day I stay here and he says if I stay the winter he thinks I will be pretty well paid. Mr. Collins daguerreotyped

---

[276] The copy of the original from which we worked cut off a lot of the right side of the page. The editor has filled in here.

[277] Rev. A. D. Gillette was a stalwart friend and supporter of the Judson, Sheldon, and Anable families. Emily met Adoniram Judson in the parlor of the Gillette home in Philadelphia. Emily was staying with the Gillettes while in Philadelphia.

[278] Anna Maria Anable frequently referred in her letters to N. P. Willis as "your papa." Emily had begun to use this title as early as her visit with Willis in May as she passed through New York. She wrote that Willis had said that she was like a daughter to him, a sister to his daughter Imogen, and Emily reported that as his new daughter she had begun to refer to him as "papa."

[279] Charles Fenno Hoffman, a prominent literary figure in Philadelphia and New York, well known in literary circles as an exceptionally talented editor, poet, and writer. Emily had started a correspondence with him as Laura Linden before he discovered that she was Fanny Forester.

[280] In other references, Joseph Neal is referred to as a bachelor and "available." He would not marry until 1846. This would be his mother, with whom he lived.

[281] Fanny Anable, one of five Anable sisters. She was born April 12, 1828. At this time, she was working in the home of Hannah and A. D. Gillette.

[282] Mrs. Mitchell's mother was Mrs. Tyndale. Clara Tyndale was probably Mrs. Mitchell's sister.

me yesterday at a great rate. He took six impressions and Mr. Gillette says got three elegant ones, but I have not seen them yet. He is to keep one himself give one to Mr. G. and the other to me. I saw the one he is to give to Mr. G. before it was smoothed down coloured [sic] or anything and I had no idea that my phiz[283] [sic] did look so well. The eyes particularly are excellent. Mr. C. is delighted with his success. He says he sh'd like to catch me in an animated conversation when I did'nt [sic] know what he was about and take a series of pictures; no two would be at all alike. He tried me first in my bonnet and coat (by the way the coat is two times prettier than Mary Adams'[284]—just as beautiful as it can be) and I tho't he would'nt [sic] get another so good, but he was'nt [sic] satisfied with it. If I were rich enough I would get him to take three or four more as presents to some of my friends, he does it so well.

Source: Hanna family files.

Emily E. Chubbuck to Catharine Chubbuck, November 23, 1845—Philadelphia

Well Kit, I don't know which has the most sisterly way of doing things in the writing line, you or me; but I fancy in a measuring case I sh'd carry away the palm. I have written you once since I have been in Philadelphia but you have not written me at all. Don't you feel ashamed of yourself—eh, Miss? Write immediately and direct "No. 69 North 12th St." I am about making up my mind to spend the winter here—I have several invitations and could pass the time delightfully and without expense. I am at the Gillettes[285] now, but am intending to go to a Mrs. Mitchell's soon. Mrs. Mitchell[286] is a lovely woman whom Mr. Neal[287] (Joseph C. Editor of *Gazette* and author of *Charcoal Sketches*) introduced to me. She took a great fancy to me and with her husband and mother and sister immediately laid a plan for detaining me through the winter. They say I shall have a room by myself and a fire when I choose to be alone and when I prefer it shall have plenty of company. Wouldn't you stay if you were I? Neal is a real nice old bach. and he lives next door so I sh'd'nt [sic] want for a beau at any time [sic] and the weather here is perfectly delightful yet. We hav'nt [sic] seen a flake of snow. They don't have sleighing here

---

[283] Emily used "phiz" to refer to her face.
[284] Mary Adams, a friend of Emily's while at the Utica Female Academy.
[285] Rev. A. D. Gillette was a stalwart friend and supporter of the Judson, Sheldon, and Anable families. Emily met Adoniram Judson in the parlor of the Gillette home in Philadelphia. Emily was staying with the Gillettes while in Philadelphia.
[286] Mr. and Mrs. Mitchell were friends of Emily's and had offered her a place to stay while in Philadelphia.
[287] Joseph Neal was part of Emily Chubbuck's circle of literary friends when she was in Philadelphia.

but a day or two at a time in the dead of winter. You may get my black cloak from Utica if you can and I want you to forward there my new quilt chemises for them to box up and send me. Tell father[288] my staying here will make no difference—the money for the house shall be paid on the nail whenever it becomes due[289]—the fifteenth of February, I believe. You will see by the *Mirror* I send that my book was published yesterday.[290] They are to pay me a sixpence on every volume they sell on the first of July next. People tell me that the bargain is a remarkably good one. I hope to get sufficiently clear of debt by that time to give the house quite a lift. I am sorry that I can't come home to fix you up but you must do the best you can for yourself. I meant to have given you my pink bonnet but I shall want it here and shall have it sent me with a big box of things. I have an elegant Daguerreotype[291] which I shall try to get an opportunity to send you. If Wallace[292] will send me in a package by mail some of his best things (*not* poetry) I will try to dispose of them for cash. I don't know whether I can, but as I am here at the head-quarters of magazinism there is no harm in trying. I had a beautiful letter from my jewel of a papa[293] not long ago. Mrs. Graham[294] takes occasion to joke me a great deal about widowers[295] and going to Europe[296] and being a good step-mother[297] etc. but her husband[298] seems to think, what's nearest is most dangerous, and talks rather more

---

[288] Charles Chubbuck, Emily's father. Though he held varying positions over the years, he failed at most of them. With the purchase of the house for them, Emily was to continue as a significant financial contributor to the support of the family.

[289] In a September 16, 1842 letter to her brother Walker, Emily told him that she had purchased a home for her parents on Broad Street in Hamilton Village. She was able to do this from the proceeds of her writing. Emily had paid four hundred dollars for the home, payable in four payments over four years, and she was to often mention this debt, and the pressure it put upon her for continued writing, and the income derived from it. She had also incurred some debt with the Utica Female Academy, for tuition for her sister Catharine who spent several terms there.

[290] *Trippings in Author-land*.

[291] See the letter of Emily E. Chubbuck to Anna Maria Anable dated November 18, 1845.

[292] William Wallace Chubbuck, Emily's younger brother, born January 1, 1824.

[293] This is a reference to N. P. Willis, the editor of the *New Mirror*, Emily's mentor and friend. Both Emily and Anna Maria Anable used "Papa" or "Dear Papa" for him. N. P. Willis was in Europe at this time, following the death of his wife the previous March.

[294] Mrs. Graham, the wife of George Graham, who published *Graham's Magazine*. The Grahams were exceedingly kind to Emily during her stay in Philadelphia and often took her on carriage rides.

[295] "Widower" refers to widowed older men and usually suggested availability and interest in marriage. The academy girls and their teachers were always referring to "the widower" or to "widowers" in their conversations and correspondence.

[296] Earlier in the year, Emily had spoken of going to Europe, supporting herself in her travels by writing letters back to the magazines. At one point, July 2, 1845, in a letter to her brother Walker, she had said that George Graham would pay for her trip for those letters. In an August 22, 1845 letter from Robert West, the editor of the *Columbian Magazine*, we learn that Emily had asked them to publish her letters exclusively if she were to go. In the end Emily's frail health precluded any such travel.

[297] N. P. Willis had a daughter, Imogen. Correspondence from this time period indicated a deepening relationship between Willis and Emily. We know from his letters that he believed that they would be married when he returned from Europe; he returned some of Emily's letters to him edged in black, with sections underlined, saying that as she re-read her letters, she would understand why he would have had that expectation.

[298] George Graham, editor of *Graham's Magazine*, took an interest in Emily Chubbuck as Fanny Forester and paid her with the unheard of sum of five dollars a page.

of bachelors. The Utica folks are all agog about Hoffy[299] and he is a darling, but—but—I don't think there's much occasion for [ ] about anybody; though my papa has promised to take care of me beautifully when he comes home. He will be here in the winter or spring.

Mr. and Mrs. Gillette are at N. Y. now attending the convention and they will bring on Doct. Judson with them when they return.[300] I expect we shall have a great flourish then and I mean to be at the Mitchells for I hate rackets. The Mitchells are very quiet sort of people—rich but not fashionable, and fond of literature tho' not precisely what is called literary. They are people of very refined taste and warm hearts. They will take as good care of me as Aunt C.[301] would and better for one thing—they have fewer to attend to. Then the Gillettes and Grahams are here so that I shall feel quite at home. Cornelia Kirkland and Mrs. Denio have come down to spend the winter in school, both for their health—and Rosa Sheldon of Detroit is married and staying with her husband's friends till spring. So we have quite a little Utica down here. My health is very good—about the same as when I was home and it seems to be the general impression that it will be greatly benefited by my stay here. Mrs. Tyndale[302] is a Quaker and she says she knows by the movings of the spirit that my constitution will be entirely revolutionized by the change of climate. I hope she may prove a true prophet. Write me immediately—do, Kate;[303] don't you suppose I want to hear a little how you are getting along? *I reckon I dew.* [sic] Hold yourself straight before the Hamiltonians and I'll come and help you cut up a row de dow in the spring. "So no more at present" from

Nem[304]

Source: Hanna Family files.

---

[299] Charles Fenno Hoffman, a prominent literary figure in Philadelphia and New York, well known in literary circles as an exceptionally talented editor, poet, and writer. Emily had started a correspondence with him as Laura Linden before he discovered that she was Fanny Forester.

[300] There must have been some sort of a problem with these plans, for as history tells us, it was the day before Christmas when the Reverend Gillette accompanied Adoniram Judson and it was not from New York, but rather from Boston to Philadelphia. Emily Chubbuck and Adoniram Judson met for the first time on Christmas Day 1845. We smile at these comments for we know that Emily did in fact meet Adoniram Judson, that it was in the Gillette home and not the Mitchell home, and that as it turned out, the commotion that ensued around their meeting proved to be life-changing not only for the two of them, but for their family and friends, as well as to the mission movement itself, not to mention the legacy of Adoniram Judson, which she was to promote so strongly after his death.

[301] Miss Cynthia Sheldon was the administrative and finance manager of the Utica Female Academy. She was a mentor, advisor, and friend to Emily. She had become "Aunt Cynthia."

[302] Mrs. Tyndale was the mother of Mrs. Mitchell. In the November 18 letter which Emily wrote to Anna Maria Anable, we learn that Mrs. Tyndale owned an "enormous china store" on Chestnut Street.

[303] Sarah Catharine ("Kate," "Kit," or "Kitty") Chubbuck, Emily's older sister, born October 25, 1816.

[304] "Nem" or "Nemmy" was a name of endearment given to Emily by a small group of her intimate friends at the Utica Female Academy. Anna Maria Anable was "Ninny."

Sarah J. Hinckley to Emily E. Chubbuck, November 25, 1845[305]

My dear Miss Chubbuck

And so naughty one, you have concluded to stay away from your "own dear blessed house" a whole winter. Why! If you knew how much suffering your absence creates—how many hearts are silently breaking (mine for example) because "Fanny[306] has withdrawn the light of her countenance—surely would think better of it." But no I would not have you come just now—for I fear that all the bloom, Philadelphia airs may have given your cheeks—would be unconditionally, unmercifully *pinched away*, before you could say Jack Robinson.

Whew! Now it is snowing, and *a-pro-pos* to that, your "Trippings"[307] is creating a great sensation among us Seminoles. Would you believe me if I should say that for more than one noon (of night I mean) it has actually witched sleep away from even my sleepyhead? And now "Fanny" mine, there is a question I would ask. Shall I make a bold plunge, and say have you borne my case in hand? There it is. You know *why it is* that I would attempt to perpetrate a murder of the king's English. Not that I think myself dextirous [sic] at all in using the steel—but because *"the state of the finance"* demands *"un pen d'attention"* [sic].

Will you think about it and do for me—and advise me as you would a sister? If you think I had better give it up entirely tell me so. It will be only what (I am) more than half inclined to think myself. You will understand me when I say that your kindness already has soaked a fountain in my heart that springs for none but you, and believe me tho' will you not write to me soon that sis and myself may know and now my darling Miss Chubbuck—Do be careful of your health—you know how very precious it is to us all—and when the first spring breze [sic] whispers that it is coming to Utica—just mount its balmy wing and come too. Will you? "I pain for a reply"!

Your aff—Sarah

Source: American Baptist Historical Society, AJ 24, no. 1182.

---

[305] This letter is undated. The content places it at a time when Emily is in Philadelphia and has changed her mind about returning to Utica. Tuesday, December 2, 1845, fits this description and we place it on that date.

[306] Emily E. Chubbuck wrote under the *nom de plume* of Fanny Forester. Asked about it once, she said "Would anyone buy a book written by Emily E. Chubbuck?"

[307] Emily's new book, *Trippings in Author-land*, had just been published by Paine and Burgess.

Anna Maria Anable to Emily E. Chubbuck, November 28, 1845[308]

Dear Nem[309]

Courtland[310] has arrived this evening with the intelligence that Aunt U.[311] had passed through this afternoon on her way back—nobody knows wither, and that the Dr.[312] this same morning started East, and this latter intelligence is what I particularly sit up tonight to communicate to you. Before Aunt U. left hoping I suppose that by your means she might effect a reunion with her renegade spouse, she told Court that he would be found by a note or messenger at Stratton and Ley[ ]'s N. Y. 24 Winter St. N. Y. that he purposed coming up the river Friday night—i.e. if you lend your interest to hers—and persuade him to return to his abandoned home. She returns by Thursday and stops with us till Saturday, when she will return to Schenectady expecting to find there her Lord and Master and perhaps you. I am expecting a letter from you tomorrow telling me when and how you will come home, but Aunt C.[313] thought I had better let you know of this opportunity. Mr. Bright[314] also is in N. Y. and is coming out some time or other, but I hope we shall see you soon.

Your book[315] is here, and selling well I hear—Mr. Throop Martin called this evening and said he had been reading for the first time your letters—and they quite touched his fancy.

I have been reading your *Columbian* story aloud to the folks this evening.

Mrs. Prentiss of Cooperstown was here also this eve'y, and enquired very kindly for you—the folks are all well and very anxious to see you.

I must go to bed or I shall be late to breakfast again tomorrow morning.

---

[308] This letter is undated. It has only "Friday night eleven o'clock." We place it on Friday, November 28, as Anna Maria is still assuming that Emily will not be staying in Philadelphia, and instead will be returning soon to Utica. That decision was to change within the next week or so. On November 18, Emily wrote of her illness keeping her in Philadelphia for a while longer.

[309] "Nem" or "Nemmy" was a name of endearment given to Emily by a small group of her intimate friends at the Utica Female Academy. Anna Maria Anable was "Ninny."

[310] Courtland Anable, younger brother to Anna Maria Anable. He held several positions over the years and eventually studied at Hamilton College and boarded for a time with Emily's parents. In 1853, he returned to Philadelphia where he preached his first sermon at the Eleventh Baptist Church. He was "Uncle Court" to Emily Frances Judson. In 1880, Anable was listed in the Massachusetts census as an ordained minister serving in a church.

[311] Urania Sheldon Nott—formerly the literary principal at the Utica Female Academy—a mentor, advisor, and friend to Emily.

[312] Eliphalet Nott, married to Urania Sheldon Nott.

[313] Miss Cynthia Sheldon was the administrative and finance manager of the Utica Female Academy. She was a mentor, advisor, and friend to Emily. Anna Maria Anable was Miss Sheldon's niece.

[314] Edward Bright was, at this time, one of the publishers of the *Baptist Register*, a very popular Baptist paper in the New York region. In 1846, Bright became the American Baptist Missionary Union's corresponding secretary, and at the time of Adoniram Judson's death, he was instrumental in helping Emily and her family settle back in the United States. He worked with Emily on the business details of the Judson Memoir, and after Emily's death, was one of the executors of her estate. Beginning in October 1851, Adoniram and Elnathan lived with the Brights in Roxbury MA.

[315] *Trippings in Author-land* had been released from the publishers on November 22.

Good night

Ninny[316]

Source: American Baptist Historical Society, AJ 23, no. 1161.

Nathaniel Parker Willis to Emily E, Chubbuck,[317] November 28, 1845—Steventon Vicarage

My dear Emily

I wrote you from Berlin since hearing from you, and I was very sure I should get a letter by the *Great Western*. None has come, however, and there must have been at least a month during which you have not written to me. Is forgetfulness beginning to steal over you, or have you warmer affections to occupy you than your feeling for me? I am so low-spirited of late that I grow sensitive and dread new calamities in the way of feeling. But this is to be a note of reminder and not a letter.

Where are you passing the winter? Suppose I should arrive in New York by the 1st week in February should I see you before the Spring? Do not speak of the probability of my returning so early, but I think it very probable I shall do so. The *Mirror* requires my presence, and I am sick of the forc'd gayety I am obliged to keep up in my letters.

My sweet Imogen is well and wonderfully improved by her residence in England. Her aunts are very highly educated people and they are influencing her character very effectively. I wish you could see her.

My eyes are in a bad way, and I write with pain. So, my dearest friend, a kiss upon your forehead and a good night.

Yours always faithfully

N. P. W.

Source: Hanna family files.

---

[316] "Ninny" was a name of endearment given to Anna Maria Anable by her most intimate friends at the Utica Female Academy. Emily was "Nemmy."

[317] Written on the address page in the handwriting of Emily Chubbuck: "33"—this was the thirty-third letter she had received from N. P. Willis.

"Orphan" to Emily "Sweet Authoress" E. Chubbuck, November 29, 1845—Philadelphia

Sweet Authoress

I have read your last story—Willard Lawson[318]—I have just finished and I'm so deeply affected. Have you never heard of a parallel to your tale? It seems to me as though you had taken the poor misguided boy from my own life—I had such a home once! Forgive me for thus boldly addressing you [Note: There is a tear here in the paper and a piece missing.] could not refrain. You have touched a chord in my heart that shall bid it always beat in a bosom that shall ever pray for your welfare! Go on fair writer, may your labors ever be attended with success.—

Orphan

Source: American Baptist Historical Society, AJ 25, no. 1225.

Anna Maria Anable to Emily E. Chubbuck, November 29, 1845

My dearest Nemmy[319]

Can you imagine how sad I feel this afternoon, when instead of welcoming you home as I have been anticipating all the week, lonesome, I sit down to write to you about staying away all winter? It is a great disappointment to me you well know and [ ] I really think it will be better for you to stay there. We have had a regular

---

[318] The opening lines of "Willard Lawson" read:

"You will be sorry for it, Willard."

"Sorry! I tell you, Sophy, I have been in leading strings long enough; and I will go where I can, now and then, do as I choose!"

"You will be back in less than three days."

"No, not in less than three years. Come, tell me what I shall bring you from over the seas; they have all sorts of gimcracks in the Indies, and maybe, I shall go to China, or—"

"Or take a peep into Symm's hole, or a ride on the roc's back. Bring me a pair of slippers from Lilliput."

"I will bring you a pair so small that you cannot wear them, if that is what you like; and a rare India shawl, to beat cousin Meg's."

"I hope you will get your purse well replenished; I dare say you will find them in New York."

"New York!"

"Don't speak so contemptuously of our mammoth city, Will; there will be a little fading out of those handsome curls, I dare say, before you will see a larger."

"I tell you, Sophy, I am going to sea. What part of the world I may visit, I don't know; but it will be many a long year before you will see me again."

"Nonsense, Will, think of scrambling up ropes and perching in the air like a monkey! You have always had a taste that way, I know, but try it in a gale, and you would soon come to the conclusion that you had a little too much of it. Come, this freak of yours is all nonsense; be obedient, and father will be kind to you, but you know it was wrong for you to go—"

[319] "Nem" or "Nemmy" was a name of endearment given to Emily by a small group of her intimate friends at the Utica Female Academy. Anna Maria Anable was "Ninny."

consultation, quite a three hour meeting on your case, and have about made up in (our) minds to give you up till spring. Aunt C.[320] on the receipt of your first letter was quite in doubt about the Mitchells,[321] whether you would continue to like them, or find it pleasant staying with them. You know she is cautious. Well, she thinks now, if you find yourself pleasantly and comfortably situated, and feel that it would be advantageous to you to stay, why they will do the best they can without you. *Of course* you can come back whenever you want to. Jul Look[322] has the hardest task. The girls are all the time telling her how they wish Miss Chubbuck would come back etc etc. and she finds it pretty hard to hear, but she behaves nobly under it. We have had a delightful visit from Aunt U.[323] who left us this morning. I read her what you said about the Mitchells, and she thinks it will be better for you to stay. You can not [sic] imagine how kind she was—she was all interest for you, and did every thing [sic] to make the rest think you ought to stay. She thinks it would be ruinous for you to come home in this cold weather (we have three or four inches of snow on the ground) and if you find the M's as pleasant a family as you think they are now, she advises you to stay the winter.

I told her about your dresses and she says you ought to have a nice dark silk to wear out to dine or spend the afternoon. So I have been down to the store and solicited these two samples for you to choose from. We all like the blue very much as it has a younger look than the other, but I thought I would send them both. They are about $14 a pattern; of wide silk, eleven yards for a dress. Henry[324] says you may pay for it when you can afford to—and if you can't *never* afford to, why they will take you as pay, and he and Will[325] will "top up" to see which will have you to prevent a fight between "Les Freses [sic] Enemies." Every body is bewitched with your "Trippings."[326] We all took tea last even at Mrs. Martins—and several of the young fellows who came in the evening inquired after the young authoress. You were invited and they expected to meet you. We told every body [sic] you were coming home this week. Indeed I sent another letter to N. Y. for you, telling you how you could come up with the Dr.[327] I think I shall not try it again. Mr. Martin,

---

[320] Miss Cynthia Sheldon was the administrative and finance manager of the Utica Female Academy. She was a mentor, advisor, and friend to Emily. Anna Maria Anable was Miss Sheldon's niece.

[321] Mr. and Mrs. Mitchell were friends of Emily's and had offered her a place to stay while in Philadelphia.

[322] Julia Look was a student of Emily's at the Utica Female Academy, and then a fellow teacher.

[323] Urania Sheldon Nott—a mentor, advisor, and friend to Emily—was the literary principal when Emily was at the Utica Female Academy.

[324] Henry Sheldon Anable, Joseph and Alma Sheldon Anable oldest child.

[325] Born on November 6, 1816 in Albany NY, William Stewart Anable was the son of Joseph and Alma Sheldon Anable. In an August 31, 1844 letter, Cynthia Sheldon reported to Emily that William had returned home, having "doff'd his sailor garb for age." He married Olivia Williams on September 24, 1846, according to a letter written September 27 by Anna Maria Anable. They moved to Sheboygan, Wisconsin, where William opened a store. William died February 9, 1863, in Virginia CA.

[326] Emily's newly published book, *Trippings in Author-land*, which had been released November 22, 1845.

[327] Eliphalet Nott, president of Union College, married to Urania Sheldon Nott.

we have all quite lost our hearts with, and we intend visiting them a good deal this winter. Miss Martin (you remember?) sends a great deal of love to you.

I have been reading Willis'[328] letter again this afternoon and he is all I ever said of him. You have my entire consent and approbation of the match. I do believe he would "make you happy" and I think too, it is his intention to do so by making you his dear little wife, but he is too prudent and delicate and considerate to say so yet. Nevertheless he is becomingly horrified at the idea of your marrying any one else, for I suspect he knows very well that you cannot *love* any one [sic] else. It quite amuses me to hear him caution you "not to let the world see too much of you"— Jealous already? Eh, Mr. Willis? I send you the "daily" with a notice of *Imman's*'[329] of your book. He is pretty saucey [sic] but I don't blame him much.

What you say of the Grahams[330] is just what I suspected but I would carry out my independence till they *sued* for a visit from me. How many such folks there are in the world, and how soon one can see through their performances.

Miss Crafts[331] is going to write to her friend Mrs. C[ ] to become acquainted with you. She says she thinks it is too bad for you to stay away, just when she has come up into our neighborhood, and was calculating on such nice times, and yet she with the rest thinks that you are doing for the best. Out of spite to you I am going to make love to her with all my heart this winter. She is a blessed good soul. We don't hear anything from Mary Barber yet.[332] Aunt C. has had an excellent letter from Dr. Gregory thanking her for her kindness to all of his girls and hoping that she would someday find her reward for so much benevolence. It was expressed in such a way that we thought he understood matters for petty, and felt as if some one [sic] ought to make up for Mary's ingratitude. I suspect from her prolonged silence that she has a marrying project on foot—at least Aunt U. does.

---

[328] Nathaniel Parker (N. P.) Willis was the editor of *New Mirror*, the magazine that catapulted Emily into literary fame. He became a friend, mentor, and eventually a suitor. Anna Maria Anable gives her stamp of approval for Emily's increasing involvement with Willis.

[329] John Inman was the editor of the *Commercial Advertiser* and the *Columbian Magazine*, and an early supporter and advocate for Emily.

[330] George Graham, editor of *Graham's Magazine*, took an interest in Emily Chubbuck as Fanny Forester and paid her with the unheard of sum of five dollars a page.

[331] On December 5, 1845, Anna Maria Anable wrote that Miss Crafts was a delight. "What a blessing to society it is, that she was never married. What a shame it would have been for *her* to have settled down into a mere *me* and my *husband* and my *children*!" Miss Crafts is not to be confused with Mrs. Augusta Crafts, who was noted as having a sharp disposition and a gossipy tongue.

[332] Mary Barber, mentioned frequently in the Emily Chubbuck Judson letters, was a student and then the art teacher at the Utica Female Academy. Recently, some words spoken by Mary had proven offensive to Miss Cynthia Sheldon, and there had been no attempt at working out the issue.

What an awful thing that is about Griswold![333] Can't he get a divorce? Or would it all have to made public [sic]. Poor fellow! I don't wonder he has the "blues."

Tell me some more about the folks you see for you will of course make some new acquaintances at Mrs. Mitchell's—I like your Mr. Wall. I want to know just what kind of folks they are—what sort of room you have—if any body [sic] sleeps with you—and if any body [sic] is to take Ninny's[334] place altogether, for I feel quite jealous of you, or rather of your friends. I have made my first sacrifice in advocating your stay there—but I feel this afternoon as if it was not to be my last.

Love will get weaned from us before Spring, and tho' I do not doubt but that you will always love us—Nem I can't write any more [sic] in that strain—I have had my cry out about it and now I can be sensible again. I mean to say that it is well that it is so—you are to walk in a different path from the rest of us, and you must some time or other break loose—Well I won't indulge in my presentiments any longer—only keep a little corner of your heart all warm for

Ninny

After ten

Jul Look is sitting in your rocking-chair and we have had a nice talk. She is a dear good girl. Tell Fan[323] she must take double care of her health now—if she wants any article of dress very much let us know and she can have it. She is going out more than we expected and will very likely need a new dress—I leave all these things to your judgement [sic] if you will look after her a little. Tell [sic] she must write often.

Written upside down in the top margin of page 1: "Martha Wadsborn—She is a nice girl but not a bit companionable—Give us your address in the next letter."

Written in the right margin of page 2: "[Note: The first line is lost in the copy; the edge of the page cuts it off.] letters. Write immediately about the dress that I may send on by Mrs. [ ]. I will attend to your other commissions whenever you say so."

Written in the left margin of page 3: "Now Nemmy if I am a good girl to let you stay without teazing [sic] you [Note: The rest of the lines are cut off by the margin of the copy.]"

Source: American Baptist Historical Society, AJ 23, no. 1165.

---

[333] Reverend Rufus W. Griswold, an ordained clergyman and distinguished literary figure, had been one of Emily's suitors. Emily referred to him in a letter to Anna Maria Anable as a "widower." Apparently, the "widower" had entered into a less than successful marriage.

[334] "Ninny" was a name of endearment given to Anna Maria Anable by her most intimate friends at the Utica Female Academy. Emily was "Nemmy."

[335] Fanny Anable, one of five Anable sisters. She was born April 12, 1828. At this time, she was working and living in the home of Hannah and A. D. Gillette in Philadelphia.

Cynthia Sheldon to Emily E. Chubbuck, November 30, 1845[336]

Dear Emily,

Although we have been talking till a late hour in my room—I cannot give up writing or saying a few words—we are truly disappointed about your return home but have no doubt of its being best for you to remain there this winter[337]—Heavens grant you health—all other blessings seem to be in your pathway—you cannot think how eagerly we catch every thing [sic] Anna M.[338] will read to us. The paragraphs passed over in a wide field for conjecture. Time will probably make revelation so I let it pass—I am on the whole quite reconciled to your staying on Fanny's[339] account—her letters assure us more than you can imagine. She is stepping up in the world by rapid strides—If she improves her rare chance this winter well—she will be a prodigy in the Spring—but the *heart* that spring [sic] of immortal joys I fear is in great danger of being choked up with the vanitie [sic] which surround her—to know that each day was clearing away the rubbish causing her to look on this short life as a day of probation for immortal bliss how it would gladden our hearts.

Your account of her doings is extremely gratifying—say to Mr. and Mrs. G.[340] that we feel deeply all their kindness to her—the Music I am afraid will be too much—still feel willing she should try full lessons with the proviso that Mr. W. will not charge when is not able to go [sic]—or the weather such as to make going imprudent—her health is every thing—to be taken sick now would seem sad indeed—her unfortunate Muslin dress has no pieces here. Anna M. sent all the scraps—I hope she will find them—has Clarkson Potles [sic] yet delivered the package—we think the dress now sent will be strong and look pretty in the evening—I wish we could have it made for her—Mr. Gratiot[341] will send it on this week from N. York—by Mr. Purderville a Batchelor who visited us when Mr. G. first came—if he calls play the agreeable he has seen a great deal of the world—Mr. and Mrs. G. mean to see you in two weeks from now—he is a whole souled westerner—she is a jewel if not sparkling—it was a kind providence that placed them with us in the winter—I want to fill a sheet to Fanny but cannot write a word—we

---

[336] This letter is undated. Because of its content, we place this at the very end, the last Sunday and the last day, of November 1845.

[337] In her letter of November 23, 1845, to her sister Catharine, Emily said that she had "about decided" to spend the remainder of the winter in Philadelphia.

[338] Anna Maria Anable was the niece of the Urania and Cynthia Sheldon, the daughter of Joseph and Alma Sheldon Anable; she was Emily's closest friend at the Utica Female Academy.

[339] Fanny Anable, one of five Anable sisters. She was born April 12, 1828. At this time, she was working and living in the home of Hannah and A. D. Gillette in Philadelphia.

[340] Rev. A. D. Gillette was a stalwart friend and supporter of the Judson, Sheldon, and Anable families. Emily met Adoniram Judson in the parlor of the Gillette home in Philadelphia. Emily was staying with the Gillettes while in Philadelphia.

[341] Charles Gratiot married Ann Sheldon, who was a cousin of Cynthia Sheldon, Urania Sheldon Nott and Alma Sheldon Anable.

did not conclude to send the package until your letter last evening—thought we must wait till Wednesday—the reason for now to Fanny from the girls—say to Mrs. G. that Mrs. Minor failed to get her corset done by this chance—she run [sic] to death as she says—the by chance were obtained made for others—heaven bless you all—I love to think of you in the circle—had you best go to the Mitchell's[342]— you know best of course. Perhaps I am selfish on Fanny's account—she must continue to write often

Your attached friend

C. S.

Three Dolls[343] for Fanny.

Source: American Baptist Historical Society, AJ 26, no. 1261.

Emily Chubbuck on Horace Binney Wallace,[344] November 1845[345]

He is a man of talent, a scholar, and a perfect gentleman; refined, high-bred, delicate, and manly. He is not handsome; that is, there is nothing striking in his appearance; but he has a very intellectual look, and a peculiarly sweet expression. He is about as large as—; has an easy, gentlemanly carriage, and never does any thing awkward.... He is an excellent critic, not only of books, but of painting, sculpture, etc. his conversation is more improving and interesting (combining the two beautifully) than any man's I ever met.

Source: A. C. Kendrick, *The Life and Letters of Mrs. Emily C. Judson*, 136.

---

[342] Mr. and Mrs. Mitchell were friends of Emily's and had offered her a place to stay while in Philadelphia.

[343] Three dollars.

[344] Horace B. Wallace, a member of high Philadelphia Society, a literary critic, he was a part of an intimate circle of friends when Emily was in Philadelphia in winters 1844–45, 1845–46. He was both Emily's mentor in her literary pursuits, and a strong friend, as evidenced by the correspondence between them. His letters of March 1, and June 28, 1846, are especially instructive. Of him Kendrick wrote in the *Life and Letters of Mrs. Emily C. Judson*: "His polished and gentlemanly bearing, his broad culture and sound judgment, his ripened knowledge of the world, his taste at once enthusiastic and discriminating, made a profound impression on her fresh and susceptible intellect, while he in turn perceived all the delicate beauty, and as yet half-latent capacities of her opening genius" (136). Kendrick also quotes an analysis of "Fanny Forester" taken from Wallace's "Literary Criticisms." For more on Wallace, see A. C. Kendrick, *The Life and Letters of Emily C. Judson*, 135–38.

[345] Emily E. Chubbuck wrote these lines about Horace Binney Wallace, one of her prominent literary friends from Philadelphia. See June 1845, for a piece Wallace had written about Fanny Forester for his magazine, *Literary Criticisms*.

Charles Fenno "Hoffy" Hoffman to Laura Linden,[346] December 1, 1845[347]

"Fanny"[348] shall be taken care of dearest Laura. I had already attended to her when I got your letter this morning. I shall have a notice in the *Excelsior* which appears on the 20th and you will probably see one in an evening paper of Thursday or Saturday next.[349]

Why even I rest in that *chair* just before thou sister's room? Yet I don't know—Laura own—those kisses would certainly be *twelve* and *the* ab[ ] one might think them too eager if conscience did not—and then how long should I not [ ] them one day for dull—no I don't know that it would be good for me to be in that chair—just now—just at this very hour. Laura I wish. I [ ] not altogether of thy philosophy about "calling our better natures" into action! The very best and highest part of science in [ ] with so much that is impassioned or [ ] that I am always afraid of it. The noblest [ ] that take root in my vocal [ ] shoot toward heaven with the most generous vigor always seem to coosy up with [ ] [ ] [ ] poisonous vine. My *apple* trees of [ ] are low bowing [ ] and respectable sort of trees enough. I could set out orchards of them with safety. But the nature fondle growth always drags up all sorts of wild [ ] to deform the top-most boughs. Yet I know that [ ] [ ] growth to be the best part of me, while [ ] experiences tell me that it [ ] be stifled. I think I would have made a Capital *Saint*—but it would have been at the Court of Charles II where some qualities were so little shared or mellowed, that considerateness might pass for religious principle and [ ] for sanctity. This is [ ] [ ] [ ] and illustrating from self-consciousness only—But Laura dear I believe thou are few [ ] of affluent souls who can "afford" to "call their better natures into action"— few who had not better rest content with the exercise of those qualities of character which [ ] them "favor with the world." My own *better nature* Laura [ ] thy purity and radiant womanly nature would impel me to fold thee to my bosom and press again and again thy lips with a brother's fondness—But I know—I know my o*ther* nature would [ ] [ ] could the beating of thy heart too long and [ ] the [ ] till thou [ ] [ ] [ ] [ ]—Laura one thing I insist upon—that you would not forget that you are my *elder* sister—that you would keep her in [ ]—have things your own way—and take all responsibility off my hands by holding your little brother full in the mode and to the degree that you think the child ought to be indulged. The

---

[346] Charles Fenno Hoffman, a prominent literary figure in Philadelphia and New York, well known in literary circles as an exceptionally talented editor, poet, and writer. Emily had started a correspondence with him as Laura Linden before he discovered that she was Fanny Forester. The gaps in this letter are proof of the quality (or lack of) in his handwriting.

[347] All eight of the Laura Letters are undated.

[348] Fanny Forester, Emily Chubbuck's *nom de plume*.

[349] *Trippings in Author-land*, a collection of Emily's stories, had been published in November. Here, and in a letter we have dated December 14, Charles Fenno Hoffman promises her that a review of her book by him will appear in the pages of the *Excelsior*, which will come out just before Christmas.

muscles of my mind are all [ ] with wearing the [ ] of considerateness. My very soul is weary with the [ ] task of sifting its "better natures" from "its world [ ]" and I want the whole duty taken off my hands by some sisterly soul with winnowing house as single-hearted as theirs. Well my Laura this is really throwing off my most careless thoughts towards thee—no, 'tis carelessly throwing off my most earnest thoughts—I am writing a novel dear and it just enters my head that I will fashion the head upon this idea of a character of strong and opposing phases continually at war with each other—There was a time when I would have [ ] love the blessed solv[ ] which should fuse them happily together—But there again I come to my own self-consciousness and love—so much love is within me a [ ] of madness—its [ ], its prof[ ]ly, its all submissiveness was more or less unintelligible to its object who at one moment would put a [ ] into the fountain were it gushed [ ] [ ] and at another stood back in awe when the torrent [ ] too overwhelming for another to guide or regulate its flow. The affection which was [ ] almost at the cost of Reason [ ] from devoted considerateness only—That affection was deemed coldness—while that which would not be controlled overwhelmed with alarm and something like dismay when the heart became agonized into [ ]—yet [ ] as we were—I and that warmest of friends. I know we much love each other and she [ ] herself if she thinks any other impress can efface him—But my own Sweet Sister I meant not to allude again to these things—You read me rightly in thinking that I am not happy—I fear I never can be happy Laura—for though my [ ] [ ] on sometimes as [ ] as ever, I fear [ ] much that my health is sapped, and I know by the [ ] eagerness with which I catch at anything to occupy [ ] [ ] or sentiment, and the difficulty I find in enlisting any prospec[ ] places of life not to say of ambition, which I long sense outlived, I know that some springs much have bent too far if not broken entirely—But what a novel of egotism is this—How readily have I caught at thy ministering offen [sic]—put up thy lips girl that I may kiss them—another—another yet. Then sweet sister [ ] and good night—wont you say "good night" Laura? Was that kiss too earnest? Could thee take it back—Take all kisses back—and [ ] [ ] [ ] Good Night.

Source: Hanna family files.

Sarah Bell Wheeler to Emily E. Chubbuck, December 1, 1845[350]

My dear cousin Nemmy[351]—you don't know how much disappointed we are to learn that you have *really* made up your mind to spend the winter in P.—

How much you will enjoy yourself, and the number of hearts you break we hope to find out from your letters. How much I'd like to see you in Ninny's[352] room this morning. Wouldn't you tell me some cunning stories about Hoffman[353] and others. [ ] says she will write in a letter Anna Maria[354] will send tomorrow.

She has had any quantity of things to do this morning. I presume Miss Fan[355] has told you of Lauries [sic] marrying before this. I had a letter from her a week since and she is *very happy* of course. Susan Avery has sent for me to spend the holidays at Aurora with [ ]. Won't we have nice times? I intend to break the heart of one of those old Bachelors. Perhaps I'll do as well as [ ] [ ]! They say that Mr. Williams is to marry Helen Munson[356]—are *you* very sorry? I wish you could see the quantity of snow on the ground although I suppose you prefer doing without it. Mr. Gratiot[357] gave us a fine sleigh ride Thanksgiving day. Molly Gregory is with us. She left Cleveland last week, and has been with us since Friday. She sends much love to you.

I hope you will be very happy all winter, and if you cannot have Ninny to take care of you when you get sick, I hope you will find many many kind friends. Do write one a letter now, one of these days. You have the love and best wishes of

Sarah Bell

You don't know how sorry all the people are to hear that you have concluded to stay away all winter. Do let us see your phiz as soon as warm weather comes.

Sarah Bell

---

[350] This letter is undated. December 1 would have been the first Monday after Thanksgiving, which is mentioned here in the letter.

[351] "Nem" or "Nemmy" was a name of endearment given to Emily by a small group of her intimate friends at the Utica Female Academy. Anna Maria Anable was "Ninny."

[352] "Ninny" was a name of endearment given to Anna Maria Anable by her most intimate friends at the Utica Female Academy. Emily was "Nemmy."

[353] Charles Fenno Hoffman, a prominent literary figure in Philadelphia and New York, well known in literary circles as an exceptionally talented editor, poet, and writer. Emily had started a correspondence with him as Laura Linden before he discovered that she was Fanny Forester.

[354] Anna Maria Anable was the niece of the Urania and Cynthia Sheldon, the daughter of Joseph and Alma Sheldon Anable; she was Emily's closest friend at the Utica Female Academy.

[355] Fanny Anable was one of five Anable sisters. At this time, she was working and living in the home of Hannah and A. D. Gillette in Philadelphia.

[356] Jimmy Williams, often mentioned in Anna Maria Anable's letters. Helen Munson was his fiancée.

[357] Charles Gratiot married Ann Sheldon, who was a cousin of Cynthia Sheldon, Urania Sheldon Nott and Alma Sheldon Anable.

Give my best love to Fan. Tell her I'm very anxious to hear her voice already.

Source: American Baptist Historical Society. A file reference and reference number cannot be found.

Anna Maria Anable to Emily E. Chubbuck, December 5, 1845[358]

Dear Nem[359]

I don't owe you anything in the way of a letter or note but as there has been a letter here for a week waiting for you to come home and I must forward it. Now, I won't let it go alone—I forgot it when I sent the last package.

Now Nem by all that's forlorn and lonesome and desolate and deserted sit right down and write me something to cheer me up—I've been sick ever since last Friday when your letter came saying you weren't coming back, but I would not tell you so then, for I felt unselfish and didn't want to make you feel bad, but there is nothing like a real hard old fashioned orthodox *cold* to call out one's selfishness and incline one to test one's friend's benevolence.

All day Saturday and Sunday I lay tucked up on the lounge a wheezing and sniffling and coughing like old December himself—and didn't I feel *forlorn* without my Nemmy to pet me, or my Fanny[360] to get nice things for me and keep me covered up and [ ] and put the wood in the stove? Martha is a nice child, but she is no more companionable than the broom and knows no more how to pet than the tongs. Nora Westcott[361] and Martha Hooker[362] and the rest pet too much and I have to entertain them when they come in, so *that* ain't [sic] pleasant. I tell you I feel forlorn and you needn't tell me I am getting well, because I grumble—I ain't a-getting well [sic]—I'm down sick and I mean to come right off to Philadelphia and see if I can't get somebody to take care of me.

There has been a hen-fight [sic] tonight over to Mrs. Bacon's and *all* the teachers were invited—to entertain each other. Interesting wasn't it? Well, I felt

---

[358] This letter is undated. We place it on Friday, December 5, 1845, mainly because of the reference Anna Maria's comment that the week before was when they had heard that Emily would stay in Philadelphia, and that decision had been made the very end of November.

[359] "Nem" or "Nemmy" was a name of endearment given to Emily by a small group of her intimate friends at the Utica Female Academy. Anna Maria Anable was "Ninny."

[360] Fanny Anable, one of five Anable sisters. She was born April 12, 1828. At this time, she was working and living in the home of Hannah and A. D. Gillette in Philadelphia.

[361] Nora Westcott was one of the girls from the Utica Female Academy. On January 17, 1847, Anna Maria Anable noted that Nora was in Mississippi, though dying of consumption. In November 1849, Sarah Hinckley spoke of her death.

[362] Martha Hooker knew Emily through the Utica Female Academy. There are two early letters from Martha Hooker to Emily Chubbuck in April 1845 and May 1846. Then in September 1852 she wrote to Emily Judson saying that she too had responded to God's call to missionary Service, and that she was going as a missionary teacher to Illinois. In this letter she also asked Emily for an autograph for a friend.

secure in my cold for an excuse—but no! Just at dusk Jane Kelly[363] came up in the greatest "stew" and said not one of her girls but herself and I knew Mrs. B. and if I had any bowels of compassion I would go over just for an hour or two and help her introduce the girls. Oh! Me! That was most *too* much to ask of me, but I went Nem, and my good nature had like to have been the undoing of me. As it was, I was obligated to come home at eight, with an addition ticked on to my old *cold*. Oh, how cross I feel! I want some one [sic] to rant at, you little angel, and I want *you*. Yes, Nemmy, Ninny[364] does want you—without you she feels as if she had lost her *Abbo*! [sic] her part and parcel, her other half. Oh, here comes Miss Crafts[365] with her pleasant good-souled face. It would be a sin to be cross to her, and I must sub up a smile.

You may hope for the next page to be good-natured, for I am quite revived by a half hours chat with Miss C.—What a blessing to society it is, that she was never married. What a shame it would have been for *her* to have settled down into a mere *me* and *my husband* and *my children*! I wonder if I should ever make such a good old maid! Nay, I tron [sic] not. It's too late to begin now.

Do you want to hear something that will make you thank your stars that you are in the mild city of brotherly love? In coming home tonight Aunt C.[366] pitched into a snow-bank nearly as high as her head, and came down on all fours. The weather has done nothing but snow since Saturday morning. Nem, I am curling my hair at a great rate and very becomingly the folks say—and I don't wear my spectacles hardly ever, and I have a cunning little eye-glass that you would quite envy if you were here. The folks hardly knew me tonight. I mean to go away somewhere and come out fresh, as a new belle. Do you know Jimmy is really engaged to Helen M?[367] He hasn't been to see me yet, and he came home last Sat. Oh, love! love! Even a seven year friendship must fade before thy potent spell. Little did I think tho' that Jimmy would be faithless.

Miss Crafts and all the rest of the "worthies" are working their fingers off for another fair for the orphan asylum—that orphan asylum that has but one orphan in it! By the way speaking of orphans reminds me of a letter that come to you yes-

---

[363] Jane Kelly was Emily Chubbuck's friend at the Utica Female Academy. Jane was the literary principal at the Utica Female Academy. In fall 1848, she followed Cynthia Sheldon as headmistress.

[364] "Ninny" was a name of endearment given to Anna Maria Anable by her most intimate friends at the Utica Female Academy. Emily was "Nemmy."

[365] Speaking of Miss Crafts here, Anna Maria Anable reflected that Miss Crafts was a blessing to all and she wondered is she herself could attain those same qualities as late in life. We note a distinction between Miss Crafts and Mrs. Crafts, who at one point was accused of having a gossipy tongue.

[366] Miss Cynthia Sheldon was the administrative and finance manager of the Utica Female Academy. She was a mentor, advisor, and friend to Emily. Anna Maria Anable was Miss Sheldon's niece.

[367] Jimmy Williams, often mentioned in Anna Maria Anable's letters, usually just as "Jimmy." His fiancée was Helen Munson.

terday from Philadelphia addressed *Miss Chubbuck School teacher*, Utica. Aunt C. thought it must be an application for a pupil, so I took the liberty of opening it before sending it back to you. It was from a boy very much affected by the similarity of Willard Lawson's[368] early history and his own, and was signed *Orphan*. Ah! Nem, your turn for anonymous correspondents has come now, and you deserve to be bored, don't you?

Written in the right margin of the address page: "I don't know your address yet at the Mitchells[369] so shall forward this to Mr. Gillette.[370] Did you not say you were going there last Thursday?

"Tell Fan I shall answer her letter and attend to her wants as soon as possible. Mr. Gratiot[371] came back today—and I don't know when he will be back again, but probably soon so you must write immediately if you want your things sent on."

Written in the bottom margin of the address page: "I meant to keep this among [ ] letters to send when I wrote again, but I can use it as an envelope. Blessings on the new postage law! I don't feel as if I was going to impoverish you if I *do* write often enough to bore you."

Written along the left margin of the address page: "Good night! Mother[372] has just been in to hurry me off to bed."

Source: American Baptist Historical Society, AJ 23, no. 1137.

Cynthia Sheldon to Emily E. Chubbuck, December 5, 1845[373]

Dear Emily,

We have conned the content of your letter with the deepest interest. On some accounts it appears greatly to your advantage to comply with the Mitchells[374] entreaty—but as we cannot always tell by appearance I am about to suggest your

---

[368] "Willard Lawson" was a story written by Emily Chubbuck for publication. It appeared as well in *Alderbrook*, vol. 1I. See the letter from "Orphan" dated November 29, 1845.

[369] Mr. and Mrs. Mitchell were friends of Emily's and had offered her a place to stay while in Philadelphia.

[370] A Philadelphia minister, Rev. A. D. Gillette was a stalwart friend and supporter of the Judson, Sheldon, and Anable families. Emily met Adoniram Judson in the parlor of the Gillette home in Philadelphia. Emily was living with the Gillettes while in Philadelphia.

[371] Charles Gratiot married Ann Sheldon, who was a cousin of Cynthia Sheldon, Urania Sheldon Nott and Alma Sheldon Anable.

[372] Alma Sheldon Anable, sister of Cynthia Sheldon and Urania Sheldon Nott and married to Joseph Hubbell Anable. The Anables had nine children.

[373] This letter is undated. We place this on December 5, 1845; often Miss Sheldon and Anna Maria Anable enclosed letters in the same mail, and Anna Maria has a letter of that date. Also, the issues addressed in this letter conform to the short time after Emily had decided to stay in Philadelphia, but still was thinking of staying with the Mitchells.

[374] Mr. and Mrs. Mitchell were friends of Emily's and had offered her a place to stay while in Philadelphia.

acceptance for a few weeks—Mr. Gratiot and cousin Ann[375] will be there on their way to Washington in about four weeks or less from this. They will spend one week with his Uncle Gen. Gratiot at W.—return through P. giving you the best company in the wide world for your homeward jaunt. You will know all about your new friends by that time—we will do the best we can without you but talk confidentially of your coming then. I perceive Fanny[376] dear girl should have a five Dollar in this—but cannot spare it—can you let her have it for me[377]—Will you also regulate the matter of her teaching—would not from 9 to 11 and one hour after dinner be all sufficient for the good of the children—particularly if it is varied with a little music—

It will not do for F. to have all her hours taken up—her own practice must have a place—you will see how near to right I am—and whatever you think and say to them will I am sure be acceded to. I am very much afraid she will be in some way overtaxed—

Heaven grant you may both be preserved to set in in [sic] health. It is too late to write more—

Remember me kindly to each of the dear family—a world of love to Fanny and yourself—

Your truly attached friend,

C.— Source: American Baptist Historical Society, AJ 26, no. 1264.

Charles Fenno "Hoffy" Hoffman to Laura Linden,[378] December 8, 1845[379]

"For my lips were never made for wise words" quoth my Laura. What were they made for then dear? Were those kisses within reach of kisses at this moment [ ] thou shouldst learn! But I must not write [ ] to thee excellent friend, for next I would be telling thee of all my dreams last night, how we sat on the root of an old tree over a spring, or rather I sat on the tree but you Laura [ ] to have placed your-

---

[375] Ann Sheldon was a younger cousin of Cynthia Sheldon, Alma Sheldon Anable, and Urania Sheldon Nott. She married Charles Gratiot, the son of a prominent army officer and engineer who had opened up the port of St Louis. Because Charles and Ann Gratiot often lived with the Sheldon—Anable families, both at Utica and in Philadelphia after 1848, they were very often mentioned in the correspondence. We learn of the birth and growth of their six children (one born very close to the birth of Emily Frances Judson), Charles Gratiot's journeys to California in search of gold, and his religious awakening.

[376] Fanny Anable, one of five Anable sisters. She was born April 12, 1828. At this time, she was working and living in the home of Hannah and A. D. Gillette in Philadelphia.

[377] In a letter we have dated November 30, 1845, Sheldon had enclosed three dollars for Fanny.

[378] Charles Fenno Hoffman, a prominent literary figure in Philadelphia and New York, well known in literary circles as an exceptionally talented editor, poet, and writer. Emily had started a correspondence with him as Laura Linden before he discovered that she was Fanny Forester.

[379] All eight of the Laura Linden letters are undated.

self in my lap in a matter of course way and pulled the arm furtherst round that encircled you. We talked and chucked pebbles in the spring and kissed in between while as if to silty [sic] and calmly enjoying belonged to us as naturally as the air we believed it seemed to be in fact the matter-of-course repetition of previous happy hours that we had often thus enjoyed together. But then though the morning [ ] to [ ] around us. Yet evening seemed also to be there. My darling Sister thought it better to wend homewards but I [ ] without saying anything to [ ] [ ] her to the spot she was [ ] and if not angry confused and abashed. I then [ ] with which I clasped her. Yet she did not return the pressure—and then quickly disentangling herself exclaimed "This is but the overflowing of a tenderness which belongs to another." Then she burst into tears. I kissed those tears, kissed them till she trembled all over with agitation. It thrilled her in that dream, Laura—of which I must not tell thee now my [ ] friend—of which I ought not to have told thee this. But how otherwise could I make thee fully comprehend the [ ] and hallowed feeling which thy most delicate sisterly and refined letter awakened to chasten these wild images of the fevered night. Besides would I blot out all that dream from memory? would I keep all to myself of that which is its pleasure and its pain was shared between us—and did it not come to me as the [ ], the masculine, of that dainty vision of thee among the strawberry blossoms and buttercups—that sweet feminine picture disfigured by none of the throes of affection perverted into passion which haunted her—Laura how I'd like to write thee all—everything—everything girl, but variant as thou art [ ] sin for any but my better nature to go forth to thee at my waking moments. Yet this [ ]lty out one's soul—this revel of [ ] up thy mouth—my that is too deliriously delightful.

"Well what of it"—are we not children—children of the heart—would either of us harm the others—would not either shield—Laura a false columface [sic] come between the paper and me on that instant—I will not stop to interpret its holy reproachful look—yet why should it look reproachful? Each word of endearment that flies to my pen I write to thee Sweet Sister. Each [ ] all are cold—very cold—measured either by thy [ ] or by contrast with that which have at times overwhelmed her. Laura I should have [ ] between thee to death by [ ] one had I been thy lover. The droplet of Anglo Saxon in my [ ] seems to float on the surface without [ ] with the fountain of [ ] and Provencal that give their yesty qualities to the mongrel puddles. Surely I cannot help it if other blood than the Anglo Saxon rushes to my lips when they glow upon thine. How excellent is that lecture upon the last page of your letter. Do I not think that Laura would make a good physician? Surely does thy brother so think. Do not be "sad" about my health dear. I have been leached since I wrote and find myself much better from this application of the principle of old local remedies. I shall send you the *Excelsior* containing the enclosed notice of Fanny's[380] book[381] so soon as it is published, observe when you get the [ ] how on page third you are clasped in the heart of "bondel." A clever friend of mine promised to take care of her in the *Evening Gazette*, but his paragraph though complimentary in the [ ] [ ] [ ] [ ] from a <u>Mal-p-</u>propos side cut at Mr. Willis[382] who has been so cordially and efficiently your literary friend. My own notice would have been longer and gone [ ] into the variety of the book for which I thought full room had been reserved in the *Excelsior* but at the last moment we were obliged to cut down our [ ] and put much of it in a smaller type than had been contemplated originally and I put Fanny into as pithy a shake as possible. The *Excelsior* will appear at Christmas and so Laura you only added one to the Number when returning my three kisses for good night—Well dear if what one was as *long* and *close* a one as I now give thee it comes with a dozen of common kisses.

Written along the right margin of page 3: "Which would Miss G[ ] say if she saw our lips thus clinging together in [ ]. Good night."

Source: Hanna family files.

Emily E. Chubbuck to Catharine Chubbuck, December 13, 1845

My love kitty,

I will answer your nice long letter when I get time but now I am in great haste. Meanwhile write me very often. I don't send you the Daguerre[383] because I have concluded to spend the winter here and Anna Maria[384] wants it—you have the miniature you know. I got a steel bracelet and pin as they are very fashionable just now and will answer all purposes. You must put the comb inside your braid and then make the basket as large as the hair is long. Put the brau [sic] inside and the other thing on top. I send you a pocket-handkerchief to save your laud one. I am cutting up high here and have just the cutest and biggest beau in the city—Mr. Wallace,[385] nephew of Horace Binney. My papa[386] would be jealous if he knew

---

[380] Fanny Forester, Emily Chubbuck's *nom de plume*.

[381] *Trippings in Author-land*, a collection of Emily's stories, had been published on November 22. Here, and in a letter we have dated December 14, Charles Fenno Hoffman promised Emily that a review of her book by him will appear in the pages of the *Excelsior*, which will come out just before Christmas.

[382] Nathaniel Parker (N. P.) Willis was the editor of *New Mirror*, the magazine that catapulted Emily into literary fame. He became a friend, mentor, and eventually a suitor.

[383] See the letter of Emily Chubbuck to Anna Maria Anable dated November 18, 1845.

[384] Anna Maria Anable was the niece of the Urania and Cynthia Sheldon, the daughter of Joseph and Alma Sheldon Anable; she was Emily's closest friend at the Utica Female Academy.

[385] Wallace was the nephew of Horace Binney Wallace. An attorney, whom Emily called aristocratic and privileged, he called on Emily regularly during winter 1845 when Emily was in Philadelphia, and then after Emily's engagement to Adoniram, he became a trusted friend and advisor.

[386] Emily and Anna Maria Anable often referred to N. P. Willis, editor of the *New Mirror*, as "my papa" or "your papa." Willis was in Europe with his daughter at this time, following the death of his wife in late March 1845.

what great friends we are. I hear from my good N. P.[387] often—he is to return in March. Hoffy[388] is engaged. What do you guess? People here call me beautiful and fascinating and all those nice things. Think of *my* being beautiful—there's nothing like getting your name up, darlin'. I shall have oceans to tell when I see you but I can't write it. We have no snow but the weather is pretty cold and the ground freezes. I would send you a nice frock if I could, but I am as poor as a rat. More, by and by—In haste,

Your very loving sister

Nem[389]

Source: Hanna family files.

Charles Fenno "Hoffy" Hoffman to Laura Linden,[390] December 15, 1845[391]

A week—nay two of them have elapsed since I wrote the within in [ ] reply to your last scorch 5 [sic] by letter. I will not look it over because that would cheat you of a first reading—besides the chance is I would not then mail it—and like myself I know you like first impressions of a friend's mind. Well my dear after with holding [sic] my letter under the expectation of seeing you last week I find myself now compelled to put off my visit to Phila till after the hollidays [sic]. Laura own I think that will double the number of kisses to console thy brother for his disappointment. I [ ] a notice of [ ] friend Fanny[392] other [ ] this morning but as it has to be a stereotyped it will not reach thine eye for ten days to come. The title to Fanny's book has not helped it here and I have taken the liberty [ ] that the choice was the publisher's office. Still I hear that thy family like "trippings" are doing well.[393] By the way I wish you would tell Emily Chubbuck that I heard the other day that she had some time ago written and published some remarkably clever children's books! I do think Laura that you Emily and Fanny are the [ ] set at witching

---

[387] Nathaniel Parker (N. P.) Willis was the editor of *New Mirror*, the magazine that catapulted Emily into literary fame. He became a friend, mentor, and eventually a suitor.

[388] Charles Fenno Hoffman, a prominent literary figure in Philadelphia and New York, well known in literary circles as an exceptionally talented editor, poet, and writer. Emily had started a correspondence with him as Laura Linden before he discovered that she was Fanny Forester.

[389] "Nem" or "Nemmy" was a name of endearment given to Emily by a small group of her intimate friends at the Utica Female Academy. Anna Maria Anable was "Ninny."

[390] Charles Fenno Hoffman, a prominent literary figure in Philadelphia and New York, well known in literary circles as an exceptionally talented editor, poet, and writer. Emily had started a correspondence with him as Laura Linden before he discovered that she was Fanny Forester.

[391] All eight of the Laura Letters are undated.

[392] Fanny Forester, Emily Chubbuck's *nom de plume*.

[393] Emily's book, published on November 22, 1845, was *Trippings in Author-land*.

the world glancing like sun-beams or Spring airs everywhere. O if I were only now alone in a room with all three of you. But [ ] those my elder sister would be there and check me. I know you would—if too forward with Emily or Fanny! I should not be more afraid of Emily's demure gravity than of Fanny's wit, but Laura's tendency would mould [sic] me instantly to her will, and I should turn from teasing the sensible E or romping with the spirited F. to receive an elderly caress for my good behavior from the affectionate L.

And "your Mother" sparkling Laura "is still your best love"! dearest friend may he who succeeds to the Mother's care have all a Mother's tenderness for thee in addition to every manly quality which thy heart would desire. Remember Sweet Sister that I must know of the [ ] the instant he is born to thy soul. Know of this or ought else that interests or concerns the darling sister of they affectionate H.

Source: Hanna family files.

Mary R. Adams[394] to Emily E. Chubbuck, December 16, 1845

"The day was cold and dark and dreary"—and so had been the day before, and the day before that, and the one before that, and so on as far back, as I can remember (my memory by the way was always remarkably short, never being able to contain or rather retain, the moral law or the multiplication tables). At any rate it rained and rained and rained, till all the streets were covered, and where the people walked, and ladies rode it was nothing but mud, mud, mud! Now though I am blest with the lightest of all light hearts, I could not hold out against three weeks of such diabolical weather, and my spirits sank day by day, as the doleful reply of my "little maid" to my material question of, "What's the weather? "Dreadful bad weather miss." was sounded in my ears 'till I had passed through all the variations of the blues from the sky down to the "deeply darkly"—While in the "widigo" [sic] sitting all alone—in my little chamber, I conclude to console myself by "tripping" with Fanny Forester[395] in Author Land;[396] so turning over the leaves, I hit upon the "Bank Note"[397]—well I read on a few pages, wished little Rosa

---

[394] Mary Adams, a friend of Emily's while at the Utica Female Academy.

[395] Fanny Forester, Emily Chubbuck's *nom de plume*.

[396] Emily's new book, published on November 22, 1845, was *Trippings in Author-land*.

[397] "The Bank Note" was a story written by Emily Chubbuck; it was also published in *Trippings in Author-land* and in vol. 1 of *Alderbrook*.

Warner and her pink barege [sic][398] "to the devil" (politely and in French) and wondered why people had the face to publish such stupid stories, but still the pale faced seamstress, looked out on me from the page, and I followed Rosa on tip toe through the dark streets and looked with her upon the dead mother, and the starving little ones, and then, what then? Why, my eyes being weak and the solar' being particularly bright, there came a film over my sight, and the tears they come "trickling down, down, down." If people will write stupid stories (they might at least have them decently printed so as not to put people's eyes out—So much for "Tripping with Fanny Forester"—she treads daintily and her footsteps are light and true, flowers spring in her path, and she scatters bright jewels around her—

It must be a blessed gift—that of the frock—when all is dull and dark around—when you are walled up in the dirty town, not one green leaf near yours, to be able to create for yourself a world of beauty—to dress the fields, wake up the streams, call to life the race of flowers, and make the birds sing on the "balancing branches"—

The blessed sun has shone today again, and I wandered out to the skirts of the town, and I stopped to smell the fresh earth as the men turned it up with their spades, and looked up into the clear blue sky, and drew in long breaths of the balmy air, and wondered how I ever could have had the "blues"—

"Our eldest" was married last night, she was a beautiful bride, but the groom—alas! The vogoues [sic] of love are exceeding strange—oceans of tears were shed and seas of champagne were drunk, the ring was put on the finger, the prayers were mumbled over in Latin—and so the Miss was made a Madam—Hatty[399] has been ill for some days, but is better now, an euretie [sic] administered this morning, has worked wonders—she is so near me that I can see her daily. Loo [sic] is still in the country, Mr. Roman[400] is very ill and his recovery is doubtful, which renders it uncertain whether they will come to town. Now Emily Chugup,[401] [sic] the fire has gone out and the lamp seems to be following its example, Babet is snoozing on the floor…

---

[398] The first two paragraphs of "The Bank Note" read:

> "A pink barege, with tucks—or a flounce—no! I like tucks better; let me think—how many? Half a dozen little ones look fixed up; one deep one, doubling the whole skirt, is very suitable for mamma, but it would be rather too heavy, too dignified for me; then two of moderate size—oh! they are so common! Never mind! Madam Dufraneau shall decide that matter. But I will have the dress, at any rate, and it shall be pink—just the palest and most delicate in the world—but pink it shall be, because of my dark eyes and hair, and fair complexion."
>
> So soliloquized pretty Rosa Warner, a good-natured, thoughtless miss, of some thirteen summers, whose only troublous reflection was occasioned by the distance of bright sixteen, when her mother had promised she should be allowed to abolish short dresses, and gather up her jetty curls into a comb. And this would, indeed, be quite an era in the life of the little lady; —for she had no small pretensions to beauty, and was, moreover, the only child of a very wealthy father and a very fashionable mother. Oh! what visions she had of the future!

[399] Harriet ("Hatty," "Hattie," or "Hat") Anable, one of the five Anable sisters. She had been teaching in a private residence in the New Orleans area.

[400] Harriet or "Hatty" Anable worked with the family of Roman.

[401] Mary Adams had used this spelling of Emily's name in her previous letter of October 12, 1845.

Written in the right margin of the address page: "…and my sleepy eyes put me in mind that at two o'clock this morning I was still eating oranges—I wish I could throw one of the immense ones from "our plantation" into your mouth, and a bucket…"

Written in the left margin of the address page: "…of violets and jasmine at your nose—and kiss you good night, the last I [ ] you to do for me. My love to Mrs. Gillette[402] and Fanny[403]—and do when you can spare an hour for charity's sake give it to me your Dear Caring

Mary R. Adams."

Source: American Baptist Historical Society, AJ 22, no. 1092.

Nathaniel Parker Willis to Emily E. Chubbuck,[404] December 17, 1845—London

My dear Emily,

Your sweet, earnest letter of Nov. 24 reached me last night. It came very opportunely, as I had left my sweet Imogen that morning in the country and had a lonely and wretched evening before me in the solitude of heartless London. You can conceive neither the desolation to which you ministered, nor the value and charm of your tender ministry. With scores of acquaintances within reach of a visit, there was not one whose society would not have been a burden to me, and, but for your letter, I should have sat alone over my fire, sad and without a comforter. The world is so dreadfully disenchanted to me that everything which comes from the level of its *surface* tires and sickens me. I look in vain for a beginning of a return to my former taste for it. Any thing [sic] to interest me must come from the *heart*-level, and there is so little of that, that I feel in a desert. For the last three weeks I have lived in solitary lodgings in the country a mile from my daughter, (unwilling to burden the hospitality of my kinsman for so long a visit) and with the exception of two hours of her prattle each day, I have been in complete loneliness, yet much happier there than in the gayeties of London. I was compelled to be about my work, however, and here I am. Now the angels, who know what *Spirit*-recognition is, know *why* it is that, of all the people whose natures have been read by me, yours

---

[402] Hannah Gillette was the wife of the A. D. Gillette. Hannah would play an important part in preparing Emily for life in Burmah.

[403] Fanny Anable, one of five Anable sisters. She was born April 12, 1828. At this time, she was working and living in the home of Hannah and A. D. Gillette in Philadelphia.

[404] Written on the address page in the handwriting of Emily Chubbuck: "34"—meaning that this was the thirty-fourth letter from N. P. Willis she had received.

is the most palatable to my present state of mind—the most genuine, the most worthy of trust and affection. Your *kind is rare* dearest Emily, and if circumstances were to put your qualities to the trial, the world would find that there had been stuff for a heroine lock'd up in your partial development by literature. *I have read you,* however. I know you. I prize the discovery of you, and while my life lasts I shall draw what sweetness you will permit from the *soul's well* within you. It is the assurance in your letter that this bountiful spring is open to me that made me last night so happy.

I like the title of your new book,[405] and I would have written a preface[406] if I had not thought my other recommendation was the better way—to let *some one* [sic] *else* write the preface and *embody in it* the mention I made of you in one of my public letters. Did you get my letter recommending this? You make no mention of it. My object was to avoid the apparent *protege*-ship and shield you from the ill-will of my literary enemies, who would either slur or neglect you as an avow'd disciple of mine. In this, and all other respects, my dear friend, you will be much better lov'd by the world the less they see of your leaning toward me. I carry quite too full and easy a sail of notoriety to please the envious—(to whom, however, I would gladly make over all my unsought title to it)—and you need not be a sufferer by their malice.

Where shall you be when I return? If not living in New York, I can only, at best, have a glimpse of you. I *may* go home this winter—but I *may* stay till April. Do not stop writing to me. Your last letter has probably gone to Germany, as I have not yet received it.

God bless you, dearest Emily. I should strain you to my bosom like a last hope, if you were here.

Ever yours affectionately,

N. P. W.

I am sadly distracted between my *aching* desire to take my child home with me, and the apparent expediency of leaving her with her aunts. I really fear I should go crazy, alone in New York. My brain is not a strong one, and I am strangely nervous of late and subject to terrible depressions. I need a home, and a solitary room at a hotel looks intolerable to me. I shall decide probably in the course of this month. Her aunts here are such very superior women, and she is so carefully taught and cared-for here, that I scarce dare take her home again. Her angel mother wish'd her left with the sister who has now the charge of her.

---

[405] *Trippings in Author-land* had been published on November 22, 1845.

[406] Emily had originally asked Willis to write the Preface for *Trippings*. She thought also of several others after not hearing from Willis, but eventually wrote it herself.

Written in the right margin of the address page: "Direct always to London, care of Mrs. Kelly, No 2 Vigo St."

Written in the left margin of the address page: "I have written three letters to your one—I hope they reached you. I directed to Utica Academy."

Source: Hanna family files.

Cynthia Sheldon to Emily E. Chubbuck, December 17, 1845[407]

Dear Emily,

Your letters always make us happy for the time—but what can compensate for the absence of one we want to chat with every hour on some topic—nothing save the conviction that absence is for the best good of the friend—then we pass on hardly time enough on hand to write a note here after Sunday efforts to get your things safe in care of Mr. Gratiot[408] without avail—we find they can go by express for one Dollar. Our information before led us to think it would be three dollars. It will not do to put your Johnson[409] in this. I am sorry—but hope you can be furnished by your good friends. Anna M.[410] did not think of it until Mr. G.'s trunk was fairly gone—Mr. Griswold[411] can certainly raise one for you—how surprisingly useful he is to you. Do bring on his daughter[412] if you can—I will take her for $100 per year while she is in the juvenile Department, except her current expense for wardrobe, books and washing—Your dear Mr. Watson—I see by the *Mirror* in him your past friend—am fully prepared to have you bind him as you like—we hear many fine things about him—how I do wish Anna M. had the privilege of Society with you this winter. I am bent on her having her day yet. If she gets a moment for you there is no need of my saying anything about parties. They have a large one at Mrs. Walcott this evening.

---

[407] We know from a letter of Emily Chubbuck written on the 23rd of December that Gillette was to return the next day and that he would have Dr. Judson with him. It was on this trip from Boston that A. D. Gillette was to give the great missionary a copy to read of *Trippings in Author-land*, a new book out by Fanny Forester. Sheldon wrote in this letter that she had heard from the Gillettes and she expected them to be in Boston. Her letter was written on a Wednesday—it would be the Wednesday prior to December 23—and in this way are we able to put the date of December 17 on this letter.

[408] Charles Gratiot married Ann Sheldon, who was a cousin of Cynthia Sheldon, Urania Sheldon Nott and Alma Sheldon Anable.

[409] Emily had been looking for her Dictionary.

[410] Anna Maria Anable was the niece of the Urania and Cynthia Sheldon, the daughter of Joseph and Alma Sheldon Anable; she was Emily's closest friend at the Utica Female Academy.

[411] Reverend Rufus W. Griswold, an ordained clergyman and distinguished literary figure, had been one of Emily's suitors. Emily referred to him in a letter to Anna Maria Anable as a "widower," and "crazy to get married." On November 29, 1845, Anna Maria had suggested in a letter that Griswold had gotten married and that something had gone wrong. "Can't he get a divorce?" Anna Maria asked.

[412] This is the first information we have that Rufus Griswold has a daughter, and that she would possibly be attending the Utica Female Academy.

The concert in our church by the choir comes off next Monday evening—we are all screwing up forces to buy the house—cannot tell yet how it will come out—you may know it's a hard run. When I had to stand for five hundred dollars—now my girl if you put down any sum over fifty you have five years to make out the sum in equal yearly payments can you trust to providence and give a lift—just tell me what to say to Horace[413] about it. I promised him to write you—we have just had the mail come in—Mrs. G.[414] wrote from N. York. They are probably in Boston today. You will likely see them next week with your muff and Hood.

A missionary box is to be packed tonight and a letter to Boston inventory etc. beside one to Mrs. G. must go in the morning—could we have known Fanny's[415] dress would be detained so long—it should have been washed nicely. I hope you got the valise last week. I am writing in the greatest haste—have really been sick or should have got my writing ahead last night—tell dear Fanny I could fill a sheet to her for her good long letter. This party business for her takes us all *aback*—but you are there. I leave it—only do not fail to curb her if required—I am greatly relieved in your decision to stay with the dear friends who always have my love,[416] whether put on paper or not give it to them

Your truly attached friend

C—

Source: American Baptist Historical Society, AJ 26, no. 1262.

Robert A. West to Emily E. Chubbuck, December 17, 1845—South Brooklyn[417]

December 17, 1865

My dear friend,

I ought to have written you some days ago in acknowledgment of the receipt of your article for the January number[418]—so kindly intended to serve us, but which, alas! proved too late for the fulfillment of your benevolent purpose. We hesitated

---

[413] Horace H. Hawley was enormously helpful to Emily as she published her early stories and books.

[414] Hannah Gillette was the wife of the A. D. Gillette. Hannah would play an important part in preparing Emily for life in Burmah.

[415] Fanny Anable, one of five Anable sisters. She was born April 12, 1828. At this time, she was working and living in the home of Hannah and A. D. Gillette in Philadelphia.

[416] As she had the prior spring, Emily was staying with the family of the Reverend and Mrs. A. D. Gillette; Mr. and Mrs. Mitchell, neighbors of Joseph Neal and his mother, had extended very generous hospitality to Emily, and Emily in past correspondence, had thought very seriously of moving to their spacious accommodations.

[417] This letter has a postmark of December 28, 1845, so it was held by West or his office for eleven days after it was written. Emily would not have received it until December 29 or 30.

[418] West was the editor of the *Columbian Magazine*.

about keeping back two articles already in type, which would have been necessary to have made room for yours, but finally decided against that as it would have rendered the number materially less varied in its content, and knowing you to be a most reasonable lady, we at length ventured to leave yours until the February, whence it is already in type as the leading article. I took the liberty, however, so far to represent your interests in which I hope I did no wrong, as to stipulate that so far as dollars and cents are concerned, the articles should be considered as published when the January number appeared, which will be in a day or two. Unless therefore you repudiate the arrangement, you will consider your good self as already our creditor and make your claim upon us where and with any way you think fit. I ought to have written you on this subject at the time and as I have only the old stereotyped excuse to plead in defense, multiplicity of engagements etc. I throw myself on your mercy. And "we" do the same in reference to the icon appearance of the article in the January, only pleading that under the circumstances, we seemed to have no alternative. Perhaps here again I am to blame in not remembering that as our January and February numbers are stereotyped they necessarily go to press a long time in advance of publication, as well as for other business reasons.

Mr. Inman[419] showed me your letter respecting the notice of *Trippings in Author-land* in the *Commercial*, and much grieved I was that you were grieved about it. He said he would write to you on the subject. If he has done so, he has not shown me the letter or apprized [sic] me of the nature of his communication. And herein I am placed in an unpleasant position. It is known to not a few that, with rare exceptions, I write all the book notices with *Commercial* and if that should come to your knowledge and Mr. I. neglect to write you, it might lower me in your estimation, a woe I should sincerely deprecate. If he writes he is too honorable and honest not to tell you the facts in relation to that individual notice, and I feel equally reluctant to forestall his explanations. I will therefore only say that he is senior editor of the Comm!—can give instructions or make emendations when he chooses to exercise that right and that it must be obvious to you that the alleged facts mentioned in the former part of the notice, and which have grieved you, could not be within my knowledge. More I will not say until you demand it of me.

Believe me, my dear friend, I sincerely rejoice at the home-feeling which you seem to enjoy at Philadelphia. Do you intend to Winter there? I hope your visit there will tend to "settle, establish and confirm" you in health of body and perennial happiness. If I knew that it would be any gratification to you I would send you during your stay, our semi-weekly paper to keep you in mind of your New York friends, and give you "the run" of New York affairs. Let me know if it will.

---

[419] John Inman was the editor of the *Commercial Advertiser* and the *Columbian Magazine*.

With the exception named, I think you will like our January number. Don't forget that we are in your debt, or that you may command, at all times any service you like from

Yours very truly

Robert A. West   Source: American Baptist Historical Society, AJ 27, no. 1300.

Emily E. Chubbuck to Urania Sheldon Nott, December 23, 1845

My Dear Mrs. Nott,—

I meant to have written you a long time ago, and really commenced a letter; but I have been O, so busy! Did you receive the magazine which I sent you, containing the story of Willard Lawson?[420] Well, I have been requested to re-write it for a Sunday-school book, and have been engaged in that, and some magazine things, hardly giving myself thinking time. I am very agreeably situated in Mr. Gillette's[421] family, rooming with F—.[422] They are dear, good people, amiable, kind, and warm-hearted, and we could not have a pleasanter place to stay. I had intended to leave them and stay with another family,[423] but they would not hear to it at all… Mr. Gillette has been to Boston, and we are expecting him back tomorrow with Dr. Judson.[424] We are promising ourselves a rare treat in the company of the good missionary… My health is very good indeed, though not quite equal to what it was when I left Utica. The cold weather is rather hard upon me, and indeed, I don't know what I *should* have done there, away among the snows. It has been severely cold here for a few days past, and it quite shrivels me up.

Mrs. Gillette and F—both send love, and more kind wishes than they seem to know exactly how to put into words. Please remember me kindly to your good Doctor,[425] and believe me, my dear Mrs. Nott,

Ever sincerely and affectionately yours,

E. Chubbuck

Source: A. C. Kendrick, *The Life and Letters of Mrs. Emily C. Judson*, 138–39.

---

[420] "Willard Lawson" was one of Emily's stories that was published in the magazines, and later in vol. 2 of *Alderbrook*. For a sense of its personal impact, see the letter from "Orphan" to Emily E. Chubbuck dated November 29, 1845.

[421] Rev. A. D. Gillette was a stalwart friend and supporter of the Judson, Sheldon, and Anable families. Emily met Adoniram Judson in the parlor of the Gillette home in Philadelphia. Emily was staying with the Gillettes while living in Philadelphia.

[422] Fanny Anable, one of five Anable sisters. She was born April 12, 1828. At this time, she was working and living in the home of Hannah and A. D. Gillette in Philadelphia.

[423] Mr. and Mrs. Mitchell were friends of Emily's and had offered her a place to stay while in Philadelphia.

[424] It is to be noted that this letter was written two days before she was to meet Adoniram Judson on Christmas morning, and her life was to dramatically change.

[425] Eliphalet Nott, president of Union College, married to Urania Sheldon Nott.

Anna Maria Anable to Emily E. Chubbuck, December 23, 1845

Dear Nem[426]

Your and Fanny's[427] letter came this eve'y and weren't we glad to get them? I had one from Kate[428] too, in answer to an inquiry I made about sending your cloak. I shall pack off your old de Laine and some other things of yours to her. We are a little disturbed about Fanny's cough—Aunt U.[429] wrote that Clarkson told her she had a hard cough and if Fan has had to have a physician she must be a good deal out of sorts. Is it her old cold or a new one? Aunt C.[430] is going to write to her and do up some powers for her. I sh'd write but I shall not have time. I am going out to Western to morrow with Mary Brayton to visit her Ma' and Aunts and *Uncles*. I shall return by Monday next at furtherest and hope to find a letter from you.

I am heartily glad that you are not going to write for the magazines so much. Imman[431] gives Sarah Gold and I suppose anybody that asks it five dollars a page. Besides—every body [sic] seems to be hoping something a little more solid from you. That Memoir of Mrs. Judson[432] is just the thing to please every body [sic] *here*—and I guess the soberer sort of people elsewhere—while the gay will read it because F. F.[443] wrote it and it may do good. I do really hope you will write it.

---

[426] "Nem" or "Nemmy" was a name of endearment given to Emily by a small group of her intimate friends at the Utica Female Academy. Anna Maria Anable was "Ninny."

[427] Fanny Anable, one of five Anable sisters. She was born April 12, 1828. At this time, she was working and living in the home of Hannah and A. D. Gillette in Philadelphia.

[428] Sarah Catharine ("Kate," "Kit," or "Kitty") Chubbuck, Emily's older sister, born October 25, 1816.

[429] Urania Sheldon Nott—a mentor, advisor, and friend to Emily—was the literary principal at the Utica Female Academy when Emily arrived in October 1840. In late summer of 1842 Urania married Eliphalet Nott, the president of Union College in Schenectady NY.

[430] Miss Cynthia Sheldon was the administrative and finance manager of the Utica Female Academy. She was a mentor, advisor, and friend to Emily. Anna Maria Anable was Miss Sheldon's niece.

[431] John Inman was the editor of the *Commercial Advertiser* and the *Columbian Magazine*.

[432] Adoniram Judson was looking for someone to write the memoir of Sarah Hall Boardman Judson, his second wife. Sarah had died at the Isle of St. Helena on September 1, 1845 as they were returning to America.

Conventional wisdom tells us that Adoniram Judson was introduced to Fanny Forester through *Trippings in Author-land*, Emily's recently published book which was given to him on December 24, 1845 as he rode the train from Boston to Philadelphia. A. C. Kendrick relates this story in *The Life and Letters of Mrs. Emily C. Judson*, and Courtney Anderson wrote similarly in *To the Golden Shore: The Life of Adoniram Judson*. The suggestion has always been that the idea of Fanny Forester writing the memoir came from his reading of Emily's book, and it was for this purpose of meeting the author and ascertaining her competence that he came to the home of the Reverend A. D. Gillette on Christmas morning, 1845. With this meeting the idea soon became a plan.

This comment here in this letter by Anna Maria, however, indicates some earlier conversations on this matter, not necessarily with Adoniram Judson, but certainly between Emily and Anna Maria and the circle of friends at the Utica Female Academy. It is possible that A. D. Gillette had returned from the Triennial Convention in New York a few weeks previous speculating on the possibility. Judson was originally to have returned with Gillette at that time, and while making plans something might have been said about a desire for a memoir.

We are not able to definitely tie down the lineal progression of the idea. At the same time, Anna Maria's comment does lead us to believe that there was wider conversation and speculation than what has previously been suggested.

[433] Emily Chubbuck wrote under the *nom de plume* of Fanny Forester. Asked about it once, she said "Would anyone buy a book written by Emily E. Chubbuck?"

Mrs. Witman was here last night, and she is in a great teaze [sic] to have you put F. F. to your little books and have them come out now. She thinks they would sell wonderfully—More people than Hoffman[434] would be astonished at your *variety* of talent.

What has come over me—to write so abominably the need to write plain enough.

I never did you the compliment to suppose you his *first* love, deary—only supposing him "engaged." I thought his affaire [sic] with Laura[435] might well be [Note: Several words are lost in a tear in the letter fold.] engagement—unless he is a believer in a seven years courtship. Any way [sic], that you are his *last love* there is no doubt, and if the old fellow goes to P. I reckon he'll find it out—particularly if those kisses are in reality "all his fancy pictures them."

Poor Galusha![436] I suspected as much, when I [ ] him—And you really intend to victimize Wallace?[437] Preney garde! [sic] ! The biter may get bit—your day will come yet.

Have you had any more letters from your European *correspondent*?[438] You are real good to send me the letters and I'll keep dark.[439]

Tell Fan to be prudent, and do you take good care of yourself for I should not like my daughter[440] to *love in* [ ] this winter.

Good night—from tired as most to death

Ninny[441]

That was all true what Clark said of G. The Dr. said it was the best examination he had over heard—he said it at the dinner table before all the family.

---

[434] Charles Fenno Hoffman, a prominent literary figure in Philadelphia and New York, well known in literary circles as an exceptionally talented editor, poet, and writer. Emily had started a correspondence with him as Laura Linden before he discovered that she was Fanny Forester.

[435] In late 1843, Emily had written to Hoffman as "Laura Linden," and they exchanged a number of letters before his discovery that "Laura" was in reality Fanny Forester or Emily Chubbuck.

[436] Elon B. Galusha, son of Governor Jonas Galusha of Vermont, was ordained to the Christian ministry at a young age and spent many years at the town of Whitesborough, which was near Utica. Afterwards Galusha served in Utica, which would have put him in the social circles of the Utica Female Academy and Emily E. Chubbuck. According to the *Baptist Encyclopaedia*, "He was one of the most unselfish and devout of Christians. He was a father and a leader in Israel, whose memory has a blessed fragrance." In a short letter written to Fanny Forester in September 1844, he quoted Hallock, "None know thee but to love thee/ Nor named thee but to praise."

[437] Wallace was the nephew of Horace Binney Wallace. An attorney, whom Emily called aristocratic and privileged, he called on Emily regularly during winter 1845 when Emily was in Philadelphia, and then after Emily's engagement to Adoniram, he became a trusted friend and advisor.

[438] Nathaniel Parker (N. P.) Willis was the editor of *New Mirror*, the magazine that catapulted Emily into literary fame. He became a friend, mentor, and eventually a suitor. He left for Europe on June 1 and was to return in March.

[439] It is interesting to note that Emily shared the letters from N. P. Willis with her friend Anna Maria Anable.

[440] "Daughter" was a reference to Emily. Anna Maria often referred to herself as "mother-in-law."

[441] "Ninny" was a name of endearment given to Anna Maria Anable by her most intimate friends at the Utica Female Academy. Emily was "Nemmy."

Miss Crafts[442] is going to spend the holiday with Aunt U. I should like to go but can't afford it. I hope you have rec'd the other package before this. I sent you all the things I could find that I thought you would need.

AM

Source: American Baptist Historical Society, AJ 23, no. 1160.

Anna Maria Anable to Emily E. Chubbuck, December 30, 1845

What under the sun are you all about Nem?[443] I expected a letter from you to night [sic], but, as I did not get it, I do the next most agreeable thing—write to you. Will[444] brought me *The Mirror* to night. What do Willis[445] and Morris[446] mean by retiring from the *Mirror* and that they quarreled with Fuller or—is Nidio going to live in Europe always? or what is to pay? Hank told me a long rigmarole about Willis bearing dispatches to England from Austria and I can't make head nor tail of what he is about. Has he written to you lately? I am all curiosity and I can't get satisfied. I guess he is going to live in Europe, and I think he would less be appreciated here if he would—but—I don't want you to go clean off there to live and I expect you will somehow.[447] Tell me all about it right off. Has Fuller soft-soaped you enough to get a letter out of you? I suspect he thinks he has. What have you been writing for Hoffman's[448] paper? If you can spare it—send it to me for I don't suppose I can get it here.

Nem, I have had my oyster supper, and talked with Mr. Gratiot[449] and the boys till it's most eleven. I do wish I could jump into Mr. G's trunk and run down and

---

[442] On December 5, 1845, Anna Maria Anable wrote that Miss Crafts was a delight. "What a blessing to society it is, that she was never married. What a shame it would have been for *her* to have settled down into a mere *me* and my *husband* and my *children*!" Miss Crafts is not to be confused with Mrs. Augusta Crafts, who was noted as having a sharp disposition and a gossipy tongue.

[443] "Nem" or "Nemmy" was a name of endearment given to Emily by a small group of her intimate friends at the Utica Female Academy. Anna Maria Anable was "Ninny."

[444] William Stewart Anable was the son of Joseph and Alma Sheldon Anable.

[445] Nathaniel Parker (N. P.) Willis was the editor of *New Mirror*, the magazine that catapulted Emily into literary fame. He became a friend, mentor, and eventually a suitor.

[446] George P. "General" Morris, was N. P. Willis's partner at the *New Mirror* and a prominent literary figure in New York and Philadelphia.

[447] There is a wonderful irony here. We know that, at this point Emily had known Adoniram Judson for five days, and in one of those great mysteries, Emily was about to move hemispheres, but in an entirely different direction than Anna Maria anticipated. Anna Maria was thinking England and the Continent with N. P. Willis. Whoever would have thought of Burmah? Well, in fact as history is about to unfold—God—and Adoniram Judson.

[448] Charles Fenno Hoffman, a prominent literary figure in Philadelphia and New York, well known in literary circles as an exceptionally talented editor, poet, and writer. Emily had started a correspondence with him as Laura Linden before he discovered that she was Fanny Forester.

[449] Charles Gratiot married Ann Sheldon, who was a cousin of Cynthia Sheldon, Urania Sheldon Nott and Alma Sheldon Anable. At times they lived with the Sheldon-Anable families.

make you a visit. He leaves to-morrow morning, and will call and see you if he can the first of next week. He is one of the noblest hearted men that ever lived and if he calls I want you and Fan[450] to be particularly kind to him.

We had a right nice visit out to Western. There was a family dinner party on Christmas, consisting of about thirty persons. Sarah[451] and I were the "distinguished strangers" and I was the hand organ of the whole family. Such a constant demand as there was for my poor services from Uncle Milton down to the youngest child I never met with before. They fairly ground all the music out of me and I shan't want to visit in a musical family again for some months. With all my drumming however, I don't believe I played myself into the affections of Uncle George who is "the catch," as the owner of the homestead—the richest of the brothers etc etc. Nem your advice with regard to this Dr. is very good, but not *practicable*. He is after somebody, but I don't know who—some say Marie Farwell—some Mary S. but under cover of visits to the other house. Have I told you that G. Spencer is really smitten with Kate Curtenious? And that we think he *will* succeed—in time.

I found a letter from Mary Adams[452] on my return. She says she "shall expire with vexation if Jimmy does wind up with marrying that stupid little Helen Munson.[453] To think that he might have had you—or me! Oh, that men would only live up to their privileges!" Now when I look around on the rest of the beaux and think of what Jimmy used to was [sic] I feel a sort o' sympathy with Mary. *N'importe*. As Mary Barber[454] says "Who cares? He's no great shakes." Aunt U.[455] writes she is having a nice visit with Miss Crafts[456] who is spending the holidays with her.

I see by the papers that Mr. Judson is to be with you to-morrow.[457] Will you write those Memoirs[458] think you? Some folks here think you are getting transcen-

---

[450] Fanny Anable, one of five Anable sisters. She was born April 12, 1828. At this time, she was working and living in the home of Hannah and A. D. Gillette in Philadelphia.

[451] Sarah Bell Wheeler was a teacher at the Utica Female Academy, and an intimate friend of Emily Chubbuck.

[452] Mary Adams, a friend of Emily's while at the Utica Female Academy. She was from New Orleans.

[453] Jimmy Williams, often mentioned in Anna Maria Anable's letters, usually just as "Jimmy." Helen Munson was not viewed as a suitable partner for Jimmy Williams by the teachers and students of the Utica Female Academy.

[454] Mary Barber, mentioned frequently in the Emily Chubbuck Judson letters, was a student and then a teacher at the Utica Female Academy. She had had a falling out with Cynthia Sheldon which had yet to be reconciled.

[455] Urania Sheldon Nott—formerly the literary principal at the Utica Female Academy—a mentor, advisor, and friend to Emily.

[456] On December 5, 1845, Anna Maria Anable wrote that Miss Crafts was a delight. "What a blessing to society it is, that she was never married. What a shame it would have been for *her* to have settled down into a mere *me* and my *husband* and my *children*!" Miss Crafts is not to be confused with Mrs. Augusta Crafts, who was noted as having a sharp disposition and a gossipy tongue.

[457] This letter was written some five days after Adoniram Judson and Emily Chubbuck had met at the home of the Reverend A. D. Gillette. Apparently this reference is to something that Adoniram Judson was doing, probably in the Eleventh Baptist Church where A. D. Gillette was the pastor, or in the Philadelphia Baptist Association. Mr. Gillette had just returned from Boston, having brought Adoniram Judson to Philadelphia for meetings.

[458] It had been Adoniram Judson's plan to ask Emily to write a memoir of Sarah Hall Boardman Judson, his second wife, who had died on September 1, 1845, as they returned to America. She was buried on the Isle of St. Helena.

dentalist. What do they mean do you suppose? I guess it's because you say "God-gifted" and "inner light." If a body advances an original idea now-a-days one is transcendentalist. Good night. I wish you could be here to hop into bed with me. I shall be all alone if Molly Jerome don't [sic] come home from the sick room

Ninny[459]

Source: American Baptist Historical Society, AJ 23, no. 1145.

Anna Maria Anable to Emily E. Chubbuck, December 31, 1845[460]

What a glorious morning this is! O dear, how I do want to go with Mr. Gratiot[461]—I must to do something, go anywhere, anything but stay here in this stupid Utica. Do write as often as you can find time for I hear nothing else to interest me and its awful poky here.

Emily Chubbuck

Source: American Baptist Historical Society, AJ 23, no. 1145.

Nathaniel Parker Willis to Emily E. Chubbuck,[462] December 31, 1845 —Steventon Vicarage

My dear Emily

There is but an hour left of *my* 1845. There are five hours and half left of yours—(by the difference of longitude.) Your two letters from Philadelphia did their best to arrive *this* year—for they came in from the Railway Station half an hour ago. There is a letter for you still waiting to start from London, but I must send you a line while my heart is warm, so you will receive two together.

Your letters breathe the full fragrance of the spirit I recognized for one of Heaven's richest combinations, and it would be impossible for anyone to read them without loving you. I have been thinking over what I have worth living for, with the parting year, and nothing beside my child is sweeter to me than the link I have to your bountiful heart and sweet passionate imagination. I mean that you shall

---

[459] "Ninny" was a name of endearment given to Anna Maria Anable by her most intimate friends at the Utica Female Academy. Emily was "Nemmy."

[460] This segment was an addendum to Anna Maria Anable's letter of December 30, 1845.

[461] Charles Gratiot married Ann Sheldon, who was a cousin of Cynthia Sheldon, Urania Sheldon Nott and Alma Sheldon Anable.

[462] Written on the address page in the handwriting of Emily E. Chubbuck: "35"—meaning that this was the thirty-fifth letter from N. P. Willis that Emily had received.

always love me, dearest Emily. I shall carefully *garden* you and fence you in, for a hallowed retreat for my weary heart when world-worn.

As I wrote you ten days ago, I am preparing to sail for home. My brother-in-law Mr. Dennett, is to be married again on the 18th, and he and his wife, my child and nurse, embark with me. We shall probably take a sailing-packet as more comfortable and safer for Imogen, tho' of longer passage. The *Prince-Albert* is the one we now propose to sail in. Do not mention it till you hear of it elsewhere, however, as "the public" might wonder too soon.

Since I have been writing to you, one of the homeless locks on my temple nearest the light, has importunately fallen between my eyes and paper, and I send it you to serve as an *avant-courier* in case I bring you the rest of me, or as a momento of me if I should not arrive. The sea is treacherous, and Hope seems looking but a short way ahead. In the latter case, dear Emily, believe that you were the dearest to whom it could go when it was sever'd.

God bless you. I must leave this letter before the New Year. I will *bite* a kiss where my signature should be. Ever yours affectionately

Source: Hanna family files.

Index

Adams, Mary, 466, 511
Allen, Eliza C., 177, 191, 201, 326
Allen, Lydia Ann, 52, 57, 88
Anable, Anna Maria, 96, 208, 219, 221, 222, 223, 225, 227, 230, 231, 239, 243, 276, 281, 286, 287, 288, 293, 295, 327, 329, 333, 334, 336, 338, 340, 344, 353, 359, 361, 364, 369, 371, 372, 375, 377, 382, 383, 386, 391, 392, 396, 398, 401, 404, 406, 410, 412, 453, 456, 457, 473, 477, 480, 483, 485, 486, 493, 495, 504, 519, 521, 523
Anable, Harriet, 119
Arthur, Timothy Shay, 462, 463
Barber, Mary, 349
Bates, Marie Dawson, 56, 61, 67, 85, 86, 89, 101, 112, 123, 128, 130, 135, 147, 299, 302
Bates, Emilius, 124
Blair, John, 47
Blodgett, Jane, 141, 157
Chubbuck, Catharine, 35, 36, 38, 102, 110, 114, 121, 138, 160, 167, 168, 184, 214, 309, 320, 332, 337, 351, 366, 414, 416, 440, 461, 489, 509
Chubbuck, Emily,
   Childhood memories, 13-18
   Family History, 9-11
   Letters From, 9, 24, 26, 29, 33, 35, 36, 38, 43, 47, 51, 55, 56, 67, 71, 77, 80, 86, 101, 102, 103,106, 108,110, 112, 114, 121, 128, 133, 135, 138, 149, 151, 153, 158, 160, 165, 166, 167, 168, 175, 184, 186, 188, 198, 199, 212, 214, 215, 221, 222, 223, 234, 237, 240, 246, 293, 302, 309, 320, 332, 336, 337, 359, 361, 366, 386, 391, 414, 416, 417, 422, 425, 433, 434, 440, 446, 461, 486, 489, 509, 518
   Letters To, 45, 47, 50, 52, 54, 57, 59, 61, 69, 74, 75, 76, 82, 83, 85, 88, 89, 117, 118, 119, 120, 121, 123, 124, 125, 130, 137, 141, 143, 144, 145, 147, 156, 157, 159, 162, 163, 164, 169, 170, 172, 173, 175, 177,182, 183, 187, 191, 192, 193, 200, 201, 202, 205, 206, 207, 208, 214, 217, 219, 225, 227, 228, 229, 230, 231, 232, 237, 239, 241, 242, 243, 244, 245, 248, 249, 250, 252, 253, 255, 256, 258, 260, 269, 270, 273, 274, 276, 277, 280, 281,283, 284, 286, 287, 288, 295, 298, 299, 300, 301, 302, 304, 305, 306, 307, 308, 311, 312, 313, 315, 319, 324, 326, 327, 329,332, 333, 334, 338, 340, 341, 342, 344, 346, 347, 349, 351, 353, 355, 357, 364, 369, 370, 371, 372, 373, 375, 377, 378, 380, 382, 383, 386, 389, 392, 394, 395, 396, 398 399, 401, 403, 404, 406, 407, 408, 410, 412, 413, 419, 421, 422, 436, 438, 442, 443, 444, 447, 448, 450, 452, 453, 456, 457, 458, 460, 462, 463, 464, 466, 468, 469, 471, 473, 475, 476, 477, 479, 480, 483, 485, 492, 493, 494, 495, 499, 500, 501, 503, 504, 506, 507, 510, 511, 513, 515, 516, 519, 521, 523
   Teaching, 18-21
Chubbuck, J. Walker, 26, 29, 32, 33, 43, 47, 51, 71, 77, 80, 103, 106, 108, 133, 149, 246, 434
Chubbuck, Wallace, 32
Colgate, Mary, 480
Composition,
   A Sketch of Female Character, 91
   The importance to Ladies of cultivating a Talent for Conversation, 99-101
Conant, H. C., 298
Corey, D. G., 206
Cousin 'Bel', 425
Damaux, Eugenia, 274
Dawson, Marie, 24, 54, 55,
Dean, William, 23
Dexter, C. W., 269
Dodge, H.M., 141, 159
Forester, Fanny, 216,
   Essay, *Underhill Cottage*, 278
   Fiction, *Dora'*, 262
   Horace Binney Wallace on F. F., 428
   Letter to *New Mirror*, 212, 215
   Lines to Fanny Forester, 322
   N. P. Willis on Fanny Forester, 217
   Preface, *Trippings*, 427
   To Cousin 'Bel'
Galusha, Elon B., 244
Gillespie, William M., 444, 458
Gillette, Hannah, 433, 436
Gillette, Abram Dunn, 438, 448
Graham, George R., 245, 250, 253, 305, 324, 326
Gregory, Mary, 256
Griggs, E. M., 45, 75, 76
Griswold, Rufus Wilmot, 96
Harriet, death of, 17
Hawley, Horace H., 475
Hinckley, Sarah J., 492
Hoffman, Charles Fenno, 183, 349, 357, 373, 389, 501, 507, 510
Hooker, Martha, 378, 403
Inman, John, 201, 205, 217, 258, 311
"J", 332
Jones, Morven M., 468
Josslyn, E. T., 193

Judson, Adoniram, 9
Kelly, Jane, 347, 370,
Kendrick, A.C., 23
Lavinia, death of, 12-13
Lillybridge, Lydia, 173
Lightbody, J.M., 476
Linden, Laura, 501
Loomis, I.M., 469
Loucks, H., 447, 452
Loxley, B. R., 175, 202, 249, 253
Luce, Harmony, 164
Luce, N, 163
Marble, Louisa B., 172
Minnie, 137
Morrisville Newspaper, 67 – 68
Mother's Journal,
    The works of God the best teachers, 179
New Mirror, 212, 213, 215, 262, 278, 317, 322, 323, 425
Noble, Mary Florence, 322
    Poem from Sarah J. Clark, 323-324
Nott, Urania Sheldon, 151, 153, 156, 158, 165, 166, 167, 169, 170, 186, 187, 198, 199, 200, 243, 255, 273, 300, 380, 422, 479, 518
"Orphan", 495
Paine and Burgess, 469
Poem
    A Dialogue, 6-9
    A morning scene at Utica Fem. Acd., 97-99
    A portrait drawn for my cousin, 1
    Apostrophe to the Moon, 5-6
    Can't you come this way, 250
    For Miss Damaux, 132
    Grandfather, 94-96
    Happy, happy! Earth is gay, 87
    Mary Anable, May Queen, 106
    Ministering Angels, 170
    Miss U. Sheldon
    Morning Thoughts, 68-68
    Parting Ode, 24-25
    Stanzas, 41-43
    Thanksgiving, 25-26
    Thanksgiving Hymn, 270
    The Caged Robin, 178-9
    The Little Girl's Soliloquy, 2-4
    The midnight air is filled, 32
    The Old Man, 92-93
    The Salem Murder, 22
    The Spirit Voice, 26
    The Weaver, 317-319
    To Hatty, 105
    To Maria on Her Marriage, 56
    To Mrs. Nott, 155-56
    To my brother, 41
    To Sarah, - Love, 9
    To the coin in her purse, 4-5
    Where Are the Dead?, 116-117
    Why not attend church, 44-45
    Written on the day I left school, 21
Post, J., 280, 313
Randall, Hannah, 59, 125
Randall, Roswell, 50
Redfield, James W., 69, 74, 82, 83
Reynolds, Caroline, 118, 145
Rhees, M. I., 143, 144, 169
Sheldon, Cynthia, 117, 120, 162, 175, 182, 187, 188, 207, 227, 229, 232, 234, 237, 240, 241, 302, 342, 355, 399, 417, 419, 446, 499, 506, 515
Sheldon, Urania, 90, 121
Swett, L. S., 125
Taylor, Alfred, 341
Taylor, Sophia, 407
Wallace, Horace Binney, 428, 500
West, Robert, 408, 450, 516
Westcott, Nora, 395
Wheeler, Sarah Bell, 346, 503
Williams, J. Watson, 192, 202, 442
Willis, Nathaniel Parker, 212, 213, 214, 215, 228, 242, 248, 252, 256, 260, 270, 277, 283, 284, 301, 304, 306, 307, 308, 311, 312, 315, 317, 319, 324, 351, 372, 394, 413, 421, 422, 442, 443, 447, 464, 471, 494, 513, 523
Wilmarth, M., 460